Publications of The Pennsylvania German Society

Volume XVI

The Lutheran church in Schwaigern was built in parts during several centuries, as is true of many churches of its size in Germany. The oldest part, the Romanesque tower, was built about 1200, together with the "old church"—now the northern side of the nave. In the 16th century the church was vastly expanded to its present form, with a purely Gothic nave and choir added, just on the eve of the Reformation. The church was dedicated to St. John the Baptizer, St. Anna and St. Mary. It became Lutheran in the mid-sixteenth century and much of its art work was retained at that time.

The baptismal font, to the right of the high altar, is one of the oldest pieces in the church. It was there during the eighteenth century and therefore held the water for hundreds of baptisms cited in this book. The records of this and of several dozen other churches in the Kraichgau have been the basis for the information in this volume about over 600 families who left the area to come to Pennsylvania, to the "new land."

Photo: J. Godshall

Eighteenth Century Emigrants from German-Speaking Lands to North America

Volume I: The Northern Kraichgau

by
Annette Kunselman Burgert

Breinigsville, Pennsylvania
The Pennsylvania German Society
1983

The cover design is a panel from a chest made by Christian Seltzer who was born in 1749 in Michelfeld. The floral decorations on the pages of the text are from *Fraktur* documents made by John Conrad Gilbert who was born 1734 in Hoffenheim.
Cover design and floral decorations by Robert G. Hostetter
Maps by J. William Long

This volume was prepared for distribution to members of The Pennsylvania German Society during 1982. Subsequent volumes in this series will be offered from time to time.

I dedicate this volume to my husband,
Richard A. Burgert, Sr.
His patience and understanding made
it possible.

Contents

Illustrations

Maps

Preface

A complete history of the migration of Germans to Pennsylvania has not been written. A comprehensive history of this migration would have to include information from all German-speaking areas of central Europe: Germany, part of France, part of Switzerland, and Austria. Several volumes would be required to publish the available material and indeed several volumes containing immigrant data have already been published. The first geographical area with documented emigrant information to be published was some of the German-speaking area of Switzerland. Emigrants from the cantons of Zurich, Bern and Basel were published in 1925 in two volumes by the National Genealogical Society edited by A. B. Faust and M. G. Brumbaugh. *Lists of Swiss Emigrants in the Eighteenth Century to the American Colonies* is a good starting point for a study of Swiss emigration, but more research could and should be done. Volume I, the Zurich lists, covers only a ten year period (1734–1744) and much direct and indirect emigration from that canton occurred both before and after these dates. Emigrants from the canton of Schaffhausen were published in Volume 16 of the Pennsylvania German Folklore Society in 1951. The next area to be represented by a published list of emigrants was Zweibrücken. Volume I of the Pennsylvania German Folklore Society (1936) contained a list of emigrants from Zweibrücken territories, 1728–1749, followed by volume 16 (1951) containing lists from 1750–1771. The Gerber lists of emigrants from Wuerttemberg appear in volume 10 of this Society (1945). The Langguth list from the county of Wertheim appeared in volume 12 (1947). All of the lists published by the Pennsylvania German Folklore Society have been reprinted by Don Yoder in one volume, *Pennsylvania German Immigrants 1709–1786* (Baltimore, 1980).

Numerous additional magazine articles, pamphlets and monographs containing new immigrant origins have been published for many years in the United States. Some of the later lists were enhanced by the addition of ship identification and Pennsylvania documentation. Many of these have also been consolidated and reprinted in volumes that are currently on the market. A three-volume index compiled by P. William Filby and Mary K. Meyer, *Passenger and Immigration Lists Index* (Detroit, 1981), is an excellent finding aid for families in all of these previously published lists.

Moreover, in addition to lists published in America, other material from European archival sources published by German genealogists has not been translated. Four names stand out in this field: Fritz Braun, long-time director of the Heimatstelle Pfalz; Friedrich Krebs, archivist in the Palatine State Archives at Speyer; Adolf Gerber, professor at Earlham College until he returned to Germany to engage in research; and Werner Hacker, a director of the German federal railways and amateur genealogist. The work of these four men provided valuable background material to the present volume, and their prior identification of passengers in the Pennsylvania lists supplied the basis for further identification.

In almost all cases, the previously published lists have been compiled from civil sources or from church records that specifically state that the destination of an emigrant was Pennsylvania or the new land, many including the year of emigration. In some areas, manumission records exist. When this information is given, identi-

fication of an immigrant in the Pennsylvania ship lists can be made with a reason-
able degree of accuracy. A few of the previously published articles contain names
of emigrants from the northern Kraichgau, the area covered in this volume, but
only those for whom civil documents exist.

In 1977 the Board of Directors of the Pennsylvania German Society, under the
leadership of Mahlon H. Hellerich, Ph.D., then president of the society, commis-
sioned a study to locate the European origins of as many of the Pennsylvania
German families as possible. 1983 marks the three hundredth anniversary of the
arrival of the thirteen Mennonite families from Krefeld at Philadelphia. In the days
after their arrival Germantown was established, and in the years that followed
thousands of German-speaking families came to Pennsylvania. Other than the fact
that they were called frequently "Palatines," no general documentation of their
homes exists. The original goal of this study was to produce a volume bringing
together the following information:

1. Data from previously published lists about European origins.

2. Notations in Pennsylvania church records with reference to villages of birth.

3. Information from several other sources such as family genealogies, private
knowledge, tombstone inscriptions, wills.

4. Information from German sources, including untranslated articles not readily
available in the United States.

5. Supplementary data that could be found in various European church records.

All five sources of information have been utilized in compiling this volume, but
the last was soon found to be the most important and productive source of new
material. We soon realized that it would require several volumes to publish all of
the materials that could be found in this one source.

This study of the emigration differs from the other published works mentioned
above, therefore, in one important respect. The emigrants identified here are for
the most part either those who did not ask permission to leave or those about whom
such records no longer exist. In a few cases pastors made notations in the German
church records about individuals who had gone to the new world and these are
cited throughout the text. However, for a large majority of the families in the
following text, no such notations were located; they could be established in fact as
immigrants only by the judicious use of supporting evidence. When a familiar
name was located in a German church record, a series of research steps then
produced the following additional information:

1. The family in question disappears from the German records at a certain date.

2. The name appears in Pennsylvania records or the existing ship passenger lists
about the same time.

3. If located in the ship lists, arrival with other families from the same village
or general area.

4. Supporting evidence from Pennsylvania records, showing association with
other families from the same European area, a coinciding date of birth, a corre-
sponding list of children, a wife with the same given name as that found in the
German record.

Step four was no easy task. Children often died young and their deaths were not always recorded. Sometimes the wife and children died on the voyage, and the immigrant remarried after arrival. We have collected data on many potential immigrants who are not included here because we could not find sufficient supporting evidence to verify the emigration. Such common names as Ziegler, Schneider, Müller, Klein, Bender, Wolff, Meyer, and Geiger are prevalent in the northern Kraichgau, and in some cases we have located proveable immigrants with these surnames. It is hoped that publication will encourage further studies of these families and perhaps reveal additional Pennsylvania German pioneers.

The decision to limit the volume to one relatively small geographical area was difficult, knowing that families who came from other, equally important areas would not be represented this time. But the amount of information found made that decision inevitable. Eventually an area that included villages, as they existed prior to the post-World War II revisions of political jurisdiction, was selected for inclusion in this study. A few places which may not be considered a part of the Kraichgau today are included and occasionally records of adjoining villages not thoroughly studied in this book were examined for data about families who moved around.

It would not be accurate to claim that this volume names every emigrant from the northern Kraichgau to Pennsylvania. There are some persons in Pennsylvania with names and association so close to known emigrants from the area that one would guess their origin was there, but all efforts to locate them have failed. Undoubtedly some have simply been overlooked. As others are discovered, subsequent volumes in the series will include them.

Since the material was obtained by an examination of church records, something should be said about the nature of the primary source used. Congregations of Lutherans, Reformed and some Roman Catholics existed in the area, depending upon the overlord of the village in question. Each of these religious denominations required their pastors to keep records of the pastoral acts they performed involving their parishioners or others who came to them for ministry. They preserved, therefore, registers of baptisms, marriages, burials, confirmations, and communicants. In some instances registers of the congregation arranged by family were also kept. In every village such records were probably begun shortly after the Reformation in the sixteenth century, but not all of the records still exist from that period. The Thirty Years' War (1618–1648) and subsequent conflicts contributed to the destruction of some records. Occasionally pastors began a new book to replace the destroyed one by listing the families in the village and telling what persons knew about their own age, marriage, and so on. The situation in the Kraichgau is further complicated by these factors: 1) some church buildings changed hands as the result of political changes of administration; sometimes new records were begun by the pastor of the new confession, sometimes the old was simply continued in use, sometimes the last pastor of the old confession took the record with him for use in his next appointment. After the Lutherans lost many congregations in the area, they began new ones in the same villages where they had been represented earlier; 2) pastors then as ever since have sometimes simultaneously served two or more congregations which adjoined one another. The result is that parishioners sometimes had their ministerial acts performed in either of the congregations the pastor served; 3) people moved about far more than American researchers often realize. Fortunately some pastors noted former home villages in making entries in the records.

In only a few cases the original church books were used. The majority of the documentation from Germany provided here was compiled from microfilms of the records made by the Genealogical Society of Utah. When a record is microfilmed some of the quality of the original is lost. Some records are thick books with the dates entered close to the inner margins of the pages. These are lost in microfilming, and if there is a questionable date in the text below, it might be more clearly legible in the original record. Faded entries might also be more legible in the original. Handwritings vary in legibility as well and styles of German script changed considerably as time went on. Sometimes there are periods of years when no records were entered.

All of which is a way of saying that researchers finding a family of interest in this book are urged to consult the original records (most of them now in the archives of the Baden Church in Karlsruhe). An intensive study of the family in the village cited here and in neighboring villages will undoubtedly be fruitful. The student should be aware that the data given here on a family is not intended to be complete. Only enough has been cited to identify the immigrant and his *Heimat* (hometown). Some of the records are so complete that if a family was native to the village, by no means always the case, several more generations can be added to the lineage. What is more, there are very likely civil records available in some of the German villages which we did not touch, such as probate, land and tax records from which a fuller picture of the immigrant and his family might be gained.

All dates are given as they appear in the old records, both German and Pennsylvanian, with no transposition for the change from the Julian to the present Gregorian calendar. That change seems to have taken place about 1697 in the Kraichgau. English lands, including the colonies made the change in 1752, at which time 11 days were dropped from the calendar here. In some of the church records only one date is given for the children without any statement as to whether the date is for birth or baptism. When this is the case, since most of the books are baptismal records, the date is given here with *bp.* preceeding it, signifiying that it is a baptismal record. In a few instances, however, it might actually be the date of birth (and in some, of course, of both, since it was customary to baptise at once). Some of the records contain both a date of birth and a date of baptism. When this was found, the date of the actual birth has been given preference.

Throughout the text, the spelling of both village names and surnames are given as they appear in the records. Although the old spelling of place names is maintained, the modern version, complete with zip code identification (in German, *die Postleitzahl*) is given in each family entry. Neckarbischofsheim usually appears as Bischofsheim or sometimes as Bischofsheim in the Kraichgau in old records. There are three other towns named Bischofsheim in the German *Postleitzahl* directory; having the number is essential for precise location.

One of the reasons that some emigrants from these villages may not be included here is simply because the name could not be found in the ship lists and Pennsylvania records. Martine Kearstuter on the *Molley* in 1727 (S-H 13) could correctly be identified as the Johann Martin Kirstatter who married in 1727 in Neckarbischofsheim because his marriage record mentions that he is going to Pennsylvania. He later appears in Pennsylvania records with the correct spelling of his surname. In some instances enough information could be found in both German and American records to narrow the probable time of immigration to within a year or two. When this was the case, a thorough search of the ship lists for those years was often rewarding. Using this method, Caspar Elias Diller from Gauangelloch was located in the lists as Casper Elias Taylor on the *Samuel* in 1733 (S-H 106). The second volume of Strassburger-Hinke, which unfortunately was not reprinted with the others some years back, was frequently consulted and proved to be invaluable. Several of the immigrants were located by using the signature lists rather than the printed translation. This does not intend any criticism of Hinke's monumental task of transcribing those lists. One reason the signatures were published was because of the problems in reading them. Hinke himself commented in the introduction to *Pennsylvania German Pioneers*, "in some cases no man living can decipher with certainty the awful scribbles of some of the writers." Any person working with this old handwriting is going to have a margin of error in interpreting certain letters. No translation of these records can be completely accurate, since the translator is limited by many factors: old faded ink, torn pages, ink that bled through the paper making both sides of the page illegible. Most of all the translator is limited by the writer's ability to make clear, distinct and consistent letters. This is not only true of the signatures on the ship lists, of course, but it is a valid comment on some of the German script church records in both Germany and Pennsylvania.

In preparing the family entries, I have tried to locate some evidence of the precise year of arrival. For those who appear in the ship lists, the page reference in Strassburger and Hinke, *Pennsylvania German Pioneers*, Volume I, is given. The useful abbreviation S-H is used to indicate this source. The page number is cited, along with the ship's name and year of arrival, because in a few instances, ships' names are duplicated in the lists. Two *Neptunes* arrived in 1751, so that the page numbers become important. The immigrants arriving before 1727 when the ship lists start are designated prelist in the text. For some of these prelist immigrants a definite year of arrival could be determined from other sources and when available it is noted.

The Pennsylvania documentation involved the use of hundreds of records, both published and unpublished sources. Charles Glatfelter's *Pastors and People*, Volume I, identifies 525 Lutheran and Reformed congregations that existed at some time or other between 1717 and 1793. Not all of these records were searched, but many of them, especially the earliest ones, were. To simplify the task of citing these sources, certain key words are used to identify the congregational records. *Hill Lutheran KB, Lebanon co*. is used to designate the Lutheran church book of the congregation located in North Annville township, Lebanon county, also known as Quitopahilla, Quittapahilla, and Hill. A separate record for the Reformed congregation here is listed as *Hill Reformed KB, Lebanon co*. KB is a standard German genealogical abbreviation for *Kirchenbuch*, church record volume. There were other Hill churches, but only one in Lebanon county. Researchers who are not familiar with the exact location or history of the early congregations mentioned in the text should refer to the two volumes by Glatfelter already mentioned.

Where will and probate record citations are used, I have relied, of necessity, quite heavily on previously compiled abstracts and indices. Some contain errors and omissions and the original wills should be consulted. The decision to include this material was difficult, but the knowledge that a probate record exists outweighed the disadvantage of using secondary sources.

The Pennsylvania research has been compiled from previously translated or transcribed sources and is also subject to any errors of transcribing that might have been made. It would have been more satisfactory to work entirely from primary sources, but neither time nor the availability of the original records permitted such research. The Pennsylvania documentation on these families is not intended to be exhaustive. On some families the available information is far too extensive to publish here in its entirety. On other families only the arrival on the ship list was found and no other information could be located. A thorough search of all county estate records, deeds and assessment lists would probably yield much more information about some of these families. The few Pennsylvania records presented here are offered as a guide for others who might be interested in developing the family's history. The researcher should be aware that ages given in the ship lists and dates of birth given on tombstones or in church records in obituary notices are often incorrect.

One historian has commented that detailed genealogical interest overshadows the general historical evaluation of such a migration as that of the Pennsylvania Germans, that it is a mistake to point out the trees instead of describing the forest. My view is that you cannot have a forest without trees, nor can you describe a forest adequately without extensive knowledge of the trees therein. The families from the northern Kraichgau were among the earliest to come to Pennsylvania. Their names occur in the earliest Lutheran and Reformed church records in Pennsylvania. Their pastors and schoolmasters came with them, and they pioneered new settlements and established congregations that had not previously existed. Many of them may rightly be considered the architects of Pennsylvania German folk culture.

We have not attempted to glorify any outstanding individuals, nor have we concealed human frailties. If more information is given about one family than another, it is simply because more information was found. If a family fondly cherishes an illustrious ancestor and the facts presented here do not support the tradition, we apologize for the disenchantment. But we do not apologize for presenting the facts found in the old records.

With all the limitations stated, we present the following list of 624 emigrant heads of households, being fully aware that there may be errors in identification. There are three Bernhart Gilberts in the S-H index; there are five Bernhart Gilberts in the Hoffenheim records during the same time period. Exact identification requires extensive study of the families. The repetition of both given and surnames in some villages makes unquestionable identification impossible in some cases. As is true in all of the questionable areas, or in incomplete entries, additions or corrections to the material here will be welcomed and so far as practicable attention will be called to errors in subsequent volumes.

This work would not have been possible without the help of some very special people.

Pastor Frederick S. Weiser, editor of the Pennsylvania German Society, has provided consistent encouragement, valuable suggestions, and helped in so many ways that it is impossible to express my gratitude adequately. He had the most difficult task of editing the manuscript. He added naturalization information and other materials to many of the entries; he provided illustrations and captions and the historical introduction. He made records available and wrote many letters to obtain material needed for the research. His total contribution could not be summed up in a few words.

Helen Snyder of Harrisburg helped from the beginning of this project and almost to the end. Her unfailing willingness to aid whenever and wherever help was needed will be remembered for a long time. I regret that she did not live to see the publication of the book. She spent many hours in both the Pennsylvania Archives and the State Library reading wills and deeds on microfilm and garnering details.

Peggy Joyner of Portsmouth, Virginia, provided extensive notes on the families who moved into the Shenandoah. Her tireless indexing of some of the source materials was an essential part of the task.

Indexing became a vital part of this project at an early time. Many manuscript records had never been indexed. The following people have provided help in this area: Bernice Simon, Frances Taylor, and Shirley Pahl.

Klaus Wust provided several interesting documents from the archives in Holland concerning the emigrants and several hours of stimulating conversation about the emigration.

Hank Jones, whose main interest is the 1709 New York migration of Germans, generously shared many notes in his files about later immigrants to Pennsylvania.

Carla Mittelstaedt-Kubaseck researched in records not available here on microfilm, particularly Berwangen, Bonfeld, Treschklingen, Fürfeld, and Dühren. We also thank John P. Dern for making the results of her research in Berwangen available to us.

Pastor Larry M. Neff provided editorial assistance. His seemingly endless patience with revisions and his ability to catch little inconsistencies between entries have been invaluable.

Raymond E. Hollenbach's translations and transcriptions of early Pennsylvania records and cemeteries were a great help in providing documentation.

Photographs and illustrations greatly enhance a text. I am grateful for the pictures of the villages from which the emigrants came, most of which were made by Jeff Godshall. The files of the Pennsylvania German Society provided other illustrations. Poist Studio in Hanover was most helpful in preparing the pictures for the press.

I would like to express especially my deep gratitude to the Genealogical Society of Utah. Their collection of German church records on microfilm made the European research possible, and their generous cooperation made this research material available. I am especially thankful to Noel R. Barton, supervisor of the correspondence section, for his many efforts and his patient replies to my frequent questions. The staff of the branch library in Reynoldsburg, Ohio, have always responded most graciously to my many requests.

Franz Rink and Roland Paul of the Heimatstelle Pfalz in Kaiserslautern have helped by making available material from the Heimatstelle files and by answering many questions.

Karl Diefenbacher of Ladenburg and Dr. Hermann Lau of Karlsruhe, active genealogists of Kraichgau families, responded generously to pleas for help.

The following persons provided information on one or more of the families in this volume from their own genealogical research; their correspondence has been appreciated, although not always promptly acknowledged: Monroe Fabian, Jane Adams Clarke, Rev. Harry Miller, Schuyler Brossman, Fred Houts, Mary Harter, Ray Wolff, Grace Thompson, Betty R. Massman, Clarice Z. Fisher, Eugene R. Sweigert, Sue Adams, Jane Evans Best, Alan G. Keyser, Janice Eichholtz Rodriguez and Helen Seubold. Many others have contributed information on families who are not from the area covered in this volume. Bill Grenoble has spent many hours at work in the films of other villages which will be included in other studies, but his deep interest in this project has been an encouragement.

A group of persons made financial contributions which enabled us to have research done in records not available on microfilm. These were: The Hon. Carl Albert, former Speaker of the House of Representatives, United States Congress, whose generous initial contribution established the research fund; Nancy and Jerry Myers, David Pope, Dr. William Rader, Nettie Schreiner-Yantis, Junia Stambaugh, Dr. Benjamin B. Weisiger III, Helen Seubold, Pastor Frederick S. Weiser.

Whether time, research materials, funds, or a good word, each contribution was important to the success of this book. It has been an enriching experience to work with all of these people.

I owe more than I can say to my husband and my children for their understanding. They have listened to each day's marvelous discoveries and cared enough not to resent the time that the research demanded. I hope that, in return, they have gained an appreciation of their heritage.

Annette K. Burgert

Worthington, Ohio
December 1982

Abbreviations

A.	acres
Adm.	administration, administrator
appt.	appointed
b.	born
bp.	baptized
bu.	buried
ca.	circa (about)
CH	Switzerland (Confederatio Helvetica). Used in connection with a four-digit number it designates a Swiss postal code
ch.	child or children
co.	county
conf.	confirmed
d.	died
decd.	deceased
exr, exrs.	executor(s)
Joh.	Johann (the form of Johannes used preceding another name, as Johann Martin; an alternative is Hans. The full name alone is Johannes.)
KB	Kirchenbuch, church book or parish register. This term is used to designate any form of church record in Germany or America.
m.	married
Md.	Maryland
mo.	month(s)
nat.	naturalized
Pa.	Pennsylvania
q.v.	which see (refers to another emigrant listed in the text)
sp.	sponsors at baptism
twp.	township
Va.	Virginia
w.	weeks
wit.	witnesses, witnessed
Wurtt.	Württemberg
y.	year(s)
*	the person emigrating

Short citations

Blumer's records:

Unpublished nineteenth century copy of records of marriages and burials by Abraham Blumer, Reformed clergyman. The original appears to be lost; copy in the Historical Society of the Evangelical and Reformed Church, Philip Schaff Library, Lancaster Theological Seminary, Lancaster.

Chalkley:

Lyman Chalkley, *Chronicles of the Scotch-Irish Settlement in Virginia: Extracted from the Original Court Records of Augusta County, 1745–1800*. 3 vols. (1912; reprinted Baltimore, 1974). Usually cited as Chalkleys Chronicles.

Glatfelter:

Charles H. Glatfelter, *Pastors and People: German Lutheran and Reformed Churches in the Pennsylvania Field, 1717–1793. 2 vols.* (Breinigsville, 1979, 1981).

Krebs:

Friedrich Krebs, "Palatine Emigration Materials from the Neckar Valley, 1726–1766," *Pennsylvania Folklife* XXIV (Spring 1975), 15–44; reprinted in Don Yoder, *Rhineland Emigrants*, Baltimore, 1981.

Muhlenberg's Journals

Theodore G. Tappert and John W. Doberstein, trans and ed., *The Journals of Henry Melchior Muhlenberg*. 3 vols. (Philadelphia, 1942–1958; reprinted, 1982).

PA:

Pennsylvania Archives, together with the *Colonial Records* a 135-volume set published between 1838 and 1935 in several series in many volumes each.

Rupp:

I. Daniel Rupp, *A Collection of Thirty-Thousand Names of German, Swiss, Dutch, French, Portuguese and other immigrants in Pennsylvania, chronologically arranged* 1727 to 1776 (Harrisburg, 1856, reissued and revised Philadelphia 1876, numerous reprints; also printed with a German text, most recently Leipzig, 1936)

S-H

Ralph Beaver Strassburger and William John Hinke, *Pennsylvania German Pioneers*. 3 vols. (Norristown, 1934). All citations in this text are to Volume I.

Shultze's Journals

Andrew S. Berkey, *The Journals and Papers of David Shultze*. 2 vols. (Pennsburg, 1952–53).

Schumacher's records: Frederick S. Weiser, "Daniel Schumacher's Bap-
                          tismal Register," in *Publications of The Pennsyl-
                          vania German Society* I (Breinigsville 1967), 185–
                          407.

Stoever's records: [F.J.F.Schantz, trans.] *Records of Rev. John Cas-
                          per Stoever, Baptismal and Marriage*, 1730–1799
                          (Harrisburg, 1896; reprinted Baltimore 1982). This
                          translation contains errors and omissions. The
                          original record was consulted in questionable
                          cases. See Charles H. Glatfelter and Frederick
                          S. Weiser, *The Ministry of John Casper Stoever* (in
                          process, 1983).

Annotations

The German church records have been studied either in person by a professional
reader or by the author on films made by the Utah Genealogical Society, all of
which are available to other students through the genealogical society's branch
library system. Most of the originals are in the Protestant Church Archives in
Karlsruhe.

The Pennsylvania Church records have been studied from existing translations
and/or microfilms of the originals in various libraries and archives.

Naturalizations: 1) Pennsylvania: Acts of the colonial legislature in *Statutes at
Large*; M.S.Giuseppi, *Naturalizations of Foreign Protestants in the American and
West Indian Colonies* (London, 1921; reprinted Baltimore 1964, 1969, 1979). See
also Pennsylvania Archives, Second Series, 2:347–486; 2) Maryland: Jeffrey A.
Wyand and Florence L. Wyand, *Colonial Maryland Naturalizations* (Baltimore,
1975).

Newspaper citations: All of the newspapers cited in the text have been micro-
filmed. A handy guide to references to Germans in them: Edward W. Hocker,
*Genealogical Data relating to the German Settlers of Pennsylvania and Adjacent
Territory* (Baltimore, 1981).

As an accommodation to American readers, the entries have been arranged and
indexed without reference to umlauts. These two marks above an *a*, *o* or *u* amount
to adding an *e* behind them. In German alphabetizing these letters are treated as
ae, *oe* and *ue*.

Deeds   References to deeds are abstracted as follows:
                          Deed book references; date of transaction; seller,
                          his occupation, his residence, his wife, to pur-
                          chaser, his occupation, his residence, acreage or
                          lot number, location of land sold; how seller ac-
                          quired it.

Patent deeds

References to patent deeds (originals in Pennsylvania Land Office, Harrisburg) are abstracted as follows: Patent book references; warrant, date and to whom; recital of warrant sales if any; patentee; date of transaction; size and location of acreage.

Wills

References to wills are abstracted as follows: (Since many German wills were not recorded, references to dockets have been ignored) Decedent's name, location, occupation (date of will/date of probate). Wife; children (or other heirs). Witnesses; Executors.

Volume I

The Northern Kraichgau

1. The Kraichgau today

Introduction

It is easier to write the history of the Kraichgau than to describe its boundaries. Everyone agrees that it is an area on the east side of the Rhine between the Schwarzwald (Black Forest) and the Odenwald (Oden Forest). This much is visible to a traveler going northwards or southwards along the Rhine. South of Heidelberg the forested hills become lower for some miles before they rise again into the Black Forest. It is also obvious that the Neckar River makes a great bend to the west from its northerly flow a few miles north of Heilbronn, making a great arc around that land between Schwarzwald and Odenwald. The Neckar enters the Rhine just west of Heidelberg. A careful eye will even note a little creek on the map of the area called the Kraich, which flows northwesterly into the Rhine. But further boundaries fail in the precise sense, so that one wag has commented, "Everyone knows where the Kraichgau is not, but no one knows where it really is." In a word *Kraichgau* is a concept as much as an area; it is not a political unit in Germany and has not been since the Middle Ages, when the word described far less of an area than it encompasses today.

The most commonly accepted territory called the Kraichgau may be seen on Map 1, a contemporary German map in fairly widespread use based on recent topographical grouping of Germany. Topographical regions are defined in terms of homogeneous land contour, soil types and native flora. The Kraichgau consists of 1602 square kilometers (about 1000 square miles) of hilly land, whose loamy soil covers both limestone cliffs along stream-carved valleys and red marl, or keuper, hills which project up within it, such as the Eichelberg, which gave its name to one of the families which emigrated from the vicinity to Pennsylvania.

It is a well-watered, rich area, not unlike Pennsylvania in soil, appearance, and climate.

Emigrants from a small portion of the total Kraichgau (see map 3) are the concern of this volume. This area was arbitrarily chosen and no one but the framers of this book consider it a unit. For lack of a better designation for it, the term "northern Kraichgau" has been selected. To be quite honest the unit was created by the expediency of having found enough emigrants from within it to constitute one volume! Emigration did not cease at its borders in any direction. The evidence is already at hand to suggest that from the Palatinate on the other side of the Rhine to the Württemberg villages across the Neckar, up into the Odenwald, and down into the rest of the Kraichgau, the lure of Pennsylvania had its effect.

The villages studied intensively here each possess definite and frequently very old boundaries. In German this territory is called a *Gemarkung*. In recent times, since World War II, many villages have consolidated politically into larger units, especially those around Sinsheim and Eppingen, two of the largest towns in the area. Since the villages are still generally separated physically from one another, they retain their identity. They are listed "Steinsfurt = 6920 Sinsheim" in the text below because in the eighteenth century they were all independent political units. Today they are frequently designated as "Sinsheim-Steinsfurt" and so on. It is good to understand that within each village's territory are the village itself and the fields, meadows and woodlands around it. There may also be a tiny settlement, or *Hof*,

3

somewhere outside the village: a fairly large farm with a handful of houses and
farm buildings for the persons working there. These *Höfe* played an important role
in the emigration to Pennsylvania. There are also some mills, each of which has a
name, scattered along the creeks in the countryside. A few castles or the ruins of
them stand watch here or there over the valleys. Every hill, every field, every
forest, every geological feature of any distinction bears a name, names which
appear in the records sometimes concerning an emigrant. (See Map 7 with entry
542.)

The villages whose emigration to America in the eighteenth century is studied
in this volume, together with their current German zip code and name, are:

> Adelshofen (7519-Eppingen-Adelshofen)
> Adersbach (6920 Sinsheim-Adersbach)
> Asbach (6951 Obrigheim-Asbach)
> Babstadt (6921 Babstadt)
> Bammental (6901)
> Berwangen (6926 Kirchardt-Berwangen)
> Bockschaft (6921 Bockschaft)
> Bonfeld (6927 Bad Rappenau-Bonfeld)
> Daisbach (6923 Waibstadt-Daisbach)
> Daudenzell (6955 Aglasterhausen-Daudenzell)
> Dühren (6920 Sinsheim-Dühren)
> Ehrstädt (6920 Sinsheim-Ehrstädt)
> Eichtersheim (6921 Angelbachtal-Eichtersheim)
> Elsenz (7519 Eppingen-Elsenz)
> Epfenbach (6921 Epfenbach)
> Eppingen (7519)
> Eschelbach (6920 Sinsheim-Eschelbach)
> Eschelbronn (6925)
> Fürfeld (6927 Bad Rappenau-Fürfeld)
> Gauangelloch (6906 Leimen-Gauangelloch)
> Grombach (6921)
> Hasselbach (6921)
> Helmstadt (6928 Bargen-Helmstadt)
> Hilsbach (6921)
> Hoffenheim (6920 Sinsheim-Hoffenheim)
> Ittlingen (6921)
> Kirchardt (6926)
> Massenbach (7101)
> Mauer (6901)
> Meckesheim (6922)
> Michelfeld (6921 Angelbachtal-Michelfeld)
> Mönchzell (6922 Meckesheim-Mönchzell)
> Neckarbischofsheim (6924)
> Neidenstein (6921 Elsenzgau-Neidenstein)
> Obergimpern (6921)
> Bad Rappenau (6927)
> Reihen (6920)

Rohrbach bei Sinsheim (6920 Sinsheim-Rohrbach)
Schatthausen (6908 Wiesloch-Schatthausen)
Schluchtern (7101)
Schwaigern (7103)
Sinsheim (6920)
Stebbach (7519 Gemmingen-Stebbach)
Steinsfurt (6920 Sinsheim-Steinsfurt)
Tairnbach (6909 Mühlhausen-Tairnbach)
Treschklingen (6927 Bad Rappenau-Treschklingen)
Waibstadt (6923)
Waldangelloch (6920 Sinsheim-Waldangelloch)
Zuzenhausen (6921)

The area in question in this volume consists of the drainage system of several creeks. The first of these is the Elsenz, which rises from a spring in the town of the same name. As it flows on its 57 kilometer course to meet the Neckar at Neckargemünd, it receives the Himmelreichbach, Hilsbach, Sulzgraben, Insenbach, Lobbach, and the Schwarzbach (which has itself received the Asbach, Forellenbach, Forstbach, Wartschaftbach, Krebsbach, and the Epfenbach). The second parallels the Elsenz a few miles west of it. This is the Angelbach, which eventually enters the Leimbach and the Rhine. A third is the Lein, or the Gartach, which flows to the east and enters the Neckar at Neckargartach. Since the settlement of villages was nearly always located with respect to streams and since paths, roads and highways usually followed them, the direction of the flow of water frequently became the route of emigration.

2.

In the eighteenth century the population of this area consisted of a mixture of peoples, mostly Germanic, who had settled there in ancient times.

When the continent was a tropical forest 500,000 years ago, the Neckar made a great loop to the south east of the Elsenz as far as Mauer's location today and then encompassed the path of the Elsenz as it returned to what is its current bed. As the river changed to its present course, it left a sandy, fossil-rich area behind. Late in the nineteenth century workers in sand quarries and archeologists found fragments of the remains of prehistoric animals from tropical climates as well as the smaller skeletal remains of frigid climate zones left from the ice age which followed the tropical times. Scholars reasoned that human remains might also be found and on 21 October 1907 they were discovered. Workers in a quarry near Mauer watched while Daniel Hartmann pulled out the lower jaw of a human. Scientists promptly dubbed the creature "Heidelberg Man." His age is dated to 200,000 to 500,000 years ago. He was one of the first group of humans to live in Europe, but his tenure there was cut short by the return of the ice. Hartmann, Pennsylvanians will be glad to learn, told his comrades in the tavern, "Isch hab de Adam gfunne."

When the ice retreated again, Neanderthal man lived for 100,000 years in western Europe until about 40,000 years ago. Though no direct evidence of him seems to exist from the Kraichgau, he did know how to use fire and how to make it from flintstone, whose sole German deposit is in the southern Schwarzwald. In

2. Germany's western part, the *Bundesrepublik*, showing the Kraichgau

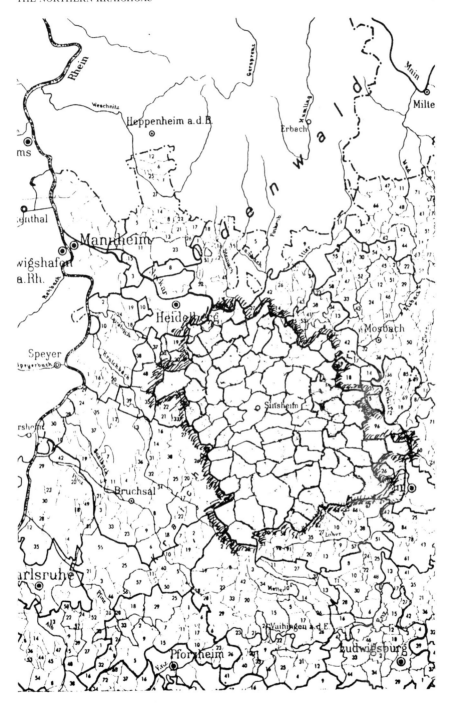

3. The Kraichgau showing the area covered by this book

Neolithic times—the late stone age—people did live in the Kraichgau again, who left artifacts from their life behind in the soil. The first of these were the *Bandceramiker*—the band potters—named by the shape of their vessel decoration. They were farmers, they lived in wooden houses, they grouped their houses together in primitive villages. They were replaced by the *Schnurceramiker,* who impressed a string into the neck of their jars as decoration. Like other Germanic peoples after them they came from the northeast. They too lived in wooden houses covered with straw, they learned to bore through stones and had the wheel; they had priests and, to judge from their grave mounds, they had some belief in an after-life. The Celts succeeded them during what is called the bronze age which began ca. 800 B.C. and was followed by another time of glacial descent until the beginning of the Christian era. Celtic bronze, gold and silver objects reached a high level of achievement, but archeologists have been able to piece together the story of the way they lived only gradually. About 100 years before the birth of Christ tribes of Swabians came from the Elbe and drove the Celts further south. Some of them remained behind, however, so that the population became a mixture of Celtic and Germanic folk under the Suebian control.

At the same time, the Romans began to push their way northward across the Alps. By 15 B.C. they extended the northern border of their empire along the Danube westward to its source and jumped a line from there to Lake Constance, from which point the imperial border followed the Rhine. Strassburg and Mainz were originally Roman settlements. In the first Christian century the Romans pushed their sovereignty east and north to the Neckar. By 117 A.D. they had completed fortifications from Wimpfen on the Neckar north to Wörth on the Main. From there it was only a few kilometers east again to the *Limes,* the fortification the Romans had built to keep the wild Germanic tribes behind it out. Within the area of Roman control military veterans settled in residences which bore all the accoutrements of their culture from hot and cold baths to sub-floor heating. They farmed the fields, some of them already opened by the *Bandceramiker,* sometimes in tracts as large as entire *Germarkungen.* An archeological find bears evidence that a Roman provinicial subdivision was named *Alisinensis,* an ancient Latin form of the Germanic word which is now the name of the Elsenz.

About 260 A.D. and in some areas earlier Alemanni tribes broke through the Roman fortifications and drove the Romans out, to the south and to the west across the Rhine. The battles lasted until the fall of Rome. Since most of the names of natural features in the Kraichgau are Germanic, scholars believe that the population under Roman sovereignty was never purely Roman so that the Alemanni found Germanic folk living here and there when they arrived. They organized themselves into districts, each of which was a *Gau.* In the whole Kraichgau, as the name is used today, there were many such *Gaue,* frequently named for a creek. In the area covered in this volume there were parts of the Kraichgau itself, the Elsenzgau and the Gartachgau. By a fluke of history the term *Kraichgau* survived into modern times. Farther south the term *Breisgau* also continued to be used. The university town of Freibourg and its Münster church reign over it.

It was the clans, who together formed the *Gau,* who created and occupied the villages. Since there had been Romans in the area, one might have expected their settlements, their residences, to become the basis for Germanic villages. The

Alemanni did assume use of the fields the Romans had farmed. Field names (in German, *Flurnamen*) are often substantial clues to the settlement history of an area, somewhat as pottery remains are in archeological investigations. Some *Flurnamen*, such as *Haidenacker* (heathen field) are direct links to the Romans. The Romans also had roads for communication and commerce and military transport. But both roads and farmsteads crumbled into ruins before the Germans and sometimes the forest grew right over them. The discovery of ruins and artifacts continues to illumine the extent of Roman culture in the area. But about all their successors used them for was as a source of stones to scavenger for household construction once the wood supply ran low and as paths to lead their herds about.

In fact factors closely related to the economic use of the land determined where the new owners created their towns. They were initially cattle breeders, even before the movements of these tribes brought them into the Kraichgau. Cultivating soil was adjunct to breeding, although it was more important than hunting or fishing. But this cultivation was a wild, unregulated field-grass economy by which a piece of land was planted for a year and then allowed to lie fallow until it could be used again. Plowing was only superficial, fertilizing unknown, and the fallow fields over which the cattle went to pasture far outnumbered the plowed ones. Hogs were even more important than beef in their economy, but the hogs preferred the moist wooded meadows into which they and the beef were driven. With a lifespan of about two years, Alemanni hogs survived well in the forests of the Kraichgau which then produced a good acorn crop every three years. Keeping cattle over the winter was a problem, too, though the relatively mild and snow-free winters of the Kraichgau simplified it. Hay was cut and kept; in the town name *Bargen*, the Alemanni word *parac*, hay hut, is preserved, as reflected in the English word *barracks*, one of whose meanings is a hay storage building. Spelt was the prevalent grain, but herbs and textile fibers were raised near the houses of the people and fruit trees, such as crabapples and wild pears, were planted around the villages.

Forests were also important as sources of wood, for housing and energy, as well as of berries, fruit and honey. It was, however, the valleys with their good meadows and dependable water supplies which determined the places villages appeared. A good site was near the meadow, forest, a clean stream, and the loamy fields. Valleys also provided some protection against the wind, important since Alemanni houses were also built entirely of wood and roofed with straw or reeds and fire was always a threat. Thus we find the earliest settlements on the valley slopes at the end of the loamy topsoil, frequently near the spot a creek enters a larger stream of water. The valley of the Elsenz with wide expanses was ideally suited for settlement. The Alemanni soon learned to fertilize the soil perhaps by observing what happened when rain washed the lime-rich loam onto the fields.

The Merovingian Franks under their ruler Chlodwig conquered the Alemanni shortly before the year 500 and superimposed themselves on the population. Once again there were remnants of the earlier stock which remained. The Franks adopted the *Gau* system of territorial organization, they added royal control of forests and of militarily significant places and major town sites, such as Eppingen, and their nobles gained ownership of other significant towns such as Sinsheim. In time they introduced the three-field-economy which they had learned from the Romans. They also brought Christianity (in its Roman form and not in the Arian variation some other Germanic tribes adopted), but the poorly trained and overworked priests faced a difficult task in making the faith a reality among the people. Sometime between 600 and 650 Christianity came into the area of this volume, by way of the bishopric at Worms, but missionary work continued until the year 1000. Church buildings were not erected until about the year 750 and cemeteries were laid out with them. Until then Christians were buried in the old heathen cemeteries, but their graves are to be distinguished when excavated by the lack of burial gifts in them. In the time of the Carolingian Franks monasteries began to appear; at one at Lorsch many documents about the area were written and preserved. Between the 760s and the year 800, sixteen of the villages studied here are mentioned for the first known time in these codices.

Even more villages appeared in Carolingian times as the population grew. As they separated themselves from existing towns, the newer settlements had to be content with fewer forest or meadowlands and a greater percentage of fields. Sometimes even their names suggest this, as in the case of Michel*feld*. In this time too ownership of villages by cloisters, dioceses, and noble or royal families became a fixed pattern. A few of the newer towns, such as Neidenstein, were built at the foot of a castle, sprawling down a hill.

Cities developed somewhat later, but usually in connection with an older village alongside which they grew up and which they eventually eclipsed. Two factors were responsible for the development of these cities: an old, highly developed agricultural economy, which created an internal market; and traffic routes, some of which brought merchants, customers and wares from afar together. A weekly market provided the greatest impetus to city development. The monarchy reserved the right to dispense the market privilege, as indeed it later elevated cities to that status. Neither Sinsheim, Eppingen or Bischofsheim had the significant roads necessary to develop into great cities, but before the Middle Ages had run out, each was designated imperially as a city. The rebuilding of roads through the Kraichgau, which had fallen into decay after the Romans left, enhanced its natural character as a cross-roads land. While these brought commerce, they would also bring marauding armies in time.

The feudal system settled down on the Kraichgau under Frankish rule. At its peak was the Holy Roman Emperor, the successor of Charlemagne; at its bottom, the serf. Though much pagaentry and pomp surrounded the emperor, he can be called sovereign over his vast domain only in a relative sense of the term. Actual power lay with the owners of the many territories within the empire, one of which was the church. One of the landowners in the Kraichgau was the elector of the Palatinate, the *Kurfurst*, one of the seven persons who selected the emperor. Others were the bishop of Speyer and the ducal family in Württemberg. But many of the villages were owned by noble families, the knights of the Ritterkanton of the Kraichgau as it was called: proud, but really petty rulers of various tracts a few miles square in size here and there. These families came and went, with time, but there was always someone to inherit their lands. Trading towns or parts of towns back and forth by sale, swap, or as part of a dowery became common between all these landowners. It is difficult and for our purposes unnecessary to trace all of these deals, but they can be extremely important to the genealogist as time rolls on, for in order to locate records of a civil nature, one must know the sovereign who ruled over the place. By the eighteenth century the picture as presented on Map 5 is essentially valid. Only the Napoleonic reorganization of Europe early in the nineteenth century totally eradicated the mottled Medieval picture by replacing smaller units with simpler, but larger ones.

The Reformation came to the Kraichgau, including its northeastern villages, by way of the religious preferences of these various village owners. Already in 1555, at the end of one series of religious wars, a principle was enunciated which had far-reaching implications for German religious history: whoever had political sovereignty over an area could determine its religious faith. This principle was reinforced again and again, at the same time that at first only two and then only three confessions were given legal recognition. These were the Roman Catholic, the Lutheran and, after some time, the Reformed. In the Palatinate the latter took on a Zwinglian tone, rather than stringently Calvinistic one, and the Heidelberg Catechism (1563) became its basic handbook. All three legally admitted forms of the Christian faith came into the Kraichgau (See Map 6). In essence, those villages owned by the Bishopric of Speyer remained Catholic. The villages belonging to the petty nobility were Lutheran, as were those belonging to Württemberg. The Palatinate was another story.

The Palatinate became Lutheran in 1556, Reformed in 1563. By Palatinate here we mean the territories owned by the Elector, not all of the area called "Palatinate" today, which latter was, like the Kraichgau, owned by various sovereigns, and parts of which also frequently changed hands. During the Thirty Years' War a recatholicization of the Palatinate set in, which was only partly reversed by the settlement at the end of the war. The Lutherans then did retain their rights to the knightly towns and were even permitted to conduct worship according to the Lutheran rite at the request of a minority of Lutherans in a given village. But many areas were not returned to the Reformed at all. When the Palatine royal family of Pfalz-Simmern died out in 1685, their Catholic successors, the Pfalz-Neuburg line declared (1698) that the entire Palatinate would henceforth have the *Simultaneum* (use of one church building by both Catholic and Reformed congregations). In 240 places Catholic worship was inaugurated and 100 Reformed pastors were removed from their parishes. Under political pressure from Prussia, England, Holland and Sweden, the "Palatine Church Division" of 1705–1707 was effected. According to its terms, 5/7 of the parishes became Reformed, 2/7 Catholic and none Lutheran. Twenty-seven congregations on the right side of the Rhine became Catholic; any residue of Reformed members was served by nearby Reformed pastors. The Lutherans could preserve their existence only by raising funds in other parts of Germany and for a long time their small congregations were filials of distant or even non-Palatine Lutheran parishes. Gradually in the eighteenth century they were able to establish modest congregations again in some towns. Even then the Reformed clergy could collect fees for pastoral acts Lutheran pastors performed and record them in their own records, although the 1707 agreement had allowed each group to keep its own record. This fact accounts for two congregations in some towns, like Sinheim or Eppingen, and for Lutheran pastoral acts to be recorded in Reformed records, such as at Kirchardt. In the nineteenth century the Lutheran and Reformed churches in Baden, to which most of the Kraichgau now belonged, united to form one Evangelical or Protestant church there. About the same time,

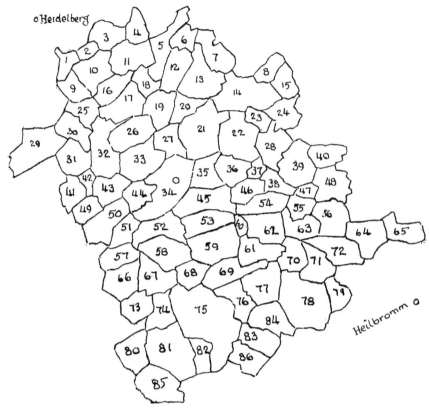

4. The northern portion of the Kraichgau, showing the *Gemarkungen*, or village boundaries, included here.

1. Gaiberg	30. Baiertal	59. Ittlingen
2. Waldhilsbach	31. Dielheim	60. Bockschaft
3. Neckargmünd	32. Horrenberg	61. Berwangen
4. Dilsberg	33. Hoffenheim	62. Kirchardt
5. Lobenfeld	34. Sinsheim	63. Fürfeld
6. Waldwimmersbach	35. Rohrbach	64. Biberach
7. Reichartshausen	36. Adersbach	65. Obereisesheim
8. Daudenzell	37. Hasselbach	66. Odenheim
9. Gauangelloch	38. Untergimpern	67. Elsenz
10. Bammental	39. Obergimpern	68. Adelshofen
11. Wiesenbach	40. Siegelsbach	69. Richen
12. Spechbach	41. Mühlhausen	70. Massenbachhausen
13. Epfenbach	42. Tairnbach	71. Massenbach
14. Helmstadt	43. Eschelbach	72. Kirchhausen
15. Asbach	44. Dühren	73. Landshausen
16. Mauer	45. Steinsfurt	74. Rohrbach am Giesshübel
17. Meckesheim	46. Ehrstädt	75. Eppingen
18. Mönchzell	47. Babstadt	76. Stebbach
19. Eschelbronn	48. Bad Rappenau	77. Gemmingen
20. Neidenstein	49. Eichtersheim	78. Schwaigern
21. Waibstadt	50. Michelfeld	79. Schluchtern
22. Neckarbischofsheim	51. Waldangelloch	80. Zaisenhausen
23. Flinsbach	52. Hilsbach	81. Sulzfeld
24. Bargen	53. Reihen	82. Mühlbach
25. Schatthausen	54. Grombach	83. Niederhofen
26. Zuzenhausen	55. Treschklingen	84. Stetten am Heuchelberg
27. Daisbach	56. Bonfeld	85. Kürnbach
28. belonged to Bad Wimpfen	57. Eichelberg	86. Kleingartach
29. Wiesloch	58. Weiler	

political subdivisions began to keep records of births, marriages and deaths as well.

One event not quite a century before the great emigration played as important a role in the population history of the Kraichgau as the emigration itself did. That was the series of battles between 1618 and 1648 which are known as the Thirty Years' War. This was the end of the military attempt to settle the religious division the Reformation had caused. It was also a devastating demolition of many towns and caused the death of many people. For our study it is significant to note that as a result only six church records from before 1650 survive among the villages here listed, whereas all would have had them from the time of the Reformation on. Eschelbronn was totally depopulated by 1648 and only nine persons remained in Zuzenhausen. In Ittlingen, only the stump of the church tower remained.

This gap in population was surprisingly rapidly filled by immigrants from other areas of Germany, but especially from over-populated Switzerland. The latter wave of people included many Anabaptists, or *Wiedertäuffer*, as the records also call them—Mennonites to use their current name today. Although adherents of an officially illegal religion, they were tolerated at first because of their skills as farmers. Often settling on a secluded *Hof*, they practiced their religion quietly, sometimes even with fairly good relations with the Lutheran or Reformed clergy. In time, of course, they suffered losses by conversion to the sanctioned faiths, sometimes occasioned by intermarriages. In time, too, the exemptions from military service and church fees were cancelled. Presently special assessments were added as fees for permission to practice a religion not lawfully allowed. These amounted to increasing oppression, as did another regulation which did not permit their number in any one place to increase. Added to the promise of religious freedom and cheap, abundant land in Pennsylvania, these repressive stipulations drove many Mennonites to emigrate alongside their Lutheran and Reformed neighbors. But whereas the Lutherans and Reformed left records by which it is generally possible to determine who emigrated, the Mennonites did not, making the problem of finding their homes in the Kraichgau a tantalizingly difficult one. (See Appendix A)

The coming of refugees after the Thirty Years' War, many of them Swiss, was the last major movement of new peoples into the Kraichgau until after World War II. The coming and going of people and the rebuilding of society and the villages of the Kraichgau was in process in the first half of the eighteenth century when the persons named in this volume left for America. Without question they left for a new land and a new start, with much building and social change there. In a sense one could argue that the world they left behind was really not much different.

3.
Most of the persons who emigrated were peasants. Notable exceptions were three clergymen: Lutherans Joshua Harrsch/Kocherthal, Anthony Jacob Henckel and Reformed George Michael Weiss. To them one might add a few schoolmasters. It is important for us to know something about village society in the eighteenth century and something about village life.

The clergy and the schoolmasters, as the only educated persons within the village, were at the top of their society. Whereas a pastor had to be a university scholar, schoolmasters had to pass an examination in which they demonstrated

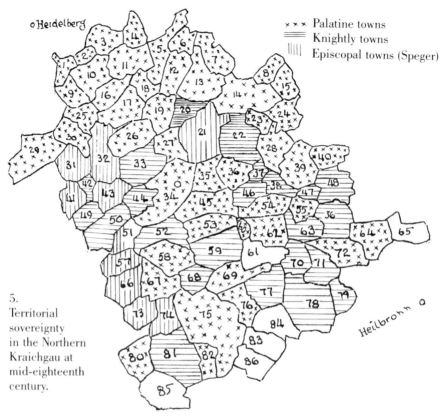

o Heidelberg

××× Palatine towns
≡≡≡ Knightly towns
||||| Episcopal towns (Speger)

5.
Territorial
sovereignty
in the Northern
Kraichgau at
mid-eighteenth
century.

their skills in writing, reading, fancy penmanship and singing. Their position, bolstered by the latter two skills, generally afforded them a high standing. But schoolmasters frequently had supplementary occupations such as weaving or tailoring, and they were responsible for the parish organ and the church's bells. They worked the *Schulland*, a tract of ground owned by the congregation for their support. They always lived in the schoolhouse. School itself was frequently only a wintertime event. The income of the schoolmaster was derived from tuition (*Schulgeld*), the church and the political community, but many, especially popular schoolmasters received gifts in kinds (*Naturalien*) from the parents.

The miller was a highly placed member of the community, as was the innkeeper, especially if they held considerable land. Each inn had its own name, and in many cases inns remain with the same names they bore in the eighteenth century. The records often designate the innkeeper (*Wirt* or *Gastwirt*) by the name of his inn, such as the *Adlerwirt* (innkeeper at the sign of the eagle) or the *Engelwirt* (innkeeper at the sign of the angel). The rich peasant farmer could come near the top of society if he had much land; his position varied according to his wealth. Crafts which demanded both skill and preparation, such as butcher or baker, dyer or wagonmaker, or saddler, not each of which would be present in every village, fell next in the hierarchy of standing. A *Chirurgus* was a non-university trained doctor who treated minor wounds or kicks from animals. Shoemakers, smiths, tailors were less highly esteemed and linenweavers too; these were the lower crafts. Below them

x x x Reformed
=== Lutheran
||||| Roman Catholic

6. Religious
   dominance
   in the
   Northern
   Kraichgau at
   mid-eighteenth
   century.

in village social order were the servants (*Dienstboden, Dienstknechte,* or *Dienst-mägde*), day workers (*Taglöhner*), and depending upon how transient they were the peddlers (*Hausierer*). Herdsmen were at the fringe of society; a *Rindehirt* or *Viehhirt* (cattletender) was somewhat better off than a *Schäffer* (shepherd) or a *Schweinehirt* (hogkeeper). These people moved about frequently seeking better opportunities, as, ironically, schoolmasters—in spite of their higher standing—also did.

Seen from the political point-of-view, a citizen (*Bürger*) had full rights in a village. The right to such citizenship could be purchased as one made his way up in life, or inherited, and was variously difficult to obtain. A mere inhabitant (*Inwohner or Einwohner*) had fewer rights than citizens and obviously less wealth and prestige. Other terms, *Hintersasse* or *Schutzverwandten* can have various meanings. There was no uniform constitution for the area. The government of daily life in a village rested with a *Gericht*, a term which means *court* in modern German, but which entails more in eighteenth century village life. The *Gericht* consisted of three to seven persons from the village, the richer farmers and citizens, generally able to read and write. They served without pay to perform minor judicial and legislative functions. They judged in minor cases, wrote inventories, set precedents as necessary and had authority over citizens, inhabitants and strangers in the place alike. German records refer to these persons by several designations which have no difference in meaning: *des Gerichts* (literally, of the *Gericht*, i.e., a member), *Gerichtsmann, Gerichtsverwandten, Gerichtsschöffe*. To translate these terms *jury-*

man, court official, court representative, councilman may only confuse American readers with their concept of neat division of government into executive, legislative and judicial branches. For this reason all of these terms have been left untranslated below, for in fact no one word conveys the entire picture. To refer to a *Gerichtsver-wandt* as a judge simply creates a false, and inflated, picture.

In some places there was an adjunct to the *Gericht*, an *Ausschuss* of 12, 18 or 24 more citizens.

At the head of the *Gericht*, as its chairman, but at the same time as the executive, was the *Schultheiss*. Perhaps mayor would convey the meaning of this term, or president of the town council; but it is best to leave the German word untranslated, as has been done in this book, rather than falsely simplify the matter. If a village was owned by two landlords there could be a *Gericht* and *Schultheiss* for each part, but the designation of a *Schultheiss* by an adjective formed from the name of the overlord family also points to the fact that the owners had their representatives, too, in village affairs. Sometimes these men are called *Anwalt;* they too were part of the *Gericht*. They were the alternatives to the *Schutlheiss* and since they were selected by the owners, they had the responsibility to look out for the owners' interests. Though a *Rechtsanwalt* today is an attorney, and the shorter form of the word means the same thing, to translate it as attorney or lawyer here misses the point. The landlords also had an *Amtsmann* who worked on their behalf. All of these terms and others were frequently entered by the clergy as designations of citizens. A fondness for title and position, for a place under the sun, plays a role here too. One should understand the terms all to describe relatively minor officials in village life.

The medieval system of vassalage still prevailed at the time of emigration, but its days were already numbered. This means that the peasants were bound as serfs to the nobility who in theory gave them military protection in return for their compulsory labor (*Frondienst*) on the estates of the nobles. In one village, for instance, the owners of the farms were obliged to provide twelve days of labor a year with two oxen or horses, for which they received compensation and expenses. The vassalage was not entirely dissolved until the nineteenth century. A tithe was also collected, originally and ostensibly for the church, but the rights to the tithe were sold or traded, against the will of both papacy and church councils, so that only a part of it went for the support of the local church and schools. Tithes too were finally discontinued early in the nineteenth century. Tithed were the produce of the fields (the "great" tithe), of the garden (the "small" tithe, of cabbages, beets, fruits, flax, peas, lentils, and beans) and animals (the "blood" tithe of geese, little pigs, calves, fillies). Finally ground rents were also collected, which were cancelled in the nineteenth century by settlement with the nobility. In sum, the peasant was not a free man. He was bound to a master, as the whole manumission process which so many emigrants simply ignored suggests. Nor did he really own any land outright, but only the right to its use.

The church congregation also had a governing body composed of elders *(Älteste or Kirchencenzor)* and deacons *Vorsteher*) and other officials. The *Almosenpfleger* was the administrator of the parish finances, which could be greater than the political community's; the *Heiligenpfleger* was responsible for church-owned buildings and their maintenance. Strict regulations governed the moral life of the community, requiring church attendance, forbidding pastors other than the one of the village from performing marriages or baptisms, controlling how closely related persons marrying one another dared to be or how soon after a spouse's death the survivor could remarry, and punishing the not-infrequent cases of premature "*concubitum*," as pregnancy before marriage was termed.

To learn a craft or trade, a youth attended school for six years. He then was apprenticed to a master, whom his father paid, to learn whatever it might be. The term was generally for two to three years and protective legislation surrounded the procedure. Given adolescent nature, there was inevitable conflict, running away and punishment. But the youth who completed his training became a *Gesell*, which really meant in the village that he was trained, let us say, as a baker. The title *baker* would only become his if he amassed sufficient capital to acquire it—or happened to marry the widow of a former baker. This explains the reason that some women were older than their husbands. Lacking money or a convenient marriage, one might remain a *Gesell* for life.

Only in the larger towns were there guilds of craftsmen (*Zünfte*). There, too, there were also higher classes of citizens called patricians (*Patrizier*). The guild member and patricians do not figure in the story below.

While one would expect the lower classes of society to emigrate, the picture is told accurately in the panoply of occupations listed below. Schoolmaster, Chirurgus, butcher, baker, even candlestickmaker (in the form of the wives) are all here. If there seem to be many persons with no named occupation, who were therefore farmers, and more weavers and tailors, there were more of them in the world. Not only economic circumstances drove people to emigrate. Personal moral untowardness, the death of a spouse, even the lure of adventure and the unknown played their role, too. The chance to start over, the opportunity for personal improvement, the promise of a "new" world all intertwined in the motives of these more than one thousand souls who left *Haus* and *Hof* for Pennsylvania, for America. That not all were satisfied with what they found is attested by records here of those who returned to stay. That some prospered is also attested by return trips to Germany, in one instance to acquire a second wife. That communication between old home and new was lively is attested by the notations Pastor Schoder made in the Ittlingen church record in 1749 about the persons from the place who died at sea en route to America.

It should be understood that relatively few bothered with the formality of obtaining the necessary manumission—permission to forsake their medieval obligations. Most left, as the Germans say, *bei Nacht und Nebel*, under cover of night or fog. But, in fact, their departure was often no great secret. Pastors often wrote out a *Taufschein*, baptismal certification, to accompany them. Ironically perhaps the naive peasants assumed that proof of legitimacy and Christianity would be needed in their new homeland. At any rate, these documents were often the only proof the emigrants were who they said they were and often, too, their last memento of their old *Heimat*.

4.

For many of the villages included in this study there exist local histories in the German language, often rich in details that might be of value and surely would be of interest to genealogists. A partial bibliography of them is given here. American readers will understand the motivation behind some works which appeared in the 1930s, but which are generally useful for the facts they offer.

Daisbach

H. Steidel, *Ortsgeschichte von Daisbach* (Heidelberg, 1919)

Dühren

Karl Schuhmacher, *Geschichte von Dühren* (Sinsheim, 1931).

Ehrstädt

Friedrich Hub, *Ehrstädt und Schloss Neuhaus* (1967)

Eichtersheim

G. Schlechmann, *Chronik von Eichtersheim* (Eppingen, 1948)

Epfenbach

J. E. Zaph, *Unsre Heimat und Sitte, Geschichte von Epfenbach und seine Bewohner* (Heidelberg, 1936)

Fr. Blink, *Heimatbuch der Gemeinde Epfenbach* (Epfenbach, 1927)

Elsenz

Franz Gehrig, *Dorf und Pfarrei Elsenz* (1960)

Eppingen

A. Braun, *Geschichte der Stadt Eppingen* (Eppingen, 1914)

A. Wirth, *Kirchengeschichte von Eppingen* (Karlsruhe, 1879)

Eschelbronn

W. Sambel, *Eschelbronn* (Eschelbronn, 1931)

Helmstadt

W. Senges, *Geschichte des Kraichdorfes Helmstadt* (Helmstadt, 1937)

Hilsbach

Franz Gehrig, *Chronik von Hilsbach* (Hilsbach, 1979)

Hoffenheim

H. E. Neu, *Aus Vergangenheit und Gegenwart von Hoffenheim* (Hoffenheim, 1953)

Ittlingen

Gustav Neuwirth, *Geschichte der Gemeinde Ittlingen* (1981)

Kirchhardt (Berwangen and Bockschaft)

Gustav Neuwirth, *Geschichte der Gemeinde Kirchhardt, und der Ortsteile Berwangen und Bockschaft* (1978)

Meckesheim
F. Zimmermann, *Ortsgeschichte von Meckesheim* (1937)

Neidenstein
R. Heid, *Burg und Dorf Neidenstein* (Eschelbronn, 1928)

Bad Rappenau
K. Noll, *Ortsgeschichte von Rappenau* (1907)
Gustav Neuwirth, *Geschichte von Bad Rappenau* (1978)

Richen
Heinrich Meny, *Geschichte des Dorfes Richen* (1928)

Schatthausen
A. Pfisterer, *Chronik von Schatthausen* (Schatthausen, 1955)

Sinsheim
Wilhelmi, *Geschichte von Sinsheim* (1856)

Waldangelloch
K. Keller, *Aus Waldangellochs Vergangenheit* (Eppingen, 1935)

The most recent of these histories is that of Ittlingen, from which an unbelievably large number of persons emigrated. We will publish several lists of names of residents of Ittlingen included in this volume as an example of what material one may find in such local chronicles. Then we will relate one incident from the community's history which illustrates the sort of event which may have encouraged people to emigrate. (* = Family names represented among emigrants)

Ittlingen residents named in 1579

Peter Johann
Martin Eberhardt
*Hans Conrad
Hans Gurrer
Daniel Hermann

Kaspar Volz
Wendel Fell
Hanns Eberhard, butcher
Hans Mezger, baker

Ittlingen Hof-names which pre-date 1648

Hofmannshof
Kellershof
Kurtzenhof
*Eichelbergerhof
Ottenhof
Kräutershof
Pflügersdorferhof
*Schweizerhof
Flockenhof
*Bärenhof
Mosershof

Mayleshof or Meilshof
*   *   with the Konradhof*
*Bernhardshof
Fleckenhof
Hahnenhof
*Romigshof
Schottenhof

Ittlingen residents named in 1695

Hans Martin Oberacker
Johann Adrian Michel
Hans Wittner, miller at the lower mill
Peter Moser
Jost Bützle

Ittlingen residents named in 1718
(The leading citizens signed a document and added their seals which are described)

Johann Dietrich vom Berg, Kronenwirt	(unclear)
Johann Heinrich Schuchmann, smith	(horseshoe, tongs, file)
Caspar Caspari, *Schultheiss*	(aged 85, did not sign)
Andreas Wagner, *Anwalt*	(horseshoe)
Anastasius Fleck, Sr., *Hofbauer*	(plowshare, 6-pointed stars)
*Hanss Adam Romich	(Wheeled plow)
Johann Dietrich Schuchmann	(3 flowers with stem)
*Erasmus Uhler	(plowshare)
Andreas Betz	(figure 8 on its side on a ring—pretzel?)
Jost Frank	
Johann Ihle	(unclear)
Anastasius Fleck, Jr.	(same as A. Fleck, Sr.)
Johann Martin Schuchmann	(horse)
*Jacob Conrad	(human figure)
*Jerg Huber	
Adam Komert	
*Hans Georg Schweitzer	

1751

(In 1751 the two landlord families decided that a new survey of the boundaries of Ittlingen should be made and new boundary stones set, in order to end strife with neighboring villages. 192 new stones were needed! Witnesses to the process, according to ancient rights, were named in a document worth our attention.)

Johann Martin Schuchmann, *Schultheiss*
Johann Jakob Schuchmann, *Verwalter* for the
Gemmingen-Hornberg family
Ferdinand vom Berg, *Jäger* (hunter) from Gemmingen

Old Citizens (Alte Bürger)

Michael Voltz	Andreas Blank
*Jacob Bernhard	Joh. Heinr. Schuchmann, Sr.

Field judges (Feldrichter)

*David Hottenstein, *Anwalt*
Hans Georg Fischer

*Balthasar Romig or Romich
*Andreas Uhler

Younger Citizens (Junge Bürger)

Gemmingen side
Hans Georg Fuchs
Johann Martin Fritschle
Ernst Funk
Andreas Voltz
Jacob Meyer
Jeremias Vollmer, Jr.

Hornberger side
*Valentin Uhler
*Georg Schweitzer, Jr.
Wilhelm Strudel
*Heinrich Uhler
Sebastian Reinhard
Jakob Ziegler

Single sons of citizens (Ledige Bürgersöhne)

*Jacob Hottenstein
Johann Jakob Griner
Peter Blank
*Jacob Weber
Georg Wilhelm Reych

Michael Voltz
Andreas Kappis
*Heinrich Schweitzer
Johann Dietrich Schuchmann
Hyronimus Keller
*Georg Michael Weber

Schoolboys (Schulknaben)

Georg Heinrich Schuchmann
*Michael Uhler
*Johannes Romig (Romich)
Johannes Schuchmann
Johann Adam Kappis
Johannes Raupp
Christoph Heiser

*Johann Leonhard Hottenstein
Friedrich Gruner
Andreas Lilli
Georg Michael Keller
Conrad Landschab
*Michael Klemm
Daniel vom Berg

1752

(A list of citizens exists which contains the names of the twelve members of the *Gericht*, 24 members of the *24er Ausschuss*, a lesser council, and other citizens. Not all the names could be read because of water damage. Missing numbers represent illegible names. At the end of the list, not surprisingly, are a dozen Jewish persons, four Mennonites and 21 widows. There are 140 heads of families, from which Neuwirth assumes a population of about 630 souls. By his factor, the 64 emigrating families would have accounted for 288 additional persons.)

1. Johann Martin Schuchmann, Schultheiß
*2. David Hottenstein, Anwalt (Vertreter des Schultheißen)
*3. Jacob Bernhard
4. Heinrich Floch
*5. Balthes Romig
*6. Ulrich Uhler
*7. Johannes Geiger, Schneider

8. Ludwig vom Berg, Löwenwirt
9. Jacob Blanck, Sattler
10. Michael Volz (Voltz)
11. Georg Klein, Krämer
12. Ludwig Keller
13. Andreas Blanck
14. Heinrich Schuchmann, alt
*15. Georg Schweizer, alt
16. Heinrich Schuchmann, jung, Ochsenwirt
17. Jakob Fritschle
18. Valentin Floch
19. Andreas Barth
20. Jeremias Vollmer, alt
*21. Andreas Uhler
22. Hannß Jerg Fischer
23. Johannes Röckle, barber
24. Johannes Raupp
27. Johannes Raupp
28. Caspar Bauer
29. Christoph Ziegler
30. Friedrich Wirth
31. Jacob Grimmerdinger
32. Philipp Ziegler
33. Heinrich Funk, Schütz
*34. Hannß Jerg Schumacher
35. Christian Hoffmann
36. Andreas Umberger
37. Hannß Jerg Limbach
38. Leonhard Schweizer
39. Mathäus Schiller
40. Georg Weuber
41. Valentin Uhler
42. Ludwig Schulz
43. Hannß Uhler
44. Michel Wendling
45. Dietrich Schuchmann
46. Georg Michael Keller
47. Abraham Schwiz
48. Conrad Seubert
49. Andreas Volz
50. Jakob Wuber (Weber?)
51. Georg Wagner
52. Wilhelm Klein
*53. Jacob Uhler alt
58. Martin Volz
59. Jacob Schlauch
60. Andreas Brenner

61. Jacob Singer
*62. Michel Maag
*63. Johann Georg Maag
64. Johann Georg Würster
65. Ernst Funk
66. Jakob Meyer, Adlerwirt
67. Wilhelm Strudel, Straußwirt
68. Hannß Jerg Rothacker
69. Martin Fritschle
70. Anastasius Friedle
71. Abraham Arbeither
72. Jeremias Vollmar, jung
*73. Johann Heinrich Uhler
74. Jacob Ziegler
75. Johann Guckholz
76. Michel Saiffert
77. Heinrich Fleck
78. Valentin Fleck
*79. Michael Hofmann
80. illegible
81. Michel Aigenmann
82. Heinrich Fritschle
83. Jacob Keller
84. Johannes Waibel
85. Jacob Groner (Grumer?)
86. Wilhelm Pflaum
87. Michael Lille (Liller)
88. Christian Roth
89. Jacob Sieber
90. Michael Link
91. Peter Diem
92. Jacob Bachmann
93. Michael Ebert
*94. Johann Kilian
95. Sebastian Reichert
*96. Georg Wendel Romig
97. Hannß Martin Wageneck
98. Conrad Lutz
99. Andreas Straub
*100. Jakob Bernhardt, jung
101. Johann Jacob Schuchmann, Verwalter
102. Andreas Crumreyh
103. Hannß Georg Böhringer

JEWS

104. Jung Marx
105. Alt Marx

106. Marx Gerpon
107. Marum
108. Jeßel
109. Caijum (auch Cajum)
110. Jankoff
111. Salomon
112. Seligmann
113. Samuel
114. Jung Cajum
115. Darich

MENNONITES

116. Jakob Krautter (auch Krauter)
117. Jakob Krautter, jung
118. Martin Krautter
119. Hannß Gräß

In order to provide a perspective that these lists frankly could not give, we name here the emigrants from Ittlingen identified in this book. Those whose family names occur in the lists above are starred. The fact that many emigrants' surnames do not occur as recently after their departure as 1752 indicates several things: they were members of families all of whose members migrated out; they were members of highly mobile social classes; the population, as Gustav Neuwirth says, "fluctuated greatly." The landlords of the village brought servants and tenants from their widely scattered possessions, who married into existing families of the village.

Elias Aff
Michael Allgayer children
*Joh. Ulrich Bär
Matthaeus Bender
Joh. Dietrich Benedict
Melchior Benedict
*Hans Henrich Bernhard
Conrad Bissecker
Joh. Gottlieb Breuninger
Joh. Martin Breuninger
*Hans Martin Conrad
Joh. Jacob Dambach
*Friedrich Eichelberger
*Joh. Georg Eichelberger
Philipp Adam Endler
*Jacob Geiger
*Joh. Georg Geiger
*Joh. Valentin Geiger
Johannes Grob
Paulus Hartman
Joh. Henrich Hartmann
*Henrich Hoffmann
*Christoph Hoffman
Johannes Holl

Andres Holtzbaum
Andreas Honetter
*Joh. David Hottenstein
*Joh. Jacob Hottenstein
*Joh. Jacob Hottenstein
*Andreas Huber
*Balthasar Huber
*Joh. Jacob Huber
*Ludwig Huber
*Philip Dietrich Huber
Adam Kautzmann
Joh. Heinrich Kautzmann
*Michael Killian
Frantz Klebsattel
*Hans Adam Klem
*Joh. Conrad Klemm
*Joh. David Klemm
*Joh. Michael Maag
Joh. Michael Österle
Joh. Reichelsdörffer
Hans Jonas Reiffel
Friedrich Reiffel
Joh. Adam Reiffel
Daniel Rieb
*Joh. Adam Romich
*Jacob Roth
Pleickard Dietrich Sailer
Hans Peter Sailer
Jurg Leonhard Schiele
Heinrich Schmidt
Johannes Schröttlin
*Andreas Schuhmacher
*Matthaeus Schweitzer
*Anastasius Uhler
*Joh. Valentin Uhler
*Joh. Dietrich Uhler
*Heinrich Weber
*Joh. Valentin Weber
Sebastian Winterbauer
Andreas Wolff
Alexander Zartmann
Hans Heinrich Zirkel

Three more comments may be made: 1) The rare given names *Anastasius* and *Pleickard* result from the custom of the sponsors giving the name to the child at baptism. Persons named Anastasius occur in Ittlingen rather frequently; Pleickard was the given name of one of the noblemen. 2) For persons who were not longstanding citizens, these individuals founded quite a number of prominent Pennsylvania

German families or were themselves successful in the new world. Hans Heinrich Zirkel, for instance, could never have been patron of the parish in the sense that he was for the Indianfield Lutheran church had he remained in Ittlingen; and it is doubtful that Friedrich Eichelberger's three sons would have been tavernkeepers, or the descendants of John Jacob Hottenstein a family of physicians into the twentieth century. 3) From all of these names it should be quite clear that, at least in the case of Ittlingen, perhaps only a few families—the Conrads, the Eichelbergers, the Bärs, Schweitzers and the Bernhards—could have traced themselves to residence there before the Thirty Years' War.

The story of the "Ittlinger Schweinekrieg"—the Ittlingen hog war—of 1720/21 illustrates some of the frustrations of the peasants prior to the height of emigration. The story is summarized from the Neuwirth book already mentioned.

From before anyone's memory the peasants had the right to drive their hogs into the forest to find nourishment. In the middle of the sixteenth century the right was reduced to the time of acorn and beechnut harvest, from Michaelis (29 September) to Thomasius (21 December). Later, due to harm to the forests, the number of swine per household was restricted. Then a fee for use of the forest was added. By 1720 this was three Batzen per hog. In that year suddenly the two landlord families united and demanded a higher fee than the Dorfordnung (village regulations) of 1584 allowed. The villagers, under the leadership of the proprietors of the Ochsen and the Krone, two of the taverns, filed a protest with the next higher judicial authority, the council of the knights, which sat at Heilbronn, and refused to pay the levy.

The nobles then took matters into their own hands in a crafty way. Wanting to make the villagers appear in the wrong, they took advantage of another stipulation which required everyone to be at worship on Sunday morning. Sunday 1 November 1720, witnesses swore that the villagers had driven more hogs into the forest than was allowed. They ordered the Gemmingen gamesman to tell the swine herdsman not to let the hogs go the normal Saugrund, but to take them higher into the woods of the von Gemmingen-Gemmingen family. All the while the Ittlinger were in church, where they were expected to be. Suddenly a representative of the von Gemmingen clan called to the herdsman, "The hogs must get out of the forest, for a roe buck is there. The nobles are here and want to slay it."

The herdsman was hardly out of the forest when he was surrounded by 20 armed men who forced him to drive all 160 hogs to the nearby town of Gemmingen, a two-hours' walk away.

The same afternoon, as the sun shone a little, the farmers took their customary walk into the "Aicheln," the wooded area in which their hogs foraged. They noticed with alarm as they approached that no grunting was to be heard—all was silence. Gradually it dawned on them: the landlords had stolen their pigs. Some of the younger men followed the tracks to Gemmingen and returned some hours later confirming the suspicions. In the meantime the whole village was stirred up and people were standing in groups together cursing and scolding. The Schultheiss, old Caspar Caspari, summoned all the villagers to the town hall. Some wanted to take the swine back by force, but Caspari counselled seeking justice in Heilbronn. Consequently on 11 November a complaint was filed. The knights' directorium responded three days later by fining the noblemen and ordering the immediate return of the hogs. The nobility did not respond. Soon a butcher who had been in Gemmingen brought word that cheap hogs could be bought there.

In Gemmingen gossip spread that the Ittlinger were marching to get their hogs back, but when a team of twenty men, twelve of them armed, set out to meet them, no one was to be found. Meanwhile, a second complaint was filed in Heilbronn and a third one in Wetzlar, where the imperial chamber court met. The herdsman returned to Ittlingen presently with word that one night the *Schultheiss* of Gemmingen had come to the nobles' kitchen and instructed the maid to heat water since he had orders to stick some of the hogs of the *Kronenwirt*. The *Schultheiss* kindly told the herdsman not to worry, that he would at least have a sausage out of it. Other news reported that the sale of hogs was brisk in Gemmingen. Individuals' attempts to negotiate return of their animals only failed and provoked threats from the nobles, who allowed that they would murder the two innkeepers and punish anyone else who came, even if to ask pardon.

The matter worsened when, on 15 November at 9 p.m. twenty men from Gemmingen, one of them on horseback, went to Ittlingen, broke into the sheep pen and began to drive the sheep away. The noise awakened the villagers, who managed, even after the mounted man shot at them, to get the sheep back in place.

More protests to Heilbronn, another admonition to the knights to return the hogs at once and to appear at the *Ross* (horse) tavern in Heilbronn on 25 November followed. A warning that the case would go as far as Vienna, if necessary, was added. The villagers sent their deputation to Heilbronn. The knights' directorium stated the grievance against the nobility, but one blamed the other, claimed ignorance, or accused one of their number not present because he was already under arrest on another charge.

Finally one of them, Pleickard von Gemmingen zu Gemmingen, took the guilt upon himself. When the villagers were brought in, they were told that they had evaluated the hogs too highly and that one Gulden less per hog would be paid, but that restitution would be made. The villagers protested that their fellows would be angered by the reduced price, but they said they would accept it for the sake of peace with their masters. It was finally agreed that the hogs still alive should be returned, together with those lying in salt and that 350 Gulden and eight days later another 40 Gulden should be paid for the 86 hogs which were sold or butchered. The living hogs and 237¾ pounds of salted meat were returned. The villagers were fined thirty Gulden because there were more hogs in the forest than regulations allowed.

After a reminder from the chamber court had to be solicited, payment was finally made on 24 December 1720. Since one of the knights was under arrest, his share was paid by sending two large containers of wine and nine loads of beets!
Further considerations by the court in Heilbronn debated additional punishment against the nobility, but since the villagers were satisfied with the restitution, nothing more was done to them. The townsfolk knew that, after all, they did have to live with their overlords; and so they, who were basically innocent in the whole proceedings, bore their loss quietly and, no doubt, added it to their list of grievances.

5.

What the emigrants carried with them as luggage is anybody's guess, in spite of many claims and some documentary evidence. But what they brought in their persons is another story. And the evidence is clearer than might have been the case had the book before you never been compiled. For one thing, the language they were speaking, a Frankish dialect that became more Alemannish the farther east one went, survived in America as Pennsylvania Dutch or Pennsylvania German, still spoken two and a half centuries later. When Johannes Schaeffer returned to Michelfeld to get a bride in 1728, the pastor confidently wrote in the church book that he had come from "St. Johannes Stocken in Pennsylvania." That is, of course, *Conestoga:* in the dialect Johannes can emerge as *Kans* in sound, as in the word *Kansdrauwe,* currants, which ripen about 24 June, St. John the Baptizer's day. More than once we found in Kraichgau records that names like *Reinhart* or *Gebhart* have been shortened to *Reinert* or *Gebert,* precisely as the Pennsylvania Dutch pronounce them still, no matter how spelled. And Conrad Gilbert, born in Hoffenheim, used the word *Pfetterich* to name his godson in his will, a good Kraichgau dialect term.

Of course, the settlers stuck together in America, at least at first. Had German, and not English, authorities held Pennsylvania, Lancaster and York counties might well have been named for Sinsheim and Eppingen, so many Kraichgauer settled there. There is in fact a tiny hamlet in southwestern York county named Sinsheim, the only place name carried over to Pennsylvania.[1] Large numbers of the members of the Lutheran Church of the Holy Trinity in Lancaster came from the Kraichgau, from the small portion of it studied in this book. And even significant numbers of Lancaster county's Mennonites had once lived hidden and quietly on a *Hof* here or there.

An example of the remarkable way in which families from the same and neighboring villages retained ties in their new world is provided by the Müllers of Zuzenhausen, Erasmus Buggemeier, Michael Neff, John Michael Reiss of Michelfeld and Friedrich Elberscheidt of nearby Weiler and Elsenz.

Erasmus Buggemeier was born in 1695 in Michelfeld to Hans and Maria Magdalena; in 1719 he married Margaretha, the widow of Ludwig Müller who had been killed the year before in the stone quarry still being used in Zuzenhausen. Before the ship lists were kept they emigrated with her four children and presently we find them in Tulpehocken. All four Müller children are named in Erasmus's will together with the one daughter they had together. He even states that he has been holding the Müllers' father's estate ever since his death! The Müllers were Michael of Cocalico; George of Heidelberg, both in Lancaster county (the latter the miller at Millbach, from whose house built in 1752 the interiors have been removed to the Philadelphia Museum of Art); Margaret (who married Friedrich Elberscheidt in 1739 when Buggemeier wrote his will, as his second wife, but then had married Michael Reiss by the time the estate was settled; (after Margaret's death Reiss married a daughter of Andreas Krafft who had come from Waldangelloch!) and finally Anna Maria, who married Michael Neff, Jr., a first cousin of Michael Reiss.

Surely this net of affinity is not sheer coincidence: people knew former neighbors and kept contact with them. Many more examples could be cited. The index to this book, when creatively used, will show connections between immigrants the text simply could not point out. Like a monkey chain, one can follow connections between families back almost directly to Anthony Jacob Henkel and that stalwart, but still mystifying soul Joshua Harrsch, who capitalized upon his first name and changed his last to lure his countrymen to a Canaan thousands of miles and a dangerous voyage of many weeks across the sea.

---

[1]The possible exception to this statement may be in the names given to plantations when they were patented. A study of these names has not been made, but enough examples are known that it would not be surprising ot find a tract called Hoffenheim or Eschelbronn by some—could it have been?—slightly homesick emigrant. Cf. in fact entry 256, page 187!

The tiny village of Sinsheim in Codorus township, York county, is the only Pennsylvania village which bears the name of a place in the Kraichgau. A station on
the Western Maryland Railroad, Sinsheim once had a post office and a store. Today
the memory is preserved on a shed in the hamlet of about ten houses.

Photo. J. Godshall

The mark of these persons on their new home was left in nomenclature as photos
throughout the text suggest. It was also made in helping to frame a whole new folk
culture in America. Here are the Wistars, glass and buttonmakers, Christian
Seltzer, joiner and chestmaker, Conrad Gilbert, a Frakturist, and Georg Müller,
the miller just named. Here are the Rudisills, three brothers *in fact* and two others
besides, who scattered themselves all over the nation with their unmistakably Swiss
name, invariably causing every Englishman who enountered it a nightmare in
spelling. And here are the Benders and the Peters, whose names might just as well
have been English, but are not, and the Hoffmanns, Schmidts, Müllers, Kleins,
Schumachers—all so common that one stands back in admiration at the wizzardry
which recognized them as emigrants—here the Breiningers, Breneisens, Glass-
brenners, Clapsaddles, Eichelbergers, Brossmans, Dotterers and the Utzes, Uhlers
and Umbergers, names any Pennsylvania German would recognize at once, just
about any way they are spelled, as names that sound like home. Indeed they are,
many of them no longer to be found in the quiet but rapidly changing villages of
the Kraichgau their forebears left twenty five decades ago to improve their lot in
life and give their children a better start in life than they had had.

Frederick S. Weiser

Orchards were essential to a good supply of winter food. Roads in the country-side were lined with fruit and nut trees, but specially planted orchards were planted, too. An orchard is depicted here in the northwestern tip of the Kraichgau near Schatthausen.

Photo: J. Godshall

The Emigrants

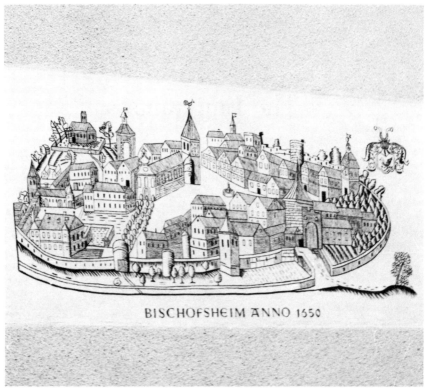

BISCHOFSHEIM ANNO 1650

Artist reproduction of Neckarbischofsheim about 1650 as seen from the south. The 5-cornered tower in the right foreground, the city church at the open market place and the "Totenkirche"—Helmstatt family memorial chapel—are all visible, together with the moated palace of the noble family on the left.

Photo: J. Godshall

1. ABENDSCHÖN, SAMUEL HEINRICH   7103 Schwaigern
ABENDSCHÖN, CHRISTIAN
ABENDSCHÖN, REINHOLD

Fane, 1749
S-H 424

SCHWAIGERN LUTHERAN KB:
m. Nov. (?) 1715 Samuel Heinrich Abendschön, citizen and wagon maker, widower, and Maria Barbara, daughter of Martin Rambacher. They had:
1. Christianus b. 9 Sept. 1716
2. Samuel Henrich b. 27 Oct. 1718; bp. 28 Oct. 1718; d. young
3. Maria Dorothea b. 24 May 1720; m. 13 Aug. 1748 Jacob Hiller
4. Maria Barbara b. 24 Apr. 1723
5. Reinhold b. 24 Oct. 1725
6. Maria Elisabetha b. 21 Apr. 1729
m. 1 May 1731 Samuel Heinrich Abendschön, citizen and wagon maker, widower, and Rosina, daughter of the late Hans Jerg Willheit, citizen and cooper.
m. 10 Nov. 1744 Christian Abendschön, son of Samuel Abendschön, wagon maker, and Catharina, daughter of Matthai Beeringer. They had:
1. Christian b. 12 Aug. 1745
2. Matthaus b. 7 Mar. 1747; d. young
3. Wilhelm b. 25 May 1749

Pennsylvania records:
PHILADELPHIA WILLS AND ADMINISTRATIONS:
Samuel Avensheen, Amity twp., [Berks co., Pa.], (24 Aug. 1756; 22 Oct. 1757) Son Reinhold, property in said twp. where Jacob Erly lives. Mentions daughter Barbara, wife of Georg Keplinger [see Leonhard Kepplinger family]; son Christian; daughter Dorothea; daughter Elisabeth, wife of John Greiner. Adm. granted to Reinhold Avensheen, son.

MERTZ LUTHERAN KB, DRYVILLE, BERKS CO.:
Christian Abendschein was a sp. in 1754
Reinhold Abendschein and wife Hanna:
1. Anna Marcretha b. 10 Jan. 1760; bp. 20 Apr. 1760

Reinholt Abendshen, Berks co., nat. Philadelphia 24 Sept. 1755.

2. ACKERMANN, JOH. WENDEL   6924 Neckarbischofsheim
ACKERMANN, JOH. GEORG

Osgood, 1750
S-H 445

ADERSBACH LUTHERAN KB:
m. 11 May 1697 Hans Georg Ackerman, citizen and smith at Bischofsheim, and Anna Maria, daughter of Thomas Gerlach, "Schultheiss" at Hasselbach.

NECKARBISCHOFSHEIM LUTHERAN KB:
Hans Jerg Ackermann, farrier, and Anna Maria had:
Johann Wendel b. 5 Jan. 1703

m. 4 Sept. 1725 Joh. Wendel Ackermann, farrier and armorer, son of the late Hans Georg Ackermann, and Anna Maria, daughter of the late Joh. Georg Schick. Children:

1. Joh. Henrich b. 13 Aug. 1726
2. Joh. Georg b. 17 Sept. 1728
3. Joh. Leonhard b. 3 Aug. 1730; d. young
4. Maria Barbara b. 1 Oct. 1732
5. Georg Balthasar b. 19 May 1736
6. Maria Christina b. 18 Dec. 1739

Pennsylvania records:
TRINITY LUTHERAN KB, LANCASTER:
Maria Barbara Ackermännin, single, m. 27 Apr. 1755 Joh. Georg Federhaaf from [7131] Lomersheim in Württemberg.
Joh. Georg Ackermann, single, m. 22 Jan. 1758 Catharina Danningerin from Düren near Bretten [7531 Dürrn]
D. 31 Mar. 1764 Wendel Ackermann, farrier, a married man aged 61 y. 2 mo. 7 days; buried the following day.
Bu 27 May 1769 Georg, little son of Georg Ackermann and his wife Catharina, aged 1 year, 6 mo. and 29 days. D. of smallpox.

WALDSCHMIDT RECORDS:
Balser Ackermann, son of the late Wendel Ackermann, m. 18 June 1771 Elisabeth, widow of Gorg Albrecht. _____

Geo. Ackerman and Baltzer Ackerman, Lancaster twp. Lancaster co., nat. Philadelphia, Fall 1765, not taking an oath.

3. ADAM, NICOLAUS   Eichtersheim =
William & Sarah, 1727   6921 Angelbachtal
S-H 8 (2 persons)

EICHTERSHEIM LUTHERAN KB:
m. 23 Nov. 1719 Nicolaus Adam and Juliana Schweickhardt. Nicolausen Adam, potter, and wife Juliana Bernhardina had:
1. Jonas Paul b. 3 Feb. 1725; sp.: Jonas Donner [q.v.] and wife Juliana and Paul Kurtzenhauser and wife Anna Margretha

Pennsylvania records:
MUDDY CREEK LUTHERAN KB, LANCASTER CO.:
Nicolaus Adam had:
1. Johannes b. 29 Sept. 1729
2. Joh. Bernhardt b. 14 Mar. 1731
3. Juliana Margaretha b. 6 Nov. 1733; sp. Jonas Donner [q.v.] and Juliana
4. Susanna b. 17 Aug. 1736; sp. Joh. Philipp Schweickert [q.v.] and wife Susanna
5. Christina

m. 2 July 1748 Georg Bräckle and Juliana Adamin (Earltown)
m. 24 Feb. 1751 Bernhardt Adam and Margaretha Derrin (Cocalico)
m. 8 Apr. 1751 Johannes Adam and Maria Eva Schmidin (Muddy Creek)

BERGSTRASSE LUTHERAN KB, LANCASTER CO.:
Bernhard Adam and his wife had:
1. Joh. Adam b. 9 June 1751; sp. Johan Adam and Cath. Dörrin
2. Juliana Margreta b. 12 Feb. 1753; sp. Johann Adam and his sister Juliana Margreta, now Fastnacht
3. Anna Maria b. _____ July 1756
4. Nicolaus b. 5 July 1758
5. Maria Margreta b. 14 June 1760
6. Joh. Bernhard b. 28 Aug. 1763
7. Lea b. 16 Apr. 1765

LANCASTER CO. ORPHANS' COURT DOCKET I:
5 Mar. 1754, Christena and Dorothea Adam, orphan children of Nicholas Adam, deceased, choose John Gehr as guardian. Susanna Adam, an orphan daughter of Nicholas Adam, chooses Bernard Adam, her brother, as guardian.

STOEVER'S RECORDS:
m. 26 Sept. 1748 Jonas Adam and Anna Eva Meixel, Earltown.

4. AFF, ELIAS
6921 Ittlingen

Prelist

ITTLINGEN LUTHERAN KB:
Elias Aff and Anna Catharina had one child bp. at Ittlingen:
1. Maria Catharina bp. 26 Sept. 1709

Pennsylvania records:
Land purchase May 24, 1720, Hanover twp., 150 A from John Henry Sprogell. Signed petition for the division of Hanover twp. in March 1731. In March 1723, a petition for a road from Limerick twp. through Falkner Swamp, to Oley. Elias Aff was one of the signers. 13 Jan. 1742—Elias Affe and Anna Catrina, his wife, sold 125 A to John Benner (part of the 1720 land purchase.)

5. ALDORFFER, FRIEDERICH age 18
Steinsfurt =
6920 Sinsheim, Elsenz
Samuel, 1733
S-H 106, 110, 112

STEINSFURT REFORMED KB:
Leonhard Altorffer, son of the late Hans Altorffer, married (1) 20 Nov. 1703, Magdalena, widow of the late Hans Wurffel. They had 4 children bp. at Steinsfurt. Leonard Altorffer m. (2) Barbara ca. 1714 (no marriages recorded at Steinsfurt 1713 to 1715)

Their son:
  Friederick bp. 19 May 1715. Sp. Friederick Leipi (q.v.) Conf. 1729, age
14½.
[Earlier Altorffer families in the villages in this area were from CH-8302 Kloten,
ZH (Kirchardt KB) and CH-8303 Oberwil b. Bassersdorf, ZH (Richen KB)]

Pennsylvania records:
Salford Mennonite cemetery, Harleysville, Montgomery co., Pa.:
  Frederick Alderfer, b. in the Palatinate May 18, 1715, died Nov. 7, 1801
His wife Anna Alderfer (nee Detwiler), b. 1712, is also buried here. There are
more than 100 other Alderfers and wives buried in this cemetery.

Frederick Alderfer, Philadelphia co., nat. Philadelphia April 1743 a "Quaker."

6. ALLGEŸER   6921 Ittlingen
Prelist

ITTLINGEN LUTHERAN KB:
Michael Allgaÿer and wife Maria Catharina had:
  1. Hans Oster bp. 29 May 1701
  2. Maria Elisabetha b. 30 Mar. 1704
  3. Joh. Wolfgang b. 6 Apr. 1707
  4. Ulrich b. 23 June 1710
  5. Johannes b. 22 July 1714

Pennsylvania records:
TRINITY LUTHERAN KB, LANCASTER:
Joh. Wolff Allgeyer had:
  Maria Eva b. 25 Apr. 1736; sp. Wilhelm Albert and wife Maria Eva

STOEVER'S RECORDS:
m. 14 Oct. 1735 Maria Eva Allgeyer and Joh. Wilhelm Albert (Leacock)

Johannes Allgeyer nat. Annapolis 12 Sept. 1759

7. ANSEL, JOH. PETER   Eschelbach, Baden =
                                                6920 Sinsheim, Elsenz
Anderson, 1752
S-H 489

ESCHELBACH LUTHERAN KB:
m. 24 June 1742 Peeter Ansel, shoemaker, son of Joh. Michel Ansel, shoemaker
in Maichingen, Böblinger Amts, Wurtemberg [= 7032 Sindelfingen], and Anna
Margretha Schaller, daughter of the late Michel Schaller, citizen. Children:
  1. Joh. Leonhard b. 15 Aug. 1743; d. 1744
  2. Joh. Leonhard b. 28 June 1745; "Is in the new land."
  3. Maria Magdalena b. 20 Dec. 1748

American records:
LOUDOUN CO., VA., WILLS F: 52:
Leonard Ansel witnessed the will of George Thomas in Loudoun co., Va. in 1798.

8. ARNOLD, JOH. GEORG age 34   6921 Zuzenhausen

Elizabeth, 1738
S-H 243, 244, 245

ZUZENHAUSEN LUTHERAN KB:
m. 17 Oct. 1724 Hans Georg Arnoldt from [6921] Epfenbach, and Anna Maria
Barth. Children:
    Joh. Marthin bp. 16 July 1731
    Joh. Diterich bp. 25 Feb. 1735

Krebs, "Palatine Emigration . . . ," p. 26:
In 1738 Johann Georg Arnold of Zuzenhausen (Kreis Sinsheim) received permission to emigrate to America with his wife and children, on payment of 10 florins
manumission tax.

American records:
Frederick, Md., Lutheran KB:
A Georg Arnhold and wife Anna Maria sp. a child of Ludwig Kümmerer in 1743.

9. ARNOLDT, JOH. GEORG   Treschklingen =
                                                6927 Bad Rappenau
William & Sarah, 1727
S-H 8
                    (Hans Jerig Arldnold, dead)

TRESCHKLINGEN LUTHERAN KB:
m. 24 Nov. 1685 Joh. Georg Arnoldt, journeyman carpenter, and Barbara, dau. of
the late Joh. Frey, tenant farmer. Children:
    1. Catharina Barbara b. 19 Oct. 1686
    2. Catharina b. 7 Aug. 1690; d. 2 Oct. 1701
    3. Hans Georg bp. 30 Mar. 1696
    4. Cathar. Margretha b. 25 June 1699
Barbara, wife of Hans Georg Arnold, d. 12 Jan. 1707
m. (2) 3 Jan. 1708 Joh. Georg Arnoldt and Anna Catharina, widow of the late Joh.
Felix Greb, formerly a tailor at [7519] Eppingen.
"In May 1727 this Hs. Georg Arnold, with his family, went to Pennsylvania."

Pennsylvania records:
One George Arnold appears in the Goshenhoppen Catholic KB. There are references to one George Arnold in the St. Michael and Zion Lutheran KB, Philadelphia. These may refer to the Hans Georg b. 1696.

One George Arnold, Albany Twp., Berks co., nat. Philadelphia Fall 1765.

10. BAFFENMEYER, MATTHAEUS

Massenbach =
7103 Schwaigern

Royal Union, 1750
S-H 433

MASSENBACH LUTHERAN KB:
m. 23 Jan. 1725 Jerg Wendel Poffenmeier, son of Fridrich Poffenmeier, citizen and
"des Gerichts," and Maria Eva, daughter of Hans Jerg Bikel, tailor. Children:
1. Rosina Catharina b. 19 Oct. 1725
2. Georg Tobias b. 13 Apr. 1728
3. Anna Barbara b. 13 Dec. 1730; d. young
*4. Mathaus b. 10 July 1733
5. Hans Jerg b. 29 Apr. 1737; d. young
Jerg Wendel Poffenmeier died, and his widow m. (2) Johannes Würtz [who also
appears on this ship's list as Hans Weertz.]

Pennsylvania records:
TRINITY LUTHERAN KB, LANCASTER:
m. 3 Dec. 1754 Matthaeus Boffenmajer from Massenbach, single, and Maria
Elisabet Millerin, single. Children:
1. Eva Margaret b. 18 Oct. 1756
2. Anna Margaret b. 24 Feb. 1758
3. Maria Elisabeth b. 10 Feb. 1762
4. Heinrich b. 23 Oct. 1763
5. David b. 26 July 1766
6. Johannes b. 2 June 1769

Mathew Buffenmeyer, Hempfield twp., Lancaster co., nat. 10 Apr. 1765.

11. BALL, TOBIAS

7519 Eppingen

Dragon, 1732
S-H 96, 98, 99

EPPINGEN REFORMED KB:
Tobias Baal and his wife Apolonia had:
Anna Maria bp. 2 Mar. 1730; sp. Teathores (Theodorus?) Fechtner and his
wife Anna Maria

Pennsylvania records:
ST. PAUL'S (BLUE) LUTHERAN KB, UPPER SAUCON TWP., NORTHAMPTON CO.:
Communicants' list May 1750:
Johann Jacob Reich, servant to Tobias Baal

TOHICKON REFORMED KB, BUCKS CO.:
Tobias Baal d. 10 May 1759, bu. 12 May.

12. BALMER, CARL age 20
BALMER, CHRISTIAN age 24

6924 Neckarbischofsheim

Samuel, 1732
S-H 60, 64, 65
[Translated Carl Diedrich (?) Balmer on B and C list; actually Carl Friedrich
Balmer]

Eppingen's narrow streets lined with *Fachwerk-Gebäude*—half-timber constructed buildings—look much like they did when the pioneers left there in the eighteenth century.

Photo: J. Godshall

NECKARBISCHOFSHEIM LUTHERAN KB:
bp. 8 June 1721 two Anabaptists (Mennonites); one was 22 years old and the other was 18 years. The father was Johann Balmer, tenant farmer at the Büchelhoff (Biegelhof), and the mother was Christina nee Majer, a Mennonite from Switzerland. The sons were named:
1. Carl Friderich
2. Christian Eberhardt

Pennsylvania records:
WARWICK MORAVIAN KB, LITITZ, LANCASTER CO.:
Carl Palmer, infant, bu. in 1750.
Carl Frederick Palmer, age 10 mo., bu. in 1757.
Andrew Palmer, infant, bu. in 1764.
Eberhard Palmer, son of Christian and Barbara, d. 1769, age 11 y.
Christian Palmer, b. Aug. 1703 near Sinsheim, came to this country 1733 and m. widow Susanna Brunck. They had 6 children. He m. (2) widow Barbara Pichler and they had 7 children. He d. 8 Mar. 1778, age 74 years.

WARWICK LUTHERAN KB, LANCASTER CO.:
Christian Balmar had:
1. Anna Christina b. 27 Oct. 1734
2. Joh. Michael b. 28 Dec. 1735
3. Joh. Christian b. 17 Apr. 1737

4. Anna Barbara b. June 1743
[The first 3 children are also recorded in the Muddy Creek Lutheran KB.]

Christian Palmar, Hamfield twp., Lancaster co., nat. Philadelphia 24 Sept. 1755 without taking an oath.

13. BÄR, JOH. ULRICH   6921 Ittlingen
Dragon, 1732
S-H 97, 98, 99

ITTLINGEN LUTHERAN KB:
Felix Bär and wife Margaretha had:
    Johann Ulrich bp. 23 Apr. 1689
Joh. Ulrich Bär and wife Anna had:
    1. Susanna Agatha bp. 9 Dec. 1716
    2. Maria Agatha b. 28 Feb. 1720
    3. Joh. Martin b. 19 Jan. 1722
    4. Maria Barbara b. 3 Aug. 1723
    5. Anna Elisabetha b. 16 Aug. 1725; d. young [sic; obviously an error.]
    6. Joh. Ulrich b. 15 Nov. 1727; d. young
    7. Anna Barbara b. 31 Jan. 1729
    8. Anna b. 7 Dec. 1730; "married 16 Feb. 1751 Joh. Heinrich Uhler, wagon-maker, son of Joh. Ulrich Uhler, and Anna Bär, daughter of the late Ulrich Bär, *colonist in Pennsylvania*."
KIRCHARDT REFORMED KB:
m. (1) 19 Nov. 1715 Hans Ulrich Bähr, son of Felix Bähr of Ittlingen, and Anna, daughter of Hans Michael Klein, citizen and judge at Kirchardt.
m. (2) 28 Aug. 1731 Ulerich Bär, citizen and inhabitant at Üttlingen, widower, and Anna Schupp, daughter of Christoph Schupp.

Pennsylvania records:
Several documents recorded in Lancaster co. Deed books contain detailed (and sometimes conflicting) information on the descendants of this immigrant.

LANCASTER CO. DEEDS:
GG:2:170–172: 17 Sept 1771—Elizabeth Wolf of Lancaster Co., widow, died intestate leaving no children, but the following Relations and Kinsmen:
    1. Maria Agatha Geesy, her full sister (with same father and mother), wife of Conrad Geesey of York Co.
    2. Catharina Snavely, her sister (with the same father and different mother), wife of Henry Snavely of Lancaster Co.
    3. George Bare   } all brothers (same
    4. Martin Bare   } father, different mother)
    5. Adam Bare, deceased leaving 4 children }
    6. Michael Wolf, the only brother of Samuel Wolf, her late husband. She had 80 A. of land in Elizabeth twp., Lancaster co., and the above mentioned persons were listed as her heirs.
LANCASTER CO. DEEDS:
GG:2:313–316: 17 Dec.1787—this deed also concerns this estate, but contains a conflicting statement to the above deed. On p. 315, it states that Agatha Geesy was the only child of Elisabetha and Samuel Wolff.

LANCASTER DEEDS:
T:3:169–174: document dated Ittlingen in the Suabian Canton of Craichgau,
7 May 1804, recorded in Lancaster deed book 14 Nov. 1805: Extract from the
church books at Ittlingen:

Ulrich Bar, formerly a citizen of this place, who afterwards emigrated to
America with his family, his youngest daughter Anna excepted, was married in the
year 1715 with Anna, daughter of Hans Michael Klein of Kirchhard; with this wife
he had children:
1. Anna Elizabetha b. 16 Aug. 1725
2. Johann Ulrich b. 15 Nov. 1727
3. Anna Barbara b. 31 Jan. 1729
4. Anna b. 7 Dec. 1730
As the mother of the above mentioned Anna died in 1730, the father Ulrich Bar
then married 21 Aug. 1731 Anna, daughter of Christoph Schupp of Kirchhard,
and shortly afterward emigrated to America, the youngest child, Anna, remaining
in Ittlingen. Anna Bär m. 16 Feb. 1751 Johann Henrich Uhler and she d. 2 Mar.
1792. Her husband d. 8 Feb. 1795. They had 4 children (named in the document)
of whom 2 were deceased. The surviving children were:
Johann Heinrich Uhler b. 30 Oct.1756
Andreas Uhler b. 7 July 1759
These two Uhler sons appointed Mr. Peter Ulrich, merchant in Philadelphia, as
their attorney to collect their inheritance from the estate of their aunt, Elizabeth
Wolf, nee Barin.

14. BART(H), JOH. GEORG   6926 Kirchardt
Prelist

SINSHEIM LUTHERAN KB:
m. 26 Nov. 1715 at Kirchardt Joh. Georg Barth, son of Johannes Barth of Tieffen-
bach in Franckenland [one of these possibilities: 7181 Tiefenbach, today part of
the city of Crailsheim, or 7101 Tiefenbach, today part of the city of Gundelsheim,
or 8541 Tiefenbach, part of the community of Thalmässing], and Anna Barbara
Klein, daughter of Joh. Wolf Klein of Kirchardt. Children:
1. Anna b. 21 Oct. 1717
2. —(n.n.) b. 13 May 1719
3. Zacharias b. 4 Jan. 1721

Pennsylvania records:
TRINITY LUTHERAN KB, LANCASTER:
Joh. Georg Bart and wife Anna Barbara had:
Anna Catharina b. 2 Sept. 1730 ⎫ all sponsored by
Anna Maria b. 1 Apr. 1734   ⎬ Georg Klein and wife.
Georg Philipp b. 2 June 1736   ⎭

m. 23 Aug. 1748 Adam Leitner and Anna Barbara Barth, daughter of Johann
Georg Barth
Bu. 3 Aug. 1769 4 miles from the city Georg Barth, father of Zacharias Barth, age
89 y. 3 mo. less some days.
_____

John George Beard, Lancaster co., nat. by Act of March 29, 1735.

15. BASSLER, HENRICH

Elsenz =
7519 Eppingen

Dragon, 1732
S-H 96, 98

ELSENZ REFORMED KB:
m. 12 Jan. 1723 Henrich Bassler, linenweaver, and Anna Barbara, widow of Joseph Hauser. (M. 29 Aug. 1719 Joseph Hauser, widower, and Barbara, widow of Friederich Elbescheid.) There was one child, surname Hauser, by her marriage to Joseph Hauser:
Johannes bp. 24 Nov. 1721

Pennsylvania records:
FIRST REFORMED KB, LANCASTER:
Henry Basler and wife Barbara nee Boehler sp. several children from 1736–1747.

Johan Henry Basseler and Henry Basseler, Lancaster co., nat. by Act of 19 May 1739.

16. BAUER, JOH. MARTIN

7103 Schwaigern

Johnson, 1732
SH-72, 76, 77 (with Susanna Bower and Helena, under 14)

SCHWAIGERN LUTHERAN KB:
m. 7 July 1700 Hans Martin Bauer, tailor, son of Erasmi Bauer, tailor, and Margreta, daughter of Ulrich Platter
Hans Martin Baur and wife Margretha had:
Hans Martin b. 24 Aug. 1707
Hans Martin Bauer and wife Susanna Maria had:
Helena Christina bp. 25 Mar. 1732

Pennsylvania records:
ST. MICHAEL'S AND ZION LUTHERAN KB, PHILADELPHIA:
Joh. Martin Bauer appears on a list of communicants dated 1733.

STOEVER'S RECORDS:
Martin Bauer (Codorus) had:
A child b. 2 May 1741; bp. 26 June 1741 (No name given in record)

Martin Bower, Manchester twp., York co., nat. Philadelphia 11 Apr. 1751

17. BAUM, JERG SIMON

Shirley, 1751
S-H 454

Hoffenheim =
6920 Sinsheim, Elsenz

HOFFENHEIM LUTHERAN KB:
m. 9 Nov. 1700 Georg Peter Peter (Petri), widower, and Anna Catharina, dau. of
Henrich Vögele. Their daughter:
Anna Catharina b. 28 Jan. 1708
m. 7 Nov. 1724 Simon Baum, son of Jacob Baum, and Anna Catharina Peter, dau.
of Georg Peter Peter. [This surname appears in the records as both Peter and Petri.]
Children:
1. Anna Barbara b. 22 Sept. 1727; m. 20 June 1747 Joh. Elias Horch [q.v.]
2. Georg Peter b. 19 July 1731
3. Johann Jacob b. 25 Dec. 1734
4. Anna Magdalena b. 9 Sept. 1737

Pennsylvania records:
ST. DAVID'S (SHERMAN'S) KB: WEST MANHEIM TWP., YORK CO.,:
m. 16 Apr. 1754 Johann Georg Peter Baum, son of the late Georg Simon Baum,
and Anna Susanna Margaretha Zapfin, daughter of Daniel Zapf. Children:
1. Joh. Georg Peter bp. 15 Aug. 1755

George Simon Baum nat. Annapolis 11 Apr. 1759
George Peter Baum nat. Annapolis 9 Sept. 1761

18. BAUM, JOH. JACOB

Nancy, 1750
S-H 443

Hoffenheim =
6920 Sinsheim, Elsenz

HOFFENHEIM LUTHERAN KB:
m. 23 Nov. 1717 Jacob Baum, widower, and Anna Maria Röder, dau. of Joh.
Friederich Räder of Reÿhen. Children:
1. Anna Elisabetha b. 15 Oct. 1718
2. Elisabetha b. 16 Oct. 1719
3. Anna Maria b. 21 Aug. 1721
4. Joh. Niclas b. 3 Jan. 1725
5. Johanna Margaretha b. 26 Sept. 1727
*6. Joh. Jacob b. 26 Jan. 1729
Anna Maria (Röder) Baum m. (2) Frantz Kühlewein [q.v.]

Pennsylvania records:
ST. MICHAEL'S AND ZION LUTHERAN KB, PHILADELPHIA:
Johann Jacob Baum and wife Elisabetha had:
1. Johan Adam b. 26 Sept. 1753; bp. 28 Oct.; sp. Joh. Adam Probst [q.v.]
and wife Maria Magdalena.

Jacob Baum "Northern Liberties," nat. Philadelphia Oct. 1765.

The "Baumann'sche Haus," built in 1582–3 by a wealthy citizen in Eppingen, is marked by a date stone inscribed
    "Ich will nicht sterben, sondern leben
    und die Werke des Herrn verkundigen. 1583"
    "I shall not die, but live,
    and proclaim the works of the Lord. 1583" [Psalm 118:18]
and by a lion's face (*Fratze*) dated 1582. One of the most impressive half-timbered
structures in Germany and surely the finest in the Kraichgau, this house was never
stuccoed over, as were many others. It is so fancily decorated with carving that one
must study the facade carefully to discover all the motifs represented. Such buildings were built and occupied by persons on social levels which did not need to
emigrate to improve their lot.

Photo: J. Godshall

19. BAUMANN, HANS GEORG   7519 Eppingen

William & Sarah, 1727
S-H 7 (appears on list: Hans Jerrick Bowman—1 person)

EPPINGEN REFORMED KB:
Jacob Bawmann and wife Barbara had;
    Hans Georg bp. 10 Feb 1700
    Hans Georg Baumann conf. 1713.

Pennsylvania records:
Hans Jerg Bauman was a member of the Reformed congregation at Skippack in
1730. He signed the letter dated 10 May 1730 to the Classis of Amsterdam [see
Hinke, *History of the Goshenhoppen Reformed Charge*, PGS Proceedings, XXVII:
56–59]. This congregation was served by the Reformed pastor Georg Michael
Weiss, also from Eppingen.

20. BAUMGARTNER, GOTTFRIED

7103 Schwaigern

Fane, 1749
S-H 424

SCHWAIGERN LUTHERAN KB:
m. 23 Jan. 1700 Hans Jacob Baumgartner, smith, son of Jerg Baumgartner, citizen
and smith, and Catharina, daughter of Michel Wilheit. Jacob Baumgartner and
Anna Catharina had:
Gottfried bp. 6 June 1719

ADELSHOFEN LUTHERAN KB:
Andreas Frick and wife Anna Elisabetha had:
Anna Maria b. 16 Apr. 1713; "Went to the new land."
m. 17 Nov. 1744 Gottfried Baumgartner, shoemaker, son of the late Jacob Baumgartner of Schwaigern, and Anna Maria, daughter of Andreas Frick of Adelshofen.
Gottfried Baumgartner and Anna Maria had:
1. Maria Veronica b. 29 Aug. 1745

Pennsylvania records:
STOEVER'S RECORDS:
m. 28 May 1750 Gottfried Baumgaertner and Anna Catarina Kueffer, Lebanon.
Gottfried Baumgaertner (Bethel) had:
1. Joh. Jacob b. 7 Dec. 1751; bp. 22 Dec. 1751

Pennsylvanische Geschichts-Schreiber, Germantown, 1 Jan. 1751, mentions Gottfried Baumgaertner, Battleton township, on the Little Swatara, Lancaster co.; wife
Anna Catharina, daughter of Vallentin Kiefer.

21. BAUSEL, JACOB

7519 Eppingen

William & Sarah, 1727
S-H 9

SINSHEIM REFORMED KB:
m. 30 June 1711 Joh. Jacob Pausel from Eppingen and Anna Catharina Schwab.

EPPINGEN REFORMED KB:
Hans Pausel and wife Elisabetha had:
Hans Jacob bp. 23 Mar. 1687
Hans Jacob Baussel, son of Hans, and wife Anna Catharina had:
1. Hans Jörg bp. 25 Mar. 1712; d. 19 July 1712
2. Apollonia bp. 19 July 1713; d. 18 Dec. 1714
3. Agnesa Barbara bp. 5 Feb.1716
4. Joh. Georg bp. 22 June 1718
5. Georg Jacob bp. 8 Jan. 1721; d. young
One Jacob Pause, 2½ in family, appears on the A list, S-H p. 7. Jacob Bausel
signed the B list.

American records:
Chalkley III; 314:
One Jacob Pousel with wife Barbara sold 314 A. on Jumping Run, 10 Aug. 1753.

22. BECK, JOH. WEŸRICH

Dragon, 1749
S-H 414

Eschelbach =
6920 Sinsheim
6921 Michelfeld

ESCHELBACH LUTHERAN KB:
Johann Georg Ziegler, a linenweaver residing in Eschelbach, son of Hans Ziegler, m. (1) 20 Nov. 1714 Anna Margretha Zimmerman; m. (2) 6 May 1736 Margaretha Günther, a widow (who died in 1737); and m. (3) 5 Apr. 1739 Eva Catharina Britz(in) from [6927] Fürfeld, Gemmingischer Herrschafft. Children of the third marriage:
1. Joh. Stephan b. 27 Dec. 1739; d. young
2. Joh. Georg Ulrich b. 19 Feb. 1742; d. young
3. Anna Elisabetha b. 20 Aug. 1732; d. 1744
4. Eva Catharina b. 22 May 1745 (In her bp. record there is a note by her mother's name: "this woman went to the new land in 1749.")
m. 2 Nov. 1745 Joh. Weÿrich Beck, son of Leonhard Beck, citizen at Michelfeld, linenweaver, and Eva Catharina, widow of Hans Jerg Ziegler. "N.B.: gave this Beck a marriage certificate and they left in 1749 for the new land."
[Note: the Michelfeld KB gives the date of marriage as 2 Nov. 1748.]

23. BELSNER, SIMON

Dragon, 1732
S-H 96, 98

Adelshofen, Baden =
7519 Eppingen

ADELSHOFEN LUTHERAN KB:
Simon Beltzner was a sponsor in 1731 for a child of Georg Ludwig Schütz (also an immigrant on this ship.)
m. 18 Apr. 1730 Simon Pölstner, son of Johann Matthias Pölstner, citizen at Leonbrunn [= 7129 Zaberfeld], widower, and Anna Elisabetha, widow of Ernst Bernhard Schlauch, former citizen and "des Gerichts". Ernst Bernhard Schlauch married his third wife on 17 Nov. 1705, Anna Elisabetha Frick, dau. of Hans Martin Frick. Their children were:
1. Joh. Andreas Schlauch [q.v.] b. 25 Feb. 1708
2. Joh. Philipp Schlauch [q.v.] b. 11 June 1710
3. Johanna Cath. b. 1 Mar. 1712
4. Augusta Maria Magdalena b. 2 Mar. 1714
5. Joh. Jacob b. 3 Aug. 1715; d. 14 Mar. 1716
6. Joh. Jacob b. 14 Mar. 1717
7. Joh. Michael b. 14 Mar. 1717; d. 23 Apr. 1717
8. Anna Elisabetha b. 21 June 1721
9. Anna Margaretha b. 16 Jan. 1724; d. 18 Feb. 1726
Ernst Bernhard Schlauch d. 9 Nov. 1726, age 61 y. 7 weeks
Simon Peltzner (Belsner) appears on the *Dragon*, 1732, with step sons Philip and Andreas Schlauch [q.v.] and step-son-in-law Jerg Ludwig Schütz.

Simon Belzener, Philadelphia co., nat. Philadelphia April 1743.

24. BENDER, GEORG MICHAEL age 55
Friendship, 1739
S-H 265, 268, 271

Steinsfurt =
6920 Sinsheim, Elsenz

STEINSFURT REFORMED KB:
Hans Georg Bender and Catharina had a son Georg Michel bp. 3 Aug. 1682.
m. 14 Aug. 1703 Georg Michael Bender, son of Hans Georg Bender, and Anna
Elÿsabetha, dau. of Eberhard Raudenbusch. Children:
1. Anna Elisabetha bp. 18 May 1704
2. Georg Michel bp. 16 Nov. 1705
3. Eva bp. 29 Feb. 1708
4. Adam Ludwig bp. 17 Apr. 1709; conf. 1725
5. Anna Margretha bp. 18 Feb. 1711; d. 1721
6. Anna Maria bp. 26 Nov. 1715
7. Joh. Heinrich bp. 12 Apr. 1718; conf. 1734
8. Anna Elisabetha bp. 24 Apr. 1720

Ludwick Bender, Douglass twp., Berks co., nat. Philadelphia Sept. 1762

25. BENDER, GEORG NICLAUS
Rawley, 1752
S-H 500 (J. Nickolas (xx) Bender)

Eschelbach, Baden =
6920 Sinsheim, Elsenz

ESCHELBACH LUTHERAN KB:
Joh. Caspar Bender and wife Anna Catharina had:
Georg Niclaus b. 7 June 1730 conf. 1745. By his bp.: "1752 *Taufschein*
given—going to the new land."
Georg Nicolaus Bender and wife Maria Eva had:
Georg Nicolaus b. 24 June 1747
Under the parents' names: "Moved to the new land."

Pennsylvania records:
ST. MICHAEL'S AND ZION, PHILADELPHIA, KB:
M. 7 Jan. 1759 Georg Nicolaus Bender and Anna Barbara Beck. One of the
witnesses at the marriage was Georg Henrich Penz (Bentz) [q.v.], a fellow passenger from Darmbach [today Tairnbach = 6909 Mühlhausen, Kraichgau.]

Nicholas Penter, Northern Liberties, Philadelphia co., nat. Philadelphia 1765.

26. BENDER, HANS ADAM
Dragon, 1732
S-H 96, 97, 98 (George Adam on A list)

Adersbach =
6920 Sinsheim, Elsenz

ADERSBACH LUTHERAN KB:
m. 22 Apr. 1732 Johann Adam Bender, son of Michael Bender, wagonmaker at
[6920] Steinsfurt, and Maria Veronica, dau. of the late Carl Sauter, formerly of
[6920] Hasselbach. [Brother-in-law of Thomas Sauter, q.v.]

Across Pennsylvania the names of Kraichgau families may be found on towns, churches, businesses, and, of course, in city directories. Benders Church, established about 1781 in Butler township, Adams county, was a union church, consisting of Lutheran and Reformed congregations, until the Reformed withdrew in 1926. The building whose main entry is pictured here was begun in 1811. The earliest register of this congregation, opened in 1786, contains the family names Bender, Eichholtz, Gilbert, Hertzel, Rudisill, Spengler, and Wirth, among others, which are listed in this volume. These people were the third or fourth American generation of these families, in some instances; they had migrated together from Europe, migrated together within Pennsylvania; and their descendants today are extensively intermarried and still a part of the Adams county community.

Pennsylvania records:
LANCASTER CO. ORPHANS' COURT DOCKET:
1 Mar. 1757: Adam Bender and David Bender, orphan and minor children of Adam Bender, both over 14 years, choose Nathaniel Lightner and John Bare as guardians.

NEW HOLLAND LUTHERAN KB:
Adam Bender had:
Joh. Adam b. 5 Mar. 1739; bp. 23 Apr. 1739

PENNSYLVANIA PATENTS:
AA-1:461: Adam Painter (Bender) obtained the right on a warrant, 24 July 1736, for 140 acres in Earl Twp., Lancaster co. Painter, by name of Bender, d. and left a will dated 13 Nov. 1744, leaving ⅓ of estate to wife Fronica (Veronica) and ⅔ of estate to his 5 children: John, Adam, David, Elizabeth and Maria. Of these, Adam and Elisabeth Bender died as minors without issue. John Bender, the eldest son, obtained a release from John Bear, guardian of David Bender, and Adam Miller, husand of Maria Bender. John Bender obtained a patent 13 July 1761, recorded 15 July 1761.

27. BENDER, JACOB

Molly, 1727
S-H 12, 13

Eschelbach, Baden =
6920 Sinsheim, Elsenz

ESCHELBACH LUTHERAN KB:
Jacob Bender, citizen and inhabitant, and wife Apolonia had:
1. Joh. Jacob b. 21 June 1721
2. Joh. Caspar b. 15 Nov. 1722. Under the parents' names: Moved to the new land.

28. BENDER, JOH. JACOB

1752

Eschelbach, Baden =
6920 Sinsheim, Elsenz

ESCHELBACH LUTHERAN KB:
Michael Bender, citizen, and wife Margaretha had:
Johann Jacob b. 17 Oct. 1693, "Anno '52 given Taufschein—to new land."

29. BENDER, JOHANNES

Prelist ca. 1727

6926 Kirchardt

KIRCHARDT LUTHERAN KB:
Johannes Bender and wife Anna Veronica had:
Anna Catharina b. 21 Apr. 1726

Pennsylvania records:
A Johannes Bendter was a sp. in 1730 at Trinity Lutheran, Lancaster.

WARWICK MORAVIAN KB, LITITZ, LANCASTER CO.:
bu. 17 Apr. 1749 Verona Bender, wife of John Bender aged 42 y.
d. 10 Apr. 1781 John Bender, born in Kirchardt, Baden Sept. 1701. Came to this

country in 1741 (none listed in S-H that year.) United with the Brethren in 1760. Aged 81 y. 9 children.
bu. 1783—Anna Margaret Bender b. 27 Sept. 1711 in the Palatinate. Second wife of John Bender. She had one child, a son, who survived her.

d. 1757 Catharina Bender, infant daughter of John Bender. One year.

LANCASTER CO. WILLS:
John Bender, Warwick twp. (14 Mar. 1775/31 May 1782). Wife, Margaret. Only children named are John and Elisabeth.

MUDDY CREEK LUTHERAN KB, LANCASTER CO.:
Johannes Bendter (Warwick) had:
1. Johannes b. 9 Aug. 1733; sp. Joh. Heinrich Klein
2. Anna b. 21 Sept. 1735
3. Susanna   ⎱ twins b. 19 Sept. 1739
4. Margaretha ⎰ [all sp. from Kirchardt]
5. Anna Barbara b. 19 July 1742
Johannes Bender and his wife Veronica were sp. in 1737 at Muddy Creek. The immigration date of 1741 given in his obituary is wrong.

Johannes Bender, Philadelphia co., nat. by Act of 19 May 1739.

30. BENDER, LEONHARD   6926 Kirchardt
Prelist

SINSHEIM LUTHERAN KB:
Hans Wolff Bender and wife Anna Ursula had:
Hans Leonhard b. 10 Oct. 1703 in Kirchardt

Pennsylvania records:
TRINITY LUTHERAN KB, LANCASTER:
Leonhardt Bender had:
1. Johann Leonhardt b. 30 Aug. 1730
2. Joh. Michael b. 1 Mar. 1734
Margaretha, wife of Leonhardt Bender, of the Mennonites or Anabaptists, "confessed our pure Evangelical Lutheran Religion," was bp. 16 Oct. 1737. Sp. were Michael Korr and Georg Bart and wife.

LANCASTER MORAVIAN KB:
Leonhard Bender (b 19 Sept. 1705 in Kirchard, Pfalz, a Lutheran; d. 13 Oct. 1779). In 1725, he married Maria Margaret Baer (an Anabaptist who received baptism from the Lutherans 16 Oct. 1737, and d. 15 Jan. 1771, aged 58 y. 10 mo.) In 1748, he joined the Moravian congregation in Lancaster. Two sons and two daughters survived him. Ch:
1. Joh. Leonhard m. (1) 27 June 1758 Maria Susanna Farni; m. (2) 19 Nov. 1776 Catharina Loesch (b. 24 June 1748 in Oberfliersheim, Pfalz [= 6509 Ober-Flörsheim])

2. Joh. Michael m. 13 Feb. 1759 Maria Margaretha Taubenberg (b. 23 Sept. 1737 in [6954] Neckar Mühlbach, Pfalz)
3. Maria Margaret b. 26 Sept. 1745; m. 10 Oct. 1762 John Nicolas Müller
4. Barbara m. 6 Jan. 1751 Georg Michael Laubinger [q.v.]

Leonhard Bender, Lancaster co., was naturalized by Act of 19 May 1739

31. BENDER, LEONHARD

Anderson, 1752

S-H 488

Eschelbach, Baden = 6920 Sinsheim, Elsenz

ESCHELBACH LUTHERAN KB:
Joh. Jacob Bender and wife Maria Elisabetha had:
Johann Leonhardt b. 28 Mar. 1728; conf. 1741

Pennsylvania records:
TRINITY LUTHERAN KB, LANCASTER:
m. 1 Jan. 1756 Leonhart Binder from Eschelbach in the Palatinate, and Catharina Haugin, single, from [7404] Ofterdingen.

32. BENDER, MARIA AGNESIA

(Agnes Egenlauf)
1751

Tairnbach = 6909 Mühlhausen, Kraich-gau

DARMBACH (TAIRNBACH) LUTHERAN KB:
Anna Maria Bender had an illegitimate child (father not named):
Maria Agnesia b. 10 Mar. 1725, "1751 given Taufschein—going to new land."
m. 7 Jan. 1749 Johannes Egenlauf, citizen and wagonmaker, and Maria Agnes, the illegitimate daughter of Anna Maria Bender. A note added to the record later that same year (1749) indicates this Agnes committed adultery with another married man, the so-called "Schloss" Jerg Hartlieb, who went to the new land, and she with him. Her husband divorced her and an additional note indicates he died there in Dec. 1750.

33. BENDER, MATTHÄUS   6921 Ittlingen
Prelist

ITTLINGEN LUTHERAN KB:
Matthäus Bender and wife Catharina had:
1. Johann Georg b. 15 July 1703
2. Johann Georg b. 31 March 1707
3. Anna Barbara b. 15 Nov. 1708
4. Catharina Barbara b. 27 Aug. 1711
5. Alexander b. 12 Nov. 1713

Pennsylvania records:
Mattis Bender signed a petition in 1730 for the division of Hanover twp. He was
residing in Falkner Swamp.

TRAPPE LUTHERAN KB, MONTGOMERY CO.:
Joh. Georg Bender had:
Joh. Adam b. 173 ; bp. 4 Jan. 1734

NEW HANOVER LUTHERAN KB, MONTGOMERY CO.:
Alexander and Maria Margareth Bender had:
Joh. Christian b. 31 Mar. 1746

PHILADELPHIA COUNTY WILLS:
Mathias Bender, New Hanover Tp. "am an old man and sickly and uncertain of my
living. (June 25, 1743/Feb. 13, 1744/45). Wit: Daniel Shirdley and Frederick
Richards. Wife, Anna Catharine, sole exr. After wife's decease my son, Frederick,
who is born in Penna. shall be sole Exr. and then he shall give the third parts of
sd. plantation to other 3 ch: John, Alexander, and Anna Barbara, wife of Adam
Reader.

Mathias Pender, Philadelphia co., nat. Philadelphia 1740.

34. BENEDICT, JOH. DIETRICH age 30   6921 Ittlingen
Two Sisters, 1738
S-H 209, 211.

ITTLINGEN LUTHERAN KB:

Joh. Dieterich Benedict was b. 11 June 1710, son of Melchior Benedict and Maria
Elisabetha.
Joh. Dietrich Benedict and wife Anna Barbara had:
1. Anna Margretha b. 30 Nov. 1736

Pennsylvania records:
TRINITY LUTHERAN KB, LANCASTER:
Dietrich Benedict and wife were sp. in 1743.
b. 8 Oct. 1757 Barbara, wife of Dietrich Benedict, age 51 y.
m. 27 Dec. 1757 Dieterich Benedict, widower, and Sophia Maria Brehm, single.
Child:
1. Georg Jacob b. 29 Jan. 1759
d. 19 Feb. 1763 Johann Dieterich Benedict, a married man, aged 52 y., 8 mo., 8
days.

35. BENEDICT, MELCHIOR

6921 Ittlingen

Dragon, 1749
S-H 413
ITTLINGEN LUTHERAN KB:
Melchior Benedict and wife Maria Elisabetha had:
1. Joh. Jacob b. 12 May 1703
2. Anna Catharina b. 2 Oct. 1704
3. Maria Catharina b. 12 Jan. 1707
4. Joh. Dieterich b. 11 June 1710 [q.v.]
5. Joh. Bernhard b. 18 Sept. 1712
*6. Joh. Melchior b. — May 1716
7. Maria Magdalena b. 17 Nov. 1720
8. Joh. Heinrich b. 25 Aug. 1724

m. 10 May 1746 at Zuzenhausen:
Joh. Melchior Benedict, linenweaver, son of the late Melchior Benedict, and Maria Margaretha, dau. of Christoph Hofmann of Zuzenhausen. One child bp. at Ittlingen:
1. Anna Susanna b. 5 May 1747, died on the sea, to Penna. 1749

In the KB there are two communicants lists, one dated 1747 and the other dated 1749, that mention people who are leaving for Pennsylvania. The 1747 list contains the name of Joh. Heinrich Benedict. His name does not appear on the ship's lists and he may have died on the voyage. The 1749 list contains the following members of this family "who are going to Pennsylvania":

Maria Magdalena Benedictin, single
Johann Melchior Benedict and wife (the wife died)
Elisabetha Benedictin, widow (she also died on the voyage)

Pennsylvania records:
TRINITY LUTHERAN KB, LANCASTER:
m. 10 March 1752 Melchior Benedict, widower, and Maria Catharina Quickel, dau. of Philip Quickel.
m. 19 Feb. 1754 Johann Jacob Guth, single, from Schopfloch in Württemberg and Magdalena Benedict from Ittlingen.

36 BENTZ, GEORG HEINRICH

Tairnbach =
6909 Mühlhausen,
Kraichgau

Rawley, 1752
S-H 500

ESCHELBACH LUTHERAN KB:
Conf. 1740 at Darmbach [= Tairnbach] Georg Heinrich Bentz b. 30 Aug. 1727, son of Jerg Michel Bentz

DARMBACH LUTHERAN KB: (TAIRNBACH)
m. 18 Jan. 1752 Georg Heinrich Bentz, son of Jerg Michel Bentz, and Maria Helena, daughter of Hans Jerg Theuer, citizen and cooper. "They left in the month of May for the new land."

Pennsylvania records:
ST. MICHAEL'S AND ZION LUTHERAN KB, PHILADELPHIA:
Georg Heinrich Penz (Bentz) was a witness at the 1759 marriage of Georg Nicolaus Bender, another emigrant from Eschelbach.

37. BENTZ, JOH. WEYRICH

James Goodwill, 1728

Adelshofen, Baden =
7519 Eppingen

S-H 22, 23 (Name on list: Hans Veery Bants, Hans Virech Bontz)

ADELSHOFEN LUTHERAN KB:

m. 27 Apr. 1728 Joh. Weyrich Bentz, son of the late Joh. Jacob Bentz, former citizen at [7519] Elsens, Reformed, and Anna Barbara, dau. of Joh. Georg Schlauch, "Gerichts und Kirchen Vorsteher" here. "Both are going to Pennsylvania."

Pennsylvania records:

MUDDY CREEK LUTHERAN KB, LANCASTER CO.:

Joh. Weyrich Benns sp. 1733 a ch. of Joh. Adam Moser.

Anna Barbara Bentz, Weyrich Bentz's wife, sp. 1730 a ch. of Johannes Schäffer.

WALDSCHMIDT RECORDS:

Conf. 1754 at Seltenreich's church:

Elisabetha, daughter of Weyerich Benss, b. 1 Aug. 1739

Anna Maria Benss, daughter of Weyrich Benss, m. 21 Jan. 1766 Gorg Ruth, son of Peter Ruth.

Catharina Benss, daughter of Weirig Benss, m. 15 Apr. 1755 Jacob Keller, son of Joh. Lehnhart Keller.

Georg Benss, son of Weyrich Benss, m. 8 Dec. 1761 Maria Elis. Holsinger.

YORK CO. WILLS:

Whyrick Bentz, Yorktown, (18 Apr. 1782/11 Apr. 1783) Exrs: Henry Wolf and John Hay. Wife: Anna Maria; Children: Whyrick; Jacob; Peter; Catharine, wife of Jacob Heller; Anna, wife of Georg Rudy; Susanna, wife of Abraham Trostle; Elisabeth, wife of Peter Deckart; Lizzie, wife of Jacob Sidler; Ursula, wife of Henry King.

_____

Wyrick Pence, Lancaster co., nat. Philadelphia, April 1744.

38. BERINGER, ELIAS age 24

Elizabeth, 1738

7103 Schwaigern

S-H 244, 245

SCHWAIGERN LUTHERAN KB:

Hans Georg Beringer, son of Martin Beringer, m. 3 Mar. 1705 Euphrosina, daughter of Hans Jung from Oberndorf, Pastor at Rüdelsberg.

Hans Georg Beringer and wf. Euphrosina had:

Elias bp. 22 Nov. 1712

m. 18 Feb. 1738 Johann Elias Beeringer, weaver, son of Johann Georg Beeringer, and Maria Barbara, daughter of Hans Kober, citizen. (No ch. bp. there.)

ADELSHOFEN LUTHERAN KB:

Hans Georg Beringer, a day laborer, b. in Schwaigern, and wife Euphrosina had:

Catharina Barbara b. 1 Sept. 1716

39. BERINGER, PAUL

Phoenix, 1743

7103 Schwaigern

S-H 346

SCHWAIGERN LUTHERAN KB:

Matthäus Beringer, b. 12 Mar. 1692, son of Hans Jerg Beringer and Barbara; m.

The Neipperg family residence and park and the church form one of two foci of the old portion of Schwaigern. The ruling household demonstrated its wealth in its palace and in the Lutheran church to which they converted during the Reformation. The other focus of town life was the market place, not visible to the right of this picture. Hardly a square as in rectilinear Pennsylvania towns, it shared the same function as scene of regular weekly market activity. Like most German villages, streets wind and twist their narrow way according to factors far removed from modern concepts of city planning.

Photo: Metz

Apr. 1715 Anna Catharina, daughter of Johann Paul Boger and Anna Margaretha. Their children:
1. Hans Jerg b. 14 July 1715
2. Matthäus b. 20 Feb. 1717
3. Johann Dietrich d. 5 Mar. 1719, ¼ year old
4. Anna Catharina b. 14 Apr. 1720 m. 10 Nov. 1744 Christian Abendschön [q.v.]
*5. Johann Paulus b. 25 Sept. 1721
6. Maria Margaretha b. 17 Jan. 1723
7. Maria Elisabetha b. 25 Sept. 1724
8. Joh. Martin b. 8 Dec. 1726; d. 24 Feb. 1729
9. Maria Barbara b. 5 July 1729
10. Maria Dorothea b. 8 Nov. 1732
11. Joh. Matthäus b. 29 Sept. 1735

American records:
MEYNEN'S BIBLIOGRAPHY, ENTRY #6143:
John Paul Barringer, born in Duchy of Würtemberg, Germany June 4, 1721; to Pa. 30 Sept. 1743—settled in North Carolina

40. BERNHARD, HANS HEINRICH   6921 Ittlingen

Molly, 1727
S-H 12, 13 (Henrick Penhart)

ITTLINGEN LUTHERAN KB:
Hans Heinrich Bernhard and wife Anna Catharina had:
1. Anna Margaretha b. 31 Aug. 1720
2. Anna Catharina b. 4 July 1722
3. Joh. Georg b. 24 Feb. 1724
4. Sabina b. 26 Mar. 1725; d. young
5. Anna Barbara b. 16 Mar. 1727

Henry Bernhart, Bucks co., nat. by Act of 19 May 1739
Jno. Geo. Bernard, Easton, Northampton co., nat. Philadelphia Fall 1765.

41. BESINGER, ANDREAS age 24   6928 Helmstadt—Bargen

Hope, 1733   Hoffenheim =
S-H 116, 120, 121 (Name on A list: Besenar, B list: 6920 Sinsheim, Elsenz
Besinger)

HOFFENHEIM LUTHERAN KB:
m. 26 Feb. 1733 Andreas Besinger, born in Helmstadt, and Maria Barbara Ritzhaupt, daughter of Adam Ritzhaupt.

Pennsylvania records:
Pennsylvanische Berichte, 13 Feb. 1761: Land of the Pennsylvania Land Company is advertised for sale. Among the occupants: Lampeter and Manheim twps, Lancaster co. Andreas Bersinger.

Andreas Bersinger of Lancaster co. was nat. by Act of 19 May 1739.

42. BESSERER, JOH. CHRISTOPH   Massenbach =
BESSERER, SIMON, dumb.   7103 Schwaigern

Dragon, 1732
S-H 97, 98, 99

MASSENBACH LUTHERAN KB:
Joh. Christoph Besserer and wife Maria Magdalena had:
1. Euphrosina Magdalena b. 2 Jan. 1706
2. Maria Euphrosina b. 27 Aug. 1707
*3. Joh. Christoph b. 19 Jan. 1710
*4. Joh. Simon b. 4 Oct. 1711
5. Joh. Michael b. 5 Sept. 1713
6. Maria Magdalena b. 9 Sept. 1714
7. Joh. Simon b. 26 Oct. 1715; d. young
8. Joh. Georg b. 27 Jan. 1717, d. young
9. Maria Catharina b. 6 Feb. 1720; d. young
10. Joh. Michael b. 12 Dec. 1722; d. young
11. Wilhelm 1725; d. young

Pennsylvania records:
CHRIST LUTHERAN KB, STOUCHSBURG (TULPEHOCKEN), BERKS CO.:
d. 11 Jan. 1773 Simon Beshore, son of Christoph, b. 4 Oct. 1711 in the illustrious

city of Massebach near Heilbron in Germany. Age 61 y. 3 mo. 5 days. Bu. in Heidelberg church yard.
Christoph Besher appears on a list of members of this congregation, dated 1743.

43. BEYERLE, ANDREAS age 23

Charming Nancy, 1738

S-H 246, 247, 248

Rohrbach, Kraichgau =
6920 Sinsheim, Elsenz

ROHRBACH REFORMED KB:
Hans Martin Beÿerle (Bäuerlein) and wife Anna Sara had:
1. Hans Andreas bp. 26 June 1713
2. Hans Michael bp. 7 January 1717
3. Susanna, b. 1 November 1724
Hans Martin Beyerle was a brother of Hans Daniel Beyerly of Sinsheim whose sons Michael (44) and Jacob (45) follow.

Pennsylvania records:
TRINITY LUTHERAN KB, LANCASTER:
Anno 1743, October 24, Johan Michel Beyerle, at the time a single baker, donated the Baden-Durlach Evangelical Lutheran Liturgy to the church.
Joh. Michael Beyerle and wife Anna Maria (in one record he is called Johan Michael Jr.) serve as sponsors for the children of Andreas Beyerele and of Susanna Tochtermann in the 1750s.
Johann Michael Beyerele, a married man, baker, died December 10, 1766, aged 50 years.

Andreas Beyerely and wife Maria Catharina are sponsors in 1743. He and sister Susanna are sponsors in 1743.
Andreas Beyerle and wife Beatrix, Reformed, nee Kuhlin, had:
1. Michael, b. 7 Dec. 1748
2. Catharina Eisabetha, b. 9 Nov. 1750
3. Maria Elisabetha, b. 7 Apr. 1752
4. Johann Frantz, b. 4 Mar. 1754

Jacob Friedrich Tochtermann and wife Anna Susanna are sponsors in 1749. They had:
1. Anna Maria, b. 3 Feb. 1751
2. Rosina Susanna, b. 4 February 1753
3. Georg Friedrich, b. 12 July 1755
4. Christina Margaret, b. 30 Dec. 1757, d. 31 Jan. 1759
5. Christina Sophia, b. 30 Dec. 1759
6. unnamed child, b. 22 Aug. 1762

LANCASTER CO, WILLS:
Hans Michael Beyerle, Lancaster, tavernkeeper (24 November 1766/22 December 1766). Brother Hans Martin in Germany; sister Anna Maria in Germany; brother Andrew in America; Trinity Lutheran Church in Lancaster (50 pounds); wife Anna Maria; Maria Elisabeth, daughter of Andrew; children of stepsister Susannah, wife of Frederick Daughterman.

VIRGINIA RECORDS:
Chalkley III: 53
Andrew Byarly bought items at Vendue at Michael Stumps on South Fork in Hampshire Co., (W) Va.

44. BEŸERLE, HANS MICHAEL   6920 Sinsheim, Elsenz

Alexander and Anne, 1730
S-H 36, 37

SINSHEIM REFORMED KB:
m. 8 Feb. 1695 Joh. Daniel Beyerlen, son of Hans Daniel Beyerlen, citizen and baker, and Anna Maria, daughter of Hans Jacob Muller.

SINSHEIM LUTHERAN KB:
Johan Daniel Beÿerle and wife Anna Maria had:
    Hans Michael b. 12 May 1698; conf. 1711
This Michael Beyerle seems to have migrated to Shepherdstown, Berkeley County, West Virginia, where he died in 1781.

Pennsylvania records:
TRINITY LUTHERAN KB, LANCASTER:
Michael Beyerle and wife Anna Catharina appear as sponsors from 1733 to 1738.

Michael Byerly, Lancaster co., nat. by Act of 29 March 1735.

45. BEYERLE, JOH. JACOB   6920 Sinsheim, Elsenz
                                           6924 Neckarbischofsheim
Dragon, 1732
S-H 97, 98, 99

SINSHEIM REFORMED KB:

m. 8 Feb. 1695 Joh. Daniel Beyerlen, son of Hans Daniel Beyerlen, citizen and baker, and Anna Maria, daughter of Hans Jacob Muller.

SINSHEIM LUTHERAN KB:
Joh. Daniel Beÿerlin and wife Anna Maria had:
    Hans Jacob b. 22 Mar. 1703 at Sinsheim; conf. 1716

NECKARBISCHOFSHEIM LUTHERAN KB:
m. 23 Oct. 1725 Joh. Jacob Beyerlin, baker, son of Johann Beyerlin of Sintzheim, and Maria Rosina Juliana, daughter of the late Herr Joh. Georg Seybold, former barber. Children:

SINSHEIM LUTHERAN KB:
    1. Joh. Henrich b. 7 Sept. 1726   ·
    2. Maria Margretha Friederica b. 10 Apr. 1728
    3. Joh. Friedrich b. 24 Mar. 1730
    4. Maria Elisabetha b. 23 Sept. 1731

Pennsylvania records:
TRINITY LUTHERAN KB, LANCASTER:
Jacob Beyerle had:
    5. Joh. Ludwig b. 22 May 1735

The Kraichgau countryside is strikingly similar in topography to many parts of southeastern and central Pennsylvania. The cloister buildings at Sinsheim house a youth hostel today, the town itself nestled in a valley below along the Elsenz creek.

Photo courtesy I. Doll Buchhandlung, Sinsheim

6. Maria Rosina b. 13 Mar. 1738; d. young
7. Maria Rosina b. 8 Dec. 1740
Margaretha Friederica Beyerlin was a sp. there in 1739.

St. Michael's Lutheran KB, Germantown:
m. 23 May 1758 Nicolaus Knecht, a smith from Lancaster, and Maria Rosina Bayerle, daughter of Jacob Bayerle.
m. 15 Mar. 1761 Jacob Bayerle and Anna Maria Geisser.

St. Michael's and Zion Lutheran KB, Philadelphia:
d. 20 Nov. 1768 M. Rosina Juliana Beyerle, wife of Jacob Beyerle, nee Seyboldt, daughter of Christoph and Eva Rosina (nee Bräumer) Seyboldt from Bischofsheim in the Unter Pfaltz, in vicinity of Creichgau between Heidelberg and Philipsburg. She was b. 1703 and m. Jacob Beyerle at Sintzheim in Amt Bretten, Unterpfaltz ober Heidelberg on 23 Oct. 1725. Came to America in 1732 with 3 children. Had 10 children, 4 sons and 6 daughters, of whom 2 sons and 3 daughters are living.

Reading Lutheran KB, Berks co.:
d. 21 Jan. 1776 Joh. Jacob Bayerly, b. about 1701 in Senssheim, Wurtt, son of Joh. Georg and Anna Maria; during his married life he begat 2 sons and 5 daughters of whom 2 sons and 1 daughter survive. Age about 75 y.
[Note by compiler: a thorough search of the Sinsheim record reveals no Joh. Georg Beyerle, so possibly an error was made in recording this obituary. Hans Jacob Beyerle b. 1703 at Sinsheim, son of Joh. Daniel Beÿerlin, was a brother of Hans Michael Beyerle, an earlier emigrant who also settled at Lancaster.]
bu. 2 June 1794 at Reading Joh. Henry Beyerle, son of Jacob Beyerle, b. 7 Sept.

1726 in Sinsheim, Pfalz. Unmarried. d. 31 May at the house of Paul Beyerle, a son of Ludwig. Age 67 y. 8 mo. 23 days.

Jacob Byerly, Lancaster co., nat. by Act. of 29 March 1735.

46. BICKEL, JOH. CHRISTOFF age 48   Massenbach =
    BICKEL, JOH. PHILIP age 16   7103 Schwaigern

Mary, 1732
S-H 94, 95, 96 (on A list Pickle)

MASSENBACH LUTHERAN KB:
Hans Jacob Bickel and Ursula had:
    Christoph b. 27 Nov. 1682
m. 8 Aug. 1715 Joh. Christoff Bikel, son of Hans Jacob Bikel, "Gerichtsverwandten," and Maria Rosina, daughter of the late Thomas Sehner of [7103] Stetten.
They had:
    1. Joh. Philipp b. 8 Aug. 1717
    2. Margretha Rosina b. 17 Jan. 1720
    3. Jacobina Fridricca b. 1 June 1722
    4. Ludwig Adam b. 1 Apr. 1725
    5. Philippina Rosina b. 14 Sept. 1730

STETTEN AM HEUCHELBERG LUTHERAN KB: [= 7103 SCHWAIGERN]
m. 30 Jan. 1677 Georg Thomas Sohner, widower and "Gerichtsverwandten," and
Anna, daughter of Hans Joost, citizen and tailor at [7103] Niderhofen. Their
daughter:
    Anna Rosina bp. 4 Sept. 1690

Pennsylvania records:
OLD GOSHENHOPPEN LUTHERAN KB, MONTGOMERY CO.:
Johann Christoph Bickel, age 69 years, b. 27 Nov. 1682, d. 1756. Father was
Johann Jacob Bickel and mother was Ursula. On 8 Aug. 1715 he m. Rosina
Soehner, b. 4 Sept. 1690 from Stetten, below Heuchelberg in the county of Wir-
tenberg. Her father was George Soehner and her mother was Anna, both Lutheran.
In 1732 they came to America. Children:
    1. Joh. Philipp b. 1716; married, lives across the river in Jersey.
    2. Rosina Margr. b. 17 Jan. 1720; wife of Joh. Dottinger, dwelling in Falckner
       Schwamm.
    3. Jacobina Fredrica b. 1 June 1722; has married a Quaker, Jams Tschah,
       dwelling near the river.
    4. Ludwig Adam b. 1 Apr. 1725; married in 1751 Barbara, daughter of Georg
       Michael Schweinhard and Magdalena of Falckner Schwamm. (Note: Has
       moved away.)
    5. Philippina Rosina b. 14 Sept. 1730; d. 1732 in Rotterdam.

TRAPPE LUTHERAN KB:
d. 10 Dec.1756 Christoph Bukel, father of Ludewig, b. Massebach 27 Nov. 1682.
m. 1715, came to Pennsylvania 1732 with 5 children who were baptized there by
Pastor König.

Ludwig Pickle, Douglass twp., Philadelphia co., nat. 24 Sept. 1755.

47. BICKEL, JOH. FRIDRICH

Jacob, 1749

Massenbach =
7103 Schwaigern

S-H 417 (Buckel on list)

MASSENBACH LUTHERAN KB:
Joh. Georg Bikel and wife Anna Maria had:
Joh. Fridrich b. 5 Oct. 1723
m. 17 July 1742 Joh. Friderich Bikel, son of Hans Jerg Bikel from Massenbach, and Eva Dorothea, daughter of Michael Müller, wagonmaker and citizen. [In one bp. record her name is given as Catharina Dorothea and in another bp. record she is named Maria Dorothea. Joh. Michael Müller and wife Catharina Elisabetha had a daughter Catharina Dorothea b. 3 Oct. 1714.]
Joh. Friederich Bickel, weaver, and wife (Catharina) Dorothea had:
1. Joh. Jacob b. 16 June 1744
2. Maria Elisabetha b. 23 Mar. 1748

Pennsylvania records:
BINDNAGLE'S LUTHERAN KB, LEBANON CO.:
John Frederick Bickel, b. 5 Oct. 1723 in Massenbach, son of Joh. Georg Bickel and wife Anna Maria. m. to Catharina Dorothea Müller for 45 y. 3 mo. and had 7 children. In Nov. 1788 he m. Mrs. Elizabeth Berger, widow. No children to second m. He d. 10 Aug. 1794, age 71 y. 10 mo. 5 days.

TRINITY LUTHERAN KB, LANCASTER:
Friedrich Bickel and wife Dorothea had:
3. Antoni b. 25 Aug. 1750

48. BINDNAGEL, JOHANNES age 31

Loyal Judith, 1732

Ehrstädt =
6920 Sinsheim, Elsenz

S-H 89, 91, 92

EHRSTÄDT LUTHERAN KB:
m. 14 Sept. 1728 Johannes Bindnagel, single son of Adam Bindnagel, former citizen and "des Gerichts" and Maria Regina Mantz, single daughter of the late Jacob Mantz citizen in Zaisenhausen [= 7119 Mulfingen, Jagst], Württemberg. No children bp. at Ehrstädt.

Pennsylvania records:
STOEVER'S RECORDS:
John Bindtnagel (Swatara) had:
1. Anna Sabina b. 11 Sept. 1733
2. Johannes b. 7 Feb. 1735
3. Joh. Martin b. 7 Sept. 1736
(These bp. also recorded in Hill Lutheran KB, North Annville twp., Lebanon co.)

TRINITY LUTHERAN KB, LANCASTER:
Johannes Bindtnagel and wife Maria Regina sp. 1736 and 1738 two children of Joh. Georg Dörr.

HILL LUTHERAN KB:
m. 9 Oct. 1750 Johann Wolff Kissner and Anna Sabina Bindtnagel

Hans Bindnagel, who was married in 1728 in Ehrstädt near Sinsheim and emigrated in 1732, was one of the founders of a Lutheran congregation at the juncture of the Swatara and the Quitopahilla creeks in what is now Lebanon county. The church bears his name. The building now standing dates from 1803 and is one of the most perfectly preserved churches of its period. It probably replaced a church built in the 1750s, for whose use Bindnagel donated a large piece of brown cloth which has been traditionally called an altar cloth. It bears the date 1754 and the initials HBN, which in German fashion refer to *H*ans *B*ind*n*agel.

Photographs:
J. Godshall and A. Keyser

On 27 Jan. 1753 John Bindnagel deeded about 5 A. to the trustees of the "Lutheran congregation at Great Swetara in Derry twp." for a church, burial ground and school house. [See Charles H. Glatfelter, *Pastors and People*, I:330 for additional details of this congregation, known as Bindnagel's Church.]

DAUPHIN CO. DEEDS:
A-I:163: John Penagle warranted 199 A. in Londonderry twp. on 26 Oct. 1753. He d. leaving issue: Martin, only son, and Sabina, wife of John Kisner. John and Sabina Kisner released to Martin Penagle on 22 Feb. 1785. Martin Penagle and wife Elisabeth sold to Charles Barger.

DAUPHIN CO. WILLS:
Martin Bindnagel of Paxton twp., Dauphin co. (12 Sept. 1792/2 Oct. 1792). Wife Maria Elizabeth, children: son John, daughters Christina Elisabeth Dilmann, Catharina Dorothea, and Maria Barbara. Wife and Jacob Zollinger, exrs.

49. BISCHOFF, JOH. GEORG age 20

Halifax, 1753
S-H 560, 561, 563

Elsenz =
7519 Eppingen

ELSENZ REFORMED KB:
Daniel Bischoff, shoemaker, and wife Walburgis had:
Joh. Georg bp. ——— 1733 (exact date missing from side of page.)

Pennsylvania records:
Pennsylvanische Berichte, 23 May 1760:
Georg Bischoff or perhaps Dicken Albrecht, from Elsens in the Pfaltz had last year his residence in Weitmarsch and at the end of last May went away from there. If he sees this, he shall come for his chest and clothing as the landlord has paid out a small sum for him.

50. BISCHOFF, MARIA BARBARA
    BISCHOFF, ANNA MARGARETHA
    BISCHOFF, ANNA MARIA KUNIGUNDA

Hasselbach and
Adersbach =
6920 Sinsheim, Elsenz

Probably on *Friendship*, 1739 with Jacob Frank and others from area.

ADERSBACH LUTHERAN KB:
Georg Philipp Bischoff was b. 28 May 1667 son of Jacob Bischoff and wife Agnes at Hasselbach. With his first wife Catharina he had:
1. Georg Adam b. 13 Oct. 1692
2. Maria Barbara b. 27 Jan. 1695
3. Joh. Michael b. 13 July 1697
4. Maria Margretha b. 29 Dec. 1698
5. Maria Christina b. 15 Feb. 1701
6. Maria Catharina b. 7 Jan. 1708
The mother, Catharina, died 5 days after the birth of this child.
With his second wife Barbara he had:
7. Anna Margaretha b. 18 Sept. 1709

    8. Anna Christina b. 2 Apr. 1711
    9. Bernhard Andreas b. 28 Mar. 1714
   10. Maria Kunigunda b. 5 Apr. 1718

Dietrich Saltzgeber, Reformed (b. 27 Jan. 1705, son of Johann Ferdinand Saltzgeber and Barbara, nee Ringer), m. at Dühren 9 May 1730 Margaretha Bischoff,
daughter of Georg Philipp Bischoff and Barbara, nee Wezel in Adersbach. Their
children:
    1. Maria Magdalena b. 29 Jan. 1731
    2. Margaretha b. 10 Dec. 1732
    3. Susanna Esther b. 23 Jan. 1736
    4. Johann Reichardt b. 1 Mar. 1737
Dietrich Saltzgeber emigrated with wife and four children in March/April 1738 to
Pennsylvania.

Pennsylvania records:
PHILADELPHIA WILLS:
Maria Barbara Zeigler, Boro of Lancaster, widow. 16 Apr. 1753/12 Feb. 1756; Exr.
bro-in-law Jacob Frank. To loving sister Anna Marigretha, wife of Diterick Saltzgeber, £5. To Jacob Frank, city of Philadelphia, cordwainer, "my brother-in-law,
lot and messuage in Boro of Lancaster during his natural life, and at his death, to
his heirs lawfully begotten upon the body of my dear sister, Anna Maria Kunigunda,
his lawful wife." Balance of estate to Jacob Frank during his natural life and then
to his said children. Wit. by Jacob Wise and Peter Miller, Jr.

LANCASTER MORAVIAN KB:
Jacob Frank, b. 28 July 1714 in Sinsheim, d. 13 Apr. 1787 at Lancaster; m. 1740
at Philadelphia Anna Maria Bischoff, b. 5 Apr. 1718 in "Bedersbach, Zinzen" [=
Adersbach near Sinsheim]. She d. 7 Dec. 1804. Children:
    1. Anna Margaretha b. 7 Dec. 1740 at Philadelphia; m. 1758 Friedrich Lutz.
    2. Daniel b 2 Feb. 1747
    3. Elisabetha b. 16 Mar. 1752
    4. Peter b. 20 May 1756
d. 6 Feb. 1756 Maria Barbara Ziegler, a widow, aged 61 y. 10 days.

Christ Lutheran KB, York:
Dietrich Saltzgeber and wife had:
    Engel Elisabetha b. 6 Apr. 1742
    Joh. Caspar b. 28 Feb. 1747

51. BISECKER, JACOB age 46   7519 Eppingen

Plaisance, 1732
S-H 78, 80, 81, 82 (with Anna Mare age 20)

EPPINGEN REFORMED KB:
m. 12 Jan. 1712 Jacob Bisecker, single son of Jacob Bisecker, citizen and inhabitant, and Anna Maria, daughter of the late Johann Klotz, citizen and mason at [6927] Treschklingen, Gemmingen jurisdiction. Children:
1. Joh. Christoph bp. 2 July 1713
2. Hans Jacob bp. 19 Sept. 1714
3. Juliana bp. 28 Nov. 1719; d. 6 Jan. 1722

Pennsylvania records:
NEW GOSHENHOPPEN REFORMED KB; MONTGOMERY CO.:
Jacob Biseker and wife Anna Maria had:
Johan Niclaus bp. 24 Sept. 1740

OLD GOSHENHOPPEN LUTHERAN KB, MONTGOMERY CO.:
d. 27 Mar. 1754 Jacob Bisecker, b. 1687. bu. in the Old Goshenhoppen cemetery 29 Mar. His father was Jacob Bisecker from Manheim, Reformed. In his first marriage he lived 17 years and had 5 children, of whom only a son survives. He lived in his second marriage 22 years and had 3 children, who survive along with their mother. He came to America in 1733.

52. BISSECKER, CONRAD   6921 Ittlingen

Restauration, 1747
S-H 365

ITTLINGEN LUTHERAN KB:
m. 26 Jan. 1745 Conrad Bissecker, son of Joh. Jacob Bissecker from Menzingen (= 7527 Kraichtal), and Eva, dau. of Joh. Michael Funck. They had:
1. Johann Jacob b. 3 Jan. 1746
On a communicants' list dated 1747, a group of people are mentioned as "going to the new land." Joh. Conrad Bissecker and wife appear on this list.

Pennsylvania records:
INDIANFIELD LUTHERAN KB, FRANCONIA TWP., MONTGOMERY CO.:
John Conrad Bisecker and wife Eva had
Anna Barbara b. 22 Feb. 1754

WILLIAMS TWP. CONGREGATION, NORTHAMPTON CO., PA.:
Conrad Piesäcker and wife Anna Maria (?) had:
Georg b. 5 Dec. 1758; bp. 29 March 1759; sp. Georg Hauer and Catharina

DRYLAND UNION CHURCH, NAZARETH TWP., NORTHAMPTON CO.:
Jacob Bisecker and wife Catharine had:
1. Maria Catharina b. 26 Feb. 1778; sp. Conrad Bisecker and Maria Eva
2. Barbara b. 7 July 1784
3. John b. 12 Nov. 1787
4. Frederick b. 13 Feb. 1790

53. BISWANGER, PETER   Hoffenheim =
                                                  6920 Sinsheim, Elsenz
Thistle, 1730
S-H 31, 32, 33

HOFFENHEIM LUTHERAN KB:
Caspar Biswanger and wife Maria Elisabetha had:
    Georg Peter b. 19 July 1705; conf. 1721

Pennsylvania records:
STOEVER'S RECORDS:
m. 7 Jan. 1734 Geo. Peter Bisswanger and Justina Elis. Riess, Germantown. They
had:
    1. Maria Barbara b. 7 Jan. 1735; bp. 7 Apr. 1735
Justina Biswanger m. (2) 25 May 1747 Carl Evald at St. Michael's and Zion,
Philadelphia
Elisabeth Biswanger m. 8 Dec. 1757 Peter Lamferd
Barbara Biswanger m. 23 Oct. 1760 Joh. Martin Roh

54. BLATTNER, MICHEL age 23   Waldangelloch =
                                                  6920 Sinsheim, Elsenz
Britannia, 1731
S-H 47, 49, 50, 51 53 (with Maria Katherina, age 27
and Georg Michel, age 2 and Katherina Bladner, age
36 Anna Maria, age 20)

WALDANGELLOCH LUTHERAN KB:
Hans Jerg Blatner and wife Apollonia had:
    1. Michael bp. 2 Feb. 1708 at (?) Pappenheim [? = 8834 Pappenheim]
    2. Anna Maria bp. 24 July 1711
m. 3 Nov. 1726 Hans Michel Blatner and Maria Catharina, dau. of Hans Jerg
Rennert (Reinhard elsewhere in the records.) Children:
    1. Jerg Michel b. 12 Mar. 1729
    2. Anna Margaretha b. 30 Aug. 1730
Hans Michel Blatner's wife Maria Catharina was bp. 5 June 1701, dau. of Hans
Gerg Rennert (Reinhard) and wife Susanna Heinsin.
Apollonia, wife of Hans Jerg Blatner, d. 19 Dec. 1728
(Note: The Katherina Bladner, age 36, on the ship's list is not identified in the
Waldangelloch KB—it is possible that Hans Jerg Blatner married again after the
death of Apollonia in 1728, perhaps in a nearby village.)

Pennsylvania records:
CHRIST "LITTLE TULPEHOCKEN" LUTHERAN KB:
Michael Plattner had:
    1. Joh. Conrad b. 24 Jan. 1738; sp. were Joh. Conrad Scharpff and wife.
    2. Eva b. 1 Oct. 1739; sp. Michael Busch and wife.
    3. Joh. Michael b. 2 July 1741; sp. Joh. Michael Busch and wife.
m. 12 Jan. 1736 George William Riegel and Anna Mary Plattner

———————

Michael Platner, Richmond tp., Berks co. nat. Philadelphia 24 Sept. 1762

55. BLEYMEIER, MARTIN

Jacob, 1749

S-H 418

Massenbach =
7103 Schwaigern

MASSENBACH LUTHERN KB:

m. (1) 6 May 1732 Georg Martin Bleymeier, son of Hans Jerg Bleymeier, citizen at [7103] Stetten, and Johanna Fridricca, daughter of Joh. Ulrich Schmaltzhaff. They had:

1. Joh. Georg b. 9 June 1733
2. Joh. Abraham b. 7 Sept. 1734
3. Joh. Jacob b. 23 Dec. 1737
4. Christianus b. 3 Apr. 1741.

(2) 10 May 1746 Martin Bleÿmeyer, "des Gerichts," widower, and Catharina, daughter of the late Leonhardt Rüb, former citizen at [7103] Stetten an dem Heuchelberg. They had:

5. Maria Elisabetha b. 20 Nov. 1746; d. young
6. Georg Martin b. 14 Aug. 1748; d. young

Pennsylvania records:

TRINITY LUTHERAN KB, LANCASTER:

Georg Friedrich, little son of Martin Bleymeier and Catharina, b. 15 July, bp. the same day, d. 3 Nov. 1750.

BLIMYERS UNION KB, HOPEWELL TWP., YORK CO.:

Jacob Bleimeyer (Bleymeyer) and wife Catharine had:

1. Joh. Jacob b. 26 Dec. 1766
2. Anna Elisabeth b. 13 Dec. 1768
3. Bernhard b. 10 May 1771
4. Sophia b. 12 Apr. 1774
5. Georg Martin b. 28 May 1776
6. John b. 7 May 1779
7. Rosina b. 22 Apr. 1781

Christian Bleymeyer and wife Maria Elisabeth had:

1. John Christian b. 13 May 1770; one of the sp.: Martin Bleymeyer
2. Magdalena b. 1 Nov. 1771
3. Conrad b.   Jan. 1774
4. John Jacob b. 22 Mar. 1782

Abraham Bleimyer of York twp., York co., nat. at York 20 May 1768

56. BÖCKLE, GOTTLIEB

Richmond, 1764

S-H 696

7103 Schwaigern

SCHWAIGERN LUTHERAN KB:

Jacob Böckle was b. 17 May 1702, son of Hans Jacob Böckle and Anna Margretha Kober. He m. 19 June 1731 Catharina Frey. Jacob Böckle and wife Maria Catharina had:

Joh. Gottlieb b. 18 Nov. 1738

57. BÖCKLE, HANS JACOB age 46   7103 Schwaigern
BÖCKLE, CHRISTOPH age 20
BÖCKLE, MATTEUS age 17
BÖCKLE, ULRICH age 19
BÖCKLE, HENRICK age 12

Samuel, 1732
S-H 59, 60, 61, 63, 64 (with Barbara, age 42; Katharina, age 8; Barbara age 11.)

SCHWAIGERN LUTHERAN KB:
m. 31 May 1701 Hans Jacob Böckle, son of Jacob Böckle, and Anna Margretha,
daughter of Christoph Kober. They had:
1. Jacob b. 17 May 1702; m. 19 June 1731 Catharina Freÿ; remained in
   Schwaigern
2. Hans Jerg b. 1 Dec. 1703
3. Christoph b. 19 June 1705
4. Hans Ulrich b.   Dec. 1707
5. Mathias b. 12 Aug. 1712
6. Heinrich b. 5 Apr. 1716
7. Anna Barbara b. 17 May 1719
8. Maria Catharina b. 30 Mar. 1723
d. 24 May 1724 Anna Gretha, Jacob Böcklin's wife
m. 5 Dec. 1724 Hans Jacob Böcklin, widower, and Maria Barbara, daughter of the
late Peter Ebermann. They had:
9. Joh. Bernhard b. 20 July 1726; d. 7 May 1727

Pennsylvania records:
ST. MICHAEL'S AND ZION LUTHERAN KB, PHILADELPHIA:
The following members of this family appear on communicants' lists in the specified
year:
      Maria Barbara Böckler 1733
      Matthias Bockle 1734
      Ulrich Bockle 1734
      Maria Barbara Bockle 1734
      Maria Barbara Bockle, Jr. 1734
      Matthias Bockle 1735
      Heinrich Bockle 1735

MUDDY CREEK LUTHERAN KB, LANCASTER CO.:
In 1737 Heinrich Böckel is a sponsor
Ulrich Böckle had:
1. Margaretha Dorothea b. 11 June 1733
2. Catharina Charlotta b. 28 Mar. 1735
3. Joh. Heinrich b. 22 Nov. 1740
4. Maria Margaretha b. 29 Apr. 1743
m. 30 May 1743 Matheis Böckle and Maria Dorothea Riedt, Earltown (Stoever's
records) They had:
1. Catharina Barbara b. 29 May 1749
2. Mattheis b. 2 Nov. 1751

58. BOGER, JOH. PAUL age 40   7103 Schwaigern
BOGER, PHILIP age 18

Samuel, 1732
S-H 60, 61, 62, 64, 65 (Others on ship: Eva Bogerin
age 35, Mathias age 13, Michael age 12, and Justina
age 5)

SCHWAIGERN LUTHERAN KB:
m. 1710 (no date given) Paulus Boger, son of Pauli Boger, citizen and butcher, and
Eva, daughter of Paul Fux (Fuchs), citizen. They had:
1. Hans Paulus b. 30 Mar. 1712
2. Joh. Philipp b. 18 June 1714
3. Matheus b. 21 Nov. 1716
4. Joh. Michael b. 15 Apr. 1719
5. Anna Catharina b. 22 Nov. 1721; d. young
6. Joh. Georg b.   July 1724; d. young
7. Justina b. 17 Oct. 1726
8. Joh. Jacob b. 12 Aug. 1730

Pennsylvania records:
PHILADELPHIA CO. WILLS:
N:245: Paul Boger, Whitemarsh twp., Philadelphia co. (8 Feb. 1765/15 Mar.
1765). Wife Christianna and ch. Margaret, Elizabeth and Daniel. Executor to issue
a deed to brother Martin Boger for tract of about 82 acres in Gwinned sold to him.

STOEVER'S RECORDS:
Mattheis Boger m. 7 Jan. 1746 Anna Magdalena Wampfler, Lebanon.

JORDAN LUTHERAN KB, LEHIGH CO.:
Matthias Boger and wife Magdalena had:
      Hans Michel b. 28 Sept. 1746; sp. were Michael Wamffler and Anna Veronica
m. 16 May 1742 Philip Boger and Anna Margaretha Fix.

Mathias Boger, Lebanon tp., Lancaster co. nat. Philadelphia Fall 1765

59. BOGER, MARTIN   7103 Schwaigern

Pennsylvania Merchant, 1731
S-H, 43, 45, 46

SCHWAIGERN LUTHERAN KB:
Paul Boger, butcher, and wife Anna Margretha had:
      Martin b. 23 July 1703

Pennsylvania Records:
Named in will of his brother Paul (1765) as owner of 82 A. tract in Gwinned.

Martin Boger, Long Swamp twp., Berks co., nat. Philadelphia 10 April 1755

The base of the Lutheran church tower in Eschelbach dates to early times. The village itself is first mentioned in 1071. It became Lutheran in 1555 and its earliest church book was begun in 1616. Eschelbach belonged to the bishopric of Speyer in the eighteenth century.

60. BOGNER, MARIA HELENA (ELISABETHA)   Eschelbach, Baden =
                                                             6920 Sinsheim, Elsenz
1753

ESCHELBACH LUTHERAN KB:
Joh. Georg Christoph Bogner, organist and schoolmaster, and wife Maria Magdalena had a dau.:
      Maria Helena b. 6 Dec. 1722. "Given Taufschein in 1753—going to the new land."
In the conf. record, 1736, her name is given as Maria Elisabetha.

61. BOPENMEIR, STEPHEN   Massenbach =
Francis & Elizabeth, 1742   7103 Schwaigern
S-H 327, 329

MASSENBACH LUTHERAN KB:
m.   Nov. 1700 Friderich Poffenmajer, the younger, and Anna Barbara, daughter of Christoph Besserer. Fridrich Poffenmeier, the younger, and Maria Barbara had:
      Joh. Philipp Stephanus b. 26 Dec. 1721

Pennsylvania records:
DILLINGERSVILLE LUTHERAN KB, LEHIGH CO.:
Stephan Bobbenmeyer and Maria Sophia Thürrin sp. 1746 a child of Michael

Floris.
Philipp Stephan Poppenmeier and wife Sophia had:
1. Gabriel b. 2 Dec. ; bp. 15 May 1749; sp. Gabriel Köhler [q.v.] and wife Anna Elisabeth
2. Anna Elisabeth b. 4 Dec. ; bp. 16 Dec. 1750; sp. Gabriel Köhler and wife Anna Elisabeth
3. Maria Margrete bp. 15 Feb. 1756
Communicants 22 Apr. 1751:
Philipp Stepan Poppenmeyer and wife Sophia

Stephan Poppenmyer, Upper Milford twp., Northampton co., nat. Fall 1765

62. BOPP, JOH. GEORG

Bonfeld = 6927 Bad Rappenau
7141 Grossbottwar

1717
Bonfeld Emigrant List: Hans Jerg Bopp, Lanio (Lanius = Butcher) with wife

BONFELD LUTHERAN KB:
m. 28 Feb. 1716 Johann Georg Bopp, butcher, son of Gottlieb Bopp, citizen and butcher at Grossen Bottwar, and Anna Felicitas, daughter of Abraham Merckle [q.v.]. Joh. Georg Bopp and wife Anna Felicitas had:
Jacob b. 25 July 1716; bp. 26 July; d. 26 Feb. 1717, age 7 mo.
"Hans Jerg Popp, butcher, son-in-law of Abraham Merckle, emigrated with his wife in 1717."

Pennsylvania records:
ST. MICHAEL'S AND ZION LUTHERAN KB, PHILADELPHIA:
bu. 19 Oct. 1773 widow Anna Felicitas Bob, daughter of Abraham Merckle from Bohnfeld in the Oberpfaltz; b. 6 Jan. 1689; bp., conf. and m. there to Johann Georg Bob. Was 40 y. in this land. Had 2 sons and 1 daughter. Husband d. in 1740. She lived with her son, Joh. Georg Bob. d. 18 Oct., age 84 y. 9 mo.

63. BÖRINGER, STEPHAN

6921 Michelfeld = Angelbachtal

St. Andrew, 1738
S-H 237, 238, 239

MICHELFELD LUTHERAN KB:
Stephan Boringer, son of the late Jacob Boringer, citizen at Eckwaldes, Kirchheimer Ambts an der Teck [= 7321 Eckwälden], m. 6 May 1732 Anna Catharina, daughter of Weÿerich Mittebühl. (Weÿerich Mittenbühl, son of Sebastian M. and wife Maria Catharina, daughter of Weÿrich Seltzer, had a dau. Anna Catharina b. 18 Feb. 1711.) Böringer children:
1. Maria Philippina b. 7 May 1733
2. Johann Michael b. 2 Jan. 1736
3. Johann Jacob b. 13 Feb. 1738
"This family went to Pennsylvania 6 May 1738."

Pennsylvania records:
MUDDY CREEK LUTHERAN KB, LANCASTER CO.:
Stephan Böringer and wife Catarina sp. two children of Johannes Schäffer, another emigrant fromMichelfeld, and brother-in-law.
Stephan Böringer of Warwick had:
  4. Joh. Michael b. 15 Feb. 1742; bp. 28 Mar.; sp. Johannes Schäffer and wife
  6. Joh. Philipp b. 22 Feb. 1746; bp. 23 May; sp. Joh. Phillipp Schäffer and wife

WARWICK (BRICKERVILLE) LUTHERAN KB; LANCASTER CO:
  5. Barbara, b. 2 December 1743; bp. 14 Feb. 1744; sp. Leonhardt Bender, Jr., and Barbara Schäfferin
  7. Christina, b. 22 Mar. 1748; bp. 13 Mar. [sic]; sp. Jacob Thomas and Barbara Schäfferin
  8. Joh. Jacob, b. 15 Apr. 1750; bp. 22 Apr.; sp. Johannes Schäffer and wife Catarina

64. BRAUN, JOHANNES   6924 Neckarbischofsheim

Robert & Alice, 1738
S-H 212, 214, 215

NECKARBISCHOFSHEIM LUTHERAN KB:
m. 22 Apr. 1738 Joh. Braun, linenweaver, son of the late Friederich Braun, farmer, born at "Niederhochstatt in dem Stiff Hombach," and Maria Catharina, daughter of Thoma Remler, citizen. "This married couple went to the new land."
[They were married on the same day as Johann Wendel Heft, q.v., and notations in the KB indicate that both couples left for the new land. Hans Wendel Heft arrived on the *Two Sisters*, 1738.]

Pennsylvania records:
HILL LUTHERAN KB, NORTH ANNVILLE TWP., LEBANON CO.:
A John Brown had:
  1. Johannes b. 15 Apr. 1744; sp. Johannes Bindtnagel [q.v.] and wife
  2. Joh. Valentin b. 7 Apr. 1748
  3. Eva Maria b. 30 Jan. 1751
  _____

John Brown, Lebanon twp., Lancaster co., nat. Philadelphia Fall 1765 without taking an oath.

65. BRAUS, HANS ADAM   Asbach, Baden =
                              6951 Obrigheim, Baden
St. Andrew, 1738
S-H 237, 238, 240

ASBACH REFORMED KB:
m. 18 Nov. 1732 Hans Adam Braus, son of Hans Peter Braus, and Anna Catharina, daughter of the late Hans Georg Kuch, church elder.
[See Marcus Adam Braus for family record.]

Children:
1. Maria Margaretha b. 18 Nov. 1733
2. Maria Barbara b. 2 Feb. 1737
Hans Georg Kuch (Reformed) and wife Barbara (Lutheran) had:
1. Maria Barbara [m. Bernhard Wannemacher, q.v.]
2. Anna Maria [m. Marx Adam Braus, q.v.]
3. Anna Magdalena
4. Anna Catharina b. 25 Oct. 1711
Hans Georg Kuch, judge and church elder, d. 30 Sept. 1727, aged 53 y.

Pennsylvania records:
Adam Brauss witnessed the will of Egidius Grim of Macungie twp., Northampton co. on 28 Jan. 1760.

ZIEGEL UNION KB, WEISENBERG TWP., LEHIGH CO.:
Johan Adam Brauss and wife Anna Catharina had:
3. Joh. Adam b. 17 Dec. 1739
4. Anna Catharina b. 16 Feb. 1742
5. Susanna Margaret b. 26 Mar. 1745
6. Anna b. 1 July 1747
7. Anna Christina b. 17 Nov. 1749
8. Joh. Georg b. 26 May 1751
9. Anna Maria b. 8 Oct. 1755

JOH. HEINRICH HELFFRICH'S RECORDS:
Anna Catharina Brauss d. 4 May 1793, aged 81 y. 6 mo. and 1 week.

Adam Brosse, Maccungy twp., Northampton co., nat. Philadelphia 24 Sept. 1762.

66. BRAUS, MARCUS ADAM

Asbach, Baden =
6951 Obrigheim, Baden

St. Andrew, 1738
S-H 237

ASBACH REFORMED KB:
Family register dated 1709 at beginning of church book: Peter Braus and wife Anna Catharina, Reformed, had:
1. Anna
2. Maria Catharina
3. Marcus Adam
4. Hans Adam
5. Maria Barbara
m. 1 May 1727 Marx Adam Braus, son of Hans Peter Braus, schoolteacher at Asbach, and Anna Maria, dau. of Hans Georg Kuch, "des Gerichts" and church elder. Children:
1. Joh. Philipp b. 21 May 1727
2. Joanna b. 1 Aug. 1729
3. Barbara Joanna b. 14 Aug. 1731
4. Anna Magdalena b. 26 July 1734
5. Bernhard b. 11 Sept. 1736

67. BRECHT, JOH. JACOB
1749

Eschelbach, Baden =
6920 Sinsheim, Elsenz

ESCHELBACH LUTHERAN KB:
m. 8 June 1723 Jorg Adam Brecht, widower, and Maria Esther, daughter of Balthasar Bender. Their son:
Joh. Jacob b. 21 July 1725; conf. 1738. "Given Taufschein 1749, going to the new land."

68. BRECHT, JOH. JACOB
1752

Eschelbach, Baden =
6920 Sinsheim, Elsenz

ESCHELBACH LUTHERAN KB:
Thomas Brecht and Anna Margareth had a son Johann Jacob b. 3 July 1718.
m. 23 Sept. 1742 Johann Jacob Brecht, son of the old Joh. Thomas Brecht, and Maria Ursula Bender, daughter of Joh. Jacob Bender. "Anno 1752 to the new land." Their children:
1. Johann Christoph b. 18 Mar. 1743; d. young
2. Maria Magdalena b. 23 Apr. 1745; d. May 1749
3. Maria Barbara b. 4 Mar. 1747; d. Aug. 1747

69. BRENEISEN, JOH. VALENTIN
Alexander & Anne, 1730
S-H 36

Adelshofen =
7519 Eppingen

ADELSHOFEN LUTHERAN KB:
m. 8 Nov. 1724, after premature concubitum, Valentin Brenneisen, servant of Samuel Bär, Anabaptist, and Margaretha Hertzler (Catholic), daughter of Andreas Hertzlin of Gimbert. Joh. Valentin Breneisen, day laborer at the Dammhoff, and wife Anna Margaretha (Catholic) had:
1. Joh. Friedrich b. 23 June 1726
2. Joh. Rudolff b. 21 Sept. 1728

Pennsylvania records:
MUDDY CREEK LUTHERAN KB, LANCASTER CO.:
Valentin Brenn Eisen, deceased, had:
1. Joh. Martin b. 4 Sept. 1731
2. Joh. Jacob b. 17 Sept. 1733
3. Joh. Cunradt b. 1 Feb. 1736
Joh. Valentin Brenneisen and wife Margaretha sp. 1736 a child of Philipp Schweickert.
m. 13 Sept. 1737 Johannes Ulrich and Margaretha Brenn Eisen, surviving widow of Valentin.

STOEVER'S RECORDS:
m. 17 Jan. 1749 Rudolph Brenneisen and Anna Barbara Schaeffer, Cocalico

PENNSYLVANIA PATENT BOOK AA-2:518
Warrant dated 30 Apr. 1746, surveyed 13 Dec. 1748, A 154 A. tract in Earl twp., Lancaster co. to Hans Urigh. Urigh died, leaving land to two step-sons, Conrad

and Valentine Breneisen. Valentine released his right to Conrad on 15 Mar. 1758. Patented 13 Feb. 1762, recorded 19 Feb. 1762.

Rudolph Breneisen nat. Philadelphia 10 April 1760.

70. BRENNEISEN, GEORG MICHAEL   6920 Sinsheim, Elsenz

Alexander & Anne, 1730
S-H 35, 36

EICHTERSHEIM LUTHERAN KB:
Hans Georg Brenneisen and wife Ann Ursula had:
   Geörg Michael b. 9 Dec. 1702
"Went to Pennsylvania 2 Apr. 1730."

SINSHEIM LUTHERAN KB:
m. 23 Nov. 1723 at Hilspach Georg Michael Brenneisen, son of the late Joh. Georg Brenneisen, citizen and "des Gerichts" at Euchtersheim [Eichtersheim = 6921 Angelbachtal], and Anna Margretha, daughter of the late J. Georg Klein, court recorder in [6926] Kirchardt. Children:
   1. Gottfried b. 1 Dec. 1724 at Weiler
   2. Maria Barbara b. 6 Mar. 1727 at Sinsheim
   3. Joh. Jacob b. 12 Aug. 1729 at Sinsheim

Pennsylvania records:
STOEVER'S RECORD:
m. 26 Sept. 1743 John Peter Wampler and Anna Barbara Brenneiss, Swatara
m. 13 Jan. 1747 Jacob Brenneiser and Anna Veronica Wampfler, Lebanon

HILL LUTHERAN CHURCH, NORTH ANNVILLE TWP., LEBANON CO.:
Jacob Brenneissen and wife Veronica had:
   1. Joh. Michael b. 6 Oct. 1747
   2. Joh. Jacob b. 28 Sept. 1749
   3. Anna Elisabetha bp. 28 Oct. 1750
("Renounced Evangelical truth and the Lutheran Church and became Dunkers.")

Jacob Brenniser, Lebanon tp., Lancaster co., nat. Philadelphia Fall 1765, without taking an oath.

71. BRENNER, HANS PHILIP   Daudenzell =
                                        6955 Aglasterhausen
Patience, 1749
S-H 408

DAUDENZELL LUTHERAN KB:
Hans Georg Brenner, Jr. and wife Anna Catharina nee Klenk (Glenck) had a son:
   Johann Philipp b. 8 Dec. 1712
m. 17 Nov. 1738 in Breidebrunn [6955 Breitenbronn, Baden] Johann Philipp Brenner, son of Hans Görg Brenner, inhabitant of Daudenzell, and Maria Catharina Klein, dau. of Christoph Klein of Breidebrunn.
Hans Philipp Brenner of [6951] Aspach and wife Maria Catharina had:
   1. Elisabetha Margretha b. 10 Nov. 1740
   2. Catharina Veronica b. 7 Sept. 1743

3. Anna Catharina b. 16 July 1745

Krebs, "Palatine Emigration . . . ," p. 34, Philip Brenner of Asbach received permission to emigrate in 1749 on payment of the tithe.

Pennsylvania records:
TRINITY LUTHERAN KB, LANCASTER:
Philipp Brenner and wife Anna (Maria) Catharina, nee Klein, had:
   1. Philipp Adam b. 8 Jan. 1750
   2. Joh. Philipp b. 2 Dec. 1752
m. 26 Feb. 1760 Philipp Brenner, widower, and Anna Elisabet Kempferin, widow
m.   Apr. 1763 Johannes Gorner, locksmith, single, and Elisabet Margaret Brenner _____

Philip Brenner, Lancaster co., nat. Philadelphia May 10, 1769.

72. BRENNER, PHILIP ADAM

Patience, 1749
S-H 408

Daudenzell =
6955 Aglasterhausen

DAUDENZELL LUTHERAN KB:
Hans Görg Brenner and wife Anna Catharina of Daudenzell had:
   Philipps Adam b. 22 Aug. 1721
He was a brother of Philipp Brenner, also a passenger on this ship.

Pennsylvania records:
TRINITY LUTHERAN KB, LANCASTER:
m. 18 Sept. 1751 Philip Adam Brenner, single, and Anna Maria, daughter of Philip Rudisill. Children:
   1. Joh. Philipp b. 1 Dec. 1752
   2. Joh. Georg b. 4 Feb. 1754
   3. Maria Catharina b. 14 Feb. 1759

ST. JOHN'S LUTHERAN KB, MAYTOWN, LANCASTER CO:
Conf. 22 Dec. 1771 Philip Brenner, son of Philip and Maria (she deceased), age 19.

73. BREUNINGER, JOH. GOTTLIEB age 33
BREUNINGER, JOH. MARTIN age 35

Two Sisters, 1738
S-H 209, 211 (with Elizth Brininger age 30 and Barbara Brininger age 28)

6921 Ittlingen
Massenbach =
7103 Schwaigern

ITTLINGEN LUTHERAN KB:
Joh. Gottlieb Bräuninger and wife Maria Elisabetha had:
   1. Maria Susanna b. 27 Apr. 1737; bp. 30 Apr., sp. Joh. Martin Bräuninger

MASSENBACH LUTHERAN KB:
Joh. Martin Breuninger and wife (Catharina) Barbara had:
   1. Joh. Michael b. 18 Oct. 1733

2. Joh. Paulus b. 17 Jan. 1736; sp.: Paulus Breuninger, his brother, Joh.
   Kober and Michel Hornung from Schwaigern
3. Maria Eva b. 8 Nov. 1738

Pennsylvania records:
Pennsylvanische Geschichts-Schreiber, 16 May 1745:
Johann Gottlieb Braeuninger, born at Erlingen near Sinsheim, arrived in this
country in 1738 with his brother Martin. They were separated, and Johann Gottlieb, who is now in Anweil (N.J.) seeks news of his brother.

TRINITY LUTHERAN KB, READING:
bu. Maria Elisabetha Breuninger, widow of Joh. Gottlieb; b. 7 May 1707 in Bruck-
enheim, Wuertemberg. Married for 30 years and had 9 ch., 4 of whom are living.
A widow for 30 years. Blind. Bu. in Cumru twp. cemetery near Riem's Tavern. d.
15 Oct. 1794, bu. 17 Oct. Age 87 y., 7 mo., 8 days.
m. 30 Oct. 1770 Georg Brenninger, second son of Joh. Gottlieb, deceased, of
Cumry twp. and Maria Catharina Schmel, oldest daughter of Adam Schmel of
Roscommänner twp.

BERKS CO. WILLS AND ADM.
John Godlieb Breininger, Cumru, 4 Mar. 1768. Adm. granted to George Breinin-
ger, a son in whose favor Elizabeth, the widow and Francis, eldest son, renounced.
Martin Breininger, Cumru, 29 May 1777. Adm. to Magdalena Breininger, the
widow.
Anna Magdalena Breninger, Cumru (widow of Martin) (1 Feb. 1802/20 Apr. 1802).
Dau. Anna Catharine, wife of Nicholas Miller. Grandchildren: John, Nicholas and
Peter Miller. Son-in-law John Gelsinger. Trusty neighbor Frederick Weitzell, exr.

John Godlin Bryninger and Jno. Martin Brininger, nat. Philadelphia, Sept. 1761,
of Cumru, Berks

74. BROSSMANN, FRANTZ age 45

Waldangelloch =
6920 Sinsheim, Elsenz

Friendship, 1739
S-H 265, 268, 271

WALDANGELLOCH LUTHERAN KB:
m. 18 Nov. 1680 Hans Jerg Rudolph and Catharina Margretha Fessler. They had:
   Clara Elisabetha bp. 11 Mar. 1700
m. 6 June 1724 Frantz Brossman, turner, and Anna Clara, dau. of the late Hans
Jerg Rudolph.
[parents of Frantz Brossman not mentioned in marriage record, but a Nicolaus
Brosmann, also a turner, died in Waldangelloch 8 Aug. 1717, age 64 years]

Pennsylvania records:
Frantz Brossman was one of the early members of Christ Lutheran Church, Stouchsburg, Berks co. Bu. 18 Oct. 1749 Franz Brosman. Lancaster co. estate records
give the name of his wife as Corlis [evidently an abbreviated form of Clara Elisa-
betha]. Their children:
   1. Anna Maria m. Johannes Nicholas Kistler
   2. Frantz Sebastian b. 28 Aug. 1728

The Elsenz valley, with its tributary the Hilsbach, is separated from the Angelbach valley by a forested hilly area in whose center the town of Waldangelloch stands. Earliest documentation is from 1228. The portions of it which belonged to Württemberg were Lutheran; the parish record begins in 1647. Nearby are the several *Höfe* which were home to Swiss Mennonites in the seventeenth and eighteenth centuries, many of whom came to America for greater freedom to practice their religion.

Photo: J. Godshall

3. Maria Appolonia b. 19 May 1730; m. Balthasar Umbenhauer
4. Anna Margaretha b. ca. 1734; conf. 14 May 1749
5. Christina Brossman b. ca. 1738; conf. 1753
6. Johannes b. ca. 1739; conf. 1754; m. Anna Maria Heilmann
7. possibly Justina who was a sp. 9 Dec. 1750

Pennsylvania records also give the occupation of Frantz Brossman as turner.

France Brosman, Heidelburg twp., Lancaster co., nat. Philadelphia Sept. 1761

75. BRUNNER, FELIX   7519 Eppingen

Dragon, 1732
S-H 97, 98, 99

Eppingen Reformed KB:
m. 13 Aug. 1720 Felix Brunner from Besserstorff, Canton Zurich [CH—8303 Bassersdorf, ZH] and Anna Barbara Güttinger from Bäretschwÿl, Canton Zurich [CH—8344 Bäretswil, ZH], both single. Children:
1. Anna Magareth bp. 9 May 1723
2. Anna Maria (Barbara, name crossed out) bp. 16 Nov. 1725

Pennsylvania records:
Felix Brunner appears on a list of the heads of families who in Great Swamp belonged to the congregation of the Rev. Georg Michael Weiss [also from Eppingen].

Felix Brunner and Barbara were sp. at Great Swamp in 1738. Anna Margreth Brunner, daughter of Felix Brunner, was also a sp. that year.

PA. PATENTS:
AA-4:185: A warrant was issued for 100 A. of land in Upper Milford twp., Bucks co. (now Northampton) on 25 Apr. 1735 to Felix Bruner. Bruner died, leaving a will dated 14 Jan. 1760. His heirs were: Anna Margaret who married Peter Linn of Philadelphia; Anna Mary, wife of John Greesemer. The widow Anna Barbara and John Adam Williams were executors. Peter Linn has since died, and Anna Margareta m. (2) Georg Schantzeuber. Anna Barbara, the widow, is also deceased. A patent requested by the daughters and their husbands; issued 17 Jan. 1763, recorded 17 Jan. 1763.
The surname Schantzeuber appears in the church records as Schansebach. It later was anglicized to Johnsonbach and Johnsonbaugh.

GREAT SWAMP REFORMED KB, LEHIGH CO., PA.:
bu. 12 May 1777 John George Schonsebach, b. 1746 (?) day unknown. His age, about 51 y. (which would indicate year of birth 1726)
buried 27 Aug. 1777 Mrs. Schansebach, born 8 May 1723, her age 54 y., 4 mo., 3 weeks.

———————

Felix Brunner, Bucks co., nat. Philadelphia as a Quaker 11 Apr. 1749.

76. BUCKEMEŸER, ERASMUS   6921 Michelfeld
Prelist

MICHELFELD LUTHERAN KB:
Hans Buckhenmayer and Maria Magdalena had:
      Erasmus b. 10 Oct. 1695
Hans Buckemeÿer died 24 June 1730 and Maria Magdalena Buckemeÿer died 7 Nov. 1735.

NECKARGEMÜND LUTHERAN KB:
m. 14 Feb. 1719 Asmus Buckenmeÿer, son of Hans Buckemeÿer of Michelfeld, and Anna Margaretha, widow of the late Ludwig Müller, des Gerichts and inhabitant at Zuzenhausen. They had one child, bp. at Zuzenhausen, recorded in the Neckargemünd KB:
      1. Maria Magdalena b. 12 Feb. 1721; bp. 16 Feb.
[See Müller, Michael, Joh. Gorg, Anna Maria Margaretha, Anna Maria.]

Pennsylvania records:
CHRIST LUTHERAN KB, TULPEHOCKEN:
Bu. Mar. 1748 Asmus Buckemeyer

BERKS CO. DEEDS:
A-I:217, 221: 22 Mar. 1755 Peter Ansbach and wife Magdalena, only child and heir of Erasmus Buggenmeyer, release to Michael Riess. (Tract of 216 A. patented to Erasmus Buggenmeyer in 1737.)

PHILADELPHIA WILLS:
Erasmus Buggenmeyer, Tulpehocken (Jan. 11, 1739/Apr. 13, 1748). Translated

Nachdem Ich Erasmus Buggenmeyer von gott mit
einer schwæren Kranckheit heimgesucht bin daß ich nichts
anders als den todt vorwarte weil es aber dessen gnadige.
fürsorge beliebet hat mir meinen völligen Verstand zu frei[?]
bis[?] ich mein Hauß bestellet habe, so bestelle ich mein[?] Ehevrau[?]
Margret zu meinem Executor und vormund der alles das
[...] die Lænder gefahr. Zustehet, welcher
[...] werden wie folgt nemlich [...]
halber Madlena peter anspach weib soll ½ theil haben als
der anderen frony oder ¼ Dritz theil von allem so wol[?]
fahrende als liegende güter (nachdem mein weib Ihr portion
heraus hat) das übrige sollen meine drei liebe Kinder
als Michel Müller, Georg Müller, Margreta [...]
anna Maria [...] welche alle mir getreulich gedienet[?] Ihr[?]
under sich theilen, nemlich ein iedes ein Gleichen theil (nach dem
mein Liebes das Ihrige oder Ihre portion davon hat) welch
theil Ihr nichts wegen zu Komm (als Ihr vätterlich bißher in
mein[?] fund geweß[?] [...]) Dieses ist mein letzter will
und testament und solches meines [...] den sollen getreulich
nach zu komm alle andere willen mündlich oder schriftlich nach
hiemit ungültig und dester soll des Komm gefallen werden[?]
Zu mehrer und wahrer Versicherung und bekräfft[?] zu mir [...]
hab ich mein Hand und Siegel dazu [...]

[several illegible lines through ink blot]

dieses geschehen [...]
meiner Hand [...] Erasmus Buggen [...]
                                    sein Handzeichen

[signatures illegible]

from German. Erasmus Buggenmeyer. Wife, Margred, sole exr. Wit: Jost (?) Dubb;
Jacob (?) Rost; Conrad Weiser. "Whereas I Erasmus Buggenmeyer am visited by
God with a Deadly Decease that I expect Nothing but Death" . . . To wife the share
to which she is entitled by Law . . . Between my children, things shall be observed
as follows: my own daughter Madlena wife of Peter Anspach shall have as much as
two of the others, that is ⅓rd of my moveable estate after my wife has her share.
Balance divided among my 4 stepchildren: Michael Miller; George Miller; Margred
Elbertscheit and Ann Maria Neff who have all served me truly . . . Each of them
shall have a *sixth* part after my wife has hers which is their just due of their dec.
father's estate which has been in my hands.

Erasmus Buckemeyer, of Lancaster co., nat. by Act of 19 May 1739.

77. BUCKENMEYER, FRIEDERICH

Waldangelloch =
6920 Sinsheim, Elsenz

St. Andrew, 1738
S-H 236, 238, 239

WALDANGELLOCH LUTHERAN KB:
Hanns Michel Buckenmeyer and wife Catharina Barbara had:
     Johannes Georgius Friedericus b. 10 Nov. 1703
m. (1) 11 Nov. 1726 Jerg Frid. Buggenmeÿer and Anna Elisabetha, daughter of
Hans Michel Werner.
m. (2) 16 May 1730 Jerg Friderich Buggenmejer and Maria Magdalena Popp, born
in Bittelbronn [One of these is possible, most likely the first: 7109 Bittelbronn,
part of the city of Möckmühl, or 7452 Bittelbronn, part of the city of Haigerloch,
or 7241 Bittelbronn, part of the city of Horb at the Neckar.]
An infant of Frid. Buggenmeyer was b. 3 Aug. 1728. No name recorded, possibly
died at birth.

Pennsylvania records:
CHRIST LUTHERAN KB (TULPEHOCKEN), STOUCHSBURG:
m. May 26, 1748 Werner Stamm, son of John Adam Stamm, and Catharina Elisabeth, daughter of George Friderich Bachemeyer, both from Northkill.

78. BÜKLE, JOH. ADAM

6921 Epfenbach
6921 Spechbach

St. Andrew, 1751
S-H 458 (The next name on the ship's list is translated
in Hinke as Johann Gottfridt Stückle—examination of
the signature list in Vol. II: p. 536 shows Bückle)

NECKARGEMÜND REFORMED KB:
m. 6 Apr. 1706 Joh. Adam Bückle, widower, Reformed schoolmaster at [6901]
Wiesenbach, and Maria Veronica, daughter of Valentin Wildt. Joh. Adam Bükle,

---

Erasmus Buggemeyer made his will in 1739 in anticipation of death, but lived
nearly a decade longer. Step-father of four children whom he regarded faithfully,
he carefully provided for them. The original will is filed in the county of Philadelphia.

schoolmaster at Wiesenbach, and wife Maria Veronica had:
*1. Joh. Adam bp. 4 May 1708
 2. Anna Barbara b. 21 Mar. 1710
 3. Joh. Peter b. 10 Feb. 1712
 4. Maria Magdalena b. 9 June 1714
 5. Jörg Adam b. 17 Mar. 1715
 6. Eva Maria b. 27 Mar. 1721
 7. Susanna Elisabetha b. 22 Mar. 1723; m. Georg Gantzhorn (q.v.) of Bammental
 8. Maria Veronica b. 27 Dec. 1725; d. 1729

EPFENBACH REFORMED KB:
m. 14 Feb. 1730 at Spechbach Johann Adam Bükle, schoolmaster, son of the schoolmaster at [6901] Wiesenbach, Adam Bükle, and Maria Catharina, daughter of Matheus Strauss, citizen at Spechbach. Children:
 1. Gottfried bp. 25 Oct. 1730
 2. Benigna bp. 6 Apr. 1732
 3. Anna Barbara bp. 11 Oct. 1733
 4. Maria Barbara bp. 7 Feb. 1735
 5. Anna Barbara bp. 13 Sept. 1737
 6. Georg Adam bp. 30 Apr. 1739
The following children with wife Elisabetha:
 7. Joh. Jacob b. 10 Feb. 1743
 8. Georg Adam b. 22 Feb. 1744
 9. Georg Heinrich b. 28 Oct. 1745
Krebs, "Palatine Emigration . . . ," p. 37. Permitted with wife and children to emigrate gratis in 1751, on account of his poverty

Pennsylvania records:
WALDSCHMIDT RECORDS:
m. 19 Dec. 1768 Heinrich Buckle, son of Adam Buckle, and Gerteraub (Gertraud), daughter of Johann Engel Braun.

TRINITY LUTHERAN KB, READING:
d. 3 Nov. 1738 Johann Adam Bueckle, b. 1 May 1708 at Wiesenbach, Oberamt Heydelberg, Unteramt Dillperg, son of Joh. Adam Bueckle, a Reformed schoolmaster there, and Veronica. In 1729 he was called as schoolmaster to "Stechtbach in the Palatinate" and remained there 22 years. In 1741 he married a 2nd time to Elisabeth Bernion of Germersheim, Palatinate. Had 4 children of whom 1 son is living. Buried on the Reformed cemetery 5 Nov. 1783

79. BURKHARD, MARIA SOPHIA   Massenbach =
      1732   7103 Schwaigern

MASSENBACH LUTHERAN KB:
Lorentz Frederich Burkhard from [6927] Bonfeldt and wife Maria Margretha had:
    Maria Sophia b. 19 Aug. 1704

Pennsylvania records:
OLEY HILLS LUTHERAN KB (ST. JOSEPH'S), BERKS CO.:
Family register:
Conrad Böhm, b. 1705 in Fehrfeld [6927 Fürfeld] in Wurtenberg, son of Peter
Böhm and Anna Catharina. In 1729 he m. (1) Anna Catharina, b. 1707, daughter
of Philip Ensbach and Anna Eva. She d. 1733. They had:
    1. Anna Christina b. 25 Dec. 1730, m. 9 Feb. 1755 Georg Hartlein
He came to America in 1733. In 1734 he m. (2) Maria Sophia, b. 19 Aug. 1704,
daughter of Lorentz Friedrich Burchhard and Margaretha, from Massenbach. She
came to America without her parents in 1732. Children:
    2. Eva b. 20 Sept. 1735
    3. Joh. Jacob b. 1 Jan. 1737
    4. Joh. Balthasar b. 1 Apr. 1739
    5. Anna Maria b. 28 May 1741
    6. Maria Elisabeth b. 18 Sept. 1743

BERKS CO. WILLS:
Conrad Böhm (6 Dec. 1788/18 May 1789). Wife Eva Elisabeth. Estate to grandchildren in equal shares: the children of George Hartlein, children of David Seis-
holtz, children of Lorentz Hartlein, and children of Baltzer Böhm. Son Jacob has
received land.

80. BUSCH, JOH. JACOB age 26   Massenbach =
                                                     7103 Schwaigern
Princess Augusta, 1736
S-H 162, 164, 166

SCHWAIGERN LUTHERAN KB:
m.6   Jan. 1708 Philipp Busch, son of Georg Busch, citizen, and Maria Agnes,
daughter of Hans Leonhard Hiller, citizen at (?) Brackenheim. Their son:
    Hans Jacob bp. 14 Jan. 1709

MASSENBACH LUTHERAN KB:
Rudolff Essig [q.v.], cooper, and wife Maria Catharina had:
    Anna Elisabetha b. 8 Oct. 1708
m. 18 June 1735 Joh. Jacob Busch, apprentice tailor, son of Joh. Philipp Busch,
cooper at Schweiggen [7103 Schwaigern], and Anna Elisabetha, daughter of Rudolff Essig, cooper. They had:
    1. Hans Jerg b. 4 Mar. 1736

Pennsylvania records:
Wochentlicher Pennsylvanischer Staatsbote
11 Feb. 1772: Jacob Busch, tailor, Germantown

81. BUSCH, MICHAEL age 36

Daisbach =
6923 Waibstadt

Hope, 1733
S-H 116, 117, 118, 120, 121 (with Eieffa Busing age
36, Jurig Adam Bueys 13, Ludwick Buss 11, Maria
Margreta Buss 9, Janis Buss 7)

NECKARGEMÜND LUTHERAN KB:
Hans Michael Busch, citizen at Daÿspach, and wife Eva had:
1. Georg Adam b. 23 July 1721, bp. in Zuzenhausen

DAISBACH LUTHERAN KB:
Hans Michael Busch and Eva had:
2. Joh. Ludwig bp. 2 July 1723
3. Maria Margareta bp. 18 Nov. 1724
4. Johannes bp. 21 Sept. 1726
5. Georg Michael b. 20 July 1728
6. Anna Barbara b. 15 (Nov. or Dec.) 1730; d. 1732
7. Joh. Adam b. 16 Feb. 1733

Pennsylvania records:
CHRIST "LITTLE TULPEHOCKEN" LUTHERAN KB, BERKS CO.:
29 July 1749 Michael Busch was bu. on his own land.
m. 17 Jan. 1750 Georg Adam Busch and Dorothea Kattermann
In 1739, Michael Busch and wife Eva sp. a child of Michael Plattner

Michael Busch, Heidelberg twp. Berks co., nat. Philadelphia Fall 1765

82. BÜTTNER, MICHAEL

7103 Schwaigern

Vernon, 1747
S-H, 363

SCHWAIGERN LUTHERAN KB:
Joh. Georg Bittner, Swineherder, and wife Anna Clara had:
Michael b. 2 May 1726

Pennsylvania Records:
TRINITY LUTHERAN KB, LANCASTER:
m. 11 Nov. 1755 Michael Büttner, single, from Schwaigern and Elisabet Bucherin,
widow.
Michael and Elisabeth Büttner had:
Michael b. 30 Aug. 1756; bp. 5 Sept. 1756

83. CONRAD, HANS MARTIN

6921 Ittlingen

Robert and Alice, 1740
S-H 286, 288, 289

ITTLINGEN LUTHERAN KB:
Rudolph Conrad and wife Margaretha had a son:
Joh. Martin bp. 6 June 1716

Martin Conrad   Martin Conrad
d. 4n Mertz   March 4,
Anno 1769   1769

—Indianfield Lutheran Churchyard,
Franconia twp., Montgomery co., Pa.
Photo: J. Godshall

Pennsylvania records:
ST. PAUL'S LUTHERAN KB, UPPER HANOVER TWP., MONTGOMERY CO.;
m. 18 Jan. 1741 Martin Conrad and Mara Barbara . . . Children:
  1. Anna Eva b. 22 Feb. 1741; sp. Georg Nungesser and wife Anna Eva
  2. Johann Henrich b. 26 Aug. 1744; sp. Henrich Schmid [also from Ittlingen]
    and Anna Maria Wagenseil
  3. Eva Elisabeth b. Sept. 1746
In 1754, Martin Conrad and wife sp. a child of Conrad Bisecker [also from Ittlin-
gen] at Indianfield Lutheran, Montgomery co. Indianfield cemetery:
Martin Conrad d. 4 Mar. 1769 (a field stone, no other inscription)

84. CREINER, MARTIN   6922 Meckesheim
Alexander and Anne, 1730
S-H 35, 36

MECKESHEIM REFORMED KB:
Conf. 1717 Joh. Martin Kreiner, 15 years.
(m. record not found)

Marthin Kreiner and wife Barbara had:
1. Joh. Valenthin bp. 15 Oct. 1724

Pennsylvania records:
MUDDY CREEK LUTHERAN KB, LANCASTER CO.:
Martin Greiner (Warwick) had:
1. Joh. Cunradt b. 3 Aug. 1734; sp. Cunradt Glassbrenner [his wife was
   Margaretha Greiner from Meckesheim]
Maria Barbara Greiner sp. two of Conrad Glassbrenner's children, also recorded in
this KB.

WARWICK LUTHERAN KB, LANCASTER CO.:
Valentin Greiner a sp. 1744 a child of Adam Klemm

FIRST REFORMED KB, LANCASTER:
John Martin Kreiner and wife Barbara Klein sp. 1740 a child of John George
Wagner.

LANCASTER CO. DEED:
C:363: 16 May 1752, 128 A. Warwick twp. Barbara Gryner, widow, to Adam
Gryner.
C:366: 16 May 1752, 136 A. Warwick twp. Barbara Gryner, widow, to Valentine
Grynor. (patented 1747 to Barbara Gryner)

Valentin Kryner, Warwick twp., Lancaster co., nat. Philadelphia Fall 1765.

85. DAMBACH, JOH. JACOB   6921 Ittlingen
Albany, 1728
S-H 20, 21

ITTLINGEN LUTHERAN KB:
Joh. Jacob Dambach and wife Maria Helena had:
1. Joh. Philip Adam b. 12 July 1721
2. Fridrich Marcell b. 20 Aug. 1723
3. Frederica Elisabetha b. 23 Feb. 1726

Pennsylvania records:
NEW HOLLAND LUTHERAN KB, LANCASTER CO.:
Jacob Dambach had:
4. Anna Maria b. May, 1733
5. Joh. Marcus b. 20 Apr. 1735

TRINITY LUTHERAN KB, LANCASTER:
m. 21 Mar. 1738 Joh. Jacob Dambach and Maria Elisabetha Seyboldin
6. Jacobina b. 10 Oct. 1738

FIRST REFORMED KB, LANCASTER
m. 9 Feb. 1746 Frederick Dannbach, Lutheran and Elizabeth Spanseiler, Reformed. Children, bp. at Trinity Lutheran, Lancaster:
1. Maria Magdalena b. 15 Apr. 1748; d. 17 May 1749
2. Adam b. 9 Jan. 1754
3. Elisabet b. 10 Apr. 1756

4. Johann Friedrich b. 19 Nov. 1757; d. 5 May 1761
5. Johann Michael b. 4 Mar. 1761
6. Johann Friedrich b. 15 Jan. 1764

TRINITY LUTHERAN KB, LANCASTER:
d. 7 May 1758 Jacob Dannbach, a married man.
Joh. Philipp Adam Dannbach and Eva Regina had:
1. Benjamin b. 27 Jan. 1749
2. Johann Philipp Adam b. 9 Jan. 1751

86. DEDERER, JOHANN LUDWIG

Bonfeld =
6927 Bad Rappenau

Molly, 1727
S-H 12, 13 (Name on list: Dettery)

BONFELD EMIGRANT LIST:
"Ludwig Dederer, selb. 4," 1717.

BONFELD LUTHERAN KB:
Johann Ludwig Dederer and Anna Barbara had:
1. Philippina Dorothea b. 2 Oct. 1720; bp. 3 Oct. 1720; d. 19 Oct. 1722
2. Johanna Philippina b. 7 Mar. 1723; bp. 8 Mar. 1723; d. 1725
3. Magdalena Catharina b. 6 Oct. 1725; bp. 8 Oct. 1725; d. 1 Nov. 1725
4. Anna Margaretha b. 22 Oct. 1726; bp. 24 Oct. 1726; d. 21 Nov. 1726
Ludwig Dederer had four ch. bp. at Bonfeld, but it will be noted that they all died
there. Since no marriage record was found in Bonfeld, Ludwig and Barbara probably moved to Bonfeld from elsewhere; there could be older ch. born before their
arrival there.

Pennsylvania records:
Rupp's *A Collection* . . . , p. 472: Ludwig Dotterer paid quit rents in Frederick
Twp., Philadelpha, prio to 1734. No acreage given.

NEW HANOVER LUTHERAN KB, MONTGOMERY CO.:
A Conrad and Elisabetha Dotterer had a daughter Anna Barbara b. 18 June 1746;
bp. 20 July 1746; sp. Anna Barbara, wife of Ludwig Dotterer. There are several
other Dotterers in this church record who may have been related to this Bonfeld
family. Conf. in 1750: Zacharias Detterer, Ludwig's son, b. ca. 1732, age 18,
Maria Barbara Detterer, Ludwig's daughter, b. ca. 1735, age 15, Anna Maria
Detterer, Ludwig's daughter, b. ca. 1736, age 14

87. DIETER, GEORG

7103 Schwaigern

Molly, 1727
S-H 12, 13

SCHWAIGERN LUTHERAN KB:
m. 19 Nov. 1695 Hans Michael Dieter, son of Wolfgang Dieter, and Maria Catharina Frey. They had:
Georg b. 7 June 1699
m. 19 Nov. 1720 Joh. Georg Dieter, son of Joh. Michael Dieter, "Anwald und

Like many other prosperous towns with noble residents, Schwaigern was completely surrounded with walls. As towns grew in the late eighteenth and nineteenth centuries, the walls became a hindrance to growth and were torn away or incorporated into other buildings. One tower of Schwaigern's wall remains.

Photo: J. Godshall

Allmosenschultheissen," and Maria Margaretha, daughter of Joh. Georg Luttmann, mason. They had:
1. Joh. Michael b. 18 Sept. 1722
2. Maria Christina b. 25 Oct. 1726; d. 26 Nov. 1726
Maria Margreta, daughter of Hans Jerg Lutmann and Anna Dorothea Norta, b. 1 June 1701.

Pennsylvania records:
TRINITY LUTHERAN KB, LANCASTER:
Johann Georg Dieter had:
    Joh. Georg b. 6 Apr. 1730; bp. 7 May 1730

On 17 Apr. 1728 Georg Teter signed a petition in Philadelphia co., Pa.

On 10 Jan. 1735/36 he obtained a grant for 200 A. on Robinson River, Orange co., Va. (Va. Patent Book 16, p. 475) where he died intestate in 1744. His widow and children then moved to Rowan co., N.C. In 1760 they moved to present Pendleton co., W.Va. (see the *Henckel Genealogy* by Junkin and *Henckel Genealogical Bulletin,* 1974)

88. DILLER, CASPAR ELIAS age 37

Gauangelloch =
6906 Leimen

Samuel, 1733
S-H 106, 107, 108, 110, 111 [he did not sign lists—
the clerk wrote the name Casper Elias Taylor] (with
Anna Barbara, age 30; Philip Adam, age 10; Hans
Martin, age 8; Rosina, age 4; Christina, age 2)

GAUANGELLOCH LUTHERAN KB:
m. 23 Oct. 1719 Caspar Elias Diller, master shoemaker, and Anna Barbara Dornis,
daughter of Christian Dornis. Children:
1. Johanna Maria b. 20 Sept. 1720
2. Christoffel Peter b. 15 Oct. 1721
3. Philipps Adam b. 8 Mar. 1723
4. Joh. Martin b. 5 Apr. 1725
5. Maria Christina b. 16 July 1727; d. 1729
6. Anna Rosina b. 16 Nov. 1729
7. Maria Christina b. 19 Feb. 1732

Pennsylvania records:
NEW HOLLAND LUTHERAN KB, LANCASTER CO.:
Caspar Elias Diller had:
8. Anna Margaretha b. 13 Aug. 1734; sp. Anna Margaretha Fabian
9. Anna Maria b. 23 Nov. 1736
10. Maria Juliana b. 6 Mar. 1739
11. Eleanora Margaretha b. 29 June 1741
12. Johann Caspar b. 23 Nov. 1744
m. 21 Nov. 1749 Michael K*ei*net, son of the late Conrad K*lei*net of Württemberg,
master smith, and Anna Margaretha Diller, daughter of Caspar Diller.
m. 6 Aug. 1751 Adam Deininger, son of Leonhard, Dörren (Derry) twp, and Anna
Rosina Diller, daughter of Caspar.
Philip Adam Diller and wife Magd. nee Oelmakerin had:
Christina b. 27 Jan. 1750; sp. Martin Diller and Christina
Maria Magdalena b. 30 Sept. 1752
Leonhard b. 15 Feb. 1759
Joh. Peter b. 20 Mar. 1761
Martin Diller and wife Christina Maria Magdalena, nee Martin, had:
Philip Adam b. 31 Jan. 1751; sp. Adam Diller and Maria Magdalena
Johann Jacob b. 16 May 1754
Joh. Peter bp. 21 Nov. 1756
Michael Rein and Margaretha nee Diller had:
Johann Martin b. 27 Oct. 1751; sp. Martin Diller and Christina
There are many other later entries in this KB for these families.
Surname spelled Diller and Dieler.

STOEVER'S RECORDS:
m. 7 May 1745 Philipp Adam Diller and Maria Magdalena Ellmecker, Earltown
m. 14 Apr. 1766 Caspar Elias Diller and Eva Magdalena Meyer, Lebanon

Caspar Tiller, Lancaster co., nat. by Act of 19 May 1739

89. DÖBLER, ANTHONY

, 1761

Hoffenheim =
6920 Sinsheim, Elsenz

HOFFENHEIM LUTHERAN KB:
m. 16 Jan. 1730 Hans Georg Debler, son of Peter Debler from Anspach, and
Justina Maria Flick, dau. of the late Hans Georg Flick. (The first child was bp. 5
days after the marriage.) They had:
Hans Heinrich Antonius b. 29 Jan. 1738

Pennsylvania records:
SALEM LUTHERN KB, LEBANON:
Anthony Döbler b. 17 Jan. 1738 in the Middle Pfaltz in "Hostenheim" [Hoffen-
heim]. Came to Pennsylvania in his 23rd year. m. 1764 Magdalena Weidman and
had 13 children. d. 21 Mar. 1814, age 76 y., 2 mo., 7 days.

90. DODDERER, GEORG PHILIP

Prelist

Stebbach =
7519 Gemmingen

STEBBACH REFORMED KB:
Georg Philips Dodderer and wife Veronica (also given in record as Fronecka) had:
1. Johann   [?] Book taped on margin b. 21 Mar. 1697; sp.: Hans
   Michel, son of Hieronymi   [?] and Anna Margaretha, daughter
   of Henrich Schlieffer
2. Hans Michael b. 1 June 1698
3. Barbara b. 5 June 1701
4. Heinrich b. 9 Oct. 1705
5. Fronecke b. 4 Jan. 1708
6. Anna b. 25 Dec. 1709
7. Conrad b. 20 Sept. 1712
[It should be noted that the Stebbach KB was opened in 1708 and a notation
indicates that the earlier baptisms, dating from 1675, were entered into this new
Tauffbuch from an older book at that time. Pennsylvania records indicate the possibility that the above list is not complete.]

Pennsylvania records:
In 1724 a petition for a road through Bebber's twp. to the northern end of Sprogell's
tract from Georg Warner's mill on Swamp Creek is signed by:
Georg Philib Dodder
Michell Doderer
Hieronimus Dodrer
A 1726 petition for a road from Perkiomen Mill through Falkner's Swamp to
Wander's Mill is signed by:
Georg Filib Doddre
Michel Dottorer
Hironimus Dudder
A family history compiled by Rev. Dr. Wm. B. Duttera, *Descendants of George
Philip Duddra or Dodderer* (1929) gives the following list of children:
1. Michael b. May 1698, m. Anna Maria Fischer. He d. 6 Apr. 1786
2. Hieronimus b. ca. 1701
3. Barbara b. ca. 1704
4. Bernard b. ca. 1706

5. Anna Elisabeth b. 25 Dec. 1709
6. Conrad b. Sept. 1712—Unionville, Md. Dudderar's connection

PHILADELPHIA WILL BOOK F:258
George Philip Doderer, Frederick twp., Philadelphia co., husbandman. (19 Oct. 1740/1 Dec. 1741). Wife Veronica, youngest son Conrad. Refers to other 3 children and "my children's children." Michael, eldest son; son Barrant; daughter Anna and mentions her children by her first husband; daughter Barbara's children. Exrs: sons Michael and Barrant.

PHILADELPHIA ADM. BOOK F:471
Verony Doderer, "now pretty old." (8 June 1751/9 Dec. 1752.) son Conrad; son's wife Anna Maria Doterer; sons Michael and Bernhard; children of deceased son and daughter; children of daughter Anna; Adm. to Michael Dodderer, son of Veronica Dodderer, dec'd.
Michael Dotterer (b. 1698–d. 6 Apr. 1786) and wife Anna Maria Fischer had:
1. Anna Sophia b. Mar. 1725, m. Daniel Troxler, Adams co.
2. Anna Veronica b. 5 Sept. 1727
3. George Philip b. 30 Aug. 1729
4. Conrad b. 10 May 1731, m. Julianna Reiff, Adams co.
5. Maria Margaretha b. 27 June 1733
6. Michael b. 31 Oct. 1735 m. (1) Anna Reiff b. 1740, d. 1766 (2) Catharina Reiff
7. Jacob b. 4 July 1737
8. A son b. 22 Jan. 1739, died young
9. John and   (twins b. 18 Nov. 1741, died young)
10. Anna Maria b. 4 Jan. 1745, m. Christian Reiff, Adams co.

The following were naturalized by an Act of 19 May 1739, Philadelphia co.:
Conradt Dotterer, Bernhart Dotterer, Michael Dotterer and George Philip Dotterer.

91. DOLL, JOH. MICHAEL

6920 Sinsheim, Elsenz

Francis & Elizabeth, 1742
S-H 327, 329

SINSHEIM REFORMED KB:
m. 17 May 1707 Hans Georg Doll and Anna Maria Ziegler. Their son:
Johann Michael b. 6 Sept. 1718 Sp. Joh. Michael Laubinger

Pennsylvania records:
BETHLEHEM MORAVIAN BURIALS:
John Michael Zahm (alias Toll), 1718–1787, came from Sünzheim in the Palatinate. He taught in several Moravian schools, was ordained Deacon in 1755, preached at Lebanon and Gnadenthal, and since 1780 assisted in the management of the financial affairs of the Church as Treasurer of the "Sustentation." He was married to Regina Hantsch and had one son living in Lancaster.
Regina Zahm, nee Hantsch, 1720–1790, from Ottendorf near Herrnhut. In 1746 she married the Rev. John Michael Zahm with whom she served in several city and country congregations. She left one son living at Lancaster and one daughter married to the mason Chr. Ettwein.

92. DOLLINGER, GEORG PHILIPP

6928 Helmstadt—Bargen

Winter Galley, 1738
S-H 200, 202, 204

HELMSTADT LUTHERAN KB:
Hans Jorg Dillinger (Döllinger) and wife Margareth nee Hauck had:
1. Jörg Philipp b. 31 Aug. 1715
The mother died in 1724, and Hans Jorg Döllinger, tailor, m. Anna Margaretha
Winterbauer. They had several children bp. at Helmstadt.

Pennsylvania records:
STOEVER'S RECORDS:
m. 2 Jan. 1739 Georg Philipp Dollinger and Maria Ferry, Pequea

FIRST REFORMED KB, LANCASTER:
Georg Philip Dolinger and wife Maria (in this record her maiden name is given as
Leru and LeRou) had:
1. John Georg b. 1 Oct. 1739
3. John Philip b. 25 July 1742; sp. Philip Rudisihl and wife Susanna, nee
    Bayer

NEW HOLLAND LUTHERAN KB:
Georg Philipp Dollinger had children:
2. Joh. Michael b. 7 Sept. 1740
4. Christian b. 2 Nov. 1744

STOEVER'S RECORDS
In 1751 Jacob Etschberger (Atalhoe) had a child baptised. Sponsors were George
Philipp Dollinger and wife Maria _____

George Dollinger, Tulpyhoccon twp., Lancaster co., nat. Philadelphia 25 Sept.
1751

93. DONNER, JONAS

Eichtersheim =
6921 Angelbachtal

between 1729–1733
[not in S-H]

EICHTERSHEIM LUTHERAN KB:
m. 14 May 1715 Jonas Donner, wagonmaker, and Juliana, daughter of Hans Leonhardt Adam, potter. Children:
1. Maria Barbara b. 18 Mar. 1716
2. Maria Catharina b. 5 Nov. 1717; d. 1718
3. Maria Catharina b. 17 Mar. 1729

Pennsylvania records:
MUDDY CREEK LUTHERAN KB, LANCASTER CO.:
Jonas Donner and wife Juliana sp. a child of Nicolaus Adam in 1733.
Adam was also an emigrant from Eichtersheim.
m. 20 Dec. 1737 Jonas Donner and Anna Barbara Schreyack (Cocalico)
Jonas Donner had:
1. Juliana Margaretha b. 10 Nov. 1738; sp. Joh. Nicolaus Adam [q.v.] and
    wife Juliana

94. DOTTERER, JOH. MICHAEL
DOTTERER, RUDOLFF

Stebbach =
7519 Gemmingen

Prelist

STEBBACH REFORMED KB:
m. 29 May 1709 Joh. Michael Dotterer and Margaretha, born in [7129] Zaberfeld.
Children:
1. Rudolff b. 29 Dec 1709; bp. 1 Jan. 1710
2. Mattheus b. 17 Jan. 1712
3. Margaretha b. 26 Jan. 1713
4. Maria Barbara b. 29 June 1714
5. Matthaus b. 24 Mar. 1717

Pennsylvania records:
STOEVER'S RECORDS:
Rudolph Dotterer of Colebrookdale had:
1. John Michael b. Jan. 1732; bp. 29 Dec. 1734; sp. John Michael Dotterer
2. John George b. 23 Apr. 1734; bp. 29 Dec. 1734; sp. George Dotterer and wife

ST. JOSEPH'S (OLEY HILLS) LUTHERAN KB, PIKE TWP., BERKS CO.:
m. 31 Jan. 1758 Michael Dotterer, a son of Rudolph Dotterer, Reformed, and Catharine Lang, daughter of Theobald Lang, both from Colebrookdale twp.
Communicants' list dated 14 Apr. 1754:
Marg. Dotter, wife of Joh. Michel Dotterer

Michael Dorrerer (Dodderer), Colebrookdale, Berks co., nat. Philadelphia 24 Sept. 1753

95. DRUCKENMULLER, JOH. LUDWIG

Robert & Alice, 1743
S-H 347

Adersbach =
6920 Sinsheim, Elsenz

ADERSBACH LUTHERAN KB:
m. 23 Aug. 1735 Johann Ludwig Druckenmüller, shoemaker, son of Christoph Druckenmüller, citizen and wagonmaker, and Anna Catharina, daughter of the late Andreas Heilmann, tailor. Children:
1. Maria Margaretha b. 10 Feb. 1740; sp. Michael Druckenmüller [q.v.], single son of Christoph D., the wagonmaker; and Maria Margaretha Leckner, single.
2. Johann Michael b. 10 Dec. 1741; sp. Michael Truckemüller, journeyman wagonmaker.
3. A daughter b. 5 May 1743, d.

Pennsylvania records:
TRINITY LUTHERAN KB, LANCASTER:
Ludwig Truckenmüller and wife Catharina had:
Maria Catharina b. 25 Jan. 1749

LANCASTER DEEDS:
Ludwick Truckamiller is mentioned in Lancaster Deeds F:301; H:272; H:342b.
Melchior Schnider and wife Margaret sold part of a tract on Conestoga Creek to
Ludwick Truckamiller in 1749.

96. DRUCKENMÜLLER (TRUCKENMÜLLER), MICHAEL

Adersbach =
6920 Sinsheim, Elsenz

Francis & Elizabeth, 1742
S-H 329

ADERSBACH LUTHERAN KB:
Michael Truckemüller, journeyman wagonmaker, is mentioned in the Adersbach
KB as a sp. He was the single son of Christoph Druckenmüller, also wagonmaker,
and brother of Joh. Ludwig Druckenmüller [q.v.]

Pennsylvania records:
TRINITY LUTHERAN KB, LANCASTER:
m. 12 Jan. 1749 by royal license Michael Truckenmüller and Magdalena Walton.
Children bapt. at Lancaster:
  1. Jacob Fridrich twins b. 10 Dec. 1749
  2. Ludwig

LANCASTER DEED BOOK:
H:272 17 Dec. 1764—Middle St. Adamstown, Lancaster Boro: Jost Will (alias
Joseph Will) and wife Margaret of Lancaster Boro to Jacob Wisslar of Manor twp.
(Proprietor to John Moser, now dec'd; he to Simon Kuhn; he to Jacob Luttman; he
to Ludwig Truckemiller; he to Michael Truckemiller; he to Lodowick Stone; he to
Will.)

97. DUBS, JACOB sick

7519 Eppingen

Dragon, 1732
S-H 97

EPPINGEN REFORMED KB:
m. 6 Jan. 1711 Caspar Dubs, son of Jacob Dubs, inhabitant at "Esh by Bermen-
storff in Zurich" [CH 8904 Aesch b. Birmensdorf, ZH], and Anna Margaretha,
daughter of the late Jacob Hedinger, citizen at Eppingen.
conf. 16 Mar. 1713 Hans Jacob Dubs and his sister Barbara from Esch in Zurich.
[This identification is based on the fact that he arrived on the *Dragon*, 1732 with
Georg, Ludwig, and Frantz Seip, Felix Brunner and Michael Nusloch, all from
Eppingen. Previously compiled information on Jacob Dubs gives his birthplace as
Aesch, Birmensdorf, Zurich, but gives a birth date of 31 Aug. 1710. (see *Perkiomen
Region, Past and Present*, Vol I, p. 21.) This Jacob Dubs, conf. at Eppingen, would
have been born ca. 1699.]

Pennsylvania records:
GREAT SWAMP REFORMED KB, LEHIGH CO.:
Jacob Dups and Froneka (Veronica) had:
  1. Felix bp. 28 Feb. 1738; sp. Felix Brunner [q.v.] and Barbara

2. Barbara bp. 5 Apr. 1744
3. Margaretha bp.   1746
4. Daniel bp. 28 Oct. 1748
5. Elisabetha bp. 16 Oct. 1750

Jacob Dubes, Bucks co., nat. Philadelphia 11 Apr. 1749, without taking an oath.

Reihen on the Elsenz, a Palatine town, is first mentioned in 856. The Neippergs owned it at the time of the Reformation, but when its owners changed in 1650 so did its religion, from Lutheran to Reformed. The tavern at the center of town bears a decorated facade from the period of emigration to Pennsylvania.

Photo: J. Godshall

98. DÜRR, HANS GEORG

Reihen =
6290 Sinsheim, Elsenz

Restauration, 1747
S-H 365 (Törr on list)

REIHEN REFORMED KB:
There were three Hans Georg Dörrs born in Reihen in these years: 1704, 1705, 1711. The available information is not sufficient for exact identification.
Georg Dörr and wife Anna Margretha had:
1. Maria Eva bp. 10 Oct. 1738
2. Maria Margretha b. 3 Mar. 1741
3. Hans Görg b. 24 Apr. 1745

Krebs, *"Palatine Emigration,"* p. 33:
Hans Georg Dürr, of Reihen, was permitted in 1747 to leave for Pennsylvania, along with Johannes Knecht and Hans Adam Kauffman, both of Reihen. Because of his propertyless status, Dürr had to pay nothing to the government.

Pennsylvania records:
CHRIST LUTHERAN KB, YORK:
Maria Eva Sauer was b. in "Huelschbach coal region, Reye bey Zintze" [? Reihen by Sinsheim] in the Palatinate 28 Sept. 1737, daughter of George and Mary Margaret Derr; came to America with her parents 1746. Conf. in the Reformed religion. In the year 1757 at Whitsuntide she m. Leonard Sauer, a Lutheran, mason by trade. They had two sons and the younger survives. She d. before noon on 14 June 1757 ? [listed with 1760 burials] and was bu. near her child on her father George Derr's burial place.

99. EBERLE, HIERONYMUS
7103 Schwaigern

Charming Nancy, 1737
S-H, 188, 191, 193

SHWAIGERN LUTHERAN KB:
Andreas Eberlin and wife Regina had:
Johann Hieronymus b. 29 Jan. 1712

Pennsylvania Records:
ST. MICHAEL'S LUTHERAN KB, GERMANTOWN:
m. 6 Mar. 1756 Hyeronimus Eberle, a widower, and Rosina Dotel, widow of Georg Dotel.

100. EBERMANN, JOH. MICHEL age 56
EBERMANN, JOH. CONRAD age 23
EBERMANN, JACOB age 19

Massenbach =
7103 Schwaigern

Mary, 1732
S-H 93, 94, 95

MASSENBACH LUTHERAN KB:
Hans Michael Ebermann and wife Anna Barbara had:
1. Maria Ursula b. 25 Feb. 1704 [it is recorded that this child was born prematurely, but the m. record of parents not located.]
2. Mathaeus b. 21 Sept. 1705
3. Conrad b. ca. 1708/1709; bp. not located
4. Joh. Jacob b. 29 June 1712
5. Joh. Michael b. 13 Nov. 1714; d. young
6. Maria Eva b. 1 Aug. 1717
7. Maria Elisabetha b. 20 Dec. 1721
Joh. Conrad Ebermann and Maria Catharina Frank (Catholic religion) had:
1. Joh. Adam b. 11 Mar. 1729, seven weeks before their marriage
m. 27 Apr. 1729 Joh. Conrad Ebermann, son of Joh. Michel Ebermann, citizen, and Anna Catharina, daughter of Michel Frank. After the marriage, they had:
2. Maria Margretha b. 19 Feb. 1732

101. EBERMAN, JOHANNES
7103 Schwaigern

Johnson, 1732
S-H 72, 73, 74, 76, 77 (With Elisabeth, Johannes and Maria)

SCHWAIGERN LUTHERAN KB:
Andreas Eberman m. 26 Nov. 1682 Susanna Hoffarth. They had:
Johannes b. 21 May 1696
m. 29 Nov. 1716 Johannes Eberman, son of Andrae E., and Maria Elisabetha, daughter of Paul Hafner, gravedigger. They had:
1. Maria Dorothea b. 27 Apr. 1718
2. Maria Elisabetha b. 22 Apr. 1720; d. 1720
3. Johannes b. 18 July 1722

4. Maria Magdalena b. 17 June 1725; d. 15 Apr. 1729
5. Johann Paul b. 15 Mar. 1727; d. young
6. Maria Magdalena b. 3 Apr. 1730

Pennsylvania records:
LANCASTER MORAVIAN KB:
Johannes Eberman, b. 18 July 1722 in Schwaygern near Heilbrun, son of Johannes and Maria Elisabetha (Hoffner) Eberman. m. (1) in Lancaster 27 Dec. 1743 Juliana Schweig (Schweich) and had 4 ch. m. (2) Anna Maria Xander and had 8 ch. He d. 26 Dec. 1805.

102. EBERT, MARCELL   7103 Schwaigern

Minerva, 1769
S-H, 727

SCHWAIGERN LUTHERAN KB:
Johann Jacob Ebert and Christina Catharina had:
    Johann Marcell b. 16 Jan 1726

103. EICHELBERGER, FRIEDERICH   6921 Ittlingen

Albany, 1728
S-H 20, 21

ITTLINGEN LUTHERAN KB:
Philip Friederich Eichelberger was bp. 17 Apr. 1693, son of Johannes and Maria Barbara Aichelberger.
Philipp Friederich Eichelberger and wife Anna Barbara had:
    1. Joh. Martin b. 16 Nov. 1716
    2. Anna Margaretha b. 2 Mar. 1720
    3. Johann Friederich b. 18 Feb. 1722
    4. Margaretha Barbara b. 9 Aug. 1724
    5. Anna Barbara b. 7 Feb. 1727
(In three of these bp. records, the father is named simply Friederich Eichelberger.)

Pennsylvania records:
TRINITY LUTHERAN KB, LANCASTER:
Friederich Eichelberger had:
    6. Joh. Georg b. 22 Dec. 1729; conf. 1743
by second marriage:
    7. Joh. Adam b. 27 May 1739
    8. Hans Michael b. 16 Oct. 1740
    9. Maria Barbara b. 15 Jan. 1743

d. 1 May 1768 Friederich Eichelberger, age about 45.
m. 24 Jan. 1738 Adam Volmar and Anna Margaretha Eichelberger
m. 4 Apr. 1738 Joh. Friederich Eichelberger and Maria Magdalena Beckerin
m. 18 June 1751 Johann Georg Eichelberger and Christina Dorothea Päschin

On 4 November 1741, Martin Eichelberger, a native of Ittlingen in the Kraich-gau, purchased lot 102 in the new town of York. He had erected here the tavern which he ran until 1751, when he sold the property to an Englishman, Joseph Chambers, who built the stone building to the right on the same lot. The two properties managed to survive modernization in York until they were restored under the direction of G. Edwin Brumbaugh. The *Golden Plough* is a remarkable example of Germanic architecture in America, appropriately furnished with gifts from the collection of Titus Geesey. Photograph courtesy of Golden Plough Tavern, Historical Society of York County.

LANCASTER MORAVIAN KB:
m. 13 Mar. 1744 Hans Georg Näss and Maria Eichelberger

WARWICK LUTHERAN KB, LANCASTER CO.:
Friedrich Eichelberger had a son Leonhardt, b. 14 July 1750

CHRIST EVANGELICAL LUTHERAN KB, YORK:
Martin Eichelberger had:
1. Philip Jacob b. 12 Mar. 1744
2. Johann Bernhard b. 3 Mar. 1748
3. Benjamin b. 30 Oct. 1750
4. Anna Maria b. 18 Feb. 1752
5. Anna Catharina b. 6 May 1754
6. Johan Martin b. 28 Jan. 1759

YORK CO. WILLS:
Frederick Eichelberger, town of Hanover, (5 Feb. 1776/—). Wife, Magdalena, sons Martin, Adam; grandchildren (of daughter Anna Margaretha, m. Vincens Keafer) Magdalena Keafer, Barbara Keafer, Catharina Keafer, Sabina Keafer, Valentine Keafer, George Nease, Sr.

Magdalena Eyechelberger, town of Hanover (17 Nov. 1789/30 Apr. 1790): Sons Ludwig, Jacob, Lenard; Lenard's wife Elizabeth; granddaughters, daughters of son-in-law Andrew Hoke, Glora, Barbara, Elizabeth Hoke; granddaughter, daughter of son-in-law Jacob Smyser, Catharina Smyser; grandchildren, children of Ludwick, Frederick and Magdalena Eyechelberger.
Martin, Adam and Jacob Eichelberger were tavernkeepers respectively in York, Manheim tp. and Hanover, York co.
American sources quoting a document brought from Ittlingen in 1728 give Frederick Eichelberger's first marriage to Anna Barbara Donners on 11 Nov. 1714.

Frederick Eighelberger, Lancaster co., nat. by Act of 19 May 1739.
Martin Icleberger nat. Philadelphia 10 April 1760.

104. EICHELBERGER, JOH. GEORG age 29   6921 Ittlingen

Hope, 1733
S-H, 116, 117, 120, 121 (with Julian age 29—no children listed)

ITTLINGEN LUTHERAN KB:
Johannes Eichelberger and wife Maria Barbara had:
    Joh. Georg b. 16 Apr. 1704
Joh. Georg Eichelberger and wife Juliana had:
    1. Joh. Hieronymus b. 21 June 1728
    2. Christian Ludwig b. 19 Oct. 1730

ADELSHOFEN LUTHERAN KB:
m. 26 Nov. 1726 Joh. Georg Aichelberger, shoemaker at Ittlingen, son of the late Johannes Aichelberger, and Anna Juliana Catharina, dau. of the late Andreas Illgen (Illig), former citizen here.
Anna Juliana Catharina, b. 29 Sept. 1702, dau. of Andreas Jülig and Elisabetha.

Pennsylvania records:
BERKS CO. WILLS:
Hieronymus Eichelberger, Reading (11 Mar. 1757/17 Aug. 1761) mentions "present wife Margaretha by birth named Heicker." 2 children now living: Maria Elisabetha and John George

WARWICK (BRICKERVILLE) LUTHERAN KB:
Hans Jerg Eichelberger signed KB c. 1743. Children:
    Eva Barbara, b. 12 April 1739
    Eva, b. 18 July 1741
    Johannes, b. 22 Mar. 1744
    Maria Margaretha b. 1 Oct. 1745
Georg Michael Eichelberger, children:
    Maria Barbara, b. 20 Aug. 1760
    Magdalena, b. 21 Aug. 1763
    Christina, b. 18 Dec. 1766

105. EICHELBERGER, JOH. GEORG   Eschelbach, Baden =
                    1752   6920 Sinsheim, Elsenz

ESCHELBACH LUTHERAN KB:
m. (1) 13 Nov. 1714 Jacob Eychelberger, son of the late Jacob Eichelberger of
[6921] Ittlingen, and Anna Maria, dau. of Christopffel Bender (?)
m. (2) 29 June 1723 Jacob Eichelberger, widower, and Apolonia, dau. of Jerg
Adam Brecht. Their son:
    Johann Georg b. 15 Feb. 1730, conf. 1742. "Given Taufschein 1752—to new
    land."

106. EICHHOLTZ, JOH JACOB age 25   6924 Neckarbischofsheim
Samuel, 1737
S-H 169, 171, 172 (signed Eickholtz)
EICHHOLTZ, FRIDERICH
Ann Galley, 1746
S-H 360, 362

EICHHOLTZ, JOH. ADAM
EICHHOLTZ, JOH. MARTIN
Jacob, 1749
S-H 418

NECKARBISCHOFSHEIM LUTHERAN KB:
Maria Jacobina Aicholtz, widow of the late Hans Rudolph Aicholtz, wagonmaker,
had:
    Hans Adam b. 30 Aug. 1691
Adam Eichholtz and wife Ursula, nee Perth (? Barth) had:
    1. Joh. Jacob, b. 1 Apr. 1712, bp. 3 Apr. 1712, illegitimate son of Ursula
       Barth, Catholic religion, and Hans Adam Eichholtz. The parents were
       married at the time of the baptism.
    2. Maria Justina b. 23 July 1714
    3. Maria Louisa b. 2 Nov. 1715
    4. Eva Maria b. 9 Jan. 1718
    5. Maria Elisabetha b. 4 Mar. 1720
    6. Joh. Friederich b. 4 May 1723
    7. Joh. Martin b. 3 Nov. 1726
    8. Maria Ursula b. 2 Aug. 1729; m. 6 June 1749 at Worms [Worms Reformed
       KB] Joh. Adam Hildenberger [see Hiltenbeittel]

Pennsylvania records:
LISCHY'S RECORDS:
Friederich Eichholtz and wife Magdalena had:
    Joh. Jacob bp. 4 May 1755
A Martin Eichholtz had 2 daughters, Barbara and Susanna, who appear in the
marriage records of Waldschmidt.(PA, Sixth Series, 6:217)

Martin Eichold, Heidleburg, Lancaster, nat. Philadelphia Fall 1761.

The city church in Neckarbischofsheim was built in 1543 and 1610. It served Lutheran citizens of the town, many of whom migrated to Pennsylvania in the 18th century.

Photo: J. Godshall

107. EICHHORN, JOH. JACOB age 19

7103 Schwaigern

St. Andrew, 1743
S-H 348, 350, 351

SCHWAIGERN LUTHERAN KB:
m. 27 Oct. 1722 Georg Melchior Eichhorn, widower, son of Joh. Wolffgang
Eichhorn, citizen and gunsmith at [7110] Öhringen, and Anna Barbara, widow of
the late Wilhelm Willheit, cooper. They had:
    Johann Jacob b. 13 Mar. 1724

108. ELBERSCHEIDT, FRIDERICH age 24

Weiler = 6920 Sinsheim
Elsenz = 7519 Eppingen

Joyce, 1730
S-H 37, 38, 39 (with Margret Elversite age 23)

WEILER REFORMED KB:
Conf. 1722, age 14 Frederich Elberscheidt of Elsenz
m. 13 Jan. 1728 at Weÿler Frederich Elberscheidt, a tailor, and Margretha, dau.
of Ulrich Peter of Weiler. Child:
    Elisabetha Barbara bp. 16 Nov. 1728

Pennsylvania records:
TRINITY LUTHERAN, LANCASTER:
Joh. Friederich Elberscheidt first appears in this record as sp. 20 Dec. 1730 for a
child of Joh. Georg Ziegeler.
Joh. Friederich Elbescheidt and wife Margaretha are sp. in 1735 for a child of
Johannes Gorner.
It appears that his first wife Margretha Peter died and he m. (2) Margaretha Müller,
step daughter of Erasmus Buggenmeier (q.v.)

Frederick Elberschidt, Lancaster co., nat. by Act of 29 March 1735.

109. ENDLER, PHILIPP ADAM

6921 Ittlingen

Snow *Molly,* 1737
S-H 173, 174, 175

ITTLINGEN LUTHERAN KB:
Joh. Michael Endler and wife Anna Catharina had:
    Philipp Adam bp. 23 Jan. 1717

Pennsylvania records:
CHRIST LUTHERAN KB, YORK:
Philipp Adam Endler had:
    1. Joh. Martin b. 28 Mar. 1742; bp. 7 Apr.; sp. Martin Weigel and wife
    2. Anna Maria b. 28 Aug. 1743; bp. 18 Sept.; sp. Joh. Martin Eichelberger
        and Anna Maria
Philip Endler's wife Margretha sp. 1750 child of Martin Weichel.
Margaret Entler, b. 13 Mar. 1715, daughter of the late Michael Geiss, a shoemaker
of Lidolsheim in Durlach, and his wife Rosina. She came to Pennsylvania in 1738

without her parents and m. 10 Apr. 1739 Philip Entler who survives. They had 6 sons and 3 daughters of whom 5 sons and 2 daughters are living. After ten days sickness of feverish chills she d. at 4 a.m. 21 Nov. 1762. Bu. in our churchyard Nov. 22.

STOEVER'S RECORDS:
m. 10 Apr. 1739 Philipp Adam Endtler and Margaretha Gaeiss, Leacock. The same marriage is recorded in the New Holland Lutheran KB, Lancaster co. with the surname spelled Zendtler.

Philip Entler nat. Philadelphia 10 April 1760

110. ENGLER, CHRISTOPH   7103 Schwaigern

Johnson, 1732
S-H 72, 76, 77 [Hinke translated the name as England; Rupp translated it Englert.]

SCHWAIGERN LUTHERAN KB:
m. 16 Aug. 1729 Christoph Engler, son of the late Joh. Jacob Engler, "Gerichtsver-wandten" and cooper at [7107] Nordheim, Wurttemberg, and Anna Catharina, daughter of the late Hans Jurg Nellinger, linenweaver. They had:
1. Maria Elisabetha b. 2 July 1730
2. Maria Barbara b. 5 Mar. 1732; d. 14 Mar. 1732

Pennsylvania records:
TRAPPE LUTHERAN KB, MONTGOMERY CO.:
Christoph Engelardt (Coventry) had:
3. Anna Catharina b. 1 June 1735; bp. 4 June 1735
Christoph Engelardt sp. ch. of Michael and Sabina Gebert in 1734 and 1735. (Their wives were sisters, both daughters of Hans Jurg Nellinger.)

111. EPPLER, JOHANNES age 39   6901 Gaiberg
                                                 6901 Bammental
Samuel, 1737
SH 169, 170, 172

BAMMENTAL REFORMED KB:
m. 26 Nov. 1720 Johannes Epler and Anna Barbara Wüster. He was conf. 1708, from Geüberg.
Johannes Eppler, citizen at Geÿberg, and wife Anna Barbara had:
1. Hans Görg b. 21 Mar. 1722; sp. Hans Görg Bauer of Meckesheim and Maria Barbara (nee Wüster), his wife
2. Joh. Valentin b. 26 May 1723
3. Joh. Jacob b. 5 Aug. 1725
4. Anna Barbara b. 2 May 1728; d. 1729
5. Joh. Adam b. 23 Apr. 1730
6. Maria Barbara b. 16 Aug. 1732; sp. Maria Barbara, widow of the late Georg Bauer of Meckesheim
7. Anna Barbara b. 7 July 1736

Pennsylvania records:
John Epler owned more than 600 A. of land in the vicinity of Epler's Church in Bern twp., Berks co. as early as Apr. 1740. (Berks Co. Deeds 60, pp. 641–3, 102) For a history of Epler's Church, see Glatfelter, *Pastors and People*, I:242.
A Barbara Epler of Bern twp. was the wife of the Reformed minister John William Boos.

BOOS' RECORDS:
Jacob Eppler, Bern twp., b. 1 Aug. 1725, d. 29 Aug. 1792. [He left a will, probated at Reading 1 Oct. 1792 naming wife Magdalena, daughter Magdalena Hehn, son John and his son John. Other children who are not named. Exrs: wife Magdalena and Jacob, son of Valentin Epler.]
"My mother-in-law (Epler)" b. 19 Dec. 1729, d. 27 Sept. 1784

BERN REFORMED CHURCH, BERN TWP., BERKS CO.:
Felty (Valentin) Ebler and wife had a daughter Anna Mar. bp. 2 Dec. 1750 Iacob Ebler and wife had a son Joh. Adam bp. 8 Mar. 1752; sp. was Joh. Adam Ebler.

Adam Epler, Reading, Berks co., nat. Philadelphia 24 Sept. 1760
Valentine Epler, Bern twp., Berks co., nat. Phildelphia April 1761
Jacob Epler, Bern twp., Berks co., nat. Philadelphia April 1761

112. EPPRECHT, GEORG ADAM   6928 Helmstadt—Bargen

possibly prelist

HELMSTADT LUTHERAN KB:
Georg Adam Epprecht, saddler, and wife Eva nee Flitzsch, both Reformed religion, had:
1. Hans Adam b. 3 Sept. 1710
2. Hans Georg b. 24 Sept. 1712
3. Andreas b. 27 Jan. 1715; d. 20 Apr. 1718
4. Joh. Paul b. 4 Sept. 1717
5. Hans Philipp b. 4 Nov. 1720
6. Johann Jacob b. 11 Aug. 1723

Pennsylvania records:
MUDDY CREEK REFORMED KB, LANCASTER CO.:
Georg Adam Ebrecht signed the Doctrine, 1743.
Philip Ehebrecht sp. 1758.
Paul Ehbrecht and wife had a daughter bp. in 1760.
bu. 25 Apr. 1769 Eva, widow of George Adam Epprecht, age 85 y.

Jacob Eppricht warranted 100 A. of land in Bethel twp. (now Lebanon co.) 23 June 1753.

STOEVER'S RECORDS:
m. 10 Feb. 1747 Paul Ebrecht and Barbara Margaretha Sauter, Warwick

LANCASTER CO. DEEDS:
D:58, 23 June 1753—Jacob Epprieht (Tavernkeeper) of Bethel twp. a mortgage to Daniel Benezet of Philadelphia.
D:329, 25 June 1755—152 A. in Earl twp.: Philip Epright (Eppricht) of Earl twp. and wife Elisabeth, mortgage to John Gear (satisfied 1759).
H:115, 30 Apr. 1759—112 A. plus 152 A.: Philip Epprecht of Brecknock twp. and wife Elisabeth to David Shoerk of Earl twp., cordwainer.
H:369:5 Nov. 1766—50 A. in Bethel twp.: Paul Eppreight of Bethel twp. to Georg Dollinger, Jr. of same place. _____

Philip Epright, Earl twp., Lancaster co. nat. as a "Quaker" 10 April 1754.

113. ERCHENBRECHT, HANS GEORG age 45

Mary, 1732
S-H 93, 95

Daudenzell =
6955 Aglasterhausen
Steinsfurt =
6920 Sinsheim, Elsenz

SINSHEIM LUTHERAN KB:
m. 18 Jan. 1707 at Steinsfurt Hans Georg Erchenbrecht, son of the late Hans Adam Erchenbrecht of Daudenzell, and Ursula, dau. of David Metzger of Steinsfurt. Children:
1. Hans Georg b. 18 Apr. 1709; conf. 1723
2. Anna Katharina b. 16 July 1712
3. Catharina b. 14 Aug. 1713
4. Maria Catharina b. 11 Nov. 1715
5. Maria Elisabetha b. 17 July 1717
6. Joh. Martin b. 13 Nov. 1719

Pennsylvania records:
STOEVER'S RECORDS:
John George Ergebrecht (Lebanon) had:
   Catarina b. 26 Mar. 1733
   Anna Elisabetha b. 20 Feb. 1735
m. 21 Mar. 1736 George Michael Koch and Anna Catarina Ergebrecht, Warwick
m. 22 Feb. 1737 George Stephan Laumann and Maria Catar. Ergebrecht, Warwick

114. ERNST, HANS MICHAEL

Snow *Bettsey*, 1739
S-H 257, 260, 262

Hoffenheim
Waldangelloch =
6920 Sinsheim, Elsenz

HOFFENHEIM LUTHERAN KB:
m. 8 Nov. 1701 at Hoffenheim Hans Michel Ernst, son of the late Georg Martin

Ernst of Angloch, and Anna Dorothea, dau. of the late Herr Hans Bernhard Gobel, "Ahnwalt".
Their children: [Waldangeloch Lutheran KB:]
    1. Anna Margaretha bp. 27 Nov. 1702; m. 1728 Jerg Thomas Sautter [q.v.]
 *2. Hans Michel bp. 15 May 1706
    3. Hans Jacob bp. 30 June 1709; d. young
    4. Regina Barbara bp. 7 Feb. 1712
    5. Maria Regina bp. 15 June 1714
    6. Anna Eva bp. 14 Mar. 1717
m. April 1733 Hans Michael Ernst and Christina, dau. of the late Ludwig Bosch, "Anwald."

Pennsylvania records:
NEW HOLLAND LUTHERAN KB, LANCASTER CO.:
Joh. Michael Ernst had a son Georg Thomas b. 15 Nov. 1739. One of the sponsors was Georg Thomas Sautter.

115. ERNST, JOH. LUDWIG

Hoffenheim =
6920 Sinsheim, Elsenz

Shirley, 1751
S-H 454

HOFFENHEIM LUTHERAN KB:
m. 8 June 1722 Joh. Adam Ernst, son of Wolf (?) Ernst, inhabitant at Dehles, Churpfaltz, and Maria Elisabetha Horsch, widow of Philip Heinrich Horsch.
Joh. Adam Ernst and wife Maria Elisabetha had:
    1. Joh. Ludwig b. 10 June 1723; conf. 1737
[several other passengers on this ship from Hoffenheim]

116. ESSIG, RUDOLPH age 70
ESSIG, GEORGE age 40 (Jerg Abraham on
B list)
ESSIG, HANS MICHAEL age 30

Massenbach =
7103 Schwaigern

Princess Augusta, 1736
S-H 162, 164, 166

MASSENBACH LUTHERAN KB:
Rudolff Essig, cooper, and wife Maria Catharina had:
    1. Joh. Georg b. ca. 1696
    2. Maria Margaretha bp. 4 July 1700
    3. Anna Catharina b. 24 Oct. 1702
    4. Johann Michael b. 27 Jan. 1706
    5. Anna Elisabetha b. 8 Oct. 1708 [see Joh. Jacob Busch]
m. 1 July 1721 Joh. Georg Essig, son of Rudolff Essig, cooper, and Maria Anna, daughter of "H. Johann Georg N. fendrichs beÿ Röthlen zu Nördlingen." She is mentioned as Catholic at the baptisms of her children. They had:
    1. Juliana b. 15 Apr. 1722
    2. Maria Anna b. 31 Mar. 1725

m. 1 May 1731 Johann Michel Essig, son of Rudolff Essig, and Justina Catharina, daughter of Martin Sigler from [7107] Nordheim. They had:
1. Joh. Georg b. 15 Sept. 1732

Pennsylvania records:
AUGUSTUS LUTHERAN KB, TRAPPE, MONTGOMERY CO.:
Conf. 7 May 1747 Maria Anna Essig, daughter of Jürg, age 21 y.
m. 7 Feb. 1754 Heinrich Pietermann (Reformed) and Maria Anna Essig. A *Jacob* Peterman and wife Maria Anna had:
1. Jacob bp. 13 Apr. 1755
2. Johannes b. 27 Mar. 1761; sp. Jürg Essig
Michael Essig and wife Justina Catharina had:
1. Johann Jurg conf. 14 May 1749, age 16
2. Michael conf. 13 May 1753, age 19
3. Anna Catharina conf. 12 Apr. 1752, age 14
4. Rudolph conf. 6 June 1756, age 15; m. 8 Mar. 1767 Maria Berger
5. Margreth conf. 6 May 1759, age 15
6. Anna Maria b. 22 Feb. 1747
7. Eva Cathrina b. 18 July 1749
d.   Aug. 1759 Michael Essig. bu. in Providence by Pastor Schaum.
d. 31 Jan. 1760 wife of Jürg Essig, senior. Age 70 y. b. a Roman Catholic, received into the Lutheran church 2 y. ago. A pious soul.

MUHLENBERG'S JOURNALS III:472:
1732 Feb. 8, 1782 (Friday) Georg Essig, the oldest member of the Providence congregation passed away. He was bu. Feb. 9.
Joh. Georg Essig (b. 15 Sept. 1732 at Massenbach, son of Joh. Michael) m. 21 Oct. 1756 at Trappe Anna Maria Jung. Muhlenberg's Journals, III:347, 348 contains her obituary. She was b. Apr. 1729 in Gensingen near Creutzenach and came to America with her parents in 1749. Joh. Georg and Anna Maria Essig had 11 children, 9 living.

117. ETZBERGER, JACOB   6921 Zuzenhausen
Prelist

ZUZENHAUSEN LUTHERAN KB:
m. 23 Jan. 1683 Jacob Etzesberger, son of Job Etzesberger from Rütlingen, Zurich,
Switzerland, and Elisabetha Krafft, daughter of Niclaus Krafft, former "Gerichts-
Schoepffen."
m. 14 Aug. 1683 Joh. Görg Schöffer, son of Hans Schöffer, and Anna Maria,
daughter of the late Peter Krafft, "Schultheiss." Their daughter:
     Maria Dorothea bp. 6 July 1698
conf. 1703 Jacob Etsperger
m. 12 May 1722 Jacob Etsperger and Dorothea, daughter of Hans Georg Schaffer.
Joh. Jacob Etzberger was bp. 14 Oct. 1688, son of Jacob Etzberger and wife
Elisabetha.

Pennsylvania records:
PHILADELPHIA WILLS:
John (Jacob) Ertsberger, Tulpehotton, Lancaster co. (Tulpehocken) (10 Nov. 1743/
18 Aug. 1745) Wife: Dorothea; children: sons Jacob and Philip, daughters Magdalena, Maria, Catrina and Margaretha. Codicil added 18 Nov. 1743—at that time
daughter Margaretha was under 12 years. None of the daughters were married when
he wrote the will. Exrs. were: Valentin Herckelroth and Franz Wenerick.

CHRIST LUTHERAN KB, STOUCHSBURG, BERKS CO.:
Dorothea Etsbergerin appears on a list of 1743 members.
conf. 1745 Magdalena Etsberger
conf. 1748 Anna Maria Etsberger, age 19 y. 7 mo.

m. Tues. after Dom. 3 p. Trin. 1745 John Gottfried Röhrer, single son of the late
John Röhrer [q.v.], and Maria Magdalena Etschberger, single daughter of Jacob
Etschberger.

m. 15 Nov. 1748 Leonard Anspach, son of Balthes Anspach, and Anna Maria
Etsberger, orphan daughter of Jacob Etsberger

LANCASTER CO. ORPHANS COURT DOCKET:
10 Nov. 1747: At the instance of Dorothea, the mother of Anna Catrina and Anna
Margaretta Ersberger, orphan and minor children of Jacob Ertsberger, dec'd, that
guardians may be app't over said children. Ordered that Georg Miller and Jacob
Seibert be app't their guardians.

TRINITY REFORMED, TULPEHOCKEN, CEMETERY:
Jacob Etschberger b. 13 Feb. 1724 d. 12 Aug. 1806 (Revolutionary Soldier)
Esther Etschberger wife of Jacob b. 28 June 1730 d. 12 Sept. 1811

BERKS CO. ADMINISTRATIONS:
Philip Etschberger, Tulpehocken, adm. granted 29 May 1769 to Jacob Etschberger,
eldest brother.
_____

Jacob Etschberger, Lancaster co., nat. by Act of 19 May 1739

The neatest farmers in the Kraichgau even square the edges of the manure piles at the edge of their barns. Limited resources of farm acreage, meadow and forest taught the people a thriftiness which became equally well embedded in Pennsylvania German consciousness.

Photo: J. Godshall

118. FABIAN, GEORG MICHAEL age 23   6922 Meckesheim, Baden

Pleasant, 1732
S-H 100, 101

MECKENSHEIM REFORMED KB:
m. 22 Apr. 1732 Georg Michael Fabian and Maria Margretha Seltenreich (No parents mentioned in record)

Pennsylvania records:
Anna Margaretha Fabianin sp. 1734 at Trinity Lutheran, New Holland, Lancaster co. a child of Caspar Elias Diller.

119. FABIAN, JOSEPH age 41   6901 Mauer

Molley, 1741
S-H 310, 311, 312

SCHATTHAUSEN LUTHERAN KB:
m. 6 Nov. 1694 Hans Jacob Fabian from Mauer and Anna Maria, daughter of Master Georg Strohen. Hans Jacob Fabian and Anna Maria had:
    Hans Joseph b. 4 Mar. 1700 [Mauer Lutheran KB]

MAUER LUTHERAN KB:
m. 20 Feb. 1719 Joseph Fabian, son of Hans Jacob Fabian, and Maria Dorothea Müller, daughter of the late Joh. Steffan Müller. Children:
   1. Johann Valentin b. 7 Oct. 1720
   2. Maria Barbara b. 13 July 1723

3. Anna Regina b. 17 Nov. 1725
4. Johann Valentin b. 24 Nov. 1728
5. Maria Eva b. 1 June 1730
6. Johann Joseph b. 1 Jan. 1733
7. Eva Katharina b. 28 Dec. 1735; d. 1738
8. Johann Valentin b. 28 Sept. 1738
9. Maria Ernestina b. 2 Feb. 1741

Krebs, "Palatine Emigration . . . ," p. 27–29. Request for immigration indicated 1741.

Pennsylvania records:
NEW GOSHENHOPPEN REFORMED KB, MONTGOMERY CO.:
Joseph Fabion sp. 1742 a ch. of Georg Michel Kolb [q.v.]

Pennsylvanische Berichte, 16 APR. 1749:
Joseph Fabian, 15 y. old, has been indentured to a trade three times by his guardian, Georg Welcker [q.v.], Goshenhoppen (Montgomery Co.), but ran away each time.

120. FABIAN, MICHAEL age 30; Favon, sick   6921 Meckesheim
                                                  6921 Epfenbach
Pleasant, 1732
S-H 100

MECKESHEIM REFORMED KB:
Hans Michael Fabian, b. 11 Nov. 1696, son of Conrad Fabian and Magdalena (daughter of Hans Georg Herbold of [6921] Spechbach).

EPFENBACH REFORMED KB:
m. 20 Feb. 1729 Michael Fabian, citizen at Meckesheim, son of the late Conrad Fabian, and Anna Dorothea, daughter of Matheis Welz, citizen.

MECKESHEIM REFORMED KB:
Hans Michael Fabian and Anna Dorothea had:
    1. Anna Barbara b. 27 Feb. 1731

Pennsylvania records:
Michael Fabian and wife Dorothea had:
    1. Maria Barbara b. 24 Feb. 1734, bp. by Stoever
    2. Anna Catharina bp. 20 June 1736 at New Goshenhoppen
    3. Joh. Caspar bp. 21 Aug. 1737 at New Goshenhoppen
    4. Anna Margaret bp. 24 Sept. 1740 at New Goshenhoppen

ST. PAUL'S LUTHERAN KB, UPPER HANOVER TWP., MONTGOMERY CO.:
m. 12 Jan. 1742 Michael Fabian, widower, and Anna Catharina Eissenmann.

Pennsylvaniche Berichte, 16 MAR. 1751:
Michel Fabian, above the Delaware Forks (above Easton).

121. FERNSLER, GEÖRG CASPER

Townsend, 1737
S-H 185, 186, 187

Berwangen, Kraichgau =
6926 Kirachardt

BERWANGEN LUTHERAN KB:
m. 6 Feb. 1714 Georg Caspar Förnsler, son of Friedrich Förnsler, citizen and saddler, and Anna, daughter of Abraham Heydinger, inhabitant and forester. Children:
1. Anna Margaretha b. 12 Mar. 1718; probably d. young
2. Johann Conradt b. 26 Mar. 1721: d. young
3. Anna Rosina b. 30 Apr. 1724. Communicants register: the father "with this child went to Pennsylvania in 1737." The mother, Anna, d. in Berwangen 23 July 1736.

122. FINK, SEBASTIAN

6926 Kirchardt

William & Sarah, 1727
S-H 7 [surname on list: Vink 2 persons]

KIRCHARDT LUTHERAN KB:
m. 14 May 1726 Sebastian Finck, citizen and widower, and Anna Maria, daughter of Hans Jacob Meÿer, former citizen.

Pennsylvania records:
TRINITY LUTHERAN KB, LANCASTER:
Sebastian Finck and wife had:
1. Johannes b. 3 Jan. 1730; sp. Johannes Bendter
2. Joh. Martin b. 6 Oct. 1733; sp. Joh. Georg Bart
3. Anna Barbara b. 2 (?) Nov. 1734; sp. Joh. Georg Bart and wife
4. Anna Maria b. 2 Mar. 1737; sp. Joh. Georg Bart and wife
5. Christina b. 8 May 1738; sp. Joh. Georg Bart and wife [All sp. from Kirchardt]

FIRST REFORMED KB, LANCASTER:
Sebastian Finck and Christina had:
John Michael bp. 23 Dec. 1739; sp. John Michael Barth and wife Barbara Klein

Sebastian Fink was nat. by Act of 19 May 1739

123. FISCHER, ULRICH age 28

7103 Schwaigern

Samuel, 1732
S-H 60, 61, 62, 64, 65 (With Maria Fisherin age 28; Kathrana age 4)

SCHWAIGERN LUTHERAN KB:
m. 21 Nov. 1724 Georg Ulrich Fischer, son of Hans Martin Fischer, shoemaker at Nöderhall [= ? 7119 Niedernhall], and Anna Maria, daughter of old Paul Boger, butcher. They had:

1. Joh. Paul b. 3 Feb. 1726
2. Catharina b. 18 Dec. 1727
3. Maria Barbara b. 18 May 1730

Pennsylvania records:
Ulrich Fisher, Tulpehocken twp., Berks co., nat. Philadelphia, Fall 1765.

124. FISSLER, FELIX age 50   7519 Eppingen

Pink *Plaisance*, 1732
S-H 79, 80, 81, 82 (with Barvil Fisler age 48)

EPPINGEN REFORMED KB:
Joseph Fissler and wife Anna had:
    Felix bp. 27 Nov. 1681
Felix Fissler and wife Barbara had:
    Leonard bp. 14 Aug. 1728
[An earlier Fissler record indicates that the family came from "Folgen in der Schweitz, Zurich geb."—that is CH 8451 Volken, ZH]

Pennsylvania records:

FIRST REFORMED KB, PHILADELPHIA:
John Jacob Fisler and wife Sophia, daughter of Jacob Klein, had:
    Maria Magdalena b. 24 Dec. 1746; bp. 26 Mar. 1749; sp. Felix Fisler and
    wife
d. 14 Oct. 1762 Leonard Fissler from Eppingen, Palatinate, age 33 y. 2 m. 8
weeks
d. 15 Feb. 1770 Felix *Fischer*, age 88 yrs. 3 mo.

Feelix Fesler, Philadelphia, nat. Philadelphia Sept. 1740

125. FLINSBACH, ANTHONIUS age 35   Grossgartach =
Friendship, 1739   7105 Leingarten
S-H 265, 268, 271   7117 Bretzfeld

SCHLUCHTERN LUTHERAN KB:
m. 28 Apr. 1739 Anthonius Flinsbach from Gr. Garttach, and Maria Barbara Mohl
from Bretzfeldt (were married with permission)

Pennsylvania records:
TRINITY LUTHERAN KB, LANCASTER:
Antoni Flinsbach and wife Barbara sp. in 1750 Antoni Bickel, son of Friedrich
Bickel [q.v.] and wife Dorothea.
A Johann Philipp Flinspach, 22 years old, arrived on the ship *Brothers*, 1753 (S-H
551, 552, 554). Philipp Flennspach, single, from Gross Gartach, m. 22 Dec. 1754
Margaret Simmethingerin from Walzheim in Württ.
A Melchior Flintschbach, 24 years old, also arrived on the *Brothers*, 1753, also
from Gross Gartach. He married prior to emigration at Lauffen am Neckar Sophia

Catharina Rembold. A list of their children is found in the Adolf Gerber lists. He and his wife Sophia Catharina also appear in the Trinity Lutheran KB, Lancaster, and later Flinshbachs appear in York co. and Westmoreland co. records.

126. FLORI, ENGELHARDT
6908 Wiesloch

WIESLOCH REFORMED KB:
m. 29 Jan. 1710 Engelhardt Flori, shoemaker and widower, and Eva Schlegel, dau. of Christian Schlegel, "des Gerichts' at [6909] Waldorff. Their son:
Engelhard bp. 23 Aug. 1716
The father d. 21 May 1717.

Pennsylvania records:
CHRIST 'LITTE TULPEHOCKEN" KB, BERKS CO.:
m. 11 Oct. 1741 Engelhard Flory and Elisabeth Zerwe

127. FRANCK, JACOB age 25
6920 Sinsheim
Friendship, 1739
S-H 265, 268, 271

SINSHEIM REFORMED KB:
m. 30 June 1711 Peter Franck and Anna Catharina Ziegler. Their son:
Hans Jacob bp. 29 Aug. 1714

Pennsylvania records:
LANCASTER MORAVIAN RECORDS:
Jacob Frank (b. 28 July 1714 in Sinsheim, Pfalz, died 13 Apr. 1787) m. 1740 at Philadelphia Anna Maria Bischoff [q.v.] (b. 5 Apr. 1718 in "Bedersbach, Zinzen," d. 7 Dec. 1804). She came to America in 1739. 5 children, 3 surviving.
1. Anna Margaretha b. 7 Dec. 1740 in Philadelphia; m. (1) Friedrich Lutz, m. (2) Nicholas Groll
2. Daniel b. 2 Feb. 1747; m. 8 Apr. 1768 Anna Margaretha Kunz, widow Yeiser
3. Elisabeth b. 13 Mar. 1752; m. 23 Apr. 1771 Johannes Eberman [q.v.]
4. Peter b. 20 May 1756; d. 3 June 1760

Jacob Frank, Philadelphia co., nat. Philadelphia 11 Apr. 1749 as a "Quaker."

128. FREY, ANDREAS
6924 Neckarbischofsheim
Samuel, 1733
S-H 106, 107, 109 (Andreas Fry age 35, with Catharina Barbara Fry age 30 with children Elizabeth age 9, Christopher age 8 and Mettelina age 3)

NECKARBISCHOFSHEIM LUTHERAN KB:
Joh. Andres Freÿ and wife Catharina Barbara nee Ritter, had:
1. Joh. Leonhard b. 9 Mar. 1726

2. Anna Catharina b. 10 Sept. 1727; d.
3. Maria Catharina b. 21 Oct. 1728
4. Maria Magdalena b. 10 June 1730
5. Johannes b. 2 Aug. 1732

Pennsylvania records:
MOSELEM LUTHERAN KB, BERKS CO.:
Andreas Frey and wife Catharina Barbara nee Ritter had:
    John Mattheus b. 10 July 1747
Conrad Grimm and Maria Elisabeth nee Frey had Joh. Georg bp. in 1750. Sp.
were Andreas Frey and wife Catharina Barbara.
Christoph Frey and Anna Maria nee Wanner had Andreas b. 26 Nov. 1750.
Antonius Bentzinger and wife Magdalena Frey had Joh. Jacob bp. in 1753. They
had other children bp. there.

MERTZ'S CHURCH, DRYVILLE, ROCKLAND TWP., BERKS CO.:
m. 15 Nov. 1749 Christoph Frey, unmarried son of Andreas Frey, and Anna Maria
Wanner, unmarried daughter of Martin Wanner.
m. 2 Sept. 1750 Antonius Benzinger, master tailor from Germany, and Magdalena
Frey, single daughter of Andreas Frey.

129. FREY, JOH. JACOB   Tairnbach =
                                              6909 Mühlhausen,
Rawley, 1752   Kraichgau
S-H 499

DARMBACH (TAIRNBACH) LUTHERAN KB:
m. 3 Dec. 1720 Jorg Henrich Bentz, son of Hans Jerg Bentz, and Maria Catharina,
daughter of Hans Michel Schweitzer. Their daughter:
    Maria Elisabetha b. 9 May 1731 "1751 given Taufschein, to new land."
m. 24 Aug. 1751 Johann Jacob Frey, son of Jerg Michel Frey, citizen and smith at
Eschelbach [6920 Sinsheim, Elsenz], and Maria Elisabetha, daughter of Jerg Heinrich Bentz, citizen.

130. FREY, TOBIAS   Weiler =
                                              6920 Sinsheim, Elsenz
William and Sarah, 1727
S-H 8, 9 (number of persons: 4)

WEILER REFORMED KB:
Hans Frey and Margaretha had:
    Tobias bp. 1 June 1684; conf. 1700 age 15½
m. 17 July 1709 Tobias Freÿ, wagonmaker, and Anna Maria Peter from Epping(en).
Children:
    1. Martin b. ca. 1710; conf. 1724 at Weiler
    2. Conrad bp. 10 Mar. 1715
    3. Gottfried bp. 4 Aug. 1721
    4. Anna Maria bp. 16 Dec. 1722

EPPINGEN REFORMED KB:
Anna Maria Peter was bp. 3 June 1688, daughter of Heinrich Peter and Anna
Agatha.

Krebs, "Palatine Emigration . . .," p. 22. Tobias Frey paid 65 florins 18 Kreuzer
as emigration tax in 1727.

Pennsylvania records:
TRINITY LUTHERAN KB, LANCASTER:
m. 15 Apr. 1735 Martin Frey, legitimate son of Tobias Frey, and Maria Magdalena
Willheut, daughter of Friederich Willheut, both coming from across the Susquehanna. They had:
Joh. Martin b. 6 Sept. 1739; sp. Gottfried Frey and Eva Margaretha Diel
Cunradt Frey had:
1. Joh. Bernhardt b. 11 Aug. 1738; sp. Bernhardt Spengler and Anna Maria
   Frey
2. Joseph b. 19 June 1740
(also recorded in Christ Lutheran KB, York)

STOEVER'S RECORDS:
m. 31 July 1742 Gottfrey Frey and Margaretha Linn, Codorus

CHRIST LUTHERAN KB, YORK:
Gottfried Frey and wife had:
1. Gottfried b. 12 Jan. 1744
2. Maria Catharina b. 22 July 1745
3. Anna Maria b. 11 Nov. 1746
4. A son (possibly Bartel) b. 20 Aug. 1748

Martin Fry, Strasburg twp., York co., nat. Philadelphia, April 1764
Godfrey Fry, York twp., York co., nat. Philadelphia, 24 Sept. 1762

131. FRIEDBURG, LUDWIG JACOB

Francis and Elizabeth, 1742
S-H 329

Massenbach =
7103 Schwaigern

MASSENBACH LUTHERAN KB:
m. 24 Nov. 1722 Joh. Jacob Fridburg, *Provisar*, son of Andreas Fridburg from
Stammen [? 7260 Stammheim], and Maria Barbara, daughter of Joh. Jacob Nellinger, schoolmaster. [She was bp. 12 June 1701, daughter of Joh. Jacob Nellinger
and wife Sybilla.] Children:
1. Ludwig Jacob b. 25 Sept. 1723
2. Bernhardina Dorothea b. 9 Jan. 1727
3. Juliana Catharina b. 24 May 1728
4. Carlina Juliana b. 2 Nov. 1729
5. Joh. Wilhelm b. 13 July 1731; d. young
6. Carlina b. 4 Nov. 1732
7. Christina Catharina b. 26 June 1735, eleven weeks after the father died.

Joh. Jacob Fridburg, schoolmaster, d. 18 Mar. 1735, age 33 y. 10 mo. 5 days
Maria Barbara, widow of Joh. Jacob Fridburg, the former schoolmaster, had an
illegitimate child:
  Catharina Margretha b. 3 Sept. 1740
Recorded on the last page of this KB: "The widow Fridburgin with her children
went to Pennsylvania in the new land."

Pennsylvania records:
ST. MICHAEL'S AND ZION LUTHERAN KB, PHILADELPHIA:
m. 2 Feb. 1748 Ludwig Frieburg and Susanna Elisabeth Hartmannin. [One of the
witnesses at the marriage was Friedrich Reis, also from Massenbach.] They had:
  1. Anna Maria b. 11 Aug. 1751
  2. Susanna Elisabeth b. 11 Dec. 1753
m. 31 May 1747 Jacob Bender and Dorothea Friedbergerin. They had:
  1. Ludwig b. 14 Aug. 1749; sp. Ludwig Freyberg and wife
  2. Elisabetha Barbara b. 17 Nov. 1750
  3. Joh. Jacob b. 28 Feb. 1753; sp. Ludwig Freyburger and Elisabetha
  4. Johann b. 15 Feb. 1755
m. 11 Aug. 1750 John Reich and Carolina Frieburgin
D. 16 Nov. 1781 Ludewig Jacob Freiburger from Massebach, age 57 y. 5 mo.

MUHLENBERG'S JOURNALS, I: 639:
11 June 1763 buried Anna Elisabeth, Ludewig Freyburger's wife, age 34 y. 7 m.
and several d.

132. FRIEDEL, BERNHARD age 25

Friendship, 1739

S-H 265, 268, 271 (Name of list: Bernd Fridtel, Fredel)

Daisbach, Baden =
6923 Waibstadt

DAISBACH LUTHERAN KB:
m. 27 Nov. 1736 Bernhard Friedle, son of Ludwig Friedle, formerly a citizen at
Hoffen[heim] who has gone to the new world, and Helena Dorothea Hönnig, daughter of David Hönnig, "Gerichtsverwandten."

Pennsylvania records:

STOEVER'S RECORDS:
Bernhardt Friedel (Swatara) had:
  Susanna b. 16 May 1743
  Jacob b. 15 Apr. 1745
  Joh. Martin b. 25 June 1747
  John Bernhardt b. 27 Dec. 1749
  Elisabetha b. 20 Dec. 1757

133. FRIEDEL, LUDWIG

Johnson Galley, 1732

S-H 71, 73, 74, 76, 77 (with Anna Maria Friddele,
Jacob Friddele, Maria and Maria Franciscos Friddele)

Hoffenheim =
6920 Sinsheim, Elsenz

HOFFENHEIM LUTHERAN KB:
m. (1) 9 Aug. 1712 Ludwig Friedle, son of Nicolaus Friedle, and Catharina, daughter of Bernhardt Sohns (bp. 20 June 1688). Children:
1. Joh. Martin b. 19 Oct. 1713
2. Bernhard [q.v.]
3. Joh. Jacob b. 14 Jan. 1718
4. Anna Margaretha m. 26 May 1744 Sebastian Wetzel. This marriage record mentions that her father Ludwig Friedel had gone to Pennsylvania.
5. Eva Maria bp. 7 Apr. 1726 at Schwaigern
6. Anna Maria b. 22 July 1728
m. (2) 17 June 1731 Ludwig Friedel and Anna Maria Saltzgeber, daughter of Florin Saltzgeber of Dhurn.

Pennsylvania records:
STOEVER'S RECORD:
Georg Ludtwig Friedtel (Swatara) had:
    John Georg b. 31 Mar. 1737 (?)
    Maria Magdalena b. 28 Apr. 1739

Virginia records:
CHALKLEY I: 32
19 Nov. 1747 Ludwig Freedly complains that John Sigismund Hanley has clandestinely carried out of the Colony his daughter Magdalene Freedley, about nine years old. The girl had been bound to John Harmon, son-in-law of Hanley, and Harmon had lately died intestate in this colony and no person has administered. Hanley required to enter into bond for producing the child in May next.

CHALKLEY III: 10, 11
15 Feb. 1748 Ann Mary Freedley's bond as admx. of Lewis Freedley (shown also as John Lewis Freedley). Surety: Peter Gartner.
10 May 1749 Ludwick Freedley's appraisement

CHALKLEY I: 47
29 Aug. 1751 Peter Cartner complains that Màry Freedly, admx. of her dec'd husband's estate is since married to Nicholas Brock and they waste the estate.

134. FROMM, FRIEDERICH age 29   6901 Bammental
Samuel, 1737
S-H 169, 170, 172

BAMMENTAL REFORMED KB:
Bernhard Fromm and wife Anna Barbara had a son, Görg Friederich b. 24 Jan. 1710.
m. 23 June 1733 Friederich Fromm, son of Bernhard Fromm of Bammenthal, and Maria Barbara, daughter of Johannes Himmelmann, former "Anwald" at Geÿberg. [6901 Gaiberg] Children:
1. Anna Barbara b. 28 Sept. 1733
2. Geörg Bernhard b. 20 Feb. 1735
3. Anna Margareta b. 21 Dec. 1736

Pennsylvania records:
WALDSCHMIDT RECORDS, LANCASTER CO.:
Friedrick Fromm and wife Christina had:
    Magdalena b. 19 Apr. 1782
This father is probably a son of the immigrant.
Conf. 17 Mar. 1765 in Berne twp. at Appler's, Friedrich From's son

BOOS BURIALS:
Maria Barbara Fromm b. 21 Nov. 1712, d. 9 Nov. 1798

BERKS CO. WILLS:
Frederick Fromm, Bern twp. (22 May 1773/2 Apr. 1781). Wife: Maria Barbara.
Daughter Maria Barbara, wife of Christian Klöh. Grandchildren Conrad and George
Frederick Ernst, children of deceased daughter Anna Barbara. Two sons Frederick
and Johannes. Son Frederick exr. Wit. by Ulrich Moser and John Ebler.

BERN REFORMED CHURCH, BERN TWP., BERKS CO.:
Frederick From and wife Mary Barbara had:
    John Adam bp. 3 Aug. 1746
    John bp. 4 Nov. 1753

Frederick From nat. Philadelphia 10 April 1760

135. FUNCK, HANS   Bonfeld =
1709/10   6927 Bad Rappenau

BONFELD LUTHERAN KB:
    The name of Hans Funck, Anabaptist, appears on a list of emigrants from this
village recorded in the Lutheran Church book.

Pennsylvania Records:
    One Hans Funck appears among the very early Mennonite settlers in Cones-
toga, Lancaster Co., Pa.
    His name appears on the 1718 Conestoga assessment list.

John Funk of Lancaster co. nat. by Act of 14 Feb. 1729/30, having immigrated
between 1700 and 1718.

136. FUNCK, HEINRICH   Bonfeld =
     FUNCK, MARTIN   6927 Bad Rappenau
1717

BONFELD LUTHERAN KB:

    A list of emigrants from the village of Bonfeld appears in the Lutheran Church
book there. Under the date of 1717 are the following:
    Heinrich Funck with wife and children
    Martin Funck with wife and children

Pennsylvania Records:
Henry Funk appears on the 1718 Conestoga Assessment list, Lancaster Co.
A Martin Funck signed a petition in 1724 for a road in Bebber's Twp. to the Northern end of Sprogell's tract (Philadelphia Co. Records) and he signed another petition in the same area in 1726.

Henry Funk, Lancaster co., nat. by Act of 14 Feb. 1729/30, having immigrated between 1700 and 1718.

137. GANTZHORN, HANS GEORG 6901 Bammental

Brothers, 1750
S-H 437

BAMMENTAL REFORMED KB:
m. 5 Jan. 1746 Hans Georg Gantzhorn, single, born in Bammenthal, and Susanna Elisabetha Bückle, single, from Wessenbach (Wiesenbach)

Krebs, "Palatine Emigration . . .," p. 36
Johann Georg Gansshorn, from Bammental (Kr. Heidelberg), baker, may emigrate gratis, 1750

Pennsylvania records:

LISCHEY'S PRIVATE RECORDS AND STRAYER'S OR SALEM'S REFORMED KB, DOVER TWP., YORK CO.:
Georg Ganshorn and wife Susanna Elizabeth had:
1. Joh. Jacob bp. 1 Mar. 1752
2. Joh. Niclaus bp. 2 Dec. 1753
3. Joh. Görg bp. 1 Feb. 1756
4. Joh. Philip bp. 25 June 1758
5. Maria Barbara bp. 3 Aug. 1760

138. GAUGER, HEINRICH Bonfeld =

1727 6927 Bad Rappenau

BONFELD LUTHERAN KB:
Henrich Gauger b. 8 Feb. 1682, son of Melchior and Ursula (Dorckler?) Gauger.
Henrich Gauger m. 23 Jan. 1714 Anna Maria, daughter of the late Matthai Eberli, of Flein. They had:
1. Maria Margaretha b. 19 Nov. 1714; d. 1715
2. Joh. Ludwig b. 30 Apr. 1716
3. Joh. Andreas b. 25 Oct. 1718; d. 1719
4. Joh. Friedrich b. 2 Mar. 1720
5. Joh. Michael b. 25 Mar. 1722
The church book records that Henrich Gauger left Bonfeld in 1727, with Gsell, Reppert and Detterer. These 3 appear in the ship's lists in 1727 but Gauger does not.

139. GEBERT, FRIDERICH   7103 Schwaigern

Pennsylvania Merchant, 1731
S-H 43, 44, 45, 46 (Passengers on ship: Frederick
Gybert (Geberth), Women: Catrina, Eliz., Children: Ju-
lian [Reiner], Barnet [Reiner], Sabina and Mathias.)

SCHWAIGERN LUTHERAN KB:
Joh. Friderich Gebert b. 10 Apr. 1699, son of Peter Gebert and Anna Barbara, nee
Mächtlin from [7129] Zaberfeld.
m. 12 Apr. 1723 Friderich Gebhard (sic), son of Peter Gebert, and Susanna
Catharina, widow of the late Michael Reiner, former citizen and cooper.
Her first marriage: m. 1711 (no date recorded) Michael Reiner, son of Ludwig, and
Susanna Catharina, daughter of Michael Boger. Children, surname Reiner:
     1. Elisabetha Dorothea b. 1714; d. ?
     2. Gottlieb bp. 2 Feb. 1716
     3. Juliana bp. 21 Oct. 1718
     4. Johann Bernhard Ludwig bp. 22 Apr. 1722
(These last 2 ch. appear on the ship's list with their stepfather's surname.)
Frederich Gebert and Susanna Catharina had:
     1. Sabina bp. 9 Oct. 1724
     2. Joh. Friedrich bp. 6 Jan. 1727; d. 4 Feb. 1727
     3. Matthias bp. 24 Feb. 1728
     4. Maria Magdalena bp. 24 July 1730

Pennsylvania records:
STOEVER'S RECORDS (ALSO RECORDED IN TRINITY LUTHERAN KB, LANCASTER):
Friderich Gebert (Shenandoah) had:
     Susanna Catarina b. 27 June 1736; bp. 29 Aug. 1736

Facing the center of Schwaigern is a building which was erected in 1659, as a date on its cornerstone attests—the Stadt Kelter, or city wine press. Religious officials began planting vines on the hills in the Kraichgau and the produce from the area still makes an acceptable dinner wine. The Stadt Kelter proclaims

Sich regen bringt Segen
Moving oneself brings blessing.

Photos: J. Godshall

140. GEBERT, MICHAEL   7103 Schwaigern

Pennsylvania Merchant, 1731
S-H 43, 44, 45, 46 (Passengers on ship: Michail Gybert (Geberth), Sabina (Women), Godlieb)

Schwaigern Lutheran KB:
Peter Gebert and Anna Barbara had:
    Hans Michel b. 17 Nov. 1702
m. 19 Aug. 1727 Michäel Gebert, hand tailor, son of Peter Gebert, and Sabina, daughter of the late Hans Jörg Nellinger, former weaver. Hans Michael Gebert and wife Anna Sabina had:
    1. Anna Elisabetha bp. 2 Mar. 1729
    2. Gottlieb bp. 22 June 1730

Pennsylvania records:
Stoever's records:
Michael Gebert, Coventry, and wife Anna Sabina had:
    3. Johannes b. 26 Nov. 1734; bp. 10 Jan. 1735
    4. Michael b. 23 Nov. 1735; bp. 29 Nov. 1735
Sp. for both bp. was Christoph Engelardt (Engler).

141. GEIGER, GEORG   Berwangen, Kraichgau =
Fane, 1749   6926 Kirchardt
S-H 424

BERWANGEN LUTHERAN KB:
Johann Paul Geiger, b. 9 Jan. 1687, citizen and butcher, and wife Eva Maria had:
    Joh. Georg b. 27 Nov. 1728 (emigrated)

142. GEIGER, JACOB   6921 Ittlingen
probably *Francis & Elizabeth*, 1742
S-H 328
[Others from Ittlingen on this ship; however, there were
several other Jacob Geigers in lists.]
In Pennsylvania by 1744—sp. child of brother Valentin

ITTLINGEN LUTHERAN KB:
Jacob Geiger was bp. 25 July 1694, son of Valentin and Maria Barbara Geiger. He
was a brother of Valentin Geiger, a pre-list immigrant to Pennsylvania.
Joh. Jacob Geiger and wife Anna Elisabetha had:
    1. Maria Margaretha b. 26 Jan. 1721
    2. Hans Jacob b. 20 Apr. 1722
    3. Maria Barbara b. 23 Aug. 1724
    4. Anna Elisabetha b. 14 Sept. 1726
    5. Christiana b. 5 Jan. 1731
    6. Anna Catharina b. 5 Jan. 1731
    7. Joh. Valentin b. 22 Sept. 1732
Communicants list dated 1749 includes the names:
Joh. Valentin Geiger "aus Pensylvanien"
Jacob Geiger "aus Pensylvanien"
m. 21 Apr. 1750 Johann Jacob Geiger, born in Ittlingen, then went to Pennsylvania,
son of Johann Jacob Geiger, a baker in Pennsylvania, and Maria Margaretha
Schuchmann, daughter of Joh. Heinrich Schuchmann, Sr., smith. (They had sev-
eral children bp. there, and the family appears to have remained in Ittlingen.) At
the bp. of one child in 1754, the father is still mentioned as having been "an
English colonist in Pennsylvania."

Pennsylvania records:
Egle's *Notes and Queries*, (1897) p. 171:
Elizabeth Geiger b. 20 Sept. 1726 in "Ihlingen, bailiwick of Bretton, Upper
Palatinate, Germany," married Jacob Arndt.

NEW HANOVER LUTHERAN KB:
Bu. Jacob Geiger, 18 June 1772, age 77 y. 10 mo. 3 w. 5 d.
Jacob Geiger b. 16 July 1694, d. 18 June 1772 (New Hanover Lutheran Cemetery,
tombstone)

PHILADELPHIA WILLS:
Jacob Geiger, (17 June 1763/29 June 1772)

143. GEIGER, Joh. Georg   6921 Ittlingen

Prelist (possibly with brother Valentin Geiger in 1717)

ITTLINGEN LUTHERAN KB:
Valentin Geiger and wife Maria Barbara had children:
1. Joh. Valentin b. 21 Dec. 1685, d. 1762 in Pennsylvania
2. Andreas b. 29 Jan. 1688
3. Maria Catharina b. 21 Aug. 1689
4. Maria Elisabetha b. 6 Dec. 1691, d. young
5. Joh. Wilhelm b. 29 Dec. 1692; d. 1761
6. Joh. Jacob b. 25 July 1694
7. Maria Barbara b. 9 Mar. 1698
8. Maria Barbara b. 11 July 1699
9. Anna Margaretha b. 1 June 1701
*10. Joh. Georg b. 29 July 1702
11. Anna Maria b. 10 Apr. 1705
12. Johannes b. 22 Nov. 1707; d. 1708
13. Joh. Martin b. 3 May 1711

Pennsylvania records:
Georg Geiger signed the 1728 petition in New Hanover concerning the Indian
problems. This is not the Georg Geiger who arrived in 1727 on the *William &
Sarah*. The 1727 arrival came from Beihingen am Neckar with wife Barbara and
two children. (see Clifford Neal Smith, *German-American Genealogical Research,*
Monograph no. 11.)

The Henckel Genealogical Bulletin p. 340, indicates that the Joh. George Geiger,
b. 1702 in Ittlingen, married Maria Catharina Henckle. This George Geiger d.
prior to 24 June 1740 in Frederick co., Maryland.

144. GEIGER, JOH. JACOB   Berwangen, Kraichgau =
                                                    6926 Kirchardt
[several Jacob Geigers in S-H]

BERWANGEN LUTHERAN KB:
m. 8 Feb. 1718 Jacob Geiger, eldest son of Herr Joh. Conrad Geiger, and Maria
Elisabetha, daughter of Hans Leonhard Stein, citizen and "des Gerichts."
Their son:
    Johann Jacob b. 24 Mar. 1720
A notation in the communicants' register indicates he went to Pennsylvania.

145. GEIGER, JOH. PAUL age 23   Berwangen, Kraichgau =
                                                    6926 Kirchardt
Samuel, 1737
S-H 169, 170, 172

BERWANGEN LUTHERAN KB:
m. 19 May 1711 Georg Conrad Geiger, son of the late Georg Conrad Geiger,
"Heiligenpfleger und des Gerichts," and Maria Cathrina, daugthter of Johann Ross.

Two of their children:
1. Johann Paul b. 1 Jan. 1714; "in new land 1737"
2. Anna b. 8 Oct. 1715; "in new land"
In later records the late Herr Georg Conrad Geiger is designated *Anwald*

Pennsylvania records:
ST. MICHAEL'S AND ZION LUTHERAN KB, PHILADELPHIA:
Paul and Barbara Geiger had:
1. Anna Meyer (Maria?) bp. 23 Mar. 1746
2. Henrich b. 6 June 1748
3. Christina Barbara b. 21 June 1749
4. Georg David b. 11 Aug. 1750
Bu. 8 Oct. 1764 Anna Barbara Stern, nee Däschlerin from Westenheim, Pfalz, She m. (1) Paul Geiger, m. (2) Georg Stern (Reformed) Aged 48 y. 9 mo.

PHILADELPHIA WILLS AND ADM.:
Powell Gaiger Adm. Book G: 387 (1764)

146. GEIGER, JOHANNES

Billander [*Elizabeth*], 1751
S-H 453

Berwangen, Kraichgau =
6926 Kirchardt

BERWANGEN LUTHERAN KB:
m. 22 Feb. 1718 Paul Geiger, third son of Herr Joh. Conradt Geiger, "Gemeinschaftlichen Schultheissen" and Elisabetha, daughter of Paul Hobeling, wagonmaker. Their son:
Johannes b. 11 Sept. 1727
A notation in the family register indicates that he is in Pennsylvania.

Pennsylvania records:
TRINITY LUTHERAN KB, LANCASTER:
m. 5 July 1752 Johannes Geiger, single son of Paul Geiger in Germany, and Anna, widowed Cuntzin.

147. GEIGER, PAUL

Fane, 1749
S-H 424

Berwangen, Kraichgau =
6926 Kirchardt

BERWANGEN LUTHERAN KB:
m. 22 Feb. 1718 Paul Geiger, third son of Herr Joh. Conradt Geiger, "Schultheiss," and Elisabetha, daughter of Paul Hobeling, wagonmaker. Their son:
Johann Paul b. 15 Nov. 1723. "Emigrated 1749 to Pennsylvania"

Pennsylvania records:
BOOS' RECORDS, BERKS CO.:
Paul Geiger (Robeson) b. 15 Nov. 1723, buried 4 Aug. 1798
Maria Eva Geiger b. 6 Oct. 1724, buried 11 Feb. 1801
Tombstone inscription, St. Paul's Methodist Episcopal Church, Geigerstown, Berks co.:

Here rests the dead body of John Paul Geiger, who was beloved in life. He was born in Berwangen, Helmstadt in Germany, 15 Nov. 1723. He married Maria Eva, born Kistler and at once moved to this country with his faithful wife. They had 4 sons and 5 daughters and 35 surviving grandchildren. Married for 49 yers. Died 2 Aug. 1798; aged 74 y. 8 mo. and 17 days.
Maria Eva Geiger, born Kistler, b. 26 Oct. 1724; d. 9 Feb. 1801
Several other members of their family are buried in the same cemetery.
For inscriptions, see *National Genealogical Society Quarterly*, Vol XII, no. 2 (1923) p. 18.

New Hanover Lutheran KB, Montgomery co.:
Paulus and Eva (Maria) Geiger had:
    Paulus b. 25 May 1751; bp. 10 Nov.
    Anna Catharine b. 13 July 1756; bp. 5 Sept.; sp. Frederick Hubeli and wife
    Schoena Elisabeth b. 5 Sept. 1758; bp. 14 Oct.

Berks co. Wills and Adm.:
Paul Geiger, Robeson—(20 Aug. 1798 Adm. to Jacob Geiger, eldest son, the widow Maria Eva renouncing.)
Mary Eve Geiger, widow of Paul Geiger, Robeson, (23 June 1800/18 May 1801.) To daughter Elizabeth Penter, 15 pounds. To daughter Jane Amans, 25 pounds. Clothes to be divided among the 4 girls. Son Paul Geiger, executor.

Paul Geiger, Robinson twp., Berks co., nat. Philadelphia 10 Apr. 1767

148. GEIGER, VALENTIN   6921 Ittlingen
Prelist

Ittlingen Lutheran KB:
Valentin Geiger and wife Maria Barbara had:
    Johann Valentin bp. 21 Dec. 1685. "Died 1762 in Pennsylvania."
Valentin Geiger and wife Friderica had:
    Joh. Jacob bp. 29 May 1716

Pennsylvania records:
Valentin Geiger was a son-in-law of Rev. Anthony Jacob Henkel. They settled in Hanover twp. (now Montgomery co.) and Valentin Geiger purchased 250 A. of land 16 Apr. 1718 from John Henry Sprogell. An adjoining land owner was Anthony Jacob Henkel.
For additional materials on these families, see *Perkiomen Region, Past and Present* I: 66–68; and Glatfelter, *Pastors and People*, I: 59–61, 120–121. Also *The Henckel Genealogy 1500–1960* . . . (Spokane, 1964)

Valentine Geygar, Philadelphia co., nat. Sept. 1740

149. GEILINGER, JOH. ADAM   Berwangen, Kraichgau =
                                             6926 Kirchardt
Fane, 1749
S-H 424 (appears on list as Johan Adam (+) Keilinger)

BERWANGEN LUTHERAN KB:
m. 14 July 1710 Hans Peter Göhlinger, son of Hans Jerg Göhlinger, and Susanna,
daughter of Hans Lang, citizen at Holtz Kirchhausen in dem Hochstift Würtzburg.
[= 8702 Holzkirchhausen] (The Comm. Register indicates she was Catholic.)
Peter Geilinger, citizen, and Susanna, had:
        Johann Adam b. 3 Mar. 1726
Susanna, wife of Peter Geilinger, d. 21 Feb. 1744, aged 59 y. and 1 d.
Peter Geilinger d. 1 Jan. 1759, age 69 y. less 3 m. and 2 d.

Pennsylvania records:
PA, THIRD SERIES, XIV:
One Adam Gillinger appears on the 1769 tax list for Cheltenham twp., Philadel-
phia co.

The 1779 tax list for Germantown, Philadelphia co. contains the names of Henry
Geilinger and Michael Geilinger.

150. GEISER, CHRISTOPH   6925 Eschelbronn

Francis & Elizabeth, 1742
S-H 327, 329

ESCHELBRONN LUTHERAN KB:
m. 13 Feb. 1701 Christoph Geÿser, son of Hans Thomas Geÿser, and Anna Kauffmann from Hochdorff, [Either 7141 Hochdorf-Aldingen a. Neckar, or 7311 Hoch-
dorf] duchy of Wurtemberg. Christoph Geÿser and wife Anna had:
        Christoph b. 2 Nov. 1703, bapt. by Joshua Harrsch [alias Kocherthal], pastor
        at Eschelbronn.
m. at Adersbach 8 Jan. 1732 Christoph Geiser, son of Christoph Geiser, citizen at
Eschelbronn and Maria Barbara, dau. of Joh. Conrad Vogler. Christoph Geiser, Jr.
and wife Barbara had:
        1. Maria Barbara b. 5 Feb. 1733
        2. Joh. Christoph b. 3 Sept. 1739

Krebs, "Palatine Emigration . . .," p. 29. "In the year 1742 Christoph Geister of
Eschelbronn was released from vassalage in order to emigrate to America (Protocol
6188, p. 560).

Pennsylvania records:

SHULTZE'S JOURNALS, II; 258:
Chris. Geiser is mentioned as an adjacent landowner in a survey for 300 A. for
John Kreyder, in Philadelphia co., Feb. 3 and 8, 1769.

Christr. Gyser, Marlborough twp., Philadelphia co., nat. Philadelphia 11 Apr.
1763

151. GERNER, JOH. MATHEUS

6928 Helmstadt-Bargen

Two Brothers, 1750

S-H 438

HELMSTADT LUTHERAN KB:
m. 3 Feb. 1739 Johann Matheus Gerner, son of the late Lorentz Gerner, citizen and Anna Margretha Catharina, dau. of the late Hans Adam Laule. Children:
1. Joh. Michael b. 7 Nov. 1739
2. Maria Catharina b. 5 Jan. 1742
3. Johann Christoph b. 19 Aug. 1744; d. 23 July 1747
4. Susanna Margretha b. 20 Sept. 1746
5. Margretha Barbara b. 24 Feb. 1749, d. 6 Mar. 1749

He was a brother-in-law of Georg Michael Schupp who also appears on this ship's list.

Krebs, "Palatine Emigration . . . .," p. 36.
Johann Mathias Gerner of Helmstadt (Kreis Heidelberg) wanted in 1750 to go to the so called New Land.

Pennsylvania records:
LANCASTER CO. WILLS:
Mathias Gerner, Earl twp., (5 Dec. 1786/27 Apr. 1787.) Exrs. were Benjamin Lessle and Bernard Geiger, his son-in-law. Wife: Maria; children: Michael, Catharine, Susan, Eve, Anna and Margaret.

Matthew Gurner, Earl tp., Lancaster co., nat. Philadelphia 10 April 1765.

152. GILBERT, ANDREAS

Hoffenheim = 6920 Sinsheim, Elsenz

Snow *Louisa*, 1752

S-H 506

HOFFENHEIM LUTHERAN KB:
Georg Martin Gilbert m. 28 Feb. 1718 Maria Dorothea, dau. of Peter Precht. Two of their sons:
Johannes b. 14 Sept. 1725; conf. 1739 [Possibly the Johannes Gilbert on the ship *Shirley*, 1751, S-H 454]
Andreas b. 8 July 1728; conf. 1741

Pennsylvania records:
Andreas Gilbert, Conestogo twp., Lancaster co., nat. Philadelphia, as a "Quaker" Fall 1765.

153. GILBERT, BALTZER

Hoffenheim = 6920 Sinsheim, Elsenz

Robert and Alice, 1743

S-H 348

HOFFENHEIM LUTHERAN KB:
Hans Veltin Gilbert and wife Magdalena had:
Georg Balthasar b. 5 Apr. 1725; conf. 1739

154. GILBERT, BERNHART   Hoffenheim =
Robert & Alice, 1743   6920 Sinsheim, Elsenz
S-H 348

HOFFENHEIM LUTHERAN KB:
m. 23 Apr. 1720 Hans Wendel Gilbert, widower, and Eva Margaretha Greÿss.
Their son:
   Hans Bernhard b. 15 Sept. 1724; conf. 1738

Pennsylvania records:
PHILADELPHIA CO. WILLS: K:457: One of the Bernhard Gilberts is mentioned in
the will of Jacob Penter as a son-in-law, husband of his daughter Catharine Gilbert
in 1756

155. GILBERT, HANS GEORG   Hoffenheim =
     GILBERT, H. BERNHART   6920 Sinsheim, Elsenz
     GILBERT, JOH. GEORG
Nancy, 1750
S-H 443

HOFFENHEIM LUTHERAN KB:

m. 14 Nov. 1724 Hans Georg Gilbert and Elisabetha Gruber, stepdaughter of
Pleicard Rupp. Children:
   1. Anna Margretha b. 27 June 1726
   2. Johann Bernhardt b. 5 Dec. 1729; conf. 1741
   3. Johann Georg b. 21 Feb. 1732; conf. 1744
   4. Joh. Conrad b. 9 Apr. 1734; conf. 1749
   5. Hans Heinrich b. 17 Feb. 1736
   6. Maria Dorothea } twins b. 24 Dec. 1738
   7. Joh. Adam
   8. Joh. Adam b. 18 Jan. 1740
   9. Maria Elisabetha b. 8 Apr. 1744

Pennsylvania records:
TRAPPE LUTHERAN KB, MONTGOMERY CO.:
m. 30 Dec. 1755 at New Hanover Jurg Gilbert and Margetha Marolsin
m. 19 Apr. 1757 at New Hanover Joh. Conrad Gilbert and Elisabetha, daughter of
Christian Stöltz

NEW HANOVER LUTHERAN KB, MONTGOMERY CO.:
Joh. Adam Gilbert and Maria Elisabetha Gilbert were confirmed in 1756, children
of the late Jürg Gilbert.
Joh. Georg Gilbert d. 10 Dec. 1753.
Elisabetha, wife of Georg Gilbert, d. 8 Sept. 1766, age 64 y. 3 weeks 1 day.
Hans Heinrich Gilbert d. 3 Sept. 1814, age 78 y.
Johann Bernhard Gilbert d. 6 Feb. 1798, age 68 y. 2 mo.

ZION (RED) LUTHERAN KB, BRUNSWICK TWP., SCHUYLKILL CO.:
D. 26 Jan. 1812 Konrad Gilbert b. in Europe 29 Apr. 1734.

Bernard Gilbert and Conrad Gilbert nat. Philadelphia 24 September 1760 of Douglass twp., Philadelphia co.
George Gilbert nat. Philadelphia September 1761, of Cobebrookdale, Berks Co.

156. GILBERT, JACOB BERNHART
Hoffenheim =
6920 Sinsheim, Elsenz

Jacob, 1749
S-H 418

HOFFENHEIM LUTHERAN KB:
m. 25 Oct. 1718 Joh. Jacob Gilbert and Maria Barbara, daughter of Johann Spittelmeÿer. Children:
  *1. Jacob b. 7 Feb. 1721; conf. 1736
   2. Anna Maria b. 17 Feb. 1723
  *3. Joh. Bernhard b. 25 May 1724; conf. 1738
   4. Hans Georg b. 25 Jan. 1726; probably d. young
   5. Hans Georg b. 8 Mar. 1728
   6. Anna Dorothea b. 1 Mar. 1730
   7. Joh. Niclas [q.v.] b. 8 Nov. 1731; conf. 1745
   8. Joh. Friederich b. 2 Jan. 1739

Pennsylvania records:
A Bernard Gilbert, Cushahoppen, Philadelphia co., nat. 1765.

157. GILBERT, JOH. GEORG
Hoffenheim =
6920 Sinsheim, Elsenz

Snow *Louisa*, 1752
S-H 506

HOFFENHEIM LUTHERAN KB:
m. 30 Aug. 1718 Dietrich Gilbert, son of Joh. Jacob Gilbert, Sr., and Magdalena Kimmler, dau. of Georg Kimmler. Their son:
  Joh. Georg b. 13 Dec. 1720; conf. 1732

Pennsylvania records:
NEW HANOVER LUTHERAN KB, MONTGOMERY CO:
D. 15 June 1784 Joh. Georg Gilbert, age 64 y., 3 m.

158. GILBERT, JOH. HEINRICH
Robert and Alice, 1743
S-H 347

Hoffenheim =
6920 Sinsheim, Elsenz

HOFFENHEIM LUTHERAN KB:
Hans Veltin Gilbert and wife Magdalena had:
    Joh. Heinrich b. 8 June 1721; conf. 1736

Pennsylvania records:
ST. MICHAEL'S AND ZION LUTHERAN KB, PHILADELPHIA:
D. 31 May 1789 Joh. Heinrich Gilbert, b. 8 June 1721 in Germany. M. Catharina
Kieler and had 6 ch.
Heinrich Gilbert and wife Catharina (Catholic) had:
    1. Mathias b. 18 Jan. 1747
    2. Catharina b. 9 Feb. 1749
    3. Anna Margretha b. 9 Mar. 1750; bp. 2 Dec. 1751
    4. Jurg Michael b. 2 Feb. 1752
    5. Anna Maria b. 19 Dec. 1753; bp. 13 Mar. 1754

Henry Gilbert, nat. Philadelphia Sept./Oct. 1763 of Cheltenham twp., Philadelphia co.

159. GILBERT, JOH. JACOB
Possibly S-H 443, but other Jacob Gilberts in S-H 371,
418

Hoffenheim =
6920 Sinsheim, Elsenz

EICHTERSHEIM LUTHERAN KB:
m. 18 Nov. 1727 Joh. Jacob Gilbert, son of Hans Jacob Gilbert of Hoffheim, and
Anna Helena Adam, daughter of Geörg Henr. Adam, citizen and potter.

HOFFENHEIM LUTHERAN KB:
Joh. Jacob Gilbert, shoemaker, and wife Anna Helena had:
    1. Anna Maria b. 5 July 1729
    2. Anna Catharina b. 24 June 1732
    3. Joh. Georg b. 19 Nov. 1734, d. 23 Nov.
    4. Sebastian b. 20 Feb. 1736
    5. Joh. Elias b. 15 Oct. 1738
    6. Maria Elisabetha b. 13 July 1741
    7. Joh. Samuel b. 8 Aug. 1743

Pennsylvania records:
NEW HANOVER LUTHERAN, KB, MONTGOMERY CO.:
Conf. 1760 Elias Gilbert, son of Joh. Jacob Gilbert, age 23.
D. 2 Dec. 1786 Helena Gilbert, age 68 (?)
D. 5 June 1764 Jacob Gilbert, age 77 y. 8 mo.

FALKNER SWAMP REFORMED KB, MONTGOMERY CO.:
Bu. 2 Dec. 1786 Anna Helena Gilbert age 80 y. (also in Lutheran record, age
given as 68)

Hoffenheim on the Elsenz suffered from wars and invading armies like many Kraichgau towns. The face on the corner post is said to have been placed to drive away evil.

Photo: J. Godshall

160. GILBERT, JOH. NICOLAUS

Nancy, 1750
S-H 443 (appears on list as Joh. Colaus Gilbert)

Hoffenheim =
6920 Sinsheim, Elsenz

HOFFENHEIM LUTHERAN KB:
m. 25 Oct. 1718 Joh. Jacob Gilbert and Maria Barbara, daughter of Johann Spittelmeÿer. They had:
    Joh. Niclas b. 8 Nov. 1731, conf. 1745

161. GILBERT, JORG

Chance, 1764
S-H 689

Hoffenheim =
6920 Sinsheim, Elsenz
6928 Helmstadt-Bargen

HELMSTADT LUTHERAN KB:
Hans Caspar Winterbauer, citizen and baker, and wife Anna Barbara nee Kuhlwein had:
    Anna Barbara bp. 12 Feb. 1716

HOFFENHEIM LUTHERAN KB:
m. 19 Nov. 1743 Johann Georg Gilberth and Maria Barbara Winterbauer, dau. of Johann Caspar Winterbauer, inhabitant at Helmstadt. Children:
    1. Anna Catharina b. 29 May 1745
    2. Joh. Jacob b. 25 July 1748
    3. Joh. Niclas b. 30 Dec. 1751; bp. 1 Jan. 1752
    4. Catharina Margretha b. 31 Jan. 1754

Pennsylvania records:
ST. MICHAEL'S AND ZION LUTHERAN KB, PHILADELPHIA:
d. 12 Aug. 1783 Anna Barbara Gilbert, b. in Helmstadt; age 67 y. 6 m. and 2 d.

162. GILBERT, MATTEIS

Townsend, 1737
S-H 185, 186, 187

Hoffenheim =
6920 Sinsheim, Elsenz

HOFFENHEIM LUTHERAN KB:
Valentin Gilbert and wife Magdalena had:
    Mattheis b. 7 Jan. 1716; conf. 1730

Pennsylvania records:
NEW HANOVER LUTHERAN KB, MONTGOMERY CO.:
m. 5 Jan. 1748 Matthias Gilbert and Christina Dorothea Huber [q.v.]

TRINITY LUTHERAN KB, LANCASTER:
    1. Georg Henrich b. 1 Dec. 1748; bp. 29 July 1750
    2. Georg Michael b. 17 Feb. 1751
    3. Friederich b. 24 July 1752
d. 3 Aug. 1784 Math. Gilbert, age 68 y. 7 m.

SALEM LUTHERAN KB, LEBANON:
d. 6 July 1795 Anna Dorothea Christine Gilbert (nee Huber) b. in Sept. 1718 in
"Ztlinger [= Ittlingen]." Parents John J. Huber [q.v.] and wife Anna Barbara.
Bapt. witnesses were Philip Balser Romich and Dorothea Friedler [Friedle, q.v.].
Conf. in 1743, came to America in 1747. Married Mattheus Gilbert who d. 11 y.
ago. They had 4 children, 3 sons are living. Sickness: general debility. Aged 77 y.
less 2 mo.

163. GLASSBRENNER, GEORG age 21

Samuel, 1732
S-H, 59, 63, 65

7103 Schwaigern

SCHWAIGERN LUTHERAN KB:
M. 17 Aug. 1701 Hans Peter Glassbrenner, son of Hans Glassbrenner, citizen at
Onoltz, Crailsheim Amts, [Onolzheim = 7180 Crailsheim] and Anna Christina,
widow of H. Henrich Stumpff. They had:
    Joh. Georg b. 18 Apr. 1711

Pennsylvania records:
STOEVER'S RECORDS:
m. 7 Feb. 1738 Georg Glassbrenner and Elisabetha Fischer, Tulpehocken. Georg
Glassbrenner (Lebanon) had:
    Maria Christiana Margaretha b. 28 Feb. 1741; bp. 25 Mar. 1741

SALEM LUTHERAN CHURCH, LEBANON CO., PA.:
Georg Glasbrenner d. Oct. 1800 age 89 y. 5 mo. 11 d., son of Peter Glashbrenner
and wf., b. 23 Apr. 1711 in Germany; bp. and conf. a Lutheran; m. in his 27th
yr. Elisabeth Fisher. 12 ch., 7 are living.

DAUPHIN CO. WILLS:
George Glassbrenner, Lebanon (23 July 1799/7 Oct. 1800) From his will and the
Salem Lutheran Church records his ch. were:

1. Anna Maria m. Johannes Stohler
2. David Glassbrenner
3. Georg b. 27 Nov. 1747; m. Catharina Huber
4. Catharina Elisabetha m. _____ Büler
5. Anstel (Anastatius) b. 8 May 1752; m. Elisabeth Arz.
6. Anna Elisabetha, dec'd; m. _____ Lang
7. Peter b. 1 Dec. 1748; m. Cathrine Lenz
8. John Martin _____

Georg Glassbenner, Lebanon tp., Lancaster co., nat. Philadelphia, 24 Sept. 1762

164. GLASSBRENNER, JOH. CONRAD age 30   Daisbach =
                                                            6923 Waibstadt
Pleasant, 1732   6925 Eschelbronn
S-H 99, 100

ESCHELBRONN LUTHERAN KB:
Hans Jerg Glasbrenner and wife Anna Margretha had:
    Joh. Conrad b. 21 Apr. 1706 at Daÿspach

NECKARGEMÜND LUTHERAN KB:
m. 23 Nov. 1728 Joh. Conrad Glassbrenner from Dayspach [Daisbach], and Margaretha Greiner from Meckesheim. [She was conf. 1717 at Meckesheim, aged 14 years.] Their children:
    1. Joh. Georg b. 8 June 1730
    2. Joh. Ehrhart b. 1 June 1731

Pennsylvania records:
MUDDY CREEK LUTHERAN KB, LANCASTER CO.:
Cunradt Glassbrenner (Warwick) had:
    3. Anna Barbara b. 20 Dec. 1733
    4. Maria Elisabetha b. 18 Feb. 1735
    5. Anna Margaretha b. 26 May 1737
m. 8 Mar. 1768 Jacob, son of the late George Mayer, and Susanna, daughter of Conrad Glasbrenner of Warwick.
Buried at Brickerville, Lancaster co.:

Kunrath Glasbrener   Margaretha Klasbrenerin
b. 10 Feb. 17--   b. 1709
d. 3 Dec. 1771   died 21 June 1762
Age 71 years   Age 60 years
(The above from a typed transcript of tombstone inscriptions—if the transcript is correct and the tombstone data accurate, this may not be the Conrad Glassbrenner born in Eschelbronn.)

165. GLASSBRENNER, JOH. FRIEDRICH   7103 Schwaigern

Royal Union, 1750
S-H, 432

SCHWAIGERN LUTHERAN KB:
m. 17 Aug. 1701 Hans Peter Glassbrenner, son of Hans Glassbrenner, citizen at
Onoltz, Crailsheim Amts, [Onolzheim = 7180 Crailsheim] and Anna Christina,
widow of H. Henrich Stumpff. They had:
    Joh. Friedrich b. 9 Aug. 1705
Johann Frederich Glassbrenner and wife Maria Christina had:
    1. Joh. Ludwig Adam b. 15 Jan. 1735
    2. Maria Barbara b. 4 Mar. 1736, d. 1736
    3. Maria Catharina b. 21 Nov. 1737
    4. Joh. Christian b. 10 Apr. 1743, d. 1743
    5. Joh. Gottlieb b. 10 Jan. 1745
    6. Johannes b. 12 June 1749, d. 1749

Pennsylvania records:
STOEVER'S RECORDS:
Friederich Glassbrenner (Northkill) had:
    7. Joh. Friederich b. 30 Oct. 1751; bp. 10 Nov. 1751

CHRIST LUTHERAN KB, STOUCHSBURG, (TULPEHOCKEN), BERKS CO.:
m. 29 June 1773 John Frederick Glassbrenner, son of John Frederick Glassbrenner,
and Anna Margaret Lenig, daughter of Thomas Lenig, Heidelberg.

BERKS CO. ADMINISTRATION:
Frederick Glassbrenner of Heidelberg; adm. granted 2 June 1788 to Gotlieb Glassbrenner, eldest son.

166. GOBEL, GEORG   Hoffenheim =
Snow *Louisa,* 1752   6920 Sinsheim, Elsenz
S-H 506

HOFFENHEIM LUTHERAN KB:
m. 21 Nov. 1724 Niclas Gobel, son of the late Hans Georg Gobel, and Dorothea
Crafft. Joh. Niclas Gobel and Anna Dorothea had:
    Joh. Georg b. 10 May 1733; conf. 1747

American records:
ROWAN CO., N. C., SUPERIOR COURT MINUTES, P. 598:
Natives of Germany nat. 22 Sept. 1763: George Cobell, Jacob Cobell

167. GOBEL, HANS GEORG age 40   Hoffenheim =
Hope, 1733   6920 Sinsheim, Elsenz
S-H 116, 118, 120, 121 (Other passengers on ship:
Barbara age 38; Antony age 12; Anna Maria age 10;
Magdalena age 8; Jurg Adam age 5; Hans Georg age
3½.)

HOFFENHEIM LUTHERAN KB:
Hans Jerg Gobel and wife Eva had:
    Hans Jerg bp. 4 June 1693
m. 13 May 1716 Johann Georg Gobel, son of Joh. Georg Gobel, and Maria Barbara
Geisler, daughter of Peter Geisler, citizen. Children:
    1. Carl Antonius b. 21 Oct. 1718
    2. Maria Elisabetha b. 5 Sept. 1720
    3. Anna Maria b. 14 Aug. 1721
    4. Georg Balthasar b. 3 Mar. 1723
    5. Maria Magdalena b. 1 Jan. 1725
    6. Anna Margretha b. 23 Mar. 1726
    7. Georg Adam b. 13 Apr. 1727
    8. Hans Georg b. 12 Sept. 1728
    9. Maria Dorothea b. 13 May 1732

Pennsylvania records:
TRINITY LUTHERAN KB, LANCASTER:
Joh. Georg Gobel had:
    10. Johannes b. 28 Aug. 1734; bp. 10 Nov. 1734
This bp. is also recorded in Christ Lutheran KB, York.

CHRIST LUTHERAN KB, YORK:
Anthony Kobel and wife had:
    Maria Elisabeth b. 27 Oct. 1743

LISCHY'S RECORDS, YORK CO.:
Antoni Gobel and Anna Maria had:
    Eva bp. 11 June 1749

ROWAN CO., N. C. SUPERIOR COURT MINUTES, PP. 597–598:
Natives of Germany nat.
22 Mar. 1763—Anthony Cobble
22 Sept. 1763—Adam Cobell

Anthony Coble of Guilford co., N. C., will 24 May 1794. Wife mentioned but not
named. Children: George, Ludwick, David, Barbara Class, Lisabeth Smith, Eve
Glass, Molly Shatterly, Thorely Graves, Mary Graves, Cataren Cortner and son John
who is named executor.

FIRST REFORMED KB, LANCASTER:
Melchior Bayer and Anna Maria Kobel had:
    1. Maria Elisabetha b. 15 Dec. 1740; sp. Anthony Kobel and Maria Emig
Anthony Kobel and Anna Maria nee Emig had:
    1. John b. 15 July 1742; sp. John Emig

ST. MATTHEW'S LUTHERAN KB, HANOVER:
Georg Gobell has a son Johann Henrich, no dates given [ca. 1751], sponsored by
Georg Adam Gobell and Maria Magdalena Facklern. Georg Adam Gobel m. Anna
Margaretha Löffelin 13 May 1754. Johannes Gobel m. 17 February 1755 Maria
Barbara Stahlin.

The northern Kraichgau is a land of tidy farm villages and neatly tended fields and forests. Fruit and nut trees line the roads. The topography is not unlike Pennsylvania's which must have helped the many emigrants adjust to their new home.

Photo: J. Godshall

Wentz, *The Beginnings of the German Element in York Co., Pa.*, Appendix B: Gorrick Gobell appears on a list of names of persons for whose arrest a warrant was issued on 21 Oct. 1736 by the Maryland government. He had signed a letter of protest to the Governor of Maryland.

168. GOBEL, JOH. JACOB

Nancy, 1750
S-H 443

Hoffenheim =
6920 Sinsheim, Elsenz

HOFFENHEIM LUTHERAN KB:
m. 21 Nov. 1723 Niclas Gobel, son of the late Hans Georg Gobel, and Dorothea Crafft. Their son:
Johann Jacob bp. 26 Nov. 1730; conf. 1744

American records:
FIRST REFORMED KB, LANCASTER:
Jacob Kobel and Anna Margaret had:
  1. Jacob bp. 8 Mar. 1752

ROWAN CO., N. C. SUPERIOR COURT MINUTES, P. 598:
Natives of Germany nat. 22 Sept. 1763: George Cobell, Jacob Cobell
A Jacob Coble witnessed the 1793 will of Anthony Coble in Guilford co., N. C.

169. GRAFF, MICHAEL
Dragon, 1732
S-H 96, 98, 99

Elsenz =
7519 Eppingen

ELSENZ REFORMED KB:
Michael Graff, the miller's servant, and wife Catharina had a child bp. in 1728 (the edge of the page containing name and date of bp. is missing.)

Pennsylvania records:
TRINITY LUTHERAN KB, LANCASTER:
Joh. Michael Graff had:
1. Joh. Cunradt b. 22 Sept. 1734; sp. Joh. Cunradt Fry and wife Anna Elisabetha
by second marriage:
2. Joh. Georg b. 6 Apr. 1739; sp. Joh. Georg Graff, Jr. and wife Maria Magdalena

MUDDY CREEK LUTHERAN LB:
Michael Graff had:
Maria Catarina b. 9 Nov. 1742; sp. Maria Catarina Klein and Anna Catarina Meyer

170. GREINER, ANDREAS

6921 Ehrstädt

[Ship data not located; one appears on S-H, I, 404 in 1749, but he has been previously identified from another area.]

EHRSTÄDT LUTHERAN KB:
Joh. Andreas Greiner, b. 9 Dec. 1685, son of Hans Jacob Greiner and Maria Catharina. Andreas Greiner, shoemaker, and wife Anna Maria had:
1. Joh. Matthäus b. 15 Apr. 1721
2. Joh. Heinrich b. 19 Aug. 1723
3. Maria Margretha b. 21 Jan. 1726
4. Joh. Andreas b. 7 Feb. 1728
5. Maria Juliana Agatha b. 12 Aug. 1729
6. Maria Sabina b. 7 Mar. 1733
7. Joh. Andreas b. 20 May 1736
8. Maria Margaretha b. 13 Feb. 1738
9. Maria Margaretha b. 13 Feb. 1739
10. Joh. Michael b. 21 June 1743

Pennsylvania records:
TRINITY LUTHERAN KB, LANCASTER:
m. 21 Jan. 1766 Andreas Greiner from Ehrstatt near Sinzheim, and Barbara Jungin, single.

171. GREINER, JOH. DIETERICH
1717

Bonfeld =
6927 Bad Rappenau

BONFELD EMIGRANT LIST:
1717 Joh. Dieterich Greiner with wf. and daughter and sister.

BONFELD LUTHERAN KB:
Heinrich Greiner, son of Thoma(s) Greiner from Ehrstatt [= 6920 Ehrstädt], m.
26 Aug. 1681 Anna Barbara, daughter of Peter Grammeneck. Their son, Hans
Dieterich Greiner was b. 7 Feb. 1686; bp. 8 Feb. 1786.
m. 26 Jan. 1712 Joh. Dieterich Greiner, son of the late Heinrich Greiner and
Dorothea, daughter of the late Hans Emmert, citizen at Eberstatt [7101 Eberstadt,
Wurtt]. They had:
1. Christina Catharina b. Jan. 1713; d. 1714
2. Maria Catharina b. 14 Aug. 1716; bp. 15 Aug. 1716

The Bonfeld emigrant list indicates that a sister of Joh. Dieterich Greiner also
emigrated. There are two possibilities:
Anna Barbara Greiner b. 16 Aug. 1682; bp. 17 Aug. 1682
Maria Margaretha Greiner bp. 7 Mar. 1696
Both daughters of Heinrich and Anna Barbara Greiner.

Pennsylvania records:
BERKS CO. DEEDS:
B-2: 74; deed dated 12 Sept. *1717*, deed recorded 17 Jan. 1775: Henry Gibson of
the county of Philadelphia, yeoman, sold a tract of land containing 200 A. in said
county, adjoining John Jacob Roth, to John *Theoderick* Greiner, (at the end of the
deed): "On 25th day of 7 mo. 1731, within Henry Gibson delivered up unto with
John Theodorick Griner quiet possession and seizin of said premises."

BERKS CO. WILLS:
Book 1: 171: John Theodore Griner, Amity, (11 Mar. 1758/27 May 1765) wife:
Dorothy; ch.:
1. Catherean, wf. of John Sands
2. Barbara, wf. of John Weidner and their ch., Cathereen and John Weidner
3. Dorothy, wf. of George Weidner and their 5 ch.
4. Mary, wf. of Daniel Lodowick
5. John Griner, this son is also named executor of the estate.

Joh. Dietrich Kreiner, Philadelphia co., nat. by Act of 6 Feb. 1730/31.

172. GRIMM, EGIDIUS
James Goodwill, 1728
S-H 21, 22

Berwangen =
6926 Kirchardt

BERWANGEN LUTHERAN KB:
Family Register:
Georg Grimm and Anna Maria had:
Egydius b. 1700

Anna Maria, wife of Georg Grimm, d. 24 Sept. 1710, aged 41 years. Georg Grim, citizen, d. 4 Dec. 1712, aged 52 years.

SINSHEIM LUTHERAN KB:
conf. 1715 Egidius Grimm, son of the late Joh. Georg Grimm from Berwangen, aged 13 years.

Pennsylvania records:
STOEVER'S RECORDS (unpublished):
Egidius Grimm in Maxatanien had:
> Anna Catharina b. 15 Mar. 1730; bp. 1 July; sp. Andreas Fischer and Christina

JORDAN LUTHERAN KB, LEHIGH CO.:
Gitty Grim and Katharina Grimm sp. 1742 a child of Adam Brauss [q.v.]

MOSELEM LUTHERAN KB, BERKS CO.:
m. 16 Nov. 1750 Peter Merkle, son of Christian Merkle, and Catharine Grim, single daughter of Egitius Grim.
m. 1 Apr. 1755 Casper Merklin, master smith, son of Christian Merklin, and Elisabeth Grimm, single daughter of Egydius Grimm.

NORTHAMPTON CO. WILLS:
Gitty Grim, Macungie. (18 Jan. 1760/1 Oct. 1761) Children: Jacob, Henry, Catharina, Elisabeth, Margaretta. Wit.: Nicholas Hermany and A. Braus.

Getty Grimm, Bucks co., nat. Philadelphia September 1743

173. GRIMM, JOH. CONRADT age 20   Berwangen, Kraichgau =
Harle, 1736   6926 Kirchardt
S-H 156, 159, 161

BERWANGEN LUTHERAN KB:
m. 5 Sept. 1713 Hans Georg Grimm, single, and Anna Barbara, daughter of Paul Körbel. Their son:
> Johann Conradt b. 1 June 1716. Communicants register: to the new land or Pennsylvania in 1736; family register: "is in the new Land."

Pennsylvania records:
NORTHAMPTON CO. WILLS:
A Conrad Grim of Weissenberg twp. (18 Mar. 1763/13 Aug. 1763) Wife: Elisabeth; children: Diewald, George, Jacob, Henry, Mary, Catarina, Madelena, Susanna and Elisabeth.
There are other Conrad Grims in Pa. records. One Conrad Grim, a weaver, resided in Upper Salford twp., Philadelphia co. in 1781–1783.

MOSELEM LUTHERAN KB, RICHMOND TWP., BERKS CO.:
Conrad Grim and wife Maria Elisabetha nee Frey had:
> Joh. Georg bp. Dom 7 Trin 1750, 26 weeks old; sp. Andreas Frey [q.v.] and Catharina Barbara

174. GROB, JOH. JACOB

Massenbach =
7103 Schwaigern

Royal Union, 1750
S-H 431

MASSENBACH LUTHERAN KB:
Hans Jerg Grob and wife Anna Barbara had:
Joh. Jacob b. 18 July 1721
m. 8 Sept. 1744 Joh. Jacob Grob, son of the late Joh. Georg Grob, and Jacobina,
daughter of the late Peter Ries. They had:
1. Joh. Adam b. 16 Apr. 1745
2. Maria Eva b. 29 Nov. 1746, d. young
3. Johannes b. 27 Aug. 1748
The father's occupation is given as weaver in the bp. records.

Pennsylvania records:
ST. MICHAEL'S AND ZION LUTHERAN KB, PHILADELPHIA:
d. 6 June 1782 Johann Jacob Grob from Massenbach, age 54 y.

175. GROB, JOHANNES

6921 Ittlingen

Francis and Elizabeth, 1742
S-H 328

ITTLINGEN LUTHERAN KB:
Joh. Rudolf Grob and Cunigunda had:
Johannes b. 30 (?) May 1705
Johannes Grob and Anna Christina had:
1. Joh. Philip b. 21 Apr. 1734
2. Margaretha Maria b. 9 May 1736
3. Anna Maria b. 18 Apr. 1738
4. Joh. Philipp b. 1 Aug. 1741

Pennsylvania records:
TRINITY LUTHERAN KB, LANCASTER:
Johann Daniel Biebel, single, from Gerssdorf in Alsace (= F67360 Goersdorf near
Woerth) m. 14 May 1754 Maria Margaret Grobin from Ittlingen.
Anna Maria Grob, single, d. 6 Sept. 1757.
Christina Grop, widow, d. 23 Jan. 1762

176. GROCKENBERGER, GEORG ADAM

6921 Neidenstein,
Elsenzgau

NEIDENSTEIN LUTHERAN KB:
m. 20 Nov. 1753 Georg Adam Grockenberger, son of Georg Adam Grockenberger,
and Christina Margretha, daughter of the late Philip Pfisterer.
[see Pfisterer for details of the family.]

Pennsylvania records:
A Georg Adam Rockenberger appears in the records of St. Michael's and Zion. In
those records his wife is named Anna Catharina and her burial record gives her

maiden name as Pfisterer. If this is the same Georg Adam Grockenberger of the
Neidenstein record, it appears his first wife died and he then married her sister.
Georg Adam Rockenberger and wife Anna Catharina had:
1. Georg Adam b. 21 Oct. 1757, d. 10 Aug. 1758
2. Maria Salome b. 3 Sept. 1760
3. Samuel b. 3 Sept. 1763

Geo. Adam Rockeberger, Philadelphia, Philadelphia co. nat. Philadelphia with
Geo. Adam Pfister April 1762

177. GROS, JOHANN GEORG   6921 Michelfeld

1738

MICHELFELD LUTHERAN KB:
m. 7 Jan. 1738 Johann Georg Gros (?) and Anna Elisabetha Lütterin
"This married couple left 6 May 1738 for Pennsylvania."

178. GRUBER, HENRICH   Steinsfurt =
                                                     6920 Sinsheim, Elsenz
Dragon, 1732
S-H 96, 97, 98 [Christian Gruber also emigrated, ship
data not located]

SINSHEIM LUTHERAN KB:
Henrich Gruber and wife Elisabetha had ch. bp. at Steinsfurt:
*1. Hans Henrich b. 25 Mar. 1700
2. Hans Jacob b. 9 Dec. 1702
3. Hans Georg b. 6 July 1706
4. Georg Albrecht bp. 20 May 1709
*5. Christian b. 19 Oct. 1712

m. (2) 18 Jan. 1718 at Steinsfurt Henrich Gruber, widower, and Margretha, daughter of Peter Wanner. Children:
6. Georg Michel b. 13 Feb. 1719
7. Maria Margretha b. 11 Mar. 1722
8. Maria Magdalena b. 26 May 1723
9. Maria Margretha b. 26 Sept. 1727
10. Anna Catharina b. 1 Oct. 1730

Pennsylvania records:
CHRIST "LITTLE TULPEHOCKEN" KB, BERKS CO.:
Henry Gruber had:
1. Joh. Adam b. 19 Oct. 1735
2. Catharine Elisabeth b. 6 Feb. 1737
3. Maria Eva Rosina b. 3 Dec. 1738
4. Christian b. 18 Feb. 1740; sp. Christian Gruber and wife
5. Christopher b. 11 Dec. 1741
6. Henry b. 19 Aug. 1747
7. Elisabetha b. 10 Oct. 1749

m. 26 Jan. 1742 Christian Gruber and Anna Kunigunda Stup. Children:
1. Joh. Georg b. 16 Feb. 1743; sp. Henry Gruber and wife
2. Susanna b. 12 Aug. 1746

TOMBSTONE INSCRIPTIONS, BERNVILLE, PA.:
Christian Gruber b. 18 Oct. 1712, d. 14 Nov. 1781. m. in 1742 Anna Kunigunda
(daughter of Martin Stuep, now Stupp, and wife Anna Catharine Schultz) b. 21
Dec. 1721, d. 30 May 1799.

BERKS WILLS:
Henry Gruber, Heidelberg (10 Feb. 1773/17 June 1777) Eldest son John Adam.
Wife: Maria Euphrosina. Children: John Adam, Christian, Henry, Catharine, Eu-
phrosina and Elisabeth.

Henry Gruber, Heidleberg twp., Berks co., nat. Philadelphia, April 1761

179. GRUNER, JOH. DIETRICH

Dragon, 1732
S-H 96, 97, 98

Adelshofen, Baden =
7519 Eppingen

ADELSHOFEN LUTHERAN KB:
m. 2 May 1702 Matthias Krener, son of Matthias Krener, inhabitant at Schoten __
(?) [perhaps 6479 Schotten], and Agnes Catharina, dau. of Hans Elias Schlauch.
[The surname also appears in the record as Kroener, Gröner, Gruner.] Their son:
Joh. Dieterich b. 1 Apr. 1709

Pennsylvania records:
TRINITY LUTHERAN KB, LANCASTER:
Dietrich Gröener and Rosina had:
    Maria Magdalena b. __ Mar. 1749
    Maria Gertrud b. 18 Mar. 1754
    Anna Margaretha b. 28 Feb. 1755
    Charlotta b. 7 Apr. 1756

180. GRÜNER, JOH. KOLMAN

Robert and Alice, 1743
S-H 347

Hasselbach =
6920 Sinsheim, Elsenz

ADERSBACH LUTHERAN KB:
Joh. Andreas Kreiner at [6920] Hasselbach and wife Anna Maria had:
    Johann Collman b. 24 Feb. 1718 Sp.: Thomas Gerlach at Hasselbach and
    Joh. Collman Huber, single, from Unter Eisestheim [7107 Untereisesheim]

Pennsylvania records:
FIRST REFORMED KB, LANCASTER:
m. 10 Dec. 1745 Colman Kreiner, son of Andrew Kreiner, and Maria Ursula
Zehever, daughter of Francis Zehever.

TRINITY LUTHERAN KB, LANCASTER:
Johann Kohlmann Gruener and wife Ursula (Catholic) had children:

1. Jacob b. 24 Dec. 1748
2. Michael b. 12 Apr. 1751
3. Catharina b. 12 Feb. 1753
Colemann and Rosina Greiner had:
4. Elisabeth bp. 2 Mar. 1760
D. 17 Apr. 1752 Jacob, beloved son of Cohlman Greiner and Ursula; age 3 y. 3 m.
D. 17 Feb. 1761 a child of Colman Greiner, bu. the following day.

Colman Gryner, Lancaster twp., Lancaster co., nat. Philadelphia Fall 1765.

181. GSELL, LUDWIG

Bonfeld =
6927 Bad Rappenau

Molly, 1727
S-H, 12, 14 (Name on List: Gesell.)

BONFELD LUTHERAN KB:
M. 28 Aug. 1725 Georg Ludwig Gsell, son of Bernhard Christoph Friedrich Gsell, "Anwalt" and innkeeper and Anna Dorothea, daughter of Bernhard Hoffmann, citizen at Hochstatt. [Either 6451 Hochstadt or 8621 Hochstadt a. Main]
Georg Ludwig Gsell was b. 4 Apr. 1703; bp. 5 Apr. 1703, son of Bernhard Christoph Gsell and Maria Magdalena.
Maria Magdalena Gsell, widow of Bernhard Christopher Friedrich Gesell, d. 19 Jan. 1757, age 82 y. less 5 d.

Pennsylvania records:
Although the surname Gsell (Gesell) appears in some Pennsylvania records, no specific record about Ludwig Gsell has been located.

182. GÜLBERTH, CHRISTOPH

Hoffenheim =
6920 Sinsheim, Elsenz

Snow *Louisa*, 1752
S-H 506

HOFFENHEIM LUTHERAN KB:
Friedrich Gilbert and wife Johanna Sophia had:
Georg Christoph b. 27 Feb. 1734

Pennsylvania records:
ST. MICHAEL'S AND ZION LUTHERAN KB, PHILADELPHIA:
M. 21 Aug. 1759 Georg Christoph Gilbert and Maria Salome Stoesin. Children:
1. Anna Catharina b. 25 July 1760
2. Joh. Georg b. 23 Sept. 1761
3. Maria Sophia b. 25 Nov. 1762
4. Maria Salome b. 17 Apr. 1764
5. Joh. Jacob b. 2 July 1765
Sp. at the first three baptisms were Georg Adam Rockenberger and his wife Anna Catharina nee Pfisterer from Neidenstein.

183. GÜNTER, JOH. CASPAR

St. Andrew, 1752

S-H 486 (Ginter on list)

Eschelbach, Baden =
6920 Sinsheim, Elsenz

ESCHELBACH LUTHERAN KB:
Joh. Christoph Günter, tailor, and wife Maria Catharina had:
   Joh. Caspar b. 27 June 1730, conf. 1743. "1752—given Taufschein, going to
   the new land."

Pennsylvania records:
Caspar Ginther, Earl tp., Lancaster co., nat. Philadelphia 1765.

184. GUTH, FELIX

Molly, 1727

S-H 12, 13

Stebbach =
7519 Gemmingen

STEBBACH REFORMED KB:
Felix Guth and wife Anna Margaretha had:
   1. Anna Barbara b. 2 Oct. 1701
   2. Regina b. 11 Mar. 1704
   3. Margaretha b. 18 Dec. 1705; conf. 1720
   4. Hans Georg b. 9 May 1707
   5. Joh. Jacob b. 29 Nov. 1709
   6. Fronecka b. 23 May 1711; conf. 1726
   7. Ulrich b. 19 May 1713
   8. Regina b. 14 Jan. 1717

Pennsylvania records:
Felix Guth was a member of the Reformed congregation at Skippack in 1730. He
signed the letter dated 10 May 1730 to the Classis of Amsterdam [see Hinke,
History of the Goshenhoppen Reformed Charge, PGS XXVII: 56–59, for full text of
letter and 41 signers]. Another signer of this document, Georg Philib Dodder, was
also from Stebbach. Georg Michael Weiss, pastor of the congregation, was from
nearby Eppingen.

TRAPPE LUTHERAN KB, MONTGOMERY CO.:
Görg Guth and wife Lisabarbara had:
   1. Vehlicks b. 23 Oct. 1743, bp. 14 Jan. 1744; sp.: Velicks Guth
[Note: the published translation of this church record gives the name of the child
as Plipp (Phillip) and the sp. as Phillip Guth. However, the original record has the
child named Vehlicks (Felix ?)]

185. HAAGMEYER, JOH. MICHAEL
[ship data not located]

Waldangelloch =
6920 Sinsheim, Elsenz

WALDANGELLOCH LUTHERAN KB:
Veit Haagmayer and wife Anna Margaretha had:
Hans Michel b. 26 Sept. 1697

EPPINGEN LUTHERAN KB:
m. 4 July 1724 Hans Michel Hackmaÿer, Lutheran, son of Veit Hackmaÿer, citizen
and "des Gerichts" at Angeloch, and Anna Maria Volck, dau. of Elias Volck,
Reformed.

WALDANGELLOCH LUTHERAN KB:
Hans Michel Hagmeyer and wife Anna Maria had:
1. Hans Michel b. 13 Oct. 1725; d. 1725
2. Maria Magdalena b. 19 Oct. 1726
3. Hans Michael b. 5 May 1729

Pennsylvania records:
MUDDY CREEK KB, LANCASTER CO.:
Joh. Michael Haagmeyer m. 4 Aug. 1741 Eva Friederica Weydmann (Cocalico)

WARWICK LUTHERAN KB, LANCASTER CO:
Hans Michael Haagmayer signed membership list, ca. 1742

186. HAGENBUCH, ANDREAS
Charming Nancy, 1737
S-H 189, 190, 192, 193 (with Magdalena Hagabuck)

Grossgartach =
7105 Leingarten

SCHLUCHTERN LUTHERAN KB:
m. 26 Apr. 1737 Andreas Haagenbuch, son of the late Michael Haagenbuch, of
Gr. Gartach, and Maria Magdalena, dau. of Jacob Schmutz, citizen at _____
(faded)

Pennsylvania records:
SCHUMACHER'S RECORDS:
Andreas Hagebach and wife Margaretha had:
1. Johannes bp. 1 Jan. 1756 in Allemangle.
Confirmed in Allemangel, Albany Twp.:
    Michel Hagebuch
    Maria Hagebuchin

BERKS CO. WILLS:
Andreas Hagenbuch, Albany (9 Apr. 1785/26 Sept. 1785) Wife Maria Margareth;
Children named in will; to receive specified legacies: Henry, Catharina, Maria,
Magdalena, Ann Elizabeth, Christina, Anna Margareth, John, Anna Barbara. The
remainder of the est. divided into 10 shares, at wife's decease, to the following
children: Michael, Christian, John, Maria, Magdalena, Anna Elisabeth, Christina,
Anna Margareth, Anna Barbara, (and Magdalena Probst instead of her mother
called Catharina.) Mentions sons Michael and Christian had deeds for land. Wife
Maria Margareth, son-in-law John Reichelderfer and Michael Hagenbuch, Jr. exrs.

Andrew Hagebuck, Albany tp., Berks co., nat. Philadelphia April 1762.

A bakeoven in Adersbach with a roof to protect it from the elements attached to a house is similar to one Pennsylvania German arrangement. Adersbach is first mentioned in 1016. It belonged to the von Gemmingen-Hornberg family who converted its church to Lutheranism in 1590. It is still an agricultural village.

Photo: J. Godshall

187. HAHN, JOH. HENRY

Sandwich, 1750

S-H 449 (Haan on ship's list)

Adersbach =
6920 Sinsheim, Elsenz

ADERSBACH LUTHERAN KB:
Joh. Matthias Hehn and wife Juliana had:
  1. Johann Heinrich b. 20 Mar. 1723
  2. Maria Margaretha Barbara b. 5 Nov. 1725

Pennsylvania records:
TRINITY LUTHERAN KB, READING:
Joh. Henry Hahn, b. 20 Mar. 1723 at Adersbach, son of Joh. Matthias Hahn and Juliana. Came to America 1750; m. 1752 Catharina Reiffel [q.v.]

188. HALLER, JÖRG CHRISTOPH

1752

Eschelbronn =
6920 Sinsheim, Elsenz
7107 Bad Wimpfen

ESCHELBRONN LUTHERAN KB:
m. 27 Aug. 1709 Philips Jörg Haller, butcher, son of Hans Jörg Haller, and Johanna Mund, dau. of Hans Bernhardt Mund, citizen and potter in Wimpfen. Their son:
  Jörg Christoph b. 26 Nov. 1710

BAD WIMPFEN LUTHERAN KB:
m. 19 Apr. 1735 Georg Christoph Haller, single, and Maria Elisabetha Seuffert, dau. of Johannes Seuffert. Children:
  1. Susanna Margaretha b. 14 Feb. 1736; d. 1738
  2. Maria Elisabetha b. 21 Feb. 1737; d. 1738

3. Susanna Rosina Elisabetha b. 8 July 1738, d. 1740
4. Joh. Thomas b. 1 Jan. 1740, d. 3 Mar. 1740
5. Juliana Christina b. 13 Jan. 1742, d. 19 Mar. 1742
6. Joh. Christoph b. 7 Feb. 1743, d. 11 Mar. 1743
7. Joh. Martin b. 8 Oct. 1744
8. Susanna Margaretha b. 18 Jan. 1749

Pennsylvania records:
YORK MORAVIAN KB:
Christopher Haller of Yorktown, b. at Eschelbronn in the Palatinate 25 Nov. 1710,
Lutheran. Came to America 1752. D. 25 Mar. 1777. M. (1) 5 Apr. 1734 Maria
Elizabeth (b. at Wimpfen in the Palatinate 5 Nov. 1709, Lutheran). She d. 7 May
1758. He m. (2) 28 Jan. 1760 widow Barbara Stauffer of the Warwick congregation
(She was b. 17 Apr. 1707 at [6737] Iggelheim, daughter of Joh. Georg Kissel and
Anna Maria nee Mäny). She came to America with her parents in 1729 and m. (1)
25 Dec. 1733 Vincent Stauffer. He m. (3)—July 1770 widow Anna Maria Gerber.

Children of the first marriage:
1. Susanna Margaret b. 13 Feb. 1749; bapt. at Wimpfen; married Abraham
   Etter on Mountjoy 16 Nov. 1768. She is the sole survivor of their 12
   children.

189. HARTLIEB, JOH. GEORG

Dragon, 1749
S-H 414

Tairnbach =
6909 Mühlhausen,
Kraichgau
Eschelbach =
6920 Sinsheim, Elsenz

ESCHELBACH LUTHERAN KB:
m. 3 Jan. 1731 Joh. Georg Hartlieb from Darnbach, son of Joh. Michael Hartlieb,
and Anna Maria, dau. of Joh. Adam Schaller. No children bp. at Eschelbach.
Joh. Georg Hartlieb of Darnbach was conf. 1723. Anna Maria Schaller was b. 18
Feb. 1710, daughter of Joh. Adam Schaller and his wife Anna Elisabetha [dau. of
the late Hans Georg Krafft of Zuzenhausen.]

Pennsylvania records:
ST. MICHAEL'S AND ZION LUTHERAN KB, PHILADELPHIA:
d. 2 Oct. 1749 Anna Maria Hartlieb, wife of Hans Jurg Hartlieb, a newcomer. She
was b. 18 Feb. 1710 at Eschelbach. Buried 30 Oct. 1749.

HAMILTON UNION KB, MONROE CO.:
Hans Georg Hartlieb and wife Margaretha sp. for several children from 1769–
1774

190. HARTMAN, FRIEDERICH age 33   6924 Neckarbischofsheim
Samuel, 1732
S-H 60, 61, 64, 65 (with Rosina age 27, Georg age 8)

NECKARBISCHOFSHEIM LUTHERAN KB:
Johann Friedr. Hartman, day laborer and inhabitant, and wife Rosina Margaretha
nee Kautzmann had:
  1. Maria Magdalena b. 14 Aug. 1721
  2. Johann Georg b. 1 Apr. 1723

Pennsylvania records:
EMMAUS MORAVIAN KB, SALISBURY TWP., LEHIGH CO.:
George Hartmann, b. in Bischofsheim in the Palatinate on Apr. 13, 1723, son of
Friederick and Rosina Hartmann, both Lutherans. Occupation: farmer. He came to
Pennsylvania with his father in 1730. On Sept. 28, 1743 he m. Maria Christina
Spaus who was b. Mar. 1716 in [6571] Kellebach in Baden. Her father was Philip
Spaus and her mother was Liza Margaretha Franz. They belonged to the Reformed
church. She came to Penna. in Dec. 1740 by herself. Georg and Maria Christina
(Spaus) Hartmann had only one child:
      Rosina b. 21 Oct. 1748 in Salisbury, bp. in her father's house, 1 mile from
      Bethlehem.

191. HARTMAN, PAULUS   6921 Ittlingen
      HARTMAN, JOH. HEINRICH
Dragon, 1749
S-H 414

ITTLINGEN LUTHERAN KB:
Paul Hartmann and wife Barbara had:
  1. Joh. Dieterich b. __ Nov. 1718
  2. Philippina Elisabetha; m. 16 July 1748 Johann Jacob Roth [q.v.]
  3. Maria Barbara b. 16 Aug. 1724
  4. Christina Apollonia b. 22 Mar. 1727; d. young
 *5. Joh. Heinrich b. 14 Aug. 1729
 *6. Dietrich Paul b. 3 Jan. 1732
  7. Eva Margaretha b. 27 June 1734
A communicants' list, dated 1749, mentions the following persons who are leaving
for Pennsylvania:
      Maria Barbara Hartmann, married (died on the voyage)
      Joh. Jacob Roth and wife (a dau. of Paul Hartmann)
      Maria Barbara Hartmann, single
      Johann Heinrich Harttman, single
      Dietrich Paul Harttmann, single

Pennsylvania records:

A Henry Hartman, Northern Liberties, Philadelphia co., nat. 1765.

192. HASS, JOH. GEORG

Bonfeld =
6927 Bad Rappenau

—————————— , 1717

Bonfeld emigrant list: Joh. Georg Hass, Fab. Murarius
(Latin: bricklayer, mason) with wf.

BONFELD LUTHERAN KB:
M. 24 Apr. 1714 at Bonfeld, Joh. Georg Hass, bricklayer, son of the late Jerg Hass, citizen at Reuthin, Alperspacher Closter Ambts and parish in Hertzogthumb Württemberg, [Reutin = 7297 Alpirsbach 2] and Anna Felicitas, daughter of Hans Jerg Mercklin, citizen and tailor. They had:
Johann Andreas b. 27 July 1715; bp. 28 July; d. 13 Mar. 1717

Pennsylvania records:
PHILADELPHIA WILLS:
George Haas, Germantown, mason. (11 June 1743/27 July 1743.) "Beloved wife, Anne Elizabeth, to have and enjoy all my privilege to live in Jacob Kyser's house during her natural life and to be maintained out of my estate." 3 months after wife's death or re-marriage estate is to be divided among "my 4 daughters: Christina, Barbara, Catharine and Mary." Executors were: Dyak (Dirk) Keyser, Frederick Hesser, both of Germantown. Witnessed by Claus Rittinghause, Jacob Kyser and Christn. Lehman.
If this is the George Hass, mason, from Bonfeld, his wf. Anna Felicitas Merklin may have d. and the Anna Elizabeth mentioned in the will could be a second marriage.

193. HAUERT, JOH. GEORG

Tairnbach =
6909 Mühlhausen,
Kraichgau

1751

DARMBACH (TAIRNBACH) LUTHERAN KB:
m. 20 Feb. 1700 Georg Heinrich Hauert, son of Jacob Hauert, "Gerichtsverwandten", and Maria Margretha, daughter of Joh. Georg Schweitzer. Their son:
Joh. Georg b. 22 Mar. 1718 "Given Taufschein in 1751, to the new land."
Joh. Georg Hauert and wife Catharina nee Engelhardt from Hoffenheim had one child bp. at Darmbach:
1. Georg Heinrich b. 3 Nov. 1743, died young

Pennsylvania records:
DILLINGERSVILLE LUTHERAN KB, UPPER MILFORD TWP., LEHIGH CO.:
Johann Georg Hauert and wife Anna Catharina had:
Anna Catharina b. 19 Nov. 1751; bp. 12 Dec.; sp. Jacob Bush and wife Catharina

194. HEERBURGER, JOHANNES

Hasselbach =
6920 Sinsheim, Elsenz

Dragon, 1732
S-H 96, 97, 98

ADERSBACH LUTHERAN KB:

Johannes Heerburger, schoolmaster at Hasselbach, and wife Eva Magdalena had:
    1. Joh. Michael b. 7 Feb. 1721
Johannes Heerburger, schoolmaster at Hasselbach, and wife Juliana Barbara had:
    2. Juliana Barbara b. 9 Apr. 1728
    3. Joh. Georg b. 27 Nov. 1730

Pennsylvania records:
TRINITY LUTHERAN KB, LANCASTER:
Johannes Heerburger had:
    4. Maria Catharina b. 12 Sept. 1733
    5. Anna Maria b. 21 Aug. 1736
    6. Joh. Friederich b. 18 Feb. 1739

Joh. Heerburger and wife Juliana were sp. in 1734.

CHRIST LUTHERAN KB, YORK:
John Heerburger and wife sp. a child of Christian Groll in 1741.

The surname Herrberger later appears in Augusta Co., Va. records.

195. HEFT, HANS WENDEL age 28

6924 Neckarbischofsheim

Two Sisters, 1738
S-H 209, 211 [with Catharina Heft age 24, Anna Elizabeth age 27 Anna Maria age 30]

NECKARBISCHOFSHEIM LUTHERAN KB:
m. 13 Feb. 1700 Hans Jerg Hefft, son of the late Hans Jacob Hefft, innkeeper, and
Maria Catharina, daughter of Hanns Wagner, farrier. Their son:
    Johannes Wendel b. 14 Nov. 1711 "went to the new land 1738."
m. 22 Apr. 1738 Johann Wendel Heft, son of Hans Georg Heft, and _____
(no name recorded). It is mentioned in this marriage record that they went to the
new land.

Pennsylvania records:
PA, THIRD SERIES, 14:91:
Wendel Hefft appears on the Germantown, Philadelphia co., tax list in 1769, taxed
with ½ acre.

196. HEGI, JOHN (sick)
HEGI, JACOB (sick)
HEGI, HANS JERGI

Elsenz =
7519 Eppingen

Dragon, 1732
S-H 96, 98 (surname of A list: Hayea)

ELSENZ REFORMED KB:
Hans Jacob Hegi and Anna Margretha nee Steinmann had:
1. Hans Jorg bp. 18 Oct. 1699
2. Hans Rudolph bp. 26 Feb. 1702; conf. 1716
3. possibly Jacob b. ca. 1704; conf. 1718
4. Johannes bp. 4 Sept. 1707

Pennsylvania records:
MUDDY CREEK LUTHERAN KB, LANCASTER CO.:
Jacob Högie (Warwick) had:
1. Joh. Martin b. 14 Jan. 1736
2. Joh. Jacob b. 2 Feb. 1737
m. 20 Jan. 1736 Georg Högie and Anna Eva Frey

MUDDY CREEK REFORMED KB:
Hans Görg Hegi signed the Muddy Creek Reformed Church Doctrine in 1743.
George Hegi (also Haege) and wife Anna Eva were sponsors in 1744 and 1748.
A Johannes Hegy was a sp. at Jordan Lutheran KB, Lehigh co. in 1743.

Jacob Heagy, Lancaster co., nat. Philadelphia April 1745

Drainspouts on the Lutheran city church at Neckarbischofsheim stand in contrast to the evangelists on its pulpit and the gigantic crucifix on its altar.

197. HEIL, GEORG THOMAS age 35   6924 Neckarbischofsheim

Friendship, 1739
S-H 265, 268, 272

NECKARBISCHOFSHEIM LUTHERAN KB:
m. 27 Apr. 1728 Georg Thomas Heile, son of Joh. Thomas of Rohrbach, and Susanna, daughter of the late Joh. Martin Störtzer. Georg Thomas Heil and wife Susanna nee Störtzer had:
1. Joh. Wilhelm b. 12 Sept. 1729
2. Catharina Elisabetha b. 27 Mar. 1731
3. Catharina Susanna b. 21 Sept. 1732
4. Maria Christina b. 15 Jan. 1734; d. young
5. Joh. Daniel b. 16 Mar. 1735; d. young
6. Joh. Wilhelm Daniel b. 1 Aug. 1736
7. Maria Barbara b. 3 Feb. 1738

Pennsylvania records:
ST. MICHAEL'S AND ZION LUTHERAN KB, PHILADELPHIA:
Bu. 2 Nov. 1777 Barbara Minckel or Mangold; b. in Bischofsheim 40 y. ago, dau.
of Thomas Heil and Susanna. In this land 28 y. M. for 20 y. to Johann Minckel or
Mangold. Had 3 children, all are living.
Johannes Menckel and Barbara had:
　　1. Thomas b. 16 Nov. 1759; sp. were Thomas Heyl and wife Susanna,
　　　　grandparents.
　　2. Maria Susanna bp. 19 Oct. 1761, age 8 days; sp. Maria Susanna Heylin
　　3. Maria b. 19 Feb. 1763
confirmed 1758 Barbara Heil, age 21, formerly a Zinzendoerffer [Moravian]
conf. 1759 Philipp Heyl age 20
　　　　　　　 Georg Heyl age 18　　former Zinzendoerffers [Moravians]

Thomas Hail, Philadelphia co., nat. Philadelphia 11 Apr. 1749, as a "Quaker."

198. HEINRICH, CHRISTIAN　　　　　　　　7103 Schwaigern

St. Andrew, 1738
S-H 236, 238, 239

SCHWAIGERN LUTHERAN KB:
m. 25 Jan. 1708 Hs. Peter Heinrich, son of Ludwig Heinrich, and Margareth,
widow of Matthias Boger. (She was a daughter of Michael Kerr (?)) Their son:
　　Christian b. 8 Mar. 1717

　　The interior of the Lutheran church in Schwaigern—an unforgettable sight
very likely also to the many families who migrated from there to Pennsylvania in
the eighteenth century.

Photo: J. Godshall

Pennsylvania records:
BERKS CO. WILLS:
A Christian Henry of Rockland twp., (20 Feb. 1791/26 Apr. 1791) Children:
Conrad, Jacob, Peter, Christian, Daniel and daughter Catharine, wife of George
Neidlinger.   _____

Christian Hendrick, Rockland twp., Berks co., nat. Philadelphia, Fall 1765.

199. HEINRICH, CHRISTOPH   7103 Schwaigern

Thistle, 1730
S-H, 32, 33, 34

SCHWAIGERN LUTHERAN KB:
M. 25 Jan. 1708 Hs. Peter Heinrich, son of Ludwig Heinrich, and Margaretha,
widow of Matthias Boger (She was a daughter of Michael Kerr (?)). Peter Heinrich
and Margretha had:
     Hans Christoph bp. 30 Mar. 1712

200. HEINRICH, JERG   7103 Schwaigern

Pennsylvania Merchant, 1731
S-H, 43, 45, 46

SCHWAIGERN LUTHERAN KB:
M. 8 Nov. 1699 Hans Henrich Henrich son of Hans Henrich Henrich, and Anna
Barbara, daughter of Thomas Höll. They had:
     Hans Jerg b. 24 Dec. 1705

Pennsylvania records:
One George Hendrick, Lebanon twp., Lancaster co., nat. Philadelphia 10 Apr.
1755

201. HEINRICH, WENDEL   7103 Schwaigern

Charming Nancy, 1737
S-H, 189, 192, 194 (Passengers on ship: Vindle Henrich and Diana Henrich)

SCHWAIGERN LUTHERAN KB:
M. 8 Nov. 1699 Hans Henrich Henrich son of Hans Henric Henrich, and Anna
Barbara, daughter of Thomas Höll. They had:
     Hans Wendel bp. 23 Feb. 1712
m. 8 May 1736 Wendel Heinrich, son of Joh. Heinrich Heinrich, "des Gerichts"
and Eberhardina, daughter of the late Matthai Fuchs, citizen.

Pennsylvania records:
Wendal Hendrick, Pike tp., Chester co., nat. Philadelphia, Fall 1765

202. HENCKEL, ANTHONY JACOB

Prelist 1717

This early Pennsylvania pastor was born at [6291] Merenberg, Nassau. He was ordained at Eschelbronn 28 Feb. 1692 and served as pastor there until 1695. He also served congregations at Daudenzell, Breitenbronn, Neckargemünd, Mönchzell and Zuzenhausen prior to his emigration. The baptisms of his children can be found in the Eschelbronn and Daudenzell Lutheran KBs. For full detail on his career and family, see: Junkin, *The Henckel Genealogy* (1964) *Henckel Family Records* (14 pamphlets issued 1923–1936) Mary Harter, *Henckel Genealogical Bulletin* (1970-   ) Glatfelter, *Pastors and People*, I, 59–61.

When Henckel left the congregations at Eschelbronn and Mönchzell, he was succeeded by Pastor Joshua Harrsch, who served the congregations until February 1708. Four of Harrsch's children were baptized at Eschelbronn. He entered his last baptism there 23 Feb. 1708. He entered his last baptism in the Mönchzell record 9 Feb. 1708.

He was the Joshua Kocherthal who led the first group of 41 people in the 1708 immigration to New York. For additional detail on Harrsch see: Knittle, *Early Eighteenth Century Palatine Emigration*, pp. 243–244. Heinz Schuchmann, "Der 1708 nach Amerika ausgewanderte Pfarrer Josua Kocherthal hiess ursprünglich Josua Harrsch," *Mitteilungen zur Wanderungsgeschichte der Pfälzer* 1967/4: 121–128. Trans. as "Notes on the Origins of Joshua Kocherthal" by F. Weiser in *Concordia Historical Institute Quarterly* XLI (1968), 147–53.

Heinz Schuchmann, "Sibylla Charlotta Winchenbach die Ehefrau Josua Kocherthals," *Mitteilungen zur Wanderungsgeschichte der Pfälzer*, 1970/1: 25–28. Trans. as "Sibylla Charlotta Winchenbach, the Wife of Joshua Kocherthal" by F. Weiser in *Concordia Historical Institute Quarterly* XLIV (1971), 136–40.

Hank Jones, *The Palatine Families of New York* (in progress)

203. HENGERER, DANIEL

Peggy, 1754
S-H 637, 638, 640

Ehrstädt =
6920 Sinsheim, Elsenz

EHRSTÄDT LUTHERAN KB:
Daniel Hüngerer, tailor, and Maria Barbara had:
1. Euphrosina Sophia Margaretha b. 24 Aug. 1736, d. young
2. Eva Sophia Margaretha Jacobina b. 5 Nov. 1737

Pennsylvania records:
FALCKNER SWAMP REFORMED KB, MONTGOMERY CO.:
D. 12 Mar. 1787 Daniel Hingerer, Lutheran, aged 87 (also in Lutheran record, where age is given as 79.)

204. HENGERER, JOHANN MELCHIOR

Robert and Alice, 1740
S-H 287, 288, 289

6921 Neidenstein,
Elsenzgau
6925 Eschelbronn

DAISBACH LUTHERAN KB:
m. 24 Jan. 1723 Johann Melchior Hüngerer, forester, son of Hanns Cunrad Hüngerer, citizen and wine-grower at "Hessgen in the Dukedom Würtemberg" and Maria Elisabetha Majer, daughter of Marx Majer, citizen and "Gerichtsverwandten" at Neidenstein.
NEIDENSTEIN LUTHERAN KB:
Johann Melchior Hengerer, gamekeeper, had:
  1. Johann Friederich bp. 19 Nov. 1726

ESCHELBRONN LUTHERAN KB:
Joh. Melchior Hengerer, gamekeeper, and wife Maria Elisabeth had:
  2. Johann Peter b. 15 Feb. 1729
  3. Maria Rosina b. 24 Mar. 1731, d. young
  4. Joh. Georg b. 5 Apr. 1733
  5. Joh. Philipp b. 6 Apr. 1735
  6. Anna Barbara b. 7 Nov. 1736
  7. Maria Friederica b. 27 Dec. 1738
On the 23 Mar. 1740, a child named Johann Melchior was born to Anna Maria, the wife of Peter Münch. The record states that Peter Münch is not the father of this child. The mother herself names the father as the former "Herrschafflichen Jäger" (ducal gamekeeper-hunter) Melchior Hengerer, who left 5 months ago for Dillsperg. Melchior Hengerer evidently was also the father of Carl Ludwig b. 31 July 1738 and bp. 1 Aug. 1738 as a son of Peter Mönch and Anna Maria.

Pennsylvania records:
NEW HOLLAND LUTHERAN KB, LANCASTER CO.:
Melchior Hengerer and wife Maria Elisabetha were sp. in 1745. Friedrich Hengerer, single, sp. two children in 1746.

PENNSYLVANIA PATENTS:
AA:13:202 Warrant 28 Oct. 1746 to Melchior Hengerer, 120 A. Survey 5 Sept. 1768 to Mathias Basor, to whom said Hengerer conveyed tract (land in Hanover twp., Lancaster co.)

NEW HOLLAND LUTHERAN KB, LANCASTER CO.:
Mattheis Boesshaar m. 13 Oct. 1745 Apollonia Hengerer. Their child: Joh. Peter b. 29 Nov. 1748; bp. 25 Dec. 1748 (Suadara) by Stoever, sp. by Melchior Huengerer and wife Elisabetha.
Virginia Magazine of History and Biography, 19:169 (1911) Early settlers in Greenbrier co., Va. (now in West Va.) "1751, Apr. 25—Malr. Hanger" (Melchior Hengerer?)
Peter Hengerer (Hanger):
150 A. on Muddy Creek were surveyed for Peter Hanger on 24 Apr. 1751 (*Abstract of Land Grant Surveys, 1761–1791*, by Peter C. Kaylor): In 1762–64, 2 parcels of land on the Shenandoah River, Frederick co., Va. were surveyed for Peter Hanger.

Augusta co. Will Book IX: 248—Will of Peter Hanger (2 Jan. 1802/27 Dec. 1802). John Frederick Hengerer (Hanger): (*Abstract of Land Grant Surveys, 1761–1791*, Peter C. Kaylor) Frederick Hanger, 600 A., Branch of Greenbrier River, 1 Nov. 1752. Augusta co. Wills, Book IX: 28, (2 June 1799/probated 22 July 1799.) 13 children are named in Augusta co. File 157, Litigation in Chancery.

205. HENNIG, JOH. BALTHASAR (BALZAR HENING)

Hoffenheim = 6920 Sinsheim, Elsenz

Shirley, 1751
S-H 454

HOFFENHEIM LUTHERAN KB:
m. 12 Jan. 1717 Johann Hennig, son of Dieterich Hennig from Daispach (Daisbach, Baden = 6923 Waibstadt), and Maria Barbara Cuntzelmann, dau. of Johann Cuntzelmann (Kuntzelmann) of Hoffenheim. Hans and Barbara Hennig had:
    Balthasar b. 10 Jan. 1724; conf. 1738 age 15
m. 17 Jan. 1747 Hans Balthasar Hennig, son of Johann Hennig, and Anna Elisabetha Blum, daughter of Georg Ernst Blum, shoemaker. Children:
    1. Elisabetha Barbara b. 15 Nov. 1747
    2. Maria Susanna b. 24 May 1749
    3. Maria Catharina b. 28 Aug. 1750

Pennsylvania records:
TRINITY LUTHERAN KB, READING:
D. 20 Feb. 1770 Anna Elisabetha Hennig, b. 13 Mar. 1721 and bp. at Hoffenheim 14 Mar. 1721, daughter of Georg Ernst Blum and Margareth. She m. 17 June 1747 to Balthasar Hennig. Had 6 sons and 3 daughters. 4 sons survive.

OLEY HILLS KB, BERKS CO.:
Baltaser Häenig and wife Elisabetha appear on communicants' lists 1755, 1756. They had:
    Johann Adam b. 15 Jan. 1757

TRINITY LUTHERAN KB, READING:
Balthasar Hoenig and Elisabetha had:
    Joh. Georg b. 8 Dec. 1760

206. HERBOLDT, JOH. ADAM

Nancy, 1750
S-H 443

Hoffenheim = 6920 Sinsheim, Elsenz

HOFFENHEIM LUTHERAN KB:
m. 10 Nov. 1748 Joh. Adam Herboldt from Arphelbach or Aeppelbach (?) (Epfenbach?) and Margaretha, daughter of the late Valentin Lang. Hans Adam Herbold and wife Anna Margretha Jacobina had:
    1. Catharina Margaretha b. 3 Mar. 1749

Pennsylvania records:
NEW HANOVER LUTHERAN KB, MONTGOMERY CO:
Adam Herbold and Marcreth (Margareth) had:
1. Marcreth b. 1 May 1752
2. Frederick b. 12 July 1756

TRINITY LUTHERAN KB, READING:
Friedrick Herbold and wife Philippina (from the Forest) had:
    Adam b. 25 Nov. 1784

207. HERBST, JOHANN DAVID

Shirley, 1751

S-H 454

Hoffenheim =
6920 Sinsheim, Elsenz

HOFFENHEIM LUTHERAN KB:
m. 27 Apr. 1751 Johann David Herbst from Mindesheim in Durlach region [7121 Mundelsheim], son of the late Hans Georg Herbst, and Anna Catharina Landes, dau. of the late Sebastian Landes. They left eight days later to go to Pennsylvania.

Pennsylvania records:
NEW HANOVER LUTHERAN, MONTGOMERY CO:
David and Catharina Herbst had:
1. Marcaretha b. 7 July 1752
2. Jörg David b. 15 Mar. 1754; conf. 1768
3. Anna Barbara b. 12 Apr. 1756
4. Joh. Friderich b. 30 Sept. 1758
5. Eva b. 25 July 1761
David Herbst d. 29 Mar. 1774, age 61 y. 6 mo.

208. HERPEL, JOHANNES

Alexander & Anne, 1730

S-H 35, 36

Neckarelz =
6950 Mosbach, Baden

DIEDESHEIM REFORMED KB:
Conf. Easter 1709 Johannes Herpel, son of Johannes, age 13 years.
m. 5 July 1719 at Neckarelz Johannes Herpel and Maria Kunigunda Utz. Their children:
1. Hans Peter bp. 8 Sept. 1719
2. Jörg Peter bp. 4 Feb. 1723; d. 6 Feb.
3. Jörg Ludwig bp. 4 Feb. 1725
4. Maria Catharina bp. 17 June 1729

Pennsylvania records:
TRAPPE LUTHERAN KB, MONTGOMERY CO.:
Johannes Herpel's wife Anna Maria sp. 1747 child of Peter Buhl.

TRAPPE REFORMED KB, MONTGOMERY CO.:
Contributors to the pastor's yearly salary in 1761:
    Ludwig Herbel, Peter Herbel

MUHLENBERG'S JOURNALS III: 131:
15 Feb. 1778 bu. at Trappe Catharina Herpel, wife of Joh. Peter Herpel. B. in
Germany in 1721, daughter of Rudolph Gutman. Came to Pennsylvania 35 y. ago,
married 32 years ago. Had 5 sons and 4 daughters.

Peter Herble, Providence twp., Philadelphia co., nat. Philadelphia Fall 1765, not
taking an oath.

209. HERTZEL, HANS JERG

William & Sarah, 1727
S-H 7, 10 (no. of persons: 4)

Reihen =
6920 Sinsheim, Elsenz

REIHEN REFORMED KB:
Hans Georg Hertzel, b. 30 May 1686, son of Clemens Hertzel and Anna (see
Ulrich Hertzel for a complete record of their family)
m. 10 Jan. 1713 Hans Görg Hiertzel, son of Clemens Hiertzel, "Verwandter and
des Gerichts" and Margretha, dau. of Jacob Conradt, citizen at Ittlingen.
Hans Görg Hertzel and Anna Margretha had:
  Hans Georg b. 8 July 1714
  Hans Jacob b. 16 Feb. 1716
  Anna Margretha bp. 17 Sept (?) or Dec. (?) 1719
  Joh. Dieterich 31 Aug. 1721
  Joh. Leonhardt 29 Sept. 1726

Pennsylvania records:
Hannah Benner Roach, "Hans Georg Hertzel, Pioneer of Northampton County and
His Family," *Pennsylvania Genealogical Magazine* (24:151–181) gives the marriage
date of Hans Georg Hertzel incorrectly as "10 1m. 1703."

George Hartsell nat. Philadelphia September 1740, of Bucks co.

210. HERTZEL, HENRICH age 50

Pink *Plaisance*, 1732
S-H 79, 80, 82, 83 (Hans Leonhardt age 24, Urig, sick
(Görg) age 18 (indexed in S-H as Ulrich), Barbara age
50, Christina age 27, Jacobina)

Reihen =
6920 Sinsheim, Elsenz

REIHEN REFORMED KB:
Hans Henrich Hirtzel, bp. 25 Sept. 1681, son of Clemens Hirtzel and Anna (see
Ulrich Hertzel for complete family record)
m. 3 Feb. 1705 Johann Henrich Hertzel, son of Clemens Hertzel, "Gerichtsverwandten", and Anna Barbara, dau. of the late Rudolph Umberger, "Gerichtsver-
wandter". Children:
  1. Anna Christina b. 20 Dec. 1705
  2. Hans Leonhardt b. 5 July 1707; conf. 1726
  3. Maria Catharina b. 29 Oct. 1710
  4. Hans Görg b. 28 May 1713
  5. Jacobina bp. 31 Jan. 1717
  6. Joh. Philips bp. 4 June 1724

Pennsylvania records:
NEW GOSHENHOPPEN REFORMED KB, MONTGOMERY CO:
Christina Herzel, daughter of Mr. Herzel of Schipbach, m. 22 June 1736
Georg Peter Knecht, shoemaker.
Hans Leonhardt Herzel sp. their first child.

WILLIAMS TWP. KB, NORTHAMPTON CO:
Leonhardt Hertzel and wife Magdalena had:
   Gertraud b. 24 Dec. 1740

211. HERTZEL, HEINRICH age 40   Reihen =
                                 6920 Sinsheim, Elsenz
Pink *Plaisance*, 1732
S-H 79, 82, 83

REIHEN REFORMED KB:
Hans Heinrich Hirtzel and wife Margretha nee Rudi had a son:
   Heinrich bp. 5 Oct. 1684
m. 10 Apr. 1714 Heinrich Hertzel, son of Heinrich Hertzel, and Elisabetha, dau.
of Ludwig Schuch.
(no children bp. at Reihen.)

212. HERTZEL, MELCHIOR   Reihen =
                               6920 Sinsheim, Elsenz
Francis & Elizabeth, 1742
S-H 328

REIHEN REFORMED KB:
Christoph Hertzel b. ca. 1692, (son of Clemens Hirtzel and Anna Sinter); conf.
1706, age 14; m. 2 Feb. 1717 Magdalena, daughter of Hans Düringer of Obergimpern. Christoph Hertzel d. 16 Dec. 1734. Their son:
   Hans Melchior b. 10 Apr. 1718; conf. 1732

Pennsylvania records:
TOHICKON LUTHERAN KB, BUCKS CO.:
Melchior Hertzel and wife Esther had:
   1. George b. 18 Apr. 1752
   2. Jacob b. 1 Sept. 1751 (?)   All bp. 1 June 1755
   3. Magdalena b. 28 Sept. 1754

KELLER'S LUTHERAN KB, BUCKS CO.:
m. 29 May 1769 John Nicolai, son of Valentine Nicoläi and his wife Elisa, and
Christine Hertzel, daughter of Melchior Hertzel of Haycock twp.

213. HERTZEL, PAULUS age 50
HERTZEL, Catharina age 51
HERTZEL, Heinrich, Jr. age 17

Reihen =
6920 Sinsheim, Elsenz

Pink *Plaisance*, 1732
S-H 78, 79, 81, 82

REIHEN REFORMED KB:
Hans Paul Hertzel bp. 13 Aug. 1677, son of Hans Heinrich Hirtzel and Margretha, nee Rudi.
m. 23 Jan. 1703 Johannes Paulus Hertzel, son of Heinrich Hertzel, and Anna Catharina, dau. of Georg Wagner, "Schultheiss". Children:
1. Joh. Georg b. 25 Jan. 1706; d. age 4 y.
2. Hans Paulus b. 17 Oct. 1707; conf. 1721
3. Anna Christina b. 5 Oct. 1712; d. young
4. Görg Heinrich b. 11 Jan. 1715; conf. as Heinrich 1730

Pennsylvania records:
INDIAN CREEK REFORMED KB, MONTGOMERY CO:
Bu. Feb. 25, 1784 Old Mrs. Hertzel, 65 y., several months (Margaretha added by compiler)
June 23, 1784 Old Mr. Hertzel, 67 y. 5 m. 10 d. (George Heinrich added by compiler)

George Henry Hartsle, Bucks co., nat. Sept. 1740.

214. HERTZEL, ULRICH

William & Sarah, 1727
S-H 8 (Skippach—2 in family)

Reihen =
6920 Sinsheim, Elsenz

REIHEN REFORMED KB:
Clemens Hirtzel (b. 20 Feb. 1659, d. 25 Mar. 1707) m. 23 Nov. 1680 Anna Sinter, daughter of Hans Sinter. Their children:
1. Hans Henrich bp. 25 Sept. 1681 [q.v.—em. 1732]
2. Hans Georg bp. 30 May 1686 [q.v.—em. 1727]
3. Maria Esther bp. 9 May 1688; conf. 1702; m. 13 Jan. 1711
   Hans Leonhard Dörr; d. 20 Oct. 1714.
[their dau. Anna Maria m. Martin Schuch, q.v., em. 1751]
4. Christoph b. ca. 1692; conf. 1706 age 14; m. 2 Feb. 1717
Magdalena, dau. of Hans Düringer of Obergimpern. He died 16 Dec. 1734
[their son, Hans Melchior, q.v., em. S-H p. 328]
5. Hans Jonas b. 1 July 1694; conf. 1708; d. 1714
6. Anna Christina bp. 3 Feb. 1697; conf. 1712; d. 1714
7. Joh. Jacob bp. 27 Dec. 1699; d. 1708
8. Maria Margretha bp. 27 Dec. 1699 twins
9. Anna Margreta bp. 24 Sept. 1702; m. 1724 Johannes Leipp (Leib) [em. 1727 q.v.]
*10. Hans Ulrich bp. 21 Aug. 1705

Pennsylvania records:
NEW GOSHENHOPPEN REFORMED KB, MONTGOMERY CO:
Ulrich Hertzel and wife had:
    Johann Georg bp. 20 May 1733

OLD GOSHENHOPPEN REFORMED KB, MONTGOMERY CO:
Bu. 12 Feb. 1771 Ulrich Herzel of Old Goshenhoppen; b. 20 Aug. 1705
Age 65½ y. less 9 d.

PHILADELPHIA WILLS P-71:
John Ulrich Hertzel, Upper Salford twp., (Jan. 24, 1771/Mar. 6, 1771). "Very sick
and weak." Exrs. sons, George and Jacob. Wit.: Philip Zeigler and Johannes Egg.
Wife, Anna Margaret, £ 100 for support and shall not have share with children.
Ch. to have equal shares, girls as much as boys and the youngest shall not wait
longer than the eldest. Daughter Ann Margaret to have beforehand for household
furniture £ 1.20.0 . . . Law of land says 2 shares for eldest son "to whom I give 5
shillings in lieu of double share."

MONTGOMERY CO. DEEDS:
6: 450: 7 May 1773
Jacob Hertzel, Rockhill twp., Bucks co. and wife Catharine; Ulrich Hertzel of
Upper Salford twp., Philadelphia co. and wife Catharine; Henry Hertzel of Spring-
field twp., Bucks co., mason, and wife Sophia; Margaret Hertzel, single, of Upper
Salford twp.; Adam Smith of Upper Salford, mason, and wife Barbara; Release to
George Hertzel of Upper Salford. Tract of 150½ A. in Upper Salford twp. patented
3 July 1761 to Ulrich Hertzel who died testate leaving a will dated 24 Jan. 1771.
Heirs at time of will were: Jacob, George, Ulrich, Henry, Mark (since deceased),
Margaret, and Barbara married to Adam Smith; and his wife Margaret.

———

Ulrich Hertzel, Upper Salford twp. Philadelphia co. nat. Philadelphia 24 Sept.
1763

215. HESSER, JOH. FRIEDRICH, age 25

Loyal Judith, 1732
S-H, 88, 90, 92

Bonfeld =
6927 Bad Rappenau

BONFELD LUTHERAN KB:
Hans Bernhardt Hesser m. at Bonfeld, 1 July 1684 Anna (maiden name not given).
They had 10 ch. bp. there; the youngest one was:
    Johann Friderich b. 6 Feb. 1708; bp. 8 Feb. 1708; sp. Johann Bernhard
Gsell, butcher and innkeeper of the Ox at Bonfeld and Johannes Treiss (?), single.
    Johann Friedrich Hesser, baker, son of the late Johann Bernhard Hesser m.
27 Nov. 1731 at Bonfeld Maria Catharina, daughter of the late Johann Georg
Merckle, citizen and tailor. There were no ch. in the church record.
    Johann Bernhard Hesser d. at Bonfeld 28 Nov. 1719, age 63 yrs. His widow
Anna, d. at Bonfeld 4 Mar. 1728, age 63 yr, 3 mo.

Pennsylvania records:
ST. MICHAEL'S & ZION LUTHERAN KB, PHILADELPHIA:
Communicants' list, 8 June 1735: Friedrich Hester and Maria Catharina Hesser.

STOEVER'S RECORDS:
John Frederich Hesser of Germantown had:
   John Georg b. 21 Feb. 1735; bp. 7 Mar. 1735; sp. John Frederich Haass
(possibly this should be John George Haas, a brother-in-law of Frederich Hesser.)

ST. MICHAEL'S LUTHERAN KB, GERMANTOWN:
Johann Friederich Hesser b. 6 Feb. 1708; d. 3 July 1763.

216. HETZEL, JOH. JACOB

Neptune, 1751

S-H 466

Schatthausen =
6908 Wiesloch

SCHATTHAUSEN LUTHERAN KB:
Jacob Hetzel and wife Anna Maria had:
   Joh. Jacob b. 11 Nov. 1711
m. 7 Feb. 1741 Joh. Jacob Hetzel, single, Lutheran, and Barbara
Beisel, single and Lutheran. Children:
   1. Joh. Peter b. 1 Feb. 1742
   2. Maria Eva b. 30 June 1744
   3. Susanna b. 31 Dec. 1747
   4. Joh. Jacob b. 14 Mar. 1749

   The village of Schatthausen, a Palatine-owned town, is dateable to 1241. Its
Lutheran church records begin in mid-seventeenth century; the church itself was
built a century later, about the time two Pennsylvania German churches—Trappe
and Moselem—were built in similar architecture. A twentieth century renovation
added a tower to the building and a Biblical text to the earlier datestone.

Photo: J. Godshall

Krebs, "Palatine Emigration . . . ," p. 29.
Jacob Hezel of Schatthausen made application to go to America in 1741.

Pennsylvania records:
WARWICK LUTHERAN KB, LANCASTER CO.:
Peter Hezel and wife had:
1. Susanna b. 26 Sept. 1765; one of the sp. Susanna Hezel
2. Anna Maria b. 28 Aug. 1767
3. Joh. Jacob b. 31 Aug. 1769
4. Maria Barbara b. 14 Sept. 1771
Jacob Hezel had:
1. Christina b. 10 Apr. 1766; sp. Michael Selser and Christina Böhringer

ST. PETER'S UNION KB, PINEGROVE TWP., SCHUYLKILL CO:
Bu. 9 Aug. 1821 Anna Catharine Hetzel, b. 10 Oct. 1741, Elizabeth twp., Lancaster co., Her age 79 y. 10 m. 1d.

217. HETZER, HANS MICHAEL age 53   Gauangelloch =
Samuel, 1737   6906 Leimen
S-H 169, 170, 172

GAUANGELLOCH LUTHERAN KB:
m. 10 Feb. 1715 Hans Michael Hetzer, forester, and Susanna Sperer
(m. necessary). Children:
1. Joh. Philipp b. 14 June 1715
2. Maria Juliana Christina b. 5 Aug. 1719
3. Eleonora Friederica Charlotta b. 26 Nov. 1723

Pennsylvania records:
NEW HOLLAND LUTHERAN KB, LANCASTER CO.:
Maria Juliana Hetzer, single, sp. of child of Caspar Elias Diller [q.v.] in 1739.

Charlotta Hetzer sp. a child of Philip Breiteistein, Sr. in 1739 and a child of Joh.
Adam Müller in 1745.
Philip Hetzer had a child bapt.:
Barbara b. 18 Feb. 1746 [The child's father is said to be a Mennonite named
Philipp Schäffer]; sp. Anna Barbara Heueberger, single
Philip Hetzer and Elisabetha nee Henneberger had:
1. Charlotta b. 28 Apr. 1747
2. Georg Adam b. 4 Dec. 1748
3. Maria Christina b. 17 Mar. 1751
4. Joh. Carolus b. 18 Oct. 1752
5. Joh. Philip b. 3 May 1754
m. 12 Mar. 1745 Hanss Georg Bösshaar and Charlotta Hetzer. Children:
1. Johanna b. 25 Jan. 1746
2. Elisabetha bp. 9 Nov. 1747; sp. Philip Hezer's wife
3. Susanna Charlotta bp. 9 Nov. 1747
4. Catharina b. 2 Mar. 1752

218. HEYLMANN, JOH. ADAM age 24   6921 Zuzenhausen
Two Sisters, 1738
S-H 209, 211

ZUZENHAUSEN LUTHERAN KB:
Joh. Jacob Heilman, bp. 24 Aug. 1687, son of Hans Dieterich Heilman and Lucia.
m. 22 Feb. 1707 Jacob Hilmann and Maria Catharina (no surname given)
Children:
    1. Anna Catharina b. 28 Jan. 1708
    2. Maria Eva b. 9 May 1710
    3. Anna Maria b. 2 May 1712
  *4. Joh. Adam b. 20 Nov. 1715; conf. 1730; em. 1738
  *5. Anna Regina, b. 10 Sept. 1718; em. 1744
    6. Maria Margretha b. 12 Nov. 1720; d. 1720
    7. Anna Margretha b. 26 Dec. 1721
    8. Joh. Leonhardt b. 28 Sept. 1724; d. 24 Oct. 1724

Krebs, "Palatine Emigration . . . ," p. 31-2.
In 1744 Anna Maria (Regina) Heylmann, single, of Zuzenhausen, was permitted
to emigrate to America.

Pennsylvania records:
HILL LUTHERAN KB, NORTH ANNVILLE TWP., LEBANON CO.:
Adam Heÿlmann and wife had:
    1. Catarina b. 7 Apr. 1740
    2. Anna Elisabetha b. 2 Mar. 1742
In 1745, Hans Adam Heilemann was a church elder for the Reformed congregation
at Quittopahilla (Hill Church).
Adam Heilman and wife had:
    Anna Maria bp. 26 Aug. 1747

William H. Egle, *History of the Counties of Dauphin and Lebanon in the Commonwealth of Pennsylvania* (Harrisburg, 1883), p. 226n:
John Adam Heilman, a native of Zutzenhausen [6921 Zuzenhausen] in the Palatinate, migrated to this country in 1738 and settled in North Annville twp; was an
elder in the Reformed congregation of "Berg Kirche" in 1745. He was b. 16 Nov.
1715; d. 25 Sept. 1770.

BURIED AT HILL CHURCH:
Maria Catharine Heilman (nee Steger, wife of Joh. Adam Heilman)
b. 25 Mar. 1709, d. 12 May 1787

219. HILDEBRANDT, CONRAD age 34   Weiler =
                                                  6920 Sinsheim, Elsenz
Pleasant, 1732
S-H 99 (sick, name on A list: Connard Hellebran)

WEILER REFORMED KB:
Hans Conradt Hildebrandt, shoemaker, and wife Elisabetha Barther had:
    Hans Conrad b. 12 Feb. 1699, conf. 1713

Conrad Hildebrandt, citizen at Weÿler, and wife Susanna had:
1. Barbara bp. 16 Apr. 1722; sp.: Hans Georg Spengler and Barbara Hoffmann
2. George Michael bp. 1 Oct. 1724; sp.: Joh. Georg Spengler and Anna
   Maria Albrecht, daughter of the huntsman at Neidenstein
3. Hans Georg bp. 19 Jan. 1729; sp.: Georg Spengler and Regina Hildebrand

Krebs, *Palatine Emigration* . . . , p. 25–26.
Conrad Hildenbrand, Jr., citizen of Weiler, was reported, with others, on May 7,
1732, as "intending to go to the island of Pennsylvania". He left after sale of
property and payment of debts and the tithe (10. Pfennig) emigration taxes.

220. HILDEBRANDT, JOH. ADAM

Weiler =
6920 Sinsheim, Elsenz

Phoenix, 1750
S-H 440

WEILER REFORMED KB:
m. (2) 7 Nov. 1702 Conrad Hildebrand, citizen and shoemaker, and Anna Eva,
daughter of the late Christianus Grensiger (?), citizen and saddler at Heidelberg.
Their son:
   Hans Adam bp. 9 Apr. 1713; conf. 1729

American records:
One Adam Yeildenbrand, Frederick co., Md., nat. Annapolis 28 Sept. 1763.

221. HILLEGASS, GEORG ALBRECHT

6920 Sinsheim, Elsenz

Ann Galley, 1746
S-H 360, 362

SINSHEIM REFORMED KB:
Peter Hillegas and wife Regina had:
   Joh. Jacob bp. 11 Jan. 1693
m. 30 Jan. 1720 Jacob Hullengas, son of Peter Hullengas, wagon maker, and
Ottilia, daughter of Joh. Heinrich Kämpffer, schoolteacher at Steinforth. Their son:
   Georg Albrecht b. 5 Sept. 1723

Pennsylvania records:
FIRST REFORMED KB, PHILADELPHIA:
(George) Albrecht Hilligas and wife Catharine had:
1. George bp. 9 June 1760, d. 25 July 1760
2. Maria Margaret bp. 3 June 1761; d. 21 Feb. 1763
3. An unbapt. child buried 4 Dec. 1762
4. Maria Catharina b. 26 Apr. 1764
5. Philip b. 1 Oct. 1766
6. Joh. Jacob b. 23 Aug. 1768
7. Susanna Catharina b. 10 Nov. 1769; evidently d. young
8. Susanna Catharina b. 6 Apr. 1772
9. Daniel b. 21 July 1774

222. HILLIGAS, JOH. FRIEDRICH   7519 Eppingen

William & Sarah, 1727
S-H 7, 9
4½ in family

EPPINGEN REFORMED KB:
m. 23 Aug. 1712 Joh. Friederich Hilligas, wagon maker, son of Peter Hilligas, citizen and wagon maker at [6920] Sintzheim, and Elisabetha Barbara, daughter of the late Georg Trigel, citizen at [7519] Eppingen. Children:
1. Leopold bp. 26 Sept. 1714
2. Hans Adam bp. 6 Jan. 1717
3. A son (N.N.) bp. 2 Apr. 1719; sp: Friederich Sauer and wife Margaretha
4. Joh. Martin bp. 26 May 1721
5. Eva Elisabetha bp. 16 Nov. 1723
6. Anna Margaretha bp. ___Aug. 1726

SINSHEIM REFORMED KB:
conf. 19 Apr. 1699 Hans Friederich Hillingas age 14 years
d. 12 Oct. 1719 Peter Hüllengass, wagon maker, age 70
d. 7 Sept. 1708 Anna Regina, wife of Peter Hilligas age 53 years

A Leopold Hilligas appears on the *Alexander & Anne* in 1730 with other passengers from this area. It is possible that he is the Leopold, b. 1714 in Eppingen, son of Friederich Hilligas; he may have arrived after the rest of the family.

Pennsylvania records:
FALCKNER SWAMP REFORMED CHURCHYARD TOMBSTONE INSCRIPTION:
Margaret Reicherin nee Hillegasin b. 15 Aug. 1726 d. 6 Jan. 1773

NEW GOSHENHOPPEN TOMBSTONE INSCRIPTIONS, PUBLISHED IN *PERKIOMEN REGION. PAST AND PRESENT, I: 51*.
Friedrick Hilegas b. 24 Nov. 1685 d. 6 Jan. 1765
Elisa Barbara Hilligesen d. 4 Mar. 1759

NEW GOSHENHOPPEN REFORMED KB, MONTGOMERY CO:
Fridrich Hilligas and wife Lisabarbara had:
    Elisabetha Barbara bp. 4 June 1732
    Georg Peter bp. 9 May 1736
Johan Adam Hilligas and Eva Hilligas, his sister, were bp. sp. in 1738.
Hans Adam Hilligas, son of Fred. Hilligas, conf. 10 Oct. 1736
Marriages between 1747–1758:
    Adam Hillikas and Catharina Bitting
    Mathys Reicherdt and Creth Hillikas
    Nicolaus Jeger and Anna Hillikas
    J. Kiefer and Barbara Hillikas
    Peter Hillikas and Barbara Hornberger
Many additional records on the families appear in this church record.

PHILADELPHIA WILLS:
N: 310: Will of Frederick Hilligas, Upper Hanover twp.

(25 June 1759/31 July 1765) Exrs: son-in-law Mathias Reichard and son George Peter Hillegas. Names children:
George Peter, youngest son Conrad, eldest son Leopold, youngest daughter Barbara, Hans Adam and Frederick, older sons, Eva Elisabeth, Ann Margaret, Ann Regina, and Elizabeth Barbara. He refers to his book, and advances made to children are to be deducted from their shares.

NEW GOSHENHOPPEN REFORMED KB, MONTGOMERY CO:
Bu. 13 Mar. 1779 old Adam Hilligas b. 5 Jan. 1717 aged 62 y. 3 m. 8 days

SHULTZE'S JOURNALS I:237:
1759—Old Hillegassin d. on May 4 and was buried on the 6th.
(Editor's note states that this refers to Elisabeth Barbara Hillegass, wife of Goshenhoppen pioneer John Frederick Hillegass.)
Ibid., I: 201: Apr. 29, 1757—Divided Hillegas' plantation
[A Shultze draft in the Schwenkfelder Library Collection: "A Draught of a Tract of Land Situate in Upper Hanover Twp.—being part of a Tract of 363 acres of Land that belonged to Frederick Hillegas, who conveyed 216 acres to his son Conrad, and the above part thereof he is to convey to his son Peter Hillegas, containing 147 acres."]

Frederick Hillengas, Philadelphia co., nat. by Act of 19 May 1739; John Adam Hilligas, Upper Hanover twp., Philadelphia co., nat. Philadelphia April 1764

223. HILLEGAS, JÖRG PETER   7519 Eppingen
Greyhound, 1722

SCHATTHAUSEN LUTHERAN KB:
Peter Hillegas' wife from Sintzheim had a son Georg Peter b. 17 Nov. 1689, bp 24 Nov. 1689.

EPPINGEN REFORMED KB:
Georg Peter Hillegass, potter, and wife Anna Margaretha had:
1. Anna Margaretha bp. 30 July 1715
2. Christoph bp. 7 Aug. 1718
3. Peter bp. 26 Feb. 1721
Jörg Peter Hillegas signed a transportation contract in 1722, on behalf of 40 passengers of the ship *Greyhound*. [Rotterdam Archives, record located by Klaus Wust.]

Pennsylvania records:
Georg Peter Hillengass was an elder of the Philadelphia Reformed congregation in 1730. As such, he signed the Power of Attorney given to Jacob Reiff on 19 May 1730 to collect funds in Europe.
[See W. J. Hinke, *History of Goshenhoppen Reformed Charge*, PGS, 27 (1916)]
In 1732 George Peter Hillengus witnessed the will of Michel Emmert (Phila. Adm. book G, p. 494).
Letters of Adm. on the estate of Peter Hillegass were granted 18 Mar. 1755 to Michael Egge and Michael Deal, in Philadelphia.

Peter Hillegas, Philadelphia, nat. by Act of 29 Mar. 1735

224. HILLEGASS, MICHAEL   6920 Sinsheim, Elsenz

Prelist

SINSHEIM REFORMED KB:
Hans Peter Hilligas and wife Regina had:
    Georg Michel bp. 15 Nov. 1696; sp. Hans Michael Krämer

Pennsylvania records:
W. J. Hinke *Life and Letters of the Rev. John Philip Boehm,* (Philadelphia, 1916),
p. 216. Michel Hillegas was born in 1696. He was naturalized in Apr. 1749 and
died 30 Oct. 1749. Buried in Christ's Church (Episcopal) burial ground at Fifth
and Arch St., Philadelphia. Letters of adm. were granted to Margaretha Hillegas,
widow of Michael, and to Michael Hillegass, son of the said deceased, on 7 Nov.
1749 at Philadelphia. Michael Hillegas, Jr. was born in Philadelphia 22 Apr.
1729. He became the first Treasurer of the United States.

ST. MICHAEL'S AND ZION LUTHERAN KB, PHILADELPHIA:
Bu. 23 July 1770—The widow Hillegas with her late husband Michael in the
English Episcopal graveyard.   _____

Michael Hillegas, Philadelphia co., nat. Philadelphia 11 Sept. 1749

225. HILTENBEITTEL, JOH. ADAM   Mittel Schefflentz =
                                              6951 Schefflenz
Jacob, 1749
S-H 418   6924 Neckarbischofsheim

WORMS REFORMED KB:
"The following persons who are going to America were privately married during
their rest days here:"
m. 6 June 1749 Johann Adam Hildenberger from Mittel Schefflentz in Churpfaltz,
Oberamts Mosbach, son of Joh. Adam Hildenberger, inhabitant there, and Ursula
Eichholtz, daughter of Hans Adam Eichholtz [q.v.], inhabitant at [6924 Neckar]
Bischofsheim near Sintzheim in Churpfaltz. Married in the presence of both fa-
thers. (Evidently the minister recorded the unfamiliar surname Hiltenbeittel as
Hildenberger.)

Pennsylvania records:

FIRST REFORMED KB, LANCASTER:
Joh. Adam Hiltenbeutel and wife Anna Maria Ursula had:
    1. Catharina b. 21 Aug. 1750; sp. Ferdinand Rieder and wife Catharina

MÜHLBACH REFORMED KB, LEBANON CO.:
John Adam Hiltenbeitel and wife Maria Ursula first appear in this record as sp. in
1758.
Adam Hiltenbeitel and wife Ursula had:
    Maria Elisabeth bp. 11 June 1759; sp. Maria Elisabetha Miller
    John Jacob bp. 20 Sept. 1761; sp. John Jacob Eicholtz and Maria Barbara
Miller

226. HOFFERT, JOH. GEORG

7103 Schwaigern

Allen, 1729
S-H 27, 29, 30 (Passengers: Jorick Hoffart; under 15:
Christian Hoffart; females: Anna Margaret Hoffart, Anna
Margaret Hoffart, Jr.)

SCHWAIGERN LUTHERAN KB:
m. 24 Aug. 1702 Hans Jerg Hoffert, son of Stofel Hoffert, and Anna Margretha,
daughter of Marx Mest (?). They had:
1. Hans Ulrich bp. 29 Sept. 1703
2. Hans Georg b. 20 Mar. 1705
3. Anna Christina b. 1 Dec. 1706; m. Caspar Krieger [q.v.], 1730 immigrant.
4. Child (N.N.) b. 2 Jan. 1710
5. Christianus b. 5 Jan. 1716

Pennsylvania records:
STOEVER'S RECORDS:
John Georg Hoffert sp. 1734 ch. of Caspar Krueger [q.v.]
Pennsylvanische Berichte, 1 Feb. 1756:
Christian Hoffert, Whitpain twp. (Montgomery co.), 18 miles from Philadelphia,
offers part of his plantation for sale.

George Hoffer, Cocalico twp., Lancaster co., nat. Philadelphia 1761
Christian Hoffert, Whitpain, nat. Philadelphia April 1761

227. HOFMANN, HENRICH

6921 Ittlingen

1762 [no ship list that year]

ITTLINGEN LUTHERAN KB:
Hans Jerg Hofmann and wife Anna Catharina had:
    Joh. Heinrich b. 1 June 1742
Anna Catharina Hofmann d. 22 Apr. 1745. Joh. Dietrich vom Berg and wife Maria
Margaretha had a daughter Maria Catharina b. 24 Oct. 1712, d. 1745.

Pennsylvania records:
MUHLENBERG'S JOURNALS, I: 613:
Mar. 30, 1763 (Wednesday). Christoph Beyer reported that Henrich Hofman had
passed away at Paul Cover's last night between eleven and twelve. His age: twenty-
one years, five months. Born in Ittlingen, a baronial locality in the Palatinate, of
Georg Hofman, the crown innkeeper, and his wife Margretha, nee von Berg; six
months in this country. Funeral text Psalm 39: 5–9.

228. HOFFMAN, CHRISTOPH   6921 Ittlingen

Dragon, 1732
S-H 96, 97, 98

ITTLINGEN LUTHERAN KB:
Christoph Hofmann and wife Maria Elisabetha had:
1. Anastasius b. 3 Jan. 1731

Pennsylvania records:
TRINITY LUTHERAN KB, LANCASTER:
Christoph Hoffmann had:
2. Joh. Christoph b. 21 Feb. 1734; sp. Anastasius Uhler [q.v.] and Christina Ziegelerin
3. Maria Margaretha b. 18 Apr. 1736; sp. Joh. Jost Allgeyer and wife Maria

229. HOFFMAN, MICHAEL   Bonfeld =

Restauration, 1747   6927 Bad Rappenau
S-H 366

MASSENBACH LUTHERAN KB:
Joh. Michael Hoffmann, servant at the upper mill, b. in Bonfeld, and wife Anna Maria, b. at [7156] Wüstenroth in the Dukedom of Wurttemberg, had:
1. Margaretha b. 5 July 1744

ITTLINGEN LUTHERAN KB:
Joh. Michel Hofmann and wife, from Bonfeld, communed in 1747 before going to the New Land. [See Appendix B.]

230. HOFFMANN, JACOB   6921 Zuzenhausen

Possibly on *Rosannah*, 1743

ZUZENHAUSEN LUTHERAN KB:
m. 22 Aug. 1741 Jacob Hoffmann, master shoemaker, son of Christoph Hoffmann, "Kirchen Vorsteher" and Maria Eva, daughter of Georg Oblander.

Krebs, "Palatine Emigration . . . ," p. 36.
Jacob Hoffman, shoemaker, of Zuzenhausen, was permitted to emigrate in 1743, along with Dietrich Müller, without payment of the usual taxes because of their poverty.

231. HOFFMANN, JOH. BURCKHARD   Adelshofen, Baden =

Molly, 1727   7519 Eppingen
S-H 12, 13

ADELSHOFEN LUTHERAN KB:
m. 11 Feb. 1727 Joh. Burckhard, son of the late Joh. Martin Hoffmann, inhabitant at [7109] Widdern, and Anna Elisabetha, dau. of Joh. Bernhard Saltzgeber, inhabitant. "Both wish to go to Pennsylvania."
Joh. Martin Hoffmann of [7109] Widdern d. 3 Feb. 1727, age 57 years.
He had come to Adelshofen to attend his son's wedding.

Pennsylvania records:
ST. PAUL'S LUTHERAN KB, RED HILL, MONTGOMERY CO:
Burckhardt Hoffman and wife Anna Elisabetha had:
    Johann Heinrich b. 28 Jan. 1742
Communicants, 1754:
    Martin Hofman, of Borck Hofman
    Anna Maria Hofman
    Elisabeth Hofman

SHULTZE'S JOURNALS, II: 27:
Oct. 1768 Burghart Hoffman's wife died on the 25th and was buried on the 27th.

Burchard Hoffman, Philadelphia co., nat. Philadelphia Sept. 1743

232. HOFFMANN, JOH. MICHAEL   7519 Eppingen
[several possibilities in S-H]

EPPINGEN LUTHERAN KB:
m. 29 June 1723 Michael Hoffmann, son of Andreas Hoffmann, former citizen at
Weifertshoffen, Brandenburg, Onoltzbach region, (probably 7181 Weipertshofen
near Crailsheim) and Maria Magdalena Schweitzer, daughter of the late Johannes
Schweitzer. Children:
    1. Anna Barbara b. 30 June 1724
    2. Maria Barbara b. 15 July 1727
    3. Maria Magdalena b. 17 Sept. 1729
    4. Anna Catharina b. 21 July 1732; d.
    5. Joh. Georg b. 11 Sept. 1733; d.
    6. Joh. Georg b. 14 Feb. 1736
    7. David b. 1 Mar. 1743

Pennsylvania records:
TRINITY LUTHERAN KB, LANCASTER:
m. 12 July 1758 Georg Naegele from Steineberg in Württemberg and Mar. Magdalena Hofmännin from Eppingen.
m. 27 Mar. 1764 Georg Hofmann from Eppingen, Pfalz, and Elisabet Kümmlin.

233. HOFFMANN, WILHELM   Berwangen, Kraichgau =
                                                  6926 Kirchardt
Dragon, 1749
S-H 413

BERWANGEN AND MASSENBACH KB:
m. 30 May 1747 at Massenbach Wilhelm Hoffmann, linenweaver, son of the late
Georg Hoffmann, citizen and smith in Berwangen, and Anna Margaretha, daughter
of the late Georg Friedrich Werner, citizen at Massenbach. [She was bp. 21 Feb.
1723, daughter of Georg Fridrich Werner and wife Maria Waldpurgis.] Children:
    1. Anna Maria b. 5 Jan. 1748 in Massenbach; bp. 6 Jan. 1748 (Berwangen
    record)

Pennsylvania records:
ST. MICHAEL'S AND ZION LUTHERAN KB, PHILADELPHIA:
Bu. 26 July 1767 Wilhelm Hofmann, b. in Behrwangen near Bischofsheim in
1718. Lived here 18 y. Had 12 children, one still living. Aged 49 y.

234. HOLL, JOHANNES age 23   6921 Ittlingen

Patience, 1748
S-H 384, 386

ITTLINGEN LUTHERAN KB:
Johannes Holl, Catholic, and wife Maria Elisabetha had:
    Johannes b. 15 May 1724; bp. 17 May 1724

Pennsylvania records:
ST. MICHAEL'S AND ZION LUTHERAN KB, PHILADELPHIA:
d. 14 Oct. 1778 Johann Holl from Ittlingen, age 54 y. 4 m. and 18 d.

235. HÖLL, WENDEL age 34   7103 Schwaigern

Samuel, 1732
S-H 59, 61, 62, 64, 65 (Others on ship: Barbara Hellin
age 38, Barbara age 12, Anna age 11, Gottlib age 9,
Kathrina age 5, Maria age 4, Rosina age 3)

SCHWAIGERN LUTHERAN KB:
m. 30 Oct. 1690 Adam Höll, son of Hans Höll, and Maria Catharina, daughter of
Hans Leonhardt Betz. They had:
    Hans Wendel b. 20 (?) Apr. 1693
m. 14 Feb. 1716 Hans Wendel Höll, son of Adam Höll, vintner, and Anna Barbara,
daughter of the late Michael Anmuller, citizen at Eschenau [= 7104 Obersulm].
The marriage was necessary due to pregnancy. They had:
    1. Elisabetha Barbara b. 27 June 1716
    2. Margaretha b. 13 July 1718; d. 25 Feb. 1719
    3. Anna Dorothea b. 20 Jan. 1720
    4. Gottlieb b. 2 Jan. 1722
    5. Johann Heinrich b. 20 Dec. 1723; d. 1724
    6. Maria Catharina b. 18 Apr. 1725
    7. Maria Magdalena b. 20 Apr. 1727
    8. Anna Rosina b. 2 July 1729

Pennsylvania records:
TRINITY LUTHERAN KB, LANCASTER:
1750 Gottlieb Hill, age 25 y., d. after a very long and hard illness on Mar. 15; bu.
Mar. 16

OLEY HILLS LUTHERAN KB, BERKS CO.:
Communicants' list: Anna Rosina Hill, single daughter of Wendel Hill, dec'd
LITITZ MORAVIAN KB:
M. 12 Mar. 1745 Gottlieb Hill and Anna Maria Wetterich

Gotliff Hill, Lancaster co., nat. Philadelphia, September 1743, with Adam Hill, Philadelphia

236. HOLTZAPFEL, LEONHARD age 47   6921 Michelfeld
HOLTZAPFEL, Erazmus, age 20
HOLTZAPFEL, Anna Barbara age 57

Britannia, 1731
S-H 48, 52, 53

MICHELFELD LUTHERAN KB:
Jacob Holtzapffel and (Anna) Maria Margretha nee Klein had:
    Johann Leonhard b. 21 Feb. 1683
[His marriage and the children do not appear in this record, but he and his wife Maria Barbara sponsor a child at Michelfeld in 1717 and a daughter married there in 1730—see Adam Ruppert]

ESCHELBACH LUTHERAN KB:
Hans Lenhart Holtzapffel, citizen at Michelfeld, and wife Anna Barbara had one child bp. at Eschelbach:
    Asmus (Erasmus) b. 21 Sept. 1710; bp. 27 Sept. 1710

Pennsylvania records:
TRINITY LUTHERAN KB, LANCASTER:
Erasmus Holtzapfel had a son Joh. Jacob, b. 23 Jan. 1739, bp. 15 Feb. 1739; Sp. Jacob Rudiesiele and wife Elisabetha (also from Michelfeld.)

STOEVER'S RECORDS:
m. 14 Feb. 1738 Erasmus Holtzapfel and Christina Ruscher, Earltown
Erasmus Holzapfel (Codorus) had a child b. 25 Aug. 1740. Sponsors were John Adam Rupert [q.v.] and wife _____

Erasmus Holtapffel, Manchester twp., York co. nat. Philadelphia 24 Sept. 1763.

237. HOLTZBAUM, ANDREAS   6921 Ittlingen
                                               6908 Wiesloch
William & Sarah, 1727
S-H 8 (Name on list: Andrew Holtspan 4 in family)

WIESLOCH REFORMED KB:
Marriage proclaimed 20 May 1708; m. 5 (June?) 1708 Andres Holsbaum from "Zebis aus Bind" and Barbara Danner from Beyerthal, daughter of Hans Danner. [Baiertal = 6908 Wiesloch]

SCHATTHAUSEN LUTHERAN KB:
Andreas Holtzbaum and wife had:
    Maria Ursula b. 7 Feb. 1709; bp. 9 Feb.

ITTLINGEN LUTHERAN KB:
Andreas Holtzbaum and wife Barbara had:
    Joh. Adam b. 20 Sept. 1723

Pennsylvania records:
FIRST REFORMED KB, LANCASTER:
George Kaltenruetter of Waldmoor, Zweibrucken and his wife Anna Ursula, daughter of Andrew Holtzbaum of Sintzheim, Palatinate, residing on Little Beber Creek, had:
    John George Peter b. 2 Mar. 1747

TRINITY LUTHERAN KB, NEW HOLLAND, LANCASTER CO.:
Andreas Holtzbaum appears as a sp. in 1733.
A Cunradt Holtzbaum is a sp. in 1737 and Susanna Holtzbäumin, single, is a sp. in 1731 and 1735.

STOEVER'S RECORDS:
m. 18 Nov. 1735 Peter Becker and Susanna Holtzbaum, Conestoga

Andreas Holsbaum, Earl twp., Lancaster co., nat. Philadelphia April 1761.

238. HONETTER, ANDREAS

1742

6921 Ittlingen
Ehrstädt =
6920 Sinsheim

[He is possibly the "Andres Harter" who arrived on the *Robert and Alice*, 1742, S-H I: 331. The signature on the list appears to be possibly Anderes Honoter. Other passengers from Ittlingen and Ehrstädt appear on the *Francis and Elizabeth*, 1742.]

ITTLINGEN LUTHERAN KB:
Andreas Hohenetter and wife Maria Dorothea had:
    1. Maria Margaretha b. 2 Apr. 1740
No other records for them at Ittlingen.

Pennsylvania records:
NEW HANOVER LUTHERAN KB, MONTGOMERY CO.:
Andreas and Dorothea Honetter had:
    Bernhart b. 17 Oct. 1755
    Andreas b. 2 May 1758
Sp. for both children were Bernhart Gilbert and wife.
Conf. 17 Apr. 1756 Margaretha Honetter, Andreas' daughter, in her 16th year.
Conf. 1767 Valentin Hornetter, son of Andreas, age 15
Bu. 28 Apr. 1777 Andreas Honeter, age 65 y. 4 m. 8 days
Bu. 7 Nov. 1768 George Hornetter, son of Andreas, age 21 y. 6 m. 2 weeks 1 day.

MUHLENBERG'S JOURNALS, III: 32, 36:
On 24 Apr. 1777 Muhlenberg visited a very sick member, Andreas Honetter, who had been deacon for several years. On 28 Apr. 1777 Muhlenberg buried Andreas Honetter and recorded the following details: He was b. 1711 in Ehrstädt in a baronial district. He was baptized, brought up, instructed and confirmed and in 1737 married a Christian woman. In 1742 he came to Philadelphia with his family. Served several years as deacon of the congregation in [New] Hanover. Had 8 children, all survived.
[Note by compiler: The surname Honetter appears in the Ehrstädt record, but the baptism of Andreas does not.]

JOURNALS OF HENRY MELCHIOR MUHLENBERG, III: 481, 483:
26 Apr. 1782—Mr. Peter Lober, widower, and Mrs. Dorothea Honetter, widow, of Douglas and Providence twps. are engaged.
7 May 1782—married an older couple, Peter Lober, widower, and Dorothea Honetter.
See also III: 614, 615 for their marital difficulties and separation.

Andrew Honnetta, Douglass twp., Philadelphia co., nat. 10 Apr. 1761

239. HORCH, ELIAS
Shirley, 1751
S-H 455 (Name on list: Johan Elias (   ) Horrst)

Hoffenheim =
6920 Sinsheim, Elsenz

HOFFENHEIM LUTHERAN KB:
m. 12 July 1718 Jacob Horch, son of Claus, and Anna Elisabetha Stötzenbach, dau. of Matthais. Joh. Jacob Horch and wife Elisabetha had:
    Elias b. 24 Oct. 1718
m. 20 June 1747 Joh. Elias Horch, son of the late Jacob Horch, and Anna Barbara Baum, dau. of Simon Baum [q.v.], inhabitant. Children:
    1. Maria Elisabetha b. 20 June 1748

Pennsylvania records:
ST. DAVID'S (SHERMAN'S) KB, YORK CO.:
Elias Horch and wife Anna Barbara had:
    2. Anna Margaretha b. 25 Dec. (1752); bp. 2 Jan. 1753
    3. Maria Christina b. 8 Jan. 1756; bp. 7 Feb.

Johannes Elias Horch nat. Annapolis 11 Apr. 1749.

240. HORNBERGER, HANS BARDEL
      HORNBERGER, JOHAN CARL
Alexander & Anne, 1730
S-H 35, 36, 37

6921 Michelfeld

MICHELFELD LUTHERAN KB:
Joh. Carl Hornberger, born in [6925] Eshelbronn, who came to Michelfeld in 1701 from [6920] Eschelbach, butcher, and wife Barbara had the following children:
    1. Johann Carl b. 24 Jan. 1705
    2. Johann Bartholomaus b. _____Apr. 1707
    3. Ursula Margretha b. 1708; d.
The father, Johann Carl, d. 1728 and his wife Barbara d. 24 Mar. 1741.

Pennsylvania records:
STOEVER'S RECORDS:
m. 25 Aug. 1733 John Bartholomeus Hornberger and Anna Elisabetha Reiffen, Chestnut Hill
m. 31 Aug. 1736 John Carl Hornberger and Anna Eva Saur, Leacock. Children bp. at Muddy Creek Lutheran; Lancaster co.:
    1. Joh. Carl b. 25 Oct. 1737

2. Maria Eva b. 2 Mar. 1743
3. Joh. Carl b. 5 Sept. 1744
4. Georg Friederich b. 21 Sept. 1747

BERKS CO. WILLS:
Charles Hornberger, Brecknock (30 Nov. 1785/17 Jan. 1786)
wife Anna Eva eldest son Conrad, son Georg Frederick dec'd, dau. Maria Eva
Hunsberger dec'd, youngest son John Jacob. Mentions George Frederick's widow
Anna.

PENNSYLVANIA PATENTS
AA: 3: 229: Under a warrant of 26 June 1734, there was surveyed to Parkle
Hornberier [Bartel Hornberger], Bucks co., a tract in Lower Milford twp. containing
150 A. He died leaving children: Valentine Hornberier, his son, Mary Barbara,
wife of John Reinhard, and Anna Margaret Hornberier, his daughters. His heirs
sold the land 2 Jan. 1760 to Andrew Bayer, who obtained a patent 21 Apr. 1762.

ST. PAUL'S LUTHERAN KB, MONTGOMERY CO.:
conf. 1753 Johan Valentin Hornberger, age 14 y., 6 m., stepson of Andreas Beyer.
m. 5 Apr. 1763 Valentin Hornberger and Catharina Lamprecht

Bartholomeus Hornbergher nat. Philadelphia, September 1740, of Bucks co.

241. HORNBERGER, JOH. JACOB age 33   6920 Sinsheim, Elsenz
Pleasant, 1732
S-H 99, 100, 101

SINSHEIM LUTHERAN KB:
Friderich Hornberger and wife Anna Katharina, both Evangelical (religion) had:
    Johann Jacob b. 26/16 Dec. 1699
Johann Jacob Hornberger and wife Maria Barbara had children:
    1. Susanna Barbara b. 19 Sept. 1722
    2. Anna Maria b. 20 Apr. 1725

Pennsylvania records:
New Goshenhoppen marriages, between 1747–1758:
Peter Hillikas and Barbara Hornberger

MACUNGIE LUTHERAN KB, LEHIGH CO.:
Bu. 16 Sept. 1771 at Salisbury Maria B. Hornberger, Jacob's wife, age 68 y.

242. HORNUNG, WENDEL   7103 Schwaigern
Francis & Ann, 1741
S-H, 292, 293

SCHWAIGERN LUTHERAN KB:
Michael Hornung and wf. Eva Barbara had:
    1. Maria Dorothea b. 10 Feb. 1721
    2. Joh. Wendel bp. 29 Jan. 1723

3. Jerg Adam b. at midnight 17/18 Nov. 1725; d. 29 May 1729
4. Eva Maria b. 8 Sept. 1728
5. Anna Barbara b. 28 Aug. 1730

Pennsylvania records:
TRINITY LUTHERAN KB, LANCASTER:
   Martin Bernthäussel, widower, m. Mar. 1753 Eva Maria Hornung.
   Heinrich Stauter from Freyspach near Speyer (6721 Freisbach)
   m. 16 Sept. 1760 Barbara Hornung from Schwaigern.
Wendel and Magdalena Horning had:
   Joh. Michael b. 5 Mar. 1758
   Catharina Elisabeth b. 19 Aug. 1759

243. HOTTENSTEIN, JOH. DAVID   6921 Ittlingen
HOTTENSTEIN, JOH. JACOB

Rawley, 1752
S-H 499, 500

ITTLINGEN LUTHERAN KB:
Joh. Philip David Hottenstein, bp. 28 Sept. 1700, son of Joh. Wilhelm Hottenstein
and Maria Catharina.
m. [Bonfeld Lutheran KB] 24 Nov. 1722 Joh. Philipp David Hottenstein, shoemaker, son of the late Joh. Wilhelm Hottenstein, "Anwalt" in Ittlingen, and Anna
Barbara Braun, dau. of Joh. Leonhard Braun. Their children, bapt. at Ittlingen:
   1. Catharina Barbara b. 9 Nov. 1723; d. 1771
  *2. Joh. Jacob b. 1 Dec. 1724 (? recorded with 1725 bapt.)
   3. Agatha b. June 1728; d. 1801
   4. Wilhelm Heinrich b. 17 Jan. 1731
   5. Maria Elisabetha b. 18 Apr. 1733; d. 1737
  *6. Joh. David b. 23 Sept. 1735, "d. at sea"
   7. Joh. Leonhard b. 12 Apr. 1738
m. 25 Jan. 1752 Johann Jacob Hottenstein, son of Joh. Philip David Hottenstein,
and Sabina Elisabetha Hahn, dau. of the late Matthai Hahn of Adersbach.

ADERSBACH LUTHERAN KB:
m. 25 Jan. 1752 Johann Jacob Hottenstein, cooper, son of Herr Johann David
Hottenstein, "Anwald" at Ittlingen, and Sabina Elisabetha, dau. of the late Herr
Matthias Hahn, "Herrschaftlichen Verwalter". Married at Ittlingen.

Pennsylvania records:
TRINITY LUTHERAN KB, LANCASTER:
m. 27 Aug. 1754 Joh. Jacob Hottenstein, widower, from Ittlingen, and Barbara
Schreiner, widow. Children:
   1. Joh. Jacob b. 16 July 1755; d. 26 Aug. 1758
   2. Elisabeth Barbara b. 28 Aug. 1757; d. 30 Aug. 1758
   3. Martin b. 13 Oct. 1759
   4. Eva Catharina b. 7 Aug. 1761

Jacob Hottenstein left Ittlingen as a newly-wed in 1752 with a brother David, who died apparently about the time of their arrival. They were following their uncle Jacob who had settled in Pennsylvania before 1725. But Jacob moved to Lancaster, where his cousin Henry, the uncle's son, was a potter. A house in what is now East Petersburg over whose door there was a beam with a German inscription was identified with this immigrant.

Ich gehe aus oder ein
So sted der Dot und wartet mein
Es ist besser ein drocken bisgen
man sich vergnie
laest als ein hausvol geschlates mit hater Anno 1740

I go in or out;
Death stands there to wait for me
It is better to enjoy a dry morsel
than a house full of eating with strife. 1740
(Proverbs 17:1)

Courtesy Pennsylvania Farm Museum at Landis Valley

Photo: Will Brown, 1982, courtesy of Philadelphia Museum of Art

---

5. Joh. Philip ⎫ twins, b. 16 June 1764
6. Joh. Heinrich ⎭
7. Barbara b. 7 Dec. 1771

Jacob Hottenstein nat. Philadelphia, Sept. 1761, of Manheim twp., Lancaster co.

244. HOTTENSTEIN, JOH. JACOB

6921 Ittlingen

Prelist

ITTLINGEN LUTHERAN KB:
Joh. Wilhelm Hottenstein and Maria Catharina had:
Joh. Jacob bp. 28 Jan. 1696
Joh. Jacob Hottenstein and wife Dorothea had:
1. Catharina Barbara b. 18 Oct. 1720

Pennsylvania records:
STOEVER'S RECORDS:
Jacob Hottenstein (Maxatawny) had:
2. Jacob b. 8 Dec. 1725; sp. Jacob Berendt
3. Johanna b. 19 Feb. 1727; sp. Anna Drechsler
4. Johann Wilhelm b. 15 Aug. 1730; sp. Jacob Berend and wife

BERKS CO. WILLS:
Jacob Hottenstein, Maxatawny, (30 Apr. 1753). Wife Mary Dorothy. To 2 sons David and Henry plantation containing 400 A. and 100 A. in Allemingle (Albany twp.) Dau. Mary Catharine's share to go to her children. Letters of adm. to Jacob and William Hottenstein, sons of the testator, the widow renouncing.
Dorothea Hottenstone, Maxatawny (15 Aug. 1764/28 July 1766). To son Jacob's four children: Catharine, Mary, Plantine (Blandina) and Susanna Hottenstone, a ⅙ part of the estate. To dau. Dorothea Reiffschneider's children—Jacob, John and Catharine, ⅙ of the estate. To dau. Catharina Kepler ⅙ of estate; son William, son David and son Henry, each ⅙ of estate. Sons William and Henry, exrs.

PENNSYLVANIA PATENTS:
AA:4:398: warrant 30 Sept. 1751 to Jacob Huttenstine for 176 A. in Maxatawny twp., Berks co. In his will, 21 Mar. 1753, he devised the land to two sons, David and Henry. Henry Hottenstein, of Lancaster town, a potter, sold his share to David for £ 440. Patent to David 5 Jan. 1763. Recorded 6 July 1763.

———————

Jacob Hettlestein, Philadelphia co., nat. by Act of 6 Feb. 1730/31.

245. HUBELE, JACOB

Berwangen, Kraichgau = 6926 Kirchardt

Charming Nancy, 1737
S-H 188, 189, 191, 193 (with Catharine and Eva)

BERWANGEN LUTHERAN KB:
Hans Hobele from Effingen, Canton Bern, Switzerland [CH 5253 Effingen, AG], and wife Anna Buchlin, had:
Paulus b. 14 Aug. 1668
Paul Hobelin, son of Hans, m. 11 Feb. 1696, Susanna, daughter of Joseph Mausser.
m. 6 May 1732 Jacob Hubelin, wagonmaker, son of Paul Hubelin, and Anna Catharina, daughter of Loth. Ziegler, master miller. Children:
1. Eva Catharina b. 18 May 1733

2. Joh. Leonhardt b. 25 Aug. 1735

It is recorded in the communicant register that they went to Pennsylvania in 1737.

Pennsylvania records:
TRINITY LUTHERAN KB, LANCASTER:
Jacob Hubele had:
  3. Joh. Philipp, b. 2 Oct. 1737; sp. Philipp Firnssler and Maria Barbara
  4. Jacob (posthumously), b. 18 Apr. 1739; sp. Christoph Meyer and Rosina

PA, THIRD SERIES, 14:427:
Jacob Hubele, warrant for 150 A., Lancaster co. 1738

STOEVER'S RECORDS:
M. 9 Sept. 1739 Christoph Labengeiger and Anna Catarina Hubelin, Warwick
Christoph Labengeiyer of Swatara had 3 children with his first wife bp. by Stoever.
There was one child of this second marriage entered into Stoever's record:
  Christoph b. Oct. 1741; bp. 15 Apr. 1742; sp. Christoph Meyer and wife

246. HUBELE, JOH. FRIEDERICH age 25

St. Andrew, 1743
S-H 349, 350, 351

Adelshofen, Baden =
7519 Eppingen

ADELSHOFEN LUTHERAN KB:
An illegitimate child, Margaretha, b. 7 Nov. 1741; the mother was Frederica
Catharina Dupssin, born in Gemmingen. The father was Friedrich Hübele, born in
Berwangen [= 6926 Kirchardt]
m. 28 July 1742 after premature concubitum Johann Friderich Hubele, son of
Georg Hubele of Berwangen, and Elisabetha Barbara, daughter of Christoph Eck-
ert, weaver.

Pennsylvania records:
NEW HANOVER LUTHERAN KB, MONTGOMERY CO.:
Friederich and Elisabetha Hubele had:
  1. Sophia b. 26 Dec. 1746
  2. Maria Elisabeth b. 27 Mar. 1749
An infant daughter of Friederich Hubele was bu. 25 Apr. 1756, age 5 mo.

TRINITY LUTHERAN KB, LANCASTER:
d. 16 Mar. 1769 Joh. Friederich Hubele, aged 50 y. 10 m. 12 d.

Frederick Hubley, Lancaster, nat. Philadelphia Sept. 1764.

247. HUBER, ANDREAS

6921 Ittlingen

Two Sisters, 1738
S-H 210

ITTLINGEN LUHTERAN KB:
Johannes Huber and wife Ottilia had:
  1. Joh. Heinrich bp. 17 Oct. 1712; died young
  2. Erasmus bp. 19 Mar. 1714

3. Johannes bp. 5 Jan. 1716
4. Sabina bp. 22 Mar. 1718
5. Maria Barbara b. ___ Feb. 1720
6. Anna Maria b. 1 Dec. 1721
*7. Andreas b. 13 May 1724
8. Joh. Friederich b. 19 July 1726; died young
9. Maria Margaretha b. 5 Feb. 1729
10. Anna Maria b. 28 Jan. 1731; died young
11. Maria Barbara b. 16 Mar. 1732

Pennsylvania records:

The Andreas Huber on this ship has been previously identified as the ancestor of President Herbert Hoover. He was first identified as an immigrant from Trippstadt (*National Genealogical Society Quarterly*, Vol XV, no. 1, Mar. 1927) and then subsequently identified as an immigrant from Ellerstadt (*NGS Quarterly*, Vol XVII, no. 1, Mar. 1929). It seems more logical that the Andreas Huber who came at the age of 15 in 1738 is the Andreas b. 13 May 1724 in Ittlingen. This hypothesis is strengthened by the fact that he arrived on the same ship with Joh. Gottlieb Bräuninger, Joh. Martin Bräuninger, Joh. Michael Oesterlin, Dietrich Benedict, Hans Peter Sailer, Pleickerd Dietrich Sailer and Wolfgang Braun. All of these names appear in the Ittlingen records and several of them are provable immigrants from that village. Andreas Huber then settled for a time in Lancaster co. Later Huber immigrants from Ittlingen also settled in Lancaster. [See Hans Jacob Huber, Ludwig Huber and Philip Dietrich Huber, 1742 arrivals, S-H 327] In further support of this theory, it seems unlikely that a 15 year old boy would be travelling alone. Yet no other immigrant on this ship has ever been identified from Ellerstadt nor any village in that vicinity. There are no marriage records available for Ittlingen in this time period, but it seems possible that there might be a relationship, perhaps by marriage, with one or more of the several identifiable passengers on this ship, and the Hubers of Ittlingen. Andreas Huber later married a daughter of Michael Pfautz, an immigrant from the nearby village of Rohrbach (near Sinsheim).

It should be pointed out that the ages given on this ship list are incorrect. Dietrich Benedict, a provable immigrant from Ittlingen, is listed as age 30; he was actually born in 1710. Pleickerd Dietrich Sailer, listed as age 24, was actually born in 1719. Several other surnames on this ship appear in the records at Ittlingen and nearby villages: Ziegler, Funk, Geiger, Wagner and Schwartz. But exact identification of these immigrants with more common surnames is impossible without further supporting evidence. This is complicated by the age discrepancies on this list.

WARWICK LUTHERAN KB, LANCASTER CO.:
Andreas Huber and Catarina Klein sp. 1743 a child of Jacob Meyer [q.v.]

Andrew Hoover, Frederick co., Md., nat. Philadelphia Sept. 1761, as a "Quaker."

248. HUBER, BALTHASAR   6921 Ittlingen

Charming Nancy, 1737
S-H 189, 192, 194

ITTLINGEN LUTHERAN KB:
Joh. Jacob Huber [q.v.] and wife Anna Barbara had:
Balthasar bp. 27 Sept. 1716

Pennsylvania records:
NEW HANOVER LUTHERAN KB, MONTGOMERY CO.:
Balthasar Huber and wife Margaretha had:
  1. Catharina Elisabetha b. 26 Nov. 1745
  2. Philipp Balthasar b. 18 Sept. 1747 (posthumous)
Balthasar Huber d. Sept. 1747, age 30 y.

249. HUBER, HANS JACOB   6921 Ittlingen
HUBER, LUDWIG
HUBER, PHILIP TITTER

Francis & Elizabeth, 1742
S-H 327

ITTLINGEN LUTHERAN KB:
Joh. Jacob Huber and wife Anna Barbara had:
  1. Balthasar bp. 27 Sept. 1716 [q.v.]
  2. Anna Dorothea Christina b. __ Sept. 1718
  3. Joh. Philipp Dietrich b. 8 Aug. 1722
  4. Joh. Ludwig b. 4 Aug. 1726
  5. Joh. Jacob b. 9 May 1730

Pennsylvania records:
SALEM LUTHERAN KB, LEBANON:
Anna Dorothea Christina, nee Huber, b. 1717 in Sept. in Ztlinger [Ittlingen], dau.
of John J. Huber and wife Anna Barbara. Sp. at her bp. were Philip Balser Romich
and Dorothea Friedler. Conf. 1743. Came to America 1747; m. Mattheus Gilbert
[q.v.] who d. ca. 1784. They had 4 children. She d. 6 July 1795, age 77 y. less 2
mo. Matthias Gilbert and Christina Dorothea Huber were m. 5 Jan. 1748 at New
Hanover, Montgomery co. Children, bp. at Trinity Lutheran, Lancaster co.:
  1. Georg Henrich b. 1 Dec. 1748; bp. 29 July 1750
  2. Georg Michael b. 17 Feb. 1751
  3. Friederich b. 24 July 1752

TRINITY LUTHERAN KB, LANCASTER:
m. 1 Nov. 1748 Philipp Dietrich Huber and Regina Franck, in the presence of
their parents, brothers and sisters and various other people. Ch:
  1. Ursula b. 22 July 1749
m. 23 Jan. 1750 Ludwig Huber, a well known bachelor from our congregation and
Margaretha Graeff, b. a Mennonite, whose parents went over to the Siebentäger
(the Ephrata Group). She was bapt. by this sect, but did not remain with them. Ch:

1. Louise b. 2 Dec. 1750
m. 1 Jan. 1751 Jacob Huber, a bachelor and tailor from the town and Susanna Philippina Wetzlerin, single. One child bp. there:
Matthaeus b. 23 Mar. 1765
Johann Jacob Huber, b. 1684, d. 26 Aug. 1749, and bu. the 27th thereafter, the 14th Sunday after Trinity.
Anna Barbara Huberin, the surviving widow of Joh. Jacob Huber, followed her deceased husband rapidly the 21 Sept. (1749) and was bu. the 22nd thereafter.

250. HUTH, JOHANNES   7519 Eppingen

William & Sarah, 1727
S-H 7, 9

EPPINGEN REFORMED KB:
m. (1) 23 June 1711 Johannes Huth, son of Hans Huth, citizen at [6927] Babstatt, Boxberger Amt, and Anna Catharina, daughter of Noe Gerner. Children:
1. Fronica b. 8 Feb. 1706
2. Joh. Wolfgang b. 21 July 1708
3. H. Peter bp. 26 Apr. 1712; d. 14 May 1713
4. Elisabetha bp. 26 Aug. 1714; d. 3 July 1716
5. Catharina Elisabetha bp. 1 Mar. 1718; d. young
6. Maria Elisabetha bp. 23 May 1719
m. (2) 22 Aug. 1719 Johannes Huth, widower, and Maria Anna Sähm, daughter of Hans Jacob Sähm. Children:
7. Salomae bp. 15 Aug. 1720
8. Johannes bp. 16 Nov. 1721
9. Eva Margaretha bp. 23 Oct. 1722
10. Elisabetha bp. 27 Apr. 1725

Pennsylvania records:
NEW GOSHENHOPPEN REFORMED KB, MONTGOMERY CO:
Johannes Huth and wife had:
Johann Philip bp. 21 Sept. 1731
Conf. 10 Oct. 1736 Eva Marg. Hut, daughter of John Hut
M. between 1747 and 1758:
Philip Huth and Eva Weiss
John Huth and Barbara Zimmerman
J. Arendt Weiss and Susanna Huth
Johannes Hut appears on an early list of members.

251. HÜTTNER, JOH. GEORG age 31

Samuel, 1737
S-H 169, 170, 172

6922 Meckesheim
Waldhilsbach =
6903 Neckargemünd

MECKESHEIM REFORMED KB:
Joh. Georg Bauer, bp. 30 Dec. 1696; conf. 1710, son of Joh. Georg Bauer and Anna Clara.

BAMMENTHAL REFORMED KB:
m. 10 Jan. 1719 Hans Görg Bauer from Meckesheim and Maria Barbara Wüsten (Wüster), daughter of the forester at (Wald) Hilspach.

MECKESHEIM REFORMED KB:
Joh. Georg Bauer and wife Maria Barbara had children:
1. Maria Susanna b. 7 Nov. 1719
2. Joh. Conrad b. 12 Feb. 1721
3. Johannes b. 1 Nov. 1724
4. Anna Catharina Barbara b. 30 Nov. 1725
5. Joh. Balthasar b. 6 Apr. 1728
6. Georg Balthasar b. 31 Jan. 1730
7. Anna Christina b. 21 Apr. 1731
d. 17 Jan. 1732 Hans Georg Bauer, the younger, aged 35 years, 19 days. The widow Maria Barbara m. (2) Johann Georg Hüttner and they had one child bp. at Meckesheim:
1. Johann Georg bp. 15 Oct. 1734

NECKARGEMUND LUTHERAN KB:
m. 22 Aug. 1733 at Meckesheim Joh. Georg Hüttner, son of Friederich Hüttner of Irrlangen [? 8520 Erlangen], and Maria Barbara Bauer, widow of Georg Bauer. Ch.:
2. Maria Barbara b. 14 Jan. 1737, bp. 15 Jan. 1737 at Meckesheim

Pennsylvania records:
ST. MICHAEL'S AND ZION LUTHERAN KB, PHILADELPHIA:
Bu. 22 Jan. 1770 Maria Barbara Hütner, mother-in-law of Mr. H[einrich] Keppele, Sr.; b. 26 Feb. 1700, daughter of the late Herr Joh. Caspar Wüster, Chur Pfalzischen Jäger at [Wald] Hilspach; her mother, Anna Catharina. Her sp. at baptism was Maria Barbara, wife of Herr Justus Schäfer from Neckargemünd near Heidelberg. She m. (1) George Bauer, miller in Meckesheim and has 2 daughters living— one is Frau Keppele. She m. (2) the late George Hütner and came with him to Pennsylvania in 1737; they had 2 sons now living.

[She was a sister of Caspar Wister, 1717 immigrant.]

D. 2 July 1797 Johann Henrich Keppele, b. in Treschklingen near Heilbron 1 Aug. 1716, son of Leonhard Keppele and wife Eva Dorothea. m. Anna Catharina Barbara Bauer. Had 15 children, 1 son and 4 daughters living.
[He arrived on the *Charming Nancy*, 1738]

252. ILLIG, JOH. ANDREAS
Molly, 1727
S-H 12, 13

Adelshofen, Baden =
7519 Eppingen

ADELSHOFEN LUTHERAN KB:
m. 20 Oct. 1685 Andreas Ilg, son of Herr Reinhard Ilg, "Anwald", and Magdalena
Elisabetha Stupp, daughter of Joh. Matthaeus Stupp. Their son:
Hans Andreas b. 27 Apr. 1693
m. 23 Feb. 1727 Johann Andreas, son of the late Andreas Ilgen, citizen, and
Philippina, daughter of the respected Daniel Nord, inhabitant at Schwaigern.
[Notation in KB: "Both wish to go to Pennsylvania."]

Pennsylvania records:
CHRIST LUTHERAN KB, TULPEHOCKEN, STOUCHSBURG:
Andrew Illig and wife Philippina had:
George Michael b. 24 June 1744; conf. 1759
Confirmations:
9 Oct. 1748:
Eva Barb. Illig, daughter of Andreas; age 16 y. 2 mo.
Elisa. Margre. Illig, daughter of Andreas; age 14 y.
3 June 1750:
Eva Cath. Illig, dau. of Andreas, age 15 y.
1753: Eva Maria Illig, daughter of Andreas, age 14 y.
m. 9 Apr. 1751 Andrew Scholl and Elisabetha Illig, daughter of Andreas Illig.

253. ILLIG, JOH. PHILIPP age 36
Friendship, 1739
S-H 264, 268, 271

Hasselbach =
6920 Sinsheim, Elsenz

ADERSBACH AND NECKARBISCHOFSHEIM LUTHERAN KB:
Philipp Illick, tailor at Hasselbach, and Amalia Maria, nee Ulrich, had:
1. Catharina Margaretha b. 3 Apr. 1735; bp. at Adersbach
2. Friederich b. 15 Jan. 1738; bp. at Neckarbischofsheim

Pennsylvania records:
PHILADELPHIA MORAVIAN KB:
Amelia Illig, nee Ulrich, b. 26 Dec. 1695 at [8720?] Schweinfort, Germany.
m. 8 Mar. 1728 John Philip Illig and came with him to Penna. in 1739.

254. ILLIG, JOH. RUDOLPH
Dragon, 1732
S-H 96, 98

Adelshofen, Baden =
7519 Eppingen

ADELSHOFEN LUTHERAN KB:
Andreas Jelig and wife Anna Elisabetha had a son Hans Rudolff b. 28 July 1700
m. 16 Nov. 1728 Johann Rudolph Jilig, son of the late Andreae Jillgen, and Maria
Catharina, daughter of Joh. Auer, citizen at Emetsheim [8831 Emetzheim] belong-

ing to the episcopal region of Eichstätt. John. Rudolph Jilg and wife Maria Catharina had:
1. Joh. Georg Michael b. 7 Aug. 1729
2. Georg Friedrich b. 13 Dec. 1731

Pennsylvania records:
WILLIAMS TWP. CONGREGATION, NORTHAMPTON CO., PA.:
A Rudolph Illick with wife Magdalena had a son Johann Christoph b. 2 Jan. 1746
Rudolph Illick and wife Magdalena sp. a child of Jacob Schlauch [also from
Adelshofen] in 1743.

ST. PAUL'S LUTHERAN, RED HILL, KB, UPPER HANOVER TWP., MONTGOMERY
CO., PA. KB:
Rudolph Illick and wife Magdalena were sp. in 1743
Rudolph Illick and Magdalena had:
   Maria Christina b. 4 Dec. 1741, bp. 8 Dec.

PENNSYLVANIA PATENTS:
AA:4:204. warrant 29 Jan. 1734 for 166 acres, partly in Upper Hanover, Philadelphia co., and partly in Lower Milford twp., Bucks co. to Rudolph Julick. Julick
died intestate leaving his widow, Maria Magdalena Knedt (Knecht?), late Julick,
and 6 children: Christopher, the only son; Catharine, wife of Jacob Henning;
Elizabeth, wife of Philip Schneyder; Magdalena, wife of Philip Weichsell; Margaret, wife of John Weichsell; and Christina Julick. They sold the tract to Michael
Kli, Bucks co.; patented 27 Jan. 1763, recorded 27 Jan. 1763.

255. IMLER, MARCUS age 27   Waldangelloch =
                                                6920 Sinsheim, Elsenz
Mary, 1732
S-H 93, 94, 95

WALDANGELLOCH LUTHERAN KB:
Rudolff Schaber and wife Chatharina Barbara had:
   Ester Teresia bp. 13 Oct. 1709
m. 28 Apr. 1732 Marcus Imler and Ester Theresia, dau. of Rudolph Schabert.

Pennsylvania records:
NEW HOLLAND LUTHERAN KB, LANCASTER CO.:
Georg Marcks Imler had:
1. Andreas b. 14 Oct. 1733; sp. David Fischer, in the name of Andreas
   Krafft [q.v.]
2. Maria Esther b. 18 Sept. 1735; sp. Anna Margaretha Stürtzebachin

LANCASTER REFORMED KB:
George *Martin* Imbler and wife Esther Schaber had:
3. John William b. 13 Jan. 1740; bp. 13 Apr.; sp. Martin Barth and wife
   Sibylla Imbler.

256. JOST, JACOB

7519 Eppingen

William & Sarah, 1727
S-H 7, 9 (Number of persons—2)

EPPINGEN REFORMED KB:
m. (1) 8 Oct. 1715 Jacob Jost, saddler, single and Anna Barbara, daughter of Jac. Peter. Children:
1. Andreas bp. 16 Aug. 1716
m. (2) 12 Nov. 1720 Jacob Jost, saddler, widower, and Eva Barbara Ries, daughter of the late Lorentz Ries, former carpenter at Essklingen, Gemmingischen Herrschaft.

Pennsylvania records:
One Nicholas Yost patented a tract of land named Eppingen in Brecknock twp., Berks co., in 1766.

257. KAMP (KAMM), CASPAR

7519 Eppingen

Prelist; before 1723 (probably 1722 with others)

EPPINGEN REFORMED KB:
m. 3 Mar. 1710 Joh. Caspar Kamp, smith, son of Michel Kamp, smith, and Anna Catharina, nee Franck, b. at Bocksberg [6973 Boxberg]. Children:
1. Catharina b. __ May 1711; d. 4 June 1713
2. Maria Catharina bp. 23 Dec. 1713
3. Maria Barbara bp. 6 Oct. 1715
4. Anna Catharina bp. 1 May 1720; d. young
5. Maria Magdalena bp. 20 Mar. 1722

Pennsylvania records:
1723 petition—Caspar Kamp signed for road from Limerick twp. through Falkner Swamp to Oley.
Caspar Kamm appears on a list of early members of New Goshenhopen Reformed Church. Anna Barbara, daughter of Kaspar Kamm, sp. 1732 a child of Fridrich Hilligas, another emigrant from Eppingen.
Anna Catrina Kem and husband Kaspar were sp. in 1736 at New Goshenhoppen.

PHILADELPHIA WILLS:
Casper Kamm, Newhanover twp., blacksmith, "an old and weakly man." (3 Nov. 1741/17 Jan. 1752) Wife: Catharine, all estate. After her death, estate to be divided in equal shares among children, who were: eldest daughter Catharine Emert(on), Barbara Paltsgrav(in), and Anna Shelleberger, dec'd., whose share to her son John "at manly age" or marriage. One shilling sterling to son-in-law John Shelleberger) and youngest daughter Veronica. Exrs: Philip Emmert and Georg Paltsgrave. Wit.: Valentine Geiger and Bernhard Dodderer.

Philadelphia Wills:
George Paltsgroff (30 May 1757/1 Aug. 1757). Wife Barbara and 9 children: Christina, Henry, Eve, George, Barbara, Jacob, Mary, Fronica and Margaret. Men-

tions 125 A. of land, purchased from Michael Emert and another tract of 77 A. which exrs. are to sell to Paul [?] Bover who is married to daughter Christina.

258. KAPPLER, HANS MARTIN   6926 Kirchardt

Dragon, 1732
S-H 96, 98

KIRCHARDT LUTHERAN KB:
m. 21 Jan. 1716 Hans Martin Kappler, son of Benedict Cappler, and Susanna, daughter of Herr Hans Weidler, "Anwaldt." Children:
1. Anna Maria bp. 6 Oct. 1718
2. Anna Barbara bp. 22 Jan. 1722
3. Susanna bp. 18 Nov. 1724; d. young
4. Joh. Leonhardt bp. 14 May 1728
5. Joh. Jacob bp. 2 Aug. 1731

Pennsylvania records:
TRINITY LUTHERAN KB, LANCASTER:
Martin Kappler (Swatara) had:
6. Joh. Jacob b. 26 Sept. 1734
7. Catharina Barbara b. 12 June 1736

PHILADELPHIA WILLS:
Martin Capler, Bethel twp., Lancaster co. (1 Mar 1748/9/3 Apr. 1749.) Wife Marialis; children: Abraham, Cretle, Esely (?) and four children (who are not named by his first wife.) Exrs: Caspar Schnebly and Henry Dubs.

STOEVER'S RECORDS:
m. 7 Dec. 1741 Nicolaus Jungblut and Anna Maria Kappler, Tulpehocken

WARWICK—LITITZ MORAVIAN KB:
D. 28 July 1792 Anna Maria Jungblut, nee Kappler; b. 6 Oct. 1718 in Kirchardt. Wife of Nicholas Jungblut.

259. KATERMAN, ANNA BARBARA age 23   6921 Michelfeld

Britannia, 1731
S-H 49

MICHELFELD LUTHERAN KB:
Erasmus Katerman and wife Anna Gertrude had:
    Maria Barbara b. Dom. XIX p. Trin., 1706
A sponsor at the baptism of one of their other children in 1717 was Maria Barbara, wife of Leonhard Holtzapfel.
"Anna" Barbara Katerman appears on the ship's list with "Anna" Barbara Holtzapfel.

Pennsylvania records:
MUDDY CREEK LUTHERAN KB, LANCASTER CO.:
Maria Barbara Kattermännin sp. a child of Johannes Schäffer at Muddy Creek in

1732. (He married at Michelfeld).
She also sp. a child of Johann Adam Ruppert and his wife Anna Barbara (nee Holtzapfel) in 1733 at Muddy Creek.
m. 22 Apr. 1735 Paulus Lung and Maria Barbara Cattermännin (Cocalico)

260. KATERMAN, JOH. PHILIP age 20   6921 Michelfeld

Barclay, 1754
S-H 596, 597, 599

MICHELFELD LUTHERAN KB:
Johann Ulrich Katermann, son of Weÿrich, m. 16 Nov. 1728 Agnes Catharina, daughter of the late Hans Georg Kühlewein, former citizen. One of their sons was:
Johann Philipp b. 2 Jan. 1733

Pennsylvania records:
A Philip Katermann appears in the Christ Lutheran KB, Tulpehocken, Berks co. having children from 1770. He might, however, be a son of one of the earlier Katermann immigrants.

261. KATERMANN, DAVID   6921 Michelfeld

St. Andrew, 1752
S-H 485

MICHELFELD LUTHERAN KB:
Johann Ulrich Katermann, son of Weÿrich Katermann, m. 16 Nov. 1728 Agnes Catharina, daughter of the late Hans Georg Kühlewein, citizen. Their son:
David b. 12 July 1731, "To Pennsylvania 1752."

Pennsylvania records:
CHRIST LUTHERAN KB, TULPEHOCKEN, BERKS CO.:
David Katterman and wife Catharina had:
1. Maria Barbara b. 24 Sept. 1753
2. Catharina b. 5 Nov. 1756
3. Conrad b. 25 Mar. 1765
4. Elisabetha Catharina b. 24 Jan. 1768

262. KATTERMANN, WEŸRICH   6921 Michelfeld
KATTERMANN, HANS JACOB

St. Andrew, 1738
S-H 237, 238, 239 (Weyrich not on oath lists)

MICHELFELD LUTHERAN AND WALDANGELLOCH LUTHERAN KBs:
Weÿrich Katerman, Jr., b. 3 Jan. 1696 (son of Weÿrich and Elisabetha Katerman) married 6 Feb. 1720 at [6920] Waldangelloch Maria Margaretha Buggenmeyer. In the bapt. records of their children her name is given as Christina Margretha.
Children:
1. Hans Jacob b. 16 Feb. 1721
2. Joh. Martin b. 24 Nov. 1723; d. 19 Aug. 1731

   3. A dau. b. 9 Apr. 1727; d. at birth
   4. Anna Dorothea b. 13 Feb. 1729
   5. Johann Martin b. 4 Feb. 1735
"This family went to Pennsylvania 6 May 1738."

Pennsylvania records:
CHRIST LUTHERAN KB, TULPEHOCKEN, BERKS CO.:
Jacob Katerman, single, m. Easter Tuesday 1745 Anna Catharina Anspach, a
widow. Children:
   1. Maria Elisabeth b. 9 Aug. 1747
   2. John Weyrich b. 17 July 1751
   3. Catharina Margaretha b. 28 July 1755
   4. Maria Elisabetha b. 20 Sept. 1758
   5. Joh. Friderich b. 21 Dec. 1760

CHRIST "LITTLE TULPEHOCKEN" LUTHERAN KB, BERKS CO.:
m. 17 Jan. 1750 George Adam Busch and Dorothea Kattermann

BERKS CO. WILLS:
Michael Rith (15 Mar. 1754/11 Oct. 1754) names daughter Anna Catharina mar-
ried to Jacob Katerman and mentions children she had by first husband Georg
Anspach.

_____

Jacob Katterman, Tulpyhoccon twp., Lancaster co., nat. Philadelphia 25 Sept.
1751.

263. KAUTZMANN, ADAM   6921 Ittlingen
      KAUTZMANN, JOH. HEINRICH
Royal Union, 1750
S-H 432

ITTLINGEN LUTHERAN KB:
Adam Kautzmann and wife [in some records she is named as Eva Margretha, in
others Anna Margretha] had:
   1. Catharina Barbara b. 20 Sept. 1730; d. young
   2. Joh. Heinrich b. 8 Nov. 1731
   3. Joh. Jacob b. 31 Oct. 1738; d. young
   4. Eva Margaretha Barbara b. 1 Apr. 1740
   5. Anna Elisabetha b. 2 Sept. 1742; d. young
   6. Maria Barbara b. 23 Aug. 1745; d. 1748

Pennsylvania records:
TRINITY LUTHERAN KB, LANCASTER:
Joh. Adam Kauzmann d. 27 Apr. 1775, age 65 y.

LANCASTER CO. WILLS:
Adam Kautzman, Lancaster borough (28 Apr. 1774/8 May 1775). Wife Margaret
Kautzman.

_____

Adam Kowsman, Lancaster, nat. Philadelphia Sept. 1761

264. KAŸSER, CHRISTOPH age 36

Waldangelloch =
6920 Sinsheim, Elsenz

Mary, 1732
S-H 93, 94, 95 (Name on list: Kizer, Kiser)

WALDANGELLOCH LUTHERAN KB:
bp. 25 Nov. 1698 Maria Agnetha, daughter of Gottfried Krafft and Johanna, nee Fessler.
m. 15 Nov. 1718 Christoph Kaÿser, shoemaker, born "von Weltzen?" and Ananias, daughter of Gottfrid Krafft [q.v.] (Note: In the bp. records her name is given as Agnesa and Ananias.) Children:
1. Hans Willhelm bp. 5 Mar. 1721
2. Justina Catharina b. 3 June 1722
3. Joh. Michael b. 28 Dec. 1725
4. Hans Michel b. 28 June 1727
5. Jerg Friderich b. 14 May 1730

Pennsylvania records:
CHRIST "LITTLE TULPEHOCKEN" LUTHERAN KB, BERKS CO:
m. 12 June 1739 Andrew Kochendoerfer and Justina Catharine Kaeyser. Children:
1. Andrew b. 23 June 1742; sp. was Andrew Craft [Andreas Krafft q.v.] and wife
2. Geo. Philip b. 8 Apr. 1746
Justina Catharina Kaÿser was sp. for one of Andreas Krafft's [q.v.] children.

CHRIST LUTHERAN KB, TULPEHOCKEN, BERKS CO:
m. 13 Aug. 1749 Michael Keiser, son of Christoph Keiser, and Anna Maria Muller, daughter of Peter Muller.
William Keiser and wife Anna Margaret had:
1. John Michael b. 25 Dec. 1746
2. Maria Elisabeth b. 22 June 1749
3. Eva b. 2 Jan. 1751   _____

Christopher Keiser nat. Philadelphia, April 1761 of Tulpehockon twp., Berks co.

265. KEHL, GEORG DIETRICH age 46

Waldangelloch =
6920 Sinsheim, Elsenz

Britannia, 1731
S-H 48, 49, 50, 52, 53 (with Maria Ursela Kehl age 40, Katharina Margerita age 16, Philip Christoph age 11, Hans Georg age 7.)

WALDANGELLOCH LUTHERAN KB:
Georg Dieterich, bp. 2 Sept. 1685, son of Christoph Cöehl and Elisabetha. Ursula Maria, bp. 3 Feb. 1690, daughter of Michel Buckhenmeÿer and wife Catharina.
m. 17 Jan. 1713 Georg Dieterich Kehl, son of Christoph, and Maria Ursula Buckenmaÿer, daughter of Michael Buckenmaÿer here. Children:
1. Catharina Margaretha bp. 5 Apr. 1715
2. Johann Christian b. 8 Dec. 1717
3. Margaretha Barbara b. 28 June 1719

4. Philip Christoph b. 7 Nov. 1722
5. Hans Jerg b. 16 Apr. 1726
6. Maria Barbara b. 21 May 1729; d. 26 May 1729

Pennsylvania records:
PHILADELPHIA WILLS:
George Dieter Kehl, Adm. Book D: 65 (estate # 117) 1738

CHRIST LUTHERAN KB, TULPEHOCKEN, BERKS CO:
m. 13 Dec. 1748 John George Kehl and Anna Elisabeth Wagner
John George Kehl and Elisabeth had:
1. Peter b. 4 Feb. 1751; sp. Peter Anspach and wife
2. John b. 22 May 1756
3. Georg Nicholas b. 4 Mar. 1760

A Michal Köhle was conf. at Tulpehocken in 1745. Michael Kehl appears as a bp. sponsor in 1752.

Joh. Michael Kehl (Koehl) and wife Maria Catharina had:
1. Jacob b. 1 Sept. 1756
2. John Michael b. 22 Aug. 1758; sp. Michael Reiss and wife
3. Joh. George b. 18 Oct. 1760; sp. George Koehl and Elisabeth
4. Anna Catharina b. 21 July 1762; sp. Henry Kettner and wife
5. Justina (twin) b. 21 July 1762; sp. Henry Shepler and wife Justina Catharina
6. Joh. Peter b. 12 Mar. 1764; sp. Peter Albert and Eva Kettner, both single

This Michael Kehl is probably a son of the immigrant Georg Dietrich Kehl.

John George Kehl nat. Philadelphia 11 Apr. 1751 of Tulpehocken twp., Lancaster co.

266. KELLER, CARL   Weiler =
Alexander & Anne, 1730   6920 Sinsheim, Elsenz
S-H 35, 36

WEILER REFORMED KB:
Hans Martin Keller and wife Margretha nee Löscher had:
Carl b. 14 Apr. 1702
[See Johannes Keller, 1732 immigrant, for complete detail on family.]

Pennsylvania records:
FIRST REFORMED KB, LANCASTER:
Carl Keller and his mother are sp. in Lancaster in 1737.
Carl Keller and his wife had:
1. Carl Frederich bp. 1 May 1737

Charles Keller, Lancaster co., nat. by Act of 19 May 1739

The sandstone church in Weiler—near the Steinsberg, a high promonotory called the "compass of the Kraichgau" on which a fortress, in ruins today, was erected—was Reformed, although the von Venningen family owned the town. Earliest reference to Weiler is dated 1268.

Photo: J. Godshall

267. KELLER, JERG age 20   Weiler =
                                                       6920 Sinsheim, Elsenz
Pleasant, 1732
S-H 99, 100, 101

WEILER REFORMED KB:
m. 11 Jan. 1702 Bastian Keller, son of the late Johannes Keller, and Elisabetha Hildebrand, dau. of J. Hildebrand, shoemaker at "Meltzingen in Hessen." [3508 Melsungen] Children:
  1. Jacob b. 21 Sept (?) 1702
  2. Anna Catharina b. 22 Jan. 1705
  3. Anna Maria b. 7 ___ (?) 1707
  4. Maria Catharina bp. 4 Apr. 1709
  *5. Hans Georg bp. 17 May 1711; conf. 1724
  6. Maria Elisabetha bp. 3 Dec. 1713
  7. Andreas bp. 15 Dec. 1715; d. young
  8. Anna Margretha bp. 9 July 1718
  9. Anna Elisabetha bp. 6 July 1721
  10. Johannes bp. 17 Feb. 1726; d. 20 Aug. 1731

Krebs "Palatine Emigration . . .," p. 26
"Bastian Keller's widow is listed with other citizens of Weiler in a document dated 7 May 1732 as intending to go to the island of Pennsylvania."

Pennsylvania records:
FIRST REFORMED KB, LANCASTER:
Georg Keller and wife had:
  John Carl b. 7 June 1736; one of the sp. was Elisabeth Keller

268. KELLER, JOHANNES age 32   Weiler =
Pleasant, 1732   6920 Sinsheim, Elsenz
S-H 99, 100, 101

WEILER REFORMED KB:
Hans Martin Keller, b. 15 Feb. 1674, son of the late Hans Keller, married 14 Jan.
1698 Margretha, daughter of the late Samuel Löscher, former citizen at Weiler.
(Samuel Lischerd (Lescher, Löscher), son of Christian L. from "Landsburgk, Ber-
ner Geb." [CH 5600 Lenzburg, AG] m. 12 Sept. 1665 Barbara, daughter of Veltin
Meÿer, carpenter at Weÿler. Their daughter Maria Margretha was born in 1670.)
Hans Martin Keller and wife Margretha had:
  1. Maria Elisabetha b. 2 Nov. 1698
  2. Johannes b. 6 May 1700; conf. 1713
  3. Carl b. 14 Apr. 1702; [q.v.]
  4. Maria Barbara b. 25 Feb. 1704, married Joh. Georg Senck, [q.v.]
  5. Martin b. 11 July 1706
  6. Joh. Jacob b. 21 Feb. 1712

Krebs, "Palatine Emigration . . .," p. 26
"The widow of Martin Keller is listed among other citizens of Weiler, in a document
dated May 7, 1732, as intending to go to the island of Pennsylvania."

Pennsylvania records:
FIRST REFORMED KB, LANCASTER:
Carl Keller and his mother are sp. in 1737.

STOEVER'S RECORDS:
m. 19 Apr. 1737 Martin Koeller and Magdalena Leitner, Leacock. [They resided
in Cocalico twp. and his will (23 May 1772/10 June 1772) names children Martin,
George, Conrad, Henry, Elisabeth, Barbara, Magdalena, Margaretta and John.]

LANCASTER WILLS:
Margaret Keller, widow of Martin (4 Aug. 1737/14 Oct. 1737). Children: John,
Mary, wife of George Sevic [Senck?] and Charles [Carl] Exr.: Charles Keller.

269. KEMPFF, CONRAD age 48   Untergimpern =
     KEMPFF, CHRISTIAN age 18   6924 Neckarbischofsheim
     KEMPF, GILBERT age 16
Samuel, 1733
S-H 107, 108, 109, 111, 112 (Other passengers: Anna
Maria, age 38; Frederick, age 8; Hans Peter, age 6;
Catharine, age 2)

Obergimpern Lutheran KB:
Conrad Kempff, citizen and judge at Untergimbern, Reformed, and wife Anna
Maria had:
Joh. Fridrich bp. 28 Feb. 1725
Joh. Petrus bp. 2 Nov. 1727
Anna Catharina b. 15 Dec. 1731
[The baptisms of the two older sons who appear on the ship list are not found in
this record, but may be located in a nearby record since the father is mentioned as
a citizen.]

Pennsylvania records:
New Holland Lutheran KB, Lancaster co.:
Joh. Cunradt Kempff had:
Maria Sophia b. 13 Oct. 1734
Anna Maria, wife of Cunradt Kämpff, sponsor in 1738.
Christian Kempff was a sponsor in 1735 and with his wife again sponsored in 1744.
Christian Kämpff had:
1. Joh. Ludwig b. 23 Feb. 1738; sp. Joh. Gilbert Kempff
2. Elisabetha b. 28 Sept. 1744; sp. Anna Maria Kempff, grandmother

Schultz, *First Settlements of Germans in Maryland* (Frederick, Md., 1896),
pp. 43–4.
Conrad Kemp settled in the neighborhood of the present town of New Market where
he subsequently laid out the village of Kemptown in that vicinity.
Early warrants for land in the vicinity of Frederick, Md.:
Christian Kemp:
10 Feb. 1743, 230 A. called "Despatch"
20 Feb. 1743, 100 A. called "Kemp's Delight"
20 Feb. 1743, 150 A. called "Good Luck"
Mar. 1746, resurvey of "Kemp's Delight"
20 June 1753, resurvey of "Good Luck," 539 A.
4 Aug. 1752, Kemp's Long Meadow, 600 A.
31 Oct. 1754, 25 A., called "Meadow Recovered"
20 June 1753, 82 A., called "Great Desire"
Conrad Kemp:
12 Mar. 1745, 30 A., called "Wilber Sign"
Mar. 1746, 50 A., called "Peace and Quietness"
19 Sept. 1750, 100 A. called "Kemp's Delight"
30 July 1750, 10 A., called "Kemp's Lot"
Gilbert Kemp:
30 July 1750, 50 A. called "Kemp's Discovery"
10 Nov. 1752, 150 A. called "Home House"
Frederick Kemp:
patent 14 Aug. 1754, 55 A., called "Kemp's Bottom"

Conrad Kemp nat. Annapolis 10 Apr. 1743, having received Communion at the
Reformed church of "Monackese"
Christian Kemp and Gilbert Kemp nat. Annapolis 27 Sept. 1746

270. KEPLINGER, HANS GEORG   Berwangen, Kraichgau =
                                    6926 Kirchardt
Jacob, 1749
S-H 417

FAMILY REGISTER BERWANGEN LUTHERAN KB:
Johann Georg Keplinger with 4 children came from Gartach [Neckar Gartach =
7100 Heilbronn]. Joh. Georg Keplinger, weaver, and wife Maria Margaretha went
to the new Land.

Pennsylvania records:
A George Keplinger appears on the first assessment list of Berks Co. (ca. 1752–
1754) in Longswamp twp.

271. KEPPLINGER, LEONHARD   7103 Schwaigern
     KEPPLINGER, JOHANNES
Thistle of Glasgow, 1730
S-H, 31, 33, 34

SCHWAIGERN LUTHERAN KB:
Leonhard Kepplinger and wife Maria Elisabetha had:
    1. Johannes b. 1 June 1713
    2. Joh. Georg b. 27 Feb. 1719
    3. Joh. Paul b. 7 Nov. 1721
    4. Joh. Leonhard b. 20 Jan. 1724
    5. Maria Elisabetha b. 17 Mar. 1726
    6. Christian b. 14 May 1728; d. 20 May 1728

Pennsylvania records:
MOSELEM LUTHERAN KB, BERKS CO:
M. 23 Apr. 1749 Paul Kepplinger, single son of Leonard Kepplinger, and Maria
Catharine Kuhn, single daughter of Christoph Kuhn.
M. 28 Nov. 1749 Joh. Leonhard Kepplinger, Jr., single son of John Leonhard
Kepplinger, Sr., and Anna Maria Rausch, single daughter of Georg Rausch.
Geo. Kepplinger and wife Maria Elisabetha Umbenhauer had:
    1. Johan Leonhard b. Easter 1745; sp. Leonard Kepplinger and wf.
    2. Johan Georg b. Oct. 1746; bp. 14 Nov. 1746
    3. Johannes bp. Dom. Judica (1748?)
Jacob Rausch and wife Maria Elisabeth nee Keplinger had:
    1. Johan Paulus b. 26 Nov. 1747
    2. Jacob bp. Dom. 7 Trin. 1750
    3. Johannes b. 27 Nov. 1751
Paul Keplinger and wife Catharina nee Kuhn had:
    1. Johan Christoph b. 29 June (1750?)
    2. Maria Catharina b. 11 Dec. 1751
    3. Anna Maria b. 13 June 1754
Johan Leonard Keplinger and wife Anna Maria Rausch had:
    1. Johannes b. 3 Jan. 1751

Leonard Keplinger, Cumry tp., Berks co., nat. Philadelphia, 24 September 1766.

272. KESSLER, CASPAR   7519 Eppingen

Neptune, 1751
S-H 469

EPPINGEN REFORMED KB:
m. 10 Apr. 1731 Caspar Kessler, son of Jacob Kessler, and Anna Margaretha
Menzinger, daughter of Martin Menzinger. Children:
1. Margaretha b. 16 Mar. 1732
2. Hans Michel b. 13 Nov. 1733
3. Barbara b. 19 Feb. 1735
4. Catharina b. 25 Nov. 1739
5. Child b. 22 Jan. 1741, died
6. Anna Maria b. 3 Nov. 1742
7. Anna Maria b. 6 May 1745
8. Michael b. 29 Aug. 1748
Caspar Kessler was a brother-in-law of Leonhard Mentzinger, also a passenger on
this ship.

Pennsylvania records:
A Caspar Kessler—Philadelphia co. tax list 1774 Germantown 12 acres. A Michael Kessler on 1779 tax list, Frederick twp., Philadelphia co.

273. KETTNER, JOHANNES age 40   Waldangelloch =
                                          6920 Sinsheim, Elsenz
Charming Betty, 1733
S-H 134, 135, 136 (Other passengers on ship: Feron-
ica, age 34; Georg, age 18; Johan Henrich, age 9;
Henrich Adam, age 8; and Maria, age 11.)

WALDANGELLOCH LUTHERAN KB:
Johannes Kettner was b. 24 Dec. 1683 in "Sächseckher (?) Herrschaft, Nägelstatt"
[DDR—5821 Nägelstedt], son of Michael Kettner and Susanna. (This entry was
written into the margin of the KB page at a later date.)
Veronica Burkhart was bp. 13 Oct. 1692, daughter of Claus Burkhart and Maria
Barbara.
1711, no date given, Claus Burkardt's daughter Veronica married Joh. Kettner.
Johannes Kittner and Veronica had children:
1. Ester Chatharina bp. 5 Mar. 1712; d. 27 Apr. 1713; father is a "Dragoner
   in the hochfürstl. Sachsen Gothieschen Dragones Regmt."
2. Georg Michael bp. 12 Dec. 1714
3. Maria Margaretha bp. 27 Apr. 1719
4. Joh. Heinrich b. 7 Feb. 1723
5. Heinrich Adam b. 15 Oct. 1725

Pennsylvania records:
CHRIST "LITTLE TULPEHOCKEN" KB, BERKS CO:
m. 8 Feb. 1738 John Kittner and Barbara Heinrich.
m. 27 May 1740 George Michael Kittner and Mary Catharine Friedrich
   a dau. Mary Eve b. 7 Apr. 1741

a son John Michael b. 3 Oct. 1746 [Christ, Stouchsburg]; Sp. John Kettner and wife.

Communicants, 1761:

George Michael Kettner   Mary Eve Kettner
Catharina Kettner   Anna Mary Kettner
Mary Margrt. Kettner

Conf. 1761: Elisabeth Kettner age 17 Mary Catharina Kettner age 15

STOEVER'S RECORDS:
Heinrich Kittner (Northkill) had:
1. Johanna Catarina b. 25 Oct. 1750
2. Joh. Jacob b. 29 Mar. 1752
3. Joh. Nicolaus b. 24 Apr. 1754
4. Christina Catarina b. 2 May 1756
5. George Adam b. 12 Oct. 1758

BERKS CO. WILLS:
George Michael Kättner, Tulpehocken, (16 Jan. 1769/1 May 1769). Wife who is not named; eldest son John Michael to have the plantation. Mentions four daughters, only two are named: Anna Margaretha and Maria Eva. Brother Henry Kättner and Valentine Lang, exrs. Wit. by Henry Schädler and Andreas Kraft.

Henry Ketner, Bern (17 Nov. 1789/29 May 1792) Wife Catharina. 10 children: Georg Michael, Frantz, Jacob, Nicholas, John, Catharine, wife of John Yerger, Christina, wife of Henry Ely, Elisabeth, wife of Martin Lengle, Salome, wife of John Hime, and Susanna. Son John and neighbor Abraham Stout, exrs. Letters of adm. to Stout, the other said to be in Virginia. Witnessed by Balzer Umpehocker and Anthony Shomo.

Catharine Ketner, widow, Tulpehocken, (15 July 1796/3 Jan. 1798). To eldest son Georg Michael 7 shillings 6 pence. To daughters Eve, Elisabeth, Catharine, Barbara, and Mary, and heirs of daughter Margaret, dec'd, 5 shillings each. Remainder to be divided among the following 3 children: John, Magdalena and Susanna. Son John, ex.

ZION UNION KB, ORWIGSBURG, SCHUYLKILL CO. (OLD RED CHURCH):
Heinrich Adam Kettner and wife Catharina had:
  Joh. Jacob bp. 21 Apr. 1757
d. 19 Oct. 1805 Henrich Adam Kettner, b. in Europe, aged 80 years and 12 days.
d. 16 Mar. 1806 Katharine Kettner, b. in Europe, aged 72 years.

George Michael Kettner, Tolpohocken twp., Berks co., nat, Reading, 13 May 1768.
Henry Kitner, Bern twp., Berks co., nat. Philadelphia 17 Sept. 1761.

Ittlingen, documented to 789, had two owners in the eighteenth century. Part of it was held by the von Gemmingen-Gemmingen family, part by the von Gemmingen-Hornberg. The Lutheran records there begin in 1665. With a cantilevered upper structure, this building accommodates itself to the street corner on which it stands.

Photo: J. Godshall

274. KILLIAN, MICHAEL

6921 Ittlingen

Dragon, 1749
S-H 414

ITTLINGEN LUTHERAN KB:
Johannes Kilian and Maria Elisabetha had:
Joh. Michael b. 12 Sept. 1732
Communicants' list, dated 1749, of persons who were leaving for Pennsylvania:
Johann Michael Kilian, single

Pennsylvania records:
TRINITY LUTHERAN KB, LANCASTER:
Michael Kilian and Anna Gertraud had:
1. Maria Margaret b. 10 Jan. 1758

275. KIRSTATTER, MARTIN   Obergimpern =
Molly, 1727   6927 Bad Rappenau
S-H 13 ("Martine Kearstuter" on A list)

OBERGIMPERN LUTHERAN KB:
Leonhard Kirstätter and wife Anna Ursula had:
   Johann Martin bp. 5/15 Sept. 1697

NECKARBISCHOFSHEIM LUTHERAN KB:
m. 29 Apr. 1727 Joh. Martin Kirstatter, farmhand, b. in Ober Gimpern, and
Dorothea Frey, b. in Bohnfelt [6927 Bonfeld]. They are going to Pennsylvania.

Pennsylvania records:
STOEVER'S RECORDS AND HILL LUTHERAN KB, NORTH ANNVILLE TWP., LEBANON
CO.:
Martin Kirstaetter (Lebanon) and wife Dorothea had children:
   1. Joh. Martin b. 9 Dec. 1733 (also in Lancaster Lutheran KB)
   2. John b. 3 Sept. 1739
   3. Julianna b. 25 Jan. 1741
m. (2) 19 July 1744 Joh. Martin Kirstätter and Magdalena Huckenberger
m. 11 June 1751 Sebastian Kirstätter and Magdalena Diebler
m. 5 June 1753 Joh. Michael Kirstätter and Maria Dorothea Dietz
m. 1 June 1756 Joh. Martin Kirstätter and Elisabetha Bickel
m. 4 Apr. 1758 Joh. Martin Kümmerling and Elisabetha Kirstätter
m. 21 Jan. 1760 Jacob Ziegler and Juliana Kirstetter
See also Northumberland co. and Snyder co. probate records for later generations.

276. KLEBSATTEL, FRANTZ age 32   6921 Ittlingen
Hope, 1733
S-H 119, 121 (Others on ship: Rosina Klipsegel, 34,
Migel Klipsegel, 9, Hans Jerick 7)

ITTLINGEN LUTHERAN KB:
Frantz Klebsattel and wife Rosina had children:
   1. Catharina Barbara b. 24 Jan. 1728
   2. Georg Franciscus b. 2 May 1729
   3. Johannes b. 6 Jan. 1731
   4. Anna Rosina b. 4 Jan. 1732

Pennsylvania records:
STOEVER'S RECORDS:
Frantz Klebssaddel (Conewago) had:
   Maria b. 17 Feb. 1740, bp. 20 May 1740; sp. Christian Schlaegel and wife
   Maria
Children of Michael Klebsattel are bp. at St. Matthew's Lutheran KB, Hanover,
1746–1754.

_____

Michael Klabsattle, Mt. Pleasant twp., York co., nat. Annapolis, 23 June 1765.

Narrow streets lined with half-timbered buildings in Eppingen preserve its medieval character. In 1573 one Sigmund Klebsattel erected a house on the Metzgergasse (butcher's street) on which his name is still to be seen. Frantz Klebsattel emigrated from nearby Ittlingen in 1733 and made a new home in the Conewago settlement. Descendants there today spell the name Clapsaddle.

277. KLEIN, HEINRICH 6926 Kirchardt

Dragon, 1732
S-H 96, 97, 98 (with brother Jacob Klein)

KIRCHARDT REFORMED KB:
Hans Georg Klein and wife Veronica Sachs(er) had:
    Heinrich b. 13 Mar. 1710
[See Joh. Georg Klein for complete record of the family.]

Pennsylvania records:
STOEVER'S RECORDS:
M. 25 May 1736 Heinrich Klein and Anna Maria Bettlin, Warwick. Their children, recorded in Muddy Creek Lutheran KB and Hill Lutheran KB, Lebanon co. [Quitopahilla] were:
1. Anna b. 26 Feb. 1737; sp. Georg Klein and Anna
2. Sabina b. 17 Oct. 1738
3. Maria Barbara b. 6 Apr. 1740
4. Georg b. 2 Mar. 1742
5. Joh. Georg b. 14 Nov. 1743 [Hill KB]
6. Elisabetha b. ———— 1745; 22 Aug. 1745—death record [Hill KB]
7. Catharina b. 10 Feb. 1747 [Hill KB]
8. Anna Maria b. 15 Nov. 1748 [from burial records, Salem Lutheran KB, Lebanon co.]

9. Conrad [bapt. record not located]

SALEM LUTHERAN KB, LEBANON, PA.:
D. 1 Dec. 1781 Henrich Klein, aged 71 y. 8 mo. and 20 days, bu. 3 Dec. 1781.
The burial records of three of his daughters are also recorded in this KB.

DAUPHIN COUNTY WILLS:
Maria Klein, Derry, widow of Henry, formerly of Lebanon tp. (27 May 1789/19 May 1790). Oldest son George. Son Conrad has had his share. Son-in-law Andrew Schredley mentioned in will and named executor.

Henrick Klein, Lancaster co., nat. Philadelphia 24 Sept. 1741

278. KLEIN, JACOB 6926 Kirchardt
Dragon, 1732
S-H 96, 97, 98 (with brother Heinrich Klein, q.v.)

SINSHEIM LUTHERAN KB:
Hans Georg Klein and wife Veronica Sachs(er) had a son bp. at Kirchardt:
    Hans Jacob b. 16 Aug. 1702
[see Joh. Georg Klein for complete record of the family]
m. 18 June 1726 Joh. Jacob Klein, son of Georg Klein, and Veronica, daughter of Joh. Jacob Meÿer. Children:
    1. Catharina b. 19 Apr. 1727
    2. Joh. Georg b. 5 Jan. 1729; d. 1731
    3. Anna b. 14 May 1731; d. 1731

Pennsylvania records:
PENNA. PATENTS:
AA:I:99: Warrant 23 Jan. 1737 to Jacob Klean (Clyne) 176¾ acres in Warwick twp., Lancaster co. Jacob Klean sold on 21 Jan. 1754 to Conrad Merk [his son-in-law] to whom patent was issued 7 Oct. 1760.

EMANUEL LUTHERAN KB, BRICKERVILLE, LANCASTER CO.:
(also recorded in the Muddy Creek KB)
Jacob Klein had:
    4. Joh. Georg b. 4 Jan. 1734; sp. Joh. Georg Klein
    5. Anna b. 9 May 1736; sp. Johannes Bender and wife

MORAVIAN KB, LITITZ: (PA, SECOND SERIES, IX:142)
m. 10 Nov. 1747 Conrad Merk and Catharina Klein

NORTHAMPTON CO. WILLS:
George Klein (q.v.)—one of the heirs named in his will was "Catharina Merk, wife of Conrad Merk, and daughter of my brother Jacob, deceased."

279. KLEIN, JOH. GEORG 6926 Kirchardt
Prelist, ca. 1726/27

KIRCHARDT REFORMED KB AND SINSHEIM LUTHERAN KB:
Hans Georg Klein, b. 31 Dec. 1655, son of Hans Albrecht (Albert) Klein and Anna Catharina (Reckner) Klein.
Hans Georg Klein m. 5 Oct. 1700 Veronica Sachs(er), daughter of the late Hans Sachs(er), a citizen of Richen. Children:
    1. Anna Elisabeth bp. 7 July 1701
    2. Hans Jacob b. 16 Aug. 1702 [q.v.]

3. Joh. Georg b. 12 Mar. 1705
4. Elisabetha b. 20 Sept. 1707; m. 7 May 1726 Michael Weidler [q.v.]
5. Heinrich b. 13 Mar. 1710 [q.v.]
6. Hans Michael b. 5 Oct. 1712 [q.v.]
7. Barbara bp. 29 June 1715
8. Anna Catharina b. 5 Feb. 1718 [Note: this date given in Sinsheim Lutheran KB; the Kirchardt KB gives the date 5 Feb. 1717, but the entry appears to have been added at a later date.]
9. Anna or Anna Maria [Sinsheim KB: b. 8 Apr. 1721; Kirchardt KB: bp. 4 Apr. 1720]
10. Leonhard b. 3 Aug. 1725 [q.v.]

Pennsylvania records:
Joh. Georg Klein and wife (not named) sp. 1730 at Trinity Lutheran, Lancaster, a child of Joh. Georg Bart.
Joh. Georg Klein and wife Anna were sp. in 1735 and 1738, Trinity Lutheran, Lancaster. They also appear frequently as sp. in the Muddy Creek KB.
Georg Klein, b. 12 Mar. 1705 in Kirchardt, son of Hans Georg and Veronica Klein, m. (1) Anna Bender; m. (2) Dorothea Davis. He ceded his farm to the Moravians to found the town of Lititz.

GUIDE TO THE OLD MORAVIAN CEMETERY OF BETHLEHEM; PA., (PENNSYLVANIA GERMAN SOCIETY PROCEEDINGS XXI (1912), P. 9, 77.
Row 1—married men: John George Klein, b. in Kirchardt, Palatinate 1705, d. Bethlehem, Pa. 1783. M. Anna Bender. Came to Pa. 1727.
Row 8—married women: Anna Klein, b. in Kirchardt in the Palatinate 1701, d. 1777. Maiden name Bender. M. George Klein.

"MORAVIAN GRAVEYARDS OF LITITZ, PA."

PUBLICATIONS OF MORAVIAN HISTORICAL SOCIETY, 7 (1904), P. 240
Dorothea Klein, nee Davis, b. 28 Aug. 1721 "on the Schuylkill;" d. 23 July 1783. Lived in Bethlehem but came to Lititz to have the treatment of Dr. Fahnestock of Ephrata. Her third husband was George Klein, popularly known as the founder of Lititz.

NORTHAMPTON CO. WILLS:
George Klein, Bethlehem (11 Apr. 1783/29 July 1783). Wife Dorothy; brothers: Henry, Michael and Leonard Kline. Kinswomen: Anna Bender and Catharine Nerbis (?). Daughter of deceased brother Jacob, Catharina Merk, wife of Conrad Merk. Sister: Elisabeth Weidler of Lancaster co. Children of deceased sister, Anna Fautz [Pfautz]. Friend: Daniel Neubert and wife. Exrs: wife Dorothy Kline and brother Leonard Kline; Friend, John Christian Hasse of Bethlehem.

George Kline, Lancaster co., nat. by Act of 19 May 1739.

280. KLEIN, JOH. GEORG   Berwangen, Kraichgau =
                                          6926 Kirchardt
1738
[Not in ship's lists. There is a Georg Klein who arrived
in 1738, but he is not this Georg Klein.]

BERWANGEN LUTHERAN KB:
m. 6 Aug. 1737 Joh. Georg Klein, tailor, son of Joh. Georg Klein, citizen in
Kirchardt, and Regina, daughter of Leonhardt Ziegler. Notation in Family Register:
they left 8 May 1738 for Pennsylvania.

KIRCHARDT REFORMED KB:
m. 22 Jan. 1709 Hans Görg Klein, son of Wolffgang Klein, and Anna, daughter of
Heinrich Müller of Riechen [= Richen = 7519 Eppingen]. Their son:
    Hans Görg b. 19 Mar. 1711

Pennsylvania records:
TRINITY LUTHERAN KB, LANCASTER:
Joh. Georg Klein had, born after the father's death:
    Joh. Gerog b. __ Nov. 1738; bp. 4 Mar. 1739; sp. Georg Klein and wife
    Anna

MUDDY CREEK LUTHERAN KB, LANCASTER CO.:
m. 4 Dec. 1739 Andreas Wolff and Regina Klein
[Evidently this is the widow of Joh. Georg Klein]

281. KLEIN, JOH. JACOB   6926 Kirchardt
Ship data not certain; several in S-H

KIRCHARDT REFORMED AND SINSHEIM LUTHERAN KB:
Hans Wolfgang Klein (born 15 Jan. 1660, son of Hans Albrecht Klein) and wife
Anna Maria had:
    Hans Jacob bp. 8 Nov. 1697 at Kirchardt
m. 16 Jan. 1720 Joh. Jacob Klein, son of Wolfgang Klein of Kirchardt, and
Catharina, daughter of Joh. Georg Häring. The bp. record of only one child located:
Jacob Klein and Catharina had:
    Gottfried b. 11 Nov. 1730; sp. Gottfried Lautermilch and Barbara Klein

Pennsylvania records:
TRINITY LUTHERAN KB, LANCASTER, PA.:
M. 25 Feb. 1752 Gottfried Klein, son of Jacob Klein from the town, and Rosina
Geisert, daughter of Melchior Geisert, in Dennigal [Donegal] They had:
    1. Joh. Jacob b. 29 Oct. 1758
    2. Joh. Georg b. 9 June 1764
    3. Eva Rosina b. 5 Nov. 1766
    4. Joh. Christian b. 23 Apr. 1769

LANCASTER CO. WILLS:
Gottfried Klein, Lancaster Borough, (11 Feb. 1772/19 Oct. 1772). Wife Rosina,
children: George, Christian, Rosina, Elisabeth, Philipina and Catharina.

LANCASTER CO. DEEDS:
C:30; 27 Nov. 1750—King St., Lancaster. Jacob Klyne, of Lancaster borough, wagonmaker, and wife Catharina to George Klyne. (Jacob had acquired the property in 1747.)

282. KLEIN, LEONARD   6926 Kirchardt

Ship data not located; perhaps prelist, ca. 1726/27 with brother Georg, or 1732 with brothers Jacob and Heinrich.

KIRCHARDT REFORMED KB:
Hans Georg Klein and wife Veronica Sachs(er) had:
    Leonhard b. 3 Aug. 1725
[See Joh. Georg Klein for complete record of family]

Pennsylvania records:
MORAVIAN CHURCH, LITITZ, PA.:
M. 16 Dec. 1749 Leonhard Klein and Rosina Waidlin.

LANCASTER MORAVIAN BURIAL RECORDS:
D. 2 July 1793 Leonhard Klein, b. July 1725 at Kirchardt, m. 16 Dec. 1749 to Rosina, nee Waidlin. No children.

Amalia Rosina Klein, nee Waidel (widow) d. 12 Mar. 1795, aged 62 ys. and nearly 4 m. B. 14 Nov. 1732 at Addersbach in the Palatinate. Parents were Master John Michael Waidel, schoolmaster at Addersbach, and Anna Barbara, nee Vogler. M. 1749 to Leonard Klein, saddler, who d. 2 July 1793.

LANCASTER CO. WILLS:
Leonard Klein, Borough of Lancaster, (14 Nov. 1792/22 July 1793). Wife Rosina; nephew John Fowtz; Mary Herchensleger; Jane Pastor, wife of Peter Pastor; children of kinsman Stephen Martin: Jacob, Elisabeth, Catharine and Margaret Martin; Catharine Glatz, daughter of kinsman Jacob Glatz. Balance of estate: ½ to living children of my brother Henry Klein; ½ to living children of my deceased brother Michael Klein. Exrs: wife Rosina and kinsman Stephan Martin [he was m. to Leonard's niece, Catharina Weidler.]

_____

Leonard Cline, Lancaster tp., Lancaster co., nat. Philadelphia 24 Sept. 1760.

283. KLEIN, MICHAEL   6926 Kirchardt

Ship data not located; possibly prelist, ca. 1726/27 with brother Georg Klein. One Michael Klein, age 22, on *Charming Nancy*, 1738; age possibly incorrect.

KIRCHARDT REFORMED KB:
Hans Georg Klein and wife Veronica Sachs(er) had:
    Hans Michael b. 5 Oct. 1712
[See Joh. Georg Klein for complete record of the family.]

MUDDY CREEK AND WARWICK LUTHERAN KB:
Michael Klein (Warwick) had:
  1. Anna b. 21 June 1741; sp. Georg Klein and Anna
  2. Georg b. 20 Aug. 1742
  3. Leonhardt b. Nov. 1746; bp. 1 Jan. 1749 at Emanuel Lutheran, Warwick
     twp.
  4. Magdalena b. Aug. 1748; bp. 1 Jan. 1749
  5. Nicolaus b. 10 Dec. 1749
  6. Maria Barbara b. 25 Apr. 1756
Lancaster co. Orphans' Court records, 28 Feb. 1783 and various release deeds
indicate that his wife was Dorothy, and there were additional children in the family.

284. KLEM, HANS ADAM   6921 Ittlingen

Francis & Elizabeth, 1742
S-H 328

ITTLINGEN LUTHERAN KB:
Johann Conrad Klemm [q.v.] and wife Maria Catharina had:
  Joh. Adam b. 5 Mar. 1718

Pennsylvania records:
WARWICK (BRICKERVILLE) LUTHERAN KB:
Adam Klemm has a son Valentin, b. 26 Apr. 1744

285. KLEMM, GEORG PHILIPP   Adersbach =

Snow *Francis & Ann*, 1741   6920 Sinsheim, Elsenz
S-H 292

ADERSBACH LUTHERAN KB:
Adam Clemm and wife Anna Wilhelmina had:
  Georgius Adamus b. 20 Nov. 1686
Georg Adam Klemm and wife Regina had:
  1. Maria Catharina b. 27 June 1714
  2. Anna Elisabetha b. 6 Nov. 1719
  3. Georg Philipp b. 28 June 1725

American records:
FREDERICK, MD. LUTHERAN BURIALS:
Bu. 19 Aug. 1771 Georg Philipp Klemm, b. 28 Jan. 1725 at Aderspach under
Hochfreyherr Baron Schmiedberg's rule. M. 1747 Margaretha Schweinhart and
had 4 sons and 5 daughters, of whom 2 daughters d. before the father. In his last
years, he was a drunkard and d. of pains in his limbs Aug. 17. Aged 46 y. 6 mo.
19 days.
Buried 24 Mar. 1804 Margaret Klemm, b. 1734. Parents Georg Schweinhard and
Mary Catha. Married to a man named Klemm. Had 4 sons and 5 daughters. Left
behind 3 sons and 3 daughters. Became sick with dropsy and d. 22 Mar. at 7:30
p.m., aged 75 y. 5 mo. 23 days.

The sister of Georg Philipp Klemm, Maria Catharina, b. 27 June 1714, married Michal Spohn [q.v.]

George Clem, Frederick co., Md., nat. Annapolis, April 1749.

286. KLEMM, JOH. CONRAD   6921 Ittlingen
KLEMM, JOH. DAVID

Restauration, 1747
S-H 366

ITTLINGEN LUTHERAN KB:
Joh. Conrad Klemm and his first wife Maria Agnes (nee Schlötz?) had:
1. Joh. Wilhelm b. 25 Mar. 1704
2. Joh. Conrad b. 28 Aug. 1707
3. Eva Margaretha b. 25 Aug. 1710; she m. Joh. Jacob Roth and had 7 children. She died in Ittlingen 20 Jan. 1748, and her burial record states that she is "a daughter of Joh. Conrad Klemm who lives in Pennsylvania."
4. Wolfgang Friederich b. 3 Aug. 1713
Johann Conrad Klemm and his second wife Maria Catharina had:
5. Joh. David b. 28 May 1717
6. Joh. Adam b. 5 Mar. 1718 [q.v.]
7. Maria Catharina b. _____ Dec. 1719; d. 1746
8. Maria Christina b. 23 Feb. 1722
9. Anna Maria b. 6 May 1724
10. Anna Sophia b. 5 May 1726
11. Anna Margaretha b. 21 Apr. 1728
12. Joh. Valentin b. 23 June 1729
13. Agnes Maria b. 23 Aug. 1731
14. Anna Catharina b. 22 Mar. 1733
Johann David Klemm (b. 28 May 1717) and wife Anna Maria (nee Gomar from [7519] Adelshofen) had:
1. Joh. Dietrich b. 10 Nov. 1741
2. Maria Margaretha b. 5 Nov. 1743
3. Anna Maria b. 20 Oct. 1744; d. young
4. Joh. David b. 11 Apr. 1746; d. young
5. Joh. Christoph b. 21 Mar. 1747; d. 1747
Communicants' lists, 1747 on XIX Die Dom. Vocen. Jucunditatis, "before going to the new land":
Conrad Klemm, Sr. and wife
David Klemm and wife
Maria Christina Klemm
Anna Maria Klemm
Anna Catharina Klemm
Joh. Valentin Klemm

Pennsylvania records:
TRAPPE LUTHERAN KB, MONTGOMERY CO.:
M. 2 Feb. 1752 Johannes Schilling and Anna Maria Glimmin (Klemm), former

servants of Rev. H. M. Muhlenberg.
M. 4 July 1756 Jürg Dressler and Catharina Klemm.
Both couples had children bp. there and they sponsor each other's children. Joh.
Conrad Clem is a sponsor in 1753 for a child of the Schillings.
Bu. 16 Nov. 1754 Johan Conrad Klem, age 76 y., a native of Ottlingen.

NEW HANOVER LUTHERAN KB:
Joh. David and Anna Maria Klemm had:
    Maria Catharina b. 4 Sept. 1748; sp. Anna Maria Klemm and Catharina
    Schmidt.

287. KLETLE, HANS ADAM   Adersbach
                                                      Hasselbach =
William, 1737
                                                  6920 Sinsheim, Elsenz
S-H 194, 195, 196

ADERSBACH LUTHERAN KB:
Georg Kletle(r) and wife Barbara had:
    Hans Adam b. 15 Feb. 1687
m. 11 Nov. 1710 Hans Adam Klettlin, son of the late Georg Klettlin of Hasselbach,
and Anna Catharina, daughter of Hans Michael Georg, citizen and inhabitant.
Hans Adam Klettle(r) and wife Catharina of Hasselbach had:
    1. Catharina b. 21 Oct. 1711
    2. Anna Margaretha b. 27 Sept. 1713
    3. Eva Magdalena b. 11 Apr. 1718
    4. Maria Elisabetha b. 8 Sept. 1724

Pennsylvania records:
TRINITY LUTHERAN KB, LANCASTER:
Catharina Klettel, widow, d. 12 Sept. 1760, aged 72 y. 6 m.

FIRST REFORMED KB, LANCASTER:
Georg Henry Peter's wife is named as Margaret Glettler in 1740.
Georg Michael Kerber is also mentioned in this record in 1740 with wife Anna
Magdalena Kiettli.

288. KLINGMANN, GEORG age 24   Obergimpern =
                                                      6927 Bad Rappenau
Samuel, 1732
S-H 59, 60, 63, 64 [with Thoredea Klingman age 25]

OBERGIMPERN LUTHERAN KB:
m. 23 Apr. 1731 Georg Klingmann, son of Leonhard Klingmann, citizen at [6924
Neckar] Bischoffsheim, and Anna Dorothea, daughter of Georg Schuhmann, citizen at Rappenau.

NECKARBISCHOFSHEIM LUTHERAN KB:
A Leonhardt Klingmann, son of the late Ludwig Klingmann, m. 20 Apr. 1704
Maria Barbara, daughter of the late Martin Riss (elsewhere Ries). The baptisms of
six of their children were located, but no Georg is listed.

Pennsylvania records:
Arthur K. Klingaman, *The Klingaman Family History and Genealogy* (1973), indicates that there was a relationship between this Georg Klingmann and the other Hans Jeorg Klingemann who also arrived on this ship with wife Katharina and son Pieter. They lived for a time near New Hanover [Montgomery co.] and then moved to Allemangel [Berks co.] The same source indicates that Georg and Dorothea Klingmann joined the Pequea colony [Lancaster co.] and later went to Manchester twp. [York co.].

289. KNECHT, JOHANNES

Reihen =
6920 Sinsheim, Elsenz

Restauration, 1747
S-H 365

REIHEN REFORMED KB:
Herr Peter Knecht, schoolteacher at Reihen, and wife Anna Barbara had:
Johannes bp. 1 June 1704
m. 6 June 1731 Johannes Knecht, son of the late Peter Knecht, schoolteacher, and Anna Maria, daughter of the late Jonas Dörr. Children:
1. Catharina bp. 11 _____ ? 1733
2. Maria Barbara bp. 20 Mar. 1735
3. Joh. Jacob bp. 15 Dec. 1737
4. Joh. Görg bp. 20 May 1740
5. Johannes bp. 3 Feb. 1743
6. Hans Michel bp. 10 July 1745
Krebs, "Palatine Emigration . . ., p. 33. Johannes Knecht permitted to leave in 1747 without payment.

Pennsylvania records:
LOWER SAUCON CHURCH, NORTHAMPTON CO.:
Bu. 24 Mar. 1796 Mary Magdalena Knecht, wife of John Knecht, age 82 y., 1 mo.
Bu. 12 Mar. 1798 John Knecht, age 93 years 9 mo.

ST. JOHN'S LUTHERAN KB, EASTON:
Bu. 21 Feb. 1822 Johan Georg Knecht, son of Johann Knecht and wife Anna Maria; b. 5 May 1740 in Rhein Pfalz, Europe. Married Anna Maria Moritz 1 Feb. 1775. Had 3 children, one is deceased.
Bu. 11 May 1811 Rosina Muller, daughter of John Knecht, age 60 y., 3 mo., 23 days, cancer.

John Knight, Lower Saucon tp., Northampton, co., nat. Philadelphia, Fall 1765.

290. KNECHT, JÖRG PETER age 31

Reihen =
6920 Sinsheim, Elsenz

Pink *Plaisance*, 1732
S-H 78, 81, 82

REIHEN REFORMED KB:
Herr Peter Knecht, schoolteacher at Reihen, and wife Anna Barbara had:
Georg Peter bp. 26 Nov. 1702; conf. 1718, age 16.

m. 19 Aug. 1726 *Joh*. Peter Knecht, son of the late Herr Peter Knecht, Reformed schoolteacher, a shoemaker, and Anna Eva, daughter of the late Görg Michael Lampel, former citizen at Ehrstatt. [Ehrstädt = 6920 Sinsheim] *Görg* Peter Knecht, shoemaker, and wife Anna Eva had:

1. Joh. Leonhardt b. 23 Aug. 1728; d. young
2. Johannes b. 5 Feb. 1730; d. young
3. Görg b. 19 June 1731; d. young

Pennsylvania records:
NEW GOSHENHOPPEN REFORMED KB, MONTGOMERY CO.:
m. 22 June 1736 Georg Peter Knecht, shoemaker, and Christine Hertzel of Skippack. Children:

1. Hans Leonhardt bp. 11 Apr. 1737 at New Goshenhoppen; Sp. Hans Leonhardt Herzel and Anna Maria Galmann

WILLIAMS TWP. KB, NORTHAMPTON CO.:
2. Johann Georg b. 1 June 1740

Peter Knight nat. Philadelphia 24 Sept. 1757

291. KNÖRTZER, JOH. BALTHES age 37   Treschklingen =
Charming Nancy, 1738   6927 Bad Rappenau
S-H 246, 247, 248

TRESCHKLINGEN LUTHERAN KB: (KB STARTS (1732)
Joh. Balthes Knörtzer and wife Maria Dorothea nee Maÿer had:
1. Eva Barbara b. 10 Jan. 1733
2. Johann Georg b. 29 Mar. 1735
3. Christina b. 14 Sept. 1736

Pennsylvania records:
Balthaser Knörzer and wife appear in the Christ Lutheran KB, York, as sponsors in 1740.
1742—Balthasar Knoertzer and wife Anna Catharina nee Wolff are sponsors at First Reformed, Lancaster.
In 1743, Baltzer Knürtzer and wife Maria Catharina appear as sponsors for several children.
Georg Christoph Knörtzer and wife Anna Marcreta (Reformed) have two children bp. in 1747 and 1748.

DOVER LUTHERAN KB, YORK CO:
Maria Catharina Obb, born 9 Feb. 1725 in "Troschlingen in Gemingen." Father: Joh. Balser Knörtzer Mother: Maria Dorothea. Came in 1738 with her father to America. The mother d. at sea. In 1746 she m. Peter Opp, Reformed. They had 13 children, 12 are living. She d. 12 Feb. 1770, age 45 years and 3 days. Bu. in our churchyard. (One child bp. at Christ Lutheran, York; others are recorded in Salem Reformed KB (Strayer's) Dover twp. York co.)

YORK CO. WILLS:
Baltzer Knertzer, Yorktown (15 Aug. 1767/18 Sept. 1769). Wife: Catharina. Chil-

dren: Georg, Baltzer, Catharina, Dorothea, wife of Andrew Miller. Stepson: Andrew Gruss; Grandchildren: Nicholas, Andrew, Baltzer, Margaret and Catharina, children of son Georg.

Balthazar Knoertzer Dover twp., York co., nat. Philadelphia 25 Sept. 1751.

292. KOBER, BERNHARD
Francis & Elizabeth, 1742
S-H 327

Berwangen, Kraichgau =
6926 Kirchardt

BERWANGEN LUTHERAN KB:
Wolf Bernhard Kober, son of Wolf Kober, m. (1) 20 Jan. 1691 Anna Angelica, widow of Joh. Peter Kober. She d. in 1706 and he m. (2) 2 June 1707 Anna Catharina, daughter of Hans Leonhard Stein. One of the children of the second marriage was:
    Wolfgang Bernhart b. 29 Oct. 1713. "Is in Pennsylvania."

Pennsylvania records:
TRINITY LUTHERAN KB, LANCASTER:
Bernhard and Elisabetha Cober had:
1. Andreas bp. 26 July 1749, five months old.

293. KOBER, DIETRICH
Thistle, 1730
S-H 32, 33, 34

Berwangen, Kraichgau =
6926 Kirchardt

BERWANGEN LUTHERAN KB:
Family Register and KB:
Georg Kober and wife Eva Catharina nee Hocker from [7519] Gemmingen had:
1. Paul b. 1 Apr. 1703
2. Dietrich b. 20 June 1708. "Is in Pennsylvania."
3. Georg b. 7 July 1711
m. 25 Apr. 1730 Dietrich Kober, step-son of H. Stuber, and Susanna Catharina Hubelin from Ringheim (?) [probably 6961 Rinschheim], daughter of Conrad Hubelin. "Left after the marriage for Pennsylvania."
Georg Kober, father of the immigrant, d. 2 Sept. 1714 and on 26 Nov. 1715 his widow, Eva Catharina, m. Hans Georg Stieber, son of the late Paul Stieber from Eppingen.

Pennsylvania records:
STOEVER'S RECORDS (ALSO HILL LUTHERAN KB, NORTH ANNVILLE TWP., LEBANON CO.):
Joh. Dieterich Kober had:
1. Anna Elisabetha b. 12 May 1734
2. Joh. Egidius b. 18 Dec. 1738
3. Joh. Georg b. 27 Jan. 1741
4. Anna Margaretha b. 13 May 1743
5. Joh. Michael b. 30 Nov. 1748

294. KOBER, PAUL   7103 Schwaigern

Richmond, 1764
S-H 696

SCHWAIGERN LUTHERAN KB:
m. 22 Nov. 1712 Elias Kober, son of Elias Kober, cooper, and Maria Elisabetha, daughter of Michael Dieter, the old "Anwald". Elias Kober and Anna Maria had:
Joh. Paul b. 25 Jan. 1717
Paulus Kober and wife Elisabetha Catharina had one ch. bp. at Schwaigern:
Susanna Catharina b. 9 Mar. 1742; bp. 10 Mar. 1742

Pennsylvania records:
ST. MICHAEL'S AND ZION LUTHERAN KB, PHILADELPHIA:
Bu. 27 Aug. 1794 Paul Kober, son of Elias Kober and Anna Maria; b. in "Schweigen by Heilbron" 25 Jan. 1717. M. (1) 7 Feb. 1742 Elisabetha Catharina Duffing; had one daughter by first m. M. (2) 8 June 1760 Maria Barbara Herman. Age 77 y. 7 mo. 1 day

Paul Kober, Philadelphia, nat., Philadelphia 10 Apr. 1761

295. KOBERSTEIN, JOH. GEORG   6921 Zuzenhausen

Osgood, 1750
S-H' 446

GAUANGELLOCH LUTHERAN KB:
Hans Jacob Koberstein, apprentice tile-maker, and wife Maria Magdalena had:
Hans Georg b. 3 Apr. 1726

DAISBACH LUTHERAN KB:
m. 17 June 1749 at Zuzenhausen Georg Koberstein, son of the late Joh. Jacob Koberstein, master tile-maker in Zuzenhausen, and Anna Catharina, daughter of the late Johannes Glassbrenner, inhabitant.

ZUZENHAUSEN LUTHERAN KB:
m. 22 June 1749 Joh. Georg Koberstein, tile-maker, and Anna Catharina Glassbrenner from Daispach [= 6923 Waibstadt].

Krebs, Palatine Emigrants . . . ," p. 36.
Johann Georg Koberstein of Zuzenhausen (Kreis Heidelberg) applied in 1750, along with Johann Georg Ludwig of the same place, to go to the so-called New Land with his wife Anna Catharina. He had to pay 3 florins.

American records:
Georg Koberstein nat. Baltimore 7 Sept. 1768, having received Communion in the Lutheran church of "Baltimore Town."

296. KOCHENDORFFER, ANDREAS
Loyal Judith, 1732
S-H 89, 90, 92

Hoffenheim =
6920 Sinsheim, Elsenz

HOFFENHEIM LUTHERAN KB:
Andreas Kochendorffer from "Belgesthal in the Graffl. Kirchberg [= Bölgental = 7181 Satteldorf] Hohenloischen" and his wife Appolonia had:
    Anna Maria bp. 11 May 1718
No further record here.

Pennsylvania records:
CHRIST "LITTLE TULPEHOCKEN" KB, BERKS CO:
m. 12 June 1739 Andrew Kochendoerfer and Justina Catherine Keyser [q.v.]
Children:
    1. Andrew b. 23 June 1742; sp. Andrew Craft and wife
    2. Geo. Philip b. 8 Apr. 1746
    3. John Michael b. 6 Apr. 1747 [bp. at Christ Lutheran, Stouchsburg]

297. KÖHLER, GABRIEL
Francis & Elizabeth, 1742
S-H 327, 329

Massenbach =
7103 Schwaigern

MASSENBACH LUTHERAN KB:
m. 28 Jan. 1738 Gabriel Köhler, apprentice weaver from Bonfeldt [6927 Bonfeld], and Anna Elisabetha, daughter of Joh. Friderich Poffenmeier, inhabitant. They had:
    1. Catharina Barbara b. 12 Oct. 1738
    2. Christina Margretha b. 4 May 1740
    3. Anna Margretha b. 10 Oct. 1741

Pennsylvania records:
DILLINGERSVILLE LUTHERAN KB:
Gabriel Köhler and wife Anna Elisabeth sp. children of Philipp Stephan Poppenmeier in 1749 and 1750.
d. 27 Mar. 1752 Anna Elisabetha, Gabriel Köhler's wife, bu. on the 29th. She was b. 5 May 1717.
m. 28 Nov. 1752 Gabriel Köhler and Elisabetha Rohrbachin, daughter of Jacob Rohrbach.
Gabriel Köhler and wife Maria Elisabetha had:
    4. Michael b. 27 Sept.; bp. 12 Nov. 1753; sp. Michael Helffrich and Elisabetha Poppenmeier
    5. Margrethe b. 20 Nov. 1754
    6. Joh. Peter bp. _____1756 (no other date)
    7. Johannes b. 12 May; bp. 25 June 1758
Communicants:
21 May 1750 Gabriel Köhler
8 Dec. 1750 Anna Elisabetha Köhlern, Gabriel's wife

298. KÖHLER, JOHANNES

Charming Nancy, 1737
S-H 189, 192, 194

Treschklingen =
6927 Bad Rappenau

TRESCHKLINGEN LUTHERAN KB:
m. 29 Jan. 1732 Johannes Köhler, tailor, son of the late Joh. Ludwig Köhler of Bonfeld, and Eva Maria, dau. of Georg Balthasar Steiner, "Gerichtsverwandten" and baker.

Pennsylvania records:
EMMAUS MORAVIAN KB:
Johannes Koehler, b. in Brettach in Wuertemberg 6 May 1708, son of Ludwig Koehler and Catharina, nee Eberle. On the last of February 1732 he m. in "Dreslingen" and they came together to Pa. where they arrived at Philadelphia 11 Oct. 1737. His wife Eva Maria was b. in Gregau in Swabia on 23 Sept. 1708. Her parents were Balthasar and Elisabetha Steiner. Children:
 1. Maria Elisabeth b. 13 Nov. 1735; bp. in Bonfeld; d. young
 2. Georg Friederich b. 15 Sept. 1737; bp. in Germantown
 3. Georg Balthasar b. 13 Feb. 1740; d. 7 Aug. 1758
 4. Johannes b. 30 June 1742, d. shortly after birth
 5. Anna Catharina b. 6 Aug. 1744 in Salisbury
 6. Leonhard b. 10 Aug. 1746
 7. Elisabeth b. 11 Sept. 1749
 8. Maria Magdalena b. 21 Sept. 1751
 9. Christina b. 29 Sept. 1753
They later appear in the Heidelberg Moravian KB, Berks co., Pa.

QUITOPEHILLE MORAVIAN KB:
d. 3 Sept. 1786 Eva Maria Koehler, nee Steiner, b. 23 Sept. 1708 in "Drestlingen," 3 hours from Heidelberg. m. 1732 Joh. Koehler. Had 11 children, 5 are living. Aged 78 y. less 20 d.

299. KOLB, CONRAD age 34

Pleasant, 1732
S-H 99, 100, 101

6922 Meckesheim

MECKESHEIM REFORMED KB:
Johannes Kolb, miller, and wife Margaretha had:
     Johannes Conradus b. 31 Mar. 1697
m. 13 Jan. 1722 Conrad Kolb, citizen, and Anna Elisabetha Gerichts (in) from Mostbron [Moosbrunn = 6936 Schönbrunn, Baden]. Children:
 1. Joh. Conrad b. 20 May 1723
 2. Anna Barbara b. 14 Nov. 1724
 3. Anna Elisabetha b. 6 Apr. 1726
 4. Joh. Rudolff b. 14 Apr. 1731

Pennsylvania records:
NEW GOSHENHOPPEN REFORMED KB, MONTGOMERY CO.:
Conrad Kolb was a sp. in 1732

Conrad Kolb and wife Maria Barbara had:
1. Jacob Fridrich bp. 11 Apr. 1737
2. Joh. Adam bp. 31 Dec. 1738

BLUMER'S RECORD (Northampton —Lehigh co.):
d. 15 Apr. 1781 Conrad Kolb, age 84 y. 18 days

Conrath Kolb, Philadelphia co., nat. by Act of 19 May 1739.
Conrad Kolb, Richmond twp., Berks co., nat. Philadelphia Fall 1765.

300. KOLB, GEORG MICHAEL   6922 Meckesheim

Robert & Alice, 1738
S-H 212, 214, 215

MECKESHEIM AND EPFENBACH REFORMED KBs:
Hans Adam Kolb and wife Maria Eva had:
    Georg Michel b. 17 Jan. 1709
m. 21 Sept. 1733 Georg Michael Kolb from Meckesheim and Anna Elisabetha
Meÿer from [6921] Spechbach. Children:
1. Maria Friederica bp. 22 Nov. 1733 at Epfenbach
2. Anna Eva bp. 14 Oct. 1736 at Meckesheim

Pennsylvania records:
NEW GOSHENHOPPEN REFORMED KB, MONTGOMERY CO.:
Georg Michael Kolb and wife Anna Elisabetha had:
3. Michael bp. 24 Oct. 1739
4. Joseph bp. 30 Aug. 1741
5. A son bp. 1 Sept. 1745
6. Jörg Michael bp. 1 Nov. 1746
Bu. 16 Feb. 1789 Georg Michael Kolb, aged 81 y. 25 days

George Michael Kolb, New Hanover twp., Philadelphia co., nat. Philadelphia
Sept. 1761.

301. KOLB, JOH. PETER   6922 Meckesheim

Robert & Alice, 1738
S-H 212, 214, 215

MECKESHEIM REFORMED KB:
Adam Kolb and wife Maria Eva had:
    Johann Peter b. 15 June 1721
He appears on the ship's list with his brothers Melchior and Georg Michael Kolb.

Pennsylvania records:
A Peter Kolb (Colb) and Mathias Colb appear on the first assessment list of Berks
co. (ca. 1752–1754) in Ruscombmanor twp. A Stophel Colb appears on the same
list, single.

302. KOLB, MELCHIOR

6922 Meckesheim

Robert & Alice, 1738
S-H 212, 214, 215

MECKESHEIM REFORMED KB:
Joh. Adam Kolb and wife Maria Eva had:
    Johann Melchior b. 19 Jan. 1712

Pennsylvania records:
NEW GOSHENHOPPEN REFORMED KB, MONTGOMERY CO.:
Melchior Kolb and wife Catharina had:
    Anna Catharina bp. 26 Oct. 1759
m. 2 Oct. 1770 Melchior Kolb, widower, of New Goshenhoppen, and Anna Maria
Stettler, widow, of Falkner Swamp.

Melchr. Colp, Upper Hanover twp., Philadelphia co., nat. Philadelphia without
taking an oath, Fall 1765.

303. KOLB, PHILIPP

7135 Wiernsheim

1744

Häfnerhaslach =
7123 Sachsenheim

SCHLUCHTERN LUTHERAN KB:
m. 14 Apr. 1744 Philipp Kolb, son of the late Jacob Kolb, citizen and farmer at
[7135] Wiernsheim, Maulbronner Closter Ambtes, in Herzogthum Wurttemberg, a
farm hand, and Christina, dau. of Christoph Heck, citizen and wagon maker at
Häfnerhassloch [= 7123 Sachsenheim, Wurt.]. The marriage entry adds they want
to go to Pennsylvania: "welcher willens in Pensilvaniam zu ziehen."
[See also Schetzenhöfer and Portz.]

304. KOPPENHOFER, JACOB

Mönchzell =
6922 Meckesheim, Baden

Robert and Alice, 1738
S-H 212, 214, 216

MÖNCHZELL LUTHERAN KB:
Niclaus Koppenhoffer, gamekeeper, and wife Anna Margretha had:
    Jacob b. 27 Nov. 1705
m. 3 July 1736 Jacob Koppenhofer, son of the late Nicolaus Koppenhofer, gamekeeper, and Elisabeth Catharinen, daughter of the late Hans Weider. One child bp.
there:
    1. Friedrich Ludwig b. 31 Mar. 1737

Pennsylvania records:
NEW HOLLAND LUTHERAN KB, LANCASTER CO.:
Joh. Jacob Koppenhöfer had:
    2. Joh. Balthaser b. Jan. 1741; bp. 26 Apr. 1741
    3. Johannes b. 2 Sept. 1742
    4. Sophia Catharina b. 27 Feb. 1744
    5. Scharlotta bp. 10 Feb. 1748

Elisabet Catharina Koppeheberin sp. 1768 a ch. of Johannes Tiebenbach.
m. 19 Feb. 1760 Johannes Diefenbach, son of the late Caspar D., residing on the
Cocalico, and Sophia Catharina Koppenhäfer, daughter of the late Jacob Koppenhöfer of Earl twp.

305. KRAFFT, ANDREAS

James Goodwill, 1728

S-H 21, 22

Waldangelloch =
6920 Sinsheim, Elsenz

WALDANGELLOCH LUTHERAN KB:
m. 16 Nov. (?) 1723 Andreas Krafft, single, and Maria Catharina, dau. of Ludwig
Schaeffer.
(Note: Andreas Krafft was possibly a son of Gottfried Krafft and Johanna Fessler.
His bp. record is not found at Waldangelloch, but there is a family relationship
indicated in Pa. records.)
Andreas Krafft and Maria Catharina had:
1. Joh. Carl b. 16 June 1726; d. 16 Nov. 1726
2. Anna Elisabetha b. 15 Dec. 1727

Pennsylvania records:
STOEVER'S RECORDS: (cf. New Holland Lutheran KB and Christ "Little Tulpehocken" Lutheran KB)
Andreas Krafft (Northkill) had:
1. John b. 30 Sept. 1731
2. Anna Maria b. 16 Apr. 1733
3. Anna Margaretha b. 27 Dec. 1734
4. Maria Catarina b. 15 Mar. 1736
5. Maria Elisabetha b. 17 Apr. 1737
6. Justina Cathrina b. 4 Mar. 1739; sp. Justina Catarina Kayser
7. Andreas b. 1 Feb. 1741
8. Maria Magdalena b. 7 Sept. 1742; sp. Michael Krafft and wife
9. Susanna b. 9 Apr. 1744
One other child is listed in the Christ, Little Tulpehocken, KB, Berks co.:
Joh. Jacob b. 17 May 1730; bp. 27 Oct. 1730
Andreas Krafft d. before Berks co. was erected; his will is filed at Philadelphia,
H: 74 (1745)

BERKS CO. ORPHANS COURT RECORDS,
10 Aug. 1757. The guardians of the minor children of Andreas Kraft, dec'd, and
Michael Rice and Anna Maria, his wife, one of the daughters of Andreas Kraft,
dec'd,

vs.

Jacob Geiker and Catharine, his wife, late Catharine Kraft, executrix of the will of
Andreas Kraft, dec'd. The parties to be heard 11 Nov. 1758.
17 Nov. 1758. The petition and complaint of John Kraft, Michael Rice and Anna
Maria, his wife, Michael Keill and Maria Catharine, his wife, Andreas Shad and
Maria Elisabeth, his wife, John Achen and Anna Margaret, his wife, Andreas
Kraft, Justina Kraft, Mandelin Kraft, and Susannah Kraft, and Elizabeth Shower,

all children, heirs and devises of Andrew Kraft, their late father. Exhibited on
their behalf by John Ross, Esquire, their attorney. Laid over until the next week.
Feb. 1759. The heirs of Andrew Kraft, dec'd, vs. Jacob Geiker and Maria Catharine, his wife, late Catharine Kraft, ex. of Andrew Kraft, dec'd. Persons appointed
to examine and settle the account of the executrix. (On 12 May 1759 an amicable
settlement was made and confirmed by the court.)
See Pennsylvania Patent Book AA-4: 366 for final disposition of his property in
1763.

306. KRAFFT, FRIEDERICK

Shirley, 1751

S-H 454

Hoffenheim =
6920 Sinsheim, Elsenz

HOFFENHEIM LUTHERAN KB:
m. 20 Apr. 1723 Hans Georg Kraft and Anna Margaretha, daughter of Hans Georg
Pfeil of Rüga, Churpfaltz. Their son:
      Joh. Friederick b. 12 Oct. 1733, conf. 1747; sp.: Hans Georg Gilberth and
wife Anna Elisabetha
He arrived with his brother-in-law Veit Meister [q.v.]

Decorative elements carved on a timber of a building in Hoffenheim.

Photo: J. Godshall

307. KRAFFT, HANS GEORG
1751

Hoffenheim =
6920 Sinsheim, Elsenz

HOFFENHEIM LUTHERAN KB:
m. 20 Apr. 1723 Hans Georg Kraft and Anna Margaretha, daughter of Hans Georg
Pfeil of Rüga, Churpfaltz. Their son:
    Hans Georg b. 21 May 1726
m. 3 May 1751 Hans Georg Krafft, son of Hans Georg Krafft, and Elisabetha
Barbara, daughter of Anton Sohns. They left eight days later to go to Pennsylvania.
[Note by compiler: Evidently they came on the *Shirley*, 1751, with several others
from this village, including a brother Frederick Krafft [q.v.]. Hans Georg Krafft
does not appear on this ship's list. It is possible that he was making a second trip
and had already signed the oaths. One Hans Georg Krafft arrived on the *Jacob*,
1749 (S-H p. 417) with Georg Michael Laubinger, also from Hoffenheim].

Pennsylvania records:
Johan Jurg Kraft and Elisabeth Barbara Kraft were sponsors in 1752 for a child of
Veit Meister (at St. Michael's and Zion, Philadelphia). Veit Meister's wife Anna
Elisabetha was a sister of Hans Georg Krafft.

CHRIST LUTHERAN KB, YORK:
John George Kraft and Elisabetha Barbara had:
    1. Margaret Elisabetha, 13 Nov. 1752
    2. Anna Maria, 3 June 1759, d. 1762

308. KRAFFT, HANS MICHAEL
Francis & Elizabeth, 1742
S-H 327, 329

Waldangelloch =
6920 Sinsheim, Elsenz

WALDANGELLOCH LUTHERAN KB:
Gotfrid Cropf and wife Johanna (Fessler) had:
    Hans Michael bp. 6 Sept. 1687
m. 29 Oct. 1709 Hans Michael Krafft, son of Gottfried Krafft [q.v.], and Agnes
Ursula Burckardt. Children:
    1. Joh. Friederich bp. 6 Oct. 1710; d. 18 July 1711
m. 4 Nov. 1738 Johann Michael Krafft, widower, and Maria Magdalena, dau. of
Georg Veit Rempert "Gerichtsverwandten" and joiner at Michelfeld.

MICHELFELD LUTHERAN KB:
Georg Veit Rempert (son of the late Dieterich Rempert of Waldangelloch) and wife
Anna Margaretha (dau. of Hans Georg Kühlewein) had:
    Anna Magdalena b. 26 Mar. 1715

Pennsylvania records:
Michael Krafft and wife Maria Magdalena sponsor a child of Andreas Krafft at
Christ "Little Tulpehocken" church in 1742, Oct.; her name: Maria Magdalena

PHILADELPHIA WILLS:
E: 52 Michael Kraft (1744) Adm. Book

309. KRAFT, GOTTFRIED age 63   Waldangelloch =
Britannia, 1731   6920 Sinsheim, Elsenz
S-H 48, 52, 53 (with Maria Epha (Eva) Krafft, 43)

WALDANGELLOCH LUTHERAN KB:
m. (1) 27 Apr. 1686 Gottfrid Crafft and Johanna Föslerin (Fessler). Children:
  1. Hans Michael bp. 6 Sept. 1687, son of Gottfried; m. (1) 29 Oct. 1709
     Agnes Ursula Burckardt [q.v.]
  2. Anna Catharina bp. 20 Aug. 1690
  3. Possibly Andreas [q.v.]
  4. Maria Agnetha bp. 25 Nov. 1698; m. Christoph Käyser [q.v.]
  5. Anna Margaretha bp. 7 Dec. 1701
  6. Johann Georgius bp. 25 Feb. 1703, d.
m. (2) 5 May 1726 Gottfried Krafft and Maria Eva Klein, a servant of the castle
here.

310. KRÄMER, HANS GEORG   7519 Eppingen
William & Sarah, 1727
S-H 8, 9 (3 persons)

EPPINGEN REFORMED KB:
m. 10 June 1710 Hans Georg Krämer, son of the late Hans Krämer, and Anna
Barbara, daughter of the late Hans Georg Brenneÿsen. Children:
  1. Hans Georg bp. 20 Nov. 1712
  2. Susanna Barbara bp. 19 Jan. 1716
  3. Joh. Leonhard bp. 20 Nov. 1718

Pennsylvania records:
FIRST REFORMED KB, PHILADELPHIA:
Bu. 26 Sept. 1762 Leonard Kraemer, aged 49 y.

311. KRAUS, ANNA ELISABETH   Eschelbach, Baden =
1756   6920 Sinsheim, Elsenz

ESCHELBACH LUTHERAN KB:
Jacob Kraus, inhabitant, and wife Margareth had:
  Anna Elisabeth b. 24 Nov. 1708. "1756 given Taufschein—to new land."

312. KRAUSS, JOH. JACOB   Daisbach =
Dragon, 1749   6923 Waibstadt
S-H 414

ESCHELBACH LUTHERAN KB:
m. 27 Dec. 1714 Hans Michael Krauss, son of Michael (?) Krauss, and Anna
Elisabetha Schallewey, daughter of Adam (?) Schallewey. [very faded entry] Their
son:
  Joh. Jacob b. 25 Oct. 1718

DAISBACH LUTHERAN KB:
m. 12 Feb. 1743 Joh. Jacob Grauss, son of the late Michael Grauss, former inhabitant at Eschelbach, and Anna Catharina Schupp, daughter of Jacob Schupp. [no children bapt. at Daisbach or Eschelbach]

Krebs, "Palatine Emigration . . ." p. 33
Jacob Grauss (Krauss), inhabitant of Daisbach (Kreis Sinsheim) is manumitted gratis, on account of his poverty and propertyless state, in order to go to the new land with his wife and children (1749).

Pennsylvania records:
TRINITY LUTHERAN KB, LANCASTER:
1750—Joh. Jacob Krauss, formerly a servant of Hans Moser, d. on the 19th Sept., aged 32 y., after he lost his wife and 3 children already during the sea voyage. Bu. the 20th Sept.

313. KREUTZWISSER, JOHANNES

6921 Michelfeld

Two Brothers, 1750
S-H 438

MICHELFELD LUTHERAN KB:
Johannes Creutzwisser, b. 16 July 1712, son of Mathaei and Anna Elisabetha Creutzweisser, m. 24 Nov. 1733 Anna Catharina, daughter of the late Erasmi Rökel, citizen. Anna Catharina d. 9 Apr. 1746. Children:
1. Joh. Jacob b. 16 Aug. 1734
2. Maria Magdalena b. 1 May 1737
3. Maria Elisabetha b. 17 Sept. 1739; bu. 19 Sept.
4. Johann Philipp b. 7 Nov. 1740
5. Anna Catharina b. 14 Jan. 1745
Johannes Creutzweisser m. (2) 17 May 1746 Maria Eva Rüsterholtz. She was born 13 May 1721, daughter of Hans Rüsterholtz. (Earlier records indicate that the Rüsterholtz family came to Michelfeld from Zurich, Switzerland.) Children:
6. Johann Georg b. 9 June 1747
7. Maria Catharina b. 3 July 1749; d. 11 July. "This family left for Pennsylvania 20 May 1750."

314. KRIEGER, CASPAR
Thistle, 1730
S-H 31, 32, 33

7103 Schwaigern

SCHWAIGERN LUTHERAN KB:
m. 17 Aug. 1728 Johann Caspar Krieger, weaver, son of the late Ernst Krieger,
citizen and baker at Klein Gartach [= 7519 Eppingen] and Anna Christina,
daughter of Hans Jerg Hoffert [q.v.]. They had:
1. Philipp Caspar b. 5 Sept. 1729

Pennsylvania records:
STOEVER'S RECORDS:
Caspar Krueger (Oley Mountains) had:
2. Georg Valentine b. 9 Feb. 1734; bp. 2 Mar. 1734. One of the sp. was John
Georg Hoffert [q.v.].

315. KÜHLEWEIN, FRANTZ
Nancy, 1750
S-H 443

Hoffenheim =
6920 Sinsheim, Elsenz

HOFFENHEIM LUTHERAN KB:
m. 14 July 1733 Frantz Kühlewein, now huntsman and stepson of Hans Jacob
Gilbert, and Anna Maria Baum, widow of the late Jacob Baum. No children recorded
in the KB for the Kühleweins. (Joh. Jacob Gilbert, Jr. m. 12 May 1722 Eva Maria
Kühlewein, widow of the late Joh. Gottfried Kühlewein at Dautenzell [6955 Dau-
denzell])
See Joh. Jacob Baum for a listing of the children of Anna Maria Kühlewein by her
first husband, Jacob Baum.

316. KÜHNER, PHILIP
1717

Bonfeld =
6927 Bad Rappenau

BONFELD EMIGRANT LIST:
1717 Philip Kühner with wf. and 4 ch.

BONFELD LUTHERAN KB:
Johann Philipp Kühner and wife Christina Catharina had:
Anna Dorothea b. 17 Feb. 1717; bp. 20 Feb. 1717; sp. were from Wimpfen.
Additional records on this family might be found in the Winpfen records. The
emigrant list indicates that there were other ch. in this family.

317. KÜHNLEIN, KILIAN
Prelist (ca. 1717 with Daniel Schöner, also from Ehrstädt)

6921 Ehrstädt

EHRSTÄDT LUTHERAN KB:
Georg Bernhart Kühnlein and wife Anna Eva had:
Kilianus b. 7 July 1695; bp. 8 July 1695

In the marriage record, dated Jan. 1717 just the name Kilian Kühnle is mentioned; nothing further is recorded.

Pennsylvania records:
In the history of the Lutheran Church in New Hanover, Montgomery co., Pa., (Pennsylvania German Society XX (1909): 32–33) there is a statement concerning the church property acquired by the congregation in 1719. Kilian "Kalie" was among those who attested that John Henry Sprogel "did in the year of our Lord One thousand seven hundred and nineteen freely and voluntarily give and grant the above described piece of land with the appurtinances in the presence of Us and many others then living for the proper use and behoof of a Lutheran Congregation forever."

MOSELEM LUTHERAN KB, BERKS CO.:
M. 14 p. Trin. 1745 Joh. Georg Kuehnlin, single son of Kilian Kuehnlin, and Philippina Schoener, single daughter of Daniel Schoener [q.v.]
m. 29 Sept. 1747 Jacob Petri, master shoemaker, single son of Nicholai Petri in Germany, and Anna Eva Kuehnlin, single daughter of Kilian Kuehnlin. Children:
1. Joh. Adam b. 2 Nov. 1748
2. Johannes b. 26 Aug. 1750
3. Maria Catharina b. 22 Sept. 1753
4. Heinrich b. 6 Nov. 1755
Johannes Hill and wife (Jo)Hanna Kuehnlin had:
1. Anna Catharina b. 1 Oct. 1747
2. Eva Rosina
3. Hanna Martha } twins b. 22 Mar. 1750
4. Joh. Jacob b. 11 July 1752
5. Maria Christina
6. Georg Michael } twins b. 22 Apr. 1755
7. Anna Elisabetha b. 27 Jan. 1758
Jacob Schneider and wife Barbara Kuhnlin had one child bapt. at Moselem:
1. Johannes b. 12 Jan. 1749
Adam Kuhnlin and wife Maria Elisabetha Michlin had:
1. Anna Eva b. 21 July 1754
2. Martin b. 23 Nov. 1755

318. KUMMERLIN, JACOB FRIDRICH   Massenbach =
                                                   7103 Schwaigern
Osgood, 1750
S-H 446

MASSENBACH LUTHERAN KB:
m. (1) 3 Jan. 1741 Fridrich Jacob Kummerlin from [7103] Stetten under dem Heuchelberg, son of Michael Kummerlin, and Maria Eva, daughter of Philips Adam Schmaltzhoff. They had:
1. Maria Eva b. 3 Oct. 1741
2. Joh. Adam b. 7 July 1743
m. (2) Jacob Friederich Kummerlin, widower and citizen, and Maria Magdalena, daughter of Reinhardt Schuemacher, "Gerichtsverwandten" and miller. Children:

3. Joh. Reinhard b. 22 Sept. 1745
4. Maria Catharina b. 18 Nov. 1747
(The mother is mentioned in these bp. records as Roman Catholic religion.)

Pennsylvania records:
STOEVER'S RECORD:
Jacob Friederich Kuemmerlin (across the mountain) had:
5. Joh. Michael b. 5 Mar. 1753; bp. 1 July 1753; sp. John Michael Folmer and wife Magdalena Regina

319. KUMPFF, GEORG

Asbach, Baden = 6951 Obrigheim, Baden

Dragon, 1749
S-H 414 (appears on list as Georg (x) Cump)

ASBACH REFORMED KB:
Thomas Kümpff and wife Maria Catharina had:
Johann Görg bp. 19 July 1714
m. 20 Aug. 1737 Johann Georg Kumpff, son of Thomas Kumpff, and Anna Margaretha, daughter of Johannes Wannemacher [q.v.]. Children:
1. Joh. Peter b. 14 June 1738
2. Joh. Georg bp. 15 Sept. 1740
3. Maria Barbara bp. 16 June 1745; d. young.

Pennsylvania records:
A Peter Kumpf m. 9 Oct. 1759 at New Goshenhoppen Eva Elisabetha Kiefer.

Krebs, "Palatine Emigration . . .," p. 34.
"Georg Kumpff, of Asbach (Kreis Mosbach) received permission to emigrate to the New Land in 1749 on payment of the tithe. He applied with Georg Linz and Philipp Brenner and appears with them in the ship lists as Hans Jörg Kamp (with Daniel Camp), arriving at Philadelphia on the ship *Patience*, Sept. 19, 1749 (List 134 C)."
[It is the opinion of this compiler that the 1749 Asbach emigrant, Georg Kumpff, arrived on the *Dragon*, 1749. There is no Daniel Camp mentioned in the Asbach records.]

320. KUNTZ, BERNHARD age 35

6928 Bargen, Kraichgau
6922 Meckesheim

Pleasant, 1732
S-H 99, 100, 101

NECKARGEMÜND LUTHERAN KB:
m. 24 June 1721 Hans Bernhard Kuntz, son of the late Hans Martin Kuntz, citizen at Bargen, and Agnes Rosina, daughter of Michael Burger, citizen at Meckesheim. Children:
1. Joh. Michael b. 11 Mar. 1723
2. Anna Margaretha b. 28 Aug. 1725
3. Maria Margaretha b. 23 Sept. 1728
4. Maria Apellonia b. 8 June 1730

The marriage records at Mauer also contain their marriage entry, same date, but in that record Agnes Rosina is called a daughter of Michael Burckhardt at Meckesheim.

321. KÜNTZEL, JOH. MICHAEL

Massenbach =
7103 Schwaigern

Forest, 1752
S-H 495

MASSENBACH LUTHERAN KB:
m. 8 Feb. 1729 Joh. Michel Küntzel, smith, son of Mathaus Küntzel from Rappenau, and Anna Maria, daughter of Mathaeus Schmaltzhoff. Michael Kuntzel, citizen and smith, and wife Anna Maria had:
    Joh. Michael b. 11 Sept. 1731

Ehrstädt, first mentioned in 1824, belonged to the von Degenfeld knights. It became Lutheran in 1525. The church at Neuhaus a few miles away at the end of a deeply cut valley became a filial of Ehrstädt in 1760 after a brief time as a parish. The head of the von Degenfeld clan responded to citizens' complaint about high taxes in 1766 by saying, "The thunder and lightning shall strike you all, you knaves and rascals [a mild translation: "Hundsfötter und Spitzbuben"], I will charge, stab and shoot. The directorate of the nobles has no say over us ["keinen Dreck zu befehlen"], one is my father, the next cousins, there is no one to give us orders except the Kaiser." Such attitudes encouraged emigration to avoid heavy taxation. Today Ehrstädt is a quiet farm village incorporated into the municipality of Sinsheim.

Photo: J. Godshall

322. KURR, MICHAEL

Ehrstädt =
6920 Sinsheim, Elsenz

James Goodwill, 1728
S-H 21, 23 (Surname also spelled Curr, Korr, Kohr)

EHRSTÄDT LUTHERAN KB:
Michael Curr, Jr. and wife Elisabetha (marriage record not located) had:
    1. Anna Elisabetha b. 23 Dec. 1715; sp. Anna Eva wife of Bernhard Kühn-

lein; Elias Mayer, son of the miller at Eppingen; Elisabetha Armbrustin
from Eppingen
2. Anna Margretha b. 31 May 1718; d. 22 Oct. 1719
d. 21 Nov. 1720 Elisabetha, wife of Michael Curr, daylaborer.
m. (2) 5 May 1722 Michael Curr, widower, son of Michael Curr, citizen and "des
Gerichts," and Maria Margaretha Fitler, daughter of Michael Fitler, citizen in
Bretenheim near Rottenburg an der Tauber. [= 7181 Brettheim] Children:
3. Georg Caspar b. 12 Apr. 1723; d. 4 June 1723
4. Georg Caspar b. 13 Mar. 1725
d. 29 June 1730 Ursula Maria, widow of the late Michael Curr, former citizen and
judge.

Pennsylvania records:
TRINITY LUTHERAN KB, LANCASTER:
Michael Korr had:
    Michael b. 25 June 1730
    Johannes b. 13 Nov. 1734
    Christian b. 15 Oct. 1736
An Elisabetha Korrin was a sp. in 1734.
D. 27 Jan. 1749 Michael Cor, aged 75, after a lengthy illness, aged and satisfied
with life; buried on the 29th.

LANCASTER COUNTY ORPHANS' COURT DOCKET:
5 Sept. 1749: Michael Byerly appointed guardian over Christian Core, orphan child
of Michael Core
4 June 1754—Christian Core, an orphan son of Michael Core, deceased, (being
above the age of 14 years) chooses Casper Core, his brother, as guardian.
8 Nov. 1754—Peter, John, and Elizabeth Smeltzer (over 14 years) choose John
Smeltzer, their father, as their guardian over estate bequeathed them by Michael
Core, their grandfather; and the said John Smeltzer is appointed guardian over his
children Margaret, Sabina, Jacobina and Jacob Smeltzer (under 14 years.)

BETHEL MORAVIAN KB, LEBANON CO.:
D. 28 May 1801 Georg Casper Kohr, aged 76 y. 7 mo. and 21 days; b. 7 Oct.
1724 at Erstat in the Chur Pfalz and came at the age of 3 years to this land. M. (1)
1747 at Hebron Barbara nee Orendorf and she d. 20 Nov. 1763. Child of the first
marriage:
    1. Christian b. 7 Jan. 1747; m. Catharina Neff
He m. (2) 1 May 1764 the now widowed Anna Maria nee Meilin. Children of the
second marriage:
    2. Johannes b. 17 Mar. 1765; m. Catharina Meyer
    3. Anna Barbara b. 4 July 1766; m. Jacob Stör of Yorktown
    4. Anna Rosina b. 3 May 1768; m. Jacob Knaus
    5. Maria Catharina b. 22 June 1770; m. Georg Boeshor of Hanover
    6. Maria Magdalena b. 4 Dec. 1772; m. Georg Uhrig of Müllerstown
    7. Georg Caspar b. 21 Jan. 1775; m. Magdalena nee Stättler in Sciota
    8. Michael b. 20 Oct. 1777; m. Elisabetha Schaufler
    9. Jacob Ludwig b. 27 Apr. 1780
    10. Philip Jacob b. 21 Nov. 1783

11. Anna Maria b. 2 Mar. 1786
Michael Korr (b. 1730 in Lancaster, son of the immigrant) m. Magdalena Ohrendorf, daughter of Christian Ohrendorf from Kiselberg, Freudenberg, in Nassau-
Siegen. She was a sister of Georg Caspar Kohr's first wife. Children:
1. Johanna Elisabetha b. 4 Feb. 1754
2. Johannes b. 26 Nov. 1755
3. Anna Barbara b. 3 May 1758
4. Anna Rosina b. 27 Aug. 1760 in Lebanon
5. Anna Margaretha b. 22 May 1762 in Bethel
6. Anna Catharina b. 30 July 1763
7. Maria Magdalena b. 27 Aug. 1765
8. Joh. Michael b. 16 Sept. 1767
Magdalena Kohr, wife of Michael Kohr, d. 5 Dec. 1770. She was b. 1731 in
Sonnenberg in Nassau-Siegen. (Extracts from Bethel Moravian KB and Burial
Register.)

323. LABER (LAUBER), GEORG WENDEL

Steinsfurt =
6920 Sinsheim, Elsenz

Before 1754—ship data not located

STEINSFURT REFORMED KB:
Georg Wendel Laber bp. __ Oct. 1693, son of Balthasar Lauber and Anna Elisabetha nee Wanner; conf. 1706, age 14; m. 26 Nov. 1715 Esther, daughter of the
late Michael Gansser. Children:
1. Görg Philips bp. 17 Apr. 1717; d. 1724
2. Joh. Jacob bp. 14 Nov. 1720; d. 1726
3. Hans Balthasar bp. 20 Apr. 1722; d. 1729
4. (no name) bp. 27 May 1725
5. Johann Martin bp. 4 Aug. 1728
6. Joh. Balthasar bp. 1 Apr. 1731
7. Görg Balthasar bp. 24 Apr. 1733
8. Maria Eva b. 4 Feb. 1734; d. 1736
9. Joh. Jacob b. 17 Aug. 1739
10. Maria Elisabetha b. 2 Oct. 1743; d. young
11. Maria Elisabetha b. 28 Apr. 1745

Pennsylvania records:
WALDSCHMIDT'S RECORDS:
M. 13 Mar. 1754 Balsar Laber, son of Georg Wendel Laber, and Elizabeth, daugh-
ter of Samuel Baumann
Conf. 1754 at Cocalico Elisabetha, Balser Laber's wife, of a Mennonite family.

LANCASTER CO. WILLS:
Balser Laver (3 Mar. 1774/15 Apr. 1775) Wife: Elisabeth; children: Michael and
others who are not named. Exrs: Henry Keek and Martin Bowman
Elisabetha Laver, Donegal twp. (11 Jan. 1784/prob. 5 Mar. 1784) Children: Michael; Christian, wife of Philip Holinger; Jacob; John; Frederick; Henry; and Elisabeth. Ex: Stophel Holinger.

324. LABER (LAUBER), HANS WENDEL

Dragon, 1732
S-H 96, 97, 98

Steinsfurt =
6920 Sinsheim, Elsenz

STEINSFURT REFORMED KB:
m. 22 Nov. 1686 Balthasar Lauber and Anna Elisabetha Wanner, daughter of Jacob
Wanner from Wÿla, [CH—8492 Wila, Zurich, Switzerland] and his wife Sara
Klausser from Canton Bern, Switzerland. Their children:
1. Andreas bp. 1 Aug. 1688
2. Georg Wendel bp. __ Oct. 1693 (faded) [q.v.]
3. Hans Georg bp. 11 Mar. 1696; conf. 1709
4. Anna Magdalena bp. 3 Aug. 1698
*5. Johann Wendel bp. 10 Mar. 1701; conf. 1715
6. Anna Elisabetha bp. 25 May 1703
7. Görg Balthasar b. 17 May 1706; conf. 1720 age 14
Johann Wendel Laber m. 3 Sept. 1726 Anna Margaretha, daughter of Andreas
Müller, former carpenter. Children:
1. Maria Eva bp. 25 May 1727
2. Anna Margretha bp. 27 Mar. 1729
3. Anna Maria bp. 17 Dec. 1731; d. young
[Note: the father is given in some records as Hans Wendel, in others as Johann
Wendel; the surname is spelled both Laber and Lauber.]

Pennsylvania records:
WALDSCHMIDT'S RECORDS:
M. 30 Dec. 1755 Anna Catharina Laber, daughter of the late Wendel Laber, and
Jacob Enck, son of Jacob Enck.
M. 13 Oct. 1761 Barbara, daughter of the late Joh. Wendel Laber, and Johannes
Enck, son of Jacob Enck.
M. 21 June 1757 Maria Catharina Laber, daughter of the late Hans Wendel Laber,
and Adam Kreiner, son of the late Martin Kreiner.
M. 13 Oct. 1761 Martin Laber, son of the late Joh. Wendel Laber, and Catharina,
daughter of Jacob Enck.
M. 20 Nov. 1753 Anna Margaretta Lauber, daughter of the late Johannes Wendel
Lauber, and Jacob Adam Jacobi.
The estate records of Hans Vendle Laber provide the names of 2 more children:
    Balthasar (who m. 7 Feb. 1769 Rosina Wentz)
    Susanna (over 14 on 27 Dec. 1762)

PENNSYLVANIA PATENTS:
AA:11:60 Warrant 26 Mar. 1746 to Wendal Lowbar 125 A in Cocalico twp.,
Lancaster co. Pat. 23 Mar. 1769 to his son Martin Lauber.

WARWICK (BRICKERVILLE) LUTHERAN KB AND MUDDY CREEK LUTHERAN KB:
Joh. Wendel Laber had a daughter Maria Catarina, b. 13 Apr. 1737 [sic], bp. 27
Apr. 1735, sp. Michael Kitsch and wf. Maria Catarina

Date on the church in Schaffhausen: 1748

325. LANDIS, RUDOLF

Schatthausen =
6908 Wiesloch

Molly, 1727
S-H 13, 14

SCHATTHAUSEN LUTHERAN KB:
m. 2 June 1723 Rudolff Landis, Anabaptist, and Anna Maria Gastwolf, Lutheran.
Children:
1. Christina Sharlotta b. 7 Jan. 1724
2. Juliana b. 23 Feb. 1726

C. Henry Smith, *The Mennonite Immigration to Pennsylvania* (Norristown, Pa, 1929), p. 181: A 1727 letter to the Amsterdam Committee of Foreign Needs from Mennonite elders informed the committee that at least one hundred fifty persons were preparing to leave for Pennsylvania, and that some of these were likely to need help. Among those listed is Rudolf Lanthis, five persons.

326. LANG, JOHANN GEORG

7103 Schwaigern

Christian, 1749
S-H 399

SCHWAIGERN LUTHERAN KB:
m. 7 Aug. 1701 Hans Jerg Lang, son of Herman Lang, citizen at Düren, [= 6920 Sinsheim] and Agnes Dorothea, daughter of Michel Kerr (?), citizen. Johann Georg Lang and wife Agnes Dorothea had:
Johann Georg b. 14 Apr. 1718

Pennsylvania records:
DOVER LUTHERAN KB, (STRAYER'S), YORK CO.:
Georg Lang b. 26 Sept. 1721 in "Schweryern bey Heylbronn Grafschaft Neuberg." Father Georg Lang, a vinegrower; mother: Agnes. In 1752 he m. Elisabeth, daughter of Samuel Esk. Had 11 ch. of whom 6 boys and 2 girls are living. D. 18 Dec. 1766. Bu. the 20th (Dec.) in the churchyard. Age 45 y., 2 mo. 22 days.
Georg and Elisabeth Lang had:
1. Jonathan b. 15 Sept. 1762; bp. 7 Nov. 1763
2. Maria Margretha b. 7 Aug. 1764; bp. 16 Sept. 1764

327. LANG, LEONHARD

Fane, 1749

S-H 424

Berwangen, Kraichgau =
6926 Kirchardt

BERWANGEN LUTHERAN KB:

m. 11 July 1713 Simon Lange, son of Martin Lange, and Sabina Fridauer, daughter of Hans Michael Fridauer, inhabitant at Stetten unter Heuchelberg [= 7103 Schwaigern]. Their son:

Johann Leonhard b. 17 May 1714

m. 3 Dec. 1743 Johann Leonhard Lang, son of Simon Lang, and Anna Elisabetha, widow of the late Joh. Georg Ziegler.

[Anna Elisabetha, b. 1714, daughter of Hans Leonhard Ziegler, m. (1) 1736 Joh. Georg Ziegler who was a son of Loth. Ziegler. By her first marriage she had 2 sons, surname Ziegler, and the family register indicates that they are in the new Land.

1. Georg Henrich Ziegler

2. Hans Georg Ziegler

They evidently emigrated in 1749 with their mother and step-father.] Children of Joh. Leonhardt Lang and Anna Elisabetha (Ziegler) born in Berwangen:

1. Joh. Martin b. 9 Nov. 1744

2. Joh. Carl b. 17 Apr. 1746; d. young

3. Eva Catharina b. 14 Oct. 1747

Pennsylvania records:

HILL LUTHERAN KB, LEBANON CO.:

Johannes Leonhard Lang had:

Anna Regina b. ___ Sept. 1750; bp. 9 Oct. 1750; sp. Johannes Bindtnagel [q.v.] and wife

Leonhardt b. 29 Mar. 1752

Antonius b. 8 Nov. 1753

BINDNAGEL'S LUTHERAN KB, LEBANON CO.:

d. 11 Sept. 1794 Anna Elizabeth Ramberger, b. 19 May 1714 in Berwangen, daughter of Joh. Lenhart and Margaret Ziegler. Sp. at her bp. were John Michael Werner and wife Regina. She m. (1) 3 Jan. 1736 Joh. Georg Ziegler and was blessed with two children, one son living. She m. (2) 3 Dec. 1743 Joh. Lenhardt Lang and they had 8 children, of whom 3 are living. She m. (3) in 1759 Christian Ramberger and they had 1 son, who is living. She d. aged 80 y., 4 mo., 6 days, and leaves 23 grandchildren and 3 great grandchildren.

328. LAUB, JOH. MICHAEL age 22

Friendship, 1739

S-H 265, 268, 271

Grombach =
6927 Bad Rappenau

GROMBACH CATHOLIC KB:

Christoph Friderici Laub and wife Barbara had:

Michael bp. 16 Oct. 1716

Pennsylvania records:
GOSHENHOPPEN ROMAN CATHOLIC KB, MONTGOMERY CO,:
m. 8 Dec. 1741 in the chapel in Philadelphia:
John Michael Laub and Regina ───────────── , widow. Witnesses: John
Schmidt and several others, Protestants as well as Catholics.

329. LAUBINGER, GEORG MICHAEL

Hoffenheim =
6920 Sinsheim, Elsenz

Jacob, 1749
S-H 417

HOFFENHEIM LUTHERAN KB:
Hans Bernhard Laubinger, baker, and wife Anna Maria had:

Georg Michael b. 17 Mar. 1729; conf. 1741
Johan Georg b. 20 Sept. 1731 [q.v.]

Pennsylvania records:
LITITZ MORAVIAN KB:
m. 6/17 Jan. 1751 Georg Michael Lauwinger and Barbara Bender

330. LAUBINGER, JOH. GEORG

Hoffenheim =
6920 Sinsheim, Elsenz

Snow *Louisa,* 1752
S-H 506

HOFFENHEIM LUTHERAN KB:
Hans Bernhard Laubinger, baker, and wife Anna Maria had:
Johan Georg b. 20 Sept. 1731; conf. 1743
[He arrived with Gilberts, Gobel, Scholl and Probst, all from Hoffenheim.]

Pennsylvania records:
ST. PETER'S UNION KB, PINEGROVE TWP., SCHUYLKILL CO.:
A Dorothea Laubinger, b. 18 Oct. 1738 in Herzogthum Wirtemburg, bu. 20 Aug.
1820, age 81 years 10 mo. 11 days.

331. LAUFFER, JOH. CONRAD

Massenbach =
7103 Schwaigern

Jacob, 1749
S-H 417

MASSENBACH LUTHERAN KB:
m. 26 Nov. 1743 Johann Conrad Lauffer, son of the late Christian Lauffer, former
citizen at Buchhorn [= 6967 Buchen, Odenwald], and Eva Catharina, daughter of
Joh. Michael Müller, citizen and wagon maker.
[Brother-in-law Joh. Fridrich Bikel also on ship]

"Adolf Gerber lists," *Emigrants from Wuerttemberg*, Pennsylvania German Folklore
Society, Vol. X (1945), p. 184:
Lauffer, (Johann) Conrad (2) Eberstadt (1749)

In the communicants register, under the classification "Unmarried sons and servants" at Filial Lennach-Buchhorn, is the following entry, scribbled in at the bottom: "From Dörtzbach, Molitor, going to Pennsylvania with Conrad Lauffer and others." The bp. register, three weeks previously, lists a child of Lauffers.

Pennsylvania records:
TRINITY LUTHERAN KB, LANCASTER:
Georg Adam, little son of Johann Conrad Lauffer, recently arrived, d. in his 8th month, 19 Dec. 1749, and was bu. on the 20th.

332. LAUMANN, GEORG BERNHARD   Ehrstädt =
St. Andrew, 1738   6920 Sinsheim, Elsenz
S-H 237, 238, 239

ADERSBACH LUTHERAN KB:
m. 23 Jan. 1700 Georg Bernhard Laumann, son of Georg Laumann, citizen at Sigespach, [6921 Siegelsbach] and Margretha Ursula, daughter of Joh. Heinrich Sties, citizen and *Anwald* at Hasselbach.

EHRSTÄDT LUTHERNN KB:
Georg Bernhart Laumann, gamekeeper at the Biegelhof, and wife Margretha Ursula had:
    Georg Bernhard b. 23 Apr. 1710
Georg Bernhard Laumann, turner at Unterbügelhof, and wife Anna Margaretha had children:
    1. Georg Daniel Christoph b. 28 Nov. 1734
    2. Maria Margretha b. 13 Nov. 1736

Pennsylvania records:
Bernhard Laumann and wife Anna Margretha sp. at Christ Lutheran Church, York, a child of Adam Müller in 1743. In 1744 they sp. a child of Balthasar Spengel (Spengler).

CHRIST LUTHERAN KB, YORK:
Bernhart Laumann had children bp.:
    Georg Daniel Christoph bp. 1st Advent 1735
    Maria Madalena Christina b. 18 Dec. 1748
    Anna Maria b. or bp. 12 Aug. 1741
    Johann Gottlieb no dates
[Note that the first child listed here was actually born and bp. in Germany, but he is listed in this Pennsylvania record.]

The northern part of the Lutheran church in Schwaigern was erected in Romanesque style in the 12th century. A renovation three centuries later gave the structure the Gothic character it now has, but the original nature is evident in the northern wall. Church adjoins palace even as gospel was supported by the law of the land, which legislated compulsory infant baptism, church membership and attendance in the only confession recognized in the territory.

Photo: Metz

333. LAUTENSCHLÄGER, MATHEUS   7103 Schwaigern

Chesterfield, 1749
S-H, 394

SCHWAIGERN LUTHERAN KB:
m. 12 Feb. 1715 Hans Martin Lautenschläger, son of Hans Lautenschläger, carpenter, and Maria Ursula, surviving daughter of Thomas Bromager (?). They had:
Matheus b. 2 Mar. 1716
The Lautenschlagers migrated to Schwaigern from Gechligen [CH 8214 Gächlingen, SH] Canton Schaffhausen, Switzerland.

334. LAUTENSCHLÄGER, MICHAEL   7103 Schwaigern

Phoenix, 1751
S-H 470

SCHWAIGERN LUTHERAN KB:
m. 12 Feb. 1715 Hans Martin Lautenschläger, son of Hans Lautenschläger, carpenter, and Maria Ursula, surviving daughter Thomas Bromager (?). They had:
Michael b. 29 Sept. 1723

Pennsylvania records:
NEW HANOVER LUTHERAN KB, MONTGOMERY CO.:
Joh. Michael Lautenschläger and wife Elisabetha had:
1. Joh. Peter b. 6 Nov. 1755; sp. Peter Seiler, Reformed and ----
2. Joh. Michael b. 27 Mar. 1757; sp. Michael Fridle and wife
3. Joh. Thomas b. 14 Aug. 1759

335. LAUTERMILCH, GEORG WENDEL age 27   6926 Kirchardt

Britannia, 1731   Reihen =
                                                        6920 Sinsheim, Elsenz
S-H 48, 52, 53 (with Magdalena Lautermilch age 22;
appears on A List as George William; on B List as
Wendel.)

KIRCHARDT REFORMED KB:
Georg Wendel Lautermilch, b. 12 Oct. 1705, son of Hans Melchior and Anna
Margretha Lautermilch; conf. 1720, age 14½ years.

REIHEN REFORMED KB:
m. 16 Nov. 1728 Görg Wendel Lautermilch, son of Melchior Lautermilch, shepherd at Kirchardt and Magdalena, daughter of Hans Peter Flecker, now shepherd
at Newkirchen.

Pennsylvania records:
Wendel Loutermilk warrant for 200 A. of land in Heidelberg twp. (now Lebanon
co.) dated 14 Sept. 1738.

LANCASTER CO DEEDS:
F: 255: 27 Jan. 1755, Richard Tea of Philadelphia to Wendell Lowtermilk, 48 A.
in Heidelberg twp.

_____

Wilder Laudermeligh, Heidelberg tp., Lancaster co., nat. Philadelphia April 1761,
as a "Quaker."

336. LAUTERMILCH, GOTTFRIED age 28   6926 Kirchardt

Princess Augusta, 1736
S-H 162, 164, 165

KIRCHARDT REFORMED KB:
Gottfried Lautermilch, bp. 26 May 1708, son of Hans Melchior Lautermilch and
wife Anna Margretha.

Pennsylvania records:
Gottfried Lautermilch sp. 1740 a ch. of Joh. Georg Mohr (Warwick) at Muddy
Creek Lutheran Church, Lancaster co.

STOEVER'S RECORDS:
m. 12 Apr. 1741 Gottfried Lautermilch and Anna Margaretha Meyer, Tulpehocken.

LANCASTER CO. DEEDS:
F:264:27 Jan. 1755, Richard Tea of Philadelphia to Godfrey Lowdermilk of Heidelberg twp. 36 A. in Heidelberg twp.

Warrant for 100 A. dated 11 May 1738, Heidelberg twp. (now Lebanon co.) to Godfield Lautermill.

Godfrey Laudermilk Heidleberg tp., Lancaster co., nat. Philadelphia, Fall 1765, without taking an oath.

337. LAUTERMILCH, JOHANN age 28

6926 Kirchardt

Mary, 1732
S-H 93, 94, 95

KIRCHARDT REFORMED KB:
Hans Melchior Lautermilch and wife Anna Margretha had:
  *1. Johannes b. 17 July 1701
  2. Anna Magdalena b. 31 Aug. 1703
  3. Georg Wendel b. 12 Oct. 1705 [q.v.]
  4. Gottfried bp. 26 May 1708 [q.v.]
  5. Antonius bp. 26 May 1708 (twin)

Pennsylvania records:
John Loutermilk warranted 100 A. of land in Heidelberg twp. (now Lebanon co.) on 14 Sept. 1738.

338. LAUTERMILCH, JOH. JACOB

6921 Michelfeld

Phoenix, 1749
S-H 406

MICHELFELD LUTHERAN KB:
Joh. Jacob Lautermilch, son of Joh. Valentin Lautermilch, a shoemaker, m. 21 Aug. 1725 Maria Catharina, daughter of the late Erasmus Röckel. Joh. Jacob Lautermilch d. 14 Mar. 1735. Their son:
  Joh. Jacob b. 6 June 1726

Pennsylvania records:
PA, Third Series: 5:14:667
A Jacob Lautermilch appears on the 1779 tax list of Heidelberg twp., Lancaster co., along with Melchior Lautermilch.

339. LEDERER, PAUL

7103 Schwaigern

Johnson, 1732
S-H 72, 76, 78

SCHWAIGERN LUTHERAN KB:
M. 31 Oct. 1699 Hans Thomas Lederer, son of Philip Jacob Lederer, and Anna Margreta, daughter of Peter Stumpff. They had:
  Hans Paulus b. 17 Jan. 1709
M. 3 Oct. 1730 Johann Paul Lederer, tailor, son of the late Thomas Lederer, and Anna Maria, daughter of Christian Albrecht Schlotzer, "Allmosen pfleger" and saddle maker. They had:
  Maria Magdalena b. 2 Sept. 1731

340. LEIB, JOHANNES

William & Sarah, 1727

Reihen =
6920 Sinsheim, Elsenz

S-H 8, 10 (Johannes Leyb—4 in family) [The father
Rudolph Leib (Leipp) is likely also a passenger on the
William & Sarah, 1727. In S-H I:9, the 5th name on
the list is Rudolff Beyl. However, Hinke also translated
this name elsewhere as Rudolff Leyb. [See "History of
Goshenhoppen Reformed Charge," PGS XXVII:26.] The
signature in S-H II:1 is *Leÿb*.]

REIHEN REFORMED KB:
Melcher Leip and wife Margreth Müller had:
     Hans Rudolff bp. 21 Oct. 1668
Hans Rudolph Leipp m. 2 Nov. 1689 Maria Agnes Orth. Children:
     1. Johannes b. 5 Aug. 1696
     2. Paul Christian b. 23 (?) Sept. 1698
     3. Anna Christina bp. 8 Aug. 1700
     4. Anna Catharina b. 26 Aug. 1706
m. 2 Nov. 1724 Johannes Leipp, son of Rudolph Leipp, citizen and baker, and
Margretha, dau. of the late Herr Clemens Hiertzel, "des Gerichts." Children:
     1. Johann Jonas bp. 30 Nov. 1725

Pennsylvania record:
TRINITY LUTHERAN KB, LANCASTER:
Johannes Leib had:
     Susanna Catharina b. 5 Mar. 1739

CHRIST LUTHERAN KB, YORK:
John Leib had:
     Maria Barbara b. 15 July 1743

FIRST REFORMED KB, YORK:
D. 1 Jan. 1754 Jonas Leib

YORK ORHANS COURT, 30 Aug. 1763 John Leib, late of Manchester twp., yeoman,
who died interstate. His children were:
     Jonas Leib, oldest son and heir at law
     Esther m. Leonard Hartzell
     Margaret m. Teeter (Dietrich) Mayer
     Elisabeth m. Philip Ziegler
     Catharina m. Sebastian Wigle
     Gotfrid
     Barbara m. Jacob Ament

CHRIST LUTHERAN KB, YORK:
m. 22 Dec. 1761 Johann Gottfried Leib, son of the late Johann Leib, and Barbara
Rudisill, dau. of Jacob Rudisill.

341. LEIBY, FRIEDRICH (LEYDAY) age 38

Steinsfurt =
6920 Sinsheim, Elsenz

Samuel, 1733
S-H 106, 107, 109, 110, 112 (Other passengers: Maria
Mettlina Leyday age 37; Jacob age 13; Michall age 10;
Wolrick age 4; Catharine age 1.)

STEINSFURT REFORMED KB:
Michel Leipe and wife Barbara had:
  Friederich bp. 2 Dec. 1694
Friederich Leippe, linenweaver, and wife Maria Magdalena had:
  1. Joh. Jacob bp. 20 Feb. 1721
  2. Görg Michael bp. 3 Jan. 1724
  3. Maria Catharina bp. 17 Dec. 1726; d. 1727
  4. Hans Ulerich bp. 29 May 1729
  5. Anna Catharina bp. 13 Sept. 1732
[According to the earlier Steinsfurt records, the Leÿpe family came from "Mutetz,
Basler Gebiets" (CH 4132 Muttenz, BL) before 1663].

Pennsylvania records:
DUNKEL'S REFORMED KB, GREENWICH TWP., BERKS CO.:
Jacob Leiby and wife had:
  Maria Magdalena bp. 18 Apr. 1747
George Leiby and wife had:
  Andrew bp. 19 Feb. 1749
Georg Michael Leiby and wife had:
  Barbara bp. 7 May 1752
  Joh. Georg bp. 13 Dec. 1753
Jacob Faust and Catharine Leiby had:
  Catharine bp. 14 Dec. 1750
John Frederick Leiby was a sponsor in 1755.
(There are many later entries for the family in this KB.)

DUNKEL'S CHURCH CEMETERY:
Friedrich Leibi, b. 7 May 1735, d. 28 Mar. 1817 m. 1758 Anna Jurgon; had 3
sons and 3 daughters.
Johan Georg Leibi 1788 (A fieldstone, no other inscription)
(several other later Leiby burials at this cemetery)

Jacob Leiby, and George Michl. Leiby, Greenwich twp., Berks co., nat. Philadelphia Sept. 1765.

342. LEIN, JOHANNES

Obergimpern =
6927 Bad Rappenau

prelist, before 1718

KIRCHARDT REFORMED KB AND OBERGIMPERN LUTHERAN KB:
Johannes Lein, shepherd, and wife Elisabetha had:
  1. Michael bp. 7 May 1692 at Kirchardt
  2. Anna Barbara b. ca. 1698; conf. Kirchardt 1713, age 15; m. 21 Jan. 1716
     Hans Jacob Weidler, son of Herr Hans Weidler, "Anwald". [This Jacob

Weidler was a brother of Michael Weidler who m. Anna Elisabetha Klein
and emigrated to Penna. Jacob and Barbara Weidler remained in Kirchardt.]
3. Joh. Jacob bp. 2 Mar. 1702
4. Anna Margareth bp. 24 Apr. 1706
5. Eva bp. 23 Sept. 1712

Pennsylvania records:
Johannes Lein [2 of them, evidently Sr. and Jr.] appear on the 1725/26 Conestoga
tax list. Jacob Lein also appears on this tax list.

PENNSYLVANIA PATENTS:
AA:2:384: Hans Line warrant 4 Oct. 1718 for a tract of 900 acres in Lancaster co.
between Mill Creek and Conestoga. Line conveyed 100 A. to Mathias Snyder on
16 May 1735.
The Lein family settled in the vicinity of Hill Reformed Church, Upper Leacock
twp., Lancaster co. (also called Schaeffer's or Heller's Church). John Lein was a
trustee of Hill Church in 1743 and elder in 1748.

LANCASTER CO. ORPHANS' COURT DOCKET I,
3 Sept. 1751 John Swope appointed guardian over Catherine, Conrad, Margaret
and Dorothy, his daughters and legatees under the will of John Lyne, deceased.
John Lyne is appointed guardian over Elizabeth, Margaret, Eva, Henry and Catherine Lyne, his daughters [children] and legatees under the Testament of John
Lyne, deceased. Jacob Lyne is appointed guardian over George Lyne, his son, one
of the legatees under the testament of John Lyne, deceased.

John Line, Lancaster co., nat. by Act of 14 Feb. 1729/30

343. LEISSER, ANDREAS   6921 Michelfeld
Brothers, 1752
S-H 481

MICHELFELD LUTHERAN KB:
Andreas Leÿsser m. 4 Apr. 1752 Maria Eliesabetha Merckel.

Pennsylvania records:
JORDAN LUTHERAN KB, S. WHITEHALL TWP., LEHIGH CO.:
Andreas Leisser and wife Elisabetha had:
   Theobald b. 28 Sept. 1769; sp. Theobald Höhninger and Maria Anna (Kern)

Andreas Leiser, Lowhill twp., Northampton co., nat. Philadelphia Sept. 1765.

344. LIBENSTEIN, MARTIN
LIBENSTEIN, BERNHARD

Dühren, Baden =
6920 Sinsheim

William and Sarah, 1727
S-H 9

DÜHREN LUTHERAN KB:
Gregorius Libenstein, b. in Albesrieden, Canton Zurich, Switzerland, m. 27 Oct. 1661 Anna, daughter of Philipp Ludwig Ruppert. They had:
1. Hans Andreas b. 1 Feb. 1663; m. 1688 Magdalena zur Backhoff, b. in Hochstetten, Switzerland. They had:
   1. Martin bp. 24 Feb. 1702 or 1703; "went in 1727 to Pennsylvania."
   2. Bernhard b. 1705 [No other date given.]
   3. Magdalena b. 10 Dec. 1709 [See Appendix C]
Johann Martin Liebenstein, son of Hans Andreas Liebenstein, m. 23 Jan. 1725 Juliana Auer, daughter of Christian Auer of Weiler. They had:
   1. Maria Elisabeth b. 21 May 1726

Pennsylvania records:
[The surname appears as Libenstein, Liebenstein in German records and as Löwenstein in Pennsylvania records. It was sometimes anglicized to Livingstone.]

NEW HOLLAND LUTHERAN KB, LANCASTER CO.:
Martin Löwenstein had:
1. Anna Eva b. 15 Aug. 1732
2. Anna Maria b. 30 July 1732; sp. Joh. Georg Schwab and wife Anna Maria from Sinsheim
3. Joh. Georg b. 17 Aug. 1737

MUDDY CREEK LUTHERAN KB, LANCASTER CO.:
Bernhardt Löwenstein had:
1. Maria Magdalena b. Dec. 1728, bp. 8 May 1730; sp. Maria Magdalena, wife of Benedict Strom.
2. Juliana b. 5 May 1731; sp. Nicolaus Adam and wife Juliana
3. Johannes b. 3 Aug. 1733; sp. Joh. Adam Rupert and wife
4. Lowisa Friederica b. 19 Apr. 1736; sp. Lowisa Friederica, wife of Elias Meyer.

345. LICHTNER, ANNA DOROTHEA

6921 Zuzenhausen

1744

NECKARGEMÜND LUTHERAN KB:
m. 24 July 1725 Joh. Georg Lichtner, widower, and Dorothea Etschberger in Zuzenhausen. They had:
   1. Joh. Jacob b. 24 June 1726 in Zuzenhausen

Krebs, "Palatine Emigrants . . . ," p. 32:
In 1744 Anna Dorothea, widow of Georg Licht(n)er, of Zuzenhausen, was permitted to emigrate to America with her 16-year-old son.

346. LIMBERGER, JOHANNES

Elsenz =
7519 Eppingen

Edinburg, 1753
S-H 521, 524

SINSHEIM LUTHERAN KB:
Joh. Jacob Limberger of Elsenz and wife Margretha had:
    Johannes b. 1 Aug. 1715
This same bapt. is recorded in the Adelshofen KB with the notation that the child was baptized at Elsenz by the Lutheran pastor at Sinsheim.

HILSBACH LUTHERAN KB:
m. 3 Feb. 1750 at Elsenz Johannes Limberger, son of Jacob Limberger, citizen at Elsenz, and Catharina Elisabetha, daughter of Friederich Dettinger, citizen at [7519] Sulzfeld. Children:
    1. Catharina Margretha b. 8 Nov. 1750

347. LINTZ, GEORG

Asbach, Baden =
6951 Obrigheim, Baden

Patience, 1749
S-H 408 (Jerg Lintz)

ASBACH REFORMED AND DAUDENZELL LUTHERAN KB:
Joh. Georg Lintz and wife Anna Maria had:
    Hans Georg bp. 19 Feb. 1711
[The surname also appears as Lins in the KB.]
m. 15 Nov. 1735 Hans Görg Lentz, son of the late Hans Görg Lentz of Aspach, Reformed, and Anna Elisabetha Brunn, daughter of Hans Görg Brunn of Breide-brunn. [= 6955 Breitenbronn] Children:
    1. Anna Maria b. 24 Nov. 1736 at Breidebronn
    2. Maria Catharina b. 17 Feb. 1740 at Aspach
    3. Anna Elisabetha b. 1 Dec. 1745 at Aspach

Krebs, "Palatine Emigration . . . ," p. 34.
Georg Lintz received permission in 1749 to emigrate on payment of the tithe. He also had to pay 10 florins to buy himself out of vassalage.

Pennsylvania records:
OLEY HILLS KB, BERKS CO., PA.:
Conf. 18 May 1755 Maria Catharine Lintz, daughter of Georg (Reformed) and Anna Elisabetha (Lutheran) Lintz, age 15 years.
Communicants 18 May 1755—
Elizabeth Lintz, wife of Georg (Reformed) and daughter Anna Maria
Communicants 14 Dec. 1755—
Anna Elis. Lintz, wife of Joh. Georg (Reformed) and Maria Elia., daughter
Communicants 30 May 1756—
Anna Elisabeth, wife of Johann Georg Lintz
Anna Maria, daughter
Maria Catharina, daughter
In 1761 and 1778 George Lintz and wife Anna Elisabeth sp. ch. of Christofel Kolb

and wife Catharine.
George Lintz nat. Philadelphia 24 Sept. 1756.

348. LÖFFLER, JOH. ADAM age 25   6920 Sinsheim, Elsenz

Samuel, 1737
S-H 170, 171, 173

SINSHEIM LUTHERAN KB:
m. 8 June 1736 Johann Adam Löffler, apprentice potter, son of the late Leonhard
Löffler, citizen and baker at Hohen Hassloch [Hohenhaslach = 7123 Sachsenheim, Württ.], Wurtemberg, and Anna Margretha, daughter of Herr Christoph
Trinckel, citizen and master potter. (Marriage necessary.) Ch.:
  1. Joh. Georg b. 4 Sept. 1736

Pennsylvania records:
TRINITY LUTHERAN KB, LANCASTER:
29 May 1743 Adam Löffler, along with Christoph Dränckel [his father-in-law] and
others, had the church pews under the pulpit made.
11 June 1743 Joh. Adam Löffler gave a little napkin, also on the baptismal table;
and his wife Margretha prepared the pieces which remained from the large white
altar cloth.
In 1739 Joh. Adam Löffler and wife Anna Margaretha were sponsors for a child of
Friederich Eichelberger.
Joh. Adam Löffler had:
  2. Magdalena Catarina b. 16 Nov. 1739
  3. Georg Ludwig b. 5 Apr. 1742

349. LOHRMAN, GEORG   7103 Schwaigern

Samuel, 1731
S-H 39, 40 (Passengers on ship: Men over 16 Georg;
Women 16 and over Elizabeth, Elizabeth, Barbary; Ch.
Katrena, Mary)

SCHWAIGERN LUTHERAN KB:
Hans Georg Lohrmann m. 14 May 1678 Maria Margaretha Stumpf. Their son:
  Hans Georg b. 11 Aug. 1682
m. 9 Nov. 1706 Hs. Jerg Lohrmann, son of the late Hs. Jerg Lohrmann, and Maria
Elisabetha, daughter of (not recorded) Stechmesser, citizen and "Gerichtsverwandten" at Niderhoffen in Wurttemberg [Niederhofen = 7103 Schwaigern]. They had:
  1. Maria Elisabetha b. 27 July 1707
  2. Margaretha b. Sept. 1708; d. young
  3. Maria Catharina b. 17 June 1715
  4. Anna Christina b. Dec. 1717
  5. Margaretha b. 11 July 1720; d. 22 Sept. 1720
  6. Anna Maria bp. 21 Aug. 1721
  7. Margaretha b. 23 May 1724
(The daughter Barbara who appears on the ship's list may have been born in the
1709–1714 period. There are gaps in the record in this time period.)

350. LOHRMAN, PETER

7103 Schwaigern

Charming Nancy, 1737
S-H 189, 192, 194 (Passengers on ship: Males; Peter
Lohrman, Women and Children: Margareta, Catrina,
Margareta and Maria Hannah)

SCHWAIGERN LUTHERAN KB:
Hans Georg Lohrmann m. 14 May 1678 Maria Margaretha Stumpf. Their son:
Peter b. 24 Jan. 1688
m. 25 Aug. 1711 Peter Lohrman, son of the late Hans Jerg Lohrmann, citizen, and
Margaretha, daughter of old Michael Dieter, citizen. They had:
1. Maria Catharina b. 15 July 1712
2. Jacob b. 4 May 1715, d. 1716
3. Margaretha b. 24 May 1717
4. Maria Elisabetha b. 29 Oct. 1719; d. 27 May 1720
5. Juliana b. 3 May 1721; d. 28 Apr. 1725
6. Maria Johanna b. 8 Nov. 1725

Pennsylvania records:
PHILADELPHIA WILLS:
Peter Loreman, Upper Dublin tp., yeoman. (Mar. 2 (Scotch tape over year—
illegible)/Oct. 2, 1749). Wife Margret all estate during her natural life and at her
death to 3 ch.: Margt. Swarts, Catrine Arnal ? Wan and Hannah Loreman. Exrs.
friends Peter Cleaver and Valentine Puff. Wit: Isaac Weaver and John Cleaver.

351. LUDWIG, JOH. GEORG

Hasselbach =
[3 in S-H: p. 414 (1749), p. 442 (1750), p. 486 (1752)]   6920 Sinsheim, Elsenz

ADERSBACH LUTHERAN KB;
m. 26 Apr. 1712 Hans Jacob Ludwig, son of Hans Jacob Ludwig, citizen and
saddler at Steinsfurt, and Anna Catharina, daughter of Thomas Gerlach, "Schultheiss" at Hasselbach. Their son:
Joh. Georg b. 17 Feb. 1731 at Hasselbach

Pennsylvania records:
ST. MICHAEL'S AND ZION LUTHERAN KB, PHILADELPHIA:
m. 4 Sept. 1753 Johann Jürg Ludwig and Anna Maria Elisabeth Misshattin. Children:
1. Joh. Martin bp. 26 Jan. 1755
2. Johannes b. 1 Nov. 1765
3. Maria Elisabetha b. 7 Nov. 1767
d. 2 Apr. 1769 Joh. Georg Ludwig, a butcher from Hasselbach between Heidelberg
and Wimpfen near Helmstadt in the Chur Pfaltz. Came to America in 1751. m.
1753 Anna Maria Elisabetha Mischatt. Had 7 children, 1 son and 1 daughter
living. Aged 38 y.
d. 15 Aug. 1769 Anna Maria Elisabetha Haas. Wife of Caspar Haas, nee Mischatt.
She m. (1) Georg Ludewig and had 7 children. She m. (2) 25 July 1769 Caspar
Haas. Aged 35 y.

George Ludwick, Philadelphia, nat. Philadelphia Fall 1765, without taking an oath.

352. LUDWIG, JOH. GEORG   6921 Zuzenhausen

Osgood, 1750
S-H 446

ZUZENHAUSEN LUTHERAN KB:
m. 13 Nov. 1742 Joh. Georg Ludwig, son of Valentin Ludwig, and Anna Margretha, daughter of Joh. Georg Wildt.

Krebs, "Palatine Emigration . . . ," p. 36
Johann Georg Ludwig, of Zuzenhausen (Kreis Heidelberg), applied in 1750, along with Johann Georg Koberstein, for permission to go to the so-called New Land with his wife Maria Margaretha. He paid 2 florins 30 kreuzer manumission tax.

353. LUTTMAN, EBERHARD   7103 Schwaigern

St. Andrew, 1752
S-H, 485 (Hinke translates the surname as Buttman; Rupp translates it Luttman; Luttman is correct.)

SCHWAIGERN LUTHERAN KB:
m. 22 Nov. 1718 Johann Heinrich Luttman, son of Hans Jerg Luttman, mason here and Sophia Margretha, daughter of Johann Wilhelm Lehman. They had:
    Johann Eberhard bp. 28 Sept. 1727.

Pennsylvania records:
TRINITY LUTHERAN KB, LANCASTER:
Eberhart Luttman and wf. Christina had:
    1. Joh. Georg b. 3 Sept. 1754; d. 13 March 1757
    2. Joh. Michael b. 15 Nov. 1755; d. 26 Sept. 1757
    3. Joh. Georg b. 16 July 1757; d. 22 Dec. 1757
    4. Anna Catharina b. 9 Nov. 1760
    5. Johann Georg b. 26 June 1765
d. 15 Sept. 1766 Eberhart Luttman, mason, a married man; age 39 y. 11 mo., 18 days.

354. LUTTMAN, JOH. MICHAEL   7103 Schwaigern

Royal Union, 1750
S-H 432

SCHWAIGERN LUTHERAN KB:
m. 19 Oct. 1717 Johann Georg Lutmann, son of Joh. Georg Lutmann, master mason, and Maria Barbara, widow of the late Jacob Kramer, former mason in Rappenau [= 6927 Bad Rappenau]. They had:
    Joh. Michael bp. 3 Sept. 1724.

MASSENBACH LUTHERAN KB:
m. 12 Nov. 1748 Joh. Michael Ludtmann, mason, son of Jerg Ludtmann, master

On the corner of the church in Schwaigern a carving of Christ as the *Schmerz-ensmann*—man of sorrows—looks out over the town. Grinding poverty, disease, repeated wars and destruction made this figure one of great relevance to late medieval man when it was erected (1520), as well as to persons into the eighteenth century when over 60 families left Schwaigern for the new world.

Photo: J. Godshall

mason in Schwaigern, and Elisabetha, daughter of the late Caspar Würtz. (She was bp. 4 July 1724, daughter of Joh. Caspar Würtz and wife Anna Barbara.) They had:
  1. Catharina Dorothea b. 29 Nov. 1749; d. young

Pennsylvania records:
TRINITY LUTHERAN KB, LANCASTER:
Michael and Elisabetha Luttmann had:
  2. Anna Catharina b. 7 June 1751; m. 4 Dec. 1768 Andreas Denger (Tanger)
  3. Joh. Georg b. _____1753
  4. Jacob b. 15 Nov. 1755
  5. Christina b. 3 June 1758; d. 7 Apr. 1759
  6. Eberhart b. 15 Mar. 1760
  7. Margaret (posthumous) b. 11 Oct. 1762
Michael Luttman, mason, d. in the spring or summer of 1762, exact date not given in the burial records.
d. 3 Oct. 1801 Elisabeth Luttmann, for a long time blind, 77 y. 3 mo. old.

355. LUTTMAN, PHILIP JACOB age 23   7103 Schwaigern

St. Andrew, 1743
S-H, 348, 349, 351

SCHWAIGERN LUTHERAN KB:
m. 19 Oct. 1717 Johann Georg Lutmann, son of Joh. Georg Lutmann, master mason, and Maria Barbara, widow of the late Jac. Kramer, former mason in Rappenau [= 6927 Bad Rappenau]. They had:
  Philip Jacob bp. 30 Apr. 1720

Pennsylvania records:
This immigrant evidently dropped the Philip and used Jacob exclusively after his arrival. All Pennsylvania records refer to him as Jacob or Joh. Jacob Luttmann. He purchased land in Lancaster in 1744.

TRINITY LUTHERAN KB, LANCASTER:
Jacob Luttmann (Ludman, Luthman) and wife had:
  1. Maria Margaret b. 30 _____1746
  2. Joh. Georg b. 28 July 1748
  3. Johanna Maria b. 3 Jan. 1751
  4. Johannes b. 28 Feb. 1753
  5. Johannes b. 21 Jan. 1754
  6. Anna Elisabet b. 28 Nov. 1755
  7. Anna Elisabeth b. 13 Aug. 1760
A ch. of Jacob Luttman d. 15 Apr. 1759
Bu. 4 Nov. 1780 Jacob Lutman, d. 2 Nov., age 60 y. 6 mo. and some days
Will of Jacob Luttman, made 11 Oct. 1780, prob. 28 Aug. 1787, Lancaster co. Names wife Margaretta, executor. Resided in Lancaster borough. Children: George, John, Margaretta, Mary, Elisabeth.

356. LUTZ, LEONHARD age 24

6920 Sinsheim, Elsenz

Pleasant, 1732
S-H 99 (appears on list as Lennard Lutes, sick)

SINSHEIM LUTHERAN KB:
Conrad Lutz and wife Susanna had:
Leonhard b. 22 Apr. 1704; conf. 1717

Pennsylvania records:
TRINITY LUTHERAN KB, LANCASTER:
Leonhard Lutz and Maria Catharina Brunner, both single, sp. 1733 a child of
Johann Frantz Fuchs.

NEW HOLLAND LUTHERAN KB, LANCASTER CO.:
Joh. Leonhardt Lutz sp. 3 children of Carl Seip, 1736–1739

CHALKLEY I: 294
"Leonard Lutses of Lancaster co., Pa. vs. John Martin Levinstone of Lancaster co.,
Pa. Debt-Bond. Dated 20 Jan. 1743–4."

357. MAAG (MAG), MICHAEL

Adelshofen =
7519 Eppingen

Richmond, 1764
S-H 696 (Name appears in S-H translated as Michael
May.)

ADELSHOFEN LUTHERAN KB:
m. 8 May 1764 Joh. Michael Maag from Ittlingen, single, and Susanna Charlotta,
daughter of Georg Heinrich Walz, citizen and weaver.
Michael Maag and his wife along with Johannes Seiz [Seitz—q.v.] and his bride
[who were married on the same day] left 8 days later to go to America.
Susanna Charlotta Waltz was b. 6 Oct. 1746, daughter of Georg Heinrich Waltz
and Dorothea.

358. MANN, GÖRG BERNHARDT age 31

Reihen =
6920 Sinsheim, Elsenz

Pink *Plaisance*, 1732
S-H 79, 82, 83 (Other passengers: Anna Margrit Man,
age 27; Catrin Man age 27, and Jacob, child)

REIHEN REFORMED KB:
m. 14 Sept. 1723 Görg Bernhardt Mann, smith, son of Hans Mann, citizen at
[6921] Siegelspach, and Anna Margretha, daughter of Herr Christian Geisser, "des
Gerichts."

SINSHEIM LUTHERAN KB:
George Bernhard Mann, citizen and smith at Reÿhen and wife had:
(in some records his wife is given as Catharina, Anna Catharina, Margretha.)
1. Joh. Jacob b. 3 Dec. 1724
2. Georg Bernhard b. 25 Nov. 1726
3. Maria Margreth b. 18 Dec. 1729

REIHEN REFORMED KB:
d. 29 Oct. 1730 Anna Margretha, wife of Görg Bernhardt Mann, smith; age 27 y.
9 mo. 14 days. He evidently married again, but the record has not been located.
(No marriages were recorded in the Sinsheim Lutheran KB 1723–1732.)

SINSHEIM LUTHERAN KB:
Georg Bernhard Mann of Reÿhen and wife Maria Margretha had:
    Anna Maria b. 9 Feb. 1732

Pennsylvania records:
STOEVER'S RECORDS:
George Bernhardt Mann and his wife sp. ch. of Jacob Herman at Swatara in 1739
and 1742.

NEW HOLLAND LUTHERAN KB:
Georg Bernhardt Mann had:
    Georg Adam b. 15/16 Mar. 1734
    Georg Carl b. 6 Aug. 1735
    Georg Cunradt b. 25 Apr. 1737
    Catarina b. 6 May 1739
    Catarina b. 24 May 1741
On 1 May 1744, he sold his land in Lancaster co. and went to Virginia.
On 17 Apr. 1749 Barnet Man, 320 A., lying between Shanado and the Peaked
Mountain on Stony Run.

359. MANTZ, MICHAEL age 33   Waldangelloch =
                                                6920 Sinsheim, Elsenz
Mary, 1732
S-H 93, 95, 96

WALDANGELLOCH LUTHERAN KB:
Christoff Mantz m. 28 Apr. 1696 Margretha Babara, daughter of Hans Rennert
(Reinhard). Their son:
    Johann Michael bp. 30 Mar. 1699
m. 27 Jan. 1722 Hans Michel Mantz and Margaretha Apollonia Hofmann
    1. Joh. Christoph b. 12 Dec. 1722

360. MARTIN, CHRISTIAN   Berwangen, Kraichgau =
                                                6926 Kirchardt
Prelist

BERWANGEN LUTHERAN KB:
Christian Martin, an Anabaptist from Boxhof (= Bockschaft = 6926 Kirchardt)
"went to Pennsylvania." His wife, Maria Magdalena, had:
    Johanna Justina b. 22 Feb. 1722; bp. 23 Feb.
The record mentions that the wife Maria Magdalena will probably "walk in the
footsteps of her husband" which presumably means that she intends to join him in
Pennsylvania.

Pennsylvania records:
Christian Martin appears on the list of taxables in Conestoga twp. in 1724. C. Henry Smith, *The Mennonite Immigration to Pennsylvania*, (Norristown Pa., 1929) p. 167, notes that there were many Martins in the Weaverland district, and it is a common Mennonite name today.

361. MATTERN, JOH. PETER
6920 Sinsheim, Elsenz

Dragon, 1732
S-H 96, 97, 98

SINSHEIM LUTHERAN KB:
Hans Georg Mathern and wife Anna Margretha had:
Joh. Peter b. 13 Feb. 1706
Peter Matern and wife Anna Catharina had:
1. Anna Margretha b. 21 Dec. 1729
2. Maria Rosina Juliana b. 11 Apr. 1732

Pennsylvania records:
ST. PAUL'S LUTHERAN KB, UPPER HANOVER TWP., MONTGOMERY CO.:
Peter Matern and wife Maria Catharina had:
Johann Heinrich b. 2 Sept. 1740
Johann Peter bp. 5 Sept. 1743, 4 weeks old

ZION'S LUTHERAN KB (LEHIGH CHURCH), LOWER MACUNGIE TWP., LEHIGH CO.:
d. 10 Sept. 1758 Maria Catharina Mattern, wife of Peter Mattern, aged 56 years 7 months.
Confirmations at Lehigh Church:
1756—Heinrich Matern
Peter Matern
Agnes Materin

362. MAUCH, TOBIAS
7103 Schwaigern

Fane, 1749
S-H 424

SCHWAIGERN LUTHERAN KB:
m. 11 May 1745 Tobias Mauch, shoemaker, son of the late Hans Jerg Mauch, shoemaker at Warmbronn, Leonberger Amts, [= 7250 Leonberg] and Maria Barbara, widow of the late Heinrich Busch, citizen and shoemaker. They had:
1. Maria Catharina b. 2 July 1746; bp. 2 July 1746
2. Georg Wendel b. 22 Nov. 1749; bp. 22 Nov. 1749
Maria Barbara, wife of Tobias Mauch, was a daughter of Hans Jerg Höll and Magdalena, nee Leibrand. She was bp. 31 July 1717
m. (1) 24 Sept. 1739 Heinrich Busch, shoemaker, son of the late Philipp Busch, cooper, and Maria Barbara, daughter of Johann Georg Höll, citizen and "Gerichtsverwandten." They had one ch. who survived:
1. Johanna b. 2 Nov. 1740; bp. 5 Nov. 1740

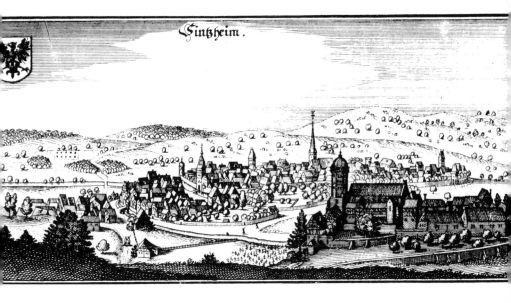

Sinsheim first is named in official documents in the 770s as "Sunnisheim." About the year 1000 a cloister of Benedictine monks was established on a hill outside the village. The village received the rights to strike coins and to hold a market weekly from Kaiser Heinrich IV in 1067. It became a free imperial city in the next centuries and in 1362 it was added to the holdings of the Palatinate. Sinsheim was completely burned in 1689. The picture from the Merian *Topographia* shows it in 1648. The *Stiftsberg* or *Michelsberg* in the right foreground shows the cloister building, still standing today, although the cloister was closed in 1565. The tall church spire in the town was on the one church shared by Reformed and Catholics: the Roman church had the choir for its worship, the Reformed the nave. In the last decade the unity of the church has been restored, the *Simultaneum* broken, and the Catholics relocated in a church building of their own. Sinsheim has grown from 2500 inhabitants about 1800, both by becoming home to refugees after World War II and by incorporating with itself eleven surrounding villages included in this study: Adersbach, Dühren, Ehrstädt, Eschelbach, Hasselbach, Reihen, Rohrbach, Steinsfurt, Waldangelloch, Weiler and the city of Hilsbach.

Photo: New York Public Library

Pennsylvania records:
OLEY HILLS KB, BERKS CO.:
Tobias Mauch b. 18 June 1722, a son of Johann Georg Mauch from Schweigern in
the principality of Neuburg; mother: Maria. In 1749 he came to America. In 1744
he m. Maria Barbara, a daughter of John Georg Hill from Schweigern and his wife
Magdalena. They had:
    1. Johanna b. 5 Nov. 1741 (Note: she was actually Johanna Busch)
    2. Catharine
    3. George Wendel, d.
    4. Anna Maria b. 23 Aug. 1755
    5. Sophia b. 31 Mar. 1758 (bp. record)
    6. Conrad b. Adv. 3rd, 1760
Conf. 18 May 1755 Johanna Busch, daughter of Heinrich (dec'd) and Barbara
Busch, now wife of Tobias Mauch; 14 years old.

363. MAŸER, ELIAS   7519 Eppingen

William & Sarah, 1727
S-H 8, 9

EPPINGEN REFORMED AND LUTHERAN KB:
Hans Görg Maÿer, miller, and wife Elisabetha had:
    Elias bp. 11 Dec. 1697
m. 2 Feb. 1717 Elias Maÿer, son of Hans Georg Maÿer, miller, and Louisa Frieder.,
daughter of Johannes Globman, smith. Children:
    1. Margretha b. 26 Nov. 1717; d. 1718
    2. Philipp b. 18 May 1719; d. young
    3. Anna Rosina b. 15 Aug. 1720; d. young
    4. Christoph b. 17 Sept. 1721; d. young?
    5. Heinrich b. 11 Sept. 1723
    6. Agnes Barbara b. 2 May 1725
    7. Maria Eva b. 27 Sept. 1726

Pennsylvania records:
Lowisa Friederica, wife of Elias Meyer, was a sp. in 1736 at Muddy Creek Church,
Lancaster co.

MUDDY CREEK LUTHERAN KB:
Elias Meyer had:
    Johann Peter b. 13 Jan. 1735
Tombstone inscription, Cocalico Reformed graveyard, Lancaster co., Pa.
Lowisa Fredericka Meyer, nee Globmann, b. in Europe in 1699 in the Pfaltz in the
city of Ettingen (Eppingen?). Was married to Elias Meyer for 40 years. Had 16
children—10 sons and 6 daughters.
d. 6 Feb. 1759, aged 60 years.

Elias Myer, Lancaster co., nat. Philadelphia April 1744.

Hier liegt begraben
Lowisa Friderricka Meuer
eine geborne Globmännin
Sie war geboren im jahr
1699 in Europa in der
Pfaltz in der Stat Etting
In der ehe hat sie gelebt
mit Elias Meuer 40 jahr
und hat 16 kinder gezeigt
10 Söhne und 6 Töchter
und verschied d. 6 Febru
1759 Ihres Alters 60 jahr

Here lies buried
Lowisa Friderricka Meuer
nee Globmann
she was born in the year
1699 in Europe in the
Palatinate in the city of Etting [Eppingen?]
She lived in matrimony
with Elias Meuer 40 years
and had 16 children
10 sons and 6 daughters
and departed 6 February
1759 her age 60 years

Cocalico Reformed Churchyard near Ephrata, Lancaster co., Pa.
Photo: J. Godshall

364. MAYER, JACOB FRIDERICH

6921 Neidenstein

Peggy, 1754
S-H 636, 638, 640

NEIDENSTEIN LUTHERAN KB:
m. 4 Sept. 1725 Hans Georg Maÿer, son of Marx Maÿer, and Maria Margretha, daughter of Hans Michael Furster. Hans Georg Maÿer, citizen, and wife Anna Margretha had:
    Jacob Friederich b. 1 May 1726
m. 28 Nov. 1752 Jacob Friederich Meyer, son of Georg Meÿer, and Anna Margretha, daughter of Balthasar Grob, "Gerichtsverwandten" in Neidenstein.

Pennsylvania records:
HEIDELBERG LUTHERAN KB, LEHIGH CO.:
A Jacob Friderich Meyer and wife Margaretha (Margaretha Barbara) had:
1. Maria Catharina b. 1 Oct. 1759
2. Carl Friedrich b. 20 Feb. 1761
3. Elisabeth Margaretha b. 4 Oct. 1762
4. Maria Magdalena b. 23 Jan. 1766; bp. 16 Feb. (b. in Heidelberg, bp. in Weisenberg)
5. Maria Eva b. 12 Jan. 1768
6. Georg Simon b. 22 Nov. 1769
7. Margaret Barbara b. 25 Nov. 1770
8. Tobias b. 16 Dec. 1773
9. Jacob Friedrich b. 18 Oct. 1775

Frederick Mayer, Heidleburg twp., Northampton co., nat. Philadelphia Fall 1765

365. MAYER, JOHANN FRIEDRICH

Fürfeld =
6927 Bad Rappenau

Johnson, 1732
S-H 72, 76, 78

FÜRFELD LUTHERAN KB:
m. 2 Oct. 1692 Hans Jacob Meyer from Tiroth (?), Canton Zurich, Switzerland, son of Hans Jacob Meyer, and Margretha Brigitin, widow of the late Adam Bischoff. (She was a daughter of Hans Wolf Betz, married first 24 Feb. 1690.) They had:
    Johann Friederich bp. 20 Oct. 1698
m. 22 Apr. 1732 Johann Friedrich Mayer, single, son of the late Johann Jacob Mayer, citizen and carpenter, and Juliana Catharina, daughter of the late Valentin Müller, citizen and shoemaker at Heintzheim [= Heinsheim, Baden = 6927 Bad Rappenau]. (She was a daughter of Johann Valentin Müller and his wife Eva Barbara nee Bullinger.)

Pennsylvania records:
OLEY HILLS KB, BERKS CO.:
Joh. Friedrich Mayer, b. 1699, son of Joh. Jacob Mayer and Margaretha from Fehrfeldt, 3 hours from Sinzheim. He m. Juliana Catharina, b. 1700, daughter of Valentin Müller and Magdalena from "Haasen am Neckar" by Gundelsheim. Came

to America in 1732. They had:
1. Elisabeth m. Bernt Gewiller
2. Maria Magdalena b. 1737; m. Henrich Schirm
3. Hanna b. Feb. 1739
4. Martin b.   1742
5. Maria Barbara b.   1745
6. Georg Friedrich b. 20 Aug. 1748

366. MAŸER, JOH. GEORG
1752

Tairnbach =
6909 Mühlhausen,
Kraichgau

DARMBACH (TAIRNBACH) LUTHERAN KB:
m. 18 Apr. 1752 Johann Georg Maÿer, son of Jacob Maÿer, and Maria Catharina, daughter of old Hans Adam Brecht.
"They left in the month of May for the new land."

367. MAŸER, MATHAUS
Robert and Alice, 1743
S-H 347 (Mattheis Meier)

Waldhilsbach =
6903 Neckargemünd

NECKARGEMÜND LUTHERAN KB:
Hans Georg Maÿer and wife Maria Barbara of [Wald] Hilspach had:
Joh. Mathaus b. 14 Jan. 1719

Pennsylvania records:
ST. MICHAEL'S AND ZION LUTHERAN KB, PHILADELPHIA:
Bu. 4 May 1775 Johann Matthaeus Mayer, son of the late Johann Georg Mayer of Hilsbach, Dilsperger Amt in the Pfalz, and his wife Maria Barbara, b. 14 Jan. 1719. In 1743 at the age of 24 years, he came single to this land. Married 1750 Esther Kroeplerin (?) [faded]. Had 4 daughters, 2 are living. Aged 56 y. 3 mo. ?? days.
m. 29 May 1750 in Samuel Hazard's house: Matthias Meyer and Esther Knöplerin
Matthew Meyer, Philadelphia, nat. Philadelphia April 1761

368. MAYER, JOH. VALENTIN
Peggy, 1754
S-H 636, 638, 640

6921 Neidenstein,
Elsenzgau

NEIDENSTEIN LUTHERAN KB:
m. 24 Jan. 1736 Thomas Mayer, son of Marx Mayer, and Eva Margretha, daughter of the late Hans Schoch, former citizen at Wald Wimmersbach. Their son:
1. Johannes Valentin bp. 27 Mar. 1737

Pennsylvania records:
TRINITY LUTHERAN KB, LANCASTER:
m. 8 June 1762 Valentin Majer from Neidenstein near Sinzen [Sinsheim] and Elisabet Haynin, single.

369. MEISTER, JOHAN VEIT

Shirley, 1751

S-H 454

Hoffenheim =
6920 Sinsheim, Elsenz
6928 Helmstadt-Bargen

BARGEN LUTHERAN KB:
m. 9 Feb. 1712 Georg Bernhard Meister, son of the late Hans Peter Meister,
inhabitant at Flinspach and wagonmaker, and Anna Maria, daughter of Quirin(us)
Ziegler, "Gerichtsverwanten." Their son:
    Joh. Veit bp. 17 Sept. 1719

HOFFENHEIM LUTHERAN KB:
m. 7 July 1744 Johan Veit Meister from Bargen and Anna Elisabetha Krafft, dau.
of Hans Georg Krafft, citizen. She was b. 20 May 1724 and was a sister of
Friederich Krafft [q.v.] and Hans Georg Krafft [q.v.]. They had:
    1. Georg Conrad b. 5 Apr. 1746
    2. Elisabetha Margaretha b. 1 Oct. 1748

Krebs, "Palatine Emigration . . . ," p. 32.
Johan Veit Meister received permission to emigrate in 1744 upon payment of 3
florins before his wedding.

Pennsylvania records:
ST. MICHAEL'S AND ZION LUTHERAN KB, PHILADELPHIA:
Veidt Meister from Hofenheim by Heidelberg and wife Anna Elisabetha (Reformed)
had:
    3. Johan Jürg b. 18 Sept. 1751; bp. 21 Sept.; sp. Johan Jurg Kraft (Lu-
        theran), Johan Jürg Hofmann, Elisabeth Barbara Kraft

370. MENTZINGER, CONRAD   7519 Eppingen

Edinburg, 1753

S-H 522, 525

EPPINGEN REFORMED KB:
m. 17 Nov. 1739 Conrad Mentzinger and Barbara Eÿermann
Hans Jörg Eÿermann, smith, and wife Anna had a daughter:
    Anna Barbara bp. 29 Sept. 1714
Jacob Menzinger and wife Margretha had a son:
    Hans Jacob Conrad bp. 17 Sept. 1715

Pennsylvania records:
HILL LUTHERAN KB, NORTH ANNVILLE TWP., LEBANON CO.:
d. Jan. 1800 Jacob Conrad Maenzinger, b. in Eppingen in the Palatinate Sept. 17,
1715; bp. and conf. as Reformed. On Nov. 17, 1739 m. Barbara Eyerman. No
children to first marriage. Came to this country in 1753. 1783 m. Barbara Ischler
and had 2 children. Sickness caused by a broken leg. Aged 84 y. and 4 mo.

Conrad Messinger, Lebanon twp., Lancaster co., nat. Philadelphia Sept. 1765.

371. MENTZINGER, LEONHART   7519 Eppingen

Neptune, 1751
S-H 468

EPPINGEN REFORMED KB:
Martin Menzinger and wife (not named) had:
    Johann Leonhard bp. 31 Jan. 1711
Leonhard Mensinger (Mentzinger) and wife Elisabetha had:
    1. Ludwig b. 28 Mar. 1736
    2. Margaretha b. 4 July 1739
    3. Catharina b. 30 Mar. 1742
    4. Ludwig b. 8 Jan. 1746
[Their marriage record not located; however, on 27 Oct. 1734 a *Bern*hard Mentzinger, son of Martin Mentzinger, m. Elisabetha, daughter of the late Elias Bär. This is possibly the *Leon*hard mentioned in the baptismal records.]

Pennsylvania records:

Ludwig Mensinger taxed in 1785, 150 acres, Penn twp., Northampton co. Ludwig Mensinger was enrolled in Company 2, Third Battalion, Northampton Co. Militia in 1778, 7th Class.

372. MERCKLE, ABRAHAM   Bonfeld =
                                                  6927 Bad Rappenau
1717

BONFELD LUTHERAN KB:
Abraham Merkle (Merklin) was b. 1 Mar. 1661, son of Jörg Merklin and his wife Eva. Abraham Merkle m. 27 July 1684 Anna Veronika (maiden name not given in record.) They had:
    1. Jeremias Andreas b. 16 May 1685; d. young
    2. Anna Maria b. 16 Jan. 1687; m. 1704 Hans Jost Haydt; em. 1709 to N.Y., later to Pennsylvania and Virginia.
    3. Anna Felizitas b. 6 Jan. 1689; m. 1716 Hans Jerg Bopp [q.v.]
    4. Anna Veronika b. 22 Aug. 1690; d. 1691
    5. Andreas Jeremias b. 9 June 1692; he remained in Germany at [7107] Bad Wimpfen and was the father of a son Georg Paul who later emigrated to Pennsylvania
    6. Anna Katharine b. 19 Mar. 1695
    7. Anna Veronika b. 3 Jan. 1697; d. 1708
    8. Regina Christine b. 20 Mar. 1699
    9. Isaac, twin b. 11 July 1701; d. young
    10. Jacob, twin b. 11 July 1701
    11. Isaac b. 22 Feb. 1704; d. young
    12. Anna Rosina b. 5 Nov. 1705
    13. Abraham b. 12 Mar. 1708; d. 1708

BONFELD EMIGRANT LIST:
1717 Abraham Merckle with wife and 5 ch. and son-in-law. [Hans Jerg Bopp, q.v.] For more extensive information on the Bonfeld Merckles, see *German Origins of*

Jost Hite, Virginia Pioneer, by Henry Z. Jones, Jr., Ralph Connor and Klaus Wust, (Edinburg, Va. 1979). Page 37 of this work also suggests several sources for additional information on the Jacob Merkle (Markley) family of Skippack, Montgomery Co., Pa. The available information is far too extensive to reproduce here.

373. MERCKLE, BALTHASAR

Bonfeld =
6927 Bad Rappenau

——————————— , 1717
Bonfeld Emigrant List: Balthasar Merckle with wf. and 3 ch.

Bonfeld Lutheran KB:
M. 2 July 1683 Balthasar Merckle, son of Jörg Merckle and Elisabetha (surname not given) from Switzerland. They had:
1. Anna Barbara bp. 17 Apr. 1687; m. 6 Sept. 1707 Joh. Peter Kauffman. They remained in Bonfeld and Anna Barbara d. in 1722. A daughter of this couple emigrated in 1732 [see Joh. Melchior Stecher].
2. Hans Lorentz bp. 27 Jan. 1691; d. 1691
3. Johann Adam b. 19 Aug. 1692; bp. 21 Aug. 1692; m. 23 July 1715 Maria Elisabetha Ancker.
4. Maria Catharina b. 4 May 1695; bp. 5 May 1695
5. Hans Jerg b. 1 Feb. 1697; bp. 3 Feb. 1697
6. a daughter b. 18 Oct. 1700; d.
7. a stillborn ch. b.   1701
8. Maria Elisabetha b. 9 June 1703; bp. 10 June 1703
According to the Bonfeld list, Balthasar Merckle emigrated in 1717 with wife and 3 ch. It would appear that the 3 ch. who left with their parents were #4, 5 and 8.

Pennsylvania records:
Old Goshenhoppen Lutheran KB, Montgomery co:
Maria Christina Hens b. 29 Nov. 1729, daughter of Hannes Hens and Maria Elisabeth. Her grandfather was Balthasar Merckley. Maria Christina Hens m. 14 Sept. 1752 Leonhard Schneider.

———————————

George Markl, Philadelphia co., nat by Act of 6 Feb. 1730/31

374. MERCKLE, JOHANNES age 26

6921 Michelfeld

Snow *Two Sisters,* 1738
S-H 209, 211, 212

Michelfeld Lutheran KB:
Hans Jacob Merckle from "Derting in Wurtemberg" [= Derdingen = 7135 Oberderdingen] m. 7 Mar. 1706 Anna Catharina Schertzer, daughter of the late Philipp Schertzer. Hans Jacob Merckle d. 29 Oct. 1753 and his wife d. in 1743. Their son:
    Johannes b. 12 June 1716. He left 5 May 1738 for Pennsylvania.

Pennsylvania records:
Jordan Lutheran KB, S. Whitehall twp., Lehigh co:

Johannes Merckel and wife Anna Catharina had:
1. Johannes b. 5 Dec. 1744
2. Elisabeth b. 6 Feb. 1747
3. Maria Agatha b. 13 Nov. 1749

John Merckle "Maccungy" nat. Philadelphia Fall 1765, twp., Northampton co.

375. METTLER, HANS GEORG
James Goodwill, 1728
S-H 22, 23

Waldangelloch =
6920 Sinsheim, Elsenz

WALDANGELLOCH LUTHERAN KB:
Hans Jerg Medler and wife Margretha had:
    Hans Jerg bp. 27 Dec. 1695
Hans Jerg Medler and wife Maria Eva had:
1. Maria Agnes Catharina b. 21 Feb. 1720; d. 1722
2. Jerg Michael b. 21 Apr. 1721
3. Ursula Catharina Margaretha (faded date) Mar. 1722
4. Hans Michel b. 23 Dec. 1723; d. 1727
5. Maria Christina b. 5 May 1726

Pennsylvania records:

Hans Georg Medler and Anna Maria Medler are on the 1733 communicants' list at
St. Michael's and Zion, Philadelphia

GUIDE TO THE OLD MORAVIAN CEMETERY, BETHLEHEM, PA.:
(Pennsylvania German Society Proceedings XXI (1912), p. 103)
Catharina Theodora Neisser, nee Medler, 1722–1807, from Waldengeloch, Würtemberg. She came to Philadelphia in 1728 with her parents. Was greatly blessed through the preaching of Whitefield and Zinzendorf. In 1745 she became the wife of Rev. George Neisser with whom she served in many city and county congregations until he departed this life in Philadelphia in 1784.

George Mettler, Bern tp., Berks co., nat. Philadelphia April 1761

376. METZGER, DAVID
Two Brothers, 1750
S-H 438 (with Hans Jacob (   ) Metziger, on board)

Eichtersheim =
6921 Angelbachtal

SINSHEIM LUTHERAN KB:
David Metzger, shoemaker at Steinsfurt, and Christina, nee Lenhard, Reformed, had:
    David, b. 20 Feb. 1704, bp. 21 Feb., sp. David Rautenbusch, Ref. from Steinsfurt

EICHTERSHEIM LUTHERAN KB:
Joh. David Metzger, a wagon maker, born in Steinsfurt, m. (1) 21 Oct. 1731 Anna

The "Wasserschloss" or moated palace at Eichtersheim, on the Angelbach, today one of the villages in the municipality of Angelbachtal. Earliest documentation of Eichtersheim is from 838; by the eighteenth century the von Venningen, who built the palace, owned the place. Eichtersheim became Lutheran in 1522, but was not a parish until nearly 1700. Today the residence is the town hall for the combined community. It is surrounded by a park containing rare and ancient trees.

Photo: J. Godshall

Margaretha, daughter of Barthel Zimmerman, a butcher. She d. in 1732, leaving no children. Joh. David Metzger m. (2) 13 Jan. 1733 Eva Catharina Muth. Children:
1. Joh. Jacob b. 26 Feb. 1734; sp. Joh. Jacob Metzger, citizen and shoemaker in Steinsfurt, and wife Barbara.
2. Anna Maria b. 28 July 1738
3. Hans Paul b. 12 Oct. 1742
4. Joh. Philipp b. 21 May 1749

Pennsylvania records:
LANCASTER CO. WILLS:
David Metzger, Conestoga twp., (13 July 1771/2 Sept. 1777) oldest son Jacob, son Paul, wife Catharina.

TRINITY LUTHERAN KB, LANCASTER:
m. 27 Nov. 1764 Jacob Mezger, single, wheelwright, and Susanna Rudesilyn, single. They had:
1. Susanna, b. 25 July 1766; d. young
2. Georg Friedrich, b. 29 Sept. 1768
3. Jacob, b. 15 Oct. 1770
4. Catharine, b. 7 March 1775

TOMBSTONE, CONESTOGA CENTRE REFORMED CHURCH:
(Trans:) Here rest the bones of Jacob Metzger. He was born February 26, 1734, united in marriage with Susanna, nee Rudisille, 1764, produced with her 4 children, died July 8, 1790.

377. MEYER, DIONŸSIUS
William & Sarah, 1727
S-H 7 (No. of persons: 5)

Reihen =
6920 Sinsheim, Elsenz

REIHEN REFORMED KB:
Hans Henrich Meyer and wife Catharina had:
Dionÿsius bp. 21 June 1678
m. 9 Nov. 1706 Dionÿsius Meyer, son of the late Henerich Meyer, former citizen,
and Anna Maria, dau. of the late Hans Dörr. Children:
1. Bernhardt b. 15 Aug. 1707; d.
2. Anna Barbara b. 30 Jan. 1709; d. age 4 years
3. Anna Maria b. 9 Feb. 1711
4. Johann Bernhardt b. 30 May 1712; d.
5. Johann Bernhardt b. 26 Sept. 1713; d.
6. Anna Barbara bp. 5 Mar. 1715; d.
7. Hans Görg bp. 23 June 1716
8. Anna Barbara bp. 24 Aug. 1718
9. Joh. Dieterich bp. 10 Mar. 1721
10. Susanna Maria bp. 27 June 1723
11. Joh. Jacob bp. 13 Apr. 1727

Pennsylvania records:

Dennis Myer signed a letter to the governor of Maryland, 11 Aug. 1736 as named
in a warrant for arrest 21 Oct. 1736. (A. R. Wentz, *The Beginnings of the German
Element in York County* (Lancaster, 1916, 203.)

A Teeter Mayer (Dieterich Meyer) is mentioned in York Orphans Court record dated
30 Aug. 1763 as a husband of Margaret Leib, dau. of Johannes Leib, another
immigrant from Reihen.

Detrick Meyer Manchester twp., York co., nat. Philadelphia, April 1762

378. MEYER, JACOB age 26
MEYER, STOFFEL age 23

6926 Kirchardt

Britannia, 1731
S-H 48, 52, 53

KIRCHARDT REFORMED KB: [NO MARRIAGES RECORDED 1685–1700]
Jacob Meÿer and wife Sabina had:
1. Joh. Georg bp. 26 Oct. 1700; sp. Hans Georg Klein and Anna Maria,
wife of Hans Jacob Hatz
*2. Joh. Jacob bp. 19 Feb. 1705; sp. Jacob Hatz and Veronica, wife of Hans
Georg Klein
*3. Stoffel b. 19 Mar. 1708; bp. 20 Mar. 1708; sp. Stoffel Geiger and
Catharina, wife of Heinrich Voll
4. Hans Heinrich b. 20 Apr. 1711

Pennsylvania records:
MUDDY CREEK LUTHERAN KB, AND EMANUEL LUTHERAN KB, WARWICK TWP,
LANCASTER CO.:
Jacob Meÿer (Warwick) had:
1. Anna Barbara b. 1 July 1734; sp. Anna Klein
2. Catharina Sophia b. 14 Sept. 1743; her bp. record mentions that the father
   is dead. Sp. Andreas Huber and Catharina Klein
m. 18 Dec. 1734 Christoph Meyer and Anna Rosina Koppenhöverin. Children:
1. Joh. Georg b. 4 Dec. 1735; sp. Joh. Georg Klein and Anna
2. Maria Barbara b. 12 Aug. 1738
3. Anna Maria b. 16 June 1742 (Stoever's personal record)
Stoever's records also contain other Meyer families, and there are some slight
indications of a possible relationship. The name is common and extensive research
would be necessary to prove the circumstantial evidence of relationship to the
Kirchardt Meyers.
Heinrich Meyer (Lebanon) had one child bp. by Stoever:
1. Christoph b. 20 Oct. 1736; sp. Christoph Meyer and Anna Rosina
Joh. Georg Meyer (Swatara) had 4 daughters bp. by Stoever:
1. Anna Barbara b. 6 Oct. 1734
2. Veronica b. 28 Feb. 1737
3. Elisabetha b. 7 Apr. 1739
4. Anna Sabina b. 3 June 1745

Christopher Meyer, Lancaster twp, Lancaster co, nat. Philadelphia Fall 1765.

379. MINIER, CHRISTIAN age 28

Mary, 1732
S-H, 93, 95

6921 Michelfeld
Lützelsachsen =
6940 Weinheim,
Bergstrasse

MICHELFELD LUTHERAN KB:
Christian Minier, son of the late Christian Minier, former citizen and smith at
Lützelsachsen, Hochfreÿh. Hundheim Herrschaft m. 13 Jan. 1728 Maria Cathar-
ina, daughter of Hans Rudi (She was b. Laetare 1706, daughter of Hans Rudi and
Anna Margaretha, nee Beilstein.) Children:
1. Joh. Heinrich b. 5 Feb. 1729

380. MINIER, DAVID (sick)

Pleasant, 1732
S-H 100 (MENEIR on list)

6921 Michelfeld
Lützelsachsen =
6940 Weinheim,
Bergstrasse

MICHELFELD LUTHERAN KB:
David Minier, son of a citizen and musician from Lietzelhassen in the Odenwald,
m. 25 Mar. 1732 Anna Maria Ziegler, daughter of the late Joh. Georg Ziegler from
Weÿler, Venningischen Herrschaft.

381. MINIER, JOH. GEORG age 26

Mary, 1732

S-H 93, 95

6921 Michelfeld
Lützelsachsen =
6940 Weinheim,
Bergstrasse

MICHELFELD LUTHERAN KB:
Johann Georg Minier (Männer), son of the late Christian Minier, former citizen and smith at Lützelsachsen, m. 23 Nov. 1728 Anna Catharina, daughter of Ulrich Maÿer, citizen. (Catharina was b. 12 May 1709 daughter of Ulrich Maÿer, formerly from Düren [= Dühren = 6920 Sinsheim], Reformed religion, and his wife Anna Elisabetha.) Children:
1. Johannes b. 20 Feb. 1730
2. Maria Catharina b. 22 Apr. 1731
"Are going to Pennsylvania 6 May 1732."

Pennsylvania records:
HEIDELBERG MORAVIAN KB, BERKS CO:
Georg Minier b. in "Lizelsasse near Heidelberg" son of Christian Minier and Anna Rosina nee Grengelbach. Georg m. 28 Nov. 1728 Catharina, daughter of Ulrich and Elisabeth Meyer of Michelfeld. Children were:
1. Johannes b. 11 Feb. 1730 (new style) in Michelfeld
2. Elisabeth b. 24 Dec. 1732 in Conestoga (old style)
3. Maria Catharina b. 2 Feb. 1734 in Conestoga (old style)
4. Heinrich b. 24 Dec. 1736 in Conestoga
5. Catharina b. 15 Sept. 1740 in Heidelberg
His first wife d. in 1745, and Georg Minier m. (2) Maria Elisabeth Strunk, daughter of Weimert Strunk, citizen of "Prendlingen in Kreuznach in the Pfalz" and his wife Catharina. Children of second marriage:
6. Christina b. 27 June 1746
7. Christian b. 30 Sept. 1747
8. Daniel b. 13 Oct. 1749
9. Maria Elisabeth b. 31 Mar. 1751

382. "MOLITOR," Anabaptist
with wife and child

1717

Bonfeld =
6927 Bad
Rappenau

BONFELD LUTHERAN KB:
There were three men mentioned in the Bonfeld church records in this time period who were designated as *Molitor* (miller) and Anabaptist. Since this emigrant is not mentioned by name and only his occupation and religion are mentioned, the information about all three is given here.
Molitor 1: Joh. Jacob Schneid(er), son of Johannis Schneid(er), miller, was bp. 21 Sept. 1710 age 19, "Anabaptista." M. 10 Feb. 1711 at Bonfeld Joh. Jacob Schneid, son of Joh. Schneid, miller, and Maria Helena (Magdalena), daughter of the late Heinrich Nischicker, former miller at the Mittlere Grundmühl. They had:
1. Johann Jacob b. 7 Apr. 1712; bu. 8 Apr. 1712
2. Anna Maria Catharina b. 22 Mar. 1713; bp. 23 Mar. 1713. In her bp.

record, the mother's name is given as Maria Magdalena. Catharina emigrated to America with her mother and m. Martin Keblinger.
3. Anna Maria Barbara b. 13 Feb. 1715; d. 24 June 1717
4. Maria Felicitas b. 10 May 1716; bp. 11 May 1716, posthumous child. The surname is given as both Schneid and Schneider in these records.
Jacob Schneid, molitor, d. 18 Dec. 1715, age 24 years less 14 days. His widow, Maria Magdalena m. (2) 27 June 1717 Joh. Matthes Ringer [q.v.] and they appear on the 1717 list.
Magdalena Ringer d. 6 Apr. 1764, age 74½ y. (New Hanover Lutheran KB, Montgomery co.)

Molitor 2: Heinrich Vollweider, son of an Anabaptist at Hasselbach, was bp. Dom. 21 p. Trin. 1706 at Bonfeld. M. 1 Nov. 1706 Heinrich Vollweider, son of the late Johannes Vollweider, Anabaptist at Hasselbach, and Anna Catharina, daughter of Johannes Bengel. They had:
1. Maria Catharina Ottilia b. 2 Nov. 1710; bp. 4 Nov. 1710
2. Maria Margaretha bp. 16 Dec. 1713, father is given as Henrich Vollweider, *molitor.*
3. Joh. Jacob bp. 21 Nov. 1716
Ernst Müller published lists of Mennonites residing in the Oberpfalz in 1731 in *Geschichte der Bernischen Taufer.* Heinrich vol Weiler's widow is on the list for Hasselbach. Therefore, there is a possibility that Henrich Vollweider may have died in Hasselbach, rather than emigrating.

Molitor 3: Johannes Wagner, son of an Anabaptist at Hasselbach, was bp. Dom. 21 p. Trin. 1706 at Bonfeld, along with Heinrich Vollweider mentioned above. M. 1 Nov. 1706 Johannes Wagner, son of the late Christian Wagner, Anabaptist at Hasselbach, and Anna Sophia Berger, daughter of Andreas and Anna Catharina Berger. Sophia Berger was bp. 2 Apr. 1675, daughter of Andreas and Anna Catharina Berger. Sophia was the sister of Andreas Berger who also appears on the 1717 Bonfeld Emigrant List.

Pennsylvania records:

One Hans Wagner signed a 1723 petition, requesting a road in Limerick twp. through Falkner's Swamp to "Oaley" (Philadelphia Co. Clerk of Quarter Sessions Records, Vol I.)

383. MOTZ, HANS
_____, 1717
Bonfeld emigrant list: Hans Motz with wife

Bonfeld = 6927 Bad Rappenau

BONFELD LUTHERAN KB:
m. 28 Feb. 1716 Johannes Motz, son of the late Galli Motz, citizen at Ditzingen, Leonberger Ambts [7257 Ditzingen], and Maria Apollonia, daughter of Johann Leonhard Maubars, citizen at Hecklingen in the Markgrafschaft Anspach [8831 Hechlingen], near Gunzenhausen. They had:
1. Johann Simon b. 28 Oct. 1716, d. 29 Oct. 1716

American records:

This immigrant has been identified by Klaus Wust as a passenger on Captain Scott's ship from London to Virginia in 1717. (*Hebron Church Register,* 1750–1825, Madison, Va., Volume I by George M. Smith. Introduction by Klaus Wust, p. XII.)

384. MÜLLER, DIETRICH

6921 Zuzenhausen

1743

ZUZENHAUSEN LUTHERAN KB:
Joh. Dieterich Müller and wife Anna Maria had:
1. Joh. Adam b. 4 Dec. 1734
2. Joh. Georg b. 23 Jan. 1736
3. Anna Maria bp. 17 Jan. 1739
4. Anna Elisabetha bp. 16 Jan. 1741
5. Anna Catharina bp. 3 Sept. 1742

Krebs, "Palatine Emigration . . . ," p. 29–30.
Dietrich Mueller of Zuzenhausen, baker, was permitted to emigrate with Jacob Hoffmann without payment of the usual taxes because of their poverty.

In Zuzenhausen on the Elsenz (first mentioned in 778), a mixed Catholic and Lutheran population dwelt. This house was built 1761 by the Schultheiss—mayor—a certain Johann Christopher Lockheimer and his wife Anna Maria. A carving of St. Christopher and the Christchild on the building reveals Lockheimer's religious faith. Although Zuzenhausen became Lutheran in 1552, it fell to the Roman Catholics at the time of the "Palatine Church Division" in 1707. After that the Lutherans were served from Neckargemünd and Daisbach, some miles away.

Photo: J. Godshall

385. MÜLLER, HANS ADAM

Weiler =
6920 Sinsheim, Elsenz

William and Sarah, 1727
S-H 7, 9 (2 persons)

WEILER REFORMED KB:
m. 22 Nov./2 Dec. 1687 [sic] Johann Christoph Müller, son of Christoph Müller, "Anwalt" at Weÿler, and Maria Barbara, daughter of the late Michael Schopf. Their son:
Hans Adam b. 8 Feb. 1700

Pennsylvania records:
YORK LUTHERAN KB:
Adam Miller and wife [also in Lancaster Lutheran KB: "across the Susquehanna"] had:
1. Joh. Georg b. 28 May 1739
2. Anna Margaret b. 5 Jan. 1743
3. Joh. Christian b. 26 Apr. 1744
Krebs, "Palatine Emigration . . . ," p. 24.
Hans Adam Miller paid 13 florins, 2 kreuzer in 1727, in order to emigrate.

386. MÜLLER, HANS GEORG

7519 Eppingen

[several possibilities in S-H.]

EPPINGEN LUTHERAN KB:
Hans Georg Müller and wife Anna Margretha had:
Hans Georg b. 18 Jan. 1720

Pennsylvania records:
ST. MICHAEL'S AND ZION LUTHERAN KB, PHILADELPHIA:
D. 22 Nov. 1787 Joh. Georg Miller, b. 20 Dec. 1720 in Eppingen in the Pfalz, son of Georg Miller and Anna Margretha. Married Marthe Hofman and had 3 children.

387. MÜLLER, JURG ADAM

Massenbach =
7103 Schwaigern

Francis & Elizabeth, 1742
S-H 327, 329

MASSENBACH LUTHERAN KB:
Joh. Michael Müller, wagonmaker, and wife Maria Elisabetha had:
Georg Adam b. 30 Jan. 1718
Hans Jerg Stocker, carpenter, and wife Anna Catharina had:
Christina Catharina b. 23 Mar. 1722

Pennsylvania records:
ST. MICHAEL'S AND ZION LUTHERAN KB, PHILADELPHIA:
D. 19 Oct. 1765 Christina Catharina Müller, wife of Jürg Adam Müller, b. 23 Mar. 1722 at Massebach.

MUHLENBERG'S JOURNALS, I: 544:
11 Aug. 1762—Georg Adam Müller reported that his little daughter Barbara (b. 11 May 1761) d. last night.

I: 580:
19 Dec. 1762—Went to Jürg Adam Müller's and bp. his little daughter, Anna Barbara, at home.

388. MÜLLER, MICHAEL   6921 Zuzenhausen
MÜLLER, JOH. GEORG
MÜLLER, ANNA MARIA MARGRETHA
MÜLLER, ANNA MARIA

Prelist, with their step-father Erasmus Buckenmeyer [q.v.]

NECKARGEMÜND LUTHERAN KB:
Ludwig Müller of Zuzenhausen and wife Anna Margretha had:
1. Michael [bp. not located, but he is mentioned as a son in Pennsylvania records. Neckargemünd KB starts in 1704 and presumably he was b. before that date.]
2. Joh. Georg b. 13 Oct. 1706
3. Anna Maria Margretha b. 20 Dec. 1711
4. Anna Maria b. 17 Sept. 1715
D. 28 July 1717 Ludwig Müller from Zuzenhausen, was struck by a stone in the quarry and killed. Bu. 29 July, aged 45 y. and 7 mo. His widow, Anna Margretha, m. (2) 14 Feb. 1719 Asmus (Erasmus) Buckemeÿer [q.v.]

Pennsylvania records:
PHILADELPHIA WILLS, BOOK G: 239
Erasmus Buggemeyer, Tulpehocken. (11 Jan. 1739/13 Apr. 1748.) Wife Margrea, daughter Madlena, wife of Peter Anspach, and 4 step-children: Michel Miller, George Miller, Margred Elbertscheit and Anna Maria Neff [see Frederick Elberscheidt, Michael Reiss and Michael Neff, Jr.]

CHRIST LUTHERAN KB, TULPEHOCKEN, BERKS CO.:
Georg Muller and wife sponsor children of Abraham Neff and Michael Neff in 1749.
Michael Muller and Anna Maria had:
Joh. Christian bp. Easter 1745

LANCASTER CO. DEEDS:
C: 170, 174. 13 May 1748. 216 A. plus 53 A., Plumton Manor. The heirs of Erasmus Buggameir: Peter Anspach and wife Madlina (daughter) and step-children: Michael Miller of Cocalico twp.; George Miller of Heidelberg twp.; Margaret, wife of Michael Reis of Bethel twp., and Anna Maria, wife of Michael Neff, Jr. of Heidelberg twp.; and Margaret Buggameir, widow of Erasmus, all released their rights to Philip Weiser.
Many other Lancaster deeds pertain to the land transactions of this family, including A-79, C-159, C-162, C-163, C-166, C-175, C-178, D-322, D-486

A mighty half-timbered structure alongside the Elsenz with an obvious complex construction history reminds us of the equally grand house erected by Georg Müller along the Millbach in Lebanon county in 1752. Müller came from Zuzenhausen with his mother and stepfather in the 1720s.

Photo: J. Godshall

MÜHLBACH REFORMED KB, MILLBACH TWP., LEBANON CO.:
Georg Müller and wife Maria Catharina were sponsors in 1749 for children of Joh. Georg Meuser and John Haack.

Date stone on the house of the miller at Mühlbach, some of whose interior features have been arranged in the Philadelphia Museum of Art.

17   JERG MÜLER   52
      MARIA CATH M.

389. MÜLLER, MICHAEL

Jacob, 1749
S-H 417

Massenbach =
7103 Schwaigern

MASSENBACH LUTHERAN KB:
Joh. Michael Müller, wagonmaker, and wife Maria Elisabetha had:
    Joh. Michael b. 16 Dec. 1725
[His brothers-in-law, Joh. Fridrich Bickel and Joh. Conrad Lauffer, are also passengers on this ship.]

Pennsylvania records:

Wochentlicher Pennsylvanischer Staatsbote, 29 Sept. 1772: Georg Adam Schmaltzhof seeks Friedrich Bickel, whose wife is the sister of Michael Mueller's wife.

390. MÜLLER, MICHAEL age 60

6901 Mauer

Molley, 1741
S-H 310, 311, 312

MAUER LUTHERAN KB:
Hans Michael Müller and Anna Catharina had:
1. Maria Catharina b. 2 Dec. 1720
2. Christina b. 12 Dec. 1722
3. Joh. Thomas b. 19 Oct. 1724
4. Joh. Peter b. 6 Nov. 1726
5. Anna Regina b. 6 Mar. 1728; d. 26 Jan. 1729
6. Joh. Andreas b. 20 Nov. 1729
7. Joh. Georg b. 30 Jan. 1734
[Note: Their marriage not recorded here—there is a Jeremias Muller b. ca. 1714 also on this ship who may be a child, bp. elsewhere.]

Krebs, "Palatine Emigration . . . ," p. 27. Michael Müller permitted to emigrate to America with wife and five children on payment of 6 florins emigration tax.

Pennsylvania records:
One Andres Müller appears on a list of members at Old Goshenhoppen Church, Montgomery co.
A Peter Müller and wife Maria had:
1. Joh. Conrad bp. 30 Aug. 1741; sp. Conrad Kolb and wife

391. MÜLLER, PHILIPP GEORG

6922 Meckesheim

Chesterfield, 1749
S-H 393 (Name on list: Pips Gorg Müller)

MECKESHEIM REFORMED KB:
Philipp Georg Müller and wife Barbara had:
1. Anna Dorothea b. 3 Apr. 1746
2. Maria Barbara b. 11 Apr. 1748

Krebs, "Palatine Emigration . . . ," p. 34.
Philipp Georg Mueller of Meckesheim (Kreis Heidelberg) was permitted in 1749 to emigrate to the New Land with wife and two children on payment of 10 florins emigration tax.

Pennsylvania records:
WALDSCHMIDT RECORDS:
Filip Gorg Muller and wife Barbara had:
Johann Jacob b. 16 Feb. 1754; sp. Jacob Hausser and wife Barbara

392. MÜNCH, JOH. CONRAD
MÜNCH, JOH. GODFRIED

Weiler =
6920 Sinsheim, Elsenz
Mechtersheim =
6725 Römerberg, Pfalz

Polly, 1765
S-H 704

WEILER REFORMED KB:
Conf. 1715 Joh. Gottfried Monig age 14.
M. 9 Nov. 1723 Johann Gottfried Münich from Weÿler, single, and Elisabetha
Lertz, daughter of Herr Dieterich Lertz, "Rathsverwandten" at Epping(en). Chil-
dren:

    1. Catharina bp. 27 Aug. 1724
    2. Georg bp. 11 Oct. 1726; d. young
    3. Simon bp. ____Apr. 1728
  *4. Joh Conrad bp. 26 Mar. 1730
    5. Johann Jacob bp. 3 Jan. 1732
    6. Johann Philipp bp. 1 Aug. 1733
    7. Maria Margretha bp. 19 Sept. 1736; d.
    8. Margaretha Elisabetha bp. 18 Oct. 1739
    9. Maria Eva. bp. 9 July 1741; d.
  10. Eva Margaretha bp. 11 Oct. 1742
*11. Johann Godfried bp. 23 Jan. 1746
D. 4 Feb. 1746 Margaretha Elisabetha Münch, wife of Joh. Godfried Münch,
Innkeeper of the "Engel" and citizen at Weiler, aged 45 y 3 mo 1 day. She was b.
in Eppingen, dau. of the late Herr Dieterich Lertz and Anna Margrethe.

PENNSYLVANIA RECORDS:
See Ella Z. Elliott, *Blue Book of Schuylkill County* (Pottsville, Pa. 1916), pp. 387–
93. According to records in this volume, Conrad Münch had a passport (in 1916
in the possession of a descendant in Long Island, N.Y.) "Conrad Münch of Mechtersheim, near Speyer, his wife and his brother Gottfried Münch do intend to settle
in the New England," 25 Apr. 1765. Also published in this volume were copies of
four letters exchanged by family members over many years. The first letter dated
Philadelphia 15 Mar. 1784 from Conrad and Gottfried Münch mentions the following relatives: Father: Gottfried, brothers Simon and Jacob, sisters Catharina and
Margaretha Elisabetha and Eva Margaretha. Brothers-in-law: Jacob Detrich and
Christophel Adolf.

393. MÜNTZ, PHILIP age 38   7103 Schwaigern

Harle, 1736
S-H, 156, 159, 161

SCHWAIGERN LUTHERAN KB:
m. 24 Jan. 1702 Ulrich Muntz, son of Sebastian Muntz, butcher, and Maria
Barbara, daughter of Hans Jerg Nellinger. They had:
    Joh. Philip bp. 7 Oct. 1707
m. 7 May 1736 Johann Philip Muntz, son of the late Ulerich Muntz, and Anna
argretha, daughter of Johann Michael Weich, citizen at Northeim [= 7107 Nord-
heim]. "And then hurriedly departed for the New Land."

Pennsylvania records:
TRAPPE LUTHERAN KB, MONTGOMERY CO. AND ZION'S LUTHERAN CHURCH,
CHESTER CO:
Joh. Philip Müntz and Anna Margretha had:

1. Margretha, conf. at Trappe 1752, age 15
2. Johan Jacob, conf. at Trappe 1754, age 15
3. Georg Christoph, conf. at Trappe 1756, age 15; (m. before 1771
Barbara _____?)
4. ·Anna Magdalena b. 14 Apr. 1749; bp. 1 July at Trappe; conf. 1764 at
   Zion's Church as Maria Magdalena Müntz, daughter of Philip, age 15.

Philip Mentz, Pikes twp, Chester co., nat. Philadelphia, Fall 1765.

394. NEFF   Bonfeld =
                                                                  6927 Bad
1717   Rappenau
Bonfeld Emigrant List, 1717:   Dühren = 6920 Sinsheim

BONFELD EMIGRANT LIST, 1717:
The Bonfeld list mentions an Anabaptist, Mennonite by the name of Neff with wife
and children. The next entry on the list is "dessen bruder" (his brother) with wife
and children. Although the given names of these two emigrants do not appear on
this list, there are two Neffs found in the records of the area and later in Pennsylvania, who might be the families in question:

DÜHREN LUTHERAN KB:
1) Franz Neff—m. 22 Apr. 1710 at Dühren Franz Neff, jr., said to be a doctor,
Anabaptist, to Barbara Ebin [or Böhm ?] born at Michelfeld. A later record mentions his intention to go to the New Land.
2) Heinrich Neff—Bonfeld Church Record: d. 1 Feb. 1717 the 7 year old son of
Heinrich Neff, named Joh. Jacob, d. and bu. the following day "mit Gesang und
Klang" ("singing and ringing"). (This entry was recorded on one of the last pages
of the KB and not with the other 1717 burials.) The wording of the burial entry
indicates that this was a Mennonite family; there was a law that forbade singing or
bells for a Mennonite burial, unless special permission had been secured. This
entry indicated that, with permission, this child was buried in the Lutheran cemetery there—"auf unserem Gottesacker." (See C. Henry Smith *The Mennonite
Immigration to Pennsylvania* (Norristown, Pa. 1929), pp. 49–53, for further reference to burial restrictions.)
The names of both Heinrich Neff and Franz Neff appear in Pennsylvania records.

Pennsylvania records:

The Mennonite Immigration to Pennsylvania by C. Henry Smith, (Norristown, Pa.,
1929), 162:
Hans Henry Neff appears on the first assessment list (1718) of Conestoga twp. (now
Lancaster co.) "John Henry Neff, known as the "Old Doctor" was a brother of
Francis Neff. He was undoubtedly the first regularly bred physician in Lancaster
Co."
1. Daniel Rupp *History of Lancaster Co., Pa.*, (Lancaster, 1844), p. 124:
Francis Neff, his sons, Francis, Jr.; Henry and Daniel and the sons of Daniel,
namely Henry and Daniel, grandsons of Francis the Elder, were all natives of
Switzerland. On account of religious persecution, being Mennonites, they fled to

Alsace, thence they emigrated to America, and settled at a very early date on a small stream, Neff's Run, which empties into the Little Conestoga." The following Neffs were naturalized by the Act of 14 Feb. 1729/30: Francis Neiff, Francis Neiff, Jr., Henry Neiff, John Henry Neiff, and John Henry Neiff, Jr.

395. NEFF, MICHAEL   6921 Michelfeld

James Goodwill, 1728
S-H 21, 22

MICHELFELD LUTHERAN KB:
Michael Neff, b. 21 Feb. 1687, son of Joh. Jacob Neff, m. 11 Nov. 1710 Anna Dorothea, daughter of Herr Hans Jacob Saur, citizen and "Gerichtsverwandten". Children:
1. Johann Michael b. 23 July 1712
2. Joh. Jacob b. 13 Feb. 1715
3. Anna Catharina b. 27 Nov. 1716
4. Georg Abraham b. 2 Oct. 1719
5. Maria Catharina b. 25 Jan. 1723; d. 1725
6. Hans Leonhard b. 8 Mar. 1725

Pennsylvania records:
NEW HOLLAND LUTHERAN KB, LANCASTER CO.:
Michael Neff had:
Joh. Georg b. 1 Dec. 1729; bp. 3 May 1730
Anna Catharina Neff, single, is a bp. sp. in 1733. She later married in Tulpehocken on 10 Sept. 1739 Michael Stump (Stoever's records)

MUDDY CREEK LUTHERAN KB, LANCASTER CO:
Jacob Neff m. 11 May 1742 Christiana Stober, Warwick. Children:
1. Joh. Jacob b. 3 Jan. 1743; bp. 14 Jan: Sp: Michael Neff, Jr. and his wife

CHRIST LUTHERAN KB, STOUCHSBURG, TULPEHOCKEN, BERKS CO.:
Joh. Jacob Nef and wife Christina had:
Maria Elisabetha b. 15 Apr. 1754
Maria Barbara b. 8 Sept. 1755
Joh. Peter b. 3 Apr. 1764
Michael Neef, Jr. and wife Anna Maria had:
1. Maria Catharine b. 5 Jan. 1749
2. Joh. Peter b. 22 Mar. 1751
Abraham Neff m. 8 June 1742 Anna Christina Loesch in Tulpehocken (Stoever's records). Children, bp. at Christ Lutheran, Tulpehocken:
1. Joh. Jacob bp. 16 Sept. 1744
2. Christina bp. 22 May 1746
3. (?) Maria Catharina bp. 16 July 1746 (? 1747)
4. Maria Magdalena b. 25 Nov. 1748
5. Joh. Georg b. 24 Feb. 1751
6. Anna Maria b. 18 May 1752
7. Abraham b. 15 July 1753
8. Joh. Georg b. 14 Jan. 1756

9. Joh. Leonard b. 10 Apr. 1757
10. Michael b. 1 July 1759
11. Anna Margaret b. 28 Aug. 1761
12. Joh. Henry b. 4 July 1764
m. 1747 Tuesday after Dom. 17 p. Trin. Leonhard Neef, single son of the church deacon Michael Neef, and Elisabeth Magdalena Feg, single dau. of the late Leonard Feg.
Lancaster co. deeds C-170, 13 May 1748, names Anna Maria [Miller] stepdaughter of Erasmus Buchemeyer [also of Michelfeld] as wife of Michael Neff.

Anna Maria Naefen, Lancaster co., wife of Michael Naefen nat. Philadelphia 26 Sept. 1748.
Abraham Netf [sic] and Jacob Netf [sic] Tulpohockon twp., Lancaster co. nat. Philadelphia April 1761.

396. NEU (NEY), H. GEORG
Shirley, 1751
S-H 454

Hoffenheim =
6920 Sinsheim, Elsenz
6921 Neidenstein

HOFFENHEIM LUTHERAN KB:
Christoph New and wife Anna Catharina had:
Johann Georg bp. 2 Dec. 1713; conf. 1728
m. 18 Nov. 1738 at Neidenstein Joh. Georg Neu, single son of Christoph Neu in Hoffenheim, and Maria Elisabetha, daughter of Andreas Horpuff, citizen in Neidenstein.
Hans Georg Neu and wife Maria Elisabetha had children bapt. at Hoffenheim:
1. Joh. Tobias b. 17 Sept. 1737; d. 1740
2. Georg Tobias b. 21 Sept. 1741; d. 1743
3. Johann b. 10 Apr. 1744, d. 1748; sp. Johann Neü [q.v.], the father's brother.
4. Joh. Martin b. 2 Apr. 1747
5. Joh. Georg b. 6 June 1750
He appears on the ship's list with several other emigrants from Hoffenheim.

397. NEY, NEU, JOHANNES
Shirley, 1751
S-H 454

Hoffenheim =
6920 Sinsheim, Elsenz

HOFFENHEIM LUTHERAN KB:
m. 29 Nov. 1707 Joh. Christophel New and Anna Catharina, daughter of Andres Jung. Their son:
Johannes b. 5 Dec. 1721
confirmed 1736 Johann Neü
m. 3 Jan. 1747 Johannes Neü, son of Christoph Neü, and Dorothea, daughter of Georg Braun from Michelfeld. Children:
1. Maria Barbara b. 24 Sept. 1747
2. Maria Dorothea b. 7 Sept. 1750

Pennsylvania records:
TRINITY LUTHERAN KB, LANCASTER:
Johannes Neu and Dorothea had:
   3. Johannes bp. (24 Mar.?) 1753
A Johannes Neu and wife Maria Magdalena had:
   Johannes b. 11 June 1769
   Elisabeth b. 8 July 1770
   Maria Magdalena b. 26 Aug. 1772
   Johann b. 15 Feb. 1774
   Catharina b. 27 Feb. 1775
   Margaretha b. 30 Mar. 1776
   Susanna b. 6 Mar. 1777
   Rebecca b. 26 Sept. 1782
   Catharina b. 13 Feb. 1786

398. NOLFF, LORENTZ

Grossgartach =
7105 Leingarten
Schluchtern =
7105 Leingarten

Charming Nancy, 1737
S-H 189, 190, 192 (with Anna Maria Nolf, Elisabetha
Nolf, Margareta Nolf)

SCHLUCHTERN LUTHERAN KB:
m. 31 Aug. 1728 Lorentz Nolff, single son of Lorentz Nolff, citizen at Grossen
Gartach, and Anna Maria, daughter of Philipp Werner, citizen and "des Gerichts".
(No ch. bp. at Schluchtern.)

Pennsylvania records:
NORTHAMPTON CO. PROBATE RECORDS:
John Knolph, adm. granted 25 May 1759 to Lawrence Knolph and Jacob Kook of
Bethlehem twp.
John Nolph of Chestnut Hill twp., adm. to Casper Nolph and Abraham Labar
26 Nov. 1762, inventory 4 July 1768 by Henrich Frantz.
Improvement in Chestnut Hill formerly belonging to Johannes Nolf, deceased,
warrant and assignment made to him by George Shaffer.

399. NOTZ, JOH. LEONHARD age 38

6921 Zuzenhausen

Two Sisters, 1738
S-H 209, 210, 211 (with Catharina Notz age 37; Dorothy age 4)

ZUZENHAUSEN LUTHERAN KB:
m. (1) 16 Nov. 1723 Leonhardt Notz and Maria Eva Barth. Children:
   1. Joh. Georg b. 28 Jan. 1726
   2. Anna Dorothea b. 22 Apr. 1733
m. (2) 26 Oct. 1734 Joh. Leonhard Notz and Anna Catharina, daughter of the late
Henrich Keÿdel. Children:
   3. Joh. Georg b. 18 Dec. 1735
   4. Joh. Michel b. 24 Jan. 1738

Durch	By
Gottes Gnad	God's grace help and
Hülff und Bey	support this
stand Haben Er	community town hall
baut Dieses Gemei	was built by Johann Willhelm Vogt,
ne Rathhaus—Johann Willhelm	(Schultheiss) Dietrich Obernese,
Vogt Schultheis—Dietrich Obernese	chairman of the Gerickt and Jo-
Burgerm. Des Gerichts und	hann Willhelm Hoffmann, chair-
Johann Willhelm Hoffmann Bur	man of the town Bürgermeister der
germeister Der Gemeind Mit Rath U	Gemeinde) with the counsel and
That Der Gantzen Gemeind All	labor of the entire town here in
heir zu Zutzenhausen Anno 1723	Zuzenhausen, Anno 1723

Zuzenhausen was plundered in 1622 and destroyed in 1634. Only nine families remained at the end of the Thirty Years' War (1648), to whom were added new immigrants from other parts of Germany and Switzerland. Hardly rebuilt, it was destroyed again in 1689 by the French. Whether he remained at home or emigrated to Pennsylvania, an eighteenth century German citizen of small towns in the Kraichgau faced a tremendous building task. Town halls often came first.

Krebs, "Palatine Emigration . . . ," p. 27. Permitted to emigrate in 1738 on payment of 28 florins.

Pennsylvania records:
SALEM LUTHERAN KB, LEBANON:
D. 31 Aug. 1799 Anna Dorothea Günther. B. 25 Apr. 1734 in Durlachishen, Germany. Parents, Leonhard Notz and wife. Bp. there. In her 5th year she came to this country. She was conf. in the Reformed Religion. In 1752 she m. Christian Günther who is dead 14 years. They had 2 ch., 1 is living. Sickness, consumption. Aged 65 y., 4 mo., 4 days

Leonard Notz estate, Lancaster co., 1758
Leonard Nutz, Lancaster co., nat. Philadelphia 24 Sept. 1746, "Quaker".

400. NUSLOCH, MICHAEL, sick

7159 Eppingen

Dragon, 1732
S-H 97

EPPINGEN REFORMED KB:
m. 3 May 1718 Hans Michael Nusloch, son of Jacob Nusloch, and Maria Catharina, widow of the late Bernhard Stierle
[no children there]

Pennsylvania records:
PA, THIRD SERIES, 24: 36:
Mich'l Nuslock, warrant for 150 acres in Philadelphia co., 4 Nov. 1734

Decorative carvings, which were polychromed, adorn many structures in Eppingen and are common to half-timbered buildings throughout the Kraichgau.

Photo: J. Godshall

401. OESTERLE, BERNHARD

Massenbach =
7103 Schwaigern

Royal Union, 1750
S-H 432

MASSENBACH LUTHERAN KB:
m. (1) 8 Nov. 1729 Johann Bernhard Österlin from [7164] Obersontheim, and Anna Maria, widow of Jerg Ludwig Harttman. She d. 28 Aug. 1735, aged 64 y.
m. (2) 29 Nov. 1735 Johann Bernhard Österlin, inhabitant and widower, and Maria Eva Weber. Comments are recorded in the KB about this couple having conceived a child just 14 days after the death of his wife. They married several weeks later.
Children:
1. Maria Catharina b. 13 June 1736
2. Maria Barbara b. 13 Sept. 1741
3. Joh. Jacob b. 21 Feb. 1744; d. young
4. Anna Dorothea b. 18 Jan. 1747; d. young
5. Joh. Georg b. 20 Oct. 1748

402. OESTERLIN, JOH. MICHAEL

6921 Ittlingen

Two Sisters, 1738
S-H 209, 211 (appears on list as Michael Easterly age
20)

KIRCHARDT REFORMED KB:
m. 20 Nov. 1708 Joh. Wolff Österle, miller, son of the late Hans Michael Österle
of Ittlingen, and Anna Catharina, daughter of Joh. Michael Klein of Kirchart
[6926].

ITTLINGEN LUTHERAN KB:
Wolfgang Oesterlin and Anna Catharina had:
    Joh. Michael bp. 2 Jan. 1710

Pennsylvania records:
The surname appears in the New Hanover Lutheran KB, Montgomery co., Pa.

403. OFFNER, JOH. MARTIN

7103 Schwaigern

Fane, 1749
S-H 424

SCHWAIGERN LUTHERAN KB:
Johann Martin Offner was b. 9 Nov. 1721, son of Conrad Offner and Maria Catharina.
m. 6 Jan. 1718 Conrad Offner, son of Hans Offner of [8803] Rotenburg an der
Tauber and Maria Catharina, dau. of Michael Hofmann, citizen.
m. 24 Oct. 1747 Johann Martin Offner, hatmaker, son of Conrad Offner, and
Veronica, dau. of Dieter Müntz. Children:
    1. Johann Paul b. 16 Nov. 1748; d. young.

Pennsylvania records:
TRINITY LUTHERAN KB, LANCASTER:
D. May 15, 1762 Martin Offner, hatmaker, a married man; age 40 y. 6 mo.
Martin and Barbara Offner had children:
    1. Johannes b. 22 Oct. 1753
    2. Catharina b. 18 Oct. 1756

LANCASTER CO. DEEDS,
D: 531: 25 Nov. 1759, Queen St., Lancaster, Martin Offner (Hatter) and wife
Barbara: mortgage to John Stoneman of Manor twp.

LANCASTER CO. WILLS:
C-I-13 Martin Offner, Lancaster, (10 Mar. 1762/7 May 1762.)
Wife: Barbara; children: John, Mathias and Catharine.

Martin Offner, Lancaster twp., Lancaster co. nat. Philadelphia 24 Sept. 1760.

404. OTTINGER, JACOB

Elsenz =
7519 Eppingen

St. Andrew, 1738
S-H 237, 238, 239

ELSENZ REFORMED KB:
Hans Ottinger and wife Dorothea had:
    Jacob b. 27 Sept. 1716

HILSBACH-WEILER REFORMED KB:
Conf. 1730 Jacob Ottinger, age 13

Pennsylvania records:
STOEVER'S RECORDS:
m. 20 Aug. 1741 Jacob Ottinger and Anna Johanna Josie, Codorus.

LISCHY'S RECORDS:
Jacob Ottinger and Anna Johanna had:
    1. Anna Ottilia bp. 26 Mar. 1749; sp. Peter Johsy and Ottilia
    2. Joh. Peter bp. 1 Mar. 1752; sp. Peter Wolff and Catharina Elisabeth
    3. Anna Dorothea bp. 17 Nov. 1754; sp. Jacob Welsch and Anna Elisabeth
    4. Johannes bp. 25 Nov. 1759; sp. Johannes Wolff and Anna

Joh. Jacob Ottinger, Manchester twp., York co., nat. Philadelphia April 1761

405. PETER, JERG

Weiler =
6920 Sinsheim, Elsenz

William and Sarah, 1727
S-H 8, 9 (2½ persons)

HILSBACH—WEILER REFORMED KB:
Hans Georg Peter and wife Anna Barbara had:
    1. Rudolph bp. 25 Oct. 1722
    2. Barbara b. 15 Apr. 1725
Anna Barbara Peter was bu. 19 Jan. 1726, aged 32.
m. (2) 7 Jan. 1727 Hans Jerg Peter and Margaretha, daughter of Johann Böhler of Reihen.

Krebs, "Palatine Emigration . . . ," p. 23.
Jerg Peter, citizen of Weiler, emigrant of 1727, had to pay 27 florins, 34 kreuzer emigration tax.

Pennsylvania records:
QUITTOPAHILLA REFORMED KB, LEBANON CO.:
Jorg Peter was a church elder in 1745
Jorg Peter and wife were sp. in 1746, 1747
Rudolf Peter and wife Maria Barbara were sp. in 1746

406. PETER, ULRICH age 24
PETER, GEORG HEINRICH age 19
Weiler =
6920 Sinsheim, Elsenz

Pleasant, 1732
S-H 99, 100, 101

HILSBACH—WEILER REFORMED KB:
m. 21 July 1693 Johannes Peter and Magdalena Grittmann. Hans Peter (in some records listed as Johannes and in one record as young Hans Peter) and wife Magdalena had:
Hans, Jr. bp. 1 Aug 1706
Hans Urich b. 18 June 1708; conf. 1722
Georg Henrich b. 7 Nov. 1713; conf. 1727

WEILER REFORMED KB:
m. 15 April 1732 Joh. Ulrich Peter and Rosina Catharina Heuschel.

Pennsylvania records:
FIRST REFORMED KB, LANCASTER:
Georg Peter and wife had:
John b. 3 Feb. 1736; sp. Georg Henry Peter
Georg Henry Peter and wife Margaret Glettler had:
1. Magdalena Barbara bp. 3 Feb. 1740; Sp. Henry Basler and wife Barbara Boehler

QUITTOPAHILA REFORMED KB, LEBANON CO.:
Jörg Heinrich Peter and wife had:
Johann Heinrich bp. 19 Apr. 1747; sp. Jörg Peter and wife
Johann Jacob bp. 2 July 1749
Barbara bp. 8 Mar. 1756
Hans Ulrich Peter and wife had:
Catrina bp. 23 Apr. 1749; sp. Heinrich Peter

407. PFAUTZ, HANS MICHAEL
Rohrbach, Kraichgau =
6920 Sinsheim, Elsenz

William & Sarah, 1727
S-H 8, 10 (5 persons)

STEINSFURT REFORMED KB:
m. 10 Jan. 1702 Hans Michael Pfautz, son of Herr Hans Michael Pfautz, Schultheiss "Freyherr Venningischen Schultheiss zu Rohrbach", and Ursula Mühlhauser, daughter of Herr Hans Jacob Mühlhauser, "Gerichtsverwandten."

ROHRBACH REFORMED KB:
Hans Michael Pfautz, innkeeper at the "Grunnen Baum," and wife Ursula had:
Anna Margretha bp. 19 June 1712
(Only one mentioned in this record.)

Krebs, "Palatine Emigration . . . ," p. 23, 24.
An entry from 1737 in the records of Dühren treats the handing over of a legacy which Pfauz "now in Pennsylvania" had made to his deceased brother-in-law Jacob Mühlhauser.

Pennsylvania records:
PENNA. PATENTS AA-3, P. 547:
AA-3: 547: A tract containing 153 acres in Leacock and Lampeter twps., Lancaster co., was surveyed to Hans Michael Poutz alias Fouts. Fouts sold the tract for 50 pounds to his eldest son Jacob. Hans Michael Fouts died intestate, leaving a widow Ursula and children: Jacob; Michael; John; Margaret, wife of Augustin Widder; and Barbara, wife of Jacob Hellar. The tract was eventually sold to Barbara Lyne of Leacock twp. Patent to Lyne 7 Apr. 1763, recorded 23 Apr. 1763

408. PFISTERER, widow of JOH. PHILIP　　　6921 Neidenstein,
　　　　　　　　JOH. ADAM　　　　　　　　　　Elsenzgau
Peggy, 1754
S-H 637, 639, 641

NEIDENSTEIN LUTHERAN KB:
Hans Philip Pfisterer, son of David Pfisterer, m. (1) 16 Jan. 1714 Anna Maria, daughter of Hans Jacob Bobel. She d. 5 Dec. 1723. His second wife was Anna Catharina, maiden name unknown. Children of first marriage:
　　1. Hans bp. 11 Sept. 1715
　　2. Anna Maria bp. 5 June 1718; m. Jacob Albert
　　3. Georg Friederich bp. 14 June 1722
[The surviving children of this marriage did not emigrate.]
Children with second wife Anna Catharina:
　　4. Georg Adam bp. 12 June 1726
　　5. Christina Margretha bp. 26 Jan. 1730
　　6. Anna Catharina bp. 23 July 1734
Joh. Philip Pfisterer d. 13 June 1750, aged 64 years.

The daughter, Christina Margretha b. 1730; m. 20 Nov. 1753 Georg Adam Grockenberger; he may appear on the ship's list, the next name after Adam Pfisterer.

Pennsylvania records:
ST. MICHAEL'S AND ZION LUTHERAN KB, PHILADELPHIA:
M. 9 Nov. 1758 Georg Adam Pfüster and Margaretha Scherin. One of the witnesses was Georg Adam ——Rockenberger
Bu. 29 Apr. 1770 Anna Catharina Rockenberger, daughter of the late Joh. Philip Pfisterer in Neidenstein, a Ritterschaftlichen town surrounded by the Pfaltz. Her mother's name was Anna Catharina. She was born ——23, 1734. Came here with her widowed mother and brother in 1754. Two years later she married Adam Rockenberger. They had 4 children, 2 are living. Aged 35 years 9 months.
Children of Georg Adam Pfisterer and wife Maria Margaretha:

　　1. Joh. Adam b. 8 Aug. 1759
　　2. Johann Georg b. 7 Feb. 1762; sp. Georg Adam Rockenberger and wife Catharina
　　3. Maria Catharina Barbara b. 10 Oct. 1764; same sponsors

Geo. Adam Pfister, Philadelphia, nat. Philadelphia, April 1762.

In Neidenstein half-timbered houses crowd by one another on hillsides. The
large house shown above, built in 1716, is in the center of the village.

Photo: J. Godshall

409. PFISTERER, MARTIN age 27

Brothers, 1753
S-H 551, 552, 554

6921 Neidenstein
Hoffenheim =
6920 Sinsheim

NEIDENSTEIN LUTHERAN KB:
Philippus Martinus Pfisterer was bp. in 1714 (date not readable), son of Friederich
Pfisterer and wife Anna Maria.

HOFFENHEIM LUTHERAN KB:
m. 10 Feb. (?) 1737 Martin Pfisterer, born in Neidenstein, and Anna Catharina,
eldest daughter of the late Ludwig Friedel. Children:
1. Anna Margaretha b. 24 July 1738, her father's occupation given as baker
2. Philip Jacob b. 6 Mar. 1740, the father's name given as Philipp Martin
3. Georg Gottfried bp. 12 June 1742
4. Joh. Georg b. 8 Apr. 1747
5. Geörg Martin b. 5 Mar. 1751

Pennsylvania records:
ST. MICHAEL'S AND ZION LUTHERAN KB, PHILADELPHIA:
Joh. Martin Pfisterer and wife Catharina had:
Johannes bp. 23 Mar. 1763, age 1 y. 3 mo.; sp. Georg Adam Pfisterer and
Anna Catharina Schwartz

MUHLENBERG'S JOURNALS I: 610:
Mar. 23, 1763 (Wednesday)—Georg Adam Pfisterer brought his cousin Martin
Pfisterer's child, one year and three months old, to be baptized, because the father
is negligent.

Picturesque Neidenstein lies at the feet of its fortress on the hills leading down to the Schwarzbach. Neidenstein dates to 1319 in old records. The von Venningen family owned it and buried some of their departed in the Lutheran church built in 1700.

Photo: J. Godshall

410. PLATNER (BLATNER), MICHL sick, age 50

Waldangelloch = 6920 Sinsheim, Elsenz

Friendship, 1739
S-H 265, 268, 271

WALDANGELLOCH LUTHERAN KB:
Hans Michel Blatner, "Hoffbauer" (Farmer) and wife Anna Magdalena had children:
1. Maria Margaretha b. 20 Jan. 1720, twin
2. Johann Caspar b. 20 Jan. 1720, twin. He d. 1725
3. Anna Magdalena b. 8 Aug. 1721
4. Anna Margaretha b. 16 Nov. 1723
5. Joh. Willhelm b. 22 Sept. 1726; d. 17 Apr. 1728
6. Maria Jacobina b. 10 May 1729; d. 10 June 1730
7. Eva Catharina b. 12 July 1731

Pennsylvania records:
CHRIST, LITTLE TULPEHOCKEN, LUTHERAN KB, BERKS CO.:
In 1741 Magdalena Plattner sp. a child of Georg Wilhelm Riegel.

NEW HOLLAND LUTHERAN KB, LANCASTER CO.:
m. 14 May 1746 Johannes Lingenfelder and Magdalena Blattner (She m. (2) 12 Feb. 1760 Adam Geissinger.)

411. PORTZ, JOHANN JACOB
1744

7519 Eppingen
6490 Schluchtern

SCHLUCHTERN LUTHERAN KB:
m. 15 May 1744 Johann Jacob Portz, son of the late Johann Helfferich Portz, former inhabitant and day laborer at Eppingen, Brettener Ambts, by profession a baker, and Maria Magdalena, daughter of Moritz Nütz, citizen and farmer in Schluchtern. They are leaving with others for Pennsylvania. [See also Schetzenhöfer and Kolb.]
Moritz Nütz d. in Schluchtern 23 Apr. 1764 age 76 y, 2 mo. and 17 days.
Maria Magdalena Nütz, wife of Moritz, d. 28 apr. 1743, age 55 y., 3 mo. less 9 days.

412. PRECHT, DANIEL
Shirley, 1751
S-H 454

Hoffenheim = 6920 Sinsheim, Elsenz

HOFFENHEIM LUTHERAN KB:
m. 23 Sept. 1731 Daniel Precht and Anna Catharina Baumgärtner
[several other passengers on this ship can be identified in the Hoffenheim records.]

413. PROBST, JOH. ADAM

Snow *Louisa*, 1752
S-H 506

Hoffenheim =
6920 Sinsheim, Elsenz

HOFFENHEIM LUTHERAN KB:
Joh. Jacob Probst and wife Rosina had:
Johann Adam b. 14 Nov. 1723; conf. 1737
m. 18 Feb. 1749 Joh. Adam Probst, shoemaker, son of the late Jacob, and Maria Magdalena, widow of the late Caspar Dietrich. Children:
    1. Joh. Michel b. 29 Sept. 1750
Maria Magdalena, dau. of Christoph Neu, married (1) 21 Oct. 1738 Caspar Dietrich. Children, surname Dieterich:
    1. Anna Barbara b. 27 Aug. 1739
    2. Johannes b. 30 Mar. 1742
    3. Maria Dorothea b. 19 Oct. 1743
    4. Joh. Jacob b. 20 Oct. 1746; d. young
    5. Joh. Jacob b. 19 Feb. 1748

Pennsylvania records:
NEW HANOVER LUTHERAN KB, MONTGOMERY CO.:
Joh. Adam Brobst and wife Maria Magdalena sp. a child of Bernhart Gilbert [q.v.] in 1757.
ST. MICHAEL'S AND ZION LUTHERAN KB, PHILADELPHIA:
Joh. Adam Probst and wife Maria Magdalena sp. a child of Joh. Jacob Baum in 1753.
Joh. Adam Probst and wife Maria Magdalena had:
    Johan Niclaus b. 21 Nov. 1753; bp. 25 Nov.

Adam Probst nat. Philadelphia 10 Apr. 1760

414. RAUDENBUSCH, PETER
RAUDENBUSCH, HEINRICH

Steinsfurt =
6920 Sinsheim, Elsenz

Dragon, 1732
S-H 96, 97, 98

STEINSFURT REFORMED KB:
m. 12 Apr. 1695 Michel Raudenbusch, son of Peter Raudenbusch of Reÿhen [6920 Reihen], and Anna Catharina, daughter of the late Hans Marthin Vogler. Two of their children:
    Joh. Peter bp. 23 Oct. 1699; conf. 1715
    Hans Heinrich bp. 6 Jan. 1712; conf. 1729

Pennsylvania records:
WILLIAMS TWP. KB, NORTHAMPTON CO.:
Peter Rautenbusch and wife Eva had:
    Johann Georg b. 11 Oct. 1740; bp. 31 May 1741

415. REBBERT, STEPHAN
Molly, 1727
S-H 12, 14 (Name on list: Raper, Reppert)
Bonfeld Emigrant List: Stephan Rebbert with wife

Bonfeld =
6927 Bad Rappenau

BONFELD LUTHERAN KB:
Melchior Rebbert, linenweaver, and his wife Barbara, Catholic, had:
  Stephanus b. 24 Dec. 1703; bp. 26 Dec. 1703
D. 6 Feb. 1721 Barbara Rebbert, wife of Melchior Rebbert, Catholic, age 50 years.
D. 27 Apr. 1731 Melchior Rebbert, linenweaver, Catholic, age 63 years.
m. 17 Sept. 1726 Stephanus Rebbert, linenweaver, son of Melchior Rebbert, and Margaretha, daughter of the late Andreas Schneider, citizen at Obersteinach. They had:
  1. Eva Barbara b. 18 Mar. 1727; bp. 19 Mar. 1727

Pennsylvania records:
GOSHENHOPPEN CATHOLIC KB, BERKS CO.:
Stephen Reppert and his wife had:
[?] 2. Melchior who m. 30 June 1761 Barbara Peter
     3. Maria Apollonia bp. 25 Dec. 1742
     4. Daniel bp. 26 May 1745
     5. James bp. 28 Sept. 1746
m. 12 May 1761 in the chapel (at Goshenhoppen) Maurice Lorentz to Mary Apollonia Reppert.

416. REFFIO, REFFIOR, CONRAD age 29
REFFIO, REFFIOR, PETER age 25

Hilsbach =
6920 Sinsheim, Elsenz

Pleasant, 1732
S-H 99 (both sick and did not sign lists—name appears on A list as Ralfure.)

HILSBACH REFORMED KB:
The father Peter Revior is mentioned as a French refugee.
m. __Aug. 1700 Peter Revio, widower, and Catharina, daughter of Hans Jacob Wimphe (?) or Wintzle. Children:
  Hans Conrad b. 5 Mar. 1705; conf. 1717
  Johann Peter (faded entries); conf. 1722, age 13

Pennsylvania records:
STOEVER'S RECORDS: (also Trappe Lutheran KB, Montgomery co.)
Cunradt Refior (Coventry) had:
  Maria Appolonia b. 9 Mar. 1735

417. REICHELSDÖRFER, JOHANNES   6921 Ittlingen
Prelist

ITTLINGEN LUTHERAN KB:
Joh. Veit Reichelsdörfer and wife Anna had children: (In the bp. records the father is given as Johannes, Veit, and Johann Veit.)
1. Joseph bp. 31 Aug. 1707
2. Anna Elisabetha bp. 30 May 1709
3. Joh. Wilhelm bp. 9 Nov. 1711
4. Joh. Heinrich bp. 30 July 1713
5. Friederich Jacob Heinrich bp. 21 Sept. 1714

Pennsylvania records:
John Reichelsdörfer signed a petition in Hanover (now Montgomery co.) dated 1728. Joh. Reichelsdörfer paid quit rent on 100 A. Hanover twp. prior to 1734. Two children of Frederick Reichelsdörfer were killed by the Indians on 14 Feb. 1756 and his property burned.

BERKS CO. WILLS:
Frederick Reichelsdorffer, Albany (20 Sept. 1759/13 Nov. 1759). Wife Christina. Mentions 4 children (only John Adam is named.) Brother Henry Reichelsdorffer and Andrew Hagebach to take care of wife and children. Letters of adm. granted 1 Dec. 1760 to Henry Neihüt and wife Christina, who was the widow of testator.

Henry Rycledorfer Albany twp., Berks co. nat. Philadelphia 24 Sept. 1762.

418. REIFFEL, HANS JONAS   6921 Ittlingen
REIFFEL, FRIEDERICH
Snow *Molly,* 1737
S-H 173, 174

ITTLINGEN LUTHERAN KB:
Joh. Jonas Reiffel and wife Anna Catharina had:
1. Maria Elisabetha bp. 16 Oct. 1702
2. Elisabetha bp. 27 Nov. 1704
3. Andreas bp. 10 Jan. 1706
4. Joh. Rudolph bp. 30 Jan. 1708
5. Joh. Adam bp. 19 Dec. 1708 [q.v.]
6. Joh. Peter bp. 19 Aug. 1711
7. Anna Barbara bp. 18 Nov. 1712 [see Joh. Adam Reiffel]
8. Friederich bp. 4 June 1715
9. Anna Catharina bp. 23 Nov. 1717
10. Joh. Ludwig b. 15 July 1719
11. Maria Barbara b. 26 Jan. 1722
12. Maria Sabina b. 27 June 1724

Pennsylvania records:
TRINITY LUTHERAN KB, READING:
D. 24 Apr. 1786 Anna Catharina Spengler, wife of Christoph, nee Reifele, age 68 y. 5 mo., bu. at Alsace 25 Apr. 1786

419. REIFFEL, JOH. ADAM   6921 Ittlingen

Hope, 1733
S-H 116, 120, 121 (with Sabina age 26, and Barbara
age 20 [his sister])

ITTLINGEN LUTHERAN KB:
Joh. Jonas Reiffel [q.v.] and wife Anna Catharina had 12 children. Among them:
    5. Joh. Adam bp. 19 Dec. 1708
    7. Anna Barbara bp. 18 Nov. 1712
Joh. Adam Reiffel and wife Maria Sabina had:
    1. Joh. Pleickardt b. 15 Jan. 1732
Maria Sabina Licht b. 24 July 1701, dau. of Jacob Licht and wife Lucia.

Pennsylvania records:
TRINITY LUTHERAN KB, READING:
Bu. 22 Sept. 1754 Maria Christina Reiffle, b. in Reading 7 June 1742, daughter
of Adam and Maria Sabina of "Winger Reder Elsassbach. (?)" She was shot by a
careless maid.

Bu. 19 Oct. 1794 John Adam Reifel, b. 19 Dec. 1708 at Itlingen in the Craichgau
beyond Heidelberg. M. Sabina, nee Lichte, who died 35 years ago. Had 8 ch., 2
daughters living: one is m. to Henr. Hahn, Sr., and the other to Joh. Baum. 21
grandchildren, 17 great grandchildren. Was blind for 12 years, then sight returned
without operation—then again blind for 2 years. Age 85 y. 10 mo. less 2 days.

Adam Rifel nat. Philadelphia 25 Sept. 1750, of Alsace twp., Philadelphia co.

420. REINER, GEORG   7103 Schwaigern
REINER, CHRISTIAN

Fane, 1749
S-H 424

SCHWAIGERN LUTHERAN KB:
m. 7 Sept. 1713 Wolfgang Reiner, son of Hans Michel Reiner, and Agnes Maria,
daughter of Joh. Paul Boger, butcher. Two of their children:
    1. Hans Jerg b. 19 Aug. 1721
    2. Christianus b. 6 May 1723

Pennsylvania records:
UPPER MILFORD LUTHERAN KB, LEHIGH CO.:
Christian Reiner and wife Catharina had:
    1. Catharina b. 11 Aug. 1757
    2. Johannes b. 23 Aug. 1759
    3. Joh. Jacobus b. 12 Sept. 1761
    4. Christian b. 7 Aug. 1763
    5. Maria Elisabeth b. 3 Sept. 1769
Georg Reiner and wife Sovia Sibilla had:
    1. Johann Christian b. 8 June 1769

2. Joh. Peter bp. 10 Nov. 1771
3. Johanna b. 26 Sept. 1774
George Reiner, Upper Milford twp., Northampton co., nat. Philadelphia 10 Apr. 1761
Christian Reyner, Upper Milford twp., Northampton co., nat. Philadelphia 24 Sept. 1763

421. REINER, JOH. DIETERICH   7103 Schwaigern
     REINER, CHRISTIAN
Fane, 1749
S-H, 425

SCHWAIGERN LUTHERAN KB:
Friderich Reiner, baker and wife Barbara had:
   Hans Diter bp. 2 Mar. 1696
Joh. Dieter Reiner and wife Maria Margaretha had:
   1. Johann Frederich b. 24 Aug. 1715
   2. Hans Dieterich b. 2 Sept. 1716
   3. Johann Christian b. 10 Apr. 1718
   4. Maria Magdalena b. 21 Sept. 1720
   5. Maria Margaretha b. 12 Feb. 1723
   6. Maria Sara b. 2 May 1724
   7. Georg Philipp b. 30 Jan. 1727; d. 31 May 1729
   8. Anna Maria b. 9 June 1728; d. 8 June 1729
   9. Johannes b. 13 July 1730
   10. Eberhard Frederich b. 23 Mar. 1733
   11. Johann Georg b. 20 Apr. 1736
   12. Maria Barbara b. 3 Dec. 1738

Pennsylvania records:

For additional details concerning the emigration of this family, see Friedrich Krebs' "Annotations to Strassburger and Hinke's Pennsylvania German Pioneers", *The Pennsylvania Genealogical Magazine*, 21 (1960): 235-248; reprinted in: Carl Boyer, *Ship Passenger Lists, Pennsylvania and Delaware* (1980), 106, 107.

422. REISINGER, HANS MARTIN   7103 Schwaigern
     REISINGER, GOTTLIEB
Charming Nancy, 1737
S-H 189, 191, 193 (Other passengers: Maria Risiger and Martin Risiger)

SCHWAIGERN LUTHERAN KB:
Martin Reisinger was b. 5 Apr. 1685. Maria Ursula, b. 30 May 1690 daughter of Hans Georg Heiss and Maria Elisabetha nee Rudel
m. 17 Nov. 1711 Martin Reising(er), son of Frantz Reising(er), former tailor, and Ursula, daughter of Hans Georg Heisch, citizen and night watchman. They had:
(Reÿsinger in bp. record)

1. Maria Barbara b. 26 Dec. 1712
2. Johann Gottlieb b. 12 June 1717
3. Maria Johanna b. 15 Nov. 1719; d. young
4. Joh. Martin b. 3 May 1722
5. Georg Adam b. 11 May 1730

D. 5 Feb. 1735 Maria Ursula, wife of Hans Martin Reisinger, tailor, aged 44 y.

Pennsylvania records:
DOVER LUTHERAN KB, YORK CO, PA.:
"Martin Reissinger b. 3 May 1722, son of Martin and the deceased Ursula Reissinger from "Schorygern am Neckar by Heylbronn." Came to America with his father in 1737. In 1747 he m. Anna Magdalena Bingemann, b. 1728, daughter of Lorentz and Anna Margretha Bingemann, both dec'd. She was b. in America. They had:

1. Johann b. 2 Aug. 1748
2. Barbara b. 2 Feb. 1750
3. Johann Martin b. 15 Dec. 1752
4. Joh. Conrad b. 26 Oct. 1753
5. Maria Magdalena b. 22 June 1756
6. Maria Margreth b. 27 Aug. 1758
7. Catharina b. 25 Oct. 1760
8. Anna Elisabet b. 7 Mar. 1762
9. Anna Maria b. 20 July 1763
10. Johann Adam b. 7 Mar. 1765 (?)
11. Eva Margretha b. 19 Feb. 1767
12. Johann Georg b. 15 Oct. 1768
13. Christian b. 27 May 1770

ST. MICHAEL'S AND ZION KB, PHILADELPHIA:
m. 20 Dec. 1747 Martin Reisinger and Anna Magdalena Biegmannin.

PHILADELPHIA WILLS:
Godlieb Reisinger, Germantown, Taylor, "weak in body." (Apr. 15, 1776/May 28, 1776). Wife Magdalena, 1¾ a lot in Germantown adj. the Lower Burying Ground on north side of Germantown Street and p.e. during her life. At her decease to daughter Catharine Kiefer (?). /S/ Godlieb Reisinger. Exr. wife Magdalena. Wit.: John Moore, Peter Schuster and Jean Dedier.

TRINITY LUTHERAN KB, LANCASTER:
D. 4 Sept. 1776 Martin Reisiner, of dysentery. He was 91 y. 6 mo. old. He always enjoyed good health. The oldest man in Lancaster.

Michelfeld is traceable to a document from the year 850. At the time of heavy emigration in the 18th century the Gemmingen-Hornbach family owned it. Farmers in the Kraichgau lived in the village and formed fields around it. Barns were attached to the houses or adjoined them around a *Hof* or courtyard. Their shape and style greatly influenced the oldest barns built by Pennsylvania Germans.

Photo: J. Godshall

423. REISS, JOH. MICHAEL age 22   6921 Michelfeld

Two Sisters, 1738
S-H 209, 211, 212

MICHELFELD LUTHERAN KB:
Hans Rudolph Reuss (b. 7 Oct. 1686, son of Martin Reuss and Anna Margaretha) m. 29 Mar. 1712 Anna Catharina, daugher of Jacob Neff. Their son:
     Johann Michael b. 1 Jan. 1713; sp. Hans Jacob Rudisile, tailor.
Notation in the KB: "Went 11 May 1738 to Pennsylvania."

Pennsylvania records:
STOEVER'S RECORDS:
Michael Reiss (Tulpehocken) had children:
1. Maria Catarina b. 28 Oct. 1743; Sp. George Mueller and wife Maria Catarina
2. Magdalena b. in 1745, bp. 22 Dec. 1745; Sp. John Peter Anspach and his wife [She was a dau. of Erasmus Buckenmeÿer, also from Michelfeld.]
3. Johannes b. 26 Oct. 1747; Sp. John Wolfart and wife Catarina Agatha
4. Anna Maria b. 8 Oct. 1749; Sp. Michael Nef, Jr. [also from Michelfeld] and wife Anna Maria
5. John Ludwig b. 16 Aug. 1752; Sp. Johannes Schaefer and second wife
6. Maria Elisabetha b. 28 Jan. 1757; Sp. John Schaefer and second wife

BERKS CO. DEEDS:
A-I:217, 221:22 Mar. 1755 Peter Ansbach and wife Magdalena (only child and heir of Erasmus Buggenmeyer) release Michael Reiss for 10 shillings. (Tract of 216

A patented to Erasmus Buggenmeyer in 1737).
According to Berks co. Orphans Court records dated 10 Aug. 1757 and 17 Nov.
1758, Michael Rice was married to Anna Maria, dau. of Andreas Krafft (q.v.).
She was a second wife.
See also Erasmus Buckemeyer and Frederick Elberscheidt

Michael Rois (Reis) nat. Philadelphia April 1747, of Lancaster co.
Margaret Reis, wf. of Michael Reis, nat. Philadelphia 26 Sept. 1748, of Lancaster
co.

424. REYER (REIHER, REIHEN), HANS MICHEL (age 45)

Rohrbach = 6920 Sinsheim, Elsenz

Loyal Judith, 1732
S-H 88, 90, 91 (with Joh. Carl Reyer, age 22 and Joh.
Martin Roir, age 16)

ROHRBACH REFORMED KB:
Hans Michel Rayen and wife Anna Maria had:
  1. Anna Sara b. 14 July 1719; bp. 16 July
  2. Maria Rosina b. 20 Aug. 1720; bp. 21 Aug.
  3. Anna Catharina b. 26 Nov. 1721; bp. 28 Nov.
  4. Anna Margaretha Brigitta b. 6 Apr. 1723; bp. 8 Apr.
  5. Maria Agnesa
  6. Anna Margaretha } twins b. 30 July 1725; bp. 31 July
  7. Maria Margreth b. 13 Aug. 1726; bp. 15 Aug.
  8. Anna Catharina b. 6 Dec. 1729; bp. 8 Dec.

SINSHEIM LUTHERAN KB:
Hans Michael Rheier of Rohrbach had:
  Maria Elisabetha bp. 4 Oct. 1709
A Christina Reÿer of Rohrbach was conf. in 1728, age 14 years.

Pennsylvania records:
GOSHENHOPPEN LUTHERAN KB, MONTGOMERY CO.:
Family register:
Joh. Michael Reiher, aged 62 years, b. 1689 son of Joh. Michel Reiher and Anna
Catharina in Rohrbach near Zinze (Sinsheim) in Wirtenberg. In 1732 he came to
America. Married (1) in 1709 Anna Maria, daughter of Dietrich Seeland and
Amalia of Nuernberg. She died in 1742 around St. John's Day. He m. (2) 1743
Maria Catharina (Reformed) b. 1713, daughter of Henrich Schneider of Aschpis-
sem, Kurpfalz. Her mother was Catharina, daughter of Abraham Schüler. She d.
in 1750. He m. (3) 12 Sept. 1751 Maria Christina, b. 18 Nov. 1718 in Borna,
Kursachsen, daughter of Georg Gerlach and Susanna (at present with her daughter.)
[Maria Christina Gerlach had married (1) Johannes Christoph Hoepler who died at
sea 18 Aug. 1750.]
Michael Reiher had children from the first and second marriages:
  1. Anna Maria, d.
  2. Johann Carl b. 15 Dec. 1711

   3. Anna Maria b. 5 Dec. 1712
   4. Joh. Martin b. 9 Jan. 1716
   5. Anna Sara b. 14 Mar. 1718
   6. Anna Cathar. b. 6 Dec. 1729
   7. Anna Barbara b. 1745
   8. Georg Phillip b. 1750
His third wife had 4 children with her first husband.
Pennsylvania Staatsbote, 16 June 1772:
Michael Reyer of Goshenhoppen died in his 86th year. He was married 3 times;
had 10 children with his first wife, 6 children with second wife and 8 children with
third wife.
Children of the third marriage, Old Goshenhoppen Lutheran KB, Montgomery co.:
   Christina Elisabetha b. 14 June 1753
   Susanna b. 14 Mar. 1756
   Maria Christina b. 25 Jan. 1761
For additional detail on the family, see *"The Perkiomen Region, Past and Present,"*
I: 153–156.

TRINITY LUTHERAN KB, READING:
d. 3 Nov. 1793 Cath. Blage, widow, nee Reier b. 8 Nov. 1729 in Rohrbach near
Sinzheim, Pfalz. Daughter of Michael and Anna Maria Reier. M. (1) Valentine
Keverper. M. (2) Michael Blage. Aged 64 y. less 6 days.

_____

Michael Ryer, Philadelphia co., nat. Philadelphia Sept. 1740

425. RIEB, DANIEL   6921 Ittlingen
1749

ITTLINGEN LUTHERAN KB:
m. 30 Jan. 1742 Daniel Rieb, son of the late Michael Rieb from _____
(faded), and Rosina Margaretha, daughter of Hans Jerg Schweitzer, Sr. Children:
   1. Catharina Barbara b. 27 June 1743
   2. Andreas Martin b. 24 Sept. 1745
   3. Elisabetha Barbara b. 25 Sept. 1748
"D. 1749, all—the father, mother, and three children, on the sea going to Pennsylvania."
Communicants' list dated 1749—leaving for Pennsylvania: Daniel Rieb and wife.

426. RIES, CHRISTOPHER   Massenbach =
RIES, FRIEDERICH   7103 Schwaigern
Johnson Galley, 1732
S-H 71, 73, 74, 75, 77 (Others on ship: Maria Kathar-
ina Rice, Elisabetha Rise, over 14; Martin Rise, under
16; Margeretta Rise, under 14.)

MASSENBACH LUTHERAN KB:
m. 12 Nov. 1710 Johann Christoff Riss, son of Hans Ris, "Gerichtsverwandten,"

and Maria Catharina, daughter of Joh. Michel Müller, citizen. (She was b. 2 Oct. 1687, daughter of Michael Müller, smith, and wife Catharina) They had:
1. Justina Elisabetha b. 17 May 1711
2. Joh. Fridrich b. 2 Apr. 1713
3. Joh. Martin Fridrich b. 2 Nov. 1718
4. Eva Margretha b. 27 Apr. 1720; d. young
5. Joh. Andreas b. 25 Aug. 1724

Pennsylvania records:
ST. MICHAEL'S AND ZION LUTHERAN KB, PHILADELPHIA:
Friedrich Reis was a witness at the 1748 marriage of Ludwig Frieburg [also from Massenbach]
Martin Ries and wife Catharina (Reformed) had:
1. Joh. Valentin b. 17 Feb. 1748
2. Anna Maria b. 19 Feb. 1751
3. Anna Maria b. 20 Aug. 1753
d. 16 June 1748 Maria Catharina Ries, wife of Joh. Christ. Ries. She was b. 2 Oct. 1687 in Massenbach in Craichgau.
d. 12 Oct. 1779 Martin Ries, b. in Massenbach, son of Joh. Christoph Ries. Age 59 y. 5 mo.
Justina Elisabetha Riess m. (1) 7 Jan 1734 Geo. Peter Biswanger [q.v.]. She m. (2) 25 May 1747 Carl Evald [Ehwald].
d. 31 Mar. 1784 Justina Elisabetha Ehwald, b. in Massenbach by Heilbrun. Age 73 years.
Justina Catharina and Carl Ewald had:
1. Johan Jurg b. 27 Dec. 1747
2. Anna Maria b. 6 Aug. 1749

427. RIESS, REINHOLD DIETRICH

Forest, 1752

S-H 495 (appears on list: Johann Dieterich Riess)

Massenbach = 7103 Schwaigern

MASSENBACH LUTHERAN KB:
m. 18 Sept. 1725 Joh. Daniel Riss, son of Daniel Riss, and Maria Eva, daughter of Joh. Michael Müller. Their son:
Reinhold Dietrich b. 4 July 1728

Pennsylvania records:
ST. MICHAEL'S AND ZION LUTHERAN KB, PHILADELPHIA:
d. 16 Aug. 1775 Reinhold Dietrich Ries, b. in Massenbach, son of Joh. Daniel
Ries and Maria Eva; b. 4 July 1728. His sp. were Reinhold Dietrich and Martin
Wagner. Came to this land in 1752. M. 19 June _____Christiana Rosina
Rohr, daughter of Friedr. Rohr. Had 6 children, 2 are deceased. Age 47 y. 2 mo.
11 days.

MUHLENBERG'S JOURNALS, II: 553:
1773—In the mont of November I wrote a letter to Massenbach for Mr. Ries. The
address was: to His Excellency Baron Reinhold Dieterich, Freiherr von und zu
Massenbach.   _____

Dietrick Rees, Philadelphia, nat. 24/25 Sept. 1764

428. RINGER, JOH. MATTHAUS   Bonfeld =
1717   6927 Bad Rappenau
Bonfeld Emigrant List: Joh. Matthaus Ringer with wife
and ch.

M. 27 June 1717 Johann Mathes Ringer, son of Wolfgang Ringer, citizen at Rappenau, and Maria Magdalena, widow of the late miller Joh. Jacob Schneider.

Jacob Schneider, miller, d. 18 Dec. 1715, age 24 y less 14 d. Since members of
his family emigrated with their mother and step-father, details of the family are
given here.

Joh. Jacob Schneid(er), son of Johannis Schneid(er), miller and Anabaptist, was
bp. 21 Sept. 1710 age 19. On 10 Feb. 1711 Joh. Jacob Schneid(er), son of Joh.,
miller, m. Maria Helena, daughter of the late miller Heinrich Nischicker, miller in
the "Mittlere Grundmühl." They had the following ch. bp. (The mother's name in
the bp. records varies from Maria Helena to Maria Magdalena and the surname
varies from Schneid to Schneider.)
    1. Johann Jacob b. 7 Apr. 1712; bu. 8 Apr. 1712
    2. Anna Maria Catharina b. 22 Mar. 1713; bp. 23 Mar. 1713
    3. Anna Maria Barbara b. 13 Feb. 1715; d. 24 June 1717
    4. Maria Felicitas b. 10 May 1716; bp. 11 May 1716

Pennsylvania records:
PA, SECOND SERIES, 19:626
Agreed with Hans George Shutz and Mathias Ringer (two Germans) for 500 A. of
land on the West side of the Schuylkill River, including the old plantation where
Peter Bizalion formerly dwelt, for which they are to pay one hundred pounds—
warrant signed, dated 20th, 11th month, 1717/18.

STOEVERS RECORDS:
m. 12 June 1733 John Martin Köblinger and Catarina Schneider, Hanover. (Catarina Schneider was the step-daughter of Mathias Ringer of New Hanover.) They had
at least 5 sons who appear in the New Hanover Lutheran bp. and conf. records.

PHILADELPHIA CO. WILLS:
Mathias Ringer, New Hanover twp., (3 Mar. 1748/9/23 Feb. 1750). Wife Maria
Magdalena. Step-daughter: Mary Catarina, wife of Martin Keplinger. Two sons:
Mathias and John Ringer. Adm. to Maria Magdalena Ringer.

NEW HANOVER LUTHERAN KB, MONTGOMERY CO.:
Magdalena Ringer d. 6 Apr. 1764, age 74½

Mathias Ringer, Philadelphia co., nat. Philadelphia, April 1743.

429. RITTER, JOHANN GORG age 17

Grombach =
6927 Bad Rappenau

Prncess Augusta, 1736
S-H 162, 164, 165

GROMBACH LUTHERAN KB:
Joh. David Ritter and wife Maria Eva had:
1. Hans Michel b. 14 June 1704
2. Hans Peter b. 22 May 1706
3. Hans Peter b. 28 Oct. 1707
4. Maria Magdalena b. 20 Oct. 1710
5. Anna Barbara b. 20 Nov. 1712
*6. Hans Georg b. 25 Oct. 1715
7. Maria Elisabetha b. 4 June 1718; d. 1720

Pennsylvania records:
ST. MICHAEL'S AND ZION LUTHERAN KB, PHILADELPHIA:
Joh. Georg Ritter and wife Margretha had:
1. Catharina b. 7 May 1745
2. Joh. Jurg b. 1 Feb. 1747
3. Peter b. 10 Feb. 1750
4. Joh. Jürg b. 14 May 1752
5. Jacob b. 18 Nov. 1754
6. Anna Maria b. 24 Nov. 1759
7. Johannes b. 24 July 1762
8. Susanna b. 1 Dec. 1764
D. 17 July 1774 Georg Ritter, son of the late David Ritter of Grumbach and Maria
Eva; b. in Grumbach 25 Oct. 1715. Has been in this land 37 years. Married for
34 years to Margareta Pop, had 11 children, 7 are living: 5 sons and 2 daughters.
D. aged 59 years, 21 days.

In 1717 a resident of Eppingen erected a baroque half-timbered structure on the Kettengasse with a mansard roof on top of an earlier gothic base. Typical of all half-timbered construction is the stone under-structure which served for cellar and other purposes. As might be expected the super structure was not as stable and could be removed and/or repaired as needed. The durability of half-timbered construction in an area of increasingly scant forests as a relatively economical building method, especially as compared to masonry, accounts for the large number of such buildings in the Kraichgau. Early German settlers in Pennsylvania used this method, too, although few such buildings remain today. Stone, log, and brick structures prevailed there.

Photo: J. Godshall

On one corner at the crossing of the Kettengasse and the Zunftgasse in Eppingen stand three half-timbered buildings which portray the entire history of this kind of construction. One of the buildings dated 1717 bears a human face similar to those seen on eighteenth century tombstones in Pennsylvania.

A renaissance half-timbered structure in Eppingen, only partly exposed, whose floor supports break through the wall and are exposed. The corner is cut back to compensate for narrow streets.

Photo: J. Godshall

In Eppingen—the Kraichgau's treasure chest—over 70 half-timbered buildings dating from the fourteenth to the eighteenth centuries have been exposed. The "Schwarzles Haus" built in 1488 by Hans Rink is Gothic in style, and constructed according to "Alemmanish" principles: the corner and binding posts stand directly on the flooring below.

Photo: J. Godshall

430. RITTER, JOSEPH   6924 Neckarbischofsheim

Jacob, 1749
S-H 417

NECKARBISCHOFSHEIM LUTHERAN KB:
Hans Georg Ritter, citizen and inhabitant, and wife Anna Margaretha nee Lutz had:
    Joseph b. 12 Nov. 1724

Pennsylvania records:
TRINITY LUTHERAN KB, LANCASTER:
Joseph Ritter from Bischofsheim in the Craichgau m. 26 June 1764 Dorothea Schober, widow.

431. RÖHRER, JOHANNES   6901 Mauer
RÖHRER, JOHANN GOTTFRIED

Robert & Alice, 1738
S-H 212, 214, 215

MAUER LUTHERAN KB:
m. 9 Feb. 1717 Johannes Dieterich Röhrer and Maria Elisabetha Müller; both single, Children:
    1. Joh. Jacob b. 2 June 1718; d.
    2. Joh. Gottfriedt b. 24 May 1720
    3. Joh. Georg b. 27 Jan. 1723
    4. Joh. Jacob b. 14 July 1725
    5. Anna Maria b. 7 Aug. 1727; d.
    6. Joh. Balthasar b. 14 Nov. 1729
    7. Anna Maria b. 25 Nov. 1730
    8. Joh. Friederich b. 26 July 1733
    9. Joh. Valentin b. 25 Feb. 1736; d. 1736
    10. Johannes   } twins b. 28 July 1737
    11. Anna Barbara   }

Krebs "Palatine Emigration . . .," p. 27.
Johannes Röhrer permitted to emigrate 1738 with wife and children on payment of 10 florins.

Pennsylvania records:
JOHN CASPER STOEVER'S RECORDS:
Jacob Roeher (Altolhoe) had:
    1. Maria Catarina b. 31 Dec. 1750
    2. Anna Margaretha b. 19 Nov. 1752
    3. Joh. Jacob b. 8 Dec. 1754; Sp. Gottfried Roehrer and wife Magdalena

STOEVER'S RECORDS:
m. 20 Feb. 1750 John Jacob Roehrer and Maria Elisab. Brosius, Atolhoe
m. 16 Sept. 1750 John Abraham Stein and Anna Maria Roehrer, Atolhoe

BERKS CO. WILLS:
Godfrey Röhrer, Tulpehocken (22 Mar. 1800/11 Sept. 1800) Mentions children: Jacob, Godfrey, Elisabeth, wife of George Snyder, Catharine, wife of Joseph Geasler, Julianna, wife of Jacob Kurr, Mary, wife of Leonard Stup, Magdalena, wife of Peter Bashore, and Hannah, wife of Jacob Brown. Wife: Magdalena, sons Jacob and Godfrey, exrs. _____

Godfret Reorher, Lancaster co., nat. Philadelphia fall 1749

432. ROMICH, JOH. ADAM   6921 Ittlingen
     ROMICH, FRIEDRICH
Dragon, 1732
S-H 96, 97, 98

ITTLINGEN LUTHERAN KB:
Joh. Adam Romich and wife Agnes Margaretha had children:
1. Anna Eva bp. 29 Sept. 1712
2. Joh. Friederich bp. 6 Apr. 1714
3. Joh. Bernhard bp. 23 Nov. 1716
4. Joh. Martin bp. 23 Feb. 1719
5. Maria Margaretha b. 18 Sept. 1721
6. Anna Maria b. 15 June 1724
7. Maria Elisabetha b. 8 Nov. 1726
8. Joh. Heinrich b. 15 Feb. 1729
9. Georg Wendel b. 8 Sept. 1731

Pennsylvania records:

ALLEMENGEL MORAVIAN KB, LYNN TWP., LEHIGH CO. AND ALBANY TWP., BERKS CO.:
Adam Romich d. 11 July 1768. He was b. 13 Feb. 1689 in the small town of Neidenstein in the Palatinate. His parents were Georg Wendel Romich and Margaretha nee Herner, both Lutherans. "In the year 1712 I married Agnes Margaretha Bernhard. In the year 1732 with my wife and children left for America. Shortly after our arrival at Philadelphia, my wife died. We had lived together 20 years and had 5 sons and 2 daughters, of whom 2 sons have died. In 1733 I married the second time to Maria Ursula Wanner [q.v.] with whom I had 2 sons and 3 daugh-

ters, 2 sons and 1 daughter died in early childhood." He was survived by 3 sons,
6 daughters, 66 grandchildren and 12 great-grandchildren. He joined the Moravian
church in 1762—prior to this he had been a deacon in the Lutheran church. He
suffered from asthma. He died the morning of July 11, aged 79 years, 5 mo. and 2
days.

Maria Margaretha Romig, b. 18 Sept. *1722* in Ittlingen, daughter of Joh. Adam
Romig; married in Pennsylvania 11 Sept. 1741 Andreas Volck.

Heinrich Romich, b. 15 Feb. 1729 in Ittlingen, son of Adam Romich. He m. (1)
Hannah Volck, daughter of Carl and Catharina Volck on 2 Dec. 1754. She d.
7 Oct. 1763. He m. (2) _____ June 1764 the widow Maria Elisabetha Xander,
maiden name Kiesel.

EMMAUS MORAVIAN KB, NORTHAMPTON CO.:
Friedrich Romig was born 4 Apr. 1713 in Ittlingen in the Palatinate of Lutheran
parents. He came to Pennsylvania in 1732. He married on Christmas 1737 Catharina Siegfried who was born 14 Nov. 1719 in Oley.

Joh. Martin Romig, born 23 Feb. 1719 in Europe. Married Anna Elisabeth Deck,
born on Good Friday, 1725. _____

Frederick Romig, "Maccungy" twp., Northampton co, nat. Philadelphia 25 Sept.
1752

Adam Romich, Philadelphia co., nat. by Act of 29 Mar. 1735.

433. ROTH, GEORG   6901 Mauer

Dragon, 1732
S-H 96, 97, 98

MAUER LUTHERAN KB:
m. 28 Aug. 1714 Hans Georg Roth, apprentice weaver, and Maria Barbara
Furstenberger. Children:
    1. Maria Dorothea b. 27 Dec. 1715
    2. Anna Dorothea b. 11 June 1717
    3. Anna Maria b. 5 Mar. 1720
    4. Joseph b. 15 Jan. 1722
    5. Joh. Jacob b. 18 Jan. 1724
    6. Maria Margaretha b. 11 Nov. 1726
    7. Anna Barbara b. 20 July 1729

Pennsylvania records:
ST. MICHAEL'S AND ZION LUTHERAN KB, PHILADELPHIA:
D. 19 Jan. 1777 Johann Jacob Roth, born in Mauer in the Churpfalz in 1724;
married (1) Maria Clara Roemer; m. (2) Susanna Weidmann. Age 53 years.
_____

Jacob Roth nat. Philadelphia September 1761 of Philadelphia tp., Philadelphia
co.

434. ROTH, JACOB   6921 Ittlingen

Dragon, 1749
S-H 414

ITTLINGEN LUTHERAN KB:
m. 16 July 1748 Johann Jacob Roth, widower, son of Joh. Georg Roth, late citizen at [7519] Zaisenhausen, born at Zaisenhausen, and Philippina Elisabetha, daughter of Paul Hartmann, shoemaker here. They had one child bp. at Ittlingen:
1. Maria Eva Barbara b. 4 Apr. 1749. D. in 1749 on the sea, going to Pennsylvania. One of her sp. was Joh. Jacob Geiger "aus Pennsylvanien."
Communicants' list dated 1749 "before their journey to Pennsylvania";
Joh. Jacob Roth and wife
Maria Barbara Hartmann, married
Maria Barbara Hartmann, single
Johann Heinrich Harttman, single
Dietrich Paul Harttmann, single

Pennsylvania records:
ONE JACOB ROTH, LEHI TWP., NORTHAMPTON CO., NAT. PHILADELPHIA 1765.

Eschelbronn, first documented in 789, was completely depopulated in 1648 when 8 families moved to it. Two pastors who played significant roles in American immigration history—Joshua Harrsch/Kocherthal and Anthony Jacob Henckel—served the Lutheran congregation in Eschelbronn whose records begin in 1648. Large barns reveal the inherent prosperity which returned when wars did not drain the economy and the people's energy.

Photo: J. Godshall

435. ROTH, JOH. ADAM   Hoffenheim =
                                                6920 Sinsheim, Elsenz
Jacob, 1749
S-H 418

HOFFENHEIM LUTHERAN KB:
Catharina Ziegler, single, and Hans Adam Roth from [6920] Eschelbronn had an illegitimate child:
1. Joh. Georg Adam b. 31 Aug. 1746
m. 17 Oct. 1746 Joh. Adam Roth from Eschelbronn and Catharina Ziegler, daughter of the late Jacob Ziegler. Child:
2. Joh. Adam b. 9 Feb. 1748

Pennsylvania records:
DILLINGERSVILLE LUTHERAN KB, LEHIGH CO.:
Johann Adam Roth and wife Maria Catharina had:
    Johannes David b. 18 July 1750; bp. 12 Aug. 1750
    Johann Jacob b. 6 Feb. 1753; bp. 19 Feb.

436. ROTH, JOHANN GEORG   6921 Michelfeld
1738

MICHELFELD LUTHERAN KB:
Johann Georg Roth and wife Anna Maria from [6901] Mauer had:
    1. Johann Valentin b. 26 Mar. 1732
"This Johann Georg Roth left for Pennsylvania with his wife and children, 6 May
1738."

437. ROTH, JOH. JACOB   Bonfeld =
1717   6927 Bad Rappenau

BONFELD EMIGRANT LIST:
Joh. Jacob Roth with his wife and two children, and sister; occupation, textor
(weaver).

BONFELD LUTHERAN KB:
Hans Ernst Roth (bp. 25 Feb. 1622, son of Jacob Roth) m. 1652 Magdalena,
daughter of the late Hanns Weyler of [7107 Bad] Wimpfen. Their son, Hans Jacob
Roth (b. 27 Nov. 1657) m. 5 June 1683 Elisabeth "von Seen aus der Schweitz"
[possibly Seen, Zh = CH 8405 Winterthur]. Hans Jacob Roth and wife Elisabeth
had their first child, Hans Jacob, bp. in 1685, the exact date is unreadable.
Johann Jacob Roth, linenweaver, son of the late Johann Jacob Roth, m. 8 Nov.
1707 Maria Barbara Weber, dau. of Michael Weber, "Anwalt" at Gellmerspach
[today Gellmersbach = 7102 Weinsberg]. Children:
    1. Johann Conrad b. 13 Nov. 1708
    2. Johann Jacob b. 11 Oct. 1711
    3. Helena Maria b. 14 Jan. 1715
The only sister of Joh. Jacob Roth located in the Bonfeld record is Anna Elisabetha
bp. 4 Jan. 1686; she m. 28 Feb. 1706 Jacob Nicholaus Hillicker. They left Bonfeld
in 1717 with four children and settled in New York.

Pennsylvania records:
OLEY HILLS LUTHERAN KB, BERKS CO.:
Matthaus Roth, born in the Fall of 1717 in America. Father: Jacob Roth from
Bonnfeld; he came to America in 1717 and died about Christmas, 1746. Mother:
Barbara. Matthaus Roth m. 18 Jan. 1741 Anna Maria Elisabetha Bayer. She was
born 1723, Candlemas [Feb. 2], dau. of Joh. Philip Bayer from Ipstein [today
Eppstein] and his wife Maria Elisabetha. Matthaus Roth's children:
    1. Catharina b. 13 Apr. 1743
    2. Maria Barbara b. 28 Dec. 1745
    3. Johannes b. 11 Oct. 1746 [New Hanover Lutheran]; d.

4. Johann b. 13 June 1748
5. Jonathan b. 18 Mar. 1751
6. Solomon b. 8 July 1757 [New Hanover Lutheran]
7. Anna Elisabetha [named in will]

NEW HANOVER LUTHERAN KB, MONTGOMERY CO.:
Matthias Roth d. 16 Mar. 1795, age 78 y. 4 mo. and 5 days

BERKS CO. WILLS:
Mathias Roth, Colebrookdale, (14 Nov. 1786, codicil 28 Dec. 1794/6 Apr. 1795).
Wife: Anna Elisabeth. Children named in will: Jonathan, Solomon, Catharine, wife
of Thomas Willson, Barbara, wife of Peter Jerger, Anna Elisabetha, wife of Peter
Bastress.
Johann Conrad Roth (b. 13 Nov. 1708 in Bonfeld) was listed as an elder of the
Oley Hills church in 1754. He married Anna Catharina, surname unknown.

BERKS CO. WILLS:
John Conrad Rood, Colebrookdale, (10 June 1780/18 Sept. 1780.) All est. to wife
Catharina, except 50 A. of warranted land to son Adam. Adm. to Cathrina, the
widow.

438. RÜCKEL, GEORG MICHAEL

6920 Sinsheim, Elsenz

Ship data not located

SINSHEIM LUTHERAN KB:
conf. 1711 Hans Georg Rückel, age 15
m. 11 Jan. 1718 Georg Rückel, son of the late Joh. Martin Rückel, smith, and
Elisabetha, daughter of Joh. Conrad Müller, gamekeeper. Their son:
    Georg Michael bp. 15 Jan. 1719

Pennsylvania records:
TRINITY LUTHERAN KB, LANCASTER:
m. 2 Jan. 1757 Georg Michael Rickel from Sinzheim, weaver, and Anna Elisebet
Bosshartin from Zürch (Zürich).

439. RUDI, BASTIAN age 24

Reihen =
6920 Sinsheim, Elsenz

Pink *Plaisance*, 1732
S-H 78, 81, 82

REIHEN REFORMED KB:
m. 8 Feb. 1701 Dieterich Rudÿ, son of Jacob Rudÿ, Gerichtsverwanten, and Anna,
daughter of Ludwig Schuch. Their son:
    Bastian b. 21 Dec. 1708

Pennsylvania records:
TRINITY LUTHERAN KB, LANCASTER:
Sebastian Rudi sp. 1734 a child of Martin Kappler.
m. 19 May 1766 Jacob Ziegler, six miles beyond Yorktown, and Susanna Rudyn,
single.

440. RUDI, HANS ERNST
William & Sarah, 1727
S-H 8, 9 (1 person; Roede on A list)

Weiler and Reihen =
6920 Sinsheim, Elsenz

HILSBACH—WEILER REFORMED KB:
M. 25 Jan. 1681 at Hilspach Hans Conrad Rudi, cooper, son of Hans Rudi of Reÿhen, and Anna Maria, daughter of the late Michael Schopff, citizen at Weÿler. Hans Conrad Rudi and wife Anna Maria had:
Hans Ernst bp. 15 Feb. 1682
M. 25 Jan. 1707 at Hilspach Hans Ernst Rudi, cooper, son of Hans Conrad Rudi, and Anna Catharina Doll, daughter of Johann Doll, "Anwald". Their children:
1. Joh. Conrad b. 21 Oct. 1707; bp. 23 Oct. 1707
2. Anna Maria bp. _____ Dec. 1708; d. young (very faded entry)
3. Maria Margretha bp. 19 Apr. 1711
4. Joh. Jacob bp. 24 Aug. 1715
5. Anna Barbara bp. _____ Feb. 1717
(May not be complete—some faded entries in KB)

Krebs, "Palatine Emigration . . ." p. 23
Ernst Rudi, citizen of Weiler, emigrant of 1727, paid 18 florins 47 kreuzer emigration tax.

441. RUDI, JOH. DIETRICH
William and Sarah, 1727
S-H 8, 10 (1 person: Roede on A list)

Reihen =
6920 Sinsheim, Elsenz

REIHEN REFORMED KB:
(no m. recorded 1697–1700)
Sebastian Rudi and wife Anna Margaretha had:
Johannes Dieterich bp. 1 Jan. 1702

Pennsylvania records:
INDIANFIELD LUTHERAN KB, MONTGOMERY CO.:
m. 20 Nov. 1753 Peter Rebbert, son of Petter Rebbert of [6600] Saarbrücken, and Margaret Rudi, daughter of Dietrich Rudi. Dietrich Rudi and wife Margaret were sponsors in 1755 for a child of Philip Zimmer.

INDIAN CREEK REFORMED KB, MONTGOMERY CO.:
Peter Reppert and wife had:
Magdalena bp. 17 Sept. 1758; sp. Dietrich Rudi and wife

Dedrick Rudey, Bucks co., nat Philadelphia Sept. 1740.

442. RUDISILE, ANDREAS
Phoenix, 1749
S-H 406 (Name on list: Rutsiele)

6921 Michelfeld

MICHELFELD LUTHERAN KB:
Hans Michael Rudisile, son of Hans Jacob Rudisile, m. 14 days after Easter, 1713,

Anna Elisabetha, daughter of Andreas Vorreuter. Children:
1. Johann Jacob b. 12 Feb. 1715
2. Andreas b. 4 Jan. 1717

Pennsylvania records:
CHRIST EVANGELICAL LUTHERAN, YORK:
Andreas Rudisill and wife Maria Margaretha had:
1. Johann Jacob b. 20 Sept. 1750; Sp. Jacob and Elisabeth Rudisill.
2. Maria Elisabeth b. 20 Aug. 1752
3. Charlotte [mentioned in brother Jacob's will, 1810]

Andreas Rudisill nat Philadelphia Apr. 1762, of Manheim twp., York co.

443. RUDISILE, JOH. JACOB   6921 Michelfeld

Mortonhouse, 1729
S-H 23, 25, 26 (Name on list: Roodlys, Roatslice)

MICHELFELD LUTHERAN KB:
Johann Jacob Rudisile b. 10 Apr. 1706, son of Johann Jacob and Cleophe (Neff)
Rudesili. See Philip Rudisile for complete record of the family.

Pennsylvania records:
FIRST REFORMED KB, LANCASTER:
Jacob Rudesili and wife Elizabeth, nee Hamsbacher had
        Anna Catharine bp. 5 May 1742

CHRIST LUTHERAN KB, YORK:
Jacob Rudesill and wife Elisabeth had
        Thomas b. 5 Nov. 1748
        Maria Dorothea b. 11 Feb. 1751

Jacob Rudesilly nat. Philadelphia Apr. 1761 of Manchester tp., York co.

444. RUDISILE, JOH. JACOB   6921 Michelfeld

Brothers, 1752
S-H 481

MICHELFELD LUTHERAN KB:
Hans Rudisile m. 30 Jan. 1665 Anna, daughter of Wendel Liebel (?) and Apol-
lonia. Their son:
        Johann Leonhard b. 5 Nov. 1679 (?) (date faded)
Hans Leonhard Rudisile, son of Hans, m. 12 Feb. 1709 Sophia, dau. of the late
Samuel Keller, former citizen and "Gerichtsverwandten" at [7923] Ochsenberg.
Sophia d. 28 Mar. 1754. Hans Leonhard d. 26 May (year not given). Their son:
        Joh. Jacob b. 12 Aug. 1715
OR
Hans Michael Rudisile [q.v.] b. 11 Mar. 1692 (son of Hans Jacob and grandson of
Hans and Anna) had:
1. Johann Jacob b. 12 Feb. 1715

m. 2 Feb. 1740 Joh. Jacob Rudesile (parentage not given) and Anna Christina Regula. Their children were:
1. Johann Ludwig b. 22 Sept. 1740 at Leimen
2. Anna Elisabetha b. 5 Nov. 1742
3. Joh. Jacob b. 23 Sept. 1745; d. 27 Mar. 1748
4. Joh. Jacob b. 30 Mar. 1748
5. Johann Leonhard b. 15 Aug. 1751

Pennsylvania records:
CHRIST LUTHERAN KB, YORK:
Jacob and Anna Christina Rudisill had:
6. Johann Leonhard b. 6 Jan. 1754, Sp. were Jacob and Elisabeth Rudisill.

YORK CO. WILLS:
Jacob Rudisill of Codorus, probated 20 Apr. 1807. Children: Ludwig, Elisabeth, wife of Abraham Roth, and a son John who had sons Jacob and Henry.

445. RUDISILE, PHILIP

6921 Michelfeld and
6920 Weiler

William & Sarah, 1727
S-H 8, 9 (name on list: Rutschly)

MICHELFELD LUTHERAN KB:
Hans Rudisile m. 30 Jan. 1665 Anna Liebel (?), daughter of Wendel Liebel (?) and Apollonia. They had:
Hans Jacob bp. 4 Oct. 1666
m. 19 Feb. 1688 Johann Jacob Rudesille, son of Hans and Anna, and Cleophe, daughter of Ulrich Neff and Catharina. Hans Jacob Riedisiele d. 16 Sept. 1748 and his wife Cleve (Cleophe) d. 6 Feb. 1758. Their ch.:
1. Anna Catharina b. 30 Oct. 1689 at [6921] Eichtersheim
2. Hans Michael b. 11 Mar. 1692 (His son Andreas [q.v.] on *Phoenix*, 1749)
3. Weÿrich b. 7 Aug. 1695 [q.v.]
*4. Philipps Heinrich b. 24 Sept. 1697
5. A dead son b. 1700
6. Hans Georg b. 7 May 1701
7. Maria Catharina b. 19 Nov. 1703; d. young
8. Johann Jacob b. 10 Apr. 1706 [q.v.]
9. Catharina b. 17 Aug. 1708; d. young
10. Joh. Philipp b. 27 Mar. 1711
11. Anna Catharina b. 27 July 1713
12. Matthaus b. Easter 1718; bp. 19 Apr. 1718

SINSHEIM LUTHERAN KB:
m. 14 Apr. 1722 at Weiler Philip Sily, son of Joh. Jacob Rudi Sili, citizen at Michelfeld, and Anna Maria, daughter of Georg Philip Schopff, "Schultheiss" at Weiler. Philip Rudi Sÿlÿ, tailor at Weiler, and wife Anna Maria had children:
1. Georg Philip b. 30 Mar. 1723; bp. 1 Apr. (evidently d. young)
2. Georg Philip b. 18 Aug. 1725; bp. 19 Aug.

Michelfeld, like many towns in the Kraichgau, and unlike nearly all in Pennsylvania, had no plan, but grew irregularly around the various *Höfe*, or farm-house combination of buildings in the village. Although many buildings standing in these villages today postdate the earliest emigration, they retain general architectural arrangements and construction techniques the emigrants knew. This house, with its central chimney and steep roof, is similar to many old Germanic buildings in Pennsylvania. Michelfeld became a Lutheran town in 1523, but as a result of destruction in the Thirty Years' War, its oldest church record begins in 1656. Today Michelfeld is part of Angelbachtal.

Photo: J. Godshall

[There is a gap in the Weiler burial records and marriage records from 1723 to 1734—the two persons on the ship appear to be Philip and son Georg Philip, since both appear in Penna. records.]

Krebs, "Palatine Emigration . . .", p. 23
Philip Rudisille's father-in-law, Georg Philipp Schopf, took over for his own use what had been sold.

Pennsylvania records:
TRINITY LUTHERAN KB, LANCASTER:
Philipp Rudisiele had:
    3. Maria Barbara, b. 12 Apr. 1730
    4. Anna Barbara below
    5. Anna Maria below
m. Philipp Rudisille and Susanna Beyerin, 29 Oct. 1734. By third marriage:
    6. Anna Catarina, 19 Aug. 1735
    7. Joh. Michael, 1 Sept. 1737
    8. Joh. Melchior, 11 Oct. 1738
    9. Susanna, 19 Oct. 1744
    10. Catharina, Aug. 1750–12 Oct. 1758
m. 29 Jan. 1751, Anna Barbara Rudisille to Joh. Georg Christoph Stech
m. 18 Sept. 1751 Philipp Adam Brenner [q.v.] to Anna Maria Rudesill

m. 27 Mar. 1758 Anna Catarina Rudisill and Henry Schenck
m. 30 Apr. 1765 Joh. Michael Rudisill to Maria Angelica Schaeffer
m. 5 May 1761 Joh. Jacob Rudisill to Barbara Wegerlin
m. 19 Oct. 1744 Jacob Metzger [q.v.] to Susanna Rudisill

LANCASTER CO. WILLS:
Philip Rudisill (23 Sept. 1755–11 Nov. 1755)

Tombstones in small cemetery on Pleasure rd., near Lancaster waterworks in
Manheim twp.:
Michael Rudisill, 11 Sept. 1737–17 Aug. 1829
Catarina, nee Bulb[?], 14 Feb. 1747, m. Michael Rudisill 23 Sept. 1769, d. 29
Aug. 1817.

Georg Philip Rudisill m. 28 Oct. 1746 at New Holland, Lancaster co., Maria
Barbara Miller. Children:
  1. Johann Michael b. 8 Oct. 1747; bp. at Trinity Lutheran, Lancaster
  2. Susanna Catharine b. 29 July 1749; bp. at Hill Church, Lebanon co.
  3. Maria Elisabeth b. Nov. 1751; bp. at Hill Church, Lebanon co.
  4. Philip Adam b. Jan. 1754
  5. Eva Catharina bp. Jan. 1756
Maria Barbara (Miller) Rudisill, b. 10 Aug. 1722, d. 4 Jan. 1813, bu. Bindnagle's
Church, Lebanon co. She m. (2) John Schulz; m. (3) Daniel Diehl.

446. RUDISILE, WEŸRICH   6921 Michelfeld
Samuel, 1737
S-H 169, 170, 172 (Name on list: Rutisieli)

ELSENZ REFORMED KB:
m. 18 Feb. 1691 Hans Peter Siegfried, son of Hans Caspar Siegfried of [6926]
Kirchart, and Anna Magdalena, daughter of Bernhard Böhli. Their daughter:
    Anna Barbara b. 9 May 1696

MICHELFELD LUTHERAN KB:
Weÿrich Rudisile, son of Hans Jacob Rudisile, citizen and tailor, m. 13 Sept. 1718
Barbara, daughter of the late Peter Siegfried, citizen and tailor at "Elsenz der
Kelleweÿ Hilspach." [= 7519 Eppingen]
[for detail on the Rudisile family, see Philip Rudisile.]
Children of Weÿrich and Barbara:
  1.
  2. Elisabetha bp. 20 Feb. 1721 (Elsenz Lutheran KB)
  3. Johann Michael b. 11 Sept. 1723
  4. Johann Weÿrich b. 29 May 1726
  5. Anna Catharina b. 12 May 1729; d. 1 July 1730
  6. Johann Georg b. 8 Feb. 1734; d. 16 Feb. 1734
  7. Philipp Jacob b. Fer Jacobi [probably 25 July] 1731; bp. the following day
  8. Johann Georg b. 3 Nov. 1735
"This Weÿrich Rudesile, with his wife and children, went to Pennsylvania 13 May
1737."

Pennsylvania records:
STOEVER'S RECORDS:
Weirich Rudiesiel (Codorus) had:
Anna Johanna b. 28 Dec. 1740; sp. Jacob Ottinger and Anna Johanna Igsin (also recorded in Christ Lutheran KB, York)
m. 21 Jan. 1746 John Rudisilli and Catharina Wagner

FIRST REFORMED KB, LANCASTER:
Johannes Rutisily and wife Anna Catharina nee Wagner had:
1. Maria Barbara b. 25 Dec. 1746; sp. Weirich Rutisily and wife Barbara
2. Johann Weinrich b. 23 Sept. 1749; sp. Weinrich Rudisill and wife
Weirich Rudisill and most of his family went to North Carolina. On 20 May 1754 he received a grant of 200 A. On 4 June 1764 John Rudisilly, eldest son and heir at law of Gerick Rudisilly, dec'd of Yourk Co., Pa. sold to Henry Dellinger, wagonmaker. Michael Rudisill and Philip Rudisill also each received grants of land in 1754.

447. RUPP, CHRISTIAN

Restauration, 1747
S-H 366

Daudenzell =
6955 Aglasterhausen

ASBACH REFORMED KB:
Joh. Christian Rupp, citizen and inhabitant from Daudenzell, and wife Margaretha had:
Joh. Christian b. 5 Oct. 1721

Krebs, "Palatine Emigrants . . .", 32, 33
Christian Rupp of Daudenzell, a citizen's son released from military service, was permitted in 1747 to emigrate "to the new land" on payment of the tithe of 11 florins plus 2 florins 40 kreuzer emergency taxes.

Pennsylvania records:
TRINITY LUTHERAN KB, LANCASTER:
A Christian Rupp and wife Maria Elisabetha had:
1. Abraham b. 4 Nov. 1751

448. RUPP, JACOB

Jacob, 1749
S-H 418

Hoffenheim =
6920 Sinsheim, Elsenz

HOFFENHEIM LUTHERAN KB:
Hans Martin Rupp and wife Maria Eva had:
1. Joh. Jacob b. 17 Mar. 1731; conf. 1744
2. Maria Dorothea b. 5 Sept. 1733; d. 1737

Pennsylvania records:
CHRIST LUTHERAN KB, YORK:
John Jacob Rupp b. Mar. 17, 1731; d. Sept. 25, 1753. Bu. Sept. 26, 1753 in the city.

449. RUPP, JONAS   Reihen =
Phoenix, 1751   6920 Sinsheim, Elsenz
S-H 471

SINSHEIM LUTHERAN KB:
Joh. Jonas Rupp of Reÿhen and wife Christina had:
   Joh. Jonas b. 3 Nov. 1729. In a different hand: "1751 nach America. Gest.
   21 Mar. 1801 in Philadelphia."
A footnote in S-H indicates that this is the parternal grandfather of I. Daniel Rupp,
the editor of the Collection of Thirty Thousand Names.

Pennsylvania records:
Wm. H. Egle, History of the Counties of Dauphin and Lebanon in the Commonwealth
of Pennsylvania (Philadelphia, 1883) contains a list of tombstone inscriptions at
Hill Church, North Annville twp., Lebanon co. Included on this list:
   Jonas Rupp, b. 16 July 1728, d. 11 Dec. 1801
   Maria Rupp (wife of Jonas) b. 2 Dec. 1732, d. 20 Feb. 1822

QUITOPAHILLA REFORMED KB, LEBANON CO.:
Jonas Rupp and wife Elisabet had a son (n.n.) b. 31 Mar. 1767; sp. Johannes
Umberger and wife.

450. RUPPERT, JOHANN ADAM age 25   6921 Michelfeld
Britannia, 1731
S-H 48, 49, 52, 54 (with Anna Barbara age 24)

MICHELFELD LUTHERAN KB:
Johann Adam Ruppert, tailor, son of Adam Ruppert, smith at [6927 Bad] Rappenau, m. 25 Apr. 1730 Anna Barbara, daughter of Leonhard Holtzapfel, citizen
here. Children:
   1. Anna Catharina b. 22 Apr. 1731
"Are going to Pennsylvania 1731"

Pennsylvania records:
MUDDY CREEK LUTHERAN KB, LANCASTER CO.:
Johann Adam Rupert had children:
   1. Catharina b. 4 June 1733 (York KB: 1 June) Sp. Maria Barbara Kattermän-
       nin
   2. Erasmus b. 6 Apr. 1736 Sp. Erasmus Holtzapfel
   3. Christina b. May 1738 Sp. Erasmus Holtzapfel and wife Christina
   4. Joh. Dieterich b. 5 Dec. 1740

CHRIST LUTHERAN KB, YORK (THIS KB CONTAINS THE ABOVE FOUR AND)
   5. Elisabetha b. 5 Mar. 1743
   6. Johann Adam b. 13 Apr. 1748; sp. Dietrich Uhler and Elisabetha
   7. Magdalena   } twins b. 4 Feb. 1751
   8. Maria Margretha   }
Joh. Adam Rupert and wife sp. 2 children of Erasmus Holtzapfel at Christ Lutheran, York.

451. SAILER, PLEICKERD DIETRICH age 24
SAILER, HANS PETER age 15

6921 Ittlingen

Two Sisters, 1738
S-H 209, 210, 211 (appears on list Bliker Tidrick Zeyler and as Michael Frederick Zeyler)

ITTLINGEN LUTHERAN KB:
Andreas Sailer and wife Maria Catharina had:
    Pleikard Dietrich b. 29 May 1719; bp. 31 May
    Joh. Peter b. 26 Sept. 1721

ADELSHOFEN LUTHERAN KB:
Conf. 1734 Pleickart Dieterich Sailer, a servant, b. at Ittlingen, son of Andreas Sailer.

American records:
CHALKLEY, I: 323:
AUGUSTA CO., VIRGINIA RECORDS:
18 Dec. 1753 James Patton to Plackard Sciler, 162 acres patented 3 Nov. 1750 on Craig's Creek.

CHALKLEY, I: 428:
9 Sept. 1764 Plackerd Sciler of Orange co., North Carolina to Nicholas Welsh of Bedford co. 162 acres for 40 pounds; patented to James Patton, deceased, 3 Nov. 1750 and by him conveyed to said Scilor 8 Dec. 1763 on Craig's Creek.

Pennsylvania records:
ST. JOHN'S LUTHERAN KB, EASTON:
A Peter Sayler d. 11 Jan. 1803 in Williams twp., age 82 y.

452. SAMPEL, ADAM

Hoffenheim =
6920 Sinsheim, Elsenz

Chance, 1763
S-H 686

HOFFENHEIM LUTHERAN KB:
Christoph Sampel and wife Dorothea had:
    Joh. Adam b. 19 Dec. 1731
    Johann Adam Sampel m. 5 May 1763 at Michelfeld Christina Mansbeck

Pennsylvania records:
PA, THIRD SERIES, 25:622:
One Adam Sambell warranted 50 acres of land in Bedford co. on 2 Nov. 1774

453. SAMPEL, CONRAD

Hoffenheim =
6920 Sinsheim, Elsenz

Shirley, 1751
S-H 454

HOFFENHEIM LUTHERAN KB:
Conrad Sampel was conf. 1738 at Hoffenheim. His bp. not located, but he was

probably b. ca. 1724. There are Sampel families having children there in that time period.
He arrived with several other emigrants from Hoffenheim.

454. SARBACH, DAVID

Robert & Alice, 1743
S-H 347

Steinsfurt =
6920 Sinsheim, Elsenz

STEINSFURT REFORMED KB:
David Sarbach and wife Maria Elisabetha had:
    Hans David bp. 29 (Feb. or Mar.) 1715; conf. 1732 age 16
m. 16 Oct. 1736 David Sarbach, son of the late David Sarbach, and Maria Margretha, daughter of Hans Görg Lackner of Aderspach. Children:
    1. Georg Balthasar bp. 22 Feb. 1738
    2. Maria Eva b. 18 June 1740
    3. Maria Barbara b. 13 Apr. 1743

Pennsylvania records:
LITITZ MORAVIAN KB:
m. 21 Oct. 1744 David Sarbach and Catharine Gennemin
David Saarbach and wife (in one record Susanna) had ch. bp. at First Reformed, Lancaster:
    1. Susanna bp. 23 Oct. 1745
    2. A son bp. 2 Apr. 1749
    3. John William b. 28 Apr. 1751

455. SARBACH, JACOB

Francis and Elizabeth, 1742
S-H 327, 329

Steinsfurt =
6920 Sinsheim, Elsenz

STEINSFURT REFORMED KB:
David Sarbach and wife Maria Elisabetha had:
    Joh. Jacob b. 20 Feb. 1721

Pennsylvania records:
YORK CO. WILLS:
Jacob Sarbach, Berwick twp. (17 June 1782/26 Sept. 1787.) Wife: Catharine. Children: Christiana, Elizabeth, Jacob, David, Susanna, Michael and Catharina, wife of Christian Rafinsberger. Exr.: Christian Sarbach.
Catharina Sarbach, Berwick twp. (14 Sept. 1795/21 Sept. 1795.) Children: Susanna, wife of John Richwine; Jacob; David; Michael; Christiana, wife of Jacob Bauin; and Elizabeth, wife of John Brown. Grandchild Catharine Bauin. Exr.: Henry Lehmer.

456. SÄTZLER, DANIEL   7103 Schwaigern

Richmond, 1764
S-H 696

SCHWAIGERN LUTHERAN KB:
Elias Setzler and Sabina nee Reiner had:
    Johann Daniel b. 2 July 1739
Daniel Setzler, son of Elias Setzler, weaver, m. 22 Sept. 1761 Dorothea, daughter
of Martin Graeslin. They had:
    1. Sabina b. 18 Dec. 1762; d. young
    2. Catharina b. 6 Feb. 1764; d. 13 Feb. 1764

Pennsylvania records:
MERTZ LUTHERAN KB, ROCKLAND TWP., BERKS CO.:
Daniel Setzler and wf. Dorothea had:
    3. Elisabetha b. 21 May 1768; bp. 3 July 1768
    4. Maria Christina b. 28 July 1772; bp. 11 Aug. 1772
    5. Susanna b. 19 July 1775; bp. 14 Aug. 1775

457. SAUDER, THOMAS   Waldangelloch =
                                                6920 Sinsheim, Elsenz
Johnson Galley, 1732
S-H 71, 73, 74, 76, 77 (Other passengers: Margaretta
Sauder, and Margaretta, under 16)

EPFENBACH REFORMED KB:
m. 15 Sept. 1699 Hans Carl Sauter, born in Stebbach [= 7519 Gemmingen], son
of Joseph Sauter, and Elisabetha Kleiner, daughter of Hans Jacob Kleiner from
Unter Mettmannstetten in Knonau region, Zurich. [= CH 8932 Mettmenstetten] at
Hasselbach, Helmstatt [= 6920 Sinsheim, Elsenz].
Joh. Carl Sautter and wife Anna Elisabetha had:
    George Thomas bp. 15 July 1704

WALDANGELLOCH LUTHERAN KB:
m. 3 Feb. 1728 Jerg Thomas Sautter from Hasselbach, Helmstatt Jurisdiction, and
Anna Margaretha, daughter of Hans Michel Ernst. (She was bp. 27 Nov. 1702.)
Children:
    1. Margaretha Barbara b. 11 Nov. 1728
    2. Joh. Friderich b. 25 Feb. 1731

Pennsylvania records:
NEW HOLLAND LUTHERAN KB, LANCASTER CO., PA.:
Georg Thomas Sauter had:
    3. Christina Barbara b. 1 Feb. 1739
    4. Joh. Bernhardt b. 5 June 1741
    5. Georg Michael b. 6 Apr. 1743
    6. Johannes b. 6 Feb. 1745
Georg Thomas Sauter and wife Margaretha are sponsors there in 1744 for a child
of Joh. Jacob Kitzmüller

STOEVER'S RECORDS:
m. 10 Feb. 1747 at Warwick Paul Ebrecht and Barbara Margaretha Sauter.

458. SAUER, JOHANN HEINRICH   6921 Michelfeld

St. Andrew, 1738
S-H 237, 238, 239

MICHELFELD LUTHERAN KB:
Johann Heinrich Sauer m. 6 Nov. 1736 Maria Elisabetha, dau. of the late Valentin
Eÿermann, citizen and miller at [6901] Nussloch. Note in KB: "6 May 1738 went
to Pennsylvania."
Johann Heinrich Sauer was b. 7 Jan. 1713, son of Philips Henrich Sauer [q.v.]

Pennsylvania records:
MUDDY CREEK LUTHERAN KB:
m. (2) 24 July 1739 Joh. Heinrich Sauer and Maria Dorothea Englert (Cocalico).
Children:
    1. Maria Dorothea b. 29 Mar. 1741
    2. Philipp Heinrich b. Feb. 1743
    3. Joh. Michael b. 6 Dec. 1746
    4. Barbara b. 5 Nov. 1748
The sp. of some of their children were also from Michelfeld.

Henry Sauer nat. Philadelphia 10 April 1760.

459. SAUER, PHILIPS HENRICH   6921 Michelfeld
     SAUER, CATHARINA, his wife
     SAUER, ANNA BARBARA, his
     granddaughter
     RÖSSLER, ANNA CATHARINA (nee Sauer),
     his daughter
     1740

MICHELFELD LUTHERAN KB AND DÜHREN LUTHERAN KB:
Philips Henrich Sauer b. 8 Feb. 1672, son of Hans Jacob and Catharina Sauer, m.
28 June 1698 Catharina. Their children:
    1. Joh. Weirich b. 11 Nov. 1699; m. 8 July 1721 Sophia Barbara, daughter
       of the late Joh. Georg Rauschenberger, former citizen at [7143] Vaihingen

an der Ens. They had a daughter Anna Barbara b. 23 Mar. 1722. "25 May 1740 went to Pennsylvania."
  2. Anna Catharina b. 1 Jan. 1704; m. 26 Jan. 1723 at Dühren Hans Georg Rössler, tailor, son of Hans Georg R., citizen at Dühren. "This Anna Catharina Rösslerin went to Pennsylvania 25 May 1740 with her father and mother and brother's daughter."
    Their children:
      1. Maria Elisabeth b. 20 May 1724
      2. Hans Jerg b. 30 Apr. 1726
      3. Johannes b. 8 Oct. 1730
      4. Johann Adam b. 1 Jan. 1736
  3. Johann Heinrich b. 7 Jan. 1713 [q.v.]
"This Philipp Heinrich Sauer went to Pennsylvania 25 May 1740 with his wife, daughter, and son's daughter."

460. SCHÄFER, JOHANNES

Prelist

6921 Zuzenhausen
6921 Michelfeld

NECKARGEMÜND Lutheran KB:
m. 20 Jan. 1722 Johannes Schafer, son of the late Hans Georg Schafer, citizen at Zuzenhausen, and Barbara, daughter of Hans Kuntz.

MICHELFELD LUTHERAN KB:
m. 1728 (no other date given) Johannes Schäfer from "St. Johannes Stocken in Pensilvanien" (evidently Conestoga is intended), former citizen at Sutzenhausen (6921 Zuzenhausen), and Maria Catharina, daughter of Weÿrich Mittenbühl.
Weÿrich Mittenbühl, son of Sebastian Mittenbühl, and his wife Maria Catharina (daughter of Weÿrich Seltzer) had a daughter Maria Catharina b. 28 Mar. 1708.

Pennsylvania records:
In 1734, Johannes Schäffer and wife Maria Catharina were sponsors for a child of Georg Minier (also an emigrant from Michelfeld) at Conestoga. (See Heidelberg Moravian Family Register—record of Georg Minier.)

MUDDY CREEK LUTHERAN KB, LANCASTER CO.:
Johannes Schäffer had:
  1. Anna Barbara b. 15 Oct. 1730
  2. Maria Catharina b. 30 Oct. 1732
  3. Joh. Michael b. 11 June 1734
  4. Joh. Georg b. 31 May 1736
  5. Anna Maria b. 28 May 1741
  6. Johannes b. 14 July 1742
  7. Maria Dorothea b. 27 Feb. 1744; bp. at Warwick Lutheran (Conestoga): sp. Maria Dorothea Etschberger [She was a daughter of Hans Georg Schaffer of Zuzenhausen.]
  8. Joh. Heinrich b. 15 Aug. 1746
  9. Rudolph b. 31 Oct. 1750
The sp. of several of these children were also from Michelfeld.

John Sheffer, Lancaster co., nat. Philadelphia April 1744

461. SCHALLENBERGER, HANS GÖRG

Reihen =
6920 Sinsheim, Elsenz

Molly, 1727
S-H 12, 14

REIHEN REFORMED KB:
m. 12 Jan. 1686 Hans Schallenberger and Anna Magdalena Rudi. Their son:
Hans Görg b. 14 Nov. 1694
m. _____ Jan. 1723 Hans Görg Schallenberger, son of the late Hans Schallenberger, and Anna Margretha, daughter of the late Hans Hug, "des Gerichts".
Children:
1. Anna Maria bp. 9 Mar. 1727
[Ulrich Shellenberger, who arrived on the same ship, is listed in Smith, *The Mennonite Immigration to Pennsylvania* (Norristown, Pa. 1929), p. 184, as a member of that denomination.]

462. SCHAUFFELBERGER, PHILIPP

6921 Michelfeld

James Goodwill, 1727
S-H 10, 11 (the name appears on the list as
Schafberger, 5 in family)

MICHELFELD LUTHERAN KB:
Joh. Jacob Schaufelberger and Elisabetha had Hans Philipp b. 24 Nov. 1682. Joh. Philips Schauffelberger conf. 1698, age 15 years. No further records of him at Michelfeld; evidently m. and had ch. elsewhere.

Pennsylvania records:
TRINITY LUTHERAN KB, LANCASTER, PA.:
Philipp Schauffelberger had a daughter Anna Elisabetha b. 28 Mar. 1730, sp. Agnes Reyer. In another record dated 1736 his wife's name is mentioned as Anna Margaretha.

LANCASTER WILLS:
Philip Shoufeberger, Manheim twp. (22 Apr. 1755/19 Oct. 1759.) Names dau.: Anna, wife of Martin Shriner. Mentions sisters: Margaret Funke and Sabina Friday. Executor: Martin Shriner. (Note: Sabina Barbara b. 6 Sept. 1686, dau. of Johann Jacob Schaufelberger and Elisabetha; she m. 1706 David Freÿtag. They had 4 children bp. at Michelfeld. David Freÿtag died there 14 Dec. 1739, and his wife Sabina died in Michelfeld 18 Dec. 1742)

TRINITY LUTHERAN KB, LANCASTER:
Philipp Schaufelberger, widower, an elder, aged 76 y. 9 mo. 23 d; d. at his own place Sept. 15, 1759, bu. the next Sunday here.

463. SCHECHTER, ANDREAS

Weiler =
6920 Sinsheim, Elsenz

Edinburg, 1753
S-H 521, 524

SINSHEIM LUTHERAN KB:

Joh. Georg Schechter of Weiler and wife Maria Dorothea had:
Andreas b. 17 Apr. 1717/18

WEILER LUTHERAN KB:
m. 11 Sept. 1742 Johann Andreas Schechter, son of Joh. Georg Schechter, citizen at Weÿler, and Catharina, daughter of Martin Rudi. Marriage necessary. Children:
1. Johannes b. 20 Nov. 1742
2. Maria Barbara b. 14 Sept. 1744
3. Joh. Martin b. 12 Jan. 1746
4. Joh. Georg b. 24 Mar. 1748
5. Anna Margretha b. 2 Oct. 1749
6. Joh. Philipp b. 17 Jan. 1752
7. A child (N.N.) b. 3 Feb. 1753

464. SCHELLING, GEORG BALTHASAR

6924 Neckarbischofsheim

Snow *Louisa*, 1752
S-H 506

NECKARBISCHOFSHEIM LUTHERAN KB:
Joh. Georg Schelling, dyer, son of Joh. Georg Schelling, m. (1) 22 Feb. 1729 Anna Catharina, daughter of Herr Joh. Philipp Schmied, baker and "Gerichtsverwandten". She died soon after this marriage and Joh. Georg Schelling, widower, m. (2) 11 July 1730 Maria Praxeta, daughter of the late Joh. Georg Schieck. (She was b. 15 Apr. 1705, daughter of Georg Schickh and Anna Barbara.) Their son:
Georg Balthasar b. 20 Feb. 1732

Pennsylvania record:
TRINITY LUTHERAN KB, LANCASTER:
m. 12 Aug. 1760 Georg Balthasar Schelling, single, from Bischofsheim, and Eva Catharina Schreiber, single. _____

Baltzer Shelling of Manheim tp., Lancaster co., nat. Philadelphia Fall 1765, refusing to take an oath.

465. SCHERTZER, JOHANN JACOB

6921 Michelfeld

St. Andrew, 1738
S-H 237, 238, 239

MICHELFELD LUTHERAN KB:
Hans Jacob Schertzer, son of Philip Schertzer, m. 1 Dec. 1711 Anna Elisabetha Seeburger. Their son Johann Jacob b. 3 Aug. 1712. Johann Jacob Schertzer, son of the late Joh. Jacob Schertzer, m. 3 Jan. 1738 Appollonia Glockenberger, daughter

An early piece of Fraktur, likely made for a child of the Georg Balthasar Schelling who emigrated from Neckarbischofsheim to Lancaster county in 1752.
"Vorschrift for Georg Baltzer Schelling
Written in the year of Christ 1769
This name is awarded me, Lord, lead me to my fatherland, to which the thief took his flight that is the beautiful Paradise to which I travel from time into sweet eternity where the chosen flock praises you eternally when the lovely voices raise a lovely hymn of praise where in a lovely scene there are twenty-four elders who give you glory at all times in the lovely eternity oh that I might at all times see how you yourself are in your loveliness and give you praise at every chance.
[the alphabet.]

Private collection

of the late Joh. Wolfgang Glockenberger, citizen and linenweaver. Children:
1. Anna Margretha b. 13 Jan. 1737
"This Johann Jacob Schertzer went on 6 May 1738 to Pennsylvania with wife and child."

Pennsylvania records:
LITITZ (WARWICK) MORAVIAN KB:
D. 16 July 1781 Anna Apollonia Sherzer, nee Glockenberger. B. 14 Dec. 1711 in the Palatinate. Came to this country with her husband Jacob Sherzer in 1738. They were the first members of the Warwick congregation. She had 5 children, Jacob, Philip and Leonhard surviving her. Age 45 (?) years.
D. 19 Jan. 1794 Jacob Sherzer, b. 3 Aug. 1712 in Michelfelde, Palatinate. Came with his wife Anna Apollonia (Glockenberger) to this country in 1738. Died on his place near Lititz. Aged 81 years.

466. SCHERTZER, JOHANN PHILIPP (age 35)   6921 Michelfeld

Barclay, 1754
S-H 596, 598, 600

MICHELFELD LUTHERAN KB:
Johann Philipp Schertzer b. 17 May 1722, (son of Hans Jacob S. and Anna
Elisabetha Seeburger), m. 19 Nov. 1743 Anna Catharina Voltz. Children:
1. A dead child Oct. 1744
2. Eliesabetha Barbara b. 26 Dec. 1745; d. 13 Apr. 1748
3. Anna Margretha b. 24 Oct. 1747; d. 13 Nov. 1750
4. Eliesabetha Barbara b. 14 Oct. 1749
5. Johannes b. 15 Sept. 1751
6. Johann Christoph b. 3 June 1753

Pennsylvania records:
A Philip Shertzer appears on the tax lists in 1772 and 1773, Manheim twp.,
Lancaster co.
Christoph Scherzer and wife Catharina had children bapt. at Trinity Lutheran,
Lancaster:
Johannes b. 12 May 1782
Philip b. 9 May 1788
Philip b. 15 July 1789
In 1790, one Philip Schirtzer witnessed a will in Shenandoah co., Va.

467. SCHERTZER, JOHANN STEPHAN   6921 Michelfeld

Shirley, 1751
S-H 454

MICHELFELD LUTHERAN KB:
Johann Stephan Schertzer b. 30 Aug. 1725, son of Hans Jacob Schertzer and Anna
Elisabetha nee Seeburger, m. 18 Feb. 1749 Eliesabetha Lechner. They had one
child bp. at Michelfeld:
1. Johann Jacob b. 12 Sept. 1750
Eliesabetha Lechner had been previously married on 20 Feb. 1748 to Joh. David
Beilstein, who had a fatal accident on 27 May 1748. By this first marriage she had
1 child:
Johann Caspar Beilstein b. 7 Dec. 1748

Pennsylvania records:
WARWICK (LITITZ) MORAVIAN KB:
Bu. 1753, John Sherzer, son of Stephen Sherzer, aged 2 y.

TRINITY LUTHERAN KB, LANCASTER:
Stephan Scherzer and Elisabeth had:
Christian b. 3 Feb. 1755
Stephan b. 19 Apr. 1757

468. SCHETTLER, ANDREAS age 29   7103 Schwaigern

Samuel, 1732
S-H 60, 61, 62, 64, 65 (with Margaretha age 27 and
Maria age 5)

SCHWAIGERN LUTHERAN KB:
Andreas Schüttler and wife Margaretha had:
    Andreas b. 6 Aug. 1730

Pennsylvania records:
PA, THIRD SERIES, 24:160,164.
Andreas Shitler warranted 100 acres in Bucks co., Pa. 25 Feb. 1734.
Andrew Shitler warranted 100 acres in Bucks co. 14 June 1745.

Andrew Shetler, York twp., York co., nat. Phila. Fall 1765 without taking an oath.

469. SCHETZENHÖFER, JOHANN PETER   7164 Obersontheim
1744   7157 Sulzbach a. d. Murr

SCHLUCHTERN LUTHERAN KB:
m. 19 Apr. 1744 Johann Peter Schetzenhöfer, son of the late Tobias Schetzenhöfer,
day laborer at Ober-Sontheim, Hochgraf. Schonburgl. Herrschaff., a blacksmith
(Hammerschmidt) and Maria Gottliebin, daughter of the late Joh. Georg Neumeis-
ter, day laborer at Sulzbach an der Murr, Lowenstein-Wertheim. Herrschaff. They
are going to Pennsylvania. (see also Portz and Kolb.)

470. SCHIELE, JERG LEONHARD   6921 Ittlingen

Ship data not located—possibly on the *Restauration*,
1747, S-H 365, 366—several others from Ittlingen on
this vessel, including Conrad Bisecker, whose wife was
a sister of Jerg Leonhard Schiele's first wife.

ITTLINGEN LUTHERAN KB:
Hans Leonhard Schiele first appears in the Ittlingen record as a sp. in 1735. He
is listed as a single man from Zaisenhausen. He appears in the record as both
Hans Leonhard and Jerg Leonhard. He last appears as a single sp. June 1737, so
his first m. was after this date.
Jerg Leonhard Schiele and wife Maria Margaretha had:
    1. Maria Margaretha b. 7 Dec. 1738
    2. Eva Catharina b. 22 May 1740
    3. Anna Maria b. 18 Dec. 1742; d. young
    4. Joh. Heinrich b. 28 Oct. 1744
D. 14 May 1745 Maria Margaretha, wife of Georg Leonhard Schule; she was b. 18
July 1712.
Maria Margaretha b. 18 July 1712 was a daughter of Joh. Michael Funk and wife
Agnes, nee Betz. Another daughter of the Funks m. Conrad Bissecker [q.v.]
(His second m. record not located.)

Georg Leonhard Schule and wife Eva, nee Stoll, had:
  Johann Michael b. 3 Aug. 1746; d. 27 Jan. 1747; one of the sp. was Conrad
Bissecker

Pennsylvania records:
SCHUMACHER'S RECORDS:
Jurg Leonhard Schilÿ and wife Eva had:
  Jürg bp. 29 May 1757, four weeks old, in Allemangle.

CHRIST LUTHERAN, YORK, BURIALS:
died 27 Aug. 1760 Georg Leonhard Schieli, b. 15 May 1759. Parents: Georg
Leonhard Schieli and Eva Catharina. Buried in the Schieli ground.

471. SCHIRM, JOH. HEINRICH

Shirley, 1751
S-H 454

Hoffenheim =
6920 Sinsheim, Elsenz

HOFFENHEIM LUTHERAN KB:
m. 15 Aug. 1722 Joh. Leonhard Schirm, son of Hans Schirm, and Elisabetha
Barbara Laubinger, daughter of Meister Jacob Laubinger, baker and "des Gerichts."
Their children:
  1. Maria Elisabetha b. 1 Nov. 1724; m. 23 May 1752 Baltzer Scholl [q.v.]
  2. Joh. Heinrich b. 17 Dec. 1730
Joh. Leonhard Schirm's widow Elisabetha Barbara m. (2) 18 Oct. 1735 Georg
Ernst Blum, widower.

Pennsylvania records:
OLEY HILLS LUTHERAN KB, BERKS CO.:
m. 2 Mar. 1755 John Heinrich Schirm, single, Lutheran, son of Leonhard Schirm
and wife Elisabetha Barbara from Hoffenheim (came to America 1752) and Maria
Magdalena Maÿer, single daughter of Friedrich Maÿer. Their children:
  1. Johannes b. 16 Jan. 1757
  2. Elisabeth b. 21 Sept. 1758
  3. Heinrich b. 9 Apr. 1761

472. SCHLAUCH, ANDREAS
SCHLAUCH, JOH. PHILIPP

Adelshofen, Baden =
7519 Eppingen

Dragon, 1732
S-H 96, 98

ADELSHOFEN LUTHERAN KB:
m. 17 Nov. 1705 Ernst Bernhard Schlauch and Anna Elisabetha Frick, daughter
of Hans Martin Frick. Children:
  1. Joh. Andreas b. 25 Feb. 1708
  2. Joh. Philipp b. 11 June 1710
  3. Joh. Jacob b. 14 Mar. 1717
  4. Joh. Michael twin, d. young

Pennsylvania records:
WILLIAMS TOWNSHIP KB:
The congregation in Saucon met at Philipp Schlauch's.
m. 1 June 1742 Jacob Schlauch and Catharine, daughter of Paul Frantz
Philip Schlauch and wife Margaretha had:
Maria Catharine b. 13 Feb. 1741
Johannes Jacob b. 14 Feb. 1743
Maria b. 17 June 1753
Jacob Schlauch and wife Catharina had:
Johann Philip b. 12 Apr. 1743; sp. Philip Schlauch and Rudolph Illick [q.v.]
and wife Magdalena

ST. PAUL'S LUTHERAN KB, RED HILL, UPPER HANOVER TWP., MONTGOMERY CO.:
Andreas Schlaug had a son:
Johann Georg bp. 6 Sept. 1743, 6 days old; sp. Ludwig Wildangel

JORDAN LUTHERAN KB, LEHIGH CO.:
Jacob Schlauch and Anna Catharina had:
Maria Susanna b. 23 Aug. 1744
Maria Magdalena b. 15 Mar. 1746
Joh. Jacob b. 29 Apr. 1748
Catharina b. 26 Mar. 1750

473. SCHLAUCH, HANS JACOB   Adelshofen, Baden =
James Goodwill, 1728   7519 Eppingen
S-H 22, 23

ADELSHOFEN LUTHERAN KB:
Joh. Georg Schlauch and wife Anna Barbara had:
Joh. Jacob b. 15 Aug. 1708

Pennsylvania records:
TRINITY LUTHERAN KB, LANCASTER:
Johann Jacob Schlauch, b. Aug. 15, 1708, m. Ursula Elisabeth Stein on Jan. 2,
1733; had 7 children, 4 are still living; died quietly and gently after a very lengthy
and agonizing illness on May 24, 1750. Buried 26 May.
Jacob Schlauch had:
1. Joh. Mattheis b. 15 Oct. 1733 [marginal note: Died Sept. 1812 in Harrisburg]
2. Joh. Georg b. 12 Apr. 1735
3. Elisabetha b. 19 May 1736
4. Maria Margaretha b. 16 Nov. 1738

Jacob Shloug of Lancaster Co. nat. by Act of 19 May 1739

474. SCHLEYHAUF, PHILIP (SHLEYHOUFF)   6921 Ittlingen
Francis & Elizabeth, 1742
S-H 328

ITTLINGEN LUTHERAN KB:
Jerg Philipp Schleyhauf and wife Catharina had:
1. Joh. Michael b. 9 May 1740; Sp. Michael Krumrein, Maria Juliana
Schuchmann, Michael Ebert, single from [7519] Gemmingen

Pennsylvania records:
ST. MICHAEL'S AND ZION LUTHERAN KB, PHILADELPHIA:
Jurg Philipp Schleyhauf and wife Anna Elisabetha had:
2. Johan Gottfried b. 30 Dec. 1745
3. Anna Maria b. 29 Dec. 1748

475. SCHLOSSER, LEONARD   Hilsbach =
SCHLOSSER, PETER   6920 Sinsheim, Elsenz
Dragon, 1732
S-H 96, 97, 98

HILSBACH REFORMED KB:
m. 11 Jan. 1701 Johann Joost Schlosser, son of the late Joh. Henrich Schlosser,
citizen at Borsdorff [?] in the Darmstatt region [6478 Borsdorf-Nidda, but this may
be 6101 Rossdorf. It is extremely difficult to read], and Margaretha, daughter of
Andreas Frey. Children:
1. Sabina b. 18 Dec. (?) 1702
2. Leonhardt b. 4 Oct. 1704; conf. 1720
3. Johannes b. 16 Oct. 1706
4. Peter b. ____Jan. 1709; bp. 25 Jan.; conf. 1722

Pennsylvania records:
A Leonhardt Schlosser and wife Anna Barbara were sp. in 1740, 1741 at Jordan
Lutheran Church, South Whitehall twp., Lehigh co.
One Peter Schlosser of Upper Milford twp., cooper, d. in Northampton co. Adm.
on his estate was granted 21 Nov. 1752 to son Peter and widow Elisabeth.
Another Schlosser (first name not given, but Leonhardt) d. in Whitehall twp.
(Unionville) and adm. was granted 10 Jan. 1756 to his widow Barbara and son
Peter.
Another Peter Schlosser appears in the records of First Reformed Church, Lancas-
ter. His wife was Anna Margaretha Weschenbach. They had:
1. Joh. Frederick bp. 24 Aug. 1737
2. Anna Barbara bp. 22 Apr. 1739; sp. Henry Basler and wife Anna Barbara
   Boehler
3. Anna Christina b. 12 Apr. 1742
Other children of this Peter Schlosser were bp. at Hill Lutheran Church, Lebanon
co. and Christ Lutheran Church, Stouchsburg, Berks co.

BLUMER'S RECORDS, NORTHAMPTON CO.:
D. 23 July 1784 Peter Schlosser, age 75 years

Hilsbach is one of the few towns in the Kraichgau built on a hill. It can be dated as early as 798. Until the "Palatine Church Division" of 1707 it was a Lutheran town; then it became Reformed. Its tower stands on its highest point with the village piled up around it. Sandstone quarries are plentiful in the neighborhood.

Photo: J. Godshall

One Peter Schlosser is buried in Sharpsburg, Maryland, with this tombstone inscription:
Here rests in God Peter Schloszer b. 20 Jan. 1710(9), d. 8 Jan. 1790. His age was
80 (changed to 81) years, 11 months and 3 days

Peter Schlosser, Lower Milford twp., Bucks co., nat. Philadelphia Fall 1765.

476. SCHMALTZHAFF, JOH. LUDWIG

Massenbach =
7103 Schwaigern

Francis & Elizabeth, 1742
S-H 327, 329

MASSENBACH LUTHERAN KB:
m. 24 Jan. 1707 Mathaus Schmaltzhaff, son of Hans Philipp Schmaltzhaff, and
Maria Barbara, daughter of Mathaus Späthern (?), citizen. Their son:
Joh. Ludwig bp. 10 June 1720

477. SCHMIDT, BASTIAN

6908 Wiesloch

William & Sarah, 1727
S-H 8 (2 in family)

WIESLOCH REFORMED KB:
m. ____May, 1727 Bostian Schmidt from Gross Bockenheim and Anna Barbara
Fessler.
Anna Barbara Fessler was bp. 19 Aug. 1701, daughter of Henrich Fessler and wife
Anna Christina.

Pennsylvania records:
MUHLENBERG'S JOURNALS, III: 94:
29 Oct. 1777—Buried at Trappe, Barbara Schmidt, widow of Sebastian Schmidt.
She was b. 10 Aug. 1702 in Wiesloch in the Palatinate. Her parents were Henrich
Vestler and his wife; they were Reformed. In May 1726 she m. Sebastian Schmidt
and came with him to America the same year. He d. on 17 Oct. 1750. They had
11 children of whom 2 sons and 3 daughters survived her death.

NEW GOSHENHOPPEN REFORMED KB, MONTGOMERY CO:
Married between 1747–1758:
Stoffel Wagner and second daughter of Bastian Schmid of Schipbach.
Confirmed 1748–1758:
Sebastian Schmid's son
Sebastian Schmid's three daughters
Bastian Schmit signed a letter in 1730, to the Classis of Amsterdam, from the
Reformed Congregation at Skippack.

478. SCHMIDT, HEINRICH age 31

6921 Ittlingen

Hope, 1733
S-H 116, 119, 121 (other passengers: Anna age 32,
Agnes (sister) age 27, Henrick age 8, and Janes [Johan-
nes] age 4)

ITTLINGEN LUTHERAN KB:
Michael Ludwig Keim and Agnes Margaretha had a daughter Anna Margaretha b. 30 Mar. 1701
Johannes Schmid, "sartor" and wife Anna Lucia had:
Heinrich bp. 20 Feb. 1704
Agnes Catharina bp. 13 Nov. 1704
Hans Heinrich Schmid and wife Anna Margaretha had:
1. Hans Heinrich b. 31 May 1725; bp. 3 June
2. Eva Catharina b. 11 Jan. 1727
3. Johannes b. 11 Mar. 1728
4. Philipp Jacob b. 6 Apr. 1730

Pennsylvania records:
OLD GOSHENHOPPEN LUTHERAN KB, MONTGOMERY CO.:
Henrich Schmidt, b. 20 Feb. 1703 from Ittlingen in Creichgau; father Joh. Schmidt, mother Anna Lucia, both Lutheran. He married (1) 11 Feb. 1723 Anna Margar. b. 30 Mar. 1701; Father Michael Ludwig Keimen, mother Agnes Margaretha. They had 4 children:
1. Johann Heinrich b. 30 May 1726
2. Johann b. 11 Mar. 1729
3. Philip Jacob b. 6 Apr. 1731
4. Johann Martin b. 1736
The first wife d. Mar. 1737 and Heinrich Schmidt m. (2) 24 June 1737 Anna Margaretha Wagner, b. 6 Oct. 1708, daughter of Georg and Magdalena Wagner. They had one child:
5. Anna Maria b. 25 Apr. 1738

Henry Schmidt, Sr., Frederich twp., Philadelphia co., and Henry Schmidt, Jr., Upper Hanover twp., Philadelphia co., nat. Philadelphia 24 Sept. 1763.

479. SCHNECK, JOH. GEORG

Polly, 1765
S-H 704

Schatthausen =
6908 Wiesloch

SCHATTHAUSEN LUTHERAN KB:
Joh. Georg Schneck and wife Maria Barbara (not m. there), both Lutheran, had:
1. Georg Peter b. 23 Sept. 1762
2. Maria Catharina b. 25 July 1764

Krebs, "Palatine Emigration . . . ," p. 42
Johann Georg Schneck of Schatthausen was permitted in 1765 to emigrate to America with his two children without paying the usual fees; presumably he was manumitted gratis on account of poverty.

Pennsylvania records:
ST. MICHAEL'S AND ZION LUTHERAN KB, PHILADELPHIA:
One Georg Schneck b. 25 Jan. 1732 in the Dukedom Wuertemberg was bu. 10

Mar. 1777, aged 45 y. [There were other Schneck immigrants, including an earlier passenger also named Georg Schneck on the *Patience*, 1750, S-H 426.]

George Schneck, Philadelphia city, nat. Philadelphia 10 April 1765

480. SCHNEIDER, CONRAD
Johnson, 1732
S-H 72, 76, 78

Fürfeld and
Treschklingen =
6927 Bad Rappenau

FÜRFELD LUTHERAN KB:
m. at Fürfeld 2 May 1724 Johann Conrad Schneider, linenweaver, single son of Johann Conrad Schneider, citizen and linenweaver at Treschklingen, and Eva Catharina, eldest daughter of Johann Sebastian Betz. (She was bp. 8 Apr. 1701 at Fürfeld.)

TRESCHKLINGEN LUTHERAN KB:
Joh. Conrad Schneider, linenweaver, and wife Eva Catharina, nee Betz, from Fürfeld had one child bp. at Treschklingen:
1. Anna Barbara b. 8 Sept. 1731

Pennsylvania records:
OLD GOSHENHOPPEN LUTHERAN KB, MONTGOMERY CO:
Elder of the church: (1751) Conrad Schneider, aged 52 y, b. 17 Mar. 1699 in Treschlingen in the Schwäbischen Kreiss. Father was Conrad Schneider, Mother, Cathar. Both Reformed. In 1732 he came to America. In 1724 he m. Catharina, b. 1700, dau. of Sebastian Betz and Eva, natives of Ferfeld. They had the following children:
1. Leonhardt b. 1 Feb. 1725
2. Eva Cathar. b. 1 May 1727
3. Elisabetha, d.
4. Anna Barbara, d.
5. Elias b. 12 Aug. 1733
6. Michael b. 18 Dec. 1735
7. Balthasar b. 16 Feb. 1738
8. Henricus b. 16 May 1740
Leonhard Schneider, b. 1 Feb. 1725, son of Conrad Schneider and Catharina. In 1732 he came to America with his parents. M. 14 Sept. 1752 Maria Christina, b. 29 Nov. 1729, dau. of Hannes Hens and Maria Elisabeth. Her grandfather was Baltasar Merckley [q.v.].
Elias Schneider, son of Conrad, m. 7 Dec. 1756 Anna Maria Nuss, dau. of Jacob Nuss and Anna Maria, both of Old Goshenhoppen.
Baltas Schneider, son of Conrad, m. 3 Dec. 1757 Sofia, dau. of Andres Vogel.

Conrad Schneider, Philadelphia co., nat. Philadelphia 11 Apr. 1749.

481. SCHOLL, BALTZER   Hoffenheim =
Snow *Louisa*, 1752   6920 Sinsheim, Elsenz
S-H 506

HOFFENHEIM LUTHERAN KB:
m. 23 May 1752 Baltzer Scholl, son of the late Baltzer Scholl, inhabitant at
Reichertshausen [= 6956 Neudenau], and Maria Elisabetha Schirm. They are
leaving for Pennsylvania.

Pennsylvania records:
DILLINGERSVILLE LUTHERAN KB:
Balthasar Scholl and wife Maria Elisabeth had
  1. Susanna b. 14 Apr. 1759; bp. 10 June 1759

482. SCHÖNER, DANIEL   Ehrstädt =
Prelist (ca. 1717)   6920 Sinsheim, Elsenz

EHRSTÄDT LUTHERAN KB:
Hans Adam Schöner and wife Eva had:
  Johann Daniel b. 25 Jan. 1686; bp. 27 Jan.
m. 17 May 1707 Hans Daniel Schöner, son of Hans Adam Schöner, the "Schultheiss" of Ehrstatt, and Maria Catharine, daughter of Hans Jörg Horn, cooper and
"des Gerichts". Children:
  1. Louisa Catharina bp. 5 Mar. 1709
  2. Johanna Christina b. 23 Dec. 1710
  3. Joh. Adam b. 20 Nov. 1712
  4. Heinrich Daniel b. 22 Dec. 1714
  5. Maria Agatha b. 18 Sept. 1716

Pennsylvania records:
Mar. 1723 Daniel Schöner signed a petition for a road from Limerick twp. through
Falkner Swamp to Oley.
Mar. 1731 signed a petition for the division of Hanover twp.
Dec. 1735 petition requesting that the boundaries of Frankfort and New Hanover
twp. be ascertained.
In 1734 Daniel Schöner was taxed for 100 A. in Hanover twp.
In 1733 Daniel Schöner was one of the three delegates sent by the United Congregations to Europe to seek financial aid for the needy Lutherans in Pennsylvania.
(see *The Lutheran Church in New Hanover*, Pennsylvania German Society Proceedings, Vol. XX (1911) 40–41; also Glatfelter *Pastors and People*, II: 31–35).
Daniel Schöner d. 25 Nov. 1741 and letters of administration were granted to his
widow Mary Catharine on 31 Dec. 1741. His will, dated 18 Oct. 1741, names the
following: wife: Mary Catharine; sons: George, Stephan, Adam, Henry; mentions
daughters, but does not name them. Will witnessed by: Matheus Bender and
Frederick Reichard.

NEW HANOVER LUTHERAN CHURCH KB:
conf. 1743 Daniel Schoener's son Daniel.
Georg Schoener and wife Margaretha, daughter of Joh. Friederick Reichard, had:

    1. Matthias b. 16 Jan. 1747
    2. Joh. Georg b. 3 Feb. 1748
His wife died in confinement at the birth of this second child.
Adam Schoener and wife (not named) had a son:
    Stevanus bp. 18 Feb. 1745, age 11 mo.

Daniel Schoner of Philadelphia co. nat. by Act of 29 Mar. 1735.

483. SCHÖNER, MELCHIOR

Ehrstädt =
6920 Sinsheim, Elsenz

Francis & Elizabeth, 1742
S-H 327, 329

EHRSTÄDT LUTHERAN KB:
Johann Balthasar Schöner, b. 29 Aug. 1687, son of Hans Adam and Eva Schöner,
citizen, and wife Johanna (Catholic religion) had a son:
    Johann Melchior b. 14 Sept. 1711
Johann Melchior Schöner and wife Anna Maria (Catholic religion) had one child
bp. in the Ehrstädt Lutheran church:
    1. Johann Peter b. 15 July 1737
[Joh. Melchior Schöner was a nephew of Daniel Schöner who emigrated ca. 1717
to Pennsylvania.]

Pennsylvania records:
NEW HANOVER LUTHERAN KB, MONTGOMERY CO., PA.:
Melchior Schoener and wife Anna Maria had:
    1. Anna Catharina conf. 1745
    2. Johannes conf. 1752
    3. Joh. Peter conf. 1753
    4. Christopher b. 19 Mar.; bp. 24 Mar. 1745; conf. 1759
    5. Andreas b. 31 July 1749; conf. 1764
    6. David b. 25 Feb. 1752
    7. Anna Maria b. 22 May 1753
    8. Joh. Jacob b. 24 May 1759
Bu. 24 June 1778 Melchior Schoener, age 67 y., 9 mo., 2 weeks and 3 days.
Bu. 28 July 1801 Anna Maria, widow of Melchior Schoener, aged 83 y. 7 mo. 3½
weeks [Her tombstone at New Hanover indicates her maiden name was Geiger and
she was b. 2 Dec. 1717]

PHILADELPHIA CO. WILLS:
Melchior "Shiner," New Hanover twp., (19 June 1778, prob. 3 July 1778). Wife
Anna Maria and children: eldest son John; Peter; George; Christophel; Catharina,
wife of Jacob Malsberger; Andrew; Anna Mary, now the wife of Georg Spengler;
and Jacob. He also mentions a granddaughter Hannah, daughter of son George.
Numerous entries for later generations of the family appear in the New Hanover
Lutheran Church records.

Melchior Shenvee (Sheener), New Hanover twp., Philadelphia co., nat. Philadelphia, April 1761

484. SCHÖRCK, HANS JACOB

Dragon, 1732
S-H 96, 97, 98

Steinsfurt =
6920 Sinsheim, Elsenz

STEINSFURT REFORMED KB:

Hans Jacob Schurck bp. 8 Aug. 1686, son of Hans Michel Schurk and Catharina (Gruber or Gucker?)
m. (1) 27 Aug. 1709 Hans Jacob Schürck, son of Hans Michael Schürck, shoe-maker, and Anna Barbara, daughter of the late Melchior Lüttig. Children:
    1. Anna Margretha bp. 9 Sept. 1711
m. (2) 2 Feb. 1712 Joh. Jacob Schurck, widower, and Margretha, daughter of Eberhardt Raudenbusch. Children:
    *2. Hans Jacob bp. 8 Jan. 1713; conf. 1729
    3. Hans Heinerich bp. 6 June 1716
    4. ? Christian or Christina b. ____Feb. 1722 (faded entry—reading uncertain)
    5. Hans Martin bp. 22 Mar. 1725
    6. Anna Elisabetha bp. 8 Aug. 1728
Margaretha Raudenbusch was bp. 4 Nov. 1691, daughter of Eberhardt Rauden-busch and Regina Esther.
A Gorg David Schurck was conf. 1734. He is possibly the Dafid Scherkh on the *Restauration,* 1747, S-H 365. [There are faded entries in this KB, and his bp. is not located.]

Pennsylvania records:
LANCASTER CO. ORPHANS' COURT DOCKET I,
26 Mar. 1752—Wendel Zwecker and David Sherk appointed guardians of Mary Elizabeth, Christina and Mary Margaret Sherk, orphan children of Jacob Sherk, deceased.

485. SCHRÖTTLIN, MARIA MARGARETHA

6921 Ittlingen

with husband:
Philip Friedrich Warth age 27
Louisa, 1753
S-H 582, 583, 584

ITTLINGEN LUTHERAN KB:
Johannes Schröttlin, chirurgus, and wife Margaretha Rosina had:
    1. Maria Margaretha b. 19 Apr. 1726
    2. Maria Elisabetha b. 24 Nov. 1727
(there are no earlier records there for this family and no later records.)

Pennsylvania records:
ST. MICHAEL'S AND ZION LUTHERAN KB, PHILADELPHIA:
m. 2 Oct. 1758 Johann Daniel Mutschler and Susanna Dorothea Schröetlin
m. 11 Sept. 1759 Michael Frick and Maria Margaretha Warth
died 8 July 1805 Maria Margaretha Rohr, dau. of Johann Schrottlin and Margaretha Rosina; born in Itlingen 19 Apr. 1726; m. 5 Nov. 1747 Philip Friedrich Wart; 2

sons and 2 daughters.
She m. (2) 11 Sept. 1759 Michael Frick.
  m. (3) 17 Nov. 1795 Johann Rohr.
The Adolf Gerber lists indicate that Philipp Friedrich Warth and wife Maria Margaretha left Pfaffenhoffen in 1753 for America.
Johan Andreas Schrödlin (*Peggy*, 1753; S-H 545, 547, 549; age 24) b. 22 or 24
Sept. 1724 in Güglinger Amt was a physician in Pa. According to family tradition
he had two sisters who came to America; one sister came with him and the other
sister came later. This immigrant brought a document (presumably a record of his
birth). Only half of the document exists today; the existing half contains the date:
22 1724; the area: Güglinger Amt; and the name: Johannes Schrödlin (the father?);
the words chirurgus allda; and the sp., Johann Adam Schoch and Andreas Uhler,
single.

486. SCHUCH, JOHANN MARTIN

Reihen =
6920 Sinsheim, Elsenz

Edinburgh, 1751
S-H 461

REIHEN REFORMED KB:
m. 13 Sept. 1740 Joh. Martin Schuch, Lutheran, son of the late Joh. Valentin
Schuch, and Anna Maria, daughter of Joh. Leonhard Dörr, Reformed, "Gerichtsverwandten." [She was b. 12 Aug. 1714, daughter of Hans Leonhard Dörr
and Maria Ester nee Hertzel] Children:
  1. Joh. Jonas b. 19 Aug. 1741
  2. Joh. Martin b. 18 Jan. 1744
  3. Joh. Georg b. 16 Feb. 1747
  4. Joh. Jacob b. 27 Nov. 1749

Krebs, "Palatine Emigration . . . ," p. 40.
Martin Schuck, of Reihen, was permitted in 1751 to emigrate to America on
payment of 4 florins for manumission and 3 florins emigration tax.

Pennsylvania records:
Pennsylvanische Berichte, 29 FEB. 1760:
Martin Schuck living in Hempfield twp., Lancaster co.; his wife Anna Maria.

Martin Shuck, Linn twp., Northampton co., nat. Philadelphia, Fall 1765.

487. SCHUMACHER, ANDREAS

6921 Ittlingen

1749

ITTLINGEN LUTHERAN KB:
Wendel Schumacher and wife Anna Elisabetha had:
  Andreas b. 24 Apr. 1717
Andreas Schumacher, tailor, and wife Anna Elisabetha nee Häberlin had:
  1. Anna Cordula b. 7 Sept. 1742
  2. Anna Catharina b. 18 Mar. 1745
  3. Johann Andreas b. 17 Aug. 1748

"They all died, parents and children, on the sea in 1749, going to Pennsylvania." Elisabetha Schumacher, widow (mother of Andreas), also appears on the 1749 communicants' list of those who are leaving for Pennsylvania. The minister later entered a cross by her name, indicating that she did not survive the voyage.

488. SCHUMACHER, JACOB

Berwangen, Kraichgau = 6926 Kirchardt

Charming Nancy, 1737
S-H 188, 189, 191, 193 (with Anna Maria, Paul, George, and Anna Maria)

BERWANGEN LUTHERAN KB:
m. 24 Nov. 1697 Jacob Schumacher, son of Andreas Schumacher, "Gerichtsverwandten," and Anna, daughter of Hans Kobelin. Their son:
Jacob b. 22 Feb. 1697
Jacob Schuhmacher and wife Anna Maria, Reformed religion, had:
   1. Paul b. 30 Apr. 1727; d. 26 Dec. 1728
   2. Paulus b. 2 Oct. 1729
   3. Joh. George bp. _____1731
   4. Maria Catharina b. 18 Dec. 1732
Jacob Schuhmacher and wife Anna Maria are listed in the Communion register with children Joh. Pauli, Joh. Georg, Maria Catharina. A notation by the entry indicates the family went to Pennsylvania in 1737.

Pennsylvania records:
Jacob Schumacher and wife Anna Maria sp. 1749 at Jordan Lutheran Church, S. Whitehall twp., Lehigh co.

BURIED AT ZIEGEL CHURCH, LEHIGH CO.:
Johann Georg Schumacher b. 31 Mar. 1731 lived in marriage for 43 years with Susanna nee Weisz; had 13 children, 7 sons and 6 daughters. D. 2 Jan. 1801, age 69 y., 9 mo. 1 day.

SCHUMACHER'S RECORDS:
Paul Schumacher and wife Eva Elisabeth had:
   1. Johann Nicolaus bp. 8 Jan. 1760 emergency bp. at Weisenberg, the child died
   2. Anna Catharina bp. 21 May 1761; b. in Lowhill, bp. in Weisenberg
   3. Eva Elisabeth bp. 20 Nov. 1763
   4. Maria Christina bp. 9 Mar. 1766; sp.: Jürg Schumacher and Catharina Grammlich, wife of Velten Grammlich
Jürg Schumacher and wife Susanna Elisabeth had:
   1. Maria Christina bp. 14 Nov. 1762 in Weisenberg
   2. Maria Margaretha bp. 28 Oct. 1767 at Ziegel Church
   3. Margaretha bp. 19 Nov. 1769 at Ziegel Church

Paul Shumaker, Lowhill twp., Northampton co., nat. Philadelphia, Fall 1765.
George Shoemaker, Weisenberg twp., Northampton co., nat. Philadelphia, Fall 1765.

Helmstadt was a Palatine town in the eighteenth century. Its Lutheran church has records dating from mid-seventeenth century. Helmstadt lies on the Schwarzbach and was mentioned as early as 782.

Photo: J. Godshall

489. SCHUPP, GEORG MICHAEL

6928 Helmstadt—Bargen

Two Brothers, 1750
S-H 438

HELMSTADT LUTHERAN KB:
m. 10 Jan. 1742 Georg Michael Schupp, son of Hans Michael Schupp, tenant farmer at the Ursenbacher Hoff [located southeast of 6921 Zuzenhausen] and Maria Margretha, daughter of the late Hans Adam Laule. The marriage was necessary. They had one child bp. at Helmstadt:
1. Joh. Adam b. 10 June 1742
He was a brother-in-law of Matheus Gerner who also appears on this ship's list.

490. SCHÜTZ, CONRAD age 30

Adelshofen, Baden =
7519 Eppingen

Samuel, 1737
S-H 169, 170, 172

ADELSHOFEN LUTHERAN KB:
Hans Leonhard Schütz and wife Anna Barbara had:
Conrad b. 24 Jan. 1706 _____

One Conrad Shutz, Lower Merion twp., Philadelphia co., was nat. 11 Apr. 1751
Another Conrad Schutz, Upper Hanover twp., Philadelphia co., was nat. 24–25 Sept. 1764

Faces turn toward the street from the corner posts and interior posts of the half-timbering in many houses in the Kraichgau. It is widely believed that these faces were placed in the aftermath of the Thirty Years' War as protection against the forces of evil, but such faces occur on older buildings, as well as in mills at the channels from which ground grain spills. Then they are called *Mehlkotzer*. The Gasthof Löwen in Neckarbischofsheim has such faces on two floors of its half-timbered overstructure.

Photo: J. Godshall

491. SCHÜTZ, FRIDERICH age 22   6924 Neckarbischofsheim

Samuel, 1732
S-H 59, 63, 65

NECKARBISCHOFSHEIM LUTHERAN KB:
Joh. Philipp Schütz, butcher, and wife Maria Margaretha had:
    Johann Friderich b. 10 Mar. 1709

Pennsylvania records:
ST. MATTHEW'S LUTHERAN KB, HANOVER:
Friderich Schütz had:
    1. John Phillip b. 6 Oct. 1743
    2. Catherine Elisabeth b. Sept. 1747

YORK CO. WILLS:
Friedrich Schütz, Heidelberg twp., (18 Nov. 1758/27 Dec. 1758). Wife Elisabetha, oldest son Friedrich and eight other children. Among other bequests he gave Elisabetha a riding horse, the choice between two named *Pantur* or *Weissschwantz*.

492. SCHÜTZ, GEORG LUDWIG
Dragon, 1732
S-H 96, 98

Adelshofen, Baden =
7519 Eppingen

ADELSHOFEN LUTHERAN KB:
Hans *Leonhardt* Schütz and Anna Barbara had:
Georg Ludwig b. 19 Feb. 1702
m. 25 June 1726 Georg Ludwig Schütz, linenweaver, son of Joh. *Bernhard* Schütz, and Anna Maria, daughter of Ernst Bernhard Schlauch, *"Heiligen Pfleger"* and *"Gerichtsverwandten"*. (She was b. 20 Aug. 1698, a daughter of his second marriage to Juliana Dorothea Fischer, daughter of Andreas Fischer.) Children:
1. Johan Georg b. 3 Sept. 1727; d. 1728
2. Catharina Ursula b. 28 Jan. 1729
3. Joh. Georg b. 8 Aug. 1731

Pennsylvania records:
WILLIAMS TWP. CONGREGATION KB:
Ludwig Schütz sp. 1741 a ch. of Philip Schlauch, his brother-in-law.

ST. PAUL'S (BLUE) KB, UPPER SAUCON TWP., LEHIGH CO.:
Catharina Schütz, daughter of Georg Ludwig Schütz, sp. 1750 a child of Johan Melchior Stecher.
m. 13 Dec. 1759 Joh. Philip Schütz, son of Ludewig Schutz from Upper Milford, and Elisabetha Margretha, daughter of Michael Schmidt, from Upper Milford.

ZIONSVILLE LUTHERAN KB, UPPER MILFORD TWP., LEHIGH CO.:
Philip Schütz had a son Johannes Georg bp. 25 Nov. 1764. Sp. were Joh. Georg Schütz and Susanna Bischoff.

Ludwick Sheetz, Lower Milford twp., Bucks co., nat. Philadelphia Fall 1765

493. SCHUTZ, JERG
1717
Bonfeld Emigrant list: Jerg Schitz, wf. and 3 ch.

Bonfeld =
6927 Bad Rappenau

BONFELD LUTHERAN KB:
m. 10 Nov. 1674 Georg Schütz, "Schultheiss", widower and Catharina Masack, daughter of Abraham Masack, "des Gerichts". She d. 1 Sept. 1683 and on 29 Jan. 1684 he m. another Catharina, surname not given in the record. He d. 20 Sept. 1690.
m. 15 Jan. 1700 Joh. Georg Schütz, son of the former "Schultheiss" Jerg Schütz, and Sophia Catharina, daughter of the late Andreae Klotz, bricklayer and Gerichtsman. They had:
1. Maria Elisabetha b. 29 Aug. 1701; bp. 30 Aug. 1701; d. 1701
2. Maria Catharina b. Dec. 1702; bp. 2 Jan. 1703
3. Maria Sophia b. 22 Apr. 1706; bp. 23 Apr. 1706
4. Maria Dorothea b. 27 Oct. 1709; bp. 27 Oct. 1709; d. 1711
5. Joh. Georg b. 23 Apr. 1712; bp. 24 Apr. 1712
6. Maria Margaretha b. 13 July 1713; bu. 14 July 1713

Pennsylvania records:
PA, SECOND SERIES, XIX: 626.
Hans George Shutz and Mathias Ringer (two Germans) warrant 20th, 11th month
1717/18 for 500 acres of land on the west side of the Schuylkill River.

494. SCHÜTZ, JOH. ADAM   Adelshofen =
Richmond, 1764   7519 Eppingen
S-H 696

ADELSHOFEN LUTHERAN KB:
m. 27 Nov. 1736 Jacob Schütz, son of the late Joh. Leonhardt Schütz, citizen, and
Anna Barbara, daughter of the late Friederich Stupp. Their son:
    Johann Adam b. 15 Dec. 1737; conf. 1751
He arrived on the *Richmond* with Johannes Seitz and Michael Maag, both recorded
in the KB as leaving Adelshofen in May 1764 to go to America.

495. SCHÜTZ, JOH. PHILIP age 21   6924 Neckarbischofsheim
Samuel, 1732
S-H 59, 63, 65

NECKARBISCHOFSHEIM LUTHERAN KB:
David Henrich Schütz, citizen and saddler, and wife Maria Barbara had:
    Johann Philipp b. 8 July 1708
They also had several other children bp. there who remained in Neckarbischof-
sheim and married there:
m. 9 Nov. 1728 Joh. Nicolaus Friedrich, son of Joh. Adam Friedrich and Anna
Catharina Schütz, daughter of the late David Henrich Schütz.
m. 28 Oct. 1732 Johann Friedrich Schütz, linenweaver, son of the late David
Henrich Schütz, saddler, and Christina Catharina, daughter of the late Joh. Georg
Schäffer.

Pennsylvania records:
LANCASTER CO. DEEDS
G: 463, 1763:
Heirs of brother Philip Schutz of Bischoffsheim (sadler) who moved to Pennsylvania
30 years ago. Philip Schutz left property by will to his brothers and sisters who
resided in Bischoffsheim. Recorded in the deed book is a power of attorney to sell
Philip's property, signed by the following heirs:
Catharine Frederick, nee Schütz, wife of John Nicolas Frederick; children of the
late Frederick Schütz—Frederick and Hans Adam; children of the late Eve Barbara
Sleher, nee Schütz, wife of Jacob Sleher—John George, Charlotte, Anna Maria,
George Philip, Maria Barbara; heirs of Nicolas Frederick and wife Catharine—
William, Balthasar, John Henry, Christina, Crieslerica, Margaret.

TRINITY LUTHERAN KB, LANCASTER:
d. 12 Apr. 1749 Anna Barbara Vislin (= Fissel), mother-in-law of Philip Schütz;
b. 4 Sept. 1689, bu. 14 Apr. 1749

d. 3 Aug. 1761 Philipp Schütz, saddler, aged 53 y. 1 mo. 22 days; separatist, buried the following day.

Philadelphia Gazette, 13 Sept. 1744:
Anna Elizabeth Schutz, wife of Philip Schutz, of Lancaster town, has eloped from her husband and gone away with one Jacob Frederick Kurtz.

496. SCHWAB, JOH. GEORG

6920 Sinsheim, Elsenz

William & Sarah, 1727
S-H 8 ("Hans Jerick Schaub, Conn., 3 in family")

This immigrant was related to the prelist Jost Schwab who emigrated from Leimen. The other Hans Jerrick Swaep with 6 persons in family who arrived on the *William and Sarah,* 1727, was a son of Jost Schwab; he was b. 19 July 1682 in Dühren and he also had a son named Georg bp. 9 Jan. 1706 in Leimen. All three George Swopes lived in Lancaster co. before 1749, and all three appear in York co. records after 1749. Researchers wishing to know more about these families should consult the following published accounts:
Morse and McLachlen, *The Swope Family Book of Remembrance* (1972). This two-volume work also includes information on Eberhard Riehm and Andreas Meixel, two prelist emigrants from Leimen who were sons-in-law of Jost Schwab.
Denniston, *Genealogy of the Stukey, Ream, Grove, Clem and Denniston Families* (1939)
Swope, *History of the Swope Family and Their Connections* (1896)

SINSHEIM REFORMED KB AND ZUZENHAUSEN LUTHERAN KB:
Marriage recorded in both church books:
m. 8/15 Nov. 1718 Johann Georg Schwab, citizen at Sinsheim, and Anna Maria, daughter of Hans (Johannes) Keÿdel, *Schultheiss* at [6921] Zuzenhausen. Children:
1. Anna Maria bp. 7 Dec. 1719
2. Anna Catharina b. 2 Apr. 1721
3. Joh. Michael b. 24 Feb. 1726

Pennsylvania records:
NEW HOLLAND LUTHERAN KB, LANCASTER CO.:
In 1735 Joh. Georg Schwab and wife Anna Maria from Sinsheim were sp. for a child of Martin Löwenstein.
George Swope, Lancaster co., nat. Philadelphia April 1744.

497. SCHWARTZ, JOH. GEORG

6903 Neckargemünd

Robert and Alice, 1743
S-H 347

NECKARGEMÜND REFORMED KB:
m. 27 Apr. 1689 Conrad Schwartz, son of Peter Schwartz, fisherman, and Anna Barbara, daughter of Hans Schmid. They had:
Joh. Jacob bp. 15 Feb. 1690
Jacob Schwartz, citizen and fisherman, and wife Maria Helena [in some records

she is named as Magdalena—m. record not located] had:
Georg b. [faded entry] Sept. 1720

Pennsylvania records:
LANCASTER MORAVIAN RECORDS:
Joh. Georg Schwartz (b. 27 Sept. 1720 in Neckargemünd, Pfalz, d. 8 Oct. 1799)
m. 1748 Maria Catharina Schweig (b. 7 Feb. 1729 at "Wolbergweilen, Dukedom
Two Brothers") [actually this should read Wolfersweiler, Zweibrücken. She was a
daughter of Hans Jacob Schweig and Maria Barbara, nee Geis. She came to America with her widowed mother in 1742.] Joh. Georg Schwartz came to America in
1743. They had 10 children:
1. Susanna b. 25 June 1750; m. (1) 24 Jan. 1775 Conrad Graff, m. (2) 1
   Jan. 1788 William Reichenbach
2. Conrad b. 22 Aug. 1752; d. 1752
3. Conrad b. 6 Sept. 1753; d. 1756
4. Joh. Georg b. 7 July 1757; d. 1757
5. Anna Maria b. 27 Aug. 1758; d. 1758
6. Jacob b. 28 Aug. 1760
7. Johannes Georg b. 26 Sept. 1762
8. Johannes b. 9 Feb. 1765; d. 1775
9. Catharina b. 29 Jan. 1767; m. Gottlob Jungman of Reading, Pa.
10. Anna Maria b. 10 June 1769

LANCASTER CO. DEEDS:
D: 49, 25 June 1753. King St., Lancaster, George Swartz, saddler, of Lancaster,
and wife Kathrin, mortgage to Sebastian Graffe of Lancaster Borough.

498. SCHWEICKHARDT, PHILIP   Eichtersheim =
                                                    6921 Angelbachtal
William & Sarah, 1727
S-H 8, 9 (2 persons)

EICHTERSHEIM LUTHERAN KB:
m. 7 Jan. 1727 Phil. Schweickhardt, son of Joh. Philip Schweickhardt, and Susanna Elisabeth Hauser from Adelshofen.

Pennsylvania records:
MUDDY CREEK LUTHERAN KB, LANCASTER CO.:
Joh. Philipp Schweickert and wife Susanna sp. a child of Nicolaus Adam in 1736
Philipp Schweickert and his wife had:
1. Joh. Philipp b. 4 Aug. 1734
2. Joh. Valentin b. 25 June 1736
3. Joh. Michael b. 16 June 1738
4. Nicolaus b. 27 May 1741
5. Susanna Margaretha b. 3 Sept. 1743
6. Susanna b. ____May 1746

499. SCHWEIGERT, SAMUEL

Bargen =
6928 Helmstadt—Bargen

Shirley, 1751
S-H 454 (Name on list: Hans Samuel Shweyart)

BARGEN LUTHERAN KB:
Georg Schweicker(t) and wife Clara had:
Samuel bp. 24 Aug. 1710
No marriage recorded for either father or son

Krebs, *"Palatine Emigration . . . ,"* p. 38:
Samuel Schweigert (Schweikert) of Bargen (Kreis Sinsheim) was permitted to emigrate in 1751, on payment of 10 florins.

500. SCHWEINFORTH, ALLBRECHT

6920 Sinsheim, Elsenz

Henrietta, 1754
S-H 649, 650

SINSHEIM REFORMED KB:
Joh. Jacob Schweinforth, cooper, and wife Anna Catharina had:
Albrecht b. 30 July 1730

Pennsylvania records:
FIRST REFORMED KB, LANCASTER:
m. 12 Aug. 1755 Albrecht Sweinford and Margaret Schneider. They had:
1. Johannes b. 17 Apr. 1758

501. SCHWEITZER, MATTHAEUS

6921 Ittlingen

Possibly on the *William*, 1737 with Sebastian Winterbauer, also from Ittlingen
S-H 194, 195, 196 [Another Mathes Schweitzer arrived in 1727 on the *Friendship*, S-H 16, 17]

ITTLINGEN LUTHERAN KB:
Joh. Georg Schweitzer and Catharina (nee Greiner) had:
Matthaeus bp. 26 Jan. 1711. "In Pensylvanien"

502. SCHWERTLE, JOHANNES

7519 Eppingen

Minerva, 1772
S-H 740 (One Jacob Schwele also appears on this ship list and he might be the Jacob Schwertle mentioned below.)

EPPINGEN REFORMED KB:
Melchior Schwerdle and wife Anna Maria had:
Johannes bp. 22 Feb. 1728, conf. 1743
m. 11 Feb. 1750 Joh. Schwertle and Eva Christina Gebhart. Johannes Schwertle and Eva Christina (Gebhard) had:

1. Jacob b. 30 Mar. 1751
2. Johannes b. 14 May 1753; conf. 1766
3. Christoph b. 17 Oct. 1754; d. young
4. Joh. Melchior b. 19 Dec. 1756
5. Joh. Georg b. 20 Dec. 1758; d. 1762
6. Georg Michael b. 16 Feb. 1761
7. Henrich b. 11 July 1762; d. young
8. Joh. Philipp b. 28 Oct. 1763

Pennsylvania records:
PA. ARCHIVES, THIRD SERIES, 16: 147.
A John Swartley was taxed in Franconia twp., Philadelphia co. in 1782.

TOHICKON REFORMED KB, BUCKS CO.:
John Schwerdtle appears on a communicants' list dated the Sunday before Easter, 1775.
Later records at this church contain the surname Swartly, Swartley, Swertly.
Record of Indentures of Individuals Bound Out as Apprentices, Servants, Etc. and of German and Other Redemptioners in the Office of the Mayor of the City of Philadelphia October 3, 1771 to October 5, 1773 (Lancaster, 1907), p. 135:
Oct. 1, 1772 John Swadley indentured to Abraham Kratz, N. Britain twp., Bucks co., 3 years.
Jacob Swadley, indentured to Henry Kephart, Bedminster twp., Bucks co., 3 years.
The youngest brother Philip Swartley is estimated to have emigrated ca. 1783/84.

LINE LEXINGTON MENNONITE CEMETERY, MONTGOMERY CO.:
Philip Swartley, Sr., b. Oct. 28, 1764, d. Sept. 23, 1840

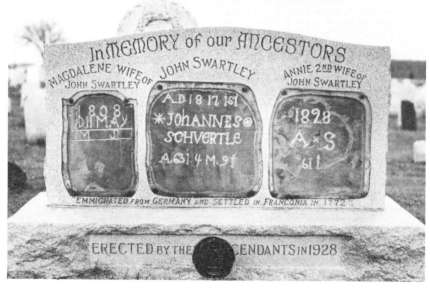

Tombstones at Franconia Mennonite Meetinghouse

503. SEIB, GEORG   7519 Eppingen
      SEIB, LUDWIG
      SEIB, FRANTZ
Dragon, 1732
S-H 97, 98, 99

EPPINGEN REFORMED KB:
Joh. Ludwig Seip and wife Christina had:
    1. Maria Margretha bp. 1 May 1701
    2. Joh. Georg bp. 30 Nov. 1702
    3. Joh. Ludwig b. 2 Mar. 1705; bp. 3 Mar.
    4. Georg Michael b. 9 Oct. 1707; d. 18 Aug. 1711
    5. Anna Barbara b. 19 Mar. 1710; d. 28 Aug. 1710
    6. Anna Maria bp. 12 Feb. 1713; d. 1 Mar. 1717
    7. Franciscus bp. 10 Mar. 1715
    8. Johannes b. 8 Aug. 1717; bp. 2 Sept.
    9. Juliana bp. 18 Feb. 1720
M. 19 June 1731 Hans Georg Seib and Anna Elisabetha Huber, both single.

Pennsylvania records:
TRINITY LUTHERAN KB, LANCASTER:
Frantz Seip had:
    Joh. Jacob b. 5 Sept. 1738; sp. Jacob Schlauch and wife Ursula Elisabetha

FIRST REFORMED KB, LANCASTER:
Joh. Adam Hoff and wife Juliana Seib had:
    1. Joh. Ludwig b. 9 Sept. 1736; sp: Ludwig Seib and wife
    2. Joh. Adam b. _____1739

YORK MORAVIAN KB:
Adam Hoff on the Codorus, born at Friedelsheim near Dürckheim an der Hard in
the Electoral Palatinate. Married Juliana Seib of Ebingen, 9 hours from Heidelberg
in the Electoral Palatinate, born 18 Feb. 1720. 5 children listed in register.

WALDSCHMIDT RECORDS:
Catharina Seib, daughter of Ludwig Seib, m. 19 Feb. 1760 Adam Schneider, son
of Daniel Schneider.

WARWICK MORAVIAN KB, LANCASTER CO.:
Bu. 24 Sept. 1749—John Philip Seip, eight months old
Bu. 3 Mar. 1750 Franciscus Seip, eight years
Bu. 1753—Anna Mary Seip, infant
Bu. 1757—John Michael Seip, one year
Bu. 1763—Franz Seip aged 48 years

504. SEIP, CARL age 27   Untergimpern =
Samuel, 1732   6924 Neckarbischofsheim
S-H 60, 61, 62, 64, 65 [with Kathrina Seyb, age 29;
and Christian(a) Beller, age 8]

OBERGIMPERN LUTHERAN KB:
M. 30 Nov. 1728 Carl Seip, son of Henrich Seip, miller at Untergimbern, and Anna Catharina, widow of the late Georg Peter Michael Beller. Children:
1. Maria Barbara bp. ___Apr. 1729
2. Maria Anna b. 25 June 1730
Anna Catharina had the following children by her first husband, Georg Peter Michael Beller, tailor and citizen at Untergimpern:
1. Christina Margaretha bp. 3 Dec. 1723
2. Georg Daniel Nicolaus bp. 31 Mar. 1725, d. 1 Jan. 1726
Georg Peter Michael Beller d. 27 Mar. 1726, age 28.

Pennsylvania records:
NEW HOLLAND LUTHERAN KB, LANCASTER CO.:
Carl Seip and wife had:
3. Anna Elisabetha b. 23 June 1734
4. Joh. Leonhardt b. 26 Apr. 1736
5. Joh. Carl b. 13 Feb. 1738
6. Anna Dorothea b. 7 June 1739
7. Joh. Peter b. 19 Aug. 1744
Carl Seip and wife sp. 1734, 1735 children of Georg Bernhardt Mann and in 1745 for a child of Emanuel Hermann.

TRINITY LUTHERAN KB, LANCASTER:
m. 23 Oct. 1737 Anna Catarina Bellerin and Joh. Jacob Franck
m. 18 Aug. 1743 Christina Margretha Bellerin and Johann Georg Schmitt

505. SEIFERT, ADAM   7103 Schwaigern
Fane, 1749
S-H 424

SCHWAIGERN LUTHERAN KB:
m. 9 Sept. 1708 Michael Seiffert, "Beysitzer" and widower (from his first m. record he was a son of Peter Seiffert), and Susanna, daughter of Leonhard Hessenauer. They had:
    Joh. Adam b. 23 May 1723
m. 9 July 1748 Johann Adam Seiffert, son of the late Michael Seiffert, former citizen, and Maria Elisabetha, daughter of Johann Frederich Schmid, citizen at Budigheim [6470 Büdingen].

Pennsylvania records:
SALEM LUTHERAN KB, DOVER TWP., YORK CO.:
Adam and Anna Maria Seiffert sp. two of Martin Reisinger's ch. [also from Schwaigern]
_____
Adam Syfert, York co., nat. York 21 May 1770.

506. SEITZ, JOHANNES

Richmond, 1764
S-H 696

Adelshofen =
7519 Eppingen

ADELSHOFEN LUTHERAN KB:
m. 8 Feb. 1729 Joh. Andreas Seitz, son of Herr Andreas Seitz, "Gerichtsverwand-ten" and church warden, and Anna Dorothea, daughter of Johann Welck, a dairy farmer for the Baron of Gemmingen at the Dammhof. Their son:
  Johannes b. 30 Jan. 1740, conf. 1753
m. 8 May 1764 Johannes Seiz, son of the late Andreas Seiz, and Anna Catharina, daughter of Johannes Ripp, citizen and mason.
"These newlyweds left 8 days later for America along with Michael Maag [q.v.] and his wife." [who were married on the same day]

507. SELTZER, HANS JACOB

6921 Michelfeld

Brothers, 1752
S-H 481

In 1752 Johann Jacob Seltzer, his wife Anna Maria and five children left Michelfeld for Pennsylvania. One of the children was Georg Christian, born in 1749. Known as Christian, he eventually settled in Jonestown, Lebanon County, where he was a joiner. The chests he made and decorated were among the first pieces of decorated furniture to be recognized by collectors of Americana. The chest here is signed by Seltzer and dated 1796.
Photo courtesy The Henry Francis duPont Winterthur Museum Object 59.2803

MICHELFELD LUTHERAN KB:
Johann Jacob Seltzer m. 9 June 1733 Anna Maria Welsin, daughter of the late Peter
Welsen, citizen and miller at Mauer. Children:
1. Maria Philippina b. 7 Mar. 1734; d. 16 May 1737
2. Susanna Maria b. 16 Oct. 1736; d. 28 Feb. 1738
3. Johann Peter b. 27 Sept. 1738; d. 7 Oct. 1738
4. Maria Eva b. 17 Aug. 1739
5. Joh. Michael b. 23 Mar. 1741
6. Philippina b. ____Dec. 1743; d. 11 Dec. 1750
7. Joh. Philipp b. 28 Sept. 1746
8. Georg Christian b. 16 Feb. 1749
9. Joh. Jacob b. 28 Oct. 1751

Pennsylvania records:
CHRIST LUTHERAN KB, STOUCHSBURG, BERKS CO.:
A Jacob Seltzer and wife Anna Maria had:
Margaret b. 29 Nov. 1754
Anna Maria b. 24 June 1761
Elisabeth b. 7 Jan. 1764
John b. 19 Nov. 1766

STOEVER'S RECORDS:
m. 19 Jan. 1772 Christian Seltzer and Maria Diewing, Bethel and Hanover

BURIED AT ZION'S CHURCH, JONESTOWN, LEBANON CO.:
Christian Seltzer, Sr. b. 16 Feb. 1749, d. 3 Feb. 1831

Jacob Seltzer, Heidleberg twp., Berks co. nat. Philadelphia 10 April 1765.

508. SELTZER, MATHIAS   6921 Michelfeld

Alexander & Anne, 1730
S-H 35, 36, 37

MICHELFELD LUTHERAN KB:
Heinrich Seltzer, son of Weyrich and Cleophe Seltzer, m. 19 Feb. 1709
Maria Catharina, daughter of Jacob Neff. Children:
1. Jonas b. 27 Oct. 1710; d. 17 Jan. 1726
2. Johann Jacob b. 16 Apr. 1713; d. 18 Aug. 1719
3. Matthaeus b. 28 May 1714
Note in KB: "This Heinrich Seltzer went to Pennsylvania with wife and one son on
the 16 May 1730."

Pennsylvania records:
RECORDS OF PASTOR JOH. CASPAR STOEVER:
Mattheis Seltzer (Moesenutten) had children:
1. John Ludwig b. 23 Feb. 1734
2. Maria Catarina b. 8 Jan. 1736
3. John Heinrich b. 12 Sept. 1737
4. Anna Christina b. in 1741 bp. 27 May 1742

(Three of these children are also recorded in the Trinity Lutheran KB, Lancaster, Pa.)

Pennsylvania records:
CHALKLEY III: 391
Augusta co. Deed Book 11: 52; 30 Jan. 1761 Mathias Celzar and Renamia of Frederick co. sold to George Cutlip; land conveyed to Mathias Celser by Peter Carr and Mary, 1 July 1754; 120 A. on Shenando.

FREDERICK CO. VA. WILLS:
Mathias Setzer (8 Sept. 1763/1 Nov. 1763)—Wife: Ruamia Setzer. Sons Lewis, Henry, John; daughters Barbara, Mary, Elisabeth. Exrs.: wife and friend Henry Miller.

509. SELTZER, WEYRICH   6921 Michelfeld

Phoenix, 1749
S-H 406 [Note: S-H lists Ulerich Seltzer; Rupp translated it as Weirich S.]

MICHELFELD LUTHERAN KB:
Hans Martin Seltzer, son of Erasmus Seltzer, m. 24 Dec. 1720 Anna Dorothea, daughter of the late Hans Zerbst, tailor from Diessel in Hessen-Cassel, Ambt Dringelburg. [Deisel = 3526 Trendelburg] Their son:
     Joh. Weyrich b. 22 July 1728

Pennsylvania records:
CHRIST LUTHERAN KB, STOUCHSBURG, BERKS CO.:
Weyrich Seltzer and Elisabeth had:
     1. Catharine b. 1 Feb. 1772
     2. Name not given bp. 13 July 1783
     3. Maria Justina b. 11 July 1785

BERKS CO. WILLS:
Weyrich Seltzer, Womelsdorf, (31 May 1796/18 Apr. 1799). Wife Elizabeth; chil-dren: Leonhard; Catharina, wife of Henry Hirsh; Christina, wife of Peter Kehl; Susanna, wife of Jacob Aulebach; Maria; Elisabetha; Justina; Elisabeth, wife of Henrich Seh. Witnessed by John Keiser and Jacob Seltzer.

Wyrick Selser, Tulpehochen twp., Berks co., nat. Philadelphia, without taking an oath 10 April 1765.

510. SENCK, JOHANN GEÖRG

Pleasant, 1732
S-H 99, 100, 101

Weiler =
6920 Sinsheim, Elsenz

WEILER REFORMED KB:
m. 9 Mar. 1730 Joh. Georg Senck, apprentice tailor, and Maria Barbara Keller.
Maria Barbara Keller b. 25 Feb. 1704, daughter of Martin and Margretha (Löscher)
Keller. See Johannes Keller, 1732 immigrant on the same ship, for complete detail
on the family.

Pennsylvania records:
TRINITY LUTHERAN KB, LANCASTER:
Georg Senck had:
  1. Anna Catarina b. 5 Feb. 1737
  2. Joh. Christian b. 7 Feb. 1739
  3. Georg Friedrich b. 3 Sept. 1743

FIRST REFORMED KB, LANCASTER:
Georg Senck and wife Anna Eva had:
  Anna Maria bp. 24 Feb. 1745; sp. H. Basler and wife

511. SETZLER, ZACHARIAS age 45

Harle, 1736
S-H 156, 159, 161

7103 Schwaigern

SCHWAIGERN LUTHERAN KB:
Hans Jacob Setzler and wife Barbara had:
  Zacharias bp. 20 July 1690
m. 5 July 1712 Zacharias Setzler, tailor, son of the late Hans Jacob Setzler, and
Johanna Catharina, daughter of the late Pastor M. Haintz, formerly at Klebronn
[7121 Cleebronn]. They had one ch. bp. at Schwaigern:
  1. Anna Barbara b. 18 Dec. 1727; d. 20 Feb. 1728
On 12 Feb. 1730 a ch. Christoph was born "partus adulterinus." The mother was
Christina Weiss and the father was Zacharias Setzler, tailor.

512. SICKMANN, JOHANNES age 40
SICKMANN, JOHANN GEORG age 20
SICKMANN, JOHANNES age 18
SICKMANN, BERNHARD age 16

Obergimpern =
6927 Bad Rappenau

Charming Nancy, 1738
S-H 246, 247, 248 (Surname appears on lists: Sigh-
man, Sigman, Zigman)

OBERGIMPERN LUTHERAN KB:
Johannes Sickmann and wife Maria Rosina had:
  1. Johann Georg
  2. Johannes
  3. Georg Bernhard

4. Georg Christoph
5. Johan Conrad
6. Johann Dieterich
"Went to the new land."

Pennsylvania records:
ST. PAUL'S (BLUE) KB, LEHIGH CO.:
Johann Sigman and wife Margaret had:
 Anna b. 26 Feb. 1749; sp. Georg Sigmann and wife Barbara

ST. JOHN'S LUTHERAN KB, EASTON, NORTHAMPTON CO.:
m. 26 Jan. 1773 Dietrich Sickman and Barbara Muller
d. 22 Sept. 1804 Maria Rosina Sigman, d. in Forks, suddenly, age 83 y.
d. 12 Mar. 1809 John Dietrich Sigman, age 64 y., 3 mo., 17 days

WILLIAMS TWP. CONGREGATION, NORTHAMPTON CO.:
Jürg and Rosina Sickman had:
 Joh. Jacob bp. XVIII after Trinitatis 1754

KELLER'S LUTHERAN KB, BUCKS CO.:
Christopher Siegmann and wife Esther had:
 Maria Esther b. 19 Apr. 1756; sp. John Hill and Catharine Schumann
 John George b. 13 Apr. 1757; sp. George Mann and wife
Anna Maria Siegman d. 9 Aug. 1757

Bernard Siegman, Tinicum, Bucks co., nat. Philadelphia Fall 1765

513. SÖHNER, GOTTLIEB   7103 Schwaigern

Fane, 1749
S-H 424

SCHWAIGERN LUTHERAN KB:
m. 23 Jan. 1714 Matheus Sehner, citizen and widower, and Barbara Sibylla, daughter of Hans Jurg Schuster, former "Hoffb. [estander]" from the Hoff Breitenau in the Lowenstein jurisdiction [= Breitenauerhof = 7101 Löwenstein] Ch.:
 Gottlieb b. 7 Apr. 1721

Pennsylvania records:
TRINITY LUTHERAN KB, LANCASTER:
M. 18 Sept. 1750 Gottlieb Sehner and Maria Barbara Klein (b. 30 Oct. 1730, d. 13 Oct. 1799)
Gottlieb Sehner and Maria Barbara had:
 1. Joh. Gottlieb b. 13 Aug. 1751
 2. Maria Barbara b. 28 Feb. 1754
 3. Jacob b. 31 Jan. 1756
 4. Friedrich b. 14 Nov. 1762
 5. Johannes b. 7 Oct. 1765

6. Maria Barbara b. 5 Aug. 1771
7. Sophia b. 16 Aug. 1773 _____

Godlip Sener, Lancaster twp., Lancaster co., nat. Philadelphia Fall 1765, not taking an oath.

514. SOLLINGER, CHRISTOPH

Mortonhouse, 1728

6921 Epfenbach
Biedersbacher Hof

S-H 18 (appears on list as Christopher Sullenger)

GROMBACH CATHOLIC KB:
Bartholomai Solinger of Grumbach had:
    Joa. Christophorus bp. 7 Dec. 1691

STEINSFURT REFORMED KB:
m. 7 May 1715 Christoph Sollinger, son of Bartholomaus Sollinger of Kirchart, and Barbara, daughter of Christian Feÿerabend

KIRCHARDT REFORMED, NECKARBISCHOFSHEIM LUTHERAN AND EPFENBACH RE-FORMED KB:
Christoph Sollinger conf. 1706, age 14, at Kirchardt.
Christoph Sollinger (Sullinger), resident at the Biedersbacher Hof, and his wife Anna Barbara, an Anabaptist, had:
    1. Catharina Wilhelmina bp. 20 Mar. 1718 (Epfenbach)
    2. Maria Barbara b. 17 Oct. 1720, bp. at Neckarbischofsheim, father mentioned as an inhabitant at the Helmhoff.
    3. Anna Margaretha bp. 31 Oct. 1723 (Epfenbach)
    4. Maria Barbara bp. 12 May 1726 (Epfenbach)

Epfenbach, on a stream by the same name, is first mentioned in the year 1286. The community was Lutheran until it became Reformed after the War of Palatine Succession (1707). A Lutheran church was reestablished in 1739. Part of the boundary of the town is an old Roman road, some of whose stones became part of the houses in the town. The half-timbered structure shown here dates from 1711.

Photo: J. Godshall

Pennsylvania records:
LANCASTER CO. WILLS:
Christopher Sollinger, Rapho twp. (20 Oct. 1769/8 Nov. 1769). Wife Barbara.
Children: Catharina, wife of J. Flory; Ann, wife of M. Martin; Elisabetha, wife of
C. Walter; and Barbara, wife of _____Frey. Grandchildren: Su-
sanna, Barbara, Mary, John and Abraham Frey; and Barbara and John Walter, Exrs:
Jacob Snyder and John Leamon.

Christopher Sullinger, Cocalico twp., Lancaster co., nat. Philadelphia without
taking an oath, September 1761.

515. SPAAR, JOH. MICHAEL

Robert and Alice, 1743

S-H 331

Steinsfurt =
6920 Sinsheim, Elsenz

SINSHEIM LUTHERAN KB:
m. 23 Nov. 1739 Joh. Michael Spaar, farmhand from Steinfurth, son of the late
Hans Georg Spaar, inhabitant at Altenburg [Altenburg = 7410 Reutlingen], Wurtemberg, and Maria Barbara, daughter of Jacob Mohr, inhabitant at Hochhausen on
the Tauber [= 6972 Tauberbischofsheim]. [The marriage entry mentions that they
had prematurely co-habited, but no child is baptized there and no further record
located at Steinsfurt.]

Pennsylvania records:
LISCHY'S RECORD:
Joh. Michel Spar and Barbara had:
   1. Maria Barbara bp. 24 Oct. 1745
A Georg Spaar, also son of the late Georg Spaar from Altenburg, 3 hours from
Tübingen, came to America ca. 1737–1740 and settled near the Dover Lutheran
Church (Strayer's or Salem) in York co., Pa. He does not appear in the ships' lists.

Michael Spaar, York, nat. at York 20 May 1769

516. SPAN (SPOHN), MICHAEL

Not in S-H; emigrated ca. 1727–1731

Ehrstädt =
6920 Sinsheim, Elsenz

EHRSTÄDT LUTHERAN KB:
Hans Martin Spohn (wife not mentioned) had:
   Joh. Michael bp. 1 June 1700
m. 3 Apr. 1720 Michael Span, shoemaker, son of Martin Span, and Anna Eva,
daughter of Conradt Gallmann, farmer at Weckelweiler, Barthenstein region [=
7181 Lendsiedel and Bartenstein = 7187 Schrozberg]. Children:
   1. Johann Georg Balthasar b. 25 Feb. 1721
   2. Anna Johanna Dorothea b. 12 July 1722
   3. Anna Margaretha b. 12 (?) Sept. 1724; d. 12 Feb. 1727
   4. Georg Philipp b. 3 Sept. 1726

Pennsylvania records:
STOEVER'S RECORDS:
Michael Spon (Maxatawney) had:
   Maria Barbara b. 10 Feb. 1732
   Johann Adam b. 1 Nov. 1735

FREDERICK, MD. LUTHERAN KB:
Bu. 24 June 1779 Maria Catharina, wife of Michel Spohn, b. 27 June 1714 in Adersbach, daughter of Georg Adam Klemm [q.v.] and Regina. She married the surviving widower in 1735 with whom she had 7 children, of whom 3 sons and 2 daughters are alive. Died of dysentery, aged 65 y. less 5 days.
Bu. 27 June 1779 Michael Spohn, b. 19 July 1701 in Erstedt [Ehrstädt, Sinsheim]. Had 9 children with his first wife, of whom 4 sons and 2 daughters are living. With the second (wife) 7 children, of whom 3 sons and 2 daughters are alive. Died of dysentery 26 June, aged 77 years, 11 mo. 7 days.

Michael Spoone, Philadelphia co., nat. Philadelphia as a Quaker April 1743

517. SPANNSEILER, HANS PHILIP age 45   6926 Kirchardt
                                                Kirnbach =
Loyal Judith, 1732   7620 Wolfach
S-H 88, 90, 91

KIRCHARDT REFORMED KB:
m. 18 Aug. 1711 Hans Philiph Spannseyler from Kirnbach, cooper, and Anna Barbara, daughter of Nicolaus Mast, citizen and *des Gerichts*. Children:
   1. Hans Jacob b. 26 May 1712; d.
   2. Hans Jacob b. 8 Feb. 1714

GROMBACH LUTHERAN KB:
Hans Philip Spannseiler and wife Anna Barbara had:
   3. Hans Georg b. 17 Dec. 1716

SINSHEIM LUTHERAN KB:
J. Philip Spannseiler and wife Barbara of Kirchardt had:
   4. Anna Barbara b. 25 Aug. 1719
   5. Andreas b. 27 Nov. 1722

Pennsylvania records:
LITITZ MORAVIAN KB:
m. 27 Dec. 1743 Andreas Spanseiler and Elisabet Liesen

TRINITY LUTHERAN KB, LANCASTER:
m. 13 Feb. 1737 Joh. Jacob Spannseiler and Elisabetha Magdalena Schmidt.
Bu. 1749 Johann Jacob Spanseiler, the last elected deacon of the Ev. Lutheran congregation; born 8 Feb. 1714, bp. the 11th; married 1737 with Elisabetha Magdalena Schmidt and had 6 children, of whom 2 sons and 2 daughters are still alive. D. after an illness of 3 weeks June 17th, bu. the 18th.
1752 Philipp Spanseiler d. Apr. 19th, bu. the 20th, having been married to his wife Barbara for 41 years. 6 children were born to them, of whom 3 died and 3 are still living. Aged 76 years.
D. Aug. 28, 1762—Old widow Spannseiler, buried the following day.

FIRST REFORMED KB, LANCASTER:
Andrew Spanseiler and wife Elizabeth Lies had:
Elizabeth bp. 8 Dec. 1745; sp. Elizabeth Spanseiler, sister of the father.

ST. MATTHEW'S LUTHERAN KB, HANOVER:
Joh. Georg Spanseler had:
a daughter Anna Margreta, b. 17 May 1743, bp. 22 May 1743; sp. Joh. Georg
Spengel and wife Anna Margreta
Georg Spanseler m. Lowwiss Lehmännin 12 Feb. 1744
Elders of the congregation 1744 Georg Spanseiler (marked deceased).

518. SPENGLER, ADAM   Steinsfurt =
                                              6920 Sinsheim, Elsenz
Prelist

SINSHEIM LUTHERAN KB:
m. 2 Feb. 1717 at Steinsfurt Adam Spengler, widower and master tailor in Steinsfurt, and Anna Maria, daughter of Peter Meckesheimer, des Gerichts. Children:
    1. Elisabetha b. 24 Aug. 1719

Pennsylvania records:
STOEVER'S RECORDS:
m. 17 Nov. 1741 John Christoph Traenckel and Anna Maria Spengler, Lancaster.
[She was the widow of Adam Spengler.]

TRINITY LUTHERAN KB, LANCASTER:
m. 27 Apr. 1752 Jacob Daudtel, a bachelor and master tanner from York, and
Anna Maria Spengler, the late Adam Spengler's single daughter and step-daughter
of Christoph Tränck (Trinckel), [q.v.]

519. SPENGLER, BALZER age 24   Weiler =
     SPENGLER, HENRICH age 26   6920 Sinsheim, Elsenz
     SPENGLER, JERG age 31

Pleasant, 1732
S-H 99, 100, 101

WEILER REFORMED KB:
Rudolph Spengler and his second wife Maria Säger had: [see also Caspar Spengler]
    1. Anna Maria b. 28 May 1693
    2. Rudolph b. 24 Sept. 1696
    3. Jacob b. 22 Sept. 1698; m. 14 June 1729 Sophia Dorothea Hoffman
   *4. Hans Georg b. 2 Feb. 1701; m. 17 Jan. 1730 Catharina Laub from
       Grombach [= 6927 Bad Rappenau]
    5. Joh. Henrich b. 1 July 1703
   *6. Jörg Henrich bp. 8 June 1704; conf. 1718; m. 17 Jan. 1730 Susanna
       Müller from [6922] Meckesheim
   *7. Joh. Balthasar b. 29 Nov. 1706; conf. 1720; m. 29 Apr. 1732 Magdalena
       Ritter
    8. Anna Elisabetha bp. 19 Jan. 1710

9. Peter bp. 19 May 1712 [He may also have emigrated—a Peter Spingler, 1 person, appears on the *William and Sarah*, 1727. Caspar Spengler [q.v.], also a son of Rudolph, arrived on that ship.]

Pennsylvania records:
PHILADELPHIA CO WILLS:
George Spengler, city of Philadelphia, butcher; (17 Oct. 1744/2 Nov. 1744) "weak and infirm." Provides for wife Catherine. Balance of estate to "my 2 brothers, Henry Spengler and Paulser Spengler."

CHRIST LUTHERAN KB, YORK:
Balthasar Spengel (Spengler) and wife Mary Magdalena had:
    Joh. Balthasar b. 16 Apr. 1735
    Mary Magdalena b. 25 Oct. 1744
    John b. 29 June 1748
In 1759, they sp. a grandchild, Joh. George, son of George and Anna Maria Spengler.
For additional information on the Spenglers, see:
Krebs, "Palatine Emigration . . . ," p. 26; Spangler, *The Annals of the Families of Caspar, Henry, Baltzer and George Spengler* . . . (1896, York, Pa.)

Bolser Spangler, York twp., York co. nat. Philadelphia without taking an oath 11 April 1752

520. SPENGLER, CASPAR   Weiler =
William and Sarah, 1727   6920 Sinsheim, Elsenz
S-H 7, 9 (4 persons)

WEILER REFORMED KB:
Hans Rudolff Spengler, son of Jacob Spengler from Schöftland [CH—5040], Aargau, Switzerland, m. (1) 16 July 1678 at Sinsheim Judith Haegis, daughter of Jacob Haegis [also given in the Weiler record as Hägi]. One of their children was:
    Hans Caspar b. 20 Jan. 1684; conf. 1700
m. 9 Feb. 1712 Caspar Spengler, linenweaver at Weÿler, and Judita Zigler, daughter of Hans Martin Zigler, innkeeper. Children:
    1. Albrecht bp. 20 Nov. 1712
    2. Jonas bp. 26 May 1715
    3. Philipp bp. 18 July 1717
    4. Bernhard bp. 2 Sept. 1719
    5. Rudolph bp. 1 Mar. 1722
    6. Anna Maria bp. 12 July 1725

Krebs, *Palatine Emigration* . . . , p. 21–22.
Caspar Spengler, citizen of Weiler, emigrant of 1727, had to pay 49 florins 5 kreuzer emigration tax.

Pennsylvania records:
CHRIST LUTHERAN KB, YORK:
Bernhard and Anna Spengler, both Reformed, had:
   Rudolph b. 10 May 1748; sp. Rudolf Spengler and wife Anna Mary, both
Reformed
Rudolph and Anna Maria Spengler had a daughter:
   Anna Maria bp. 3 Mar. 1751; sp. Michael Swoop and wife

521. SPITTELMAYER, MARTIN age 54   Hoffenheim =
     SPITTELMAYER, HANS ADAM age 18   6920 Sinsheim, Elsenz

Hope, 1733
S-H 116, 118, 120, 121 (with Maria, age 50, Anna
Maria, age 24, Anna Madlena, age 21)

HOFFENHEIM LUTHERAN KB:
Hans Martin Spittelmaÿer was bp. 13 Dec. 1677, son of Hans and Dorothea
Spittelmaÿer.
Anna Catharina Willemann was bp. 20 Mar. 1683, daughter of Heinrich and Maria
Appelonia Willemann
m. 8 May 1703 Hans Martin Spittelmaÿer and Anna Catharina, daughter of the
late Henrich Willemann, citizen. Children:
   1. Anna Magdalena b. 17 Aug. 1705
   2. Hans Martin b. 2 Nov. 1707
   3. Anna Maria b. 14 Nov. 1708
   4. Anna Magdalena b. 18 Aug. 1711
   5. Hans Adam b. 9 Mar. 1714
   6. Joh. Geörg b. 4 Jan 1718

Pennsylvania records:
MOSELEM LUTHERAN KB, BERKS CO.:
Jacob Brandstaetter and Magdalena Spitelmajer had:
   Mattheus bp. Jubilate 1746, age 6 weeks

MERTZ'S LUTHERAN KB, BERKS CO.:
m. 9 Nov. 1751 Johann Adam Spitelmajer, widower in the Olyer Mountain, and
Anna Elisabetha Manweil, widow of Georg Manweil.
_____

Adam Spittelmyer nat. Philadelphia April 1761, of Alsace twp., Berks co., not
taking an oath.

522. SPRENTZ, ANDREAS   Berwangen, Kraichgau =
                                       6926 Kirchardt
1738

BERWANGEN LUTHERAN KB:
Georg Sprentz, Schütz, and wife Anna Maria had Andreas. "Ist in Pensylv. 1738."

523. SPRENTZ, JOHANNES
1737

Berwangen, Kraichgau =
6926 Kirchardt

BERWANGEN LUTHERAN KB:
m. 24 Sept. 1720 Johannes Sprentz, son of Wolf Sprentz, and Barbara Baur, born in Schrotzberg [= 7187 Schrozberg]. No children bp. there.
The communicants' register contains the notation that they left in 1737 for Pennsylvania.
Elisabetha Sprentz, b. 13 Dec. 1703 [sister of Johannes] was m. 8 May 1730, name of spouse not given. She was pregnant. A notation in the KB: "going with each other to Pennsylvania." [No birth after this date, no year of emigration mentioned.]

524. STAHL, GOTTFRIT age 30
Samuel, 1732
S-H 59, 60, 63, 64 (with Catharina age 32, Georg age 12)

7103 Schwaigern

SCHWAIGERN LUTHERAN KB:
m. 9 Dec. 1716 Joh. Godfrid Stahl, apprentice weaver, son of the late Joh. Martin Stahl, former citizen in Gilsing (?), Marggraff Anspach, [? Giesingen] and Sibylla Catharina Jan from [7104] Eschenau, daughter of the late Niclaus Jann. (The m. was necessary due to pregnancy.) They had:
1. Joh. Jacob b. 26 Apr. 1717
2. Joh. Georg b. 12 Jan. 1719
3. Margaretha Barbara b. 13 May 1720; d. young

Pennsylvania records:
NEW HANOVER LUTHERAN KB:
Conf. 1753 Juliana Stahl, daughter of Gottfried

OLEY HILLS LUTHERAN KB:
Conf. 1753 Anna Catharina, daughter of Gottfrid Stahl

LOWER BERMUDIAN LUTHERAN KB:
Communed 30 July 1758 Gottfried Stahl, Margaretha, his wife, Juliana, his daughter, Anna Christina Stahl, wife of Georg Stahl
Communed 17 Dec. 1758 Georg Stahl
Communicants 16 Sept. 1759 Gottfried Stahl, Margaretha Stahl, his wife
Conf. 29 Apr. 1764 Isaac Stahl, age 19, Georg Stahl, age 17, Gottfried Stahl, age 15, Barbara Stahl, age 13, all ch. of Georg.
m. 11 Feb. 1759 Robert Johnston and Susanna Stahl, daughter of Gottfried Stahl.

525. STAM, CONRAD

Alexander and Anne, 1730

S-H 35, 36 [Conrad Youngman on A List!]

Elsenz =
7519 Eppingen

ELSENZ REFORMED KB:
m. 7 Nov. 1682 Marti Stamm, son of Geörg Stamm of Schlatten in Canton Schaffhausen, Switzerland, and Anna, daughter of Rudolff Frick, citizen and church elder. Their son:
Johann Conradt b. 20 Oct. 1686

Pennsylvania records:
Conrad Stamm signed a road petition in Worcester twp., Montgomery co. in 1734. He is listed as a trustee of the Worcester Mennonite meeting in 1739. He acquired land in 1743.

Smith, *The Mennonite Immigration to Pennsylvania* (Norristown, Pa., 1929), p. 192:
A Conrad Stamm was one of the pioneers of the Zionsville Church, Milford twp., Lehigh co.

Church of the Brethren, baptisms performed by Alexander Mack, Jr. at Germantown:
25 Sept. 1768 Hannah Stamm [Frederich's wife]
5 Oct. 1769 Conrad Stamm [Jr.]

PHILADELPHIA CO WILLS:
Conrad Stam, New Providence twp., (9 Dec. 1774/2 Jan. 1779). Wife Maria Catharina. Ch.: Frederick, Conrad, Balteas, Catharina, Magdalena and Salome. The daughter Magdalena is later mentioned as the deceased wife of Christian Myer. Exrs.: William Sheppard and Maria Catharina Stam.

526. STECHER, JOH. MELCHIOR

Adventure, 1732

S-H 84, 86, 87 (Even Christian Stigen, age 23, listed with women.)

Bonfeld =
6927 Bad Rappenau
6920 Adersbach

BONFELD LUTHERAN KB:
Joh. Melchior Stecher, linenweaver, son of the late Joh. Heinr. Stecher, citizen at Adersbach, m. 18 Apr. 1731 at Bonfeld, after penitence for premature co-habitation, Anna Eva Christina, daughter of Johann Peter Kauffman, wagoner at Bonfeld. Anna Eva Christina Kauffman was b. 16 Dec. 1709; bp. 17 Dec., daughter of Joh. Peter Kauffmann and wife Anna Barbara nee Mercklin. (They were m. 6 Sept. 1707 in Bonfeld.) Anna Barbara Mercklin Kauffmann was a daughter of Balthasar Mercklin, a 1717 emigrant from Bonfeld to Pennsylvania. She d. 8 Mar. 1722. Hans Peter Kaufmann was bp. 7 Mar. 1678 in Gross-Gartach, son of Frantz Thomas Kauffmann and his wife Elisabetha.
Joh. Melchior Stecher and Anna Eva Christina had:
1. Maria Eva Magdalena b. 7 Sept. 1731; bp. 9 Sept. 1731

Pennsylvania records:
NEW HANOVER LUTHERAN KB, MONTGOMERY CO.:
Melchior and Eva Christina Stecher had:
    Joh. Matthias b. 28 Feb. 1747; bp. 22 Mar. 1747

ST. PAUL'S (BLUE) LUTHERAN KB, UPPER SAUCON TWP., LEHIGH CO.:
Johan Melchior Stecker and Eva Christina had:
    Catharina Barbara b. 9 Nov. 1750; bp. 11 Dec. 1750
List of communicants, dated 1750: Melchior Steeser and wife Eva Christina.
m. 29 Dec. 1761 Adam Stecher and Margretha Rumfeld.

NORTHAMPTON COUNTY WILLS:
Melchior Stecher, Forks twp., yeoman, (13 Sept. 1785/18 Apr. 1786). Children:
Adam, Lewis, Matthew, George, Henry, Christopher, Barbara Wygant. Mentions
land in Mt. Bethel twp. Exrs: sons Adam and Lewis.
Georg Stecher m. Elisabeth Messinger, daughter of Michael Messinger of Forks
twp.
Matthias Stecher m. Christina Schneider, daughter of John Schneider of Forks twp.

ST. JOHN'S LUTHERAN KB, EASTON:
D. 25 Apr. 1772 Christina Stecher, age 62 y.

527. STEFFAN, ULRICH   Steinsfurt =
William & Sarah, 1727   6920 Sinsheim, Elsenz
S-H 8 [3 persons]

STEINSFURT REFORMED KB:
m. 5 Apr. 1712 Ulerich Steffan, son of Gabriel Steffan, "Chur Pfaltz Anwald"
here, and Anna, daughter of the late Hans Altorffer. Ch.:
    1. Anna b. 20 Mar. 1713

Pennsylvania records:
Ulrich Steffen was a member of the Skippack Reformed congregation in 1730. He
signed a letter dated 10 May 1730 to the Classis of Amsterdam [see Hinke, *History
of the Goshenhoppen Reformed Charge*, PGS XXVII: 56–59].

PA, THIRD SERIES, XXIV: 45
Ulrick Steffen warrant for 100 A. in Salford twp. 8 Jan. 1734, patent granted 1741.

Ulrick Stephan, Philadelphia co., nat. Philadelphia April 1741

528. STEGER, JOHANNES   7103 Schwaigern
Molly, 1727
S-H 13

SCHWAIGERN LUTHERAN KB:
m. 28 Apr. 1722 Johannes Steeger, widower and citizen, and Ursula Maria, widow
of the late Joh. Georg Kober, citizen and tailor at [6927] Fürfeld. They had:
    1. Joh. Michael b. 21 Jan. 1723   }
    2. Joh. Georg b. 21 Jan. 1723, d. young } twins

3. Eva Rosina b. 29 July 1724; d. young
4. Joh. Matthäus b. 19 Sept. 1725
5. Georg Christian b. 3 May 1727

Pennsylvania records:
John Steger bought land and a corn mill located in Hanover twp. now Montgomery
co. from John Henry Sprogell in 1727. Adjoining landowners were Martin Bitting
and Adam Herman.
Johannes Stager of New Hanover twp. made a will which was proven 19 Mar. 1739.
His wife's name was given as "Orshell Mary." Exrs. were Valentine Geiger and
Martin Bitting.
On Dec. 30 1751 the heirs of Johannes Stager conveyed to Valentine Geiger, Jr. 2
tracts of land (59 A. and 77 A.) in Hanover twp.
Children: Anna Maria conf. at New Hanover Lutheran in 1745; m. Jacob Isaac.
Eve, twin of Anna Maria conf. at New Hanover Lutheran 1745; m. Michael Haug.
Susanna Catharine, conf. at New Hanover 1746; m. Frederick Crissman. Hanna
m. Henry Schaff. (*Perkiomen Region Past & Present*, I: 46–47)

TRAPPE LUTHERAN KB, MONTGOMERY CO.:
Hanna Stäger, stepdaughter of Michael Haag, age 12½ y., conf. 1748

An epitaph on the memorial chapel at Neckarbischofsheim for a member of
the noble family portrays an angel in relief carving, not unlike members of the
heavenly host who adorn Pennsylvania German farmers' gravemarkers.

The Totenkirche—memorial chapel—of the Helmstatt family was built in the 12th century and has been preserved essentially as it always appeared. Frescoes on the interior walls have been exposed recently showing fine examples of medieval church decoration: scenes from the life of Christ and over the arch at the choir the five wise and the five foolish virgins. The church is at Neckarbischofsheim.

Photo: J. Godshall

529. STEIN, JACOB   6924 Neckarbischofsheim

probably on *Two Brothers*, 1750
(S-H, I, 438)
[There are two Jacob Steins in the lists, the other on S-H, I, p. 330. The one on p. 438 arrived with Christoph Albrecht, also from Neckarbischofsheim.]

NECKARBISCHOFSHEIM LUTHERAN KB:
m. 16 July 1715 Friederich Stein and Maria Magdalena Schmied (?), daughter of the late Johannes Schmied (?), tailor at Aderspach. Their son:
Hans Jacob b. 13 Sept. 1721; sp. Hans Jacob Stein from Berwangen.

Pennsylvania records:
TRINITY LUTHERAN KB, LANCASTER:
Joh. Jacob Stein from Bischofsheim m. 14 Mar. 1760 Anna Maria Kleber

530. STEIN, JOH. ESAIAS
6921 Zuzenhausen
1744

ZUZENHAUSEN LUTHERAN KB:
Hans Georg Krafft and wife Dorothea had:
1. Anna Catharina b. 25 Jan. 1725
2. Maria Catharina b. 23 Jan. 1727
3. Georg Adam b. 18 Sept. 1728; d. 1738
4. Joh. Georg b. 17 Aug. 1731; d. young
5. Maria Dorothea b. 25 Jan. 1733
6. Joh. Georg b. 9 (?) May 1736
Hans Georg Krafft d. 3 Jan. 1739, age 41 years.
m. 14 Feb. 1741 Johann Josaias Stein, a tailor by profession, son of the late Georg Adam Stein, "Schutzverwandt" at [7100] Heilbronn and Anna Dorothea Crafft, widow of the late Hans Jerg Crafft.

Krebs, "Palatine Emigration . . . ," p. 31
In 1744 Johann Esaias Stein of Zuzenhausen was granted permission to emigrate to America with his wife, a stepson, and three stepdaughters.

531. STEIN, JOH. GEORG
6924 Neckarbischofsheim
Jacob, 1749
S-H 418

NECKARBISCHOFSHEIM LUTHERAN KB:
Joh. David Stein, b. 27 Apr. 1679, son of Hans Peter and Maria Stein, and his wife Anna Elisabetha nee Wurth had:
Johann Georg b. 18 Nov. 1729

Pennsylvania records:
ST. MICHAEL'S AND ZION KB, PHILADELPHIA:
Bu. 25 Feb. 1789 Georg Stein, b. 18 Nov. 1729 in Bischoffsheim

532. STEIN, JOH. LEONHART (age 21)
Berwangen =
6926 Kirchardt
Hope, 1733
S-H 116, 120, 121

ADELSHOFEN LUTHERAN AND BERWANGEN LUTHERAN KB:
m. 13 Jan. 1711 at Adelshofen Johann Leonhard Stein, son of Joh. Leonhard Stein of Berwangen, and Anna, daughter of the late Andreas Weidknecht, former "Schultheiss" at Adelshofen [= 7519 Eppingen]. Hans Leonhard Stein and wife Anna had a son bp. at Berwangen:
Johann Leonhardt b. 15 Apr. 1712

Pennsylvania records:
TRINITY LUTHERAN KB, LANCASTER:
A Joh. Leonhardt Stein had:
Joh. Jacob b. 11 Jan. 1737; sp. Joh. Jacob Schlauch, Maria Barbara Firnssler and Maria Margaretha Wartmännin

One other Joh. Leonhart Stein arrived before 1737; this record might be for either of them.

SELTENREICH REFORMED KB, LANCASTER CO.:
A Leonard Stein and wife Anna Maria nee Lang had:
1. Joh. Ludwig bp. 26 Oct. 1746 in Earltown church; sp. Ludwig Kraft and Catharina Lang
2. John bp. 29 May 1748
Leonard Stein and wife had:
Jacob bp. 25 Feb. 1759
John Georg bp. 14 Mar. 1762
Bu. 20 July 1774 Eva Elisabeth, daughter of Leonard Stein, aged 17 y. 7 mo. and 10 days.

533. STEIN, LEONHARDT (age 46)

Princess Augusta, 1736
S-H 162, 164, 166

Berwangen, Kraichgau =
6926 Kirchardt
6924 Neckarbischofsheim

NECKARBISCHOFSHEIM LUTHERAN KB:
m. 20 Nov. 1677 at Neckarbischofsheim Hans Leonhard Stein, son of the late Weipert Stein. "Gerichtsverwandten," and Anna Magdalena, daughter of Paul Eyermann, citizen at Berwangen.

BERWANGEN LUTHERAN KB:
Hans Lonhard Stein from Bischofsheim d. 1 Dec. 1717 in Berwangen, age 65 years. His wife Anna Magdalena d. in Berwangen 10 Aug. 1732. The family register mentions that they had a son Leonhard (no birthdate given) "ist im neuen land."

Pennsylvania records:
See Joh. Leonhart Stein (1733 emigrant) for Pennsylvania records pertaining to the name.

_____

A Leonard Stone, of Earl twp., Lancaster co., nat. Philadelphia 10 April 1754 as a "Quaker."

534. STEINBRÜCKEN, JOHANNES

1744

6921 Michelfeld

MICHELFELD LUTHERAN KB:
Gabriel Steinbrücken and wife Maria Eva had:
Johannes b. 17 Mar. 1725. Left in 1744 for Pennsylvania.
Gabriel Steinbrück d. 17 Apr. 1737. His wife Maria Eva d. 21 Mar. 1743.

535. STERTZENBACH (STERSEBACH),
MICHAEL (age 42)

Steinsfurt =
6920 Sinsheim, Elsenz

Samuel, 1733
S-H 106, 107, 110, 112 (Other passengers: Crete
Stersebagh age 24)

STEINSFURT REFORMED KB:
Hans Bernhard Stetzebach and wife Elisabetha had:
    Hans Michel bp. 8 Mar. 1691
m. 1 Mar. 1729 Michael Stetzenbacher, son of Hans Bernhardt Stetzenbach, and
Margretha, daughter of Hans Görg Schnepff of Sinsheim. One child bp. at Steinsfurt:
    1. Joh. Jacob bp. 28 June 1731

Pennsylvania records:
Anna Margaretha Stürtzebach sp. 1735 at New Holland, Lancaster co., a child of
Marx Imler [q.v.]

536. STICHLING, MARIA MARGARETHA

Adersbach =
6920 Sinsheim, Elsenz

ADERSBACH LUTHERAN KB:
m. 11 Jan. 1707 Joh. Wilhelm Stichling, son of Jost Stichling from Hochhausen
[= 6954 Hassmersheim], and Maria Margareth, daughter of Wolffgang Wurm.
Their daughter: Maria Margaretha b. 16 Nov. 1723

Pennsylvania records:
TRINITY LUTHERAN KB, LANCASTER:
m. 2 Feb. 1755 Joh. Philipp Löhr from Langenbach in Weylburg and Maria Margaret Stichlingin from Aderspach

537. STIER, JACOB
STIER, MATHES

Berwangen, Kraichgau =
6926 Kirchardt

Fane, 1749
S-H 424

BERWANGEN LUTHERAN KB:
m. 11 May 1717 Christoph Stier, son of Andreas Stier, citizen, and Susanna
Taubenberger, daughter of Master Michael Taubenberger. Children:
    1. Joh. Conradt b. 28 Aug. 1719
    *2. Matthäus b. 14 Feb. 1724
    *3. Joh. Jacob b. 21 Oct. 1728
It is mentioned in the Family Register that these last 2 sons are in Pennsylvania.

REIHEN LUTHERAN KB:
m. 16 Jan. 1748 Matthias Stier, son of Christoph Stier, citizen at Berwangen, and
Anna Maria, daughter of Jacob Rupp, citizen at Reÿhen.

Pennsylvania records:
KELLER'S LUTHERAN KB, BEDMINSTER TWP., BUCKS CO.:
Matthias Stier and wife Anna Maria had:
Valentine b. 13 Sept. 1751
Susanna b. 15 Aug. 1754   sp. Valentine Philip and Susanna

PA, THIRD SERIES, 17: 427, 860:
Matthias Stier was taxed with 250 acres in Donegal twp., Lancaster co. in 1773,
and 200 acres in 1782.

PA, THIRD SERIES, 24: 766.
A Jacob Stier warranted 108 acres in Cumberland co. on 28 Aug. 1787.

538. STIESS, GEORG ADAM   Hasselbach =
                                                 6920 Sinsheim, Elsenz
John & William, 1732   Grombach =
S-H 102, 105   6927 Bad Rappenau

ADERSBACH LUTHERAN KB:
m. on Joh. Baptistae 1679 [24 June] Hans Philip Stiess at Hasselbach, and Salome,
daughter of the late Hans Multen (?) from Switzerland. Their son:
Georg Adam b. 2 Apr. 1692

SCHATTHAUSEN LUTHERAN KB:
m. 21 Sept. 1712 Georg Adam Stiess, Lutheran, from Hasselbach, and Anna
Margretha Gastwolf, Catholic. [No children in record.]
m. 30 Jan. 1725 Georg Adam Stiess, Lutheran, and Anna Catharina Gastwolf,
Lutheran.

GROMBACH LUTHERAN KB:
Georg Adam Stiess from the Obernhoff and wife Catharina had:
    1. Charlotta Barbara b. ____Apr. 1729
    2. Catharina b. ____Nov. 1730

Pennsylvania records:
TRINITY LUTHERAN KB, LANCASTER:
Georg Adam Stiess had:
    3. Joh. Jacob b. 12 Feb. 1735
m. 25 May 1735 Georg Adam Stiess and Susanna Fechterin. Children:
    4. Joh. Friederich b. 8 May 1737
    5. Joh. Adam b. 16 Sept. 1738

539. STÖRNER, JOH. GÖRG   Berwangen, Kraichgau =
                                                    6926 Kirchardt
Jacob, 1749
S-H 418

BERWANGEN LUTHERAN KB:
m. 30 June 1711 Jacob Störner, son of Sebastian Störner, "des Gerichts" and
Magdalena, daughter of Hans Jerg Faiss, also "des Gerichts." Their son:
    Joh. Georg b. 8 May 1714. "Is in the New Land, 1749"

Pennsylvania records:
ST. MICHAEL'S AND ZION LUTHERAN KB, PHILADELPHIA:
10 Sept. 1774 Joh. Georg Sterner b. 1 July 1714 in Germany,—in Berwangen.
Was m. 3 times and with his now widow, nee Jeierin, had 1 child. D. 8 Sept., aged
60 y. 1 mo. 10 days

George Starnher, Germantown, Philadelphia co., nat. Philadelphia April 1761
without taking an oath

540. STRAUS, JOH. PHILIPP

ship data not located

Massenbach =
7103 Schwaigern

MASSENBACH LUTHERAN KB:

m. 24 Apr. 1709 Joh. Caspar Strauss, citizen from the Anspach region, and Maria
Barbara, daughter of Lorentz Lösch, "Gerichtsverwandten." Joh. Caspar Straus
and wife Maria Barbara had:
Joh. Philipp b. 21 Sept. 1713

Pennsylvania records:
CHRIST "LITTLE TULPEHOCKEN" LUTHERAN KB, BERKS CO.:
m. 28 Feb. 1744 Joh. Philip Strauss and Anna Maria Reimer. Children:
1. Anna Magdalena b. 21 Dec. 1744
2. Anna Elisabetha b. 15 Sept. 1746

BERKS CO. WILLS:
Philip Strauss, Bern twp. (6 Oct. 1788/28 May 1792). Wife Margareth. 9 children:
Casper, oldest son, Magdalena, Elizabeth, Christine, Catharine, Jacob, Christian,
Mathias and Philip. Sons Caspar and Philip, executors.

Philip Straus, Tulpehoccon twp., Berks co., nat. Fall 1765

541. STRAUSS, ALBRECHT age 20

Mary, 1732
S-H 93, 94, 95

Massenbach =
7103 Schwaigern

MASSENBACH LUTHERAN KB:
m. 24 Apr. 1709 Joh. Caspar Strauss, citizen from the Anspach region, and Maria
Barbara, daughter of Lorentz Lösch, "Gerichtsverwandten." Joh. Caspar Straus
and wife Maria Barbara had:
1. Joh. Albrecht b. 31 May 1711

Pennsylvania records:
CHRIST "LITTLE TULPEHOCKEN" LUTHERAN KB, BERKS CO.:
Albrecht Strauss had:
1. Maria Barbara b. 16 Nov. 1735
2. Joh. Jacob
3. Maria Eliesabetha } twins b. 5 May 1737
4. Anna Eliesabetha b. 25 Mar. 1739

5. Joh. Caspar b. 1 Aug. 1741
6. Maria Eva Rosina b. 6 Nov. 1742
7. Maria Catharine b. 6 Mar. 1745
8. Joh. Philipp b. 4 Jan. 1748

BERKS CO. ADMINISTRATION:
Albrecht Strauss, Bern twp., Adm. granted 7 May 1787 to Samuel Strauss, third
son.
Jacob Strauss, Bern twp. (5 Mar. 1781—11 Apr. 1781). To wife Elisabeth all
estate until youngest child is 14 years old. Eldest son Albrecht, others are not
named.

Albright Straus, Bern twp., Berks co., nat. 24 Sept. 1755

542. STRAUSS, JUSTINA CHRISTINA REGINA   Ehrstädt =
                                                   6920 Sinsheim, Elsenz
1771

EHRSTÄDT LUTHERAN KB:
m. 7 Feb. 1753 in the church at Neuhaus Georg Philipp Strauss, former inhabitant
at Kalten Loch below the Eulenhof, widower, and Eva Catharina, widow of the late
Joh. Georg Graf, gatekeeper at the Neuhaus.
Philipp Strauss (possibly a son of the above widower), day laborer in the Kalten
Loch and now citizen here, and wife Anna Maria had a daughter:
    Justina Christina Regina b. 19 Feb. 1753. "Given Taufschein 2 July 1771—
going to the new land."

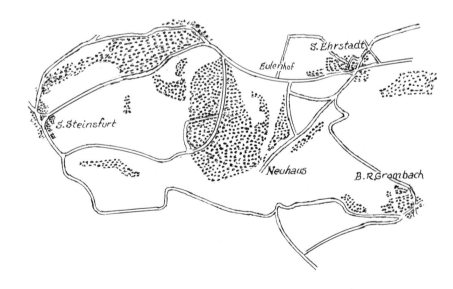

Map of the area of Steinsfurt and Ehrstädt, showing place names cited in
entry 542.

543. STROBEL, JOH. GEORG (age 21)   Berwangen, Kraichgau =
Charming Nancy, 1738   6926 Kirchardt
S-H 246, 247, 248

BERWANGEN LUTHERAN KB:
Hans Jerg Strobel, weaver, and wife Anna Maria (Catholic) had:
   Johan Georg b. 17 Oct. 1718
m. 29 Apr. 1738 Johann Georg Strobel, weaver, son of the late Joh. Georg Strobel, also weaver, and Margretha, daughter of Conrad Heberle. They both went to Pennsylvania.

544. STROHM, BENEDICT   6908 Wiesloch
William & Sarah, 1727
S-H 7

WIESLOCH REFORMED KB:
m. 19 Sept. 1719 Benedict Strohm from Switzerland and Anna Catharina Moser (marriage necessary). Child:
   1. Joh. Jacob bp. 8 Oct. 1719

Pennsylvania records:
NEW GOSHENHOPPEN REFORMED KB, MONTGOMERY CO.:
Anna Catrina, wife of Benedict Strom, was a sp. in 1737.
Benedict Strom was elected an elder in 1738.
Christian Strom and wife Anna Margaretha had a son b. 23 Jan. 1745; sp. was Benedict Strom.

SHULTZE'S JOURNALS, I: 201, 206:
Benedict Strohm's wife d. on April 13, 1757. She was bu. on the 15th.
On the 15th June 1757 Benedict Strohm married again—a girl of 15 years. He is 62 years old. [The marriage is recorded in the New Goshenhoppen record: Married between 1747–1758 Benedict Strohm and Anna Maria (N. N.)]

ST. PAUL'S LUTHERAN KB, RED HILL, MONTGOMERY CO.:
Bu. 28 Oct. 1773 Benedict Strohm, adherent of the Reformed Church, buried on the Reformed church yard, aged 78 y. 18 days

545. STÜDEL, FRANTZ age 32   Reihen =
                                             6920 Sinsheim, Elsenz
Pink *Plaisance*, 1732
S-H 79, 82, 83 (With Sharlot Stedel age 33, Andaris
Steedel (child))

REIHEN REFORMED KB:
m. 18 Feb. 1721 Franciscus Stüdel, cooper, son of the late Johannes Stüdel from Raffs in Canton Zurich, Switzerland (CH—8197 Rafz, ZH) and Charlotta, daughter of Hans Leonhardt Edelmeyer, cooper. Children:
   1. Jacob Andreas b. 8 Feb. 1722
   2. Joh. Thomas b. 11 Apr. 1723
   3. Eva Juliana b. 22 July 1725

4. Joh. Melchior   twins b. 10 Feb. 1728
5. Catharina
6. Elisabetha Barbara, d.   twins b. 9 Mar. 1730
7. Elisabetha

546. STUMPF, JOH. MICHAEL   7103 Schwaigern
Phoenix, 1743
S-H 346

SCHWAIGERN LUTHERAN KB:
m. 20 Nov. 1703 Hans Diter Stumpff, son of Gideon Stumpff, citizen and carpenter, and Anna Catharina, daughter of Bechtold Zimmerman, wagonmaker and
citizen. They had:
    1. Hans Michael bp. 16 Nov. 1705
m. 13 Nov. 1731 Johann Michael Stumpff, cabinetmaker, son of the late Dieter
Stumpff, and Anna Margaretha, daughter of Joh. Philipp Emmerich. They had:
    1. Maria Barbara b. 1 Aug. 1732
    2. Anna Rosina b. 24 Apr. 1734
    3. Anna Elisabetha b. 21 Oct. 1736
    4. Christian b. 22 Sept. 1739
    5. Johann Melchior b. 27 June 1742

American records:
FREDERICK, MD. LUTHERAN KB:
Michael Stumpff and wife Anna Margretha were sp. on 10 Oct. 1758
Bu. 1 Sept. 1794 Balthasar Bach's wife Rosina b. 24 Apr. 1734 in "Schweigen-
heim" in Germany. Parents Michael Stumpf and his wife Margareth. 30 Oct. 1753
she m. her surviving widower and had 5 daughters and 2 sons of whom 3 daughters
are dead. Died of a chest disease, complicated by typhoid fever Aug. 31, the 11th
Sunday after Trinity, 9 a.m., aged 60 years, 4 mo. and 1 week. M. 40 years, 10
mo.

547. STUPP, FRANTZ   Adelshofen, Baden =
Molly, 1727   7519 Eppingen
S-H 13

ADELSHOFEN LUTHERAN KB:
Hans Matthis Stupp and wife Anna Maria had:
    Hans Frantz b. 4 Apr. 1675
m. 3 May 1701 Frantz Stupp, son of the late Matthias Stupp, former "Gerichtsverwandten", and Maria Margretha Gressler, daughter of Hans Michael Grössler,
inhabitant at "Weÿler nach dem Steinsberg" [Weiler = 6920 Sinsheim]. Children:
    1. Jerg Andreas b. 2 May 1702
    2. Anna Barbara b. 24 May 1703
    3. Joh. Frantz b. 30 Sept. 1705; d. young
    4. Maria Agnes b. 25 Oct. 1706

5. Anna Elisabetha b. 31 July 1708
6. Anna b. 5 Oct. 1709, died 1710
7. Anna Margaretha b. 19 June 1711
8. Anna Catharina b. 6 Nov. 1712

Pennsylvania records:
NEW GOSHENHOPPEN REFORMED KB:
Johanna Elisabetha, daughter of Frantz Stupp, was a sp. in 1731.

548. SÜSS, CHRISTOPH

Snow *Ketty*, 1752
S-H 496

Eschelbach, Baden =
6920 Sinsheim, Elsenz

ESCHELBACH LUTHERAN KB:
Marcus Süss and wife Catharina had:
    Johann Christopffel b. 24 Jan. 1711; bp. 26 Jan. "1752 given Taufschein—to new land."
m. (1) 14 Jan. 1738 Joh. Christoph Süss, son of the highly respected Marcus Süss, and Maria Barbara Brecht, daughter of Joh. Thomas Brecht. Children:
1. Joh. Jacob b. 29 Dec. 1739
2. Maria Catharina b. 21 Feb. 1741
3. Joh. Martin b. 22 Feb. 1744; d. young
4. Eva Catharina b. 27 Jan. 1745; d. young
5. Maria Eva Catharina b. 15 Mar. 1746; d. 1747
6. Eva Catharina b. 25 Nov. 1748; d. young
7. Margretha b. 10 Dec. 1749, d. the following day. The mother also d. 13 days later.

m. (2) 1 Sept. 1750 Johann Christoph Süss, widower, and Susanna Anhausen from Dührn. One child bp. there:
8. Eva Catharina b. 9 June 1751

Pennsylvania records:
TRINITY LUTHERAN KB, LANCASTER:
Another Christoph Süsse, single, from [6741] Rhodt near Landau, Palatinate, m. 3 July 1759 Anna Maria Faupelin.

A Christoph Süss also appears in the Hill Lutheran KB, North Annville twp., Lebanon co. He had a child bp. there in 1748, so he cannot be this 1752 emigrant.

549. TAFFELMEYER, JOHANNES

Pleasant, 1732
S-H 100, 101 (Tablemier on A list, age 23; sister Anna Maria also possibly on ship)

6924 Neckarbischofsheim

NECKARBISCHOFSHEIM LUTHERAN KB:
Andreas Daffelmeyer, carpenter, and wife Margaretha nee Reimeth(in) had:
    Johannes b. 15 July 1709
    Anna Maria b. 21 Apr. 1713. "Ins neue land gezogen."

The interior of the memorial chapel of the Helmstatt family at Neckarbischofs-heim contains epitaphs of this noble family which presided over the countryside of this little town for centuries. From a small stone inscription to massive presenta-tions of men in full armor to inscriptions in which the dead speak of the value of true piety, as on Pennsylvania tombstones, the markers from a genealogy in stone of a family which has completely died out in modern times.

Photo: Tilly Paul

American records:

CONEWAGO LUTHERAN KB:
Johannes Taffel Meier, a daughter Maria Magdalena, b. 14 Feb. 1742; bp. March 1742; sp. Michael Scheuffele and Maria Magdalena Winterbauerin.

MANNACKES (FREDERICK, MD.) LUTHERAN KB:
Johannes Taffelmeÿer had:
    Johann Michael b. 27 Oct. 1744; bp. 5 Feb. 1745

CHALKLEY III: 502:
Michael D(a)ufflemire is mentioned in a deed dated 1770, Augusta co., Va.

550. TAUB, GEORG

Richmond, 1764
S-H 695

Berwangen, Kraichgau =
6926 Kirchardt

BERWANGEN LUTHERAN KB:
m. 30 Dec. 1728 Georg Daub, son of Johannes Daub, and Maria Catharina, daughter of Martin Lang. Their son:
Johann Georg b. 8 Apr. 1732
m. 20 Feb. 1756 Johann Georg Taub, son of Joh. Georg Taub, whitewasher, and Christina, daughter of the late Andreas Stier (marriage necessary due to pregnancy). Children:
1. Georg Gottlieb b. 28 June 1756
2. Johann Michael b. 28 Mar. 1758; d. 1758
3. Catharina Barbara b. 1 Oct. 1759
4. Johann Jacob b. 22 Mar. 1761
5. Maria Christina b. 20 Mar. 1763; d. young
6. Maria Christiana b. 30 Apr. 1764
They went to the new Land after having been manumitted: "von der Leibeigenschaft lossgekauft."

American records:
One Georg Taub appears in the Frederick, Md. Lutheran KB in 1766; however, his wife is named as Catharina.

551. THEGARTEN, ABRAHAM age 48

Harle, 1736
S-H 154, 156, 157, 158, 160 (with Aⁿ Margreth Deck-
artin age 43 and another Abraham Tiegarden on B and
C lists)

6921 Neidenstein,
Elsenzgau

NEIDENSTEIN LUTHERAN KB:
m. 17 Feb. 1716 Abraham Thegartin and _____(no other name mentioned). Abraham Thegarten, mentioned in one record as the gamekeeper's son-in-law and in a subsequent record as a gamekeeper, and his wife Anna Maria Gretha had:
1. Johannes Peter b. 9 Aug. 1716
2. Joseph Abraham b. 10 Dec. 1717
[no further mention in the records]

Pennsylvania records:
FIRST REFORMED KB, LANCASTER:
Abraham Digarten and wife:
Maria Margaret b. 15 Dec. 1736; sp. Carl Keller and his mother [q.v.]. In 1749 Abraham Degart and his wife were sp. at Frederick, Md. (Lutheran KB).

The surname eventually became Teegarden and later traces of the family are found in Westmoreland co., Pa. and Madison twp., Pickaway co., Ohio.

552. TRAUT, JACOB

Jacob, 1749
S-H 418

Hoffenheim =
6920 Sinsheim, Elsenz

HOFFENHEIM LUTHERAN KB:
m. 3 Oct. 1708 Adam Traud, son of Georg Traud from Windecken by Hanau, [=
6369 Niedderau, Hesse] and Anna Catharina, daughter of Balthasar Geisler. Adam
Traut and wife Anna Catharina had:
Joh. Jacob bp. 14 July 1709
m. (1) 5 May 1733 Johann Jacob Trauth, son of Meister Adam Trauth, "des Gerichts" and Johanna Catharina Schopfflin, oldest daughter of Hans Michael Schöpf-
fel. She d. 13 Oct. 1734
m. (2) 24 May 1735 Jacob Trauth, widower here, and Maria Eva Rupp, widow of
the late Hans Martin Rupp (d. 13 Jan. 1735)
Jacob Trauth and Maria Eva had:
1. Maria Catharina b. 10 June 1736
2. Anna Maria b. 10 Oct. 1738

Pennsylvania records:
Anna Eva Traut sp. in 1751 at Christ Lutheran, York.

553. TRINCKEL, CHRISTOPHEL age 48

6920 Sinsheim, Elsenz

Charming Nancy, 1738
S-H 246, 247, 248 (There was a Stephen Trinckel, age
20, on the ship with him who may be a close relative.
His bapt. record has not been located.)

SINSHEIM LUTHERAN KB:
m. 3 Sept. 1715 at Sinsheim Christoph Trinckel, potter, son of Ludwig Trinckel,
citizen at [7151] Allmersbach, and Susanna Laux, daughter of Michael Laux,
master potter. Children:
1. Anna Margretha b. 15 June 1716
2. Anna Elisabetha b. 4 July 1720
3. Catharina Margretha b. 30 Aug. 1723
Herr Christoph Trinckel, potter, and wife Anna Margretha had:
Johann Michael b. 8 Feb. 1737

Pennsylvania records:
TRINITY LUTHERAN KB, LANCASTER:
In 1739 Joh. Christoph Trinckel donated velvet for a collection bag. Joh. Stephen
Tränckel also appears in this church record and one of his children was sponsored
by Christoph Dränckel and wife.
D. 1 Oct. 1752 Christoph Traenkel, d. in the 62nd year of his life, he being an old
member of our church. He d. of dropsy, being sick a very long time. Buried in our
cemetery.

STOEVER'S RECORDS:
m. 17 Nov. 1741 John Christoph Traenckel and Anna Maria Spengler, Lancaster
[She was the widow of Adam Spengler (q.v.)]

LANCASTER CO WILLS:
Christopher Trinkly, Lancaster Borough, (29 Sept. 1752/9 Oct. 1752). Wife and children who are not named. Exrs: Jacob Diemer and George Hayde.

LANCASTER CO. ORPHANS' COURT,
10 JAN. 1754:
Anna Maria Trinkley, widow and adm. of Christopher Trinkley, produced the account of her Adm. There appears to be a balance of 195 pounds, 9 shillings and 4 pence, out of which the widow's legacy of 30 pounds being deducted by the noncupative will of said deceased, there remains the sum of 165 pounds, 9 shillings and 4 pence to be distributed as follows: to the widow and to Michael Ott in right of his wife Margaret, only child of the said deceased.

LANCASTER CO. DEEDS:
D: 429. 4 Aug. 1757—Widow's third, King St., Lancaster: Anna Maria Trinkle of Lancaster borough, widow of Christopher Trinkle, deceased, potter of said borough, to John Wistar of Philadelphia. (Christopher d. intestate; to his only child Margaret, late wife of Michael Ott of Lanc. bor., tailor.)

D: 434: 1 June 1757 Sheriff Sale of Michael Ott and wife Margaret, both deceased, she being only child of Christopher Trinkle, deceased. Heirs of Margaret are listed as: Catharine Ott, Lodowick Leffler, Michael Ott and Maudlina Leffler.

D: 477: 10 Sept. 1758 Middle St., Lancaster, Henry Heltzell of Lancaster borough, and wife Margaret, to Johannes Blum, organist. (Stephen Trinkle and wife Catharina to Michael Ott in 1754; Michael Ott and wife Margaret to Heltzell in 1756.) There are several other deeds recorded in Lancaster concerning the Trinckel properties.

_____

Christopher Trencle, Lancaster twp., Lancaster co., nat. Philadelphia 25 Sept. 1750.

554. TRUCKENMÜLLER, SEBASTIAN

Berwangen =
6926 Kirchardt

John & William, 1732
S-H 102, 105, 106 (with Cathrina Trookmiller)

KIRCHARDT LUTHERAN KB:
Sebastian Truckenmüller, single, from Berwangen appears in the Kirchardt record as a sp. in 1730 and 1731 for children of Leonhard Jülg. Also in 1730 Sebastian Truckenmuller, single, and Bernhard Gommer, shoemaker at Berwangen are sp. for a child of Matthies Betz at Kirchardt.
At Berwangen, Hans Bernhardt Gomer, son of Georg Michael Gomer of Adelshofen, a shoemaker, had married 9 Feb. 1720 Margaretha, widow of the late Hans Michael Truckenmüller. [Truckenmüller d. in Berwangen 7 Oct. 1717, aged 26 y. and 10 mo. Their m. not found there.]

Pennsylvania records:
NORTHAMPTON CO. WILLS:
Sebastian Druckenmiller, Upper Milford twp. (20 Oct. 1790/26 Feb. 1795). Chil-

dren: Valentine; Elizabeth, wife of Jacob Wetzel; Margaretha, wife of Peter Klock; Catharina, wife of Johannes Wetzel; Eva, wife of Peter Rothenberger; Sebastian; Jacob; and George, eldest son. Exrs: son Jacob and friend David Strauss. Some of these children appear in the later records of both the Upper Milford Lutheran and Upper Milford Reformed KBs.

Sebastian Truckenmiller, Upper Milford twp., Northampton co., nat. Philadelphia 11 April 1763

555. UHLER, ANASTASIUS (age 23)   6921 Ittlingen
Samuel, 1732
S-H 60, 64, 65

Ittlingen Lutheran KB:
Christoph Uhler and wife Anna Margaretha had:
    Anastasius bp. 14 June 1703

Pennsylvania records:
Rev. J. C. Stoever's marriage record and Trinity Lutheran KB, Lancaster:
m. 3 May 1737 Anastasius Uhler and Dorothea Ierg, Lancaster

Hill Lutheran KB, North Annville twp., Lebanon co.:
Anastasius Uhler and Dorothea had:
    1. Catharina Barbara b. 29 Oct. 1738
    2. Christoph b. 2 Feb. 1741
    3. Anna Barbara b. 20 Mar. 1743
    4. Joh. Martin b. 24 Sept. 1744
    5. Michael b. 23 Apr. 1746

Anastasius Uhler nat. Philadelphia Sept. 1761, of Lebanon twp., Lancaster co.

556. UHLER, JOH. VALENTIN   6921 Ittlingen
UHLER, JOH. DIETERICH
Charming Nancy, 1737
S-H 189, 192, 194

Ittlingen Lutheran KB:
Erasmus Uhler and wife Sabina (nee Friedlin) had ten children; among them were:
    Johann Dieterich bp. 30 Nov. 1711
    Johann Valentin bp. 4 May 1715

Pennsylvania records:
A Dietrich Uhler with wife Elisabetha were sp. in 1748 at Christ Lutheran, York, for a child of Johann Adam Rupert [q.v., from Michelfeld]
Dieter Uhler and wife Elisabetha had:
    Eva b. 6 July 1749; sp. Adam Rupert and Maria Barbara
    Erasmus b. 21 Sept. 1751; sp. Adam Ruper's wife Barbara
[Note: Is he the Johan Dietrich *Ulrich* who m. 10 July 1739 at New Holland Elisabetha Gaiss? They have 4 children bp. at York, with Rupert sponsors:

1. Rosina b. 28 Dec. 1740
2. Johann Adam b. 14 Feb. 1743
3. Maria Barbara b. 6 Sept. 1744
4. Andreas b. 9 Apr. 1747
D. 9 Feb. 1760 Andreas *Uhler*, age 12 years and 10 months.]

Valentine Uhler nat. Philadelphia 24 Sept 1762 of Forks twp., Northampton co.

557. UMBERGER, HEINRICH age 45

Hope, 1733
S-H 116, 117, 118, 120, 121 (with Hans Lenart age
18, Micgel age 15, Julian(a) age 47, Julian(a) age 12,
Jans age 10, Lisbat age 8)

Reihen =
6920 Sinsheim, Elsenz
6926 Kirchardt

REIHEN REFORMED KB:
m. 8 Nov. 1669 Rudolf Umberg, son of Conrad Umberger, and Elsbeth Wilhelm,
daughter of Conrad Wilhelm from Saffenweil, Canton Bern [CH—5745 Safenwil,
AG]. Children:
1. Maria Jacobina bp. 29 Aug. 1671; m. Hans Rudi
2. Hans Conradt bp. 9 Sept. 1673
3. Melchior bp. 12 Nov. 1676
4. Barbara bp. 14 Sept. 1679; m. 3 Feb. 1705 Joh. Henrich Hertzel [q.v.]
5. Hans Peter bp. 4 Mar. 1683; d. 27 Sept. 1684
6. Anna bp. (?) 20 Dec. 1685 (date faded); m. Joh. Görg Falckh (one Hans
Görg Falck on the *Pleasant*, 1732 with others from this area.)
*7. Hans Henrich bp. 3 Oct. 1688
Herr Rudolph Umberger, "des Gerichts", d. 28 Aug. 1691, age 45 years.

KIRCHARDT REFORMED KB:
m. 24 Jan. 1713 Heinrich Umberg, son of the late Rudolph Umberger, former
citizen at Reÿhen, and Juliana, daughter of Hans Steeger, citizen and "des Gerichts". Children:
1. Maria Elisabetha b. 18 Sept. 1713; d. young
2. Hans Leonhart b. 2 Feb. 1715
3. Hans Michael bp. 21 Mar. 1717
4. Juliana bp. 8 Jan. 1719
5. Johannes bp. 30 Sept. 1721
6. Anna Elisabetha bp. 16 May 1724
7. Anna Catharina bp. 14 Mar. 1729

Pennsylvania records:
HILL LUTHERAN KB, NORTH ANNVILLE TWP., LEBANON CO.:
Leonhardt Umberger, successor in Thao, i.e., and his wife, her second husband
had:
   Johannes b. 7 Feb. 1743; sp. Johannes Umberger and sister Elisabetha
Michael Umberger had:
1. Joh. Leonhardt b. 28 Aug. 1743
2. Joh. Michael b. 15 Feb. 1757

    3. Johannes b. 4 May 1759
m. 15 Apr. 1742 Leonhardt Umberger and Barbara Borst
m. 18 Oct. 1742 Michael Umberger and Anna Maria Rammler
m. 2 Feb. 1744 Joh. Philipp Holinger (Olinger) and Juliana Umberger
m. 10 Jan. 1751 Johannes Becker and Catarina Umberger

DAUPHIN CO. WILLS:
Henry Umberger, Lebanon (18 Feb. 1766/16 Mar. 1787).
Wife: Anna Mary Catharine; children: John; Anna Maria; Anna Margareth; eldest
son Leonard, deceased; Michael; daughter Juliana, wife of Philip Olinger, daughter
Catharine, wife of John Baker. Friend Adam Heylmann and son John, exrs.
Michael Umberger, Lebanon (16 July 1785/13 Apr. 1788). Children: Leonard;
Henry; Adam (deceased); Michael; Philip; John; Anna Margareta, wife of Jacob
Boltz, Jr.

Henry and Leonard Umberger, Lebanon twp., Lancaster co., nat. Philadelphia,
Fall 1765.

558. UTZ, GOTTLIEB   Adelshofen, Baden =
JOHANN GEORG   7519 Eppingen

Royal Union, 1750
S-H 432

ADELSHOFEN LUTHERAN KB:
m. 8 Jan. 1732 Gottlieb Utz, journeyman carpenter, son of Jacob Utz of Schotzach
(?) [Schozach = 7129 Ilsfeld], and Anna Maria, daughter of Matthias Gröner,
butcher. Children:
    1. Joh. Georg b. 17 Nov. 1732; conf. 1747
    2. Anna Catharina b. 2 Apr. 1734
    3. Anna Maria Catharina b. 16 June 1735; conf. 1750
    4. Joh. Jacob b. 28 Dec. 1737; d. young
    5. Regina b. 11 May 1739; d. young
    6. Regina Elisabetha b. 26 May 1741
    7. Anna Barbara b. 12 Mar. 1744; d. young
    8. A stillborn daughter 27 Nov. 1747
Anna Maria, wife of Gottlieb Utz, was b. 24 May 1704, daughter of Matthias
Gröner and his wife Agnes Catharina nee Schlauch.

Pennsylvania records:
M. 27 Jan. 1761 at Trinity Lutheran, Lancaster, Stephan Laumann, widower, and
Anna Maria Utzin, widow.

NEW HOLLAND LUTHERAN KB, LANCASTER CO.:
Georg Utz and wife Maria had:
    Georg b. 4 Mar. 1766
    Johannes b. 7 Jan. 1769

559. VIGELIUS, ANNA CATHARINA

6922 Meckesheim

1749

MECKESHEIM REFORMED KB:
Antoni Vigelius (also given as Anton Frans Vigelius in one record) and wife Anna Maria had:
1. Anna Margretha b. 3 Dec. 1712
2. Joh. Diterich bp. 12 Jan. 1721
3. Simon b. 30 Mar. 1726
4. Anna Catharina b. 9 Feb. 1731
Anna Catharina, daughter of Antonius Vigelius, sp. 1747 a child of Joh. Michel Vigelius.

Pennsylvania records:
ST. MICHAEL'S AND ZION, PHILADELPHIA, BURIALS:
8 Oct. 1764—Anna Catharina Klein, nee Fiegelin (Reformed). Wife of Johannes Klein. She was b. 24 July (no year given) at Meckesheim, daughter of Anthon Fiegele and wife Anna Margretha. Came to America in 1749. Married Johannes Klein 28 Sept. 1756, had five children.

Hoffenheim was home to about 50 emigrant families. It is first mentioned in 773. The Elsenz flows by it. Hoffenheim was a Lutheran town, with records beginning in mid-seventeenth century. The von Gemmingen noble family owned the town. A cellar from 1578 attests to the age of the village.

Photo: J. Godshall

560. VÖGELI, HANS HENRICK age 50
VÖGELI, MATTHIAS age 23
VÖGELI, HANS BERNHARD age 21

Hoffenheim =
6920 Sinsheim, Elsenz

Hope, 1733
S-H 117, 118, 120, 121 (Surname appears on ship's lists as Foglie, Figle, Fegley, etc.) Other passengers:

Anna Maria Figlien age 46; Catrina age 19; Anna Maria
age 16, Maria age 12, Hans Jurick age 7.)

HOFFENHEIM LUTHERAN KB:
Heinrich Vögellin and wife Elisabetha had:
   Hans Heinrich bp. 18 Nov. 1684
Henrich Vögelin, b. in Switzerland, d. 14 July 1705, age 63 y. 4 mo. and several
days.
m. 5 Feb. 1709 Johannes Vögele and Anna Maria, daughter of Jacob Gilbert, Jr.
(She was bp. 17 Jan. 1688, daughter of Hans Jacob Gilbert and Catharina.) [Note:
from this marriage entry and the baptismal records of his children, he used Hans,
Joh., Johann, Johannes as his given name.] Children of Johannes and Anna Maria
Vögele:
   1. Matthias bp. 3 Nov. 1709
   2. Georg Ludwig bp. 27 Mar. 1711
   3. Johan Bernhard bp. 31 May 1712
   4. Eva Catharina bp. 11 Oct. 1714
   5. Anna Maria b. 2 Sept. 1716
   6. Joh. Geörg b. 4 Jan. 1718
   7. Maria Margretha b. 4 Jan. 1720
   8. Johanna Maria b. 25 June 1721
   9. Hans Georg b. 24 Jan. 1726
   10. Anna Catharina b. 23 July 1729
   11. Joh. Jacob b. 14 Apr. 1732

Pennsylvania records:
NEW HANOVER LUTHERAN KB; MONTGOMERY CO.:
D. Apr. 1, 1745 Joh. Jacob Voegle, son of Heinrich, age 13 y. less 15 days.
Matthias, Bernhard and Georg Voegele all appear in the early records of this
church.

ST. MICHAEL'S AND ZION, PHILADELPHIA, MARRIAGES:
M. 17 Dec. 1746 Nicolas Graypiel and Margretha (Anna Maria) Fegelin. One of
the witnesses was Jurg Vögele.

BERKS CO. WILLS:
Bernhard Fegele, Longswamp (18 Apr. 1781/2 Apr. 1782). Eldest son Christopher.
Other children: Catharine, Anna Margaretha, Eve, Henry, Peter, Anna Maria and
youngest son John Bernard. Letters of Adm. to Christian Fegely; Wit: John Heinly
and Valentin Haupt.

———————

Bernard Fegele nat. Philadelphia Fall 1765, of Long Swamp twp., Berks co.
George Fegele nat. Philadelphia Fall 1765 of Maiden Creek twp., Berks.
George Fegele nat. Philadelphia Fall 1765 of Colebrookdale twp., Berks.

561. VOGT, JOH. GEORG

1751

Tairnbach =
6909 Mühlhausen,
Kraichgau

DARMBACH (TAIRNBACH) LUTHERAN KB:
m. 8 Jan. 1737 Joh. Georg Vogt, citizen and ropemaker from Wiseloch [6908 Wiesloch], widower, and Maria Eva Schüssler, daughter of the late Christoph Schüssler, former citizen here. (No children bp. at Tairnbach)
Christoph Schissler, linenweaver, and wife Anna Catharina had:
Maria Eva b. 3 Feb. 1720. "1751 given Taufschein—to new land."

562. VOLLWEILER, JACOB

Greyhound, 1722

7519 Eppingen

EPPINGEN REFORMED KB:
m. 5 May 1707 Joh. Jacob Vollweiler, son of Jacob Vollweiler from Mülbach, and Anna Maria, daughter of the late Thomas Dubs, former citizen.
[No children there]

ROTTERDAM ARCHIVES:
Transportation agreement for the ship *Greyhound*, 1722, signed by Jörg Peter Hillegas, *Hans Jacob Vollenweiler*, Daniel Holl and Jacob Frey, on behalf of 40 passengers on ship.
[Document located by Klaus Wust]

The *Pfeiferturm* in Eppingen was the bulwark of the city wall erected in the 12th and 13th centuries. Its original hood has been replaced with a lower tower.
Photo: J. Godshall

563. VOLTZ, HEINRICH

7103 Schwaigern

Charming Nancy, 1737
S-H 188, 191, 193

SCHWAIGERN LUTHERAN KB:
Heinrich Voltz and Maria Catharina had:
    Johann Heinrich b. 24 Mar. 1715

Pennsylvania records:
WARWICK LUTHERAN KB, LANCASTER CO.:
One Joh. Heinrich Foltz m. 25 June 1739 Maria Eva Blümin

564. VON KENNEN, BALTHASER

Steinsfurt =
6920 Sinsheim, Elsenz

Dragon, 1749
S-H 414 (Von Könne)

STEINSFURT REFORMED KB:
m. 10 Sept. 1726, Hans Michael von Kennen, son of Herr Martin von Kennen,
"des Gerichts," and Anna Elisabetha, daughter of Balthasar Laber. Their son:
    Balthasar bp. 19 Oct. 1727

Pennsylvania records:
FIRST REFORMED KB, LANCASTER:
m. 26 Nov. 1753 [Balthas]ar von Koehnen and Catharine Widder

PEQUEA REFORMED KB, NEW PROVIDENCE, LANCASTER CO.:
Balthasar von Kennen and wife Catharina had:
    Catharine b. 15 Oct. 1759
    Barbara b. 15 Oct. 1761

LANCASTER CO. WILLS:
Balser von Kennen, Leacock twp. (4 June 1776/25 June 1776).
Exrs: wife Catharina von Kennen and Michael Withers, brother-in-law. Children:
Michael, Jacob, Elisabeth, Barbara, Ann, Hannah, Catharina and Margaret.
Catharina von Kennen, widow of Balser (1 Aug. 1804/16 Oct. 1804). Children:
Barbara, wife of Michael Forney; Hannah, wife of Enoch Abraham; Margaret,
married but no name mentioned; Catharina, wife of Andrew Shower; and Jacob.
Exr: brother Michael Withers.

565. VON KENNEN, MARTIN

Steinsfurt =
6920 Sinsheim, Elsenz

Dragon, 1749
S-H 414 (von Können)

STEINSFURT REFORMED KB:
m. 16 June 1722 Hans Martin von Kennel, son of Herr Martin von Kennel, "Anwald" [name elsewhere in record von Kennen], and Anna Magdalena, daughter of
Balthasar Laber. They had:
    Hans Martin bp. 13 Dec. 1727

566. WACKER, ANDREAS

St. Andrew, 1738
S-H 237, 238, 239 (The surname appears as Walker on list A and B)

Hoffenheim =
6920 Sinsheim, Elsenz

HOFFENHEIM LUTHERAN KB:
Hans Wacker and Anna had:
    Andreas b. 14 Aug. 1708
m. 4 May 1738 Andreas Wacker, son of the late Hans Wacker, and Lucia Vogt, widow of the late Hans Adam Vogt. They left 5 days later to go to Pennsylvania.
Hans Adam Vogt m. 1731 Lucia Precht, daughter of Peter Precht. They had one child:
    1. Johann Christoph Vogt b. 1 Apr. 1734

Pennsylvania records:
ST. MICHAEL'S AND ZION LUTHERAN KB, PHILADELPHIA:
D. 9 Aug. 1780 Andreas Waker from Hoffenheim. Age 72 y.
D. 26 Jan. 1795 Catharina, daughter of Johann Hintz and Barbara Catharina, born in Ramstadt 31 May 1721; married Andreas Waaker; 3 children.
[Ramstadt: perhaps 2251 Ramstedt, Post Schwabstedt]

ST. MICHAEL'S AND ZION MARRIAGES:
m. 11 Oct. 1751 Andreas Waker and Catharina Hintzinger
Andreas Waker and wife Magdalena had:
    Anna Elisabeth b. 13 Sept. 1746
    Maria Elisabeth b. 28 Aug. 1748
Andrias Wacker and wife Cathrina had:
    Dorothea b. 23 July 1752

567. WACKER, GEORG MICHAEL (Jerg Michel Walcker)

Shirley, 1751
S-H 454

Hoffenheim =
6920 Sinsheim

HOFFENHEIM LUTHERAN KB:
Hans Wacker and Anna had:
    Georg Michel b. _____1703 (date faded); conf. 1717, age 14
m. 27 Aug. 1726 Georg Michel Wacker and Anna Maria Meyer from the Anspach region. Children:
    1. Anna Eva b. 8 Dec. 1730
m. (2) 24 May 1735 Georg Michael Wacker, widower, and Barbara, daughter of Jacob Laubinger, "des Gerichts". Children:
    1. Georg Jacob b. 18 Nov. 1740
    2. Anna Catharina b. 12 Dec. 1743
    3. Maria Elisabetha b. 9 July 1748
[several other passengers on this ship from Hoffenheim]

568. WAGENSEIL, CHRISTOPH
Prelist (?)

Weiler =
6920 Sinsheim, Elsenz

WEILER REFORMED KB:
Sebastian Wagenseil, son of Martin Wagenseil, citizen in the Reichsstatt Kauffbaur
(8950 Kaufbeuren?) m. (1) 23 Feb. 1664 Barbara, daughter of Hans Senn, an
Anabaptist at Weÿler.
Bastian Wagenseil, tile maker, widower and citizen at Weiler, m. (2) 19 Nov. 1672
at Hilsbach Rosina, daughter of Rudolph Brendtlein [another record gives this
surname as Brenneisen], former citizen at Steinfurth. They had:
    Christophel b. 7 Feb. 1686

Pennsylvania records:
Stoffel Wagenseiler paid quit-rent on 150 A. in Hanover twp., (Montgomery co.)
prior to 1734.

STOEVER'S RECORDS:
Christoph Wagenseil in Cushenhoppen had:
    Anna Maria b. 6 Oct. 1729, bp. 17 Aug. 1730
Christofell Wagenseill signed a 1734 petition for a road through Goshenhoppen

NEW GOSHENHOPPEN REFORMED KB; MONTGOMERY CO.:
m. ca. 1747 David Haag and Elisa Catharina Wagenseil

ST. PAUL'S LUTHERAN KB, UPPER HANOVER TWP., MONTGOMERY CO.:
Christopher Wagenseil and wife Christina had:
    Johannes b. 24 June 1739
Conf. 1753 Johannes Wagenseil age 14 years, son of Christoph Wagenseil

PHILADELPHIA CO. WILLS:
Christopher Wagenseil, Upper Hanover twp., (30 June 1760/27 Oct. 1762). "Of
advanced age." Wife Anna Christina, only son John, eldest daughter Anna Mary
married to John Dirr, youngest dau. Catherina married to David Haag.

569. WAGNER, HANS ULRICH age 20
WAGNER, JÖRG age 50

Reihen =
6920 Sinsheim, Elsenz

Pink *Plaisance*, 1732
S-H 78, 79, 80, 81, 82, 83 (with Orsell (Ursula) age
48 and a child Margrett)

REIHEN REFORMED KB:
m. 18 Jan. 1676 Georg Wagner, son of the late Hans Wagner, and Anna Maria
Glasser, daughter of the late Dietrich Glasser. Georg Wagner and Anna Maria had:
    Hans Georg bp. 12 Jan. 1678
m. 13 Jan. 1711 Hans Görg Wagner, the "Schultheiss", son of Görg Wagner, and
Ursula, daughter of Johann Ulerich Bär, "Gerichtsverwandten." Children:
    1. Hans Ulerich b. 21 May 1712
    2. Hans Görg b. 5 Feb. 1714; d. 8 July 1715

3. Margretha b. 9 (?) Dec. 1716

Ulrick Waggoner, Albany twp., Berks co. nat. Philadelphia Fall 1765, without taking an oath.

570. WAGNER, Johann Georg age 52   6927 Bad Rappenau
Loyal Judith, 1732
S-H, 88, 90, 91

RAPPENAU LUTHERAN KB:
m. (1) 10 Jan. 1708 Hans Jürg Wagner, son of Martin Wagner, and Maria Magdalena, daughter of Hans Jürg Körner. (She was b. 1684, daughter of Hans Georg Körner and Anna Barbara nee Schwartz.) They had:
  1. Maria Margaretha b. 6 Oct. 1708
  2. Maria Catharina bp. 27 Mar. 1711; d. 23 July 1711
His first wife d. 27 Apr. 1711.
m. (2) 3 Nov. 1711 Hans Jürg Wagner and Maria Ursula Schwab, daughter of Elias Schwab. (She was bp. 13 Mar. 1688, daughter of Joh. Elias Schwab and Anna Maria nee Födler (?).) Children:
  3. Anna Maria b. 20 Oct. 1712
  4. Anna Catharina bp. 31 Jan. 1715
  5. Catharina Barbara bp. 18 Feb. 1717; d. 13 Feb. 1718
  6. Jürg Martin b. 1 Feb. 1719
  7. Catharina b. 29 Aug. 1721
  8. Elias b. 29 Nov. 1723; d. 1723   ⎫ twins
  9. Johann Georg b. 29 Nov. 1723; d. 1723   ⎭
  10. Georg Adam bp. 21 Apr. 1725

Pennsylvania records:
OLD GOSHENHOPPEN LUTHERAN KB:
Johann Georg Wagner, age 71 yrs, b. 22 Apr. 1680, son of Martin Wagner of Rappenau. Mother was Susanna nee Scholatt. m. (1) 10 June 1708 Maria Magdalena, d. 9 Apr. 1711. Her father, Joh. Georg Kerner; mother, Anna Barbara. They had:
  1. Anna Margreth b. 6 Oct. 1708; m. 24 June 1737 Henrich Schmidt
  2. Maria Catharina b. 23 Mar. 1711; d. 23 July 1711
     m. (2) 3 Nov. 1711 Maria Ursula, b. 1687, daughter of Elias and Anna Maria Schwab from Rappenau. They had:
  3. Anna Maria b. 20 Oct. 1712; m. Paul Dietrich, Lutheran, dwelling across the Susquehanna at the Little Lehigh.
  4. Anna Catharina b. 31 Jan. 1715; m. Jacob Gruesinger in Fridrich Twp.
  5. Cathar. Barbara b. 18 Feb. 1717; d. 13 Feb. 1718
  6. Georg Martin b. 1 Feb. 1719; m. 3 May 1743 Anna Müller, b. 11 Dec. 1722, daughter of Johann and Magdalena Müller, both Mennonites.
  7. Catharina b. 29 Aug. 1721
  8. Elias b. 29 Nov. 1723
  9. Joh. Georg b. 29 Nov. 1723, twins

10. Georg Adam b. 21 Apr. 1725; m. daughter of Georg Schmidt, Lutheran, dwelling at the Blue Mountains.
11. Johann Georg b. 27 Mar. 1729
Johann Georg Wagner d. 9 Jan. 1757; age 76 yrs., 8 mo., 16 da.

571. WAIDELE, JOH. MICHAEL

Francis & Elizabeth, 1742
S-H 328

Adersbach =
6920 Sinsheim, Elsenz

ADERSBACH LUTHERAN KB:
m. 8 Mar. 1718 Johann Michael Weÿdelein, schoolmaster, and Anna Barbara, daughter of Joh. Friederich Vogler. Children:
1. Joh. Michael b. 18 Aug. 1719
2. Johannes b. 25 Mar. 1721; d.
3. Johannes b. 7 Aug. 1722
   [One of the sponsors for all of these three children was Johannes Heerburger, the schoolmaster at Hasselbach, q.v.] This Johannes remained in Adersbach and became the schoolmaster there after his father left for Pennsylvania. He m. Maria Juliana Franck in 1745, and is mentioned as the schoolmaster in the subsequent baptismal records.
4. Johann Friederich b. 1 Oct. 1724
5. Anna Maria b. 23 Feb. 1727 [surname in record: Weÿdele]
6. Maria Eva b. 17 Aug. 1728
7. Johann Christian b. 9 Oct. 1730
8. Amalia Rosina b. 14 Nov. 1732
9. Georg Adam b. 3 Feb. 1735; sp. at his baptism was Georg Heinrich Geck [who became the schoolmaster at Hasselbach when Johannes Heerberger left for Pennsylvania.]
10. Elisabetha Rosina b. 5 May 1737
11. Georg Sebastian b. 7 Aug. 1740

Pennsylvania records:
TRINITY LUTHERAN KB, LANCASTER:
In 1743, Joh. Michael Waidelin, the schoolmaster, and wife Anna Barbara are sponsors for a child of Georg Stephan Mann.
m. (1) 9 Oct. 1752 Christian Weidel, master potter, surviving legitimate son of the late Hanns Michael Weidel here in the town, and Margaretha Knecht, legitimate single daughter of Philipp Knecht.
m. (2) 21 Apr. 1761 Christian Weydtele, widower, and Barbara Schenck, single.

LANCASTER MORAVIAN KB:
D. 14 June 1744 Schoolmaster Waidelin age 63 years
D. 1 Jan. 1750 Anna Barbara Waidel

Frederick Waidle, Lancaster twp., Lancaster co., nat. Philadelphia by affirmation 24 Sept. 1760.

Half-timbered buildings, some stuccoed over and some exposed, fill the Kraichgau settlements. A building in disrepair in Michelfeld shows the woven sticks over which plaster was placed—wattle and daub construction, evident in old Germanic buildings in Pennsylvania.

Photo: J. Godshall

572. WALTER, JOH. VALENTIN   6921 Michelfeld

St. Andrew, 1738
S-H 236

MICHELFELD LUTHERAN KB:
Johann Valentin Walter, son of Joh. Philipp Walter, m. (1) 5 Feb. 1732 Anna Catharina Rudi (She was b. 9 Sept. 1704, daughter of Johann Rudi and Anna Margaretha nee Beilstein). Children:
    1. Johannes b. 1 Jan. 1733, d. 2 Jan.
    2. Jonas b. 6 Mar. 1734
Anna Catharina, wife of Joh. Valentin Walter, d. 10 Apr. 1735. He married (2) 12 July 1735 Susanna Magdalena, daughter of Lorentz Mannbecker, a mason at Michelfeld. Children:
    3. Christina Barbara b. 29 Mar. 1736
"This family left for Pennsylvania 6 May 1738."

573. WALTRICH, ANDREAS   Grombach =
Francis and Elizabeth, 1742   6927 Bad Rappenau
S-H 328

GROMBACH CATHOLIC KB:
m. (1) ___Nov. 1719 Andreas Walderich (bp. 2 Dec. 1698), son of Bernhardi and
Anna Barbara Walderich, inhabitant, and Maria Anastasia Laub (bp. 20 May
1698), daughter of Joannis Christophori and Maria Margretha Laub. Children:
1. Anna Magdalena bp. 20 Nov. 1720
2. Maria Barbara bp. 31 Dec. 1721; d. young
3. Joh. Petrus bp. 10 Mar. 1723; d. Feb. 1724
4. Maria Catharina bp. 21 Sept. 1724
5. Johannes Petrus bp. 15 Nov. 1726
6. Maria Sophia bp. 29 Apr. 1728
7. Margaretha bp. 9 July 1730
8. Johannes Andreas bp. 10 Apr. 1732
9. Anna Catharina bp. 4 Aug. 1734
m. (2) 20 Nov. 1736 Andreas Waltrich, widower, and Sibilla Maÿer. Children:
10. Franciscus Petrus bp. 28 Sept. 1737
11. Casparus Mathaeus bp. 21 Aug. 1738
12. Maria Catharina bp. 8 Nov. 1739
13. Johannes bp. 21 Nov. 1740
14. Maria Barbara bp. 30 Mar. 1742

Pennsylvania records:
GOSHENHOPPEN ROMAN CATHOLIC KB:
m. 11 Apr. 1743 in the Philadelphia chapel Paul Müller and Mary Magdalen
Walltrich; witnesses: the bride's parents and several others.

ST. MICHAEL'S AND ZION LUTHERAN KB, PHILADELPHIA:
m. 11 Aug. 1761 by license: Johannes Blume and Catharina Waltrichin

574. WANNEMACHER, BERNHARD age 40   Asbach, Baden =
Elizabeth, 1738   6951 Obrigheim, Baden
S-H 243, 244, 245

ASBACH REFORMED KB:
Family register dated 1709 at beginning of church book:
Hans Wannemacher (Reformed) and wife Maria Magdalena (Lutheran) had:
1. Hans Bernhard (Reformed)
2. Hans Conrad (Reformed)
3. Martin (Reformed)
4. Anna Margret bp. 10 Mar. 1712
m. 2 Feb. 1724 Hans Bernhard Wannemacher, joiner, son of Johannes Wannemacher, and Maria Barbara, daughter of Hans Georg Kuch, "Gerichtsverwandten"
and church elder. Children:
1. Anna b. 20 Nov. 1724
2. Marx Adam b. 6 Aug. (?) 1726

3. Joanna Barbara b. 11 May 1728
4. Anna Magdalena b. 6 Apr. 1732
5. Joh. Adam b. 25 May 1733; d.
6. Joh. Peter Frederick b. 2 July 1735

Pennsylvania records:
NEW GOSHENHOPPEN REFORMED KB, MONTGOMERY CO.:
Bernhart Wannemacher and wife had:
1. A son bp. 27 Oct. 1745; sp. Jacob Wannemacher
Bernhard Wannenmacher and wife Catharina had:
J. Casper bp. 11 Mar. 1758
m. between 1747–1758:
Marcus Wannenmacher and *N. N.*
Conf. 1748–1758: J. Wannenmacher, Anna Lena Wannenmacher, Elisa Barbara
Wannenmacher   _____

Bernard Wannemaker and Marx Wannemaker, Lynn twp., Northampton co., nat.
Philadelphia 24 Sept. 1762

575. WANNENMACHER, CONRAD

Asbach, Baden =
6951 Obrigheim, Baden

Emigration data not located

ASBACH REFORMED KB:
Family register dated 1709:
Hans (Johannes) Wannemacher (Reformed) and wife Maria Magdalena (Lutheran)
had:
1. Hans Bernhard [q.v.]
2. Hans Conrad
3. Martin
4. Anna Margret [m. Joh. Georg Kumpff q.v.]

Pennsylvania records:
NEW GOSHENHOPPEN REFORMED KB, MONTGOMERY CO.:
Conrad Wannenmacher appears on the list of members of the New Goshenhoppen
Reformed congregation compiled by Georg Michael Weiss.
Conrad Wannenmacher and Barbara had:
1. Johannes bp. 8 May 1737
2. Anna Lisabeth bp. 2 Sept. 1739
3. Elisabetha bp. 30 Aug. 1741
Buried 1 Apr. 1772 Conrad Wannenmacher, born 1701, aged 70 y. 3 mo. 20 days.
_____

Conrad Wannemacher, New Hanover twp., Philadelphia co., nat. Philadelphia Fall
1767.

576. WANNER, MARTIN age 36   Steinsfurt =
Samuel, 1733   6920 Sinsheim, Elsenz
S-H 107, 108, 109, 111, 112 (With Elizabeth Wonner
age 33; Maria Crete age 10; Anna Maria age 6; Christian age 1.)

STEINSFURT REFORMED KB:
Peter Wanner and Anna Catharina had:
    Martinus bp. 21 July 1697; conf. 1713
m. 18 Nov. 1721 Martin Wanner, son of Peter Wanner, and Maria Elisabetha,
daughter of Christian Franckh, citizen and master tailor here. Children:
    1. Friederich   { twins bp. 12 Apr. 1722   } "born 20 weeks
    2. Margaretha   { the son d. 6 days after bp. } after marriage."
    3. Maria Elisabetha bp. 5 Dec. 1723; d. 1725
    4. Anna Maria bp. 21 Mar. 1726
    5. Joh. Martin bp. 19 Oct. 1728; d. 1729
    6. Hans Martin bp. 28 Apr. 1730; d. 1731
    7. Christianus bp. 18 Feb. 1732
[The Wanner family of Steinsfurt came from CH—8492 Wila, Zurich. Emigrants
from the Canton Zurich, list dated 1661: Parish of Wÿla: "Hans Jacob Wanner, son
of Hans, is residing in Steinfurth in the Pfaltz, with wife and child."]

Pennsylvania records:
Lititz Moravian KB:
Martin Wenner (Wanner?) m. 27 Feb. 1744 Susanna Smith.

577. WANNER, URSULA   Rohrbach, Kraichgau =
1732   6920 Sinsheim, Elsenz

ROHRBACH REFORMED KB:
Mattheus Wanner and Anna Margretha had:
    Ursula bp. 27 Nov. 1696; conf. 1710
Hans Peter Kramer conf. 1695 at Sinsheim, age 14

Pennsylvania records:
ALLEMENGEL MORAVIAN KB, LYNN TWP., LEHIGH CO. AND ALBANY TWP., BERKS
CO.:
Ursula Romich, wife of Adam Romich, died 21 Dec. 1766 and was buried Dec.
23. She was born in the month of Feb. 1699 in Rohrbach near Sinsheim in the
Palatinate. Of her childhood little is known except that very early she went to live
with strangers and suffered many hardships. In 1726 she married (1) Peter Kramer,
a glazier, and in 6 years of marriage had 4 children, all four of whom died as small
children. In the year 1732 as they were coming to America her husband committed
suicide at sea. She landed in Philadelphia where she remained until 1733. She
married (2) Adam Romich with whom in 34 years of happy marriage, she had 5
children; two of the sons and one daughter preceded her in death. From the two
other children, she was survived by six grandchildren. She and her husband were
admitted as members of the Moravian church in 1762. She was sick for 10 days
with a severe cough and got pneumonia. She died at the age of 68 years.

578. WEBER, HEINRICH
WEBER, JOH. VALENTIN

6921 Ittlingen

Dragon, 1749
S-H 414

ITTLINGEN LUTHERAN KB:
Hans Heinrich Weber, bp. 1 Oct. 1699, son of Hans Heinrich Weber and Anna
Margaretha. Joh. Heinrich Weber and wife Anna Barbara had:
1. Anna Barbara b. 29 Mar. 1725
2. Joh. Heinrich b. 19 Jan. 1727; d. 29 Jan.
3. Joh. Valentin b. 5 Feb. 1729
4. Joh. Heinrich b. 30 Dec. 1730
5. Maria Margareta b. 21 Dec. 1733
6. Ludwig b. 2 July 1738
The communicants' list dated XLIII Die Dom. Cantate 1749 in the Ittlingen KB, a
list of those who took communion before their trip to Pennsylvania, includes the
names:
Johann Valentin Weeber, single
Johann Heinrich Weeber, single
Johann Heinrich Weeber and wife
Anna Barbara Weeber, single
Of these, the elder Joh. Heinrich Weeber d. on the voyage.

Pennsylvania records:
Valentine Weber, Lancaster, nat. Philadelphia, April 1762.

579. WEBER, NICOLAUS

6921 Michelfeld

1744

MICHELFELD LUTHERAN KB:
Nicolaus Weber m. 2 July 1737 Eva Barbara Steinbruck, daughter of Gabriel
Steinbruck. Children:
1. Anna Catharina b. 24 Apr. 1738
2. Johann Michael b. 2 May 1740
3. Maria Catharina b. 26 Apr. 1743
"18 Apr. 1744 to Pennsylvania." _____

A Nichs Weaver nat. Philadelphia Fall 1765, of Northern Liberties, Philadelphia
co.

580. WEIDKNECHT, MARTIN

Dragon, 1732
S-H 96, 97, 98

Adelshofen, Baden =
7519 Eppingen

ADELSHOFEN LUTHERAN KB:
Hans Dietrich Weidknecht and Anna Magdalena had:
  Hans Martin b. 14 Aug. 1693
m. 19 Feb. 1726 Johann Martin Weidknecht, son of Herr Joh. Dietrich Weidknecht, and Christiana Dorothea (surname not given), converted from Judaism and bp. in infancy in Schwaigern. Children:
  1. A child b. 10 Dec. 1726; d. after birth
  2. A child b. 9 Dec. 1727; d. after birth
  3. A child b. 8 Mar. 1729; d. after birth
  4. Johann Matthias b. 23 Feb. 1730
"Parents and son went to Pennsylvania 1732."

Pennsylvania records:
PA, THIRD SERIES, 19: 366:
Matthias Weidknecht was taxed with 100 acres in 1788, in Bethlehem twp., Northampton co.

PA, THIRD SERIES, 13: 307:
A Martin Widenecht is listed on the 1782 tax list of Milford twp., Northampton co. as single.

TRINITY LUTHERAN KB, SPRINGFIELD TWP., BUCKS CO.:
Matthias Weitknecht and wife Maria Catharina had:
  1. John Jacob b. 20 Apr. 1754
  2. Rosina b. 8 Nov. 1759

581. WEIDLER, JACOB

Dragon, 1749
S-H 414

6926 Kirchardt

KIRCHARDT LUTHERAN KB:
Heinerich Weidler and wife Ursula had:
  Joh. Jacob bp. 9 Dec. 1729
Heinrich Weidler d. 19 Sept. 1753 age 71 y. less 5 weeks.
Ursula Weidler d. 12 June 1760 age 66 y. 6 mo.

Pennsylvania records:
Pennsylvanische Staatsbote, 5 Dec. 1775:
Jacob Geiger, living at Nicholas Weber's, Philadelphia, wishes to find Jacob Weitler from Kirchard concerning a legacy.

582. WEIDLER, MICHAEL

William & Sarah, 1727
S-H 7 (Hans Mich¹ Weider, Con. 2 persons)

6926 Kirchardt

KIRCHARDT LUTHERAN KB:
m. 7 May 1726 Michael Weidler, son of the late Herr Hans Weidler, "Des
Gerichts" and Anna Elisabetha, daughter of Hans Görg Klein.

Pennsylvania records:
LANCASTER REFORMED KB:
Michael Weidler and wife Elisabetha nee Klein had:
    Michael bp. 10 Feb. 1740

HELLERS REFORMED CHURCH CEMETERY, UPPER LEACOCK TWP.:
Michael Weidler b. in Kirchart, Pfaltz Sept. 14, 1705; d. 23 July 1770, age 64 y.
10 mo. His wife Elisabetha is also buried there; her stone today is illegible.
Michael Weidler had a warrant for 185 A. of land on Conestoga Creek in 1733.

LANCASTER CO. WILLS:
Michael Weidler, Manheim twp. (14 June 1769/4 Sept. 1770). Wife Elizabeth;
children: John; Jacob; Elizabeth, wife of John Tare (Dare) to have land in York Co.;
Dorothea, wife of John Line; Barbara, wife of Jacob Glatz; Ann, wife of Michael
Wybright of York Co.; Catharina, wife of Stephen Martin.

Elizabeth Weidler, Manheim twp. (31 Aug. 1773/5 Nov. 1783). Exr: son-in-law
Stephan Martin. Same heirs as named in will of Michael, except that son John
Weidler was deceased when estate was settled.

Michael Weidler, Lancaster co., nat. by Act of 29 Mar. 1735

583. WEIGEL, MARTIN age 24   Hoffenheim =
                                                   6920 Sinsheim, Elsenz
Samuel, 1732
S-H 59, 60, 63, 65 (with Torothea, age 20)

HOFFENHEIM LUTHERAN KB:
m. 11 July 1730 Martin Weigel, carpenter, son of Veltin Weigel from "Onoltzbach-
ischen Unterthaun. aus der Orth Saalbach" [Saalbach is a small village near
Wiesenbach, Kr. Crailsheim = 7186 Blaufelden] and Anna Dorothea Friedlin,
daughter of the late Niclas Friedel, former master miller.

HELMSTADT LUTHERAN KB:
Martin Weigel, carpenter, and Anna Dorothea nee Frideli had:
    Johann Sebastian bp. 12 Nov. 1730; sp. Joh. Sebastian Hauck, son of Hans
Georg Hauck, the butcher.

Pennsylvania records:
CHRIST LUTHERAN KB, YORK:
Martin Weigel had children:
    1. Maria Juliana b. 22 Oct. 1733 (Also in Trinity Lutheran KB, Lancaster)
    2. Joh. Martin b. 11 Sept. 1735 (Also in Trinity Lutheran KB, Lancaster)
    3. Maria Elisabetha b. 31 Jan. 1738 (Also in Trinity Lutheran KB, Lancaster)
    4. Joh. Leonhard b. 2 Apr. 1743
    5. Henrich b. 18 Oct. 1747
    6. Marcretha b. 8 Apr. 1750

Bu. 2 Feb. 1759 Johann Martin Weigel, born 11 Nov. 1703. Father: Valentin Weigel from Saalbach in the Brandenburg Onoltzbach territory. He learned the carpenter trade in 1724. In the year 1729 he m. Dorothea M., daughter of Nicol. Friddel, and in 1730 he came with his wife to America. They had 11 children, 3 of whom are dead, 6 sons and 2 daughters are living. D. 31 Jan. 1759 and bu. in the churchyard at York. Aged 55 y. 2 mo. 19 d.

Sebastian Weigell, York, nat. Philadelphia Oct. 1765

584. WEISS, G. M., V.D.M.   7519 Eppingen
William & Sarah, 1727
S-H 9

EPPINGEN REFORMED KB:

m. (1) 26 Feb. 1686 Hans Michel Weiss, apprentice tailor, son of Niclas Weiss, citizen at Grosen Engersheim in the Dukedom Württenberg, [= 7121 Ingersheim] and Barbara, widow of Jacob Stierle, former citizen and tailor. Children:
    1. Maria Appollonia bp. 26 Dec. 1686
    2. Barbara bp. 7 Oct. 1689
The mother, Barbara, d. 30 June 1692.
m. (2) 16 Sept. 1692 Hans Michel Weiss, citizen and tailor, and Maria, daughter of the late Martin Frank, shoemaker at Bretten. Children:
    1. Anna Catharina bp. 11 Dec. 1695; d. 1696
    2. Eva Catharina bp. 31 July 1697
  *3. Görg Michael bp. 23 Jan. 1700
    4. Maria Elisabetha
                       twins bp. 29 Mar. 1703
    5. Christophel
    6. Maria Elisabetha b. 10 July 1705

Pennsylvania records:
see Glatfelter, *Pastors and People*, I: 160–161 for the career of this early Pennsylvania pastor.

During 1564/1565 the plague ravaged Heidelberg so that the entire University of Heidelberg moved to Eppingen to be safe from it. The patrician residence on the Fleischgasse built between 1417 and 1472 became its home giving the building the name "Alte Universität" ever since. The lower structure is built of native sandstone with Gothic fenestration—a rarity among secular structures—the half-timbered overstructure precise and artistic in its workmanship.

Photo: J. Godshall

The "Ratsschänke" in Eppingen, built in 1388, is one of the oldest half-timbered buildings in Germany. Part of its plank wall has been retained, a feature rarely seen in German buildings.

Photo: J. Godshall

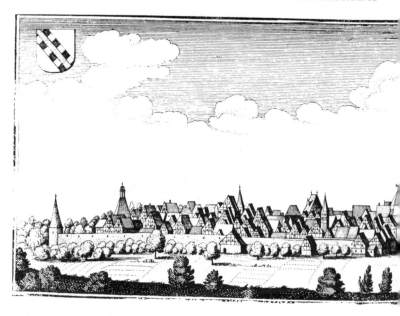

585. WEISS, JACOB

Albany, 1728
S-H 20, 21

Steinsfurt =
6920 Sinsheim, Elsenz

STEINSFURT REFORMED KB:
m. 28 Sept. 1706 Hans Jacob Weiss, son of Hans Weiss, and Barbara, daughter of
Michael Wolff, a mason at Ittlingen. Children:
1. Maria Barbara b. 31 Dec. 1706
2. Hans Jacob b. 4 July 1708 (?) (faded)
3. Maria Catharina b. 2 Aug. 1710
4. Maria Barbara b. 2 July 1713
5. Ottilia b. 14 Aug. 1714; d.
6. Maria Elisabetha b. 11 May 1716; d.
7. Maria Elisabetha b. 2 July 1717
8. Hans Martin b. 4 June 1719
9. Elisabetha b. 25 Jan. 1724
10. Georg Michael b. 25 July 1726

Pennsylvania records:
MUDDY CREEK KB, LANCASTER CO., PA.:
Jacob Weiss, Sr. had:
11. Susanna b. 8 Feb. 1730; bp. 9 May 1730; sp. Susanna Wolff

LANCASTER CO. ORPHANS' COURT DOCKET,
3 SEPT. 1754:
Jacob Wise, eldest son of Jacob Wise, deceased, petitioned the court to hold a
tract of land in Cocalico twp. containing 140 A., formerly held by his father Jacob
Wise who d. intestate. Other heirs are: Barbara Wise, the widow; George Michael

The Hilsbach and the Elsenz creeks flow together at Eppingen, the southern-most town examined in this volume. Eppingen appears for the first time in documents just before the year 1000, but by 1188 is was declared a city, in 1282 an imperial city. In 1462 the Palatinate became the owner of the city. One of the best preserved medieval towns in Germany, it numbers over 70 exposed half-timbered buildings. As pictured here in the 1640s in the Merian *Topographia*, the Pfeifer-turm (13th century) has a half-timbered hood which has since been removed. The Altstädter Church once had the *Simultaneum*, but the Protestant elements withdrew before 1900 and the church is now entirely Roman Catholic. Throughout southern Germany storks once nested on roofs and chimneys, but as swamps have been drained their food source has disappeared and they are seen less often today than at mid-seventeenth century. Eppingen today has incorporated into it nine nearby villages—Adelshofen, Elsenz, Gemmingen, Ittlingen, Kleingartach, Mühlbach, Richen, Rohrbach a. G. and Stebbach, some of them studied in this volume.

Photo courtesy New York Public Library

Wise, the other son of the said intestate. Daughters: Elisabeth, wife of Martin Widdle; Susanna; Catharine, deceased, m. (1) Michael Kitch and had: Michael, Elisabeth, Sophia and Martin Kitch; Catharine m. (2) John Berger and had: Anna, Barbara, Leonora, Margaret and Catharine Berger.

See Pennsylvania Patents AA-2: 479 for final disposition of the property of Jacob Weiss of Cocalico twp., Lancaster co., Pa.

Jacob Wise and Jacob Wise, Jr., Lancaster co., nat. Philadelphia April 1743.

586. WEISS, JACOB age 45   7103 Schwaigern

Samuel, 1732

S-H, 60, 61, 62, 64, 65. (Other passengers: Dorothea
(Torethea) age 40, Barbara age 19, Rosina age 13,
Katharina age 8, Kiliana age 10.)

SCHWAIGERN LUTHERAN KB:
  m. 16 Aug. 1707 Hans Jacob Weiss, son of the late Hans Jacob Weiss and
Dorothea, daughter of Michäel Boger, vintner. They had:
  1. Dorothea b. 4 July 1708; d. 31 Oct. 1723
  2. Maria Barbara b. 25 Jan. 1711
  3. Hans Jerg b. 21 June 1713
  4. Maria Margaretha b. 6 Dec. 1715; d. 17 Feb. 1719
  5. Maria Rosina b. 12 Mar. 1718
  6. Joh. Kilian b. 17 June 1721
  7. Maria Catharina b. 20 Apr. 1724
  8. Johannes b. 4 May 1727; d. 24 May 1727
  9. Joh. Jacob b. 21 Oct. 1728; d. Oct. 1728

A Jacob Wise, Philadelphia co., nat. Philadelphia April 1743, as a "Quaker"

587. WELCKER, JOH. GEORG   6922 Meckesheim

William & Sarah, 1727

S-H 9

MECKESHEIM REFORMED KB:
Hans Martin Welcker and wife Margaretha had:
  Joh. Georg b. 10 Feb. 1697
m. (1) 18 Feb. 1721 Hans Georg Welcker and Anna Maria Fabian. She died
12 Dec. 1721, aged 25 y. 6 mo. 17 days.
m. (2) 9 June 1722 Hans Georg Welcker and Anna Margretha Zimmermann. She
was b. 6 Apr. 1704, daughter of Andreas Zimmermann [q.v.] and Elisabetha.
Children:
  1. Joh. Jacob b. 3 Dec. 1725

Pennsylvania records:
GOSHENHOPPEN REFORMED KB, MONTGOMERY CO., PA.:
Hans Georg Welcker and wife had:
  1. Maria Susanna bp. Aug. 1731; sp. Maria Susanna Zimmermann
  2. Johannes bp. 30 Aug. 1741
  3. Joh. Jacob bp. 6 Apr. 1746

SHULTZE'S JOURNALS, II: 145, 146.
Hans Georg Welcker d. 8 Mar. 1782, aged 85.
Mrs. Welcker died 27 Feb. 1782, age 77 y., 11 mo.

Pennsylvanische Berichte, 16 Apr. 1749,

In 1749 Hans Georg Welcker was appointed guardian of Joseph Fabian, age 15.

George Wellker, Philadelphia co., nat. Philadelphia 24 Sept. 1741

Bammental lies on the edge of the conventional boundaries of the Kraichgau, but its Reformed church served the entire lower Elsenz Valley. Bammental is first mentioned in 1016. A house and barn, neatly painted, together with the other outbuildings are located close to one another in the village. The same components were built on a Pennsylvania German farmstead. While not quite as compressed, they were still built in immediate proximity in Pennsylvania, where land was plentiful, no doubt to save steps.

Photo: J. Godshall

588. WENDEROTH, CASPAR age 28

Pleasant, 1732
S-H 100, 101

6901 Bammental
6922 Meckesheim

BAMMENTAL REFORMED KB:
Joh. Jacob Wenderroth and wife Margaretha had:
 Joh. Caspar bp. 11 Dec. 1705; conf. 1720

MECKESHEIM REFORMED KB:
m. 16 Jan. 1732 Caspar Wenderoth from Bammenthal and Margretha Strep.

Pennsylvania records:
TRINITY LUTHERAN KB, NEW HOLLAND, LANCASTER CO.:
Caspar Wenderoth had:
 Anna Maria b. 9 Sept. 1733; bp. 20 Sept.; sp. Anna Maria Keller, single

Naturalized in Maryland, April Term 1753 Casparus Wintenorth (Wintenoth)

589. WERNER, JERG ADAM age 26   Massenbach =
                                                 7103 Schwaigern
Harle, 1736
S-H 156, 159, 161

MASSENBACH LUTHERAN KB:
m. 14 July 1691 Hans Jerg Werner, son of Hans Werner, and Maria Ursula,
daughter of Hans Riss, citizen and smith. Their son:
    Jerg Adam b. 22 Apr. 1711
m. 8 Feb. 1735 Jerg Adam Werner, son of the late Jerg Werner, and Augusta
Benedicta, daughter of the late Hans Jerg Brunner, former inhabitant at Bonfeldt.

590. WERNER, JOH. ADAM   Massenbach =
                                                 7103 Schwaigern
Forest, 1752
S-H 495

MASSENBACH LUTHERAN KB:
m. 14 July 1691 Hans Jerg Werner, son of Hans Werner, and Maria Ursula,
daughter of Hans Riss, citizen and smith. Their son:
    Joh. Adam b. 2 Oct. 1708

591. WETTERICH, CHRISTOPH   6924 Neckarbischofsheim

Robert and Alice, 1738
S-H 212, 214, 216

SINSHEIM AND NECKARBISCHOFSHEIM LUTHERAN KB:
m. 10 Feb. (?) 1712 at Sinsheim Christophorus Wörterich, musketeer from _____
(faded entry), and Anna Margaretha Schütz from Bischoffsheim.
Christoph Wetterich, shoemaker, and wife Anna Margaretha nee Schütz had children bp. at Neckarbischofsheim:
    1. Maria Barbara b. 30 Sept. 1715
    2. Johanna Dorothea b. 27 Dec. 1717; "went to the new land 1738."
    3. Johann Christoph b. 18 July 1720
    4. Anna Maria b. 2 Mar. 1724
    5. Johann Christoph b. 11 Feb. 1727; d. young
    6. Maria Eva b. 6 Apr. 1728
    7. Maria Barbara b. 27 May 1730

Pennsylvania records:
LITITZ MORAVIAN KB:
m. 12 Mar. 1745 Gottlieb Hill and Anna Maria Wetterich
m. 24 Apr. 1744 Joachim Burger and Marie Wetterich

592. WETZEL, CHRISTOPH   Hoffenheim =
                                                 6920 Sinsheim, Elsenz
Nancy, 1750
S-H 443

HOFFENHEIM LUTHERAN KB:
m. 10 Jan. 1713 Elias Wetzel and Margretha, daughter of the late Hans Emmrich.

The pulpit in the Lutheran Church at Neckarbischofsheim was created by Jakob Müller of Heilbronn who also saw to the rebuilding of the church which was completed in 1610. The pulpit bears the four evangelists' and St. Paul's faces and an inscription which proclaims in rhyme that it was a gift of the noble and virtuous lady Maria Magdalena of the Helmstatt family to witness to

> Ihr Lust und Lieb zu Gottes Wort
> Das sie von dieser Kanzel hort.
> All Nachkomling wird des Gedencken
> Und Got ihr ewiges Leben Schencken.

> — her joy and love for God's Word
> which from this pulpit she has heard.
> All those to come shall think thereon
> And may God give her eternal life.

Photo: J. Godshall

Elias Wetzel and wife Anna Margaretha had:
    Christoph b. 8 July 1731; conf. 1743
[Nine other passengers on this ship can be identified in the Hoffenheim records.]

593. WETZEL, JACOB   6920 Sinsheim, Elsenz

Ann Galley, 1746
S-H 360, 361

SINSHEIM LUTHERAN KB:
m. 29 Sept. 1716 Joh. Jacob Wetzel, carpenter, son of the late Joh. Michael Wetzel,
citizen and carpenter, and Anna Ursula, daughter of Joh. Michael Georg, citizen
and "des Gerichts" at Hasselbach. Children:
    1. Joh. Bernhard b. 6 Aug. 1717
    2. Joh. Martin b. 13 Nov. 1719
    3. Anna Catharina b. 20 Feb. 1724
    4. Johannes b. 13 June 1726
    5. Susanna b. 26 Apr. 1729
    6. Susanna Philippina b. 31 Aug. 1732 at Steinsfurt

Pennsylvania records:
TRINITY LUTHERAN KB, LANCASTER:
m. 12 Nov. 1749 Jacob Oberkirsch, a widower from the neighborhood, and Susanna
Wetzlerin, a single person from the vicinity.
m. 1 Jan. 1751 Jacob Huber, a bachelor and tailor from the town, and Susanna
Philippine Wetzler, a single person from the town.

FREDERICK, MD. LUTHERAN KB:
10 July 1773 Susanna Andraein, b. 26 Apr. 1729 in Sinzheim in the Oberpfalz. In
1741 she and her parents immigrated to Pennsylvania. In 1746 she m. Jacob
Oberkirsch in Lancaster and had 2 sons and 6 daughters with him, of whom 3
daughters still live. Since her first husband died, she m. Peter Andrae and had 3
daughters and 1 son with him, of whom 2 daughters are living. She died 9 July
(1773), aged 44 y. 2 mo. 13 days.

594. WETZSTEIN, ANDREAS   Gauangelloch =
1751   6906 Leimen

GAUANGELLOCH LUTHERAN KB:
m. (1) 4 Sept. 1714 Andreas Wetzstein from Wollenberg [= 6927 Bad Rappenau]
and Maria Barbara Kilian. Children:
    1. Hans Michael b. 21 Aug. 1715
    2. Maria Charlotta b. 24 Dec. 1717
    3. Joh. Michael b. 28 Aug. 1719
    4. Maria Christina b. 30 Nov. 1721

5. Phillipps Friederich b. 14 Dec. 1725
m. (2) 22 Nov. 1746 Andreas Wetzstein, widower and "des Gerichts", and Sabina
Katharina Gänsler, widow from [6901] Nusloch.

Krebs, "Annotations to Strassburger and Hinke's Pennsylvania German Pioneers,"
The Pennsylvania Genealogical Magazine, 21 (1960): 235-248: Andreas Wetzstein,
resident of Gauangeloch, district of Heidelberg, paid ten florins as manumission
fee and nine florins to satisfy the ten Pfennig tax. Permitted to emigrate with wife
and two children.

Pennsylvania records:
NEW HOLLAND LUTHERAN KB, LANCASTER CO.:
m. 20 Jan. 1752 Joh. Michael Mönch, miller and widower, and Sabina Catharina
Wettstein, widow of the late Andreas Wettstein.

595. WIDDER, AUGUSTIN

Adelshofen, Baden =
7519 Eppingen

Molly, 1727
S-H 12, 13

ADELSHOFEN LUTHERAN KB:
m. 7 Nov. 1671 Jacob Wieder and Agnes, daughter of Jorg Strohbach. Joh. Jacob
Wider and wife Agnes had:
     Augustinus Georg Hieronÿmus b. 1 Apr. 1691

Pennsylvania records:
NEW HOLLAND LUTHERAN KB, LANCASTER CO.:
Augustinus Widder had:
     Johannes b. ____1739; bp. 10 June 1739
     Augustinus b. 26 Mar. 1744
     Joh. Jacob b. 16 July 1746

TRINITY LUTHERAN KB, LANCASTER:
D. 16 Jan. 1767 Augustinus Widder, a married man, and formerly member of the
congregation here, aged 75 y., 9 mo., 15 d. Buried 18th on his place.

Augustine Widder, Strasburg twp., Lancaster co., nat. Philadelphia Sept. 1761.

596. WILCKE, RUDOLF

Weiler =
6920 Sinsheim, Elsenz

William and Sarah, 1727
S-H 8, 9 (3 persons. Name appears as A: Rudolph
Wilkes; B: Rutolff Wellecker)

WEILER REFORMED KB:
Rudolf Wilcke and wife Elisabetha had:
     1. Joh. Georg bp. 15 Dec. 1715
     2. Anna Margaretha bp. 27 Oct. 1718
     3. Joh. Gottfried bp. 6 Mar. 1721
     4. Joh. Georg bp. 29 July 1723; d. young

Krebs, *Palatine Emigration* . . . , p. 22
Rudolf Wilcke, citizen of Weiler, emigrant of 1727, paid 57 florins 21 kreuzer
emigration tax.

Pennsylvania records:
FIRST REFORMED KB, PHILADELPHIA:
Bu. 31 Jan. 1760 Anna Maria Wilki, widow of Rudolph Wilki, aged 55 years.
Bu. 12 July 1770 Joh. Georg Wilcki, aged 42 y. 5 mo.
A Joh. Georg Wilki and Anna Maria Duer were sponsors in 1750.
Joh. Georg Wilki and Anna Maria had:
    1. Daniel b. 10 Apr. 1764
    2. Anna Maria bp. 29 Dec. 1765
    3. Catharine b. 27 Mar. 1767
    4. John b. 3 Nov. 1768
A Catharina Wilkin, single, was a sp. in 1748.

ST. MICHAEL'S AND ZION LUTHERAN KB, PHILADELPHIA:
Gottfried Wilcke was a sponsor in 1746 and again a sponsor in 1748 with wife
Christina.

597. WILLHEIT, FREDERICH   7103 Schwaigern

Pennsylvania Merchant, 1731
S-H 43, 44, 45 (Other passengers: Women: Lucretia,
Magdalena, Barbara, and under 16: Elisabetha and
Frederich)

SCHWAIGERN LUTHERAN KB:
Samuel Wilheit and wife Barbara had:
    Joh. Friderich bp. 8 Jan. 1687
m. 17 Nov. 1711 Frederich Willheit, son of the late Samuel Willheit, and Lucretia,
daughter of Paul Hafner. (Her name is also given as Wilhelmina Lucretia.) They
had:
    1. Maria Magdalena b. 17 Sept. 1712
    2. Maria Barbara b. 9 Mar. 1714
    3. Johann Frederich b. 5 Aug. 1716; d. 5 Aug. 1716
    4. Maria Elisabetha b. 19 Apr. 1718
    5. Maria Catharina b. 14 Aug. 1721; d. young
    6. Georg Frederich b. 16 July 1723

Pennsylvania records:
TRINITY LUTHERAN KB, LANCASTER:
m. 15 Aug. 1735 Nicolaus Koger and Maria Elisabetha Willheutin
m. 15 Apr. 1735 Martin Frey, son of Tobias, and Maria Magdalena Willheutin,
daughter of Friederich Wilheut from across the Susquehanna.

STOEVER'S RECORDS:
m. 1 Apr. 1735 Martin Frey and Maria Magdalena Willheut, Codorus.

FREDERICK, MD. LUTHERAN KB:
Friedrich Willheit had a son bp. 10 Feb. 1751 (no name recorded).

Joh. Georg Friederich Willheit and wife Anna Maria had:
Anna Barbara b. 2 Oct. 1756
m. 25 June 1747 Friederich Willheit, the late Friederich Willheit's surviving legitimate son, and Anna Maria Weimar, Bernhard Weimar's legitimate unmarried daughter.

Frederich Wilhyde, Frederick co., nat. 1749.

598. WINTERBAUER, SEBASTIAN

6921 Ittlingen

William, 1737
S-H 195, 196, 197

ITTLINGEN LUTHERAN KB:
Sebastian Winterbauer and wife Maria Magdalena had:
1. Anna Margaretha b. 25 Feb. 1731

GROMBACH LUTHERAN KB:
Sebastian Winterbauer at the Oberbugelhoff and wife Magdalena had:
2. Maria Catharina b. 5 Sept. 1734

ADERSBACH LUTHERAN KB:
Sebastian Winderbauer from Obernbugelhoff and wife Maria Magdalena had:
3. Joh. Peter bp. 8 Feb. 1736

Pennsylvania records:
STOEVER'S RECORDS:
Sebastian Winterbauer (Conewago) had:
Maria Susanna b. 1738; bp. 1738
Sybilla b. 30 Aug. 1740; bp. 18 May 1741
These same bp. are recorded at Christ Lutheran, York.
Magdalena is also a sp. in Conewago Lutheran KB.

599. WIRTH, HANS MARTIN

Hoffenheim =
6920 Sinsheim, Elsenz

Rosannah, 1743
S-H 344, 345 (Name on ship's list: Martin Wierd)

HOFFENHEIM LUTHERAN KB:
m. 2 July 1716 Joh. Georg Wirth, born in Eberstatt [= 7101 Eberstadt], and Maria Appollonia Reuss, daughter of Frantz Reis.
Joh. Georg Wirth and wife Maria Appollonia had:
Hans Martin b. 10 Jan. 1719

Pennsylvania records:
TRAPPE LUTHERAN KB:
m. 21 Jan. 1751 at New Hanover Johan Martin Wirth and Anna Maria Grabiler.

600. WIRTH, PHILIP HEINRICH

Hoffenheim =
6920 Sinsheim, Elsenz

Jacob, 1749

S-H 418 (Name on ship's list: Henry (W) Wirdt)

HOFFENHEIM LUTHERAN KB:
conf. 1733 Philip Heinrich Wirth
m. 6 Feb. 1737 Phil. Heinrich Würth, formerly from Würtemberg but for a long
time with his cousin the late Hans Georg Würth, and Anna Eva Elisabetha Lang,
daughter of Valentin Lang. (The marriage was necessary due to pregnancy.) She
was bp. 10 Dec. 1709, daughter of Veltin Lang and Elisabetha. Children:
1. Johan Martin b. 9 Aug. 1737
2. Eva Margaretha b. 11 Mar. 1740
3. Susanna Elisabetha b. 21 May 1747
4. Christoph Henrich b. 23 Dec. 1748

Pennsylvania records:
NEW HANOVER LUTHERAN KB:
Philip Henry Wirth and wife Maria Eva had:
5. Bernhard b. 14 Dec. 1750; bp. 25 Dec. 1750; Johann Bernhard Gilbert
[q.v.] and Anna Maria Grabil.

BERKS CO. WILLS:
Philip Wirth, Robeson (26 Aug. 1798/17 Mar. 1800). Wife Elisabeth; eldest son
Martin, second son Bernhard. Wife Elizabeth and Mathias Kaler, exrs.

Philip Wirth, Union twp., Berks co., nat. Philadelphia Sept. 1764.

601. WOLFF, ANDREAS age 26

6921 Ittlingen

Plaisance, 1732

S-H 79, 82, 83 (with Anna Dority Woolf age 30)

ITTLINGEN LUTHERAN KB:
Michael Wolff and wife Anna Elisabetha had:
Andreas bp. 18 June (?) 1707
Andreas Wolf and wife Dorothea had:
1. Andreas Heinrich bp. ____Oct. 1730
[Andreas Wolf was a brother-in-law of Hans Jacob Weiss, q.v., an immigrant from
Steinsfurt.]

Pennsylvania records:
MUDDY CREEK LUTHERAN KB, LANCASTER CO., PA.:
Andreas Wolff had:
2. Joh. Georg b. 18 Dec. 1734
3. Joh. Jacob b. 22 Mar. 1736
4. Joh. Heinrich b. 22 Sept. 1737
5. Joh. Leonhardt b. 17 Dec. 1738; sp. Joh. Jacob Weiss, Jr. and wife
m. 4 Dec. 1739 Andreas Wolff and Regina Klein (Warwick). Children of the second
marriage:
6. Joh. Leonhardt b. 8 Dec. (recorded 1739 in KB, but baptism dated 26
Dec. 1740; presumably born in 1740.)

7. Joh. Valentin b. 31 Jan. 1742

Andrew Wolf, Philadelphia co. nat. Philadelphia Sept. 1744

602. WOLFF, HANS BERNHARD

William & Sarah, 1727
S-H 7, 9 (6 in family)

Steinsfurt =
6920 Sinsheim, Elsenz

STEINSFURT REFORMED KB:
Isaac Wolff m. 7 Jan. 1673 Elisabetha, daughter of Christian Ludwig. Their son:
Hans Bernhardt bp. 2 Mar. 1674
Hans Bernhard Wolff and wife Susanna had:
1. Hans Georg bp. 18 Dec. 1695 [q.v.]
2. Georg Michael bp. 11 May 1699; d. 1702
3. Johannes Bernhard bp. 11 Oct. 1701
4. Georg Michael bp. 29 Dec. 1703
5. Anna Maria bp. ____May 1706
6. Jeremias b. ca. 1708; conf. 1724, age 16
7. Hans Jacob bp. 4 Apr. 1711; d. 31 Jan. 1721
8. Susanna bp. 6 Mar. 1714
9. Anna Elisabetha bp. 22 Sept. or Oct. (?) 1716

Pennsylvania records:
LANCASTER CO. ORPHANS COURT DOCKET,
6 FEB. 1756 AND 2 MAR. 1756:
Georg Michael Wolf of Earl twp. d. intestate leaving nine children, seven of whom
are named in the Orphans Court records:
1. Georg Michael, eldest son
2. Conrad (above 14 years) chooses Jeremiah Wolf as guardian
3. Bernard (above 14 years) chooses Wendle Zwecker
4. Henry
5. Ann   All evidently minors under 14 years—
6. Abraham   guardians appointed by the court
7. Susannah
George Michael Wolf had 200 A. in Earl twp.

NEW HOLLAND LUTHERAN KB:
Georg Michael Wolff had:
Joseph b. 21 June 1734
Joh. Bernhardt Wolff was a sp. in 1737 and 1739

603. WOLFF, HANS GÖRG

William & Sarah, 1727
S-H 7, 9 (2½ in family)

Steinsfurt =
6920 Sinsheim, Elsenz

TRESCHKLINGEN LUTHERAN KB:
Anna Catharina Klenk, daughter of Michel Klenk, smith, m. (1) 24 Nov. 1716
Joh. Christoph Stecher. Children:
1. Anna Catharina Stecher bp. 22 Aug. 1717
2. Georg Adam Stecher bp. 7 Aug. 1718

Joh. Christoph Stecher d. 10 Feb. 1719
m. (2) 9 Feb. 1723 at Steinsfurt Hans Jorg Wolf, smith, and Anna Catharina, widow
of Joh. Christoph Stecher.
"(She) emigrated afterwards with her husband to Pennsylvania and when she just
arrived there, died in Philadelphia."

STEINSFURT REFORMED KB:
Hans Bernhard Wolff [q.v.] and wife Susanna had:
     Hans Georg bp. 18 Dec. 1695; conf. 1709, age 13.
Hans Görg Wolff, citizen and smith, and Catharina his wife had:
     1. Joh. Jacob bp. 2 Dec. 1723
     2. Anna Catharina bp. 21 Apr. 1727

Pennsylvania records:
TRINITY LUTHERAN KB, LANCASTER:
A Joh. Georg Wolff had:
     Joh. Philipp b. 26 Feb. 1739
He later appears in the Christ Lutheran KB, York. The name is too common to
state with certainty that this is the immigrant from Steinsfurt.

604. WOLFF, HANS PETER

Dragon, 1732
S-H 96, 97, 98

Elsenz =
7519 Eppingen

ELSENZ REFORMED KB:
m. 24 June 1679 Jacob Wolff, son of the late Elias Wolff, and Catharina, daughter
of Hans Clauser. Their son:
     Hans Peter bp. 7 Mar. 1688; conf. 1703
Peter Wolff and Anna (Maria) had:
     1. Hans Georg bp. 6 Dec. 1716
     2. Martin bp. 11 Sept. 1718
     3. Martin bp. 11 Feb. 1720
     4. Anna Elisabetha bp. 18 May 1721
     5. Joh. Henrich bp. 15 Dec. 1723
     6. Hans Peter bp. 1 Sept. 1726
     7. Caspar bp. 9 May 1728
     8. Joh. Peter bp. 4 Oct. 1730
m. 5 July 1704 Johannes Ottinger, son of the late Gregory Ottinger, and Catharina,
widow of the late Jacob Wolff

Pennsylvania records:
FIRST REFORMED KB, LANCASTER:
A Peter Wolff and wife had:
     Anna Barbara b. 10 Apr. 1737; sp. George Keller and wife
m. 3 Feb. 1745 Henry Wolf, son of Peter Wolf, and Catharine Cammer, daughter
of John George Cammer

LISCHY'S RECORDS:
Heinrich Wolff and Catharina had:
     1. Anna bp. 11 Dec. 1748; sp. Peter Wolff and Anna and Catharina Wolffin

Peter Wolff and wife Catharina Elisabeth and Johannes Wolff and wife Anna sponsor two of the children of Jacob Ottinger in 1752 and 1759.

605. WURFFEL, HANS (LEONARD) age 54   Steinsfurt =
      HANS GEORG age 18   6920 Sinsheim, Elsenz

Samuel, 1733
S-H 106, 107, 110, 112 (Others on ship: Maria Lydia
Wervell age 52, Maria Lydia age 26, Elizabeth age 17,
Leonard age 8)

STEINSFURT REFORMED KB:
m. 14 Jan. 1673 Hans Wurffel, son of Stoffel Wurffel, and Elisabetha, daughter of Hans Auchen (?)
m. 27 Nov. 1703 Hans Leonhard Würffel (bp. 9 Dec. 1679), son of the late Hans Würffel, and Maria Elisabetha, daughter of Christian Wentz. Children: [In bp. records the father is given as Hans in some of the records and as Hans Lehnhardt in others.]
    1. Maria Elisabeth bp. 21 Sept. 1704
    2. Hans Melchior b. 23 May 1706; d.
    3. Joh. Melchior [q.v.] b. 10 Nov. 1707
    4. Elisabetha b. 13 Oct. 1710; d.
    5. Elisabetha b. 17 Jan. 1712
    6. Hans Görg bp. 7 May 1715; conf. 1732 age 16
    7. Hans Görg bp. 9 Feb. 1718
    8. Hans Leonhardt bp. 9 May 1724
[Note: In the early Steinsfurt records, the Wurffel family village of origin is Wÿningen, Zurich (CH-8104 Weiningen, ZH). They were in Steinsfurt prior to 1662.]

Pennsylvania records:
FIRST REFORMED KB, LANCASTER:
John George Wuerffel and wife Maria Barbara nee Seitz had:
    1. John Henry b. 10 June 1740
    2. George b. 19 Aug. 1749 (Strasburg twp.)
Elizabeth Wuerffel m. before 1740 John Henry Weschenbach.

George Werfield, Bart twp., Lancaster co., nat. Philadelphia by affirmation 11 April 1753

606. WÜRFFEL, JOH. MARTIN   Adersbach =
                                                  6920 Sinsheim, Elsenz
Speedwell, 1749
S-H 410

ADERSBACH LUTHERAN KB:
m. 3 June 1732 Joh. Martin Würffel, son of the late Joh. Conrad Würffel, "Bestandmüller" at Wimpffen [7107 Bad Wimpfen], and Maria Dorothea, daughter of Joh. Georg Hoffman.

Pennsylvania records:
SHULTZE'S JOURNALS; II: 27:
Oct. 1768—Am to go to Martin Würfel's in Upper Milford on Christian Miller's
place on the 3rd or 4th.

607. WURFFEL, MELCHIOR age 20   Steinsfurt =
                                                 6920 Sinsheim, Elsenz
Pink *Plaisance*, 1732
S-H 79, 82, 83

STEINSFURT REFORMED KB:
Joh. Melchior Wurffel, b. 10 Nov. 1707, son of Hans Leonhard Würffel and Maria
Elisabetha nee Wentz. [See Hans Leonhard Wurffel, 1733 emigrant, for complete
detail on the family.] He was conf. 1722, age 14½.

Pennsylvania records:
FIRST REFORMED KB, LANCASTER, PA.:
Melchior Wuerffel and wife Elizabeth Gensmer had:
  1. Susanna bp. 1739 (29 June?)

        Steinsfurt—named for a Roman ford in the Elsenz—is first mentioned in a
document dated 1100. A town belonging to the Electoral Palatinate, it had a
Reformed Church. On the *Hof* of the Lerch family in Steinsfurt—hence the name
Lerchennest (lark's nest)—Frederick the Great stayed overnight on August 4/5,
1730, as he fled his enemies. Of the many families which emigrated to Pennsylvania, there are still branches of the Warfel, Wüst, Wolff, Bender, Leibe, Laber,
Schörck and Wanner in Steinsfurt today.

                                                    Photo: J. Godshall

Melchior Würffel had a daughter:
Catharina b. 6 Oct. 1745, bp. at New Holland

LANCASTER CO. ORPHANS COURT DOCKET
3 JUNE 1755:
Katharine Werfel, widow of Melchor Werfel; Melchor Werfel died intestate leaving
seven small children. Asks to sell tract of land in Bart twp. containing 150 A.

LANCASTER ORPHANS COURT
7 JUNE 1757:
Melchor Werfel—distribution of estate. Heirs were: Catharine, the widow; children: Georg, eldest son; Maria Elisabeth; Susanna; Catharine; Hans Adam; Henry
and Philippina.   _____

Melchior Werfield, Bart twp., Lancaster co., nat. Philadelphia by affirmation 11
Apr. 1753

608. WÜRTZ, HANS   Massenbach =
                                                       7103 Schwaigern
Royal Union, 1750
S-H 432 (Hans (HW) Weertz on list)

MASSENBACH LUTHERAN KB:
Joh. Caspar Würtz and wife Anna Barbara had:
    Johannes b. 17 Mar. 1720
[He was a brother-in-law of Michael Luttmann, also on this ship. His step-son,
Matthaeus Baffenmeyer is also a passenger.]
m. (1) 15 Nov. 1739 Johannes Würtz, son of Joh. Caspar Würtz, gravedigger, and
Maria Eva, widow of the late Joh. Wendel Poffenmeier. They had:
    1. Joh. Dieterich b. 24 July 1740
    2. Christianus b. 22 Mar. 1743
m. (2) 8 Sept. 1744 Johannes Würtz, citizen and widower, and Maria Barbara,
daughter of Caspar Strauss, inhabitant. Children:
    3. Joh. Caspar b. 8 July 1745; d. young
    4. Magdalena b. 14 Oct. 1747

Pennsylvania records:
BERKS CO. WILLS:
John Wertz, Tulpehocken (8 Jan. 1789/19 Aug. 1791). Wife Barbara; children:
eldest son Dietrich, Christian, Jacob, John, Barbara, Justina, Elisabeth.

CHRIST LUTHERAN KB, STOUCHSBURG, BERKS CO.:
m. 17 May 1772 Frederick Ried, son of Caspar Ried, and Barbara, daughter of
John Wurtz, Tulpehocken.
m. 9 Jan. 1776 John Werz, son of John Werz, and Catharina Miller, daughter of
Jacob Miller, both Tulpehocken.
m. 17 June 1787 Christian Gutlander and Elisabetha Werz

609. WÜSTER (WISTAR), CASPAR

Wald Hilsbach =
6903 Neckargemünd

1717

WÜSTER, JOHANNES (sick—1 person)

William & Sarah, 1727
S-H 7

BAMMENTAL REFORMED AND NECKARGEMÜND LUTHERAN KB:
Hans Caspar Wüster, (in early records, occupation "forst knecht, woodsman," in later records "Jäger", hunter), of Hilspach and wife Anna Catharina had:

*1. Hans Caspar bp. 19 Feb. 1696
 2. Dorothea bp. 22 Oct. 1697; conf. 1709
*3. Maria Barbara b. 26 Feb. 1700; conf. 1713; m. (1) Hans Georg Bauer, m. (2) Georg Hüttner [q.v.]
*4. Anna Barbara b. 22 Jan. 1702; m. Johannes Eppler [q.v.]
 5. Albertina b. 26 Dec. 1703; conf. 1717
 6. Maria Margretha b. 10 June 1707
*7. Johannes b. 7 Nov. 1708
 8. Joh. Ludwig b. 29 Jan. 1711
 9. Georg Bernhardt b. 18 Sept. 1713
[*denotes immigrants]

Pennsylvania records:
Caspar Wistar m. 25 May 1726 Catharine Jansen, daughter of Dirk Jansen of Germantown. He was a prosperous merchant who was involved in extensive land transactions. He was a brass button maker and also started the glass furnace at Wistarburg, near Salem, N.J., the first successful glass business in this country. On 10 Dec. 1745 Caspar Wistar of the city of Philadelphia, brass button maker, and Catherine, his wife, sold 100 acres of land to the trustees of Trinity Tulpehocken Church for the sum of forty pounds. This land was part of 1837 acres granted to Caspar Wistar in 1739 by Thomas Penn. (Berks co. deeds A5: 71, 72) See Caspar Wistar Haines, *Some Notes Concerning Caspar Wistar (Immigrant) and on the Origin of the Wistar and Wister Families* (Philadelphia, 1926) for additional information on the family.

_____

Caspar Wistar, Philadelphia city and John Wistar, Philadelphia city, nat. Philadelphia September 1740 without taking an oath.

610. ZARTMANN, ALEXANDER

6921 Ittlingen

Albany, 1728
S-H 20, 21

ITTLINGEN LUTHERAN KB:
Alexander Zartmann and wife Anna Catharina had:
 1. Hans Jacob b. 22 Sept. 1722
 2. Joh. Bernhardt b. 15 Oct. 1727

Pennsylvania records:
Alexander Zartman: Warrant for 179 A. 25 Apr. 1738 in Warwick twp., Lancaster co. (See Patent Book A—15: 524 and Patent Book D—6: 130.)
He was a trustee of the Emanuel congregation at Brickerville.
Alexander and Anna Catharina Zartman had:
   3. Alexander, Jr. b. 29 July 1731
Alexander Zartman, Sr. Will, Lancaster co. (6 Oct. 1762/27 Dec. 1762) wife Anna Catharina, son Alexander.

STOEVER'S RECORDS:
Jacob Zartman m. 14 Aug. 1744 Anna Margaretha Riehm. (In other records she is given as Maria Magdalena.) Children: [compiled from his will and other sources]
   1. Henry b. ca. 1745 oldest son, mentioned in will
   2. Martin b. ca. 1747; m. Susanna Fitler
   3. Jacob b. ca. 1749; m. Regina Fitler (Heidelberg twp., Dauphin co.)
   4. Susanna b. ca. 1751; m. Conrad Schreckengast (Resided in Northumber-
      land co. and later in Armstrong co.)
   5. Anna Margaretha b. 25 Oct. 1755; m. Thomas Dobson [bp. Emanuel
      Lutheran]
   6. Eva b. 1 Oct. 1758 [bp. Emanuel Lutheran]
   7. Peter b. 15 Mar. 1760; wife Catharina [tombstone Zion Cemetery, Thorn
      twp., Perry co., Ohio]
   8. Anna Maria b. ca. 1762; m. Henry Groninger
Jacob Zartmann, Sr. and wife were members of Himmel's Lutheran Church

NORTHUMBERLAND CO. WILLS:
Jacob Zartman Sr., Mahonoy twp. (11 Feb. 1793/30 Mar. 1793).
Above-mentioned wife and children.

Alexander Zartmann, Jr. m. Magdalena. Children:
   1. Joh. Michael b. 3 May 1754; m. Margaretta Eichelberger, daughter of
      Michael Eichelberger, at Zion Lutheran, Manheim 8 Aug. 1780.
   2. Alexander b. 19 Mar. 1756; m. Maria Barbara Eichelberger, daughter of
      Michael Eichelberger, at Zion Lutheran, Manheim 8 Aug. 1780.
   3. Susanna b. 11 Oct. 1759
   4. Maria Elisabetha b. 11 June 1761
   5. Catharina b. 9 Oct. 1763
   6. Emanuel b. 1 June 1765 m. Elisabeth Bassler
   7. Margareth

LANCASTER CO. WILLS:
Alexander Zartman, Warwick twp. (5 Sept. 1801/17 Dec. 1803). Wife Magdalena; children Michael, Alexander and Emanuel. (He d. 2 Dec. 1803).
For further detail on these families see: *The Zartman Family 1692–1742* (Revised ed. 1942) by Rev. R. C. Zartman. _____

   Alexr. Zartman, Warwick twp., Lancaster co., nat. Philadelphia Fall 1765.

611. ZAUCK, JOH. HEINRICH

appears on *Dragon*, 1732 as Henrich Zowck, sick
S-H 97

Hoffenheim =
6920 Sinsheim, Elsenz

HOFFENHEIM LUTHERAN KB:
m. 29 June 1717 Joh. Heinrich Zauck, youngest son of Hans Ulrich Zauck, inhabitant, and Elisabetha Schwartz, daughter of the late Martin Schwartz, citizen. Children:
1. Maria Philippina b. 15 Dec. 1718
2. Eva Rosina b. 22 Aug. 1721
3. Maria Margretha b. 4 Mar. 1724
4. Maria Eva b. 4 Jan. 1727
5. Anna Eva Barbara b. 27 Aug. 1729

Pennsylvania records:
TRINITY LUTHERAN KB, LANCASTER AND YORK LUTHERAN KB:
Heinrich Zauck had:
6. Maria Magdalena b. 28 Dec. 1734; bp. 23 Feb. 1735; sp. Martin Frey [son of Tobias, from Weiler] and his fiancee Magdalena Willheutin [daughter of Friederich Willheit from Schwaigern]
m. 22 May 1738 Joh. Jacob Scherer and Philippina Zauckin

612. ZEHNBAUER, MARTIN

Phoenix, 1752
S-H 509

7519 Eppingen

EPPINGEN LUTHERAN KB:
m. 20 June 1741 Martin Zehndbauer, from Gemmingen, and Agnes Barbara, widow of the late Herr Joh. Schmidt, "Gerichtsverwandten." Martin Zehndbauer, miller at the "unter stadt mühl" and wife Agnesa Barbara had:
1. Maria Elisabetha b. 10 July 1742
2. Eva Elisabetha b. 6 Aug. 1745; d. 24 Feb. 1749
3. Christina Barbara b. 3 Feb. 1748; d. 31 Mar. 1748

Pennsylvania records:
PA, Third Series: XVII: 143, 421.
Martin Zeneboar appears on 1771 tax list for Lebanon twp., Lancaster co.
Martin Zentbauer on 1773 tax list, same twp.

613. ZEND, JOH. JACOB

James Goodwill, 1728
S-H 22, 23 (Name on list: Sinc, Zenck)

6921 Michelfeld
Adelshofen =
7519 Eppingen

MICHELFELD LUTHERAN AND ADELSHOFEN LUTHERAN KB:
Joh. Martin Zend and wife Anna had:
Hans Jacob b. 27 Apr. 1701 at Michelfeld.
m. 4 May 1728 at Adelshofen Johann Jacob, son of Joh. Martin Zehnd, citizen and inhabitant at Michelfeld, and Anna Catharina, daughter of Matthaeus Gröner, citizen and butcher. "Both wish to go to Pennsylvania."

The Lutheran congregation at Eppingen had a church named for St. Peter in the Petersgasse built in 1520 which has long been used for secular purposes. Its churchly character is recognizable in Gothic door and fenestration still exposed. The number of Lutherans in Eppingen was always small; more members of the Reformed congregation, which shared the Altstädter Kirche with the Roman Catholics, lived there. The proportion is reflected in the number of emigrants of each faith which left Eppingen for new homes in Pennsylvania.

Photo: J. Godshall

Matthias Gröner and wife Agnes Catharina nee Schlauch had:
Johanna Catharina b. 5 Apr. 1706 at Adelshofen

Pennsylvania records:
MUDDY CREEK LUTHERAN KB, LANCASTER CO.:
Jacob Zint, died, had:
1. Joh. Martin b. 15 June 1730
2. Joh. Michael b. 4 Dec. 1732
3. Joh. Jacob b. 24 Feb. 1735; sp. Joh. Jacob Schlauch [also from Adelshofen]

614. ZIEGER, JOHANNES age 41   6924 Neckarbischofsheim

Samuel, 1732
S-H I, 60, 61, 62, 64, 65 (With: Christina Ziegerin, age 40; Margretha, age 16; Jacob, age 12; Susanna, age 9.)

NECKARBISCHOFSHEIM LUTHERAN KB:
Johannes Zieger, formerly a servant at [6928] Helmstadt, and wife Eva Catharina nee Heft had:
1. Maria Margaretha b. 11 Dec. 1714
2. Johann Jacob b. 12 Feb. 1718

3. Susanna Barbara b. 26 Jan. 1720
4. A stillborn daughter b. 9 Nov. 1722; the mother also died.

Johann Zieger, day laborer here, m. (2) 20 Apr. 1723 Anna Christina, daughter of the late Leonhard Balthasar Fischer, "Saltzträger at Zottigshoffen."

Pennsylvania records:
TRINITY LUTHERAN KB, LANCASTER:
Jacob Zieger had:
    Johann Jacob b. 16 Jan. 1743; bp. 16 Feb.

WARWICK LUTHERAN KB, LANCASTER CO.:
Jacob Zieger had a daughter:
    Catharina b. 2 Feb. 1752

ST. MICHAEL'S AND ZION LUTHERAN KB, PHILADELPHIA:
Communicants' list dated Feb. 1734
    John Zieger
    Christina Zieger

Just before the year 1000 *villa bischofsheim* appears in records; today Neckarbischofsheim on the Krebsbach preserves many of the buildings associated with the Helmstatt family of earls which owned it for seven centuries, including their memorial chapel ("Totenkirche" from the 12th century) and their residence ("Steinerne Haus" in a park setting). The town itself has not been destroyed and still has a five-cornered tower from the year 1148, part of a bastion in the medieval fortification of the place.

Photo: Tilly Paul

615. ZIEGLER, ANDREAS

Charming Nancy, 1737
S-H 188, 191, 193

Berwangen, Kraichgau =
6926 Kirchardt

BERWANGEN LUTHERAN KB:
Children of Loth Ziegler:
1. Georg Caspar m. Marg. Kuhnin
2. Georg m. Elisab. nee Ziegler. Their children:
   A. Georg Henrich ⎫ in the new land
   B. Hans Georg   ⎭
*3. Andreas "ist im neuen Land."

Pennsylvania records:
HILL LUTHERAN KB, LEBANON CO.:
One Andreas Ziegler had:
Joh. Thomas b. 15 Dec. 1745; sp. Joh. Thomas Madern and wife

616. ZIEGLER, HANS WILHELM

Dragon, 1732
S-H 96, 98

6920 Sinsheim, Elsenz

SINSHEIM REFORMED KB:
Georg Michael Ziegler, butcher and "Burgemeister", and wife Anna Maria had:
Joh. Wilhelm bp. 21 Nov. 1694; conf. 1708
Anna Maria Zieglerin conf. 1699, age 13 was possibly his sister.
[The Reformed KB starts in 1687 and her bp. was prior to that date.]
Anna Maria Ziegler m. 17 May 1707 Hans George Doll and their son, Joh. Michael
was an emigrant from Sinsheim in 1742.

Pennsylvania records:
LANCASTER CO. WILLS:
William Ziegler, Lancaster Borough (10 Jan. 1740/8 Oct. 1750). Mentions his wife
(not named). Mentions his nephew John Michael Toll.

William Ziegler nat. by Act of 29 March 1735

617. ZIEGLER, JOH. GEORG

William and Sarah, 1727
S-H 7, 10 (3 persons; appears on A list: Hans Heri^k
Siegler, B list: Hans Georg Ziegler)

Weiler =
6920 Sinsheim, Elsenz

SINSHEIM LUTHERAN KB:
Johann Georg Ziegler, joiner at Weiler, and wife Anna Maria had:
1. Anna Barbara b. 28 July 1722; sp. Anna Barbara, wife of Conrad Rudi
2. Eliesab. b. 11 July 1724; sp. Eliesabetha, wife of Gottfried Münch
3. J. Ludwig b. 15 Dec. 1726; sp. Ludwig Ziegler, "des Gerichts" and wife
   Judith Spengler
He was possibly a son of Hans Martin Ziegler who m. 23 Nov. 1680 at Hilsbach

Anna Maria, daughter of Martin Gissewein (elsewhere Gieswein). They had a son Joh. Ludwig bp. 15 Feb. 1690 and a son Hans Georg b. 16 July 1697. However, there are several other Georg Zieglers in these records and exact identification is impossible in the absence of a marriage record specifically naming his father.

Krebs, *Palatine Emigration* . . . , p. 22:
Johann Georg Ziegler, cabinetmaker, citizen of Weiler, emigrant of 1727, had to pay 126 florins 25 kreuzer emigration tax.

Pennsylvania records:
TRINITY LUTHERAN KB, LANCASTER:
One Georg Ziegler d. of old age 25 Aug. 1776, age 80 y.

618. ZIEGLER, JOH. LUDWIG   6924 Neckarbischofsheim

St. Andrew, 1751
S-H 457

NECKARBISCHOFSHEIM LUTHERAN KB:
Hans Jerg Ziegler, potter, and wife Anna Jacobina had:
    Johann Ludwig b. 26 Dec. 1702
m. 17 July 1731 Joh. Ludwig Ziegler, potter, son of Joh. Georg Ziegler, also a potter, and Maria Magdalena, daughter of Joh. Martin Schäffer, "Scheldthaisen" of Lampoltzhausen in Meckmuhler Amt [7101 Lampoldshausen]. Children:
    1. Maria Elisabetha b. 13 May 1732
    2. Maria Margaretha b. 27 Feb. 1734
    3. Maria Jacobina b. 1 June 1736
    4. Maria Catharin b. 28 Sept. 1738
    5. Joh. Georg b. 30 Jan. 1743

Pennsylvania records:
ST. MICHAEL'S AND ZION LUTHERAN KB, PHILADELPHIA:
m. 10 June 1762 Philipp Heyl and Jacobina Ziegler
m. 27 July 1762 Georg Seitz and Maria Elisabeth Zeigler, in presence of her mother, sisters and kinsmen.
Bu. 3 Jan. 1773 Maria Magdalena Ziegler, widow; mother-in-law of Georg Seits. Daughter of the late Johann Martin Schäffer, former mayor in Lamboldshausen, and his wife Elisabeth. She was b. 21 Aug. 1700; m. 14 June 1730 Johann Ludwig Ziegler, son of Joh. Georg Ziegler from Bischofsheim in the Creichgau, Unterpfaltz. Lived in wedlock 21 years and had 1 son and 4 daughters. 3 daughters are living, married names Seitz, Heil and Dietz. Came to this land in 1751. Aged 72 y., 4 mo., 10 days.

619. ZIEGLER, PHILIP   Weiler and Reihen =
                                               6920 Sinsheim, Elsenz
William and Sarah, 1727
S-H 8, 9 (5½ persons—Seigler on A list)

WEILER REFORMED KB AND SINSHEIM LUTHERAN KB:
Hans Georg Ziegler and wife Sara had:

Georg Philip bp. 1 Apr. 1677
m. ____July 1702 Philip Ziegeler, son of Hans Georg Ziegeler, citizen and "des Gerichts" at Weÿler, and Anna, daughter of the late Jacob Maÿer, citizen at Reÿhen. (Jörg) Philip Ziegeler and wife Anna had:
1. Joh. Jacob bp. 15 May (?) 1703
2. Maria Catharina b. 1 Mar. 1705
3. Barbara b. 25 July 1707; d. 1707
4. Ludwig b. 28 (?) Oct. 1708; d. 1708
5. Hans Martin bp. 12 Mar. 1710
6. Joh. Georg bp. 2 Feb. 1712
7. Joh. Philipp b. 24 Aug. 1713
8. Anna Christina b. 15 Dec. 1715

Krebs, *Palatine Emigration* . . . , p. 21
Philipp Ziegler, citizen of Weiler, had to pay 24 florins, 19 kreuzer emigration tax, intending to go to Pennsylvania.

Pennsylvania records:
STOEVER'S RECORDS:
John Philip Ziegler (Codorus) had:
    Anna Christina b. 7 Sept. 1740; sp. Jacob Ziegler and Agnes Schmidt

CHRIST LUTHERAN KB, YORK:
This church record contains numerous entries for the children of Jacob Ziegler, Philip Ziegler and Georg Ziegler.

620. ZIEGLER, REGINA wife of Georg Klein   Berwangen =
 ZIEGLER, ANNA   6926 Kirchardt

BERWANGEN LUTHERAN KB:
Hans Leonhart Ziegler, b. 15 Jan. 1683, son of Georg Zigler and Margretha, d. 14 Aug. 1743 in Berwangen. M. 22 Nov. 1707 Anna Margaretha nee Kober, daughter of Hans Peter Kober. His wife d. there 25 Nov. 1738. The family register lists their children:
1. Joh. Georg b. 2 Aug. 1712
2. Elisabeth b. 19 May 1714; m. (1) 1736 Joh. Geo. Ziegler; m. (2) 1743 Leonhard Lang [q.v.]
3. Regina b. 5 Feb. 1718; m. Georg Klein [q.v.] "is in the new Land."
4. Anna "is in the new Land."

Pennsylvania records:
see Georg Klein and Leonhard Lang

621. ZIMMERMAN, ANDREAS   6922 Meckesheim

William & Sarah, 1727
S-H 7 (8 in family)
ZIMMERMAN, HANS MICHAEL
S-H 9

MECKESHEIM REFORMED KB:
m. 24 Apr. 1703 Andreas Zimmermann and Elisabetha, widow of Andreas Freÿ-
berger. Children:
   1. Anna Margretha b. 6 Apr. 1704
   2. Hans Michael b. 16 July 1705
   3. Hans Dieterich b. 18 Aug. 1707
   4. Margretha b. 24 Aug. 1709
   5. Anna Elisabetha b. 25 Apr. 1711
   6. Maria Susanna b. 26 Sept. 1712
   7. Joh. Georg b. 6 Mar. 1714
   8. Maria Margretha b. 13 Jan. 1716
   9. Amelia Maria Catharina b. 13 Sept. 1717

Pennsylvania records:
NEW GOSHENHOPPEN REFORMED KB, MONTGOMERY CO.:
Michael Zimmermann and wife had:
   1. Joh. Michael bp. 20 May 1732; sp. Susanna Zimmermann
   2. Fronegg (Veronica) bp. 9 May 1736
   3. Georg bp. 24 Sept. 1740; sp. Georg Zimmerman

PHILADELPHIA CO. WILLS:
Michael Zimmerman, (8 Feb. 1741/4 Mar. 1740/41). "Lost all hopes of getting his
health again." Guardians of wife and children: Bernhart Doderer and George
Zimmerman. Wife Anna to have plantation until youngest son is 20, then land to
be divided between 2 sons, Michael and George. Also names daughters: Elizabeth,
Fronia and Catrina.

ST. PAUL'S LUTHERAN KB, RED HILL, MONTGOMERY CO.:
m. 6 July 1741 Jacob Kürr and Anna Zimmerman, widow of Michael Zimmerman.
m. 5 Jan. 1742 Georg Zimmerman and Anna Catharina Seidel. Children:
   1. Anna Elisabetha b. 3 Jan. 1744
   2. Anna Catharina b. 14 Oct. 1752

622. ZIRKEL, HANS HEINRICH   6921 Ittlingen

Prelist

KIRCHARDT REFORMED KB:
Johannes Lofenius Zirckel, smith, m. 2 Sept. 1670 Catharina Hirtzel. Their son:
   Henrich bp. 10 Nov. 1676

ITTLINGEN LUTHERAN KB:
Hans Heinrich Zirkel and wife Euphrosina (Eva Rosina in some records) had:
   1. Hans Martin b. 22 Aug. 1701
   2. Eva Margaretha b. 20 June 1703

The organ in the Lutheran Church in Ittlingen, a town of several thousand souls, is much like the organ cases in Pennsylvania German rural churches in the late eighteenth and early nineteenth centuries. The church in Ittlingen was built in 1732.

Photo: J. Godshall

3. Joh. Ludwig ⎫
4. Anna Maria   ⎬ twins b. 9 Oct. 1705
5. Eva Rosina b. 1 Sept. 1710

Pennsylvania records:

PHILADELPHIA CO. ADM.:
F: 173: Henry Zirkell, (8 Mar. 1745/10 Mar. 1747). Son Ludwick Zirkell and daughter Anna Mary (married to Jacob Faut), both children of first wife. All land and plantation to son Johannes (by second and present wife) and to his son. Said son, Johannes, to provide for present wife Magdalena. Son Johannes' wife: Catharine Rauch. Wife Magdalena exec., with help of Michael Burge of Francony twp., Philadelphia (Franconia) and George Henry Herzell of Rockhill, Bucks (until said Johannes shall arrive at his majority.) Witnessed by Joh. Wilhelm Straub, Dietrich Rudy, Michael Burge, and George Henry Hertzel. Adm. to Catharine the widow, and Peter Sneider, 10 Mar. 1747.

INDIANFIELD LUTHERAN KB:
m. 6 Mar. 1753 Michael Nees and Margaret Zirckel, "left for Virginia."

PHILADELPHIA CO. WILLS:
Ludwig Zirkle, "sick & weak." (28 8bris [October] 1746/17 Jan. 1746). Wife Maria Eva to have estate until youngest child is twelve, then Exec to sell it and wife to have her "Terth" and children to have two "Terths" in equal shares except eldest son George Henry to have £ 25 four years before to learn a trade. If wife

remarries, estate to be sold by Executors.—Exec.: trusty friend Peter Snider and wife Maria Eva. Witnesses Peter (X) Schnieder, Andrew Bernhart and Henry Seibel appeared at Salford. Translated by Jacob Reiff. Codicill: "I have long ago bequeathed 1 acre for use of the Proper Lutheran Church where the congregation have build one church . . . they to have and hold said land So long as the Soon and Moon a Shining . . ." On July 17, 1751 Mary Eve Hotinger [Ottinger], Zirkle's widow, deeded to Andrew Barnhart, Henry Seible and Joseph Copp the one acre. This is the Indianfield Lutheran Church.

Ludowick Cirkel, Philadelphia, nat. by Act of 19 May 1739. Henry Circle, Philadelphia co., nat. Philadelphia, April 1743.

623. ZORN, ANDREAS   7620 Kirnbach
St. Andrew, 1752   7101 Massenbach
S-H 485

SCHLUCHTERN LUTHERAN KB:
m. 13 Feb. 1744, after proclamation at Massenbach and Kirnbach, Johann Andreas Zorn from Kirnbach, servant at Massenbach, and M. Dorothea, daughter of the late Christoph Naser, citizen at Massenbach.

MASSENBACH LUTHERAN KB:
1. Eva Dorothea b. 28 July 1744; d. young
2. Eva Catharina b. 6 Oct. 1745
3. Joh. Andreas b. 23 Dec. 1747
4. Joh. Martin b. 21 Aug. 1750

Pennsylvania records:
TRINITY LUTHERAN KB, LANCASTER:
m. 15 Jan. 1754 Joh. Andreas Zorn, widower, from Kirnbach in Württ., and Catharina Zürnin

624. ZWEŸSIG, HANS VALENTIN age 49   6901 Mauer
ZWEŸSIG, JOH. DIETER age 24
ZWEŸSIG, BERNHARD age 16
Molley, 1741
S-H 310, 311, 312, 313

SCHATTHAUSEN LUTHERAN KB:
m. 13 June 1713 Hans Velten Zweÿsich from Mauer and Anna Maria Litter from here, both Lutheran.

MAUER LUTHERAN KB:
Valentin Zweÿsig b. 12 Mar. 1693, son of Alexander and wife (name not recorded)
m. 13 June 1713 Hans Valentin Zweÿsig and Anna Maria Eiether (?) of Schadhausen. Children:
1. Joh. Martin b. 19 Sept. 1714; d. 1718
2. Joh. Dieterich b. 22 Sept. 1716
3. Maria Eva b. 25 Mar. 1719; d. 1722

4. Anna Ursula b. 21 Nov. 1721; d. 1729
5. Joh. Bernhard b. 11 Mar. 1724
6. Johannes b. 21 Aug. 1726; d. 1729
7. Joh. Valentin b. 25 Feb. 1729
8. Anna Elisabetha b. 25 June 1732

MÖNCHZELL LUTHERAN KB:
m. 10 Jan. 1736 Valentin Zweisich, widower from Mauer, and Maria Elisabeth, daughter of Hans Reinhardt, citizen.

MAUER LUTHERAN KB:
9. Ursula b. 25 July 1737; d. 1737
10. Maria Dorothea b. 12 Nov. 1738; d. 1739
11. Maria Dorothea b. 28 Mar. 1740

MICHELFELD LUTHERAN KB:
m. 9 June 1741 Johann Dietrich Zweÿsig and Anna Margretha Zimmermann.

Pennsylvania records:
ST. PAUL'S LUTHERAN KB, RED HILL, MONTGOMERY CO.:
Dietrich Zweyschich and wife Margretha had:
    Maria Susanna b. 21 July 1742; sp. Maria Susanna Roeder

ZION'S (ZIEGEL) UNION CHURCH, WINDSOR TWP. (NOW PERRY TWP.), BERKS CO.:
Bernhard Zweizig and wife Margaretha had:
    Johann Bernhard b. 11 Feb. 1766

BERKS CO. ADM.:
Bernhart Zweitzig, Windsor—adm. granted 16 Mar. 1790 to John Zweitzig, eldest surviving son, and Philip Shatz, one of the creditors.
Dietrich Zweysig and wife Margaretha moved to Westmoreland co., Pa., and they appear in the records of Rev. Joh. Wilhelm Weber as sponsors in 1783, 1784 and 1785.

 Isolated farms belonged to nobility and were opened to Swiss Mennonites after the Thirty Years' War. Their reputation as good farmers ennerved the wealthy to invite them, but their religion was illegal and was practiced quietly in their homes with the eyes of the law slightly closed. Restrictions and taxes were added in the eighteenth century so that large numbers of them went to Pennsylvania, settling in both Montgomery and Lancaster counties. The Dammhof near Weiler still exists.

Photo: J. Godshall

APPENDIX A
Mennonites in the Kraichgau

After the Thirty Years' War, religious sects that were previously unwelcome in German states were invited to rebuild the devastated land. Religious persecutees from France and Switzerland came to repopulate the villages and farms. They came as early as 1651 to Sinsheim, Reihen and Hilsbach, and later are found in the records as tenant farmers on several of the *Höfe* in the area.

Their economic contribution was welcome, but their religion was not, and the tolerance lasted for a brief period. They paid special taxes, a form of protection money, and were not permitted to hold large or public meetings. By 1717, in addition to their high rents, annual tribute, and special assessments, each family was required to pay an additional three florins of military money. This taxation, along with other increased oppressions, resulted in a large migration of these people to Pennsylvania. In the five year period from 1727 to 1732, the Dutch Mennonites recorded some 3,000 Palatine brethren having passed through Holland enroute to Pennsylvania.

Excellent records exist for those Swiss families who came into this area from the canton of Zurich, deposited in the Zurich archives. There are two large volumes of documents relating to this emigration, titled *Verzeichnisse von Ausgewanderten der Zürcher Landschaft*. A few examples of the type of information found in these documents:

1651 lists:

From the Parish Wald [8636 Wald ZH]:
Hans Jacob Oberholtzer, 26 years old, a married man. With Anna Buchmann, his wife, and children:
> Hans Jacob age 4
> Samuel age 3
> Regel age 2

They went to Sintzheim in Curfurst. Pfaltz.
From the Parish Basserstorff:
Felix Altorffer, 44 years old, schoolmaster at Oberwÿl in the Parish Basserstorff, on 16 Mar. 1651 with his wife Barbara Güdel (?), age 42 years, to Reichen [Richen] in the Oberpfalz. Children:
> Jogeli age 6
> Felix age 2

1661 lists:

From the Parish Bärentschweil, Zurich [8344 Bäretswil]:
Jagli Graf, Teüfer, from Weertzweil, went in the year 1651 to the Pfaltz with other Teüffer, to Sintzheim with his wife and 7 children, [not named in record.]
Hans Jagli Graf, brother of the above, also went to Sintzheim in 1651 with his wife and one child and two young men named Hans Graf and Heinrich Brandenberger, both single. It is not known if they are Teüffer.

Other helpful sources for information on these families are:

Zumbach, Friedrich, a manuscript "Schweizer Zuwanderung in den Kraichgau nach dem 30-jährigen Krieg," of which a copy is at the Lancaster Mennonite Historical Society, Lancaster, Pa. A list of those persons specifically mentioned as Mennonites in this manuscript has been compiled and published by Lois Ann Mast, "Palatinate Mennonites" in *Mennonite Family History*, Vol I, No. I (1982). The entire Zumbach work is being edited for publication soon in Germany.

Harold S. Bender, "Palatinate Mennonite Census Lists 1664–1774" published in the *Mennonite Quarterly Review*, Vol. XIV, No. one through Vol. XV, No. one (1940–41)

For additional information on the historical background of this immigration, see:
C. Henry Smith, *The Mennonite Immigration to Pennsylvania*, Pennsylvania German Society (1929)
H. Frank Eshleman, *Historical Background and Annals of the Swiss and German Pioneer Settlers of South Eastern Pennsylvania . . .* (Lancaster, Pa. 1917)
Delbert Gratz, *Bernese Anabaptists*, The Mennonite Historical Society, Goshen, Ind. (1953)

1. Documents from the Archives of the Mennonite Church in Amsterdam

The Mennonites' Amsterdam Committee of Foreign Needs, who provided aid to the Swiss refugees in the Palatinate, received frequent requests for financial help by prospective Mennonite emigrants who did not have sufficient funds to pay their own passage to Pennsylvania.

After furnishing the necessary assistance to some emigrants, the committee became alarmed at the increasing number of emigrants and the amount needed for their aid. They sent letters into the Palatinate warning that no emigration should be attempted except by those who had sufficient means to take them to Pennsylvania. The committee could no longer provide financial aid and discouraged further emigration, citing the dangers of the ocean voyage and other factors.

In 1732, a letter was written by Mennonite ministers and elders from Grombach [= 6927 Bad Rappenau] and the nearby Immelhäuser Hof, informing the Amsterdam committee of the pending arrival of prospective emigrants, most of whom either had sufficient funds to pay their way to Pennsylvania, or were promised support from friends or relatives who were already residing in Pennsylvania.

There are two documents in the Amsterdam Archives containing information about this 1732 emigrant group. The two documents contain differences in names, place name spellings, and the number of emigrants. For purposes of comparison, these documents are cited here as list A and list B. List A is simply dated 1732 and appears to be the most accurate in names of emigrants and the number of emigrants. The A list also includes the amount of money each family had and indicates those who expect financial aid from family and friends already in Pennsylvania. List B is dated 10 May 1732. The bracketed information does not appear in these lists; it has been added from other sources.

[Copies of these two documents were provided by Klaus Wust.]

List A	List B
No.	No.
of	of
Persons	Persons

HÖSELHOFF

13   Christian Frantz
     with his wife and
     11 children

HESSELHOF

13   Michiel Frantz,
     wife and 11 children

[This place has been erroneously identified several times as Hassloch, north of Neustadt, probably based on Ernst Müller's location of this congregation "on the Haschlof one hour from Neustadt, northward," in *Geschichte der bernischen Taufer* (Frauenfeld 1895). Actually the place is Hösselinshof, north of 7106 Neuenstadt am Kocher. The family arrived on the *Samuel*, 1732, S-H 59: Christian Frants, Sr. age 47, Christian, Jr. age 26, Anna age 37, Barbara age 20, Eva age 19, Magdalena age 15, Judith age 12, John age 7, Michiel age 6, Veronica age 8, Elizabeth age 3.]

ZIMMERHOF

4   Hans Wittmer
    his wife and 2 children

ZIMMERHOF

4   Hans Wittmann
    his wife and 2 children

[He left his community without attestation and was evidently under some censorship. The Zimmerhof is located just northeast of 6927 Bad Rappenau and about 4 miles northwest of 7107 Bad Wimpfen. One Johannes Witmann arrived on the *Dragon*, 1732 with others from the Kraichgau.]

HASELBACH

6   Oswald Hochstetter
    with his wife and
    4 children

HASLEBACH

6   Oswald Hoffstetter
    with his wife and
    4 children

[today 6920 Hasselbach, southeast of 6924 Neckarbischofsheim. Ship *Samuel*, 1732, S-H 59: Oswald Hosteetter age 30, Maria Hostettin age 28, Barbara age 10, John age 10, Anna age 6, Veronica age 3.]

4   Christian Geman
    wife and 1 child and
    his brother Benedict

4   Christian Geman
    wife and 1 child
    and brother

[Ship *Samuel*, 1732, S-H 59: Chretian Geeman age 24, Benedigt Geeman age 20, Anna Gemanin age 23.]

1   Michael Dährstein

1   Michiel Dierstein

[Ship *Samuel*, 1732, S-H 59: Michiel Dierstein age 20.]

BOCKSCHAFFT   BOCKSCHAFT
4   Christian Marty   4   Christian Marty
    wife and 2 children   wife and 2 children
[Bockschaft is located between 6921 Ittlingen and 6926 Kirchardt. Pink
Plaisance, 1732, S-H 78: Christ[n] Martin age 63, Ells Marty age 60, Fravin Martin
age 16, also Martin Marta (child) and Fronik Martin (child).]

6   Hans Scherer's widow   6   Hans Scherer's widow
    with 3 children and   with 3 children
    2 sons-in-law, Ulrich   and 2 sons-in-law
    Burckhalter and Jacob Gutt
[Ship *Samuel*, 1732, S-H 59, 60: Samuel Scherer (Scheer) age 21, Jacob Guth
age 20, Ulerich Burckholter age 22, Veronica Sheer age 46, Susanna Guth age 20,
Ester Burckhalter age 20.]

1   Samuel Brant   2   Samuel Branden and his wife
[Ship *Samuel*, 1732, S-H 59: Samuel Brand age 24, Rossina Brand age 20.]

4   Samuel Meyer   4   Samuel Mayer
    his wife and 2 children   his wife and 2 children
[See below Martin Meyer for ship data.]

6   Martin Meyer   6   Martin Mayer
    wife and 4 children   wife and 4 children
[Pink *Plaisance*, 1732, S-H 78: Sam[l] Myear age 50, Martin Myear age 37,
Franick Miear age 39, Anna Mire Miar age 32, children: Jacob Miar, Martin Miar,
Christon Miar, Anna Miar.]

5   Hans Huber, widower   5   Hans Huber, wid.
    and 3 children and his   with 3 children and
    son-in-law Hans Scharer   son-in-law
[Pink *Plaisance*, 1732, S-H 78, 79: Hans Huber age 54, Hans Shear age 27,
Magdelin Sheren age 26 (? or Matelin Sharin age 20), Barbary Hufarin age 18,
Franey Hufar age 20.]

4   Hans Scharer with   4   Jacob Scherer,
    his wife and 2 children   his wife and 2 children
[Pink *Plaisance*, S-H 78: Jacob Schere age 65, Matelin Sharin age 20 (?),
Michael Share.]

MECKESHEIM   MOCKESHEIM
3   Hans Moselmann   3   Hans Muselman
    his wife and one child   his wife and one child
[Ship *Samuel*, 1732, S-H 59: John Mosiman age 23, Anna age 20. 6922
Meckesheim, located northwest of Sinsheim.]

IMMELHAUSEN   HIMELHEYSERHOF
2   Hans Behr's two   2   Hans Beer's two
    unmarried daughters   unwed daughters

[Immelhäuser Hof, located south of 6920 Sinsheim. Pink *Plaisance*, 1732, S-H 80: Magdelen Bear age 20, Frena Bear age 18.]

<table>
<tr><td>DICHELHEIM</td><td>DÖRNEN</td></tr>
</table>

	DICHELHEIM		DÖRNEN
4	Christian Huber, widower	1	Christiaen Hueber
	and 3 children		widower
	(to receive help from his friends		
	and father in Pennsylvania)		

[This place is possibly today Dühren = 6920 Sinsheim, Elsenz. Ernst Müller locates this congregation as "Thernheim, ½ hour from Sintzheim, southwest. Pink *Plaisance*, 1732, S-H 78: Christⁿ Huffer age 34, children: Hans Martin Hubar, Jacob Hubar.]

3	Jacob Oberholtz, widower	1	Jacob Obenholtzer
	and 2 children		widower

[Ship *Samuel*, 1732, S-H 59: Jacob Oberholtser age 28, Elisabeth age 6, Samuel age 3.]

List A: total 70 persons   List B: total 66 persons

2. References in the Kraichgau Church Books

In the church books of the Kraichgau, there are scattered references to Mennonites residing in the area. These references are most frequently found in the death records, but occasionally there is a marriage recorded, and in a few instances baptismal records (usually when either the mother or father is of another denomination). Various terms are used in the German records to designate these people: Anabaptist, Wiedertauffer and Mennonites. The following records were selected from the available entries, with special emphasis on those surnames that later appear in Pennsylvania Mennonite records:

ADELSHOFEN LUTHERAN KB:
Hans Michael Baer, from the Anabaptist sect to our Augustana religion, ["ab Anabaptist sect ad nostram Augustanam Relig."] m. 15 Jan. 1714 Anna Elisabetha Ott from Ittlingen.

ELSENZ REFORMED KB:
Baptized 8 Apr. 1681 Catharina Barbara, former Widertäuffer, age 18 years, daughter of Marx Oberholtzer, former Widertäuffer and tenant farmer at the Buchhoff. [today Buchenauerhof]
Conf. 1682 Catharina Barbara, age 18, daughter of Marx Oberholtzer, former Widertauffer at the Buchenhoff.
Baptized 16 Dec. 1696 Johannes Oberholtzer, son of Jacob Oberholtzer, from the Widertauffer sect in the castle; with the new religion he was given a new name:
        Kilian Casper confirmed 1697, age 16

EPFENBACH REFORMED KB:
Baptized 1 Feb. 1705 at Kloster Lobenfeld Jacob Müller, former Wiedertaufer from Ittlingen, in the 19th year of his age, became a member of the Reformed religion. He was given the baptismal name Johannes.

EPPINGEN
1703 Hans Jacob Müller, called the "Damm-Jockele," Wiedertaufer, age 35 years, at the Dammhof, since 5 years in Eppingen.

GROMBACH CATHOLIC KB:
Henrici Kindig, Widertauffer here in Grumbach, and his wife Anna _____tista, had two children baptized here against the wishes of the parents ["praeter voluntatem parent. baptizatus est."] The children were:
1. Philippus Wilhelmius bp. 5 Dec. 1691
2. Mar. Magdalena bp. 9 Jan. 1693

m. 15 Aug. 1691 Georg Jacob Wolgemuth (baptized and confesses our Catholic Religion), legitimate son of Joannes Jacob Wollgemuth, now Widertauffer in Kürchhardt, and Anna Maria Möhr, legitimate daughter of Andreas Möhr. Children:
1. Annastasia bp. 24 Apr. 1693, d. 1697
2. Anna Magdalena bp. 22 Dec. 1695
3. Dieterich Christian bp. 11 May 1698
4. Barbara bp. 16 Feb. 1701
5. Georg Christian bp. 7 Jan. 1703

HILSBACH
Buried 15 Aug. 1676 Michel Mejer, Anabaptist at Reÿhen, age 60 years.
Buried Sept. 1676 Hans Gutt, son of Jacob Gutt, Widertauffer, age 17 years.
Buried 4 Oct. 1678 Uli, son of Hans Frantz, Widertauffer at Uttlingen [Ittlingen] age 1 year
Buried 14 Sept. 1680 Marx Oberholtzer, tenant farmer at the Büchenhoff, a Widertauffer, without singing or bells. (no age given)
Confirmed 1682 Hans Jacob Lugart, age 16, son of Hans, former Widertauffer and miller at Obstatt by Brussel, now Savoy. His mother was named Barbara and was a daughter of Heinrich Mejer, former Widertauffer at Weÿler. His father was dead and this Hans Jacob was baptized at the age of 4 years.

KIRCHARDT REFORMED KB:
The deceased Widertauffer at Kirchardt, Hans Jacob Wohlgemuth, had 3 daughters and one son who were baptized 20 Apr. 1679:
1. Susanna Elisabetha age 18 years
2. Anna Barbara age 16 years
3. Anna Salome age 14 years
4. Jacob age 12 years

Buried 23 May 1718 a single fellow named Samuel Harnish, aged 20 years, son of Hans Harnish, citizen and Mennonite here.

MAUER LUTHERAN KB:
Married in the month of August, 1710: Johannes Herr, son of Christian Herr, the farmer at the Hof here, Mennonite, and Elisabetha, daughter of Johann Mair, also farmer at the Hof and Mennonite. Married in the Evangelical Lutheran Church after three proclamations.
Married 13 May 1714 Jacob Hochstätter, widower, "Hoffbauer bey Gutz Herrschafft" at Angloch [Angeloch], and Phronica [Veronica], daughter of Hans Maÿer, "Hoffbauer bey Gnädigster Herrschafft" here, both Mennonite religion.

REIHEN REFORMED KB:

Baptized 13 June 1680 Jacob Kauffman, bp. in the 24th year of his age, a former Wiedertauffer, and called Johann Jonas Jacob

Baptized 8 Apr. 1689 Elisabetha, a married woman, age 21, daughter of Jacob Kindig, a Widertauffer at Icklingen [Ittlingen].

Baptized 9 Aug. 1711 Christian Lederer, a former Wiedertauffer, a shoemaker residing at the Bochschoff; given the name Christian Jacob Philipp.

Baptized 4 June 1718 the Mennonite Jacob Schehrer's daughter, formerly called Veronica, age 18 years, named Susanna Maria.

m. 8 Feb. 1676 Samuel Meyer, son of Michael Meyer, and Anna Engelr, daughter of the late Hans Engelr of Buchheim in Switzerland.

m. 19 Feb. 1678 Hans Meyer, a Widertauffer, and (N.N.)

m. 10 May 1681 A Widertauffer Jacob Weissman and Elisabetha Rosenberger

d. 4 Mar. 1673 wife of Hans Rosenberger, Widertaufferin, age 44 years

d. 12 Jan. 1679 Jacob Rosenberger's wife, a Wid(er)tauffern

d. 13 Feb. 1679 wife of Martin Iseler, also a Widtauffern, aged 36 years

d. 2 Mar. 1682 Jacob Rosenberger, a Wid(er)tauffer, aged 66 years

d. 22 Apr. 1695 Barbara, wife of Jacob Huber, a Manistin

d. 2 Apr. 1719 Hans Meyer, citizen and Mennonist, aged 64 years and several months

d. 28 Nov. 1722 Anna Meÿer, Moennonisten, wife of Samuel Meÿer, the "Moennonisten Lehrer," aged 65 years

SINSHEIM REFORMED KB:

m. 22 Apr. 1704 the "Wiedertaufferischen Lehrer" at the Immelhausen Hoff Jacob Kundig from Ittlingen and Maria Oberholtzer.

d. 12 Nov. 1705 Samuel Oberholtzer, Widertauffer at the Immelheusener Hoff, aged 61 years

d. 8 Nov. 1708 Anna, wife of Martin Frey, Wid(er)tauffer, tenant at the Immelheusener Hoff, aged 36 years.

STEINSFURT REFORMED KB:

Baptisms:

Parents	Child
Hans Huber, a Widertäufer and Anna Scheürmann, our religion	Rudolf bp. 23 Feb. 1668
Rudolff Müller, former Widertauffer Verena Meÿer	Anna Maria bp. 15 Nov. 1669
Hans Huber, Widertäuffer Anna Scheürmann	Agnes
Vincenz Meÿer, Widertauffer Elsbeth Hassler	Samuel bp. 27 Feb. 1670
Jacob Nussli, Widertäuffer Veronica Meÿer	Maria bp. 27 Feb. 1670

Jacob Kauffman, age 14, former Wiedertauffer, bp. 21 Aug. 1681, given the name Jacob Georg Henrich.

[The first pastor of this congregation was Clemens Hirtzel from Winterthur in Switzerland. He also served the congregations at Reihen and Kirchardt. In entering the baptisms in these early records, he observed the Swiss custom of recording the mother's maiden name.]

d. 26 Aug. 1694 Hans Meyer, the elder. A Manist, in his 87th year.

d. 24 July 1702 Anna, wife of Hans Nussli of Steinsfurt, Mennonisten, aged 36 years.

d. 5 Apr. 1705 Rudy Landas aged 43 years, Mennonist.

d. 2 Nov. 1706 Hans Meÿer, Menonist, aged 62 years

d. 1 Mar. 1707 Benedict Mosemann's daughter, aged 24 years, 11 months, citizen and Menonisten.

[Note: in the following two marriage records, the Anabaptist designation is not included, but no children of these surnames appear in the baptismal records.]

m. 5 Feb. 1697 Peter Neuschwanger from Ettenweil, Bern, Switzerland, and Susanna, daughter of Georg Steffen, "Anwald".

m. 26 Jan. 1701 Christian Neuschwang, son of the late Peter Neuschwang, former citizen from Meckenmühle, Bern, Switzerland, and Anna Magdalena, daughter of Gabriel Stephan.

m. 22 Jan. 1667 Hans Huber, miller at Steinfurt and Anna Scheürmann, widow of the late Joseph Willman (?) at Weiler under Steinsberg.

m. 23 Jan. 1672 Christian Saltzgeber, born in Bundten, and Veronica, daughter of Hans Huber.

m. 18 Feb. 1679 Jacob Gutt, a Wiedertauffer, and daughter of Vincentz Meyer, the younger.

m. 18 Mar. 1679 Jacob Brechbeyl from Switzerland and Elisabetha, widow of the late MONSIEUR.

m. 13 May 1679 a Widertauffer, Hans Meyer, citizen at Mauer, and Veronica, widow of the late Jacob Rusch formerly of Gauangeloch [a marginal note adds: Rutsch in Dühren]

m. 13 May 1679 Hans Harnest, son of Martin, tenant farmer at the Bockshoff, and Anna, daughter of Hans Meyer, mason at Steinsfurt

m. 21 June 1680 Widtauffer Abraham Douscher (?) from Ziegelhausen and Maria, daughter of Vincentz Meyer, citizen at Steinfurth.

m. 22 Aug. 1682 Henrich Hauser and Ursula, daughter of the late Georg Stamm, formerly of Schlottheim

m. same day (22 Aug. 1682) Hans Meyer, son of Hans, and Elisabetha, daughter of the late Hans Jacob Hauser from Ryfferswÿl, Zurich

m. 10 June 1687 Wid(er)tauffer at Brachenberg (?) Hans Nussli and Anna Bahrin

m. 8 _____? 1687 Wid(er)tauffer at Steinfurth Jacob Gut and a Wid(er)tauffern.

m. 26 Aug. 1687 Hans Gochnauer and Anna Nussli, both Wid(er)tauffer.

m. 15 Apr. 1690 Hans Jacob Oberholtzer, son of Max (Marx?) Oberholtzer, and Maria, daughter of Jacob Nussler. These Monisten were married by their "Lehrer."

WEILER

Hans Senn, a Widertauffer at Weyler, died 8 Jan. 1666, aged 65 years. It is mentioned in his death record that "his children are of our religion." His wife

Veronica died 14 Dec. 1672, aged 46 years. After their deaths, the following children of this couple appear in the bapt. records:

Joh. Ernest bp. 9 Mar. 1675

Siegfried Samuel bp. 9 Mar. 1675

Hans Jacob bp. 2 June 1677 (his age at confirmation in 1677 23 years)

Two children of Hans Rotthe, Widertauffer at Weyler, were bapt.:

Hans Jacob, age 15 years bp. 2 June 1677

Hans Georg, age 22 years bp. 2 June 1677

Both were confirmed in 1677

m. 22 Jan. 1656 at Hilspach Hans Andreas Carl, son of Hans Jacob Carl, citizen at Obling., and Margaretha, daughter of Henrich Meÿer, a Wid(er)tauffer at Weiler. [They had seven children bp. at Weiler, and the father died there in 1675.]

m. 23 Feb. 1664 at Hilspach Sebastian Wagesiel, a tile maker, son of Martin Wagesiel in the Reichstatt Kauffbaur, and Barbara, daughter of Hans Senn, Widertauffer and citizen at Weiler.

m. 26 Apr. 1674 Jacob Frey, son of Felix Frey, farmer at the Burkenhoff [today Birkenauerhof] and Widertauffer, and Barbara, daughter of Jacob Oberholtzer, Wiedertauffer at the Immelhauser Hoff.

m. 18 Feb. 1677 Hans Ruth, widower, citizen and Widertauffer at Weiler, and Anna, widow of Georg Hegi from Dürnen [probably Dühren].

m. 18 Feb. 1677 Heinrich Ruth, son of the above Hans, and Adelheit Neÿkom, daughter of Hans Neÿkom from Hegenweil, Bern.

m. 30 July 1678 Hans Ruth, son of Hans, Anabaptista and citizen at Weiler, and Verena, daughter of Urbani Russenberger, citizen at Schlaten, Schaffhausen, Switzerland.

m. 8 Feb. 1681 at the Rauhenhoff Hans Jacob Graff, son of the late Hans Graff, former Widertauffer at the Rauenhoff in the Schmidberg jurisdiction, and Barbara, daughter of Hans Ruth, Widertauffer at citizen at Weÿler.

m. 31 Oct. 1681 Hans Landes, Anabaptista, son of Hans Jacob Landes, citizen at Weÿler, and Verena, daughter of Hans Rutt, Anabaptista and citizen at Weÿler.

m. 15 Apr. 1683 at Hasselbach Johannes Wehrlein, widower, citizen and wagonmaker at Hasselbach, Helmstatt jurisdiction, and Veronica, widow of Hans Georg Ruth of Weiler.

m. 13 May 1683 at the Immenhausenhoff Johannes Oberholtzer, son of Jacob, farmer and Widertauffer at the Immenhauser Hoff, and Anna, daughter of Felix Freÿ, former farmer and Widertauffer at the Birckenhoff.

m. 29 May 1683 Hans Ruth, widower and Widertauffer at Weÿler, and Verena, widow of Hans Jacob Graff, former citizen and Widertauffer at Sintzheim.

m. 26 June 1683 at the Birckenhoff Heinrich Freÿ, Widertauffer, son of Felix Freÿ, former farmer at the Birckenhoff, and Elisabetha, daughter of Jacob Graffe, former citizen and Widertäuffer at Steinfurth.

m. 30 Oct. 1683 Hans Jacob Landas, son of Jacob Landas, citizen and Anabaptist at Weiler, and Veronica, daughter of Hans Engel, former citizen at Östatt., Bern (Switzerland).

[all of the following are mentioned in the death records as Wiedertauffer.]

20 June 1655 a child of Hans Senn and Veronica

20 Mar. 1656 Hans Jacob Landas [no age given]

26 Sept. 1657 Hans Caspar Landas, age 13

15 June 1661 A Widertauffer's child
4 Jan. 1662 Child of Foelix Frey, farmer at the Burckenhoff
26 July 1662 a child of Foelix Frey, age 1½ years "without bells or singing"
28 Jan. 1663 a child of Hans Senn, age 8 weeks
28 Feb. 1663 a child of Hans Jacob Landas of Weiler, age ¾ year
21 Dec. 1664 a child of Hans Rudt, age 1 year
4 Apr. 1666 Hans Pistor, a Widertauffer from Weydeschwiel, Zurich, living with Hans Jacob Landas at Weiler
25 July 1666 a child of Hans Jacob Landas, age 7 years
6 Sept. 1666 a child of Hans Rüd, age ¾ years
12 _____? 1667 Hans Jacob, son of Felix Freÿ, Burckenhoff, age 18 years.
11 Jan. 1669 Christian Rudi, son of Hans, age 11
16 July 1672 Barbara, wife of Jacob Landas, died in childbirth, age 36 years
21 July 1672 Christian, son of Jacob Landas, age 5 weeks
26 Dec. 1672 Veronica, mother of Jacob Landas and widow of Hans Jacob Landas, age 70 years
5 Feb. 1675 Hans Jacob Frey, son of Jacob, at the Birckenhoff, age 11 days
29 Apr. 1675 Adelheit, wife of Hans Rudi, Wiedertauffer at Weyler, age 55 years
13 May 1675 Hans Senn age 18 years
15 May 1675 Barbara, daughter of Felix Frey
12 June 1675 Veronica, daughter of Henrich Müller, Wiedertauffer at Weiler, age 30 weeks
9 Nov. 1675 Henrich Frey, son of Felix
2 Jan. 1676 Eva, daughter of Hans Senn, age 22 years
11 Feb. 1676 Veronica, daughter of Hans Jacob Landas, age 6 years
9 Aug. 1676 Child of Felix Frey at Birkenhoff age 10 years
16 Sept. 1678 daughter of Heinrich Müller, age 4 years
24 Aug. 1682 Felix Freÿ, age 68 years, at the Burckenauerhoff
15 Dec. 1682 Anna, wife of Hans Ruth, age 40 years
_____1683 a child of Matthias Baumgartner. He is a tilemaker and farmer at the Buchenhoff [today Buchenauerhof]
19 May 1683 Hans Ruth's child, age ½ year
10 Jan. 1684 Anna, wife of Jacob Landas, in childbirth. Age 32 years.
26 Mar. 1693 Verena, wife of Heinrich Müller, age 57 years
(?) 3 Mar. 1693 Hans Ruth, born in Hessen, formerly of the Reformed religion, but became a Wid(er)tauffer. Age 73 years.
24 Nov. 1693 Hans Jacob Landas, age 31 years

Zuzenhausen Lutheran KB:
Baptized 7 Apr. 1697 a Wiedertauffer's son by name of Georg Rössel, bapt. after previous instruction and given the name: Friderich Julianus Georgius
Bapt. 19 May 1697 Veronica (no surname), a Wiedertaufferin, after instruction. Named Anna Margaretha Veronica. [The new communicants' register elsewhere in the KB indicates she was a daughter of Hans Musselmann and age 16 years.]
New communicant 1 Sept. 1686—
Christian Locher, son of a Widertauffer from Deisbach, age 30 years.

APPENDIX B

Lists of emigrants located in church records in the Kraichgau.

A. ITTLINGEN LUTHERAN KB: this church record contains 2 lists of emigrants, both in the communicants register. Earlier references to these lists are contained in the text. They are given here in their entirety:
1. Communicants list dated 1747—XIX Die Dom. Vocem Jucunditatis: The following communed before going to the New Land

    Conrad Klem and wife, Sen.
    Anna Maria Klem
    _____ Muller, single   entries faded and reading uncertain
    -Sch- and wife

    David Klemm and wife
    Anna Catharina Klemm
    Joh. Henrich Benedict
    Maria Christina Klemm
    Joh. Valentin Klemm
    Joh. Conrad Bissecker and wife
    Joh. Michel Hofmann and wife from Bonfeld

2. Communicants list dated 1749, XLIII Die Dom. Cantate: The following communed before their journey to Pennsylvania:
1. Maria Magdalena Benedictin, single
2. Elisabetha Benedictin, widow, d.
3. Anna Barbara Gschwind, single (this name crossed out—evidently did not go to Pennsylvania)
4. Anna Barbara Weeberin, single
5. Maria Barbara Hartmann, single
6. Maria Salome Gschwind, single (this name crossed out—evidently did not go to Pennsylvania)
7. Maria Barbara Hartmann, married, d.
8. Maria Margaretha Uhler, single, d.
9. Catharina Drexel, single, d.
10. Johann Michael Kilian, single
11. Johann Heinrich Harttman, single
12. Dietrich Paul Harttmann, single
13. Johann Valentin Weeber, single
14. Johann Heinrich Weeber, single
15 & 16. Andreas Schumacher and wife Elisabetha, d.
17 & 18. Joh. Jacob Roth and wife
19 & 20. Daniel Rieb and wife, d.
21. Elisabetha Schumacher, widow, d.
22 & 23. Johann Melchior Benedict and wife; wife, d.
24 & 25. Joh. Heinrich Weeber, d., and wife
26 & 27. Georg Michael Eppele and wife, d.

N.B.: in all about 40 souls from here to Pennsylvania

This group left Ittlingen on the 13 May 1749. All of the surviving male passengers appear on the *Dragon*, arriving 26 Sept. 1749 (S-H, I, p. 413, 414). The pastor later entered crosses in the communicants list, indicating the ones who died on the voyage. He also made notations in the baptismal register concerning the children who died at sea. Of the "40 souls" who left Ittlingen, 21 died.

This large 1749 emigration occured soon after the arrival of a few Pennsylvanians in Ittlingen. A 1749 communicants list, dated Die Paschatis (Easter) contains the names:

> Joh. Valentin Geiger aus Pensylvanien
> Jacob Geiger aus Pensylvanien

The record is silent about the fate of Joh. Valentin Geiger, but Jacob Geiger remained in Ittlingen, married there, and had children. This disastrous voyage appears to have discouraged further emigration. Only a few emigrants from this village have been documented after that date.

B. MICHELFELD LUTHERAN KB: although the Michelfeld church book does not contain an actual list of emigrants, there are scattered references throughout the record to various families who went to Pennsylvania. They are consolidated here in a list:

1. Weÿrich Rudisile left 13 May 1737 with wife and children
2. Joh. Valentin Walter left 6 May 1738 with family
3. Johann Georg Roth left 6 May 1738 with wife and child
4. Johann Georg Gross left 6 May 1738 with wife
5. Johann Jacob Schertzer left 6 May 1738 with wife and child
6. Johann Adam Ruppert 1731 with family
7. Nicolaus Weber 18 Apr. 1744 to Pennsylvania (with family)
8. Johannes Creutzwisser 20 May 1750 with family
9. Weÿrich Katerman left 6 May 1738 with family
10. David Katermann to Pennsylvania 1752
11. Stephan Böringer left 6 May 1738 with family
12. Johannes Schäfer from Pennsylvania m. 1728 in Michelfeld and returned to Pennsylvania
13. Anna Barbara Sauer left 25 May 1740 for Pennsylvania
14. Anna Catharina Rösslerin left 25 May 1748
15. Philipp Heinrich Sauer left 25 May 1740 with his wife, daughter (Anna Catharina Rössler) and son's daughter (Anna Barbara Sauer).
16. Johann Heinrich Sauer left 6 May 1738 with wife
17. Joh. Georg Minier left 6 May 1732 with family
18. Heinrich Seltzer left 16 May 1730 with wife and one son
19. Michael Reuss (Reiss) left 11 May 1738
20. Johannes Merckle left 5 May 1738 for Pennsylvania
21. Johannes Steinbrück(en) left 1744 for Pennsylvania
    [There were several other immigrants from Michelfeld who were not so noted in the church book.]

C. BONFELD LUTHERAN KB:
1710
Johannes Heyd with his family
Justus Heyd, his son, with his family
Michael Wägele, with his family
Simon Vogt, with his family
Sebastian Wimmer's widow with children
Hans Funck, Anabaptist
1717
Abraham Merckle and wife, with 5 children, and his son-in-law
Hans Jerg Bopp with wife, Lanio [= Lanius, butcher]
Joh. Dieterich Greiner with wife, daughter and sister
Nicolaus Hillicker with wife and 4 children
Joh. Jacob Roth with wife and 2 children and sister, Textor [= weaver]
Andreas Berger, wife and 4 children, Pisto(r) [= baker]
Jerg Schitz, wife and 3 children
Martin May, wife and 4 children, Fab. Lig. [= Faber lignarius, carpenter]
Joh. Georg Hass, with wife, Fab. Murarius [= brick layer, mason]
Anna Barbara Glotzin, Virgo [single woman]
Nicolaus Walter, _____ , with wife
An Anabaptist by the name of Neff with wife and children
His brother with wife and children
Molitor [occupation, miller] with wife and child or children, Anabaptist
Joh. Matthaeus Ringer with wife and child or children
Hans Motz with wife
Balthasar Merckle with wife and 3 children
Joh. Conrad Elleser with wife and 4 children
Joh. Conrad Dieterich with wife and 3 children
Philipp Kühner with wife and 4 children
1717 Fest Trin [= Festo Trinitatis, 23 May 1717]
Heinrich Funck with wife and children
Martin Funck with wife and children
Heinrich [no other name given] with wife and children
Anno 1727
Ludwig Dederer, selb 4 [= selbviert]
Ludwig Gsell with wife
Stephanus Rebbert with wife
Heinrich Gauger with wife and children
Anno 1738, month of May
Hans Jerg Haug with wife and 6 children
Marx Haag with wife and 3 children
Joh. Albrecht Seber with wife and 2 children
Michel Weinmann with wife and daughter

D. ESCHELBACH LUTHERAN KB:
Joh. Jacob Brecht 1752
Joh. Georg Eichelberger 1752
Joh. Jacob Brecht 1749

Christoph Süss 1752
Joh. Weÿrich Beck 1749
Georg Niclaus Bender 1752
Joh. Peter Ansel (1752)
Joh. Caspar Günter 1752

Joh. Jacob Bender 1752
Anna Elisabeth Kraus 1756
Jacob Bender
Maria Helena (Elisabetha) Bogner 1753

APPENDIX C
Emigrants from Dühren

The Dühren KB was not available on microfilm and materials on the emigrants from there were obtained from other sources. The following paper about emigrants from Dühren was sent by Prof. Dr.-Ing. Herm. Lau of Karlsruhe and arrived too late to be entered alphabetically into the preceding text. Dr. Lau's paper is presented here as he sent it, with the slight change of b., m., bp. inserted in place of the German genealogical symbols. The information in brackets has been added by the compiler of this volume.

1719 (?) Aichelberger, Jacob Valentin (family from Switzerland) m. 1 Oct. 1715 Maria Margaretha Kürtzler (b. Mönchsdeggingen) child: Anna Dorothea b. 28 Feb. 1719

1719 Allebach, Christian (Reformed or Mennonite) wife: Margaretha children: Jacob, Martin, Barbara, Esther, Elisabeth, David in America: Salford twp., Philadelphia co.
[Philadelphia Quarter Sessions Court docket:
Christian Allebach signed a petition dated 1725/26 for a township to be laid out adjoining Beeber's twp. on the northeast. He paid quit rent on 100 acres in 1732.]

1719 Bär (Behr), Hans Jacob, Mennonite, farmer; wife: Barbara children: Anna, Samuel, Veronica, Margaretha, Barbara, Jacob, Elisabeth, Magdalena

1719 Bär, Hans Michel, before 1714 Mennonite, then Lutheran), farmer wife: Anna Elisabeth children: Anna Barbara (b. 4 May 1714) Anna Eva (b. 15 Nov. 1715)

1740 (?) Bär, Lorenz Henrich (Reformed) daylaborer, son of Henrich Bär from Knonauer Amt/Zürich/Switzerland, m. at Gemmingen (Lutheran) 16 Apr. 1720 Eva Julianna Müller (bp. Gemmingen 6 Oct. 1696, daughter of Zacharias M.) children: Maria Catharina (bp. Gemmingen 9 Jan. 1721) Eva Catharina (bp. Gemmingen 29 Feb. 1724) Anna Catharina (b. Dühren 7 Oct. 1732)

1750 Bender, Johann Peter (Lutheran) b. 25 Feb. 1700, son of Joh. Georg m. Obergimpern or Untergimpern 1720 Anna Barbara _____ children: Johann Peter (?) (b. 1720 ?) Johann Georg (b. 3 May 1723) Maria Margaretha (b. 9 July 1725) Maria Elisabeth (b. 22 May 1727) Maria Eva (b. 16 May 1730) Conrad (b. 19 March 1734)   arrived 29 Sept. 1750 in Philadelphia
[The names Joh. Petter Bender, Johan Beder Benter, Conradt Bender appear on the ship list.]

1720 (?) Brentz ?, Hans Peter (b. 19 Oct. 1677), farmer, son of Hans Melchior m. (1) Michelfeld Jan./Feb. 1702 Anna Dorothea Glaser (b. Michelfeld), daugh-

ter of Hans Jacob children: Maria Catharina (bp. 12 Mar. 1704) Anna Dorothea (bp. 27 Aug. 1708) Georg Ulrich (b. 3 Feb. 1710) Eva Margaretha
(b. 19 Apr. 1712)
m. (2) Dühren 7 May 1715 Catharina Brand (or Braun) from Rappenau;
children: Anna Sabina (b. 14 Aug. 1716) Wilhelmina Juliana (b. 1 Oct.
1718)

1751 Brentz (Prinz), Johann Philipp, tailor (b. ? 1709 ?), son of Henrich m. (1)
26 June 1731 Maria Margaretha Bender (b. 28 Feb. 1712, daughter of Joh.
Georg, she d. 12 Mar. 1748) children: Anna Maria (b. 14 Feb. 1737) Johann
Philipp (b. 9 Dec. 1739) Johann Georg (b. 8 Dec. 1742) m. (2) 9 July 1748
Anna Maria Schwenzer (b. Rappenau, daughter of the late Balthasar); children: Jacob Friedrich (28 July 1749) Juliana Margaretha (b. 21 June 1750)
arrived 16 Sept. 1751 in Philadelphia

ca. 1730 Ernst, Conrad (d. 26 Jan. 1713) m. H. Cath. Rutsch (d. 22 May 1732);
children: Christian (b. 12 Apr. 1688) Johannes (b. 25 July 1698) emigrated

1720 Liebenstein, Hans Henrich, farmer (b. 28 Feb. 1683, son of Gregorius) m.
(1) 19 Aug. 1704 Eleonora Catharina Hoffmann from Adersbach m. (2) 24
May 1712 Eva Margaretha Böhl (b. _____ Feb. 1682), daughter of the minister Martin B., widow of Hans Georg Bender
Hans Henrich Liebenstein emigrated 1720 apparently without wife and children to America (Mississippi)

1727 Liebenstein, Bernhard (b. 1705), son of Hans Andreas, unmarried

1727 Liebenstein, Magdalena (b. 10 Dec. 1709), daughter of Hans Andreas,
unmarried (she married Peter Gärrer in Conestoga in Pennsylvania)

1727 Liebenstein, Johann Martin (bp. 24 Feb. 1703), son of Hans Andreas m. 23
Jan. 1725 Juliana Auer (b. Weiler a. St. 29 Jan. 1700), daughter of the
Kellermann Christian A. in Weiler a. St. child: Maria Elisabeth (b. 21 May
1726)
[see emigrant family # 344 in main text.]

before 1740 Mayle, Hans Jacob, son of the Mennonite Jacob Mayle and Anna
unmarried (?) It is not certain whether he emigrated.

before 1740 Mayle, Barbara (b. ca. 1715), daughter of the Mennonite Jacob Mayle,
who died 15 Feb. 1759 she m. in Pennsylvania Peter Böhm

1719 Neff, Franz, Mennonite, *dictus doctor* (b. ca. 1685), son of Heinrich (?) m.
22 Apr. 1720 Barbara Böhm (b. Michelfeld ca. 1690) children unknown.
Franz Neff sen. and Franz Neff jun. 1719 in Lancaster county, Pennsylvania
[see emigrant family # 394 in main text]

1740 Rössler, Hans Georg (Lutheran), tailor (b. 9 Jan. 1701, d. 25 Feb. 1739)
his widow Anna Catharina (m. 26 Jan. 1723), daughter of the *Kellermann*
Philipp Heinrich Sauer and Catharina in Michelfeld (b. Michelfeld 1 Jan.
1704) emigrated in May 1740 together with her parents and her 4 children:
Maria Elisabeth (b. 20 May 1724) Hans Jerg (b. 30 Apr. 1726) Johannes (b.
8 Oct. 1730) Johann Adam (b. 1 Jan. 1736) to Pennsylvania
[see emigrant family # 459 in main text.]

ca. 1730 Rudi (Rudy), Hans Conrad (Reformed) (b. 5 Aug. 1683), son of the tailor
Hans Rudi and Anna Dorothea nee Lang emigrated unmarried (?) and
was living in Pennsylvania in 1739

[PA Archives, Second Series, IX: 61: First Presbyterian Church, Philadelphia: m. 10-27-1725 John Conrade Rudy and Margaret Glanner.]
1738 Saltzgeber, Dietrich (Reformed) (b. 27 Jan. 1705), son of Johann Ferdinand
Saltzgeber and Barbara nee Ringer m. 9 May 1730 Margaretha Bischoff
(bp. Adersbach 18 Sept. 1708), daughter of the *Kellermann* Georg Philipp
Bischoff and Barbara nee Wezel in Adersbach children: Maria Magdalena
(b. 29 Jan. 1731) Margaretha (b. 10 Dec. 1732) Susanna Esther (b. 23 Jan.
1736) Johann Reichardt (b. 1 March 1737) he emigrated with his wife and 4
children to Pennsylvania in March/Apr. 1738
[see emigrant family # 50 in main text.]

If no other religion is mentioned, the confession is Lutheran.

The information on these emigrants will be a part of the *Ortssippenbuch
Dühren* (= kinships of the village Dühren) which will be published in 1984, and
is included here with Prof. Dr. Lau's permission.

Note on the Indexes

The first index, Index of Ships, contains the name of the ships and the year of arrival. When a more specific date of arrival is given, it is because there were two arrivals of ships with the same name in the same year. The reader is referred to Volume III of Strassburger & Hinke, *Pennsylvania German Pioneers*, pp. 215–221, for a complete alphabetical listing of the known ship arrivals.

The second index, European Place Names, contains a listing of all European villages and place names mentioned in the text. In using this index, the researcher should consider the fact that quite often place names were misspelled in both the old German and American records. An attempt has been made in the text to provide identification and location by the inclusion of the European postal code. A few place names have defied positive identification. A listing with a two-letter abbreviation following the village name indicates a village in Switzerland. The conventional Swiss postal abbreviations are used for all cantons:

AG	Aargau	GR	Graubünden
BE	Bern	SH	Schaffhausen
BL	Basel-Land	ZH	Zürich

The Surname Index should be used with care (and with some imagination). The searcher should keep in mind the sound of the names and the fact that there was no consistent spelling used in this time period. (For example, there was no difference between "Churpfalz" and "Kurpfalz;" both spellings were used for the Electoral Palatinate.) We have included some suggestions to other possible spellings. The umlaut has been ignored in the alphabetical arrangement, out of consideration for American readers not familiar with European alphabetical arrangements.

Index to Ships

Osgood, 1750: 33, 212, 233, 243, 432

Patience, 1748: 172
Patience, 1749: 75, 76, 224, 240
Patience, 1750: 325
Peggy, 1753: 329
Peggy, 1754: 154, 252, 253, 278
Pennsylvania Merchant, 1731: 69, 120, 121, 153, 398
Phoenix, 1743: 54, 364
Phoenix, 1749: 235, 302, 304, 343
Phoenix, 1750: 165
Phoenix, 1751: 233, 308
Phoenix, 1752: 408
Plaisance, 1732: 65, 112, 158, 159, 160, 209, 246, 301, 363, 378, 400, 404, 422, 423
Pleasant, 1732: 109, 110, 133, 164, 176, 193, 194, 214, 224, 246, 260, 277, 283, 344, 349, 365, 371, 393
Polly, 1765: 267, 324
Princess Augusta, 1736: 83, 106, 234, 293, 358

Rawley, 1752: 47, 53, 114, 177
Restauration, 1747: 65, 95, 170, 207, 209, 307, ?318, 328
Richmond, 1764: 67, 212, 246, 311, 334, 341, 367
Robert & Alice, 1738: 72, 215, 216, 296, 394
Robert & Alice, 1740: 84, 155
Robert & Alice, 1742: 174
Robert & Alice, 1743: 93, 127, 128, 130, 142, 253, 310, 335, 347
Rosannah, 1743: 170, 399
Royal Union, 1750: 38, 134, 140, 190, 243, 274, 372, 405

Samuel, 1731: 241
Samuel, 1732: 38, 68, 69, 111, 132, 148, 172, 208, 318, 332, 334, 339, 352, 370, 387, 392, 409, 421, 422, 423

Samuel, 1733: 35, 89, 113, 194, 237, 359, 384, 403
Samuel, 1737: 100, 103, 117, 123, 163, 184, 241, 306, 331
Sandwich, 1750: 146
Shirley, 1751: 43, 106, 127, 156, 157, 175, 218, 219, 254, 271, 281, 309, 317, 319, 337, 377
Speedwell, 1749: 403
St. Andrew, 1738: 71, 72, 73, 81, 152, 189, 232, 276, 312, 315, 377, 381
St. Andrew, 1743: 102, 180, 245
St. Andrew, 1751: 81, 412
St. Andrew, 1752: 144, 189, 243, 416

Thistle of Glasgow, 1730: 66, 153, 196, 211, 222
Townsend, 1737: 111, 132
Two Brothers, 1750: 127, 221, 257, 331, ?356
Two Sisters, 1738: 52, 76, 150, 164, 180, 256, 272, 275, 288, 309

Vernon, 1747: 84

William, 1737: 208, 337, 399
William & Sarah, 1727: 34, 37, 44, 45, 111, 114, 158, 160, 166, 173, 183, 187, 220, 236, 239, 250, 259, 264, 276, 277, 302, 304, 323, 335, 336, 350, 354, 363, 386, 388, 392, 397, 401, 406, 411, 412, 414
Winter Galley, 1738: 92

Ship unknown: 49, 51, 70, 74, 83, 90, 92, 100, 113, 119, 123, 130, 137, 140, 141, 145, 146, 149, 169, 171, 204, 205, 216, 219, 220, 227, 239, 242, 253, 263, 264, 281, 290, 300, 301, 312, 318, 329, 347, 351, 352, 357, 358, 359, 361, 362, 373, 375, 383, 384, 385, 396, 413

Index of European Place Names

Surname Index

Abendschein, 33
Abendschön, 33, 55
Abendshen, 33
Abraham, 376
Acken, 217
Ackerman, 34
Ackermann, 33, 34
Adam, 34, 35, 92, 130, 239, 336
Adolf, 268
Aff, 24, 35
Affe, 35
Aichelberger, 97, 99, 432
Aichelberger, see Eichelberger
Aicholtz, 100
Aicholtz, see Eichholtz
Aigenmann, 23
Albert, 36, 192, 278
Albrecht, 34, 63, 165, 356
Alderfer, 36
Aldorffer, 35, 36
Allebach, 432
Allgaÿer, 24, 36
Allgeyer, 36, 170
Allgeÿer, 36
Altorffer, 35, 36, 354, 419
Amans, 125
Ament, 236
Ancker, 256
Andrae, 396
Anhausen, 365
Anmuller, 172
Ansbach, 79, 288
Ansel, 36, 432
Anspach, 81, 108, 190, 192, 265, 288
Arbeiter, 23
Arldnold, see Arnoldt
Armbrust, 226
Arnal?, 242
Arndt, 122
Arnhold, 37
Arnold, 37
Arnoldt, 37
Arz, 133
Auchen?, 403
Auer, 185, 239, 433
Aulenbach, 343
Avensheen, 33
Avensheen, see Abendschön

Baal, 38
Bach, 364
Bachemeyer, 81
Bachmann, 23
Baer, 50, 423

Baffenmeyer, 38, 405
Bähr, 40, 426
Baker, (see Becker), 372
Ball, 38
Balmar, see Balmer
Balmer, 38, 39
Bants, 54; see Bentz
Bär, 24, 26, 40, 41, 74, 255, 378, 432
Bare, 40, 49
Barger, 63
Barnhart, 416
Barringer, 55
Bart, Barth, 22, 37, 41, 50, 100, 111, 186, 203, 272
Barther, 164
Bashore, 297
Basler, 42, 277, 321, 344
Basor, 155
Basseler, 42
Bassler, 42, 407
Bastress, 301
Bauer, 22, 42, 103, 184, 406
Bäuerlein, 57
Bauin, 310
Baum, 43, 175, 222, 282, 285
Bauman, 44
Baumann, 44, 227
Baumgaertner, 45
Baumgärtner, 45, 281, 428
Baur, 42, 352
Bausel, 45
Baussel, 45
Bawmann, 44
Bayer, Beyer, 92, 135, 176, 300, 305
Bayerle, Bayerly, 59
Bear, 49, 423
Beard, 41; see Barth
Beck, 46, 47, 432
Becker, 97, 174, 372
Beer, 422
Beeringer, 33, 54
Behr, 422, 432
Beilstein, 260, 317, 381
Beisel, 162
Beller, 339, 340
Belsner, 46
Belzener, 46
Bender, xv, 24, 29, 47, 48, 49, 50, 51, 52, 53, 72, 74, ?100, 116, 202, 203, 231, 326, 404, 432, 433
Bendter, 49, 50, 111
Benedict, 24, 52, 53, 181, 429
Benezet, 105
Bengel, 262
Benner, 35